Foundation Flash CS3 for Designers

Tom Green and David Stiller

friendsof

DESIGNER TO DESIGNER™

an Apress® company

Foundation Flash CS3 for Designers

Credits

CONTENTS AT A GLANCE

CONTENTS

CONTENTS

CONTENTS

FOREWORD

Like a lot of kids, I was entranced by animation. My childhood was littered with flipbooks, doodles, and at least one zoetrope I built from a kit. I even had an electronic toy called the Etch-a-Sketch Animator that let you create 12 black-and-white "pictures" on a 30×40-pixel screen and make them play back in sequence. This created possibly the worst animation ever, but to a 10-year-old it was the coolest thing!

This love for animation was lost for a few years, as I got deeper and deeper into computers. As I moved through high school and kept learning new operating systems and programming languages, I was starting to realize that one day working/playing with computers could be my career.

Then, in my sophomore year of college, I was introduced to Flash. All of the books I had read about Disney, Warner Brothers, and Hanna-Barbera came flooding back to me. With reckless abandon I learned everything I could about Flash—and was done after about a week. Flash wasn't exactly complicated in those days, and ActionScript didn't consist of much more than stop and play.

The good news was that I was in a perfect place for keeping pace with Flash as it grew—my programming background along with my love for animation let me keep on top of every new version of Flash as it was released. I was in the enviable position of being able to just ride the wave from version to version.

During that time, I spoke at and attended a lot of Flash conferences, where I was lucky enough to meet both Tom Green and David Stiller. If you're ever in a room with Tom, you'll know—the raucous laughter is your first clue. Tom has a real exuberance for learning, teaching, and life in general that is all too rare in this world. He is constantly striving to learn more and discover new ways to convey that knowledge to his students. As for David, he is from the true old school—a modern-day Renaissance man. He struck up a conversation with me about obscure board games a few years ago. The conversation wound its way through quantum mechanics, the proper brewing of Turkish coffee, and toy building, and technically is still going on today. I am proud to be able to call on him as a contractor for my company and even more proud to call him a friend.

Now, back to Flash. Recently, it has become such a huge product that I'm starting to see what folks who are new to Flash go through all over again—I'm starting to struggle a bit with the new versions. I don't have the time to peek into each new cranny of the program. I can't sit down and figure out all the new best practices. It's pretty overwhelming.

That's why I was very, very happy when I found out that Tom and David were working on this book—they have done all the research for me, so I'm not going to fall behind! I knew Tom and David would take Flash CS3 and distill everything about it into an informative and fun-to-read tome for newcomers and old hats like myself.

I'm very happy to tell you, they didn't disappoint. Enjoy the firm binding and nice new look of your new book now because I'm sure it will become well loved, dog-eared, and covered in sticky notes in no time!

Branden Hall
CTO—Automata Studios Ltd.
June 2007

ABOUT THE AUTHORS

Tom Green is currently professor of interactive media in the School of Media Studies at Humber College Institute of Technology and Advanced Learning in Toronto, Canada. He has written seven previous books on Adobe technologies and many articles for numerous magazines and websites, including Community MX, *Digital Web Magazine*, and *Computer Arts*. He has spoken at over 20 conferences internationally, including Adobe Max, NAB, FITC, MX North, Digital Design World, TODCON, and SparkEurope. You can contact Tom at tom@tomontheweb.ca.

David Stiller is an independent contractor whose portfolio includes multimedia programming and design for NASA, DOT, Adobe, major US automotive and boat manufacturers, and dozens of clients across the US and Canada. David gets a kick out of sharing "aha!" moments with others through consultation, mentoring, and regular contributions to the Adobe Flash and ActionScript forums, his blog (http://quip.net/blog/), and articles for Community MX. In off hours, his interests include unicycling, anaglyph 3D photography, finely crafted wooden game boards, Library of Congress field recordings, and Turkish coffee. David lives in Virginia with his amazing wife, Dawn, and his beguiling daughter, Meridian.

ABOUT THE TECHNICAL REVIEWER

Adam Thomas's career can best be defined as a successful hobby. Having an early interest in computers and being mostly self-taught, he decided to go to Humber College in Toronto to study computer information systems. Soon after his graduation in 2001, Adam was invited back to his school to be a professor of rich media and web development. Alongside teaching, he runs a successful web studio called Robin Hood Tech. Adam takes pride in employing former students who he has had the privilege of teaching and giving them the opportunity to gain experience and excel in a competitive field. Adam is cofounder of the Robin Hood Business Model, which advocates for justice in business. Adam strives for integrity and simplicity, but his true motivation is his wife and family, who are daily reminders of love, faith, and blessing.

ABOUT THE COVER IMAGE DESIGNER

Corné van Dooren designed the front cover image for this book. After taking a brief from friends of ED to create a new design for the *Foundation* series, he worked at combining technological and organic forms, with the results now appearing on this and other books' covers.

Corné spent his childhood drawing on everything at hand and then began exploring the infinite world of multimedia—and his journey of discovery hasn't stopped since. His mantra has always been "The only limit to multimedia is the imagination," a saying that keeps him moving forward constantly.

Corné works for many international clients, writes features for multimedia magazines, reviews and tests software, authors multimedia studies, and works on many other friends of ED books. You can see more of his work at www.cornevandooren.com, as well as contact him through his website.

If you like Corné's work, be sure to check out his chapter in *New Masters of Photoshop: Volume 2* (friends of ED, 2004).

ACKNOWLEDGMENTS

Working with a coauthor can be a tricky business. In fact, it is a lot like a marriage. Everything is wonderful when things are going well, but you never really discover the strength of the relationship until you get deep into it. When I asked David if he would share the cover with me, his response was an immediate "Am I intrigued? Umm, schyaaah!" From that point on, David and I worked together to produce this book. As we got deeper into the process, we discovered we had undergone some sort of weird "Vulcan mind-meld" where we each instinctively understood what the other was talking about and moved on from there. When David brought Peter Pan and the Tron Guy into the book, I just knew this was going to be a special project and that a rather precious writing and professional relationship, as well as deep friendship, was in place. I learned a lot from David, shared some great laughs, and the two of us produced something that went far beyond what we both envisioned. It looks like he and I are in for the long haul, and I couldn't be happier.

As we dug into this book, we realized that we could tell you what to do, but the "names" in this business could reinforce, from personal experience, what we were telling you. We deeply appreciate the help we got from Jennifer Shiman, Kristen Henry, Chris Georgenes, John Kricfalusi, and David Schroeder for sharing their experiences and insights with you.

Next up is our editor, Chris Mills. This will be the third book I have written for him, and when I explained how I wanted to move outside of the usual way of doing a *Foundation* book, he thought about it for a millisecond and told me to go for it. Chris stayed out of the way but was always there when we got stuck and needed a kick in the pants or a "have you thought of this . . . ?" idea. Even though Chris and I have a solid, professional relationship, we have also become good friends.

Finally, writing a book means I hole myself up in my office and become generally moody and difficult to be around as I mull over a technique or try to identify why something isn't quite working. It takes a very unique individual to live with that, let alone understand why—and my wife, best friend, and life partner over the past 30 years has somehow put up with it.

Tom Green

ACKNOWLEDGMENTS

Tom's the one who invited me on this tour bus, so I'd like to thank him right out the gate. From the beginning, we connected—*zing!*—on a heartfelt foundation of laughter, the kind you get from a good poke to the belly button. In fact, for months, I nicknamed our collaboration the "Tom and Jerry Show" (I was born in Germany, which makes me the Jerry . . . Tom, he's the big gray pussy cat, obviously). Humor carried us through a number of zany tribulations, including combustible early beta software and even puffs of smoke (literally) on various computers at our disposal. Humor inspired us in our analogies and illustrations, and humor kept my paws inches ahead of Tom as he chased me around the kitchen, again and again, with a cleaver (he'll never catch me!). I couldn't have asked for a better swim buddy. Thanks again, Green!

Over the years, I've learned quite a bit about programming and life in general from a dear friend who both exists and does not, and who goes by the name Uncle Chutney. "Big things are made up of lots of little things," he keeps telling me, and he's right. That proverb has gotten me out of many a jam.

Numerous people helped us write this book, from engineers at Adobe and partners at Community MX (especially Joseph Balderson and Steven Schelter) to friends ready at a moment's notice to test this-and-that, lend a pair of ears, or simply laugh (or not) at a pun. For me that list includes Noah DiCenso, Chris Georgenes, Branden Hall, Bruce Hartman, Ted Johns, Keenan Keeling, Rich Lee, Ernie Lindsey, Adam Oldham, Rothrock, Todd Sanders, and especially Amy Niebel, who often kept my head screwed on and my chin up. Thanks to Randy Constan and Jay Maynard for being so cool. Thanks, John K., for the yuks!

Near the end of this book, my wife made our backyard magical by planting a garden in it with our daughter. As always, I saw Dawn transform everyday banalities into learning opportunities for Meridian. I saw my daughter grow because of it. When I can teach as well as Dawn does, I'll be getting somewhere. These are my favorite two people in the world, and I owe them—big time—for their patience while I was writing. *Na, Bohne, jetzt ist Papi endlich fertig. Was wollen wir nun spielen?*

David Stiller

INTRODUCTION

I can remember the day as clear is if it were just yesterday. I was walking by my boss' office late one winter afternoon at the college where I teach, and he called me into his office. Sitting on his desk was a thin white box with some sort of weird swirl on it. He slid the box across to me and asked, "You know anything about Flash?"

To be honest, as a Director user, what I knew was filtered through the eyes of a Director guy, which meant I didn't know much and what I did know convinced me it was a wind-up toy compared to Director. I replied, "A bit." The boss leaned back in his chair and said, "Well learn a lot more because you are teaching it in four weeks." This was the start of one of the longest, strangest, and most exhilarating trips I have ever been on. The version was Flash 3, and I have been using and teaching Flash ever since.

In many respects, Flash CS3 completes the process started by Macromedia, now Adobe, with the release of Flash 8. That release was a "designer" release, meaning there were lots of goodies for the creatives and a few for the coders. This iteration of the application is the "developer" release. The coders are dancing in the streets, and the creatives are wondering what the hell happened.

In many respects, this release of the application marks the absorption of Flash into the Adobe product line, and Adobe didn't just toss it on the pile. As you will discover, there are some seriously cool new features that allow Flash users to take advantage of new workflows among all of the applications in the Adobe lineup including Photoshop CS3, Illustrator CS3, Fireworks CS3, Dreamweaver CS3, and even After Effects CS3 and Soundbooth CS3. The big news, of course, is the introduction of ActionScript 3.0.

This revision of the Flash scripting language will initially, in the immortal words of Ed Grimley, "Drive you mental!" The key word is "initially," because once you get used to it, you will discover everything you know about ActionScript still applies . . . just a bit differently. When Dave and I started mapping out this book, we decided to go with ActionScript 3.0 for every line of code in the book. In this way, you can learn the fundamentals and use them as a jumping-off point to further explore the power of this language.

This book is also a bit different from any Flash book you may have read or considered purchasing. From the very start of the process, Dave and I put ourselves in your shoes and asked a simple question: "What do you need to know and why?" This question led us into territory that we didn't quite expect. As we were grappling with that question early in the process, we kept bothering our network of Flash friends to be sure we were on the right track. At some point, both of us simultaneously came to the conclusion, "Why not just let them explain it in their own words?" This is why, as you journey through this book, you will encounter various experts in the field telling you why they do things and offering you insights into what they have learned. The odd thing is, at some point in their careers, they were no different from you.

One other aspect of this book that we feel is important is we had a lot of fun developing the examples and exercises in the book. The fun aspect is important because if learning is fun, what you learn will be retained. Anybody can show you how to apply a Glow filter to a line on the Flash stage. It is more effective when you do exactly the same thing to a guy wearing a Tron suit. Anybody can dryly explain 9-slice scaling, but it becomes less techie when you apply it to a guy dressed as Peter Pan. Nested movieclips are a "yawner" at best, but when they are related to a Hostess Twinkie, the concept becomes understandable. Shared libraries are an important subject. Instead of filling a library with circles and text, the concept becomes relevant when the library is populated with "Bunny Bits."

As you may have guessed, we continue to exhibit a sense of joy and wonder with Flash, and we hope a little bit of our enthusiasm rubs off on you as well.

Book structure and flow

To start, this is not a typical *Foundation* book. There is no common project that runs throughout the book. Instead, each chapter contains a number of exercises to help you develop some "Flash chops," and then we turn you loose in the "Your turn" section of each chapter.

We start by dropping you right into the application and creating a small Flash movie we call "Moonrise Over Lake Nanagook" (told you we were having fun). This chapter familiarizes you with the Flash workspace and the fundamentals of using Flash Professional CS3. Chapter 2 introduces you to working with the graphic tools and with graphics files and finishes with your creating a Monty Python–style banner ad.

Chapter 3 introduces you to symbols and libraries in Flash CS3. In this chapter, you learn how to create and use symbols, and we even let Peter Pan explain how 9-slice scaling works. With those fundamentals under your belt, we show you how to share symbols and libraries between movies, how to manipulate symbols with filters and blend effects, and along the way you travel from the Beijing Zoo to Times Square, discovering how to create some rather powerful effects in your Flash movies. The chapter finishes by showing you how to use masks to your advantage in Flash.

At this point in the book, you have pretty well mastered the fundamentals. The rest of the book builds upon what you have learned. Chapter 4 picks you up and throws you into the ActionScript 3.0 pool. Chapter 5 starts by explaining how to use audio in Flash and finishes with your constructing an MP3 player.

Chapter 6 reinforces the message that "text isn't the gray stuff that surrounds your animations." We show you how it is both serious and fun by stepping through how to create scrolling text and how to blow up your name. Chapter 7 is one of the more important chapters in the book because Flash's roots were as an animation application. You are going to learn the basics here, but don't expect to be shoving boxes and circles around. You will be banging hammers, eating apples, dropping parrots, putting on a Tron suit and lighting it up, and setting a butterfly in motion. Did we mention we believe in having fun?

From animation we move into video in Flash. In Chapter 8, we show the entire process from encoding to upload. In fact, the chapter finishes with your adding captions and a full-screen capability to a Superman movie. Along the way, you will visit heaven and also meet a rather neurotic cartoon character.

Chapters 9, 10, and 11 give you the chance to play with all of the Flash user interface components, actually style a Flash movie using Cascading Style Sheets, and explore how XML gives you a huge amount of flexibility when it comes to adding dynamic data to your movie.

Chapter 12 moves you out of Flash and into the mobile space. Device Central is a new addition to the CS3 lineup, and here you will be creating a slideshow that will appear on a cell phone.

The final two chapters focus on the end game of the design process. Chapter 13 shows you a number of the important techniques you need to know that will keep your movies small and efficient. Chapter 14 shows you how to create the SWF that will be embedded into a web page and how to keep that process as smooth as possible.

Finally, David and I are no different from you. We are learning about this application and what it can and cannot do at the same time as you. Though we may be coming at it from a slightly more advanced level, there is a lot about this application we're still learning. If there is something we have missed or something you don't quite understand, by all means contact us. We'll be sure to add it to the book's site. Our final words of advice for you are:

The amount of fun you can have with this application should be illegal. We'll see you in jail!

Tom Green

Layout conventions

To keep this book as clear and easy to follow as possible, the following text conventions are used throughout.

Important words or concepts are normally highlighted on the first appearance in **bold type**.

Code is presented in fixed-width font.

New or changed code is normally presented in **bold fixed-width font**.

Pseudo-code and variable input are written in *italic fixed-width font*.

Menu commands are written in the form Menu ➤ Submenu ➤ Submenu.

Where we want to draw your attention to something, we've highlighted it like this:

> *Ahem, don't say we didn't warn you.*

Sometimes code won't fit on a single line in a book. Where this happens, we use an arrow like this: ➡.

```
This is a very, very long section of code that should be written all ➡
on the same line without a break
```

1 LEARNING THE FLASH CS3 PROFESSIONAL INTERFACE

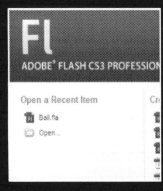 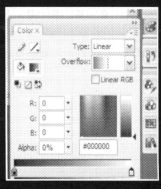 

Welcome to Flash CS3 Professional. We suspect you are here because you have seen a lot of the great stuff Flash can do and it is now time for you to get into the game. We also suspect you are here because Flash can be one great big, scary application to those unfamiliar with it. The other reason you may be here is because you are an existing Flash user and CS3 is suddenly a lot different from Flash MX 2004 or Flash 8, and you need to get yourself trained up on the new stuff in relatively short order. In either case, both of the authors have been in your shoes at some point in our careers, which means we understand what you are feeling. So instead of jumping right into the application . . . let's go for walk.

What we'll cover in this chapter:

- Exploring the Flash interface
- Using the Flash stage
- Working with panels
- The difference between a frame and a keyframe
- Using frames to arrange content on the stage
- Using layers to manage content on the stage
- Adding objects to the library
- Testing your movie

Files used in this chapter:

- Ball.fla (Chapter01/ExerciseFiles_CH01/Exercise/Ball.fla)
- Properties.fla (Chapter01/ExerciseFiles_CH01/Exercise/Properties.fla)
- Layers.fla (Chapter01/ExerciseFiles_CH01/Exercise/Layers.fla)
- MoonOverLakeNanagook.fla (Chapter01/ExerciseFiles_CH01/Exercise/ MoonOverLakeNanagook.fla)
- Nanagook.mp3 (Chapter01/ExerciseFiles_CH01/Exercise/Nanagook.mp3)

What we are going to do in this chapter is take a walk through the authoring environment—called the Flash interface—pointing out the sights and giving you an opportunity to play with the features. By the end of the stroll, you should be fairly comfortable with this tool called Flash and have a fairly good idea of what tools you can use and how to use them as you start creating a Flash movie.

As we go for our walk, we will also be having a conversation that will help you to understand the fundamentals of the creation of a Flash movie. Having this knowledge right at the start of the process gives you the confidence to build upon what you have learned. So let's start right at the beginning of the process . . . the Start page.

The Start page and creating a Flash document

The first thing you see when you launch Flash is the Start page shown in Figure 1-1. This interface, common to all of the Adobe CS3 applications, is divided into three areas. The area on the left side shows you a list of documents you have previously opened. Click one of them, and that document, provided it hasn't been moved to another location on your computer, will open. The Open link at the bottom of the list lets you navigate to a document that isn't on the list.

Figure 1-1. The Start page

The middle area of the page is where you can choose to create a variety of new Flash documents. Your choices include a blank Flash document, a project aimed at a cell phone or PDA (a mobile document), a series of code-based documents, and a Flash project.

The major change in this panel is the ability to select a new document based upon which version of ActionScript will be used in the document. Flash Professional CS3 marks the latest version of the Flash programming language named ActionScript. The previous version of this language, used in Flash MX 2004 and Flash 8, was ActionScript 2.0. We will be digging into ActionScript 3.0 in greater depth in Chapter 4.

> *From this point on, unless otherwise stated, you will be selecting the* Flash File (ActionScript 3.0) *option when opening new documents throughout this book.*

The right area of the page is reserved for a variety of templates you can use. Clicking one of the folders opens the New from Template dialog box, as shown in Figure 1-2. The Extend area at the bottom of this column contains a link to the Flash Exchange. This is a hyperlink that takes you to a page on the Adobe site where you can download a variety of tools and projects that are available for free or a nominal cost. Let's open a new document. Simply click Flash File (ActionScript 3.0) in the Create New area of the Start page to open the Flash interface.

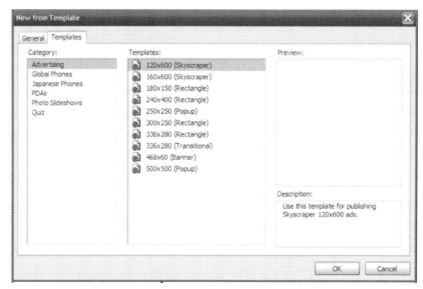

Figure 1-2. Flash contains a variety of templates designed to help you become more productive.

The interface that opens is the feature-rich authoring environment (shown in Figure 1-3) that is the heart and soul of Flash. If you are an existing Flash user, the first thing that will catch your attention is that the interface looks somewhat different from previous versions of the application.

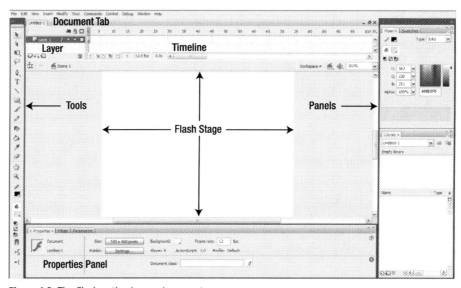

Figure 1-3. The Flash authoring environment

The **stage**, the large white area in the center of the screen, is where the action happens. A good way of regarding the stage in relation to Flash is this: if it isn't on the stage, the user isn't going to see it. There will be instances where this last statement is not exactly true, but we'll get into those later on in this book. On the left side of the screen is a set of tools that will allow you to draw, color, and otherwise manipulate objects on the stage. At the bottom of the interface is the Property inspector. We'll talk about this a little later on, but as you become more comfortable with the application, this panel will become a very important place for you.

At the top of the interface is the **timeline**. This is the place where action occurs. As you can see, the timeline is broken into a series of boxes called **frames**. The best way of regarding frames is as individual frames of a film. When you put something on the stage, it will appear in a frame. If you want it to move from here to there, it will start in one frame and end in another a little further along the timeline. That red box you see in frame 1 is called the **playhead**. Its purpose is to show you the current frame being displayed. When a Flash movie is playing through a browser, the playhead is in motion and the user is seeing the frame where the playhead is located. This is how things appear to move in Flash.

Another thing you can do with the playhead is drag it across the timeline while you are creating the Flash movie. This technique is known as **scrubbing** the timeline, and has its roots in film editing.

On the right side of the interface are the panels. Panels are used to modify and manipulate whatever object you may have selected on the stage or to even add an object to the stage. These objects can be text, photographs, line art, short animations, video, or even interface elements called components. You can use the panels and the menus to change not only the characteristics of the objects, but also how the objects behave on the stage. Panels can be connected to each other (docked) or they can float freely in the interface (floating).

Managing your workspace

As you may have surmised, the Flash authoring environment is one busy place, and if you talk to a Flash developer or designer, he will also tell you it can become one crowded place as well. As you start creating Flash projects, you will discover that real estate on your screen is a valuable commodity as it fills up with floating panels and other elements. This has all changed in Flash CS3. Here's how you manage the panels:

- At the top of the Tools panel and the Panels area on the right side of the screen is an icon that looks like a double arrow (see Figure 1-4). Click it and the panels will collapse and become icons. If you click the arrow above the tools, the Tools panel expands from a strip to a two-column layout. The process is called **panel collapse**, and is designed to free up screen space in Flash. In fact, Adobe is so thrilled with this feature that you can expect to see it added to all of the applications in the CS Studio over the next couple of years.

- Place the cursor over the bottom icon on the panel strip. The icon will change from gray to color, and a tooltip telling you what the item is will appear.

Figure 1-4. Panels can now be collapsed to give you more screen space.

- With the panel collapsed, place the cursor to the left of the icons in the panel strip. When the cursor changes to a double arrow, drag the panel strip to the left or to the right. As you drag to the left, the panel icons will expand and show you the name of the panel. As you drag to the right, the names will disappear and only the icon will be visible.

- With the panel collapsed, click an icon in the strip and the contents of that panel will fly out (as shown in Figure 1-5). Click it again and the contents of the panel will slide back. These panels that fly out and slide in are called **drawers**.

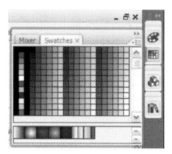

Figure 1-5. Click a panel icon and the contents slide out. Click the icon again and they slide in.

- Another method of buying some screen real estate is to collapse a panel by minimizing it. With the panel opened, click the - sign in the upper-right corner of the Property inspector or on the gray bar itself, and it will collapse and only show you the tabs. Click it again and the panel will grow to its original dimensions.

Here's a little trick that is new to the Property inspector. See that little dot beside the word Properties? *Click it, and the panel will be reduced to half size. Click it again, and the panel will collapse to just show the tabs. Click it again, and the panel will expand back to full size.*

- Click the Close button—the X—in a panel, and the panel will be removed from the group. If you do remove a panel, all is not lost. Open the Window menu and click the name of the panel you closed to restore it.

- Drag one of the panel icons onto another panel. When you release the mouse, the panel will expand to include the new panel added. This is called a **panel set**. To remove a panel from a set, just drag the panel icon to the bottom of the stack.

Though not a technique, this tip falls squarely into the "well, it's about time" category of new stuff. If you drag a floating panel over another interface element, the floating panel will become somewhat transparent and let you see what is under the panel.

Now that you have learned to become the master of the work environment, let's take a look at how you can also become the master of your Flash document.

Setting document preferences and properties

Managing the workspace is a fundamental skill, but the most important decision you will make concerns the size of the Flash stage and the space it will take up in the browser. That decision is based upon a number of factors, including the type of content to be displayed and the other items that will appear in the HTML document. These decisions all affect the stage size and, in many respects, the way the document is handled by Flash. These two factors are managed by the Preferences panel and the Document Properties dialog box.

To access the Preferences panel, select Edit ➤ Preferences (PC) or Flash Professional ➤ Preferences (Mac). There is a lot to this panel, and we'll explore it further at various points throughout this book. For now, we are concerned with the general preferences in the Category area of the window. Click General and the window will change to show you the general preferences for Flash (see Figure 1-6).

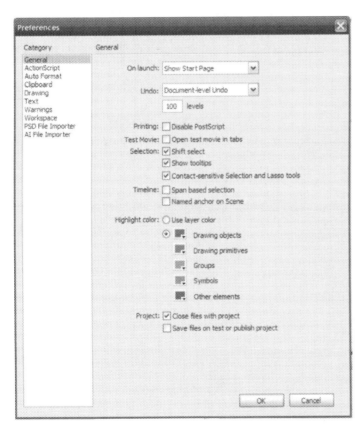

Figure 1-6. The general preferences can be used to manage not only the workspace but also items on the stage.

If you examine many of the selections, you will realize they are fairly intuitive. You can choose to see the Start page when the application starts, to see tooltips when the cursor is over a tool or object, to have a test movie appear in a tabbed window or float, how items are selected on the stage and the timeline, and even the colors that will be used to tell you what type of object has been selected on the stage. Now that you know how to set your preferences, let's look at managing the document properties. Follow these steps:

> *If you have been using Flash for a few years, you'll find that the expansion of the* Highlight color *list to include a variety of objects is a welcome addition.*

1. Click the Cancel button to close the window and return to the Flash interface.

2. Click the Size button on the Property inspector. This will open the Document Properties dialog box (shown in Figure 1-7). Other methods of opening this dialog box are as follows:

   - Select Modify ➤ Document.
   - Press Ctrl+J (PC) or Cmd+J (Mac).
   - Right-click (PC) or Ctrl-click (Mac) and select Document Properties from the context menu.
   - Double-click the box that shows 12 fps under the timeline.

> *As you have just seen, there a number of methods you can use in Flash to obtain the same result. In this case, it is opening the* Document Properties *dialog box. Which one is best? The answer is simple: whichever one you choose.*

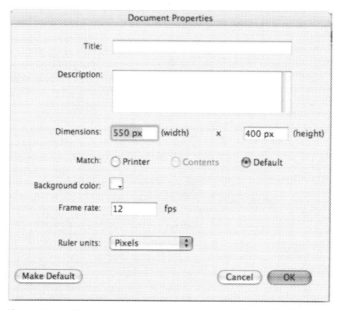

Figure 1-7. Set the stage size through the Document Properties dialog box.

The Title and Description boxes are where you can add a name for the document and write a brief description of the movie. The text you add to these two input boxes is used as the metadata that search engines can use to search your site. You can access this metadata by selecting Show Report in the Publish Options dialog box when the file that goes in the web page is created—the file is called a SWF (pronounced *swiff*).

The Dimensions input area is where you can change the size of the stage. Enter the new dimensions, press the Enter (PC) or Return (Mac) key, and the stage will change. The Match area is commonly used to shrink the stage to the size of the content on the stage. You can also change the stage color and how fast the movie plays in this dialog box. Here's how to change the stage size and stage color:

1. Enter the following values into the Document Properties dialog box:

   - Title: Pond
   - Description: My first Flash exercise
   - Width: 400
   - Height: 300
   - Background color: #000066

2. Click OK and the stage will shrink to the new dimensions and change color to a dark blue. These changes will also be shown in the Property inspector, as shown in Figure 1-8.

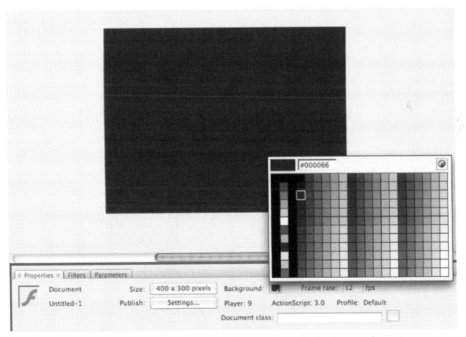

Figure 1-8. Changes made to the document properties are shown in the Property inspector.

The Property inspector

We have been mentioning this panel quite a bit to this point, and now would be a good time to stroll over to it and take a closer look.

The Property inspector is designed to make your life easy. When you select something on the stage, or select the stage itself, the panel will update to reflect the properties that can be changed in regard to what was just selected (see Figure 1-9). As you become more proficient and comfortable with Flash, this panel will become an indispensable aid to your workflow.

The panel is positioned, by default, at the bottom of the screen. You can move it elsewhere on the screen by simply dragging it into position and releasing the mouse. There are locations on the screen where you will see a shadow or darkening of the location when the panel is over it. This color change indicates that the panel can be docked into that location. Otherwise, the panel will "float" above the screen.

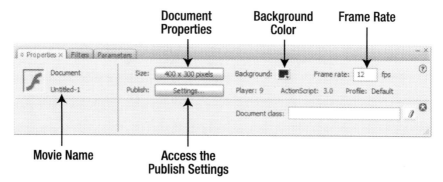

Figure 1-9. The Property inspector

When an object is placed on the stage and selected, the Property inspector will change to reflect the properties of that object that can be manipulated. For example, in Figure 1-10, a box has been drawn on the stage. The Property inspector shows you the type of object that has been selected and tells you the stroke and the fill color of the object can also be changed. As well, you can change how scaling will be applied to the object and the treatment of the red stroke around the box.

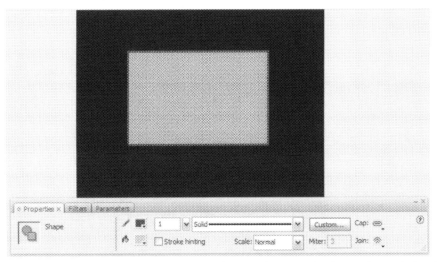

Figure 1-10. The Property inspector changes to show you the properties that can be manipulated regarding a selected object on the stage (in this case, the stroke and fill properties of the box on the stage).

Zooming the stage

There will be occasions when you will discover that the stage is a pretty crowded place. In these situations, you'll want to be sure that each item on the stage is in its correct position and is properly sized. Depending on the size of the stage, this could be difficult because the stage may fill the screen area. Fortunately, Flash allows you to reduce or increase the magnification of the stage through a technique called **zooming**.

> *Zooming the stage has no effect upon the actual stage size.*

Follow these steps to zoom the stage:

1. Click the Magnification drop-down menu near the upper-right corner of the screen (see Figure 1-11). The drop-down contains a variety of sizes ranging from Fit in Window to 800% magnification.

Figure 1-11. Select a zoom level using the Magnification drop-down.

   If you want more zoom, you can get a lot closer than 800%. Select View ➤ Zoom In to increase the zoom level to 2000%. If you want a real god's-eye view of the stage, Zoom Out allows you to reduce the magnification level to 8%. For you keyboard junkies, Zoom In is Ctrl+= and Zoom Out is Ctrl+-. On the Mac, the commands are Command++ to zoom in and Command+- to zoom out.

2. Click the 400% option, and the stage will fill the screen (as shown in Figure 1-12). Click the Show Frame option and the stage will be visible in its entirety.

Figure 1-12. Selecting a 400% zoom level brings you close to the action.

If you want a side-by-side comparison in which one image is at 100% view and the other is at 400% or 800%, follow these steps:

1. Select Window ➤ Duplicate Window. The current document will appear in a separate tab.

2. Set the new window's magnification level to 400% or 800%.

3. Select Window ➤ Tile. The two windows will appear beside each other, and any change made to the contents in one window will be reflected in the other window (see Figure 1-13). This is a handy feature if you need to really zoom in on an object or the stage to precisely position or change a property, yet want to see how your change will work with the rest of the content on the stage.

4. To close a window, click its Close button.

Figure 1-13. Duplicating a window and then tiling the open windows gives you a bird's-eye view and a detailed view of your work simultaneously.

Exploring the panels in the Flash interface

At this point in our stroll through the Flash interface, you have had the chance to play with a few of the panels. We also suspect that by this point you have discovered that the Flash interface is modular. By that we mean that it's an interface composed of a series of panels that contain the tools and features you will use on a regular basis, rather than an interface that's locked in place and fills the screen. You have also discovered that these panels can be moved around and opened or closed depending upon your workflow needs. In this section, we are going to take a closer look at the more important panels that you will use every day. They include the following:

- The timeline
- The Property inspector
- The Tools panel
- The library
- The Actions panel
- The Help panel

The timeline

There is a fundamental truth to becoming proficient with Flash: master the timeline and you will master Flash.

When somebody visits your site and an animation plays, Flash treats that animation as a series of still images. In many respects, those images are comparable to the images in a roll of film or one of those flip books you may have played with when you were younger. The ordering of those images on the film or in the book is determined by their placement on the film or in the book. In Flash, the order of images in an animation is determined by the timeline.

The timeline, therefore, controls what the user sees, and more importantly, when he or she sees it.

At its most basic, all animation is movement over time, and all animation has a start point and an end point. The length of your timeline will determine when animations start and end, and the number of frames between those two points will determine the length of the animation. As the author, you control those factors.

For example, Figure 1-14 shows you a simple animation. A ball is placed at the left and right edges of the stage. In between, the ball is at the top of the stage. From this, you can gather that the ball will move upward when the sequence starts and will continue to its finish position at the right edge of the stage once it has reached the middle of the sequence.

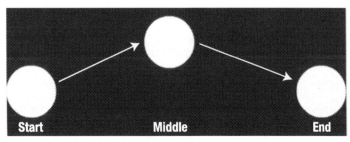

Figure 1-14. A simple animation sequence

Obviously, just having three images won't result in a ball moving. Between the start and the middle, and the middle and the end points, there needs to be a series of ball images. These will give the user the illusion of a ball moving up and returning down to its finish position. These images will represent the various locations of the ball as it moves through time (as shown in Figure 1-15).

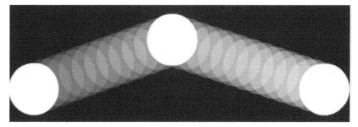

Figure 1-15. Animation is a series of frames on the timeline.

So where does time come into play? It is the number of frames between the start and middle or middle and end points in the animation. The default timing in a Flash movie—called **frame rate**—is 12 frames per second (fps). In the animation shown previously, the duration of the animation is 24 frames, which means it will play for 2 seconds. You can assume from this that the ball's middle location is the 12th frame of the timeline. If, for example, you wanted to speed up the animation, you would reduce the length of the timeline to 12 frames; if you wanted to slow it down, you would increase the number of frames to 48.

> *In the lower-left corner of the timeline, under the layers, is an icon that looks like a piece of film. It is the* Hide Timeline *button. Click it and the timeline will be minimized. Click it again and the timeline will return. If you are a Flash 8 user, note that this icon replaces the* Timeline *button that was located in the upper-left corner of the timeline.*

Let's wander over to the timeline and look at a frame.

Frames

If you unroll a spool of movie film, you will see that it is composed of a series of individual still images. Each image is called a frame, and this analogy applies just as well to Flash as it does for the film industry.

Figure 1-16. The timeline is nothing more than a series of frames.

When you open Flash, your timeline will be empty, but you will see a series of rectangles—these are the frames. You may also notice that these frames are divided into groups. Most frames are white and every fifth frame is gray (see Figure 1-16).

Flash movies can range in length from 1 to 16,000 frames, although a Flash movie that is 16,000 frames in length is highly unusual. The thing you need to keep in mind is that a frame shows you the content that is on the stage at any point in time. The content in a frame can range from one object to hundreds of objects, and a frame can include audio, video, code, images, text, and drawings either singly or in combination with each other.

When you first open a new Flash document, you will notice that frame 1 contains a hollow circle. This visual clue tells you that frame 1 is waiting for you to add something to it. Let's look at a movie that actually has something in the frames and examine some of the features of frames:

1. Open the Ball.fla file located in the Chapter 1 Exercise folder. When the file opens you will see a yellow ball, in frame 1, sitting on the stage. You should also note the solid dot in the Ball layer. This indicates that here is content in the frame.

2. Place the cursor on any frame of the timeline and right-click (PC) or Ctrl-click (Mac) to open the context menu that applies to frames (see Figure 1-17).

Figure 1-17. The context menu that applies to frames on the timeline

As you can see, there are quite a few options available to you, ranging from adding a frame to the timeline to adding code that controls the objects in the frame (code blocks added to the movie are referred to as **actions**). We aren't going to dig into what each menu item does yet, but we guarantee that by the time you finish this book, you will have used each menu item. Instead let's deal with the absolute basics.

3. Place the cursor at frame 12, open the context menu, and select Insert Keyframe. Repeat this step at frame 24 as well. What you will notice is that the timeline changes to the series of gray frames and three black dots shown in Figure 1-18.

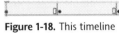

Figure 1-18. This timeline contains three keyframes.

> *If you prefer to use the keyboard, place the cursor at frame 24 and press F5. With that frame selected, press F6. The F5 command adds a frame and F6 converts the selected frame to a keyframe. If you just want to add a keyframe, select frame 24 and press F6.*

An obvious question at this point is, "So, guys, what's a keyframe?" Remember when we talked earlier about animations and how they had a start point and an end point? In Flash, those two points are called **keyframes**; any movement or changes can only occur between keyframes. In Flash, there are two types of keyframes: those with stuff in them (indicated by the solid dot shown in frame 1 of Figure 1-17) and those with nothing in them. The latter are called **blank keyframes**, and they are shown as frames with a hollow dot. The first frame in any layer, until you add something to that frame, is always indicated by a blank keyframe.

4. To navigate to specific frames in the timeline, you use the playhead. It is the red rectangle with the line coming out of it. Drag the playhead to frame 12 and click the ball on the stage. Move the ball to the top center of the stage. Drag the playhead to frame 24 and move the ball to the right edge of the stage.

> *The technique of dragging the playhead across the timeline is called scrubbing. As you scrub across the timeline, you will also see the values in the* Current Frame *and* Elapsed Time *areas at the bottom of the timeline change as well. This is quite useful in locating a precise frame number or time in the animation.*

5. Right-click (PC) or Ctrl-click (Mac) between the first two keyframes to open the context menu. Select Create Motion Tween. Repeat this step between the next two keyframes. When you release the mouse, an arrow will appear between the frames.

Simple animations are created in Flash using **motion tweens**. Flash looks at the locations of the objects between two keyframes, creates copies of those objects, and puts them in their positions in the frame. If you scrub through your timeline, you will see that Flash has placed copies of the ball in frames 2 through 11 and 13 through 24, and put them in their final positions to give the illusion that the ball is moving up and down.

> *That was interesting, but we suspect you may be wondering, "OK, guys, do tweens only work for stuff that moves?" Nope. You can also use tweens to change the shapes of objects, their color, their opacity, and a number of other properties. We'll get to them in Chapter 7.*

6. Drag the playhead to frame 12 and click the ball on the stage. Drag the ball to the bottom of the stage. If you scrub through the timeline, you will see the ball move in the opposite direction. This tells you that you can change an animation by simply changing the location of an object in a keyframe.

7. Save the movie as Ball1.fla to the Chapter 1 Exercise folder.

Using the Property inspector

Another key concept to grasp, especially if you are new to Flash, is that everything on the stage has properties that can be changed or otherwise manipulated. To understand this concept, let's step away from Flash and consider the authors of this book.

At our most basic, we are two humans on the planet Earth. In Flash terms, we are two objects on the stage. The things that describe us are our properties. For example, our height, weight, hair color, and location on the planet are properties that describe each of us. If we were somehow able to be placed on the Flash stage, those things that describe us would appear in the Property inspector. The neat thing about the Property inspector is that we can use it to change our properties. Let's wander over to the Property inspector and have a look:

1. Open the file named Properties.fla in the Chapter 1 Exercise folder. When the file opens, you will see an image of kayaks over a black background and the words Ocean Kayaks at the bottom of the stage.

2. Click the Selection tool, which is the solid black arrow at the top of the Tools panel (see Figure 1-19).

Figure 1-19. Click a tool or use the keyboard to select it.

> *Clicking tools is one way of selecting them. Another way is to use the keyboard. When you roll the cursor over a tool, you will see a tooltip containing the name of the tool and a letter. For example, the letter beside the* Selection *tool is* V. *Press the V key and the* Selection *tool will be highlighted in the* Tools *panel.*

3. Click the text once. The Property inspector will change to show you that you have selected some text and that you can change a lot of the text's properties.

4. In the Property inspector, click the Fill color chip to open the Color Picker, as shown in Figure 1-20. Click the white color, and the text will turn white. You have just changed the color property of the selected text.

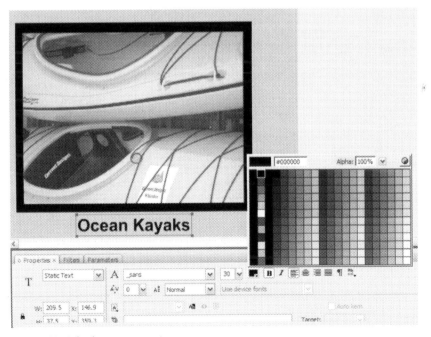

Figure 1-20. Color is a text property.

19

5. Click the gray area of the stage. The Property inspector will change to show you the stage properties. Change the stage color to a dark gray: #666666. When you select the color, the stage will change color and the color selected will appear in the Property inspector.

6. Click the black box surrounding the image. The Property inspector will change to tell you that you have selected a shape and that the fill color for this shape is black. It also lets you know that there is no stroke around the shape. At the left side of the Property inspector are four boxes that tell you the width, height, and x and y coordinates of the shape on the stage. Select the Width value and change it from 428.9 to 435. Change the Height number from 333 to 335, as shown in Figure 1-21. Each time you make a change, the selected object will get wider or higher.

Figure 1-21. The width, height, stage location, fill, and stroke are properties of objects on the stage.

The Tools panel

The Tools panel, shown in Figure 1-22, is divided into four major areas:

- **Tools**: These selections allow you create, select, and manipulate text and graphics placed on the stage.

- **View**: These allow you to pan across the stage or zoom in on specific areas of the stage.

- **Color**: These tools allow you to select and change fill, stroke, and gradient colors.
- **Options**: This is a context-sensitive area of the panel. In many ways, it is not unlike the Property inspector. It will change depending upon what you have selected.

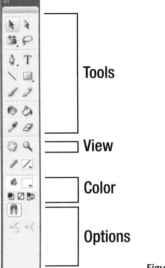

Tools

View

Color

Options

Figure 1-22. The Tools panel

If there is a small down arrow in the bottom-right corner of the tool, this indicates additional tool options. Click and hold that arrow, and the options will appear in a drop-down menu (as shown in Figure 1-23).

Figure 1-23. Some tools contain extra tools, which are shown in a drop-down menu.

The library

The library is one of those features of the application that is so indispensable to Flash developers and designers that we simply can't think of anybody that doesn't use it . . . religiously.

In very simple terms, it is the place where content that is used in the movie is stored for reuse later on in the movie. It is also the place where symbols and copies of components that you may use are automatically placed when the symbols are created or the components are added to the stage.

Let's take a look at the library:

1. Click the Library icon on the right side of the screen. The library will fly out, as shown in Figure 1-24. Inside the library, you will see that the image of the kayaks is actually a library item.

2. Drag a copy of the image from the library to the stage. Leave it selected and press the Delete key. Notice that the image on the stage disappears but the library item is retained.

3. To close the library, click the stage. Another way of opening and closing the library is to press Ctrl+L (PC) or Cmd+L (Mac).

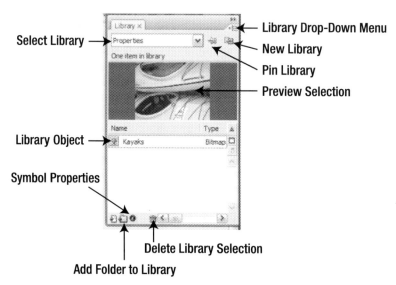

Figure 1-24. The library

Where to get help

In the early days of desktop computing, software was a major purchase and nothing made you feel more comfortable than the manuals that were tucked into the box. If you had a problem, you opened the manual and searched for the solution. Those days have long passed. This is especially true with Flash, for as its complexity has grown, the size of the manuals that would need to be packaged with the application would also have grown. In this version of Flash, the user manuals are found in the Help menu. Here's how to access Help:

1. Select Help ➤ Flash Help or press the F1 key. The Help panel that opens (see Figure 1-25) is one of the most comprehensive sources of Flash knowledge on the planet and, best of all, it's free.

The panel is divided into two areas. One the left side are 17 documents, called books. They cover a variety of subjects ranging from the use of Flash Professional CS3 to the coding languages used to program content for mobile devices. The right side is where the information you are looking for is displayed.

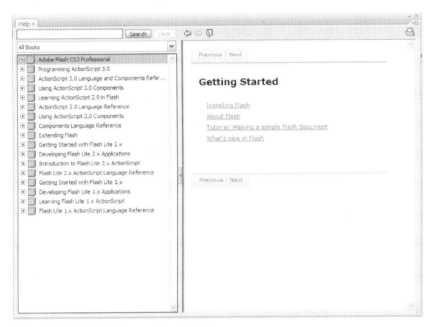

Figure 1-25. The Flash Help panel is extensive.

2. Click the Using Flash book to open it. As you can see, the books are actually collections of individual documents designed to help you learn what you need to know, along with practical examples of specific techniques.

3. To go to a specific topic, just type the word into the text input box at the top of the interface and click the Search button. For example, enter video into this area and click the button. A Working dialog box will appear, and when the progress bar finishes, all of the pages in all of the books containing the word *video* will be shown.

4. Click the first page, Getting Started. The right pane will fill with text, and the word *video* will be highlighted (as shown in Figure 1-26).

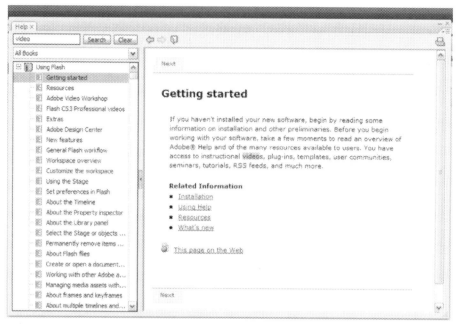

Figure 1-26. Searching a term in the Flash help documents

Using layers

The final stop on our walkabout is back at the top of the interface: the Layers feature of the timeline. There are a few things regarding layers that you need to know:

- You can have as many layers in a Flash movie as you need. They have no effect upon the file size.

- Use layers to manage your movie. Flash movies are composed of objects, media, and code, and it is a standard industry practice to give everything its own layer. This way, you can easily find content on a crowded stage. In fact, any object that is tweened must be on its own layer.

- Layers can be grouped. Layers can be placed in layer folders, which means you can, for example, have a complex animation and have all of the objects in the animation contained in their own layers inside a folder.

- Layers stack on top of each other. For example, you can have a layer with a box in it and another with a ball in it. If the ball layer is above the box layer, the ball will appear to be above the box.

- Name your layers. This is another standard industry practice that makes finding content in the movie very easy.

1

We'd like to mention one other aspect of layers, which we really won't be covering in this chapter, but will be using quite extensively in Chapters 3 and 7 (which deal with symbols and animation, respectively). Layers can also be put to very specific uses, and this is accomplished by assigning one of three layer modes to a layer. The modes are as follows:

- **Guide layer**: A guide layer contains shapes, symbols, images, and so on that you can use to align elements on other layers in a movie. These things are really handy if you have a complex design and want a standard reference for the entire movie. What makes guide layers so important is that they aren't rendered when you publish the SWF. This means, for example, that you could create a comprehensive design (or comp) of the Flash stage in either Fireworks CS3 or Photoshop CS3, place that image in a guide layer, and not have to worry about an overly large SWF being published and bloating the SWF with unnecessary file size and download time. The icon for a guide layer is a hammer.

- **Motion guide layer**: This special layer in many respects is a subset of a guide layer. A motion guide is essentially a path that you draw. This path will be the one followed by an object linked to it. For example, a small circle that meanders across the screen in a wave-like motion is, more often than not, following a motion guide. The motion guide icon looks like an atom on a path.

- **Masking layer**: The shape of an object on a masking layer is used to hide anything outside of the shape, and reveals only whatever is under the object. For example, place an image on the stage and add a box in the layer above it. If that layer is a masking layer, only the pixels of the part of the image directly under the box will be seen. The icon for a masking layer is a square with an oval in the middle of it.

> Flash Professional CS3 now allows you to optionally ignore layers that are hidden when you publish the SWF. (Guide layers aren't hidden. They are simply turned off.)

Let's start using layers—here's how:

1. Open the Layers.fla document. When it opens, you will see two colored shapes on the stage (see Figure 1-27). These shapes are sitting in one layer, and really should be moved to separate layers.

2. Open the library. You will notice that there is an object named Pentagon contained in the library. That object is a movieclip. We'll get into movieclips in a big way in Chapter 3.

3. Each object should be placed on its own layer. Click the New Layer button—it looks like a page with a turned-up corner—directly under the Layer 1 strip. A new layer, named Layer 2, is added to the timeline.

4. Select Layer 1 and add a new layer. Notice how the new layer is placed between Layer 1 and Layer 2. This should tell you that all new layers added to the timeline are added directly above the currently selected layer. Obviously, Layer 3 is out of position. Let's fix that.

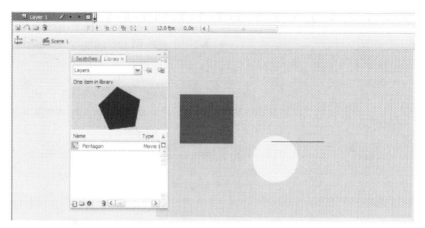

Figure 1-27. We start with two objects on the stage and one in the library.

5. Drag Layer 3 above Layer 2 and release the mouse. Now you know how to reorder layers and move them around in the timeline. Layers can be dragged above or below each other.

6. Add a new layer. Hold on—we have four layers and three objects. The math doesn't work. That new layer has to go.

7. Select Layer 4 and click the Trash Can icon under the Layer 1 strip. Layer 4 will now be deleted (and now you know how to get rid of an extra layer).

8. Double-click the Layer 1 layer name to select it. Rename the layer Box. Now that you know how to rename a layer, rename the remaining two layers Ball and Pentagon.

Content can be added to layers in one of two ways:

- Directly to the layer by moving an object from the library to the layer
- From one layer to another layer

Here's how:

1. Select the Pentagon layer and drag the movieclip from the library to the stage. The hollow dot in the layer will change to a solid dot to indicate that there is content in the frame. When moving objects from the library to the stage, be sure to select the layer, sometimes called a target layer, before you drag and drop. This way you can prevent the content from going in the wrong layer.

2. Click the ball on the stage. Notice how the layer is also selected? This is a handy way of determining the layer where an object is located.

3. Select Edit ➤ Cut, or press Ctrl+X (PC) or Cmd+X (Mac).

4. Click the Ball layer and select Edit ➤ Paste in Place (see Figure 1-28). When you release the mouse, a copy of the ball will appear in the precise location at which you cut it.

Figure 1-28. Paste in Place pastes objects in the precise location of the original object that was either cut or copied to the clipboard.

Whatever happened to a simple paste command in the Edit *menu? The* Paste in Center *command replaces it. It has always been a fact of Flash life that any content on the clipboard is pasted into the center of the stage. The change in name simply acknowledges this. The other paste command—*Paste Special*—opens a dialog box that asks you if you want the contents of the clipboard as text. This is a handy way of adding a block of text from a word processor into Flash.*

Finally, there are three icons—an eyeball, a lock, and a hollow square (shown in Figure 1-29)—above the layers. Let's see what they do:

1. Click the eyeball icon. Notice that everything on the stage disappears and the dots under the eyeball in each layer change to a red *x*. This eyeball is the Layer Visibility icon, and clicking it turns off the visibility of all of the content in the layers. Click the icon again, and everything reappears.

In previous versions of Flash, a layer's visibility did not carry into the SWF file itself. This was a feature to be used for convenience during authoring only. In Flash CS3, invisible layers may optionally be omitted from the published SWF. See File ➤ Publish Settings *and select the* Flash *tab. The preference is listed as a check box labeled* Export hidden layers.

2. This time, select the Pentagon layer, and click the dot under the eyeball. Just the pentagon disappears. What this tells you is that you can turn off the visibility for a specific layer by clicking the dot in the visibility column.

Figure 1-29. The Layer Visibility, Lock, and Show All Layers As Outlines icons. Note the Pencil icon in the Ball layer, which tells you that you can add content to that layer.

3. When you click a layer, you may notice that a Pencil icon appears on the layer strip. This tells you that you can add content to the layer. Click the Ball layer, and you'll see the Pencil icon. Now, click the dot under the lock in the Ball layer. The Lock icon will replace the dot. When you lock a layer, you can't draw on it or add content to it. You can see this because the pencil has a stroke through it. If you try to drag the pentagon symbol from the library to the Ball layer, you will also see that the layer has been locked because the cursor changes from an arrow to a circle with a line through it. Also, if you try to click the ball on the stage, you won't be able to select it. This is handy to know in situations where precision is paramount and you don't want to accidentally move something or, god forbid, delete something from the stage.

4. The final icon is the Show All Layers As Outlines icon. Click it and the content on the stage turns into outlines. This is somewhat akin to the wireframe display mode available in many 3D modeling applications. In Flash, it can be useful in cases where dozens of objects overlap, and you simply want a quick "X-ray view" of how your content is arranged. With animation, in particular, it can be helpful to evaluate the motion of objects without having to consider the distraction of color and shading. Like visibility and locking, the Show All Layers As Outlines icon is also available on a per-layer basis.

> You can change the color used for the outline in a layer by double-clicking the color chip in the layer strip. This will open the Layer Properties dialog box. Double-click the color chip in the dialog box to open the Color Picker; then click a color, and that color will be used.
>
> Want to hide the layers to buy yourself some screen real estate? Double-click the bar where you see the Scene 1 link. The stage will slide up to cover the layers.
>
> You can also click the Hide Timeline button beside the Scene 1 link to achieve the same effect. Click it again, and the layers will be revealed. Drag the bar downward and you can make more room for more layers.

You can also group layers using folders. Here's how:

1. Click the Folder icon in the Layers panel. A new unnamed folder—Folder 1—will appear on the timeline. You can rename a folder by double-clicking its name and entering a new name.

2. Drag the three layers into the folder. As each one is placed in the folder, notice how the name indents. This tells you that the layer is in a folder.

3. Next, remove the layers from the folder. To do so, simply drag the layer above the folder on the timeline. You can also drag it to the left to unindent it.

4. To delete the folder, select it and click the Trash Can icon.

Don't think you can simply select a folder and click the Trash Can *icon to remove it. Make sure that the folder is empty. If you delete a folder that contains layers, those layers will also be deleted. If this happens to you, Adobe will send a life raft in your direction. An alert box telling you that you will also be deleting the layers in the folder will appear. Click* Cancel *instead of* OK.

Now that you have had a chance to wander through the interface and try out a few things, let's put what you've learned to practical use. Moving squares and circles around the stage isn't exactly why you are here, so let's take what you have learned and hike over to Lake Nanagook.

Your turn: Building a Flash movie

In this exercise, you are going to expand on your knowledge. We have shown you where many of the interface features can be found and how they can be used, so we are now going to give you the opportunity to see how all of these features combine to create a Flash movie.

You will be undertaking such tasks as the following:

- Using the Property inspector to precisely position and resize objects on the stage
- Creating layers and adding content from the library to the layers
- Using the drawing tools to create a shape
- Creating a simple animation through the use of a tween
- Saving a Flash movie
- Testing a Flash movie

By the end of this exercise, you will have a fairly good understanding of how a Flash movie is assembled and the workflow involved in the process.

1. Open the MoonOverLakeNanagook.fla file.

2. When the file opens, open the library as well, if it isn't already, by selecting Window ➤ Library or pressing Ctrl+L (PC) or Cmd+L (Mac). As shown in Figure 1-30, you are starting with a blank stage, a few movieclips, an audio file, and a graphic symbol.

3. The specifications for the project state the stage is to be 400 pixels wide by 300 pixels high. It also calls for a dark blue stage color to give the illusion of night. Click the Size button on the Property inspector to open the Document Properties dialog box. Change the Width value to 400 and the Height value to 300.

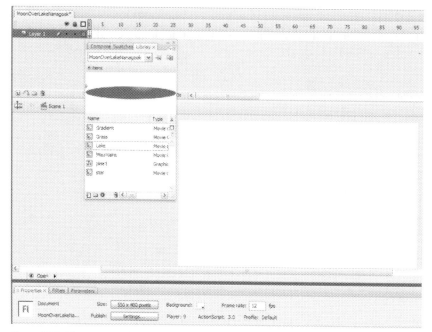

Figure 1-30. The assets are in place. It is your job to turn them into a movie.

4. Click the Background color chip to open the Color Picker. Select the color text entry area and change it from #FFFFFF to #000066 (dark blue). Click OK to accept the changes and close the dialog box. The stage will shrink to its new size and be colored a dark blue. The new size and color will now appear in the Property inspector, as shown in Figure 1-31.

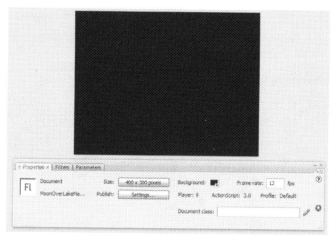

Figure 1-31. The stage is set.

5. Rename Layer 1 to gradient. Drag the Gradient movieclip from the library to the stage.

Though using your eyes for object placement on the stage is a great way to get stuff into position, your eyes aren't as precise as Flash. The gradient needs to completely cover the stage and not hang out on the pasteboard by even one pixel. Here's how you do that:

6. Click the gradient on the stage to select it. In the Property inspector, set its x and y values to 0. The object will align itself with the upper-left corner of the stage.

7. Click frame 60 of the gradient layer and press the F5 key. What this does is add a frame to the timeline; you can do this because the layer expands to 60 frames and a rectangle (indicating a frame) is shown at the end of the layer.

When Flash measures the location of an object on the stage, it uses the upper-left corner of the stage as the 0, 0 point. The actual movement is done using what is called the **registration point** of the object. In the case of this gradient, the registration point of the symbol is the upper-left corner of the symbol. If the registration point of the gradient were, say, at 200 and 150, the gradient would be placed partly on the pasteboard and partly on the stage (as shown in Figure 1-32). The registration point for the gradient symbol is the + sign you see in the upper-left corner of the symbol.

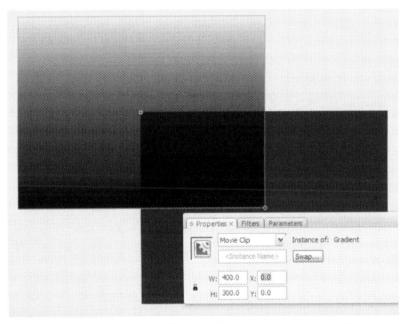

Figure 1-32. The stage and the object's registration point determine the position on the stage when using the Property inspector.

One of the really great things about Flash is that, as Flash designers, we can practice the art of illusion. If you look at the gradient on the stage, you will notice that the sky is a dark blue that gradually changes to black as it approaches the bottom of the stage. This gives the illusion of a night sky. Let's look at how this is accomplished:

8. Double-click the Gradient symbol in the library to open the Symbol Editor.

The Symbol Editor looks suspiciously like the main timeline. In fact, symbols have their own timelines that can function independently of the main timeline. You'll see what we mean by this in a couple of minutes. For now, let's just get you oriented. Beside the Scene 1 link under the layers, you will see a Movieclip icon. This tells you that you are in the Symbol Editor. Click the Scene 1 link and you will be returned to the main timeline. But for now, get yourself back to the Symbol Editor.

9. Click the gradient. The first thing you should notice is that the gradient becomes pixelated. This is a visual clue that you have selected a vector.

10. Click the Color panel to open the Color palette. When it opens you will see that the gradient is a linear gradient that runs from opaque to transparent black. The default colors for any gradient you create are black and white, but these can be changed at any time with the little arrows under the gradient strip, which are called crayons. Click the left black crayon and you will see the color appear in hexadecimal format: #000000. Note that the Alpha value is 100%. **Alpha** is Flash's term for opacity, and 100% means that the color is fully opaque; in other words, it cannot be seen through it at all. Click the right black crayon. This time, the Alpha value is 0% (as shown in Figure 1-33). Now you know how the illusion of a night sky was created.

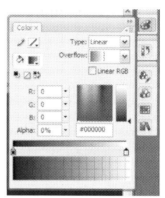

Figure 1-33. Use the Color panel to fill shapes with gradients.

The color in the gradient is rotated to fade in from transparent black to opaque black. As the color moves from the top to the bottom, the pixels become visible, hiding the blue. As they increase in number, the black takes over and the blue looks like it is transforming to black.

Adding the mountains and playing with color

With the stage prepared and the sky in place, you can now turn your attention to adding the assets to the movie. The scene involves mountains, trees, grass, a lake, and the moon. What this tells you is that the objects furthest away need to be placed near the bottom of the layering order. This means that the mountains are the next piece of content to be added.

1. Click Scene 1. Add a new layer to the movie and name it mountains.

2. With the new layer selected, open the library and drag the Mountains movieclip onto the stage.

3. With the mountains selected on the stage, in the Property inspector, set the X value to –34 and the Y value to 203. The mountain range will sit at the bottom of the stage and hang off of both sides of the stage. There is, of course, one great big problem: the mountains are black and they have been placed against a black background. Let's fix that.

4. Select the mountains on the stage and, in the Color area of the Property inspector, select Tint from the drop-down menu. The Property inspector will change to show you a color chip, a tint percentage, and the RGB color of the selected object.

Remember what we said earlier: everything on the stage has unique properties . . . including its color. Changing the tint of a selected object allows you to manipulate the color property of that instance. The original library asset's color is not affected.

5. Click the color chip, and when the Color Picker opens, select the dark gray color directly under the black chip on the left side of the picker (#333333). The mountains become a lot more distinct, but they are now too obvious.

6. With the mountains still selected, click the Tint Amount button, and when the slider appears, pull it down until the value is 50% (as shown in Figure 1-34). If you are a power user, feel free to simply double-click the value and enter 50.

7. Select frame 60 and press the F5 key to add a frame.

8. Now would be a good time to save your work. Select File ➤ Save As, and when the Save As dialog box opens, navigate to the Exercise folder for this chapter and rename the project. Click OK to close the dialog box.

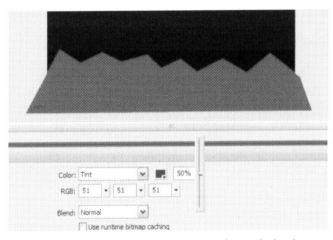

Figure 1-34. Objects can have their color properties manipulated.

Using trees to create the illusion of depth

The mountains are in place and are faintly visible against the night sky. Let's add some depth to the scene by adding a couple of trees. Here's how:

1. Create a new layer named trees.

2. With the trees layer selected, open the library and drag two copies of the Trees symbol to the stage. You may notice that the icon for the trees is different from the other symbols in the library. This symbol indicates that the tree is a **graphic symbol**. Graphic symbols are objects created with the various drawing tools in Flash—which is the case with the tree—or when a photograph is added to the library. These objects rarely get put into motion.

One of the authors read the previous sentence and wrote, "Au contraire, mon frère." In actual fact, graphic symbols' timelines are locked in step with the main timeline. This explains why graphics are the de facto symbol for JibJab-style animation (www.jibjab.com/). Complex nested symbols can be scrubbed in this way for testing, whereas movieclips could not. As you can see, there are exceptions to most rules in Flash.

A symbol placed on the stage is called an "instance."

3. The first thing you should notice is that one tree is in front of the other. This tells you that not only can you stack objects on the stage through the layering order, but you can also stack objects in layers as well.

4. Select the tree at the back.

5. Use these values to precisely place the selected tree on the stage, resize it, and darken it:

- W: 65
- H: 105
- X: 49
- Y: 178.5

- Color: Tint
- Tint Color: #000000 (black)
- Tint Amount: 48%

The tree gets smaller, moves to the left side of the stage, and darkens. Resizing the image and darkening it is what gives the illusion of depth in this scene.

6. Select the remaining tree and use these values in the Property inspector:

- W: 68
- H: 123
- X: 76.2
- Y: 160.6

- Color: Tint
- Tint Color: #000000 (black)
- Tint Amount: 26%

The tree gets a bit smaller, moves to the left side of the stage, and, due to the low tint amount, becomes a bit brighter than the tree behind it (as shown in Figure 1-35). The reason for this is that it will be lit by the moon, which you will create in a couple of minutes.

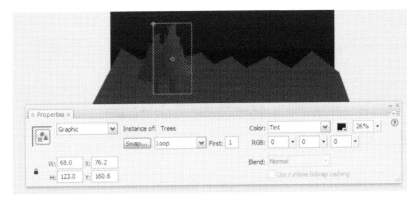

Figure 1-35. Location and size are other properties that can be manipulated using the Property inspector.

Let's finish off the scene by adding the grass and the lake.

7. Add a new layer named grass. With this new layer selected, drag the Grass movieclip to the stage. Set its X and Y coordinates in the Property inspector to −277.6 and 268.9, respectively.

8. Add a new layer named lake. With this new layer selected, drag the Lake movieclip to the stage. Set its X and Y coordinates in the Property inspector to −252 and 274, respectively.

So far, so good. It is starting to look like Lake Nanagook (see Figure 1-36), but we need to add two more elements—the moon and a twinkling star—to make it a bit more realistic. We obviously need the moon because it is reflected in the lake, and a twinkling star is a subtle bit of eye candy that will make the scene that much more interesting and catch the viewer's attention. Let's start with the star.

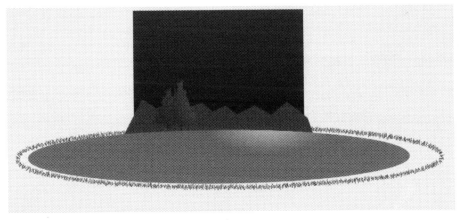

Figure 1-36. The project is starting to come together.

Using a motion tween to create a twinkling star

One of the consistent messages running throughout this chapter is that we, as Flash designers, are illusionists. In this exercise, you will discover how to create the illusion of a star twinkling in the night sky. Here's how:

1. Open the library and double-click the star movieclip to open it in the Symbol Editor. When the movieclip opens, you will see that it is composed of a layer named diamond. The shape on the stage was created using the new Rectangle Primitive tool, making the sides concave and filling the shape with #FFCC00, which is a gold color.

> *If the shape is too small, select the Magnifying Glass tool on the* Tools *panel, and click and drag it across the star. This is how you can precisely zoom in on an object on the stage.*

2. Add a new layer named diamond2. Click the star in the diamond layer and copy it to the clipboard.

3. Select the first frame of the diamond2 layer and select Edit ➤ Paste in Place.

4. Select frame 60 of the diamond2 layer and press the F6 key to add a keyframe.

5. Move the playhead back to frame 1 and click the star. This will select the star in the diamond2 layer.

6. In the Property inspector, change its color to #FFFF99, which is a faint yellow color.

7. Click anywhere between the two keyframes on the diamond2 layer.

One of the really interesting aspects of the Property inspector is that it allows you to put objects in motion. In this case, you are going to have the star rotate 360 degrees in a clockwise direction, and best of all, it only requires a couple of mouse clicks.

8. Select Motion from the Tween drop-down in the Property inspector. Select CW from the Rotate drop-down and make sure the number 1 is in the times text entry area. When you finish, you will see that a motion tween has been added to the timeline (as shown in Figure 1-37).

9. Scrub across the frames to see the rotation.

10. Double-click the Magnifying Glass tool to revert to the 100% view, and click the Scene 1 link on the timeline to return to the main timeline. Save the project.

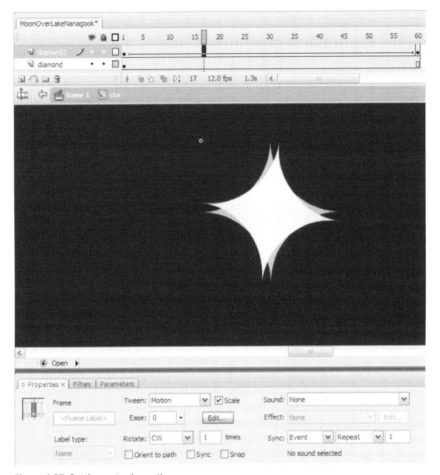

Figure 1-37. Putting a star in motion

A moon over Lake Nanagook

To this point, we have essentially handed you the assets and let you put them in place and otherwise manipulate them. It is now your turn to go solo and create the moon that rises over Lake Nanagook.

1. Start by making sure the Object Drawing button on the toolbar is not selected. Select Insert ➤ New Symbol. This will open the New Symbol dialog box. Name the symbol Moon and select Movie clip as its Type. Click OK. The dialog box will close and the Symbol Editor will open.

> *So far we have used the term* movieclip *and not put a space between the two words. Why then is the term broken into two words in the dialog box? The use of the single word has developed into a standard throughout the worldwide community when writing about Flash. The split word in the dialog box is actually one of the very few references you will see from Adobe using this terminology, which has its root back in an early release of Flash.*

2. Rename Layer 1 to bg. Add a new layer named shadow.

3. In the Tools panel, click and hold the Rectangle tool, and when the drop-down appears, select the Oval tool.

4. Click the Stroke color chip in the Tools panel to open the Color Picker. Select the red on the left as the stroke color (#FF0000). Click the Fill color chip in the Tools panel and select a light blue.

5. With the Oval tool, click the stage and drag out a circle. Select the circle, and in the Property inspector, change its width and height values to 120 and set the x and y coordinates to 0.

6. Add a new layer named Shadow. Select the moon, being careful to select both the stroke and the fill, and copy it to the clipboard.

7. Select the new layer and paste the shape on the clipboard into the new layer.

8. With the shape still selected, move it up and over the bottom layer until the intersection shape looks a bit like a football, or for those of you not in North America, a rugby ball. Click the red stroke on the object in the shadow layer to select it. Press the Delete key to remove it. You now have a solid blue circle over one with a red stroke (as shown in Figure 1-38).

9. Select the red stroke around the circle in the bg layer and cut it. Select the shadow layer and select Edit ➤ Paste in Place.

   What has happened here is that the circle you just pasted into the shadow layer has actually created the football shape for you.

10. Click the blue circle in the shadow layer, which is outside of the stroke. Press the Delete key. Now select and delete the stroke. If you turn off the visibility of the bg layer, you will see that you have created the shadow shape. Let's make it a true shadow.

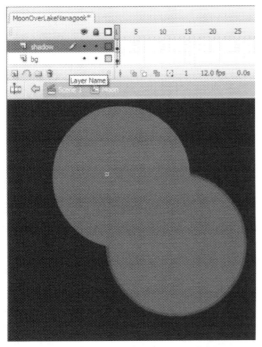

Figure 1-38. The moon shadow starts out as a couple of circles.

11. Click the shape to select it, and then open the Color panel.

12. Set the fill color to #000066 and reduce the alpha value to 36%. Turn on the visibility of the bg layer and you will see that you indeed have a shadow (as shown in Figure 1-39).

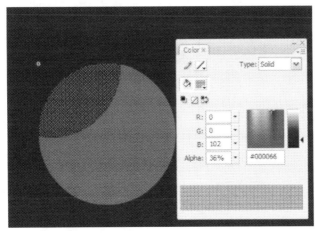

Figure 1-39. The shadow is created by using the Color panel.

The final step in the process of creating the moon is to add a gradient fill in order to give it a bit of a glow. Follow these steps:

1. Select the circle in the bg layer and open the Color panel.

2. Select Radial from the Type drop-down. The moon turns into a black-and-white radial gradient.

3. Click the black crayon to select it. Change the hex color under the Color Picker to #C4DDEE.

4. Click the white crayon and change its color to #93BDE0. The moon takes on a faint glow, thanks to the similar colors in the gradient (see Figure 1-40).

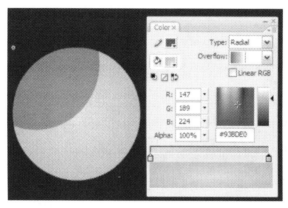

Figure 1-40. Add a radial gradient through the Color panel.

5. Click the Scene 1 link to return to the main timeline.

6. Add a layer named star and another named moon, and set their duration to 60 frames by adding a frame at frame 60 of each layer.

7. Add the star symbol to the star layer, and set its x and y coordinates to 219 and 42, respectively.

8. Add the moon symbol to the moon layer, and set its x and y coordinates to 241 and 43, respectively.

Next, let's really make the moon and the star glow in the sky over Lake Nanagook. Let's add a glow effect to both of them. Here's how:

9. Select the star on the stage and click the Filters tab on the Property inspector.

10. Click the + sign to open a pop-up menu list of the filters. Select the glow filter.

11. Use these settings in the glow filter:

- Blur X: 14
- BlurY: 14
- Strength: 418%
- Quality: High
- Color: #93BDE0

The star looks like it's about to go into supernova. Let's make it a bit smaller.

12. With the star selected on the stage, set its width and height values in the Property inspector to 13.

13. Select the moon on the stage and apply the following glow values:

- Blur X: 26
- Blur Y: 26
- Strength: 70%
- Quality: High
- Color: #93BDE0

The moon and the star should now look like they belong together in the sky (as shown in Figure 1-41).

> Filters, introduced in the previous version of Flash, can only be added to movieclips, text fields, and buttons.

14. Save the project.

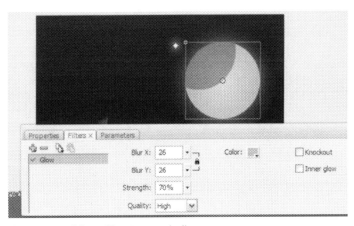

Figure 1-41. Adding a filter to a movieclip

Breaking the stillness of the night at Lake Nanagook

If we are going to have an outdoor scene, it only makes sense to add a bit of outdoor sound to the mix. Fortunately, adding audio to a Flash file is not terribly complicated.

1. Add a new layer above the star layer and name it Audio. Add a frame at frame 60 of the Audio layer.

2. Open the library and locate the Nanagook audio file.

3. Double-click the sound file in the library to open the Sound Properties dialog box (shown in Figure 1-42).

4. Click the Test button to preview the audio file. Ahh, the sounds of crickets and wolves howling in the night. Click OK to close the dialog box.

5. With the Audio layer selected, drag the sound file from the library onto the stage. When you release the mouse, the audio waveform will appear in the layer.

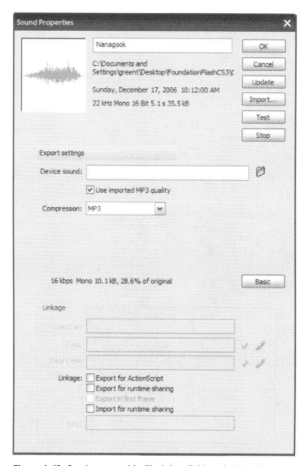

Figure 1-42. Preview sound in Flash by clicking the Test button.

Dragging a sound file from the library to the stage is how an audio file is added to the timeline. In many respects, this is not exactly regarded as a best practice because audio can be big, and when it is in the library, it can increase the SWF size. We have a whole chapter, Chapter 5, devoted to audio best practices, so for now, let's content ourselves with getting sound into the presentation and getting it to play.

6. Click anywhere on the sound's waveform in the Audio layer, and you will see the Property inspector change to show the sound properties.

7. Click the Sync drop-down menu, and select Stream (as shown in Figure 1-43).

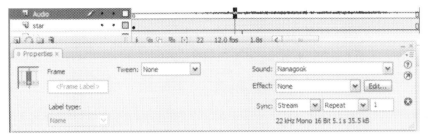

Figure 1-43. Audio on the timeline and the sound properties in the Property inspector

8. Scrub across the timeline and you will hear the audio file. Drag the playback head to frame 1 and press the Return/Enter key. The sound will start playing.

9. Save the file.

> *Picking up a pattern here? Get into the habit of saving the file every time you do something major to your movie. This way, if the computer crashes, you won't have a lot of extra work in front of you trying to reconstruct the movie up to the point of the crash.*

Testing your movie

You have created the animation and scrubbed through the timeline, and everything looks like it is in order. Now would be a good time to test your movie in Flash Player. We can't understate the importance of this step in your workflow. The procedure, as one of the authors is fond of telling his students, is, "Do a bit. Test it. Do a bit more. Test it." The reason for this is that Flash movies can be quite complex. Each element you add to your movie adds to the complexity of the movie, and developing the habit of regularly testing your work, regardless of how simple it may be, will point out mistakes, errors, or problems in the work that you've just completed. What it comes down to is this: do you really want to burrow through a complex movie and even more complex code searching for an issue, or do you want to catch it early? Here's how to test a Flash movie:

1. Press Ctrl+Enter (PC) or Cmd+Return (Mac). You will see an alert box telling you that the movie is being exported, and the movie will open in Flash Player (as shown in Figure 1-44). What you should see is the star twinkling in the sky—and that all of the stuff outside the boundaries of the stage has been trimmed off.

> *If you insist on using a menu, select* Control ➤ Test Movie.

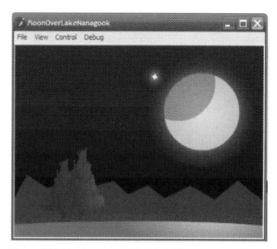

Figure 1-44. Testing a movie in Flash Player

If you open the folder where you saved the FLA file, you will see that a SWF file has also been added to the folder.

Your turn: Moonrise over Lake Nanagook

We have been constantly telling you that Flash involves the art of illusion. The other thing you need to know is that Flash developers are fanatics about detail. They pay close attention to their environment and then try and mimic it in their projects.

In this final piece of this exercise, we are going to get you up close and personal with that last statement. The plan is to have the moon rise into the night sky. On the surface, that sounds like a no-brainer: tween the motion of the moon between its start position and its finish position. Not quite.

This is a night scene, and if there is no moon, things are quite dark. They only light up when the moon is in the sky. If you look at Lake Nanagook, you can see there is a problem. The lake already contains the reflection of the moon. The lake should be dark and only start to light up as the moon rises in the sky. The other issue is the trees, which should be lit by the moon as well; they should begin dark and start to lighten as the moon rises.

Though this may all sound rather complex, this can all be handled by the Property inspector. Follow these steps to start yourself on the path to becoming a fanatic about detail:

1. The first issue is the moon itself. It is in a higher layer. This means that if you animate the moon in its current position, it will appear to rise in front of Lake Nanagook. Drag the moon layer above the gradient layer. Now the moon will rise behind the mountains.

2. Turn off the visibility of the lake layer. You will need to see what you are doing, and the lake will hide the start point of the moon rise.

3. Drag the playhead to frame 24 of the moon layer and add a keyframe. When you have added the keyframe, move the playhead to frame 1.

4. Click the moon on the stage, and in the Property inspector, set its x and y coordinates to 230 and 245.

5. Right-click (PC) or Ctrl-Click (Mac) anywhere between the two keyframes, and select Create Motion Tween from the context menu—the arrow indicating a tween will appear. If you drag the playhead across the animation, you will see the moon rise. Turn on the visibility of the lake layer.

6. Add keyframes in frames 1 and 25 of the lake layer. Return the playhead to frame 1 and click the lake on the stage.

7. With the lake selected, select Brightness from the Color drop-down. Using the slider or keyboard, reduce the Brightness value to –100%. The lake will turn black because you have essentially reduced its brightness to nothing. Add a motion tween and drag the playhead across the movie. As the moon moves upward, the lake starts to get brighter. What you can gather from this is that not only can tweens be used to animate objects, but they can also be used to tween changes in an object's property values.

8. Add keyframes in frames 1 and 25 of the trees layer.

9. Pull the playhead back to frame 1 and select the trees on the stage. Set the Brightness value to –70%. Move the playhead to frame 25, select the trees on the stage, and set their Brightness value to 3% (as shown in Figure 1-45).

10. Save and test the movie. It should look a lot more realistic . . . and you have concluded your introductory walk through Flash CS3 Professional.

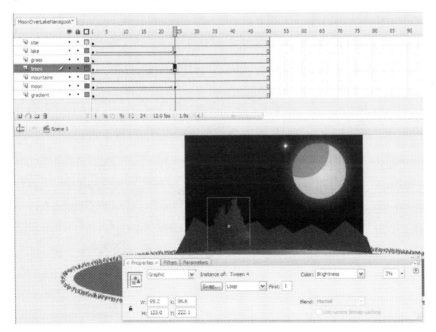

Figure 1-45. An object's properties can also be tweened.

What you've learned

- How to customize your Flash workspace
- A number of methods of manipulating objects on the Flash stage
- How to dock, undock, and minimize panels
- The importance of the Property inspector in your daily workflow
- The difference between a frame and a keyframe
- The process involved in using frames to arrange and animate content and the properties of content on the stage
- How to add, delete, nest, and rearrange layers
- How to test a Flash movie

That's a lot of stuff you've learned by taking a casual stroll through Flash CS3 Professional. In the next chapter, you'll learn how to use the tools to create content in your movies, and how Fireworks CS3, Photoshop CS3, and Illustrator CS3 are important elements in your workflow.

2 GRAPHICS IN FLASH CS3

Horizontal normal, left align
Horizontal normal, center a
Horizontal normal, right alig

Horizontal normal with war

In the previous chapter, we handed you a bunch of images and essentially said, "Here, you toss them on the stage." In this one, we dig into how those objects were created, and in fact you are going to be drawing trees, drawing the moon, creating Venetian blinds, and playing with Chinese dancers and t-shirts, among other things. We will be looking at the new Illustrator and Photoshop File Importers and also playing with JPEG and GIF images. There's a lot to cover. Let's get started.

What we'll cover in this chapter:

- Flash graphic fundamentals
- Using the drawing tools
- Managing and working with color
- Working with fills, strokes, and gradients
- Tracing bitmap images
- Image file formats and Flash
- Importing Illustrator documents into Flash
- Importing Photoshop documents into Flash

Files used in this chapter:

- GradientLock.fla (Chapter02/ExerciseFiles_CH02/Exercise/ GradientLock.fla)
- ImageFill.fla (Chapter02/ExerciseFiles_CH02/Exercise/ImageFill.fla)
- Stools.jpg (Chapter02/ExerciseFiles_CH02/Exercise/Stools.jpg)
- Dancer.jpg (Chapter02/ExerciseFiles_CH02/Exercise/Dancer.jpg)
- Trace.fla (Chapter02/ExerciseFiles_CH02/Exercise/Trace.fla)
- JPGCompression.fla (Chapter02/ExerciseFiles_CH02/Exercise/ JPGCompression.fla)
- JPGCompression.swf (Chapter02/ExerciseFiles_CH02/Exercise/ JPGCompression.swf)
- GIF.fla (Chapter02/ExerciseFiles_CH02/Exercise/GIF.fla)
- Counterforce.gif (Chapter02/ExerciseFiles_CH02/Exercise/ ICounterforce.gif)
- Fireworks.fla (Chapter02/ExerciseFiles_CH02/Exercise/Fireworks.fla)
- Clouds.png (Chapter02/ExerciseFiles_CH02/Exercise/Clouds.png)
- x-factor.ai (Chapter02/ExerciseFiles_CH02/Exercise/x-factor.ai)
- banner.psd (Chapter02/ExerciseFiles_CH02/Exercise/banner.psd)
- wheat_grass_01.psd (Chapter02/ExerciseFiles_CH02/Exercise/ wheat_grass_01.psd)
- wheat_grass_02.psd (Chapter02/ExerciseFiles_CH02/Exercise/ wheat_grass_02.psd)

- wheat_grass_03.psd (Chapter02/ExerciseFiles_CH02/Exercise/
  wheat_grass_03.psd)
- text_fields_01.psd (Chapter02/ExerciseFiles_CH02/Exercise/
  text_fields_01.psd)
- text_fields_02.psd (Chapter02/ExerciseFiles_CH02/Exercise/
  text_fields_02.psd)
- banner.swf (Chapter02/ExerciseFiles_CH02/Exercise/banner.swf)
- banner.fla (Chapter02/ExerciseFiles_CH02/Exercise/banner.fla)

Before we start, let's take a look at what you have to work with.

Graphics in Flash CS3 come in two flavors: vector or bitmap. **Vector images** are usually created in a drawing application such as Illustrator CS3 or Fireworks CS3. When you draw an object on the Flash stage, you are using the drawing tools to create a vector image. **Bitmap images** are created in such applications as Photoshop CS3 and Fireworks CS3. (Yes, Fireworks is comfortable in both worlds.)

At its heart, Flash is a vector drawing and animation tool. The great thing about vectors is their relatively small file size compared to their bitmap cousins. The other thing to keep in mind is that Flash's roots were as a vector animation tool (FutureSplash) for the Web. When it was introduced, broadband was just establishing itself, and the ubiquitous 56K modem was how many people connected to the Internet. In those days, size was paramount, and vectors, being extremely small, loaded very quickly.

What makes vectors so appealing is they require very little information and computing power to draw. In very simplistic terms, a circle of 100 pixels in diameter contains five points—four on the circle and one in the center—and those points are used in a mathematical calculation that results in the diameter of the circle. The computer also needs to know whether there is a stroke around the circle and whether the circle is being filled with a solid color. If you assume the circle is yellow and the stroke is 1 point wide and colored black, this circle really only contains eight pieces of information to draw—the five points, fill color, stroke width, and stroke color.

Its bitmap counterpart is treated a lot differently. Instead of requiring a limited amount of information to draw the circle, each pixel's location in the circle is remembered. Not only that, each pixel will require three more chunks of color information to produce the red, green, and blue values for that pixel. On top of that, the computer also needs to map and draw each pixel in the background the circle is sitting on. This means the amount of information that needs to be rendered by the computer to produce the yellow circle measures in the thousands, which explains why bitmap images on average take a bit longer to appear on the screen.

Vectors are also device independent. This means they can be scaled to 200% and still maintain their crisp edges. Scale a bitmap by that percentage, and the pixels become twice their size. The image degrades because the pixels are "tied" to the device displaying them, which in this case is a computer monitor. If you've ever printed a photograph and seen a series of blocks in it, as if a mesh had been laid over the image, you've experienced what can happen when a device-dependent format is handled by another device.

What types of graphic objects can Flash use? Flash uses four types of graphic objects:

- **Shapes**: These are usually vector drawings created using the Flash drawing tools or files imported into Flash from Illustrator CS3 or Fireworks CS3.
- **Drawing objects**: These are another sort of shape you draw using the Flash drawing tools.
- **Primitives**: These are created by using the Rectangle Primitive and Oval Primitive tools in the Tools panel.
- **Bitmaps**: These are images usually created in Photoshop CS3 and Fireworks CS3.

So much for the raw material—let's dig into drawing in Flash.

> *As you can see in this list, there is a new addition to the drawing tools in Flash: primitive shapes. In order to keep this chapter to a manageable size and not overwhelm you, we will touch on them later in Chapter 7.*

The Tools panel

The Tools panel, shown in Figure 2-1, is where all of your drawing tools are located. Used along with Flash's Property inspector, effects, blends, and Color panels, Flash's drawing tools put a pretty powerful and high-end graphics package at your disposal.

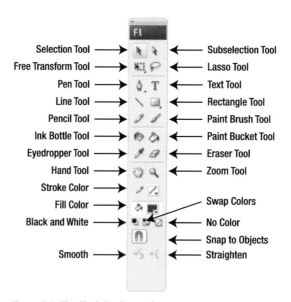

Figure 2-1. The Flash Tools panel

The lines you see separating the various tools actually group them into four distinct sections. The groupings, from top to bottom, are selecting, drawing, modification, and color selection and options.

- **Selecting**: This collection of four tools allows you select objects, select objects within objects, manipulate objects, and even select a piece of an object.

- **Drawing**: The six tools in this section can be used to draw images, create graphics and text elements, and draw shapes and lines.

- **Modification**: These four tools allow you to select strokes and fills, choose a specific color, or even remove a color or object. For example, you use the Ink Bottle tool to change the color of a stroke around the circle and the Paint Bucket tool to fill the circle or change its color. These four tools are traditionally used in conjunction with the next group of tools.

- **Color selection and options**: The tools in this area are used to zoom in and navigate around an image or object, choose fill colors and stroke colors, and even change their order. The options at the bottom change according to the tool you have selected. For example, select the Brush tool, and the options at the bottom will change, as shown in Figure 2-2, to allow you to choose the size of the brush, the type of brush, and so on.

Figure 2-2. Select the Brush tool and the tool options change.

> If you have used previous versions of Flash, you may notice that the tools have not only been regrouped, but also the names for the grouping sections have been removed.
>
> Certain tools—Free Transform, Pen, Rectangle, and the Stroke and Fill color chips—have a small triangle at the bottom right. Clicking this opens a drop-down menu that offers you either a subselection of related tool choices or the Color Picker.

The Selection and Subselection tools

The odds are almost 100% these are the tools you will use most frequently in your everyday workflow. In the previous chapter, you used the Selection tool to move objects around the stage. It does a lot more than that.

1. Click the Rectangle tool and draw a rectangle on the stage. Don't worry about colors for this exercise.

2. Switch to the Selection tool by either clicking it or pressing the V key. When you roll the tool over the square, a cross with arrows appears under the cursor. This means you are hovering over an object that can be moved by clicking and dragging.

> All tools can be selected using the keyboard. If you roll the cursor over a tool, a tooltip will appear, and the letter between the brackets is the key that can be pressed to select the tool.

3. Click the square and drag to the right. Holy smokes, you just pulled the fill out of the square (see Figure 2-3). Press Ctrl+Z (PC) or Cmd+Z (Mac) to undo that last action.

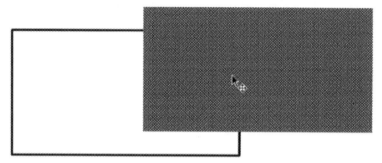

Figure 2-3. Selections in Flash aren't always what they seem.

What you have just discovered is Flash regards all objects you draw as being composed of two objects: a stroke and a fill. If you are an Illustrator, Photoshop, or Fireworks user, this may strike you as being a bit odd because in a vector universe that is not a common behavior. Give us a minute, and we'll ease you back into more familiar territory. We have a square to move.

4. To select the entire square, you have two choices. The first is to double-click the item. The second is to "marquee" the stroke and the fill by drawing a selection box around the object. To draw your selection box, click outside the rectangle near one of its corners, and then drag toward the opposite corner. Go ahead, try both methods of selection, and drag the square. You'll see the whole square move this time.

5. Now that you know objects drawn on the stage are actually composed of a stroke and a fill, we'd like to mention a third approach to selecting and moving them as a unit. Marquee the object and select Modify ➤ Group. Now, when you click the object, it is regarded as a single entity and can be dragged at will.

The Selection tool can be used for more than simply dragging objects around the stage. You can use it to also modify the shape of an object. The square on the stage, as you know, is composed of vector objects. This means they can not only be moved around the stage, but also be reshaped and still retain their crisp strokes and fills.

6. Select your object on the stage and select Modify ➤ Ungroup. Place the tip of the cursor on one of the strokes around the square. Do you see the little quarter circle, as in Figure 2-4, below the arrow? That symbol indicates you can reshape the stroke.

Figure 2-4. The shape under the cursor means the stroke can be reshaped.

7. Click and drag the stroke. When you drag the stroke, it actually bends. This tells you that the stroke is anchored, and, as in Illustrator CS3 or Fireworks CS3, if you drag a point on a line between two anchor points, the line changes its curve shape to reflect the point where you released the mouse at the apex of the curve. The other thing you may have noticed is, as shown in Figure 2-5, the fill also updates to reflect the new shape.

Figure 2-5. Both the stroke and the fill will change to reflect the new shape.

8. Select the Subselection tool or press the A key to switch to this tool. Double-click one of the corner points for the curve you have just created. The points and the handles become visible. You can further adjust the curve by either moving the handles or the points. These handles are only available on curves.

There is one other tool that allows you to manipulate objects on the stage: the Free Transform tool.

The Free Transform tool

If there is such a thing as an indispensable drawing tool in Flash, this one may just be it. What it does is scale, skew, and rotate objects on the stage. Here is how to use it:

1. Select the object on the Flash stage and select the Free Transform tool by either clicking it or pressing the Q key. The selected object sprouts a bounding box with eight handles and a white dot in the center.

2. Roll the cursor over each of the corner handles. Notice how, as in Figure 2-6, the cursor develops a rotate icon. This tells you that if you click and drag a corner, you can rotate the object. Try it out—you should also see a wireframe representation of the rotation, which is a handy feature to ensure the rotation is correct.

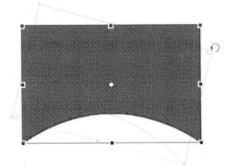

Figure 2-6. Rotating an object using the Free Transform tool

3. This time place the cursor on the bounding box. The cursor changes to split arrows. This tells you that clicking and dragging will skew (or slant) the object in the direction in which you drag. Go ahead, give it a try.

4. Now place the cursor directly over one of the handles. It changes to a double-headed arrow, meaning you can scale the object from that point.

The key to mastering this tool is to master that white dot. It is the center point of the object. Rotations use that dot as a pivot, and any of the other transformations applied using this tool are based on the location of that dot when you hold down the Alt key.

5. Click the white dot and drag it over the upper-left corner handle. Rotate the object using the handle in the lower-right corner. The rotation occurs around that white dot. Undo the change, and this time scale the object using the bottom-right corner. Again, as shown in Figure 2-7, the upper-left corner is used as the anchor for the transformation.

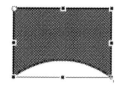

Figure 2-7. Scaling an object using the Free Transform tool

6. Now try another skew. With the white dot close to one of the corners, place the cursor on the bounding box to see the split arrows icon. Click and drag, and then hold down the Alt key and drag again. See the difference? Do the same with a scale transform.

> *Applied a couple of transformations and don't want to use them? To remove trans-formations, select* Modify ➤ Transform ➤ Remove Transform *or press Ctrl+Shift+Z (PC) or Cmd+Shift+Z (Mac). All transform actions applied to the object will be removed.*
>
> *To constrain the proportions of an object when using the mouse to scale the object, hold down the Shift key before you drag the handle. You can use Shift at the same time as the Alt key, as described previously, to both constrain and use the white dot as a pivot.*

The Gradient Transform tool

To the novice, gradients in Flash can be a little tricky. The reason is you can create the colors in the gradient, but moving them around and changing their direction is not done at the time the gradient is created. This is done using a separate tool. Here's how to create the moon that rose over Lake Nanagook in the previous chapter:

1. Select the Oval tool, deselect the stroke, and draw out a circle on the stage.

2. With the circle selected, change the width and height values of the circle to 120 and 120 in the Property inspector.

3. Click the Fill color chip to open the Color Chip panel and select the blue gradient, shown in Figure 2-8, at the bottom of the panel.

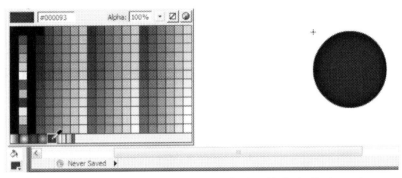

Figure 2-8. Selecting a preset gradient using the Fill color chip in the Tools panel

There are a couple of ways of changing this gradient in order to position the centered highlight elsewhere in the graphic. The first is to use the Paint Bucket tool. This tool simply fills a selected shape with the color in the Fill color chip, but it does something really interesting when the color is a gradient. Follow these steps:

1. Choose a gradient and click the Paint Bucket tool to select it or press the K key to switch to this tool.

2. Click in the upper-left corner of the circle. The center of the gradient moves to the point, where you clicked the mouse, as you can see in Figure 2-9. This occurred because the paint pouring out of the tool's icon is the hot spot for the tool. The center of the gradient will be the point where the "pour" is located.

3. Click again somewhere else on the shape to move the center point of the gradient.

Figure 2-9. The tip or "pour" point of the Paint Bucket's icon is its hot spot.

The previous technique is not as precise as this next one using the Gradient Transform tool. Here's how:

1. Click and hold on the Free Transform tool to open the drop-down menu. Select the Gradient Transform tool from the menu. Alternatively, simply press the F key to switch from the current tool to the Gradient Transform tool.

2. Click the object on the stage. When you do, it will be surrounded by circle, a line will bisect the selection, and three handles will appear as shown in Figure 2-10. The circle represents the area of the gradient fill.

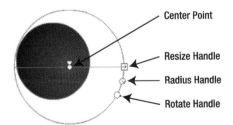

Center Point

Resize Handle

Radius Handle

Rotate Handle

Figure 2-10. The Gradient Transform tool allows you to precisely control a gradient.

Let's look at each of these controls:

- **Center point**: This is actually composed of two features. The white dot is the center point of the object and can be moved around in the usual manner. The triangle, which can only move along the line, is how the center of the gradient is moved.
- **Resize handle**: Drag this handle and you do not resize the circle—you resize and distort the radial gradient.
- **Radius handle**: Moving this one inward or outward proportionally increases the size of the gradient area.
- **Rotate handle**: Drag this and the gradient rotates around the center point. The effect can be quite subtle with a radial gradient, but you'll see a difference if you first squeeze the gradient into a lozenge shape with the resize handle.

Now that you know how to use the tool on a radial gradient, give it a try on a linear gradient. Here's how:

1. Select one of the linear gradients from the Fill color chip in the Tools panel.
2. Select the Rectangle tool and draw a square. Click the square with the Gradient Transform tool.
3. As you can see in Figure 2-11, the same controls are in place. This time rotate the gradient. Two lines will appear. These lines indicate the range of the gradient, and if you click the resize handle and drag it downward toward the top of the box, the colors in the gradient become more compressed.

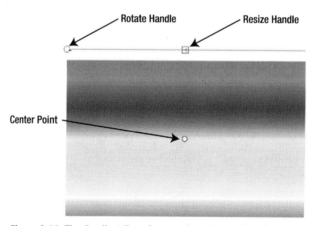

Figure 2-11. The Gradient Transform tool can be used on linear gradients as well.

Object Drawing mode

Introduced in Flash 8, the addition of the Object Drawing mode feature was greeted with wild cheering and dancing in the streets. Well, it didn't exactly happen that way, but a lot designers became seriously "happy campers" when they discovered this feature. Prior to the release of Flash 8, shapes that overlapped each other on the stage were, for many, a frustrating experience. If one shape was over another and you selected and moved it, it would cut a chunk out of the shape below it. This is not to say it was a flaw in the application. This behavior is common enough with painting applications. In Flash, once you understand the "one piece eats the other" phenomenon, it becomes a great construction tool. It can be much simpler to throw down a base shape and purposefully "take bites" out of it to achieve a complex figure than to draw the same figure from scratch.

Object Drawing mode is the opposite concept. When you select a drawing tool, such as the Oval tool, the Object Drawing icon, shown in Figure 2-12, appears in the Tools panel. Click it, and the oval you are about to draw will be drawn as a separate object on the stage and will not automatically merge with any object under it, even on the same layer.

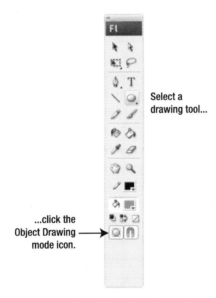

Select a
drawing tool...

...click the
Object Drawing ⟶
mode icon.

Figure 2-12. Select Object Drawing mode
to turn on this feature.

Let's see how the Object Drawing mode works:

1. Select the Oval tool, turn off the stroke in the Tools panel, and draw a circle over an existing shape on the stage. Now, select the circle and drag it off of the shape. When you release the mouse, you will see that your circle has bitten off a chunk of the shape.

2. Select the Oval tool, click the Object Drawing mode button in the Tools panel, and draw another circle over the shape. Drag it away and nothing happens, as shown in Figure 2-13. Hooray for Object Drawing mode.

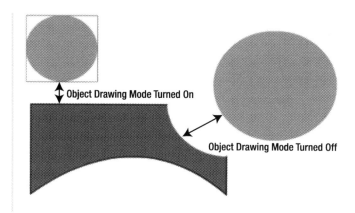

Figure 2-13. The effects of having Drawing Mode turned on or turned off

When you drew that second circle, Flash offered you a visual clue that you were in Object Drawing mode. When you selected the shape, it was surrounded by a bounding box.

Here's a little trick you can use to edit a single object in Object Drawing mode: double-click the second circle you just drew. Everything but the object clicked fades, and a drawing object appears beside the Scene 1 link. This allows you to edit the object in place without disturbing anything else on the stage. To return to the stage, click the Scene 1 link or double-click outside of the shape to go back a layer.

Your turn: Moon rise at Lake Nanagook

In this exercise, you will create the moon that was used in the exercise for Chapter 1. This exercise will review what you have learned so far plus show you how to create a custom gradient. Let's get "moonstruck."

1. Open a new Flash ActionScript 3.0 document and save it to your Chapter 2 Exercise folder as Moon.fla.

2. Select the Oval tool, turn off the stroke, and draw a circle on the stage. Click the circle, and in the Property inspector set its width and height values to 120. If you have a linear gradient filling the circle, change it to a solid fill.

3. With the oval selected, select Window ➤ Color to open the Color panel shown in Figure 2-14. This is where you can create a custom gradient for the moon.

4. Click the Type drop-down menu in the Color panel and select Radial. When you release the mouse, a gradient fills the circle.

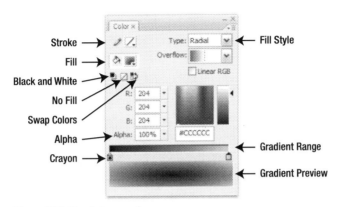

Stroke

Fill

Black and White

No Fill

Swap Colors

Alpha

Crayon

Fill Style

Gradient Range

Gradient Preview

Figure 2-14. The Color panel

Though it looks complicated, once you start using the Color panel, you will find it to be quite intuitive. The areas and controls are as follows:

- Fill Style: This drop-down list allows you to create fills using solid colors, gradients, and even photographs.

- Gradient Range: The two pointers, called **crayons**, allow you to condense or expand the colors' range.

- Gradient Preview: Drag a crayon to the right or the left, and this area will change to show you the result of the movement.

- Alpha: Move this slider up and down to increase or decrease the opacity of the fill or stroke color.

- Swap Colors: Click this, and the fill and the stroke colors are swapped with each other.

- No Fill: Click this, and the stroke or the fill color will be turned off. Click it again to restore it.

- Black and White: Click this, and the stroke color becomes black, while the fill color becomes white.

- Crayons: These are the workhorses of this panel. These controls, in an area we call the **crayon well**, slide along the Gradient Range area and condense or expand the range of the gradient. Swap their positions, and the gradient reverses. If you click anywhere between two crayons, you can add a third crayon, or more, and add new colors to the gradient. To remove a crayon, drag it anywhere outside of the crayon well and release the mouse.

5. Double-click the crayon on the left side of the Gradient Range area. This will open the color swatches and will set the color for that crayon. Enter #FFFFFF (white) as the value or click the white color swatch. Double-click the crayon on the right and change its value to #93BDE0 (light blue). The gradient will change to a light blue with a white center.

You don't have to double-click a crayon to change the color. Click the crayon and change its hexadecimal value, as shown in Figure 2-15, right in the Color panel.

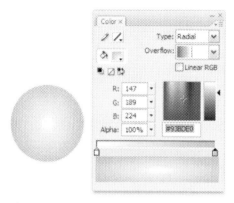

Figure 2-15. Creating custom gradient colors

6. Add a new layer and select the Oval tool. Turn off Object Drawing mode and change the stroke color to Black in the Tools panel.

7. Draw a circle and change its width and height values to 120 in the Property inspector.

8. Open the Color panel, select the Fill color chip, and enter these values:

- Type: Solid
- Color: #000066 (dark blue)
- Alpha: 36%

9. Make sure you have selected both the stroke and the fill, and drag this circle so that it covers a piece of the upper-left side of the gradient as shown in Figure 2-16.

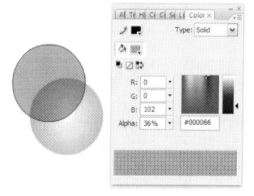

Figure 2-16. The moon shadow is created using a solid fill color with alpha transparency.

10. Click the stroke to select it, and drag it so that it surrounds the moon gradient. Where the stroke and circle overlap, you roughly get the shape of an American football.

11. Click the shadow color that is outside of the stroke. The stroke will stop you from selecting the whole shape. Because you're not in Object Drawing mode, the stroke essentially splits the solid where it intersects the solid. Press the Delete key to remove the selection.

12. Double-click the stroke to select it. Press the Delete key. You should have that football shape where the shadow is to be located.

13. Select both shapes and select Modify ➤ Convert to Symbol. When the Convert to Symbol dialog box opens, name the symbol Moon and set its type to Movie clip.

14. Save the file to your Chapter 2 Exercise folder. We'll be revisiting this file later on in this chapter.

15. Close the file.

Drawing in Flash CS3

In this part of the chapter, you are going to use the Flash drawing tools to create the tree used in the Lake Nanagook movie plus a couple of the modification tools to create the mountains and the grass around the lake. This will give you a really good opportunity to see what you can do with the tools, and along the way you will be given the opportunity to play with a few of the new drawing tools and features in Flash CS3. In this section, we will review the four main drawing tools: Pencil, Brush, Eraser, and Pen.

The Pencil tool

To start, you'll pick up a Pencil and get in touch with your inner child. What you are going to do is scribble:

1. Open a new Flash ActionScript 3.0 document. When it opens, select the Pencil tool or press the Y key.

This tool is used to draw freeform lines and shapes. When you select the tool, the Property inspector changes to allow you to set properties for the lines you will draw such as line thickness, style, and color. This tool also has a modifier that appears at the bottom of the Tools panel. Click it, and a drop-down menu gives you three modes to choose from (see Figure 2-17). These modes are important because they control how the line behaves when you draw. Also, when you select this tool, you can choose to use the Object Drawing mode.

Figure 2-17. The Pencil tool has three modes.

2. Using the Pencil tool, draw three squiggly lines. Use one of the following three modes for each line. The results will be slightly different for each.

- **Straighten mode**: Use this if you want curves to flatten.

- **Smooth mode**: Use this mode to round out kinks or otherwise smooth awkward curves.

- **Ink mode**: This is the mode that gives you exactly what you draw. If you use this mode, make sure that Stroke Hinting in the Property inspector is selected. This will ensure crisp, nonblurry lines.

3. Click the top line. Notice how you selected just a piece of it. The lines you draw with the Pencil tool are vectors.

4. Deselect the line segment, and this time roll the mouse over the line. When you see a small curve appear under the mouse, click and drag. This tells you that you can change the shape of the lines you draw by simply moving their segments.

5. Double-click one of the lines and change the thickness and line type from the drop-down menu in the Property inspector.

6. Draw a circle using the Pencil tool in Straighten mode. Select the shape, and in the Tools panel click the Smooth button, shown in Figure 2-18, a couple of times. Notice how the awkward edges of your circle are rounded. Now click the Straighten button a couple of times. Your awkward circle actually becomes a round circle. Double-click one of your lines, and click the Smooth and Straighten buttons to see how they work on nonclosed shapes.

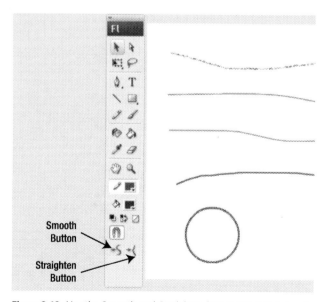

Figure 2-18. Use the Smooth and Straighten buttons to remove awkward angles.

There are preferences in Flash that will help you with your drawing chores. If you select Edit ➤ Preferences *(PC) or* Flash ➤ Preferences *(Mac), you will open the* Preferences *panel. Click the* Drawing *category and the panel will change to let you set how Flash handles the drawing tools, lines, and shapes. The* Recognize shapes *drop-down list can be set to take your hand-drawn approximations of circles, squares, triangles, and the like and replace them with truer shapes, as if drawn by the* Oval *or* Rectangle *tools.*

The Brush tool

The Brush tool feels quite similar to the Pencil tool in how it is used. The difference between the two is subtle but also quite profound. You have discovered that all objects drawn on the stage are separated into strokes and fills. The Pencil and the Brush tools follow that separation: the Pencil tool draws strokes, the Brush tool paints fills. When you select the Brush tool or press the B key to select the tool, a number of options will appear at the bottom of the Tools panel. The options are shown in Figure 2-19.

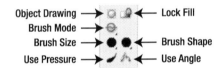

Figure 2-19. The Brush tool options

Let's review the main options:

- Lock Fill: Select this to fill multiple objects with a single gradient or some other fill. This can be useful in cases where the gradient implies a highlight, as the "lighting" will be applied evenly across all selected objects.

- Brush Mode: This controls how the strokes are painted, and the drop-down menu contains the following five modifiers:

  - Paint Normal: Paints over anything on the screen provided it is on the same layer you are painting on.

  - Paint Fills: Paints the fills and leaves the stroke alone, provided the object being painted is not a drawing object. If it is, use Modify ➤ Break Apart to turn the object into a shape, and when you finish you can put it back together by selecting Modify ➤ Combine Objects.

  - Paint Behind: Paints only on the empty areas of the layer.

  - Paint Selection: Paints only on the selected areas of the object.

  - Paint Inside: Paints only inside the area surrounded by a stroke. This mode only works if the Brush tool starts inside the stroke; otherwise, it acts like Paint Behind.

- Brush Size: Use this to change the width and spread of the brush strokes.
- Brush Shape: This drop-down menu offers a number of brush shapes ranging from round to square.
- Use Pressure and Use Angle: These two allow you to use the pressure and angle settings of a graphics tablet. This is a piece of hardware with a special drawing surface and "pen" that translates your actual hand motions into drawings on the screen.

The final control is the Smooth option on the Property inspector. This option determines the amount of smoothing and sharpness applied to an object drawn with the Brush tool. In many respects, it is the same as the Smooth mode of the Pencil tool. Try it out:

1. Select the Brush tool and select a fill color.

2. Turn off Object Drawing mode and make sure the Brush mode is set to Paint Normal.

3. In the Property inspector, set the Smooth value to 0 and draw a squiggle on the screen.

4. Set the Smooth value to 50 and draw another squiggle on the screen. Repeat this step with a value of 100. As you can see in Figure 2-20, the edges move from rough to smooth flowing. Just be aware that high values tend to remove the curves from your drawings.

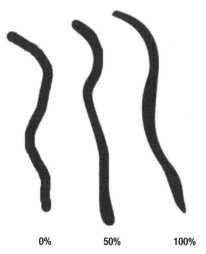

| 0% | 50% | 100% |

Figure 2-20. Smoothing brush strokes

The Eraser tool

The Eraser tool is quite similar to the Brush tool, only it erases rather than paints. Select the Eraser tool or press the E key, and the following three modifiers, shown in Figure 2-21, appear in the Tools panel:

- Eraser Mode: There are five choices in this drop-down menu, and they match those in the Brush tool.

- Eraser Shape: The choices in this drop-down menu let you select from a number of shapes for the eraser.

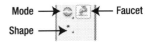

Figure 2-21. The Eraser options

- Eraser Faucet: Select this, and you can erase an entire fill or line with one click. The hot spot is the drip on the faucet.

> Here's a quick way to erase the contents of an entire layer: double-click the Eraser tool to clear your layer.

The Pen tool

If you use Illustrator, Fireworks, or Photoshop, you are accustomed to using the Pen tool. The interesting thing about this tool is that its roots aren't found in the graphics industry. It started out as a solution to a tricky problem faced by the auto industry in the 1970s.

Computers were just starting to be used in some areas of car design, and the designers involved faced a rather nasty problem: they could draw lines and simple curves, but squiggles and precise curves were completely out of the question.

The solution was to use a calculation developed by the mathematician Pierre Bezier to produce what we now know as **Bezier curves**. The difference between a Bezier curve and a simple curve is that a simple curve is composed of a number of points. A Bezier curve adds two additional pieces of data called **direction** and **speed**. These two data bits are visually represented by the handle that appears when you draw a curve with the Pen tool. Here's how to create a Bezier curve:

1. Select the Pen tool or press the P key. When you place the cursor on the stage, it changes to the pen and a small x appears next to it.

2. Click and drag. As you drag, you will see three points on the line, as shown in Figure 2-22. The center point, called the **anchor point**, is the start of the curve, and the two outer points, called **handles**, indicate the direction and degree of the curve.

Figure 2-22. The start of a Bezier curve

3. Roll the mouse to another position on the screen and click and drag the mouse. As you drag, the mouse handles and the curve get longer, and the curve follows the direction of the handle as shown in Figure 2-23.

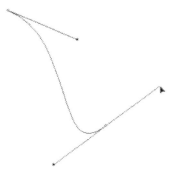

Figure 2-23. The curve shape changes based on the length and direction of the handle.

4. Click and drag a couple of more times to add a few more points to the shape.

5. Roll the mouse over the starting point of the shape. Notice the little o under the Pen tool, as shown in Figure 2-24? This tells you that you are about to create a closed shape. Click the mouse.

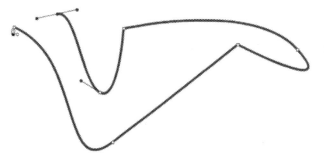

Figure 2-24. The shape is about to be closed.

There are a couple of other options available to you with the Pen tool that will allow you to edit your curves. If you click and hold the Pen tool in the Tools panel, you will see there are three extra choices:

- Add Anchor Point: Select this tool and click anywhere on the line to add an extra point.
- Delete Anchor Point: Click an anchor point to remove it. The shape will change.
- Convert Anchor Point: Click an anchor point, and the point will be converted to a corner point. Unfortunately, this conversion does not go both ways. To get your curve back, switch to the Selection tool and hover near a line that extends from the corner point. When you see the curve cursor, drag out a bit of curvature yourself, and then switch back to the Pen tool.

In previous versions of Flash, these alternative Pen tool modes were not available as separate tools, so the distinction is a nice new addition. You can, however, access the functionality of each tool from the main Pen tool itself. Here's the wrapped-up-in-one approach:

- **Adding an anchor point**: Using the Pen tool, hover over an existing line. Note how the normal x under the cursor becomes a +. Click to add a new anchor.

- **Deleting an anchor point**: Hover over a corner point, and you'll see the cursor acquire a little -. Click to delete the anchor. Hover over a normal anchor, and you'll have to click twice: once to convert the anchor to a corner point, and the second time to delete it.

- **Converting an anchor point**: Well, we just saw this in the previous bullet point. But note, in addition, that the Alt key temporarily converts the Pen tool into the Convert Anchor Point tool.

Your turn: Trees grow at Lake Nanagook

It's time to try out what you have been experimenting with. In this little exercise, you are going to draw the tree that is used in the Lake Nanagook movie from the previous chapter. Along the way, we are going to introduce you to a couple of new tools. Let's get to work:

1. Open the Moon.fla file you have saved to your Chapter 2 Exercise folder.

2. Select Insert ➤ New Symbol. When the New Symbol dialog box opens, name the symbol Trees and select Graphic as its Type. Click OK to accept the changes and to open the Symbol Editor.

3. Start with the trunk of the tree. Select the Pencil tool and, in the Smooth mode, draw a stretched oval shape. This will be the tree trunk. Select the shape on the stage and click the Smooth button a couple of times to remove the angles you may have drawn. When you finish, deselect the shape.

4. Select the Zoom tool, which looks like a magnifying glass, and click and drag over your shape. When you release the mouse, the shape will be larger and you will be able to manipulate it.

5. Refine the shape by rolling the cursor over it, and when you see the curved line under the cursor, drag the line segment you are over inward or outward to refine the shape.

> *Another way of doing this is to select the* Subselection *tool, click the shape, and manipulate the anchor points and the curves.*

6. When you finish, double-click the Zoom tool on the Tools panel to zoom out to 100% view.

7. Switch to the Selection tool, click your shape, and in the Property inspector specify these values:

   - Width: 17
   - Height: 37
   - X: 35
   - Y: 104.5
   - Stroke Color: #480000 (dark brown)

69

8. In the Tools panel, set the fill color to #480000 and select the Paint Bucket tool or press the K key. Place the tip of the bucket in the hollow part of the shape, and click the mouse. The tree trunk, as shown in Figure 2-25, will fill with the dark brown color.

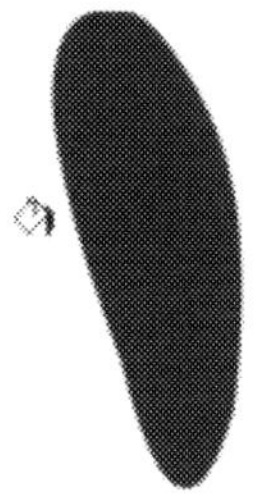

Figure 2-25. The tree trunk is filled using the Paint Bucket tool.

> *An alternative would be to select the* Brush *tool, and, using the* Paint Inside *mode, paint the fill color into the shape.*

9. Name the layer trunk, lock the layer, and add another layer. Name this new layer fir.

With the trunk in place, next you'll draw the pine tree. Think back to your youth and how you drew a pine tree. It was nothing more than a triangle filled with a gradient color. Here's how:

1. Select the new layer and select the Line tool in the Tools panel or press N on your keyboard. The Line tool draws straight lines and is great for drawing things like triangles.

2. Click and drag the tool on the stage to draw a line at an angle. Release the mouse, and the line is drawn. Repeat this step two more times to draw the three lines.

3. When you reach the start point of the first line, a circle will appear, indicating you are about to close the path. Click the mouse.

4. Select the Subselection tool and click the triangle. Notice how the stroke disappears and the anchor points become visible. Select an anchor point with the Subselection tool, as shown in Figure 2-26, and using either the mouse or the arrow keys on your keyboard, move the points until the triangle takes on the shape of a pine tree.

5. Switch to the Selection tool and roll the mouse to the bottom line of your triangle. When you see the small curve under the pointer, drag the line slightly downward. Your triangle should now look like a cone.

6. Double-click the shape to select it, and in the Property inspector set its width to 81 and its height to 114.

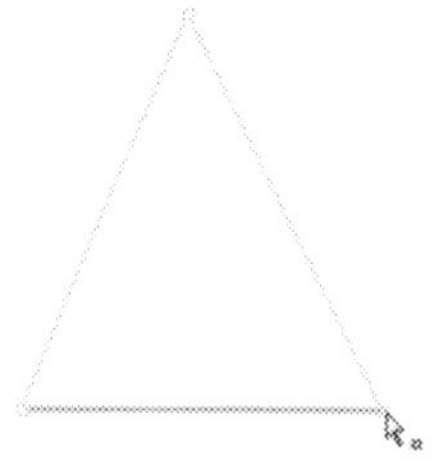

Figure 2-26. Use the Subselection tool to select and move anchor points.

7. With the object selected, open the Color panel and select Linear from the Type drop-down menu.

8. Click the left crayon and set its color value to #002211 (dark green). Set the color value of the right crayon to #004433, which is a lighter green.

9. Select the Paint Bucket tool and fill the triangle. The gradient, shown in Figure 2-27, gives the tree a bit of depth.

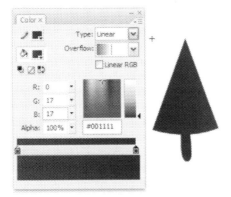

Figure 2-27. Use a gradient to give the tree some depth.

10. Switch to the Selection tool, double-click the stroke to select it, and press the Delete key. Move the tree over the trunk and lock the layer.

The final step in the process is to give your pine tree some needles. The key to this technique is to match the gradient on the tree. It is a lot easier than you may think.

1. Add a new layer named needles.

2. Open the Color panel, select the Stroke color chip, and select Linear from the Type drop-down menu. The gradient you just created is now in the stroke area of the Tools panel.

3. Select the Pencil tool and set the stroke width to 20 pixels in the Property inspector.

4. Click the Custom button in the Property inspector to customize your stroke. In the Stroke Style dialog box, specify the following settings:

- Type: Hatched
- Thickness: Medium
- Space: Very Close
- Jiggle: Wild
- Rotate: Medium
- Curve: Medium Curve
- Length: Random

5. Use the Zoom tool to zoom in on the tree. Draw four lines across the tree as shown in Figure 2-28.

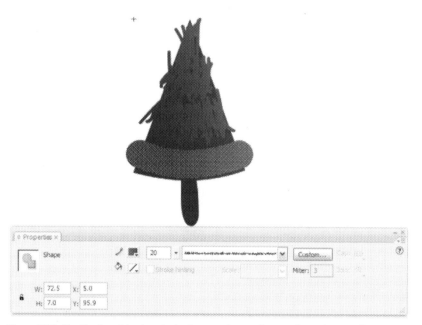

Figure 2-28. Use the Pencil tool, a stroke type, and a gradient to draw pine needles.

This should also help you to understand how we did the grass that runs around Lake Nanagook. We simply applied a smaller stroke width than the pine needles to the oval used for the lake.

A number of preset strokes already exist to the left of the Custom *button.*

Working with Color in Flash

So far you have spent some time filling objects or strokes with either a solid or a gradient color. The purpose of this section is to dig a bit deeper into the color models available to you as a Flash designer and to show you a couple of really snazzy color techniques you can use in your day-to-day workflow. What we aren't going to do is get into color theory or take color down to its molecular level. Entire books have been written on those subjects.

In Flash, you have three basic color models available to you: **RGB**, **HSB**, and **Hexadecimal**. Let's briefly look at each one.

The RGB model is the computer color model. Each pixel on your computer monitor is composed of a mixture of red, green, and blue lights. The value for each color is actually based on the old black-and-white model for computers where there were 256 shades of gray that were able to be displayed. The values started at 0 and ended at 255. The best way to imagine this is to think of 0 as being "no light," which means the color is black. This means 255 is pure white. When it comes to the RGB model, each pixel has three color values that range from 0 to 255. If you are looking at a pixel with values of 0 for red, 0 for green, and 255 for blue, you can assume the pixel is pure blue.

The letters in the HSB model represent hue, saturation, and brightness. Hue is the color, saturation is the amount of the color or its purity, and brightness (Flash uses the other term for brightness: luminosity) is the intensity of the color. The ranges for each value differ in this model. Hue goes from 0 to 360; that's one of 360 degrees around an imaginary wheel of color. Red starts at 0 (the same as 360). Green is one-third of the way around the wheel, 120. Blue is two-thirds around, 240. To see your secondary colors, shift your travel around the wheel by 60 degrees: yellow is 60, cyan is 180, and magenta is 300. Saturation and brightness are percentages. That pure blue value from the RGB model would here be hue: 240, saturation: 100, luminosity: 100.

> The RGB and HSB color modes may be switched in the top-right corner of the Color panel, just below the x that closes the panel.

The Hexadecimal model is the one commonly used on the Web. In this model, the red, green, and blue values for a pixel can either be a letter ranging from A to F, a number from 0 to 9, or a combination of the letters and numbers. In the case of our blue pixel, the hexadecimal value would be #0000FF.

The six characters in any hexadecimal color are actually three pairs of values: red, green, and blue. We humans, with ten fingers, count in decimal notation. We start with nothing and keep adding 1 to the "ones column" until we hit 9—that's a range of ten values, 0 to 9. Add one more, and the ones column can't go any higher, so it resets to 0, while the "tens column" advances by 1.

Computers aren't so simple. They have 16 fingers on each hand, so their ones column goes from 0 to 15. Columns can only hold one character at a time, so after 9, the value 10 is represented by . . . a letter—the letter A. 11 is represented by B, and so on, until 15, which is F. Add one more, and the ones column can't go any higher, so it resets to 0, while the tens column—actually, the "sixteens column"—advances by one. If your brain hasn't already turned to jelly, good, because even though this doesn't feel normal to us humans, it's not so hard.

That 1 in the sixteens column and 0 in the ones column look like 10, but in hexadecimal notation, that value is 16. 17 would be 11, 18 would be 12, and so on. A 10 in the ones column, as you now know, would be A. So what we would call 26—that is, a 1 in the sixteens column and a 10 in the ones column—would be 1A. Follow that through, and you'll see that FF refers to what we call 255 (that's 15 in the sixteens column, a total of what we call 240, plus a 15 in the ones column).

So hexadecimal notation is just another way to represent a range from 0 to 255 in each of the primary colors.

> The default color model for Flash CS3 is Hexadecimal.

When you click a color chip in Flash, the current Color palette, shown in Figure 2-29, opens. The color chips are all are arranged in hexadecimal groupings. As you run your cursor across them, you will see the hex value for the chip you are currently over. The colors on the left side of the Color palette are referred to as the **basic colors**. These are the grays and solids used most often, though we still aren't clear on how the bright pink and the turquoise at the bottom of the common colors made the hit parade.

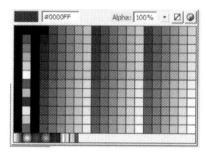

Figure 2-29. The current Color palette

> One of the authors, when he read the previous paragraph, couldn't resist and added, "I'll make an artiste out of you yet, complete with a beret." The left-hand column in that Color palette goes like this, from top to bottom: six even distributions of gray, from black to white. Then, the three primaries (red, green, blue), and finally the three secondaries (yellow, cyan, magenta). These colors, by the way, follow this hex pattern: red, #FF0000; green, #00FF00; blue, #0000FF; yellow, #FFFF00; cyan, #00FFFF; magenta, #FF00FF.

Another really useful feature of this panel is the ability to sample color anywhere on the computer screen. When the Color palette opens, your cursor changes to an eyedropper, and if you roll the cursor across the screen, you will see the hex value of the pixels you're over appearing in the Hex edit box, and the color will appear in the Preview box. This is a relatively dangerous feature because if you click the mouse over a pixel on your screen, that will be the selected color.

The Color Wheel in the upper-right corner, when clicked, opens the Flash Color Picker shown in Figure 2-30. The swatches in the top left are the basic system colors, and you probably noticed the pane on the right with all of that color that sort of looks like the Northern Lights gone haywire. This pane, called the Color window, contains all of the color you can use in your movies. Click a color, and you will see its RGB and HSB values as well as a preview of the color chosen. You can adjust that color by moving the Luminance slider up or down.

How many individual colors are available to you in the Color window? The answer is over 16 million. One of the authors once answered this question, and the student that asked the question remarked, "Is that all?" The author told him that was one seriously large number of crayons in his box, and the student responded, "What if I want more?" The author thought about that one for a couple of seconds and asked the student to imagine a crayon box with 16 million crayons. "If you have a box of crayons, are they all given a color name on the label?" asked the author. The student replied, "Of course." The author then said, "OK, you have in your hands a box containing 16 million crayons. None is labeled. Start naming them." That ended that discussion.

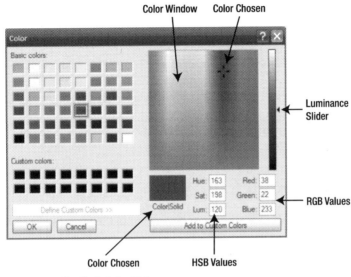

Figure 2-30. The Flash Color Picker

How do we get 16 million colors? First off, the exact number is 16,777,216. At rock bottom, computers use base 2 notation (aka binary), and millions of colors is referred to as being **24-bit color**. Each pixel is composed of 3 primary colors, and each color is defined by 8 bits (8 to the 2nd power is 256—aha, familiar number!). So that's where the 24 comes from: 3 times 8, which is the same as saying 256 to the 3rd power (256 × 256 × 256)—or 2 to the 24th power.

Things are a bit different on the Mac, as shown in Figure 2-31. Though the Color Picker may look different, it works in almost the same manner.

In the Mac-only Color Wheel, a color is chosen by clicking it in the wheel. If you want to adjust the RGB values, click the Color Sliders button at the top and select RGB Sliders, as you see in Figure 2-32, from the drop-down menu. The color picking options, to be honest, are far superior to those on the PC and well out of the scope of this book. What the Mac can't do is create multiple custom colors. You will have to mix those individually.

Figure 2-31. The Macintosh Color Picker

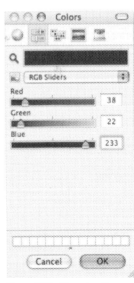

Figure 2-32. Choosing the sliders to change a color value

You don't have to click OK *on the Mac to save a color. You can drag and drop a color from the* Preview *area into the* Custom Color *boxes at the bottom of the dialog box.*

To add the color to your palette, either click the Add to Custom Colors button (PC) or click OK (Mac). Of course, things are not always wonderful for PC users. The custom color you just added appears in the Custom Colors area of the Color Picker. That's the good news. The bad news is if you add another custom color, Flash will, by default, overwrite your first color. If you are creating a number of custom colors, select the empty box before you pick your color.

So you have created a bunch of custom colors and are ready to use them in all of your projects? Not quite. They aren't automatically saved when you close Flash. If you create a bunch of custom colors and then close Flash, they will be gone—forever—when you return to Flash. The question, therefore, is how do you save your custom colors?

Creating persistent custom colors

Saving custom colors in Flash is not exactly up there in the category of "Dead Simple to Do." After you have created your custom color, you need to add it to the main Color palette and then save it as a color set. Here's how:

1. Open the Color panel, select the Fill color chip, and select Solid as the fill type. Create this color—#B74867 (dusty rose)—and make sure it is now the fill color.

2. Click the menu in the upper-right corner of the panel to open the panel's drop-down menu. Select Add Swatch as shown in Figure 2-33.

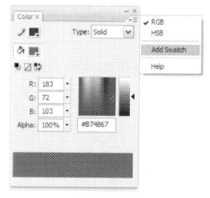

Figure 2-33. You start by selecting Add Swatch from the panel menu.

3. Click the Fill drop-down menu to open the current Color palette. Your new swatch will appear, as shown in Figure 2-34, in the bottom-left corner of the swatches. You can add as many colors as you wish, but we'll stay with the one we are using here.

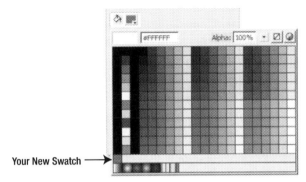

Your New Swatch ───→

Figure 2-34. Your custom color now appears on the current Color palette.

4. Open the Swatches panel by selecting Window ➤ Swatches or pressing Ctrl+F9 (PC) or Cmd+F9 (Mac).

5. When the panel opens, click the panel menu, shown in Figure 2-35, and select Save Colors. The Save As dialog box will open.

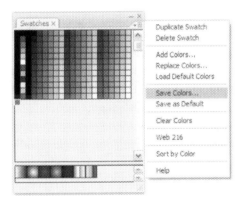

Figure 2-35. Saving a swatch

If you pay attention to the Save As dialog box, you will notice the file is being saved as a **Flash Color Set** or CLR file.

6. Name your file myFirstSet.clr and, as shown in Figure 2-36, save it to C:\ Program Files\Adobe\Adobe Flash CS3\en\First Run\Color Sets (PC) or <Hard Drive>/Users/<User Name>/Library/Application Support/Adobe/ Flash CS3/en/Configuration/Color Sets (Mac). Click OK to create the CLR file and close the dialog box.

Figure 2-36. Saving a color set

> *You don't have to use the Flash application folder for these. Just put them in a location where they will be handy. Some Flash designers stick them in their My Documents folder, and others put them in the project folder.*

7. To load the color set, simply open the Swatches panel and select Add Colors from the panel menu. Navigate to the folder containing the set and double-click it to add the set to Flash.

> *Yes, we agree that is a lot of work. Is there an easier way? In fact, there is. Why not do what the print guys do and attach a color swatch directly to the file? Let's assume you have a client who has six specific corporate colors that must always be used. Create a movieclip containing squares filled with those colors, and then simply put that movieclip on the pasteboard, which is the area just outside the stage that doesn't show in the published SWF by default. Any time you need the color, select the Eyedropper tool and sample it. If you are really lazy, don't add it to the pasteboard and simply sample the color using the Library Preview pane. If you use the colors in a lot of projects, you might even consider adding it to a shared library along with the client's logos and other common elements used in the client's Flash projects.*

Your turn: Playing with color

Here are a few tricks you can do with color. Two involve the standard use of a tool, but the other is right up there in the realm of "That is waaay cool."

The first trick involves a gradient. Did you know Flash allows you to create a variety of gradient effects with the click of a mouse? Here's how:

1. Open a new Flash document and create a big rectangle filled using the leftmost gradient in the Color Picker.

2. Switch to the Gradient Transform tool and resize the fill so it is much smaller than the rectangle. When you shorten the gradient, the black and the white areas of the gradient become larger. This is because Flash is filling the rectangle with the end colors. This process is called **overflowing**.

3. Open the Color panel and click the Overflow drop-down menu. You will see three choices, as shown in Figure 2-37.

Figure 2-37. The Gradient Overflow options

These choices, from top to bottom, are as follows:

- Extend: The default choice. The two last colors in the gradient extend to fill the shape.

- Reflect: The overflow area of the rectangle will be filled with repeating versions of the gradient. Every other version is mirrored/reflected. Select this, and the rectangle looks like stacked pipes (see Figure 2-38).

Figure 2-38. The Reflect overflow

- Repeat: The gradients aren't reflected. The result is the "Venetian blind" look in Figure 2-39.

Figure 2-39. The Repeat overflow

If you really want to rock and roll with this technique, change the gradient type to Radial, reduce the size of the gradient with the Gradient Transform tool, and select the Repeat option. As shown in Figure 2-40, the result resembles the "Looney Tunes" logo background.

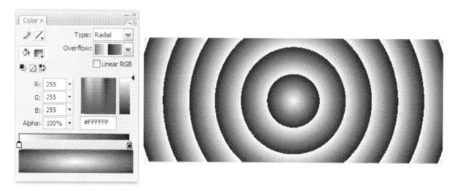

Figure 2-40. That's all, folks.

The next trick involves using a gradient fill to span across multiple unrelated objects. Here's how:

1. Open the GradientLock.fla file in your Chapter 2 Exercise folder. When it opens, you will see a long rectangle filled with a gradient and a series of shapes under the rectangle.

2. Select the Eyedropper tool and click the gradient. When you do, the icon will change to a paint bucket with a lock under it. This is the Lock Fill feature of the Paint Bucket tool.

3. Click once inside of a shape, as in Figure 2-41, and notice how the gradient fill in the object exactly matches the portion of the gradient directly above it. If you want to unlock the fills, click the Lock Fill button on the toolbar. If you click inside a shape, Flash will regard the fill as being a new gradient, not a continuation of the one above it, and the gradient color will change accordingly. When you finish, close the file without saving the changes.

Figure 2-41. The Lock Fill feature of the Paint Bucket tool

The final technique is one a lot of Flash designers tend to overlook: using an image, not a gradient or a solid color, to fill an object. There are two methods of accomplishing this, and they each have a different result. Let's try them:

1. Open the ImageFill.fla file and open the Color panel.

2. Select Bitmap as the fill type. In cases where the FLA does not yet contain imported images, an Import to Library dialog box will open at this point. In this sample file, an image already exists in the library, so you'll see the Import button instead.

3. Click the Import button, if you like, to import an image of your own. If you go this route, use the Import to Library dialog box to navigate to an image. Select the image and click OK to close the dialog box. Of course, you're welcome to use the already-imported Stools.jpg.

4. If you take a look at the Fill color chip in the Color panel, the image is in the chip and in the fill area of the Tools panel.

5. Select the Paint Bucket tool and click once inside the object on the stage. It fills, as shown in Figure 2-42, with several tiled copies of the image.

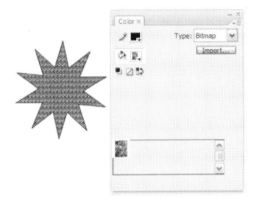

Figure 2-42. Using a bitmap as a fill

6. Select the Gradient Transform tool to adjust the tiled image in various ways. Given the minuscule size of the tiles, you may want to zoom in first.

Here's the second method:

1. Click the photo on the stage and select Modify ➤ Break Apart or press Ctrl+B (PC) or Cmd+B (Mac). The image looks cross-hatched.

2. Select the Eyedropper tool and click once in the photo. The image will appear in the Fill color chip of the Tools panel.

3. Select the Paint Bucket tool and click the object on the stage. The image, shown in Figure 2-43, fills the object.

Figure 2-43. Another way of using a bitmap as a fill

Now that you have finally had a chance to use a bitmap, let's take a closer look at how such images are used in Flash.

Using bitmap images in Flash

To this point in the book, you have been working with vectors. Though we have been telling you they are the most wonderful things in the Flash universe, we are sure our photographer friends are not exactly happy campers. Let's face it—you are going to be using bitmaps in your workflow. You can't avoid them, and they are just as important as vectors. In fact, Adobe has really improved how Flash manages images and integrates with Photoshop CS3, Illustrator CS3, and Fireworks CS3.

In this final section of the chapter, we are going to look at how you can use bitmap images in your workflow. We are going to talk about the image formats you can use; cover how to import images from Photoshop, Illustrator, and Fireworks into Flash; and even show you how to convert a bitmap image to a vector image in Flash. Let's start with the formats that can be imported.

As an Adobe application, it is not surprising that Flash can import the following formats:

- **AI**: Adobe Illustrator. This is the native Illustrator file format. This format allows Flash to preserve the layers in your Illustrator document. The good news is the Illustrator-to-Flash workflow has had its molecules rearranged and turned inside-out—in a good way.
- **GIF**: Graphic Interchange Format. This is the former standard for imaging on the Web. The upside of this format is the real small file size. The downside is the color palette is limited to 256 colors. These files come in two flavors: transparent and regular. The increasing use of Flash banner ads, with their strict file size requirements, has resulted in a resurgence of this format on websites.
- **PNG**: Portable Network Graphic. This is the native format for Fireworks. Think of PNG files as a combination vector/bitmap file. This format supports variable bit depth (PNG-8 and PNG-24) and compression settings with support for alpha channels. PNG files imported into Flash from Fireworks arrive as editable objects and will preserve vector artwork in the file, if present.
- **JPEG or JPG**: Joint Photographic Experts Group. This is the current standard for web imaging, and any image arriving in Flash will be converted to this format when the SWF is published.
- **PDF**: Portable Document Format. PDF is a cross-platform standard used in the publishing industry.
- **EPS**: Encapsulated PostScript. Think of this as a raw vector file.
- **PSD**: Photoshop Drawing. This is the native Photoshop file format. A PSD image usually contains multiple layers. Again, the workflow between Flash CS3 and Photoshop CS3 has undergone a profound change for the better.
- **PICT**: This is a Macintosh format comparable to a BMP file on the PC.
- **TIF or TIFF**: Tagged Image File Format. This is usually a high-resolution CMYK document.

A bitmap or raster image is nothing more than a collection of pixels. The reason bitmap images have taken a bit of a "bum rap" in the Flash community is because the image file needs to map and remember the location of each pixel in the image. The result is a large file size, which tends to go against the grain in a community that chants, "Small is beautiful. Small loads fast."

Use bitmaps when you need photos or lifelike images, when you need a screenshot, or when you need pictures of drawings or artwork. In fact, a good rule of thumb is to look at a bitmap image and ask, "Could I draw this in Flash?" If the answer is yes, you might want to consider that route instead.

The best advice we can give you about bitmaps is to make them as small as possible—a process called **optimization**—in the originating application. For example, Fireworks CS3 contains an Optimize panel, shown in Figure 2-44, which allows you to compare the effects of various image settings upon an image. In Illustrator CS3, see if you can reduce the number of points in your shapes, and make sure you have removed all of the stray points that aren't connected to anything. In Photoshop CS3 and Fireworks CS3, reduce the image size to fit the image size in Flash. These applications were designed to perform these tasks; Flash wasn't.

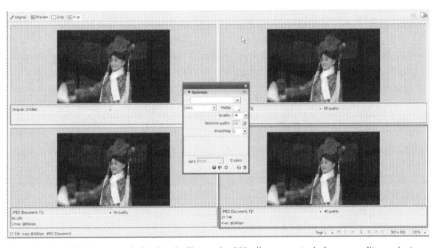

Figure 2-44. 4-Up image optimization in Fireworks CS3 allows you to balance quality against image size.

Working with bitmaps inside Flash

The decision is final. You need to use a bitmap and place it in Flash. Then you discover the color is all wrong or something needs to be cropped out of the image. It needs to be edited. How do you do it? Follow these steps:

1. Open a new Flash document and select File ➤ Import ➤ Import to Stage. When the Import dialog box opens, navigate to the Dancer.jpg file.

2. Select the file and click Open to close the Import dialog box. The image will appear on the stage and in the library, as shown in Figure 2-45.

Figure 2-45. Images imported to the stage are automatically placed in the library.

Do not delete the image from the library. This is the original bitmap, and deleting it will ripple through an entire project. If you screw something up on the stage, delete the image on the stage.

3. Right-click (PC) or Ctrl-click (Mac) the image in the library to open the context menu.

4. Select Edit with. This will launch the Open dialog box, allowing you to navigate to the application folder containing the application you will be using to edit the image. If you select Photoshop CS3, the image will launch in Photoshop. When you make your changes, select Edit ➤ Save. When you return to Flash, the change made in Photoshop CS3 will be reflected both in the image on the stage and in the library.

*Fireworks CS3 has a rather cool feature called **round tripping**. If you launch Fireworks CS3 as your editor, the image will open, and you will see a Done button, as shown in Figure 2-46, at the top of the canvas as well as notification you are, indeed, "Editing from Flash." Make your changes and click the Done button. Fireworks will close, you will be returned to Flash, and the change will be visible on the stage and in the library.*

Figure 2-46. Round-trip editing between Fireworks and Flash

Your turn: Tracing bitmaps in Flash

Tracing converts an image to a series of vectors. On the surface, this sounds like a win/win for everybody. Not quite. Yes, you get a vector image with all the benefits of scalability and so on, but you also inherit a whack of potential problems along the way. There are no hard-and-fast rules in this area, so it is best to experiment. Let's fire up the Bunsen burner:

1. Open the Trace.fla file. You will see two images of a t-shirt hanging in front of a street vendor's stall in Beijing, China.

2. Click the image over the Default Values text and select Modify ➤ Bitmap ➤ Trace Bitmap to open the Trace Bitmap dialog box. Specify the values shown in Figure 2-47.

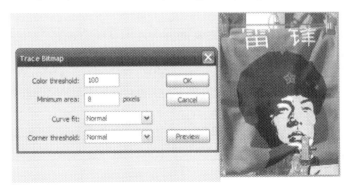

Figure 2-47. The Trace Bitmap dialog box

The settings aren't all that mysterious:

- Color threshold: The higher the number, the more colors are considered a match and the fewer the vectors.

- Minimum area: The number entered here defines the smallest size for a vector shape. If you want a really detailed image, use a low number. Just keep in mind, the smaller the number, the more the shapes, the larger the file size. In fact, extremely complex vectors can, and often do, carry a greater file size penalty than the bitmap images they're based on.

- Curve fit: Think of this as being a smoothing setting. Select Pixels, and you get a very accurate trace. Select Very Smooth, and curves really round out. Again, the fewer the curves, the smaller the file size.

- Corner threshold: This value determines how much a line can bend before Flash breaks it into corners. The fewer the corners, the smaller the file's size. (Picking up a theme here?)

3. Click the Preview button to see the effect of your choices, as shown in Figure 2-48.

Figure 2-48. A traced bitmap

> *If you have used previous versions of Flash, you will find the* Preview *button in the* Trace Bitmap *dialog box a welcome addition to Flash CS3.*

4. Click OK to apply the change and close the dialog box.

5. Now you'll see what happens when you use even closer tolerances. Select the image on the right of the stage and open the Trace Bitmap dialog box. Specify these values:

- Color threshold: 5
- Curve fit: Pixels
- Minimum area: 2
- Corner threshold: Many corners

6. Click the Preview button. The progress bar will take a bit longer this time, and when it finishes, the difference between the original image and the vector image is not readily evident. Click OK to apply the changes. You are about to find out that there is indeed a major difference between the original bitmap and the traced image.

The difference becomes evident when you optimize the image. In Flash, optimizing a drawing means you are reducing the number of corners in a traced image and smoothing out the lines in the traced image to give you a smaller and less-precise image. Though you can optimize any drawing you have in Flash, this technique is best applied to traced images. Here's how:

1. Change to the Selection tool and marquee the first image you traced. Select Modify ➤ Shape ➤ Optimize to open the Optimize Curves dialog box shown in Figure 2-49.

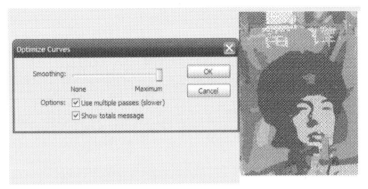

Figure 2-49. The Optimize Curves dialog box lets you reduce the size of a traced image.

2. Drag the Smooth slider to the Maximum value on the right and click OK. The process starts, and when it finishes, you will be presented with an Alert box telling you how many curves have been optimized (see Figure 2-50).

Figure 2-50. A 43% curve reduction means a significant file size reduction.

The downside is the image loses a lot of its precision, and some of the curves become spiky because Flash converted all the pixelated smoothness to vectors. If you repeat the process on the second image but only move the Smooth slider to the midpoint, the process will take a lot longer than the previous one, yet the curve reduction will be minimal. This is because you essentially created a high-resolution vector image, so there are a lot more curves to check out. The bottom line here is the decision regarding using a bitmap, tracing it, and optimizing the curves is up to you.

JPG files and Flash

The JPG, or JPEG, file format is the one used for photos. As mentioned earlier, JPEG stands for Joint Photographic Experts Group and is a method of compressing an image using areas of contiguous color. The file size reductions can be significant with minimal to moderate image quality loss. This explains why this format has become a de facto imaging format for digital media. In this exercise, you are going to learn how to optimize a JPG image in Flash.

Before you do this, it is extremely important you understand that the JPG format is **lossy**. This means each time a JPG image is compressed in the JPG format, the image quality degrades. The point here is you have to make a decision regarding JPG images before they arrive in Flash. Will the compression be done in Photoshop or Fireworks, or will Flash handle the chores? If the answer is Flash, always set the JPG Quality slider in Photoshop or Fireworks to 100% to apply minimal compression. If you don't know where the image came from or what compression was used, don't let Flash handle the compression.

1. Open the JPGCompression.fla file in your Chapter 2 Exercise folder. When it opens, you will notice the movie contains nothing more than a single JPG image, and the stage matches the image dimensions. In short, there is no wasted space that can skew the results of this experiment.

2. Minimize Flash and open the Chapter 2 Exercise folder. Inside the folder is a file named JPGCompression.swf. It is the compiled version of the FLA file, and if you check its file size, you will see it comes in at about 69 KB. Let's see if we can shed some weight from this file.

3. Return to Flash and save the open Flash file to your Exercise folder by selecting File ➤ Save As and naming the file JPGCompression2.fla.

4. Double-click the image in the library to open the Bitmap Properties dialog box shown in Figure 2-51.

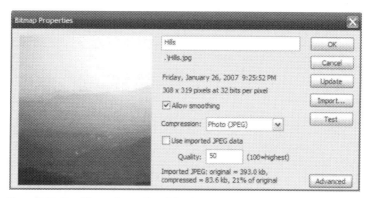

Figure 2-51. The Bitmap Properties dialog box

2

> *Be aware that any changes made in this dialog box ripple through the entire movie and will override the defaults used in the* Publish *dialog box.*

Let's examine this dialog box. To start, the image on the left side is the preview image. As you start playing with some of the settings, this image will show you the final result of your choices. This is a good thing, because changes you make in this dialog box are only visible when the SWF file is running; they won't be reflected in the image on the stage during authoring. The other areas are:

- **Name**: The name of the file. If you want to rename the file, select it and enter a new name. This only changes the name by which Flash knows the file—it does not "reach outside of Flash" and rename the original image.

- **Path, date, dimensions**: Fairly self-explanatory. There will be the odd occasion where this info will not be displayed. The reason is the image was pasted in from the clipboard.

- Update **button**: If you have edited the image without using the Edit with feature, clicking this button will replace the image with the new version. This button will not work if you have saved or moved the original image to a new location on the computer. To "reconnect" such a broken link, respecify the image file's location with the Import button, explained next.

- Import **button**: Click this, and you open the Import Bitmap dialog box. When using this button, the new file will replace the image in the library, and all instances of that image in your movie will also be updated.

- Allow smoothing **option**: Think of this as anti-aliasing applied to an image. This feature tends to blur an image, so use it judiciously. Where it really shines is when it is applied to low-res images because it reduces the dreaded jaggies.

- Compression **drop-down menu**: This allows you to change the image compression to either Photo (JPEG) or Lossless PNG (PNG/GIF). Use Photo (JPEG) for photographs and Lossless PNG (PNG/GIF) for images with simple shapes and few colors, such as line art or logos. To help you wrap your mind around this, the image in the dialog box uses Photo (JPEG) compression, and if you click the Test button, the file size is about 2.4 KB. Apply Lossless PNG (PNG/GIF) compression and click the Test button, and the file size rockets up to 142 KB.

- Use Imported JPEG data **option**: Select this check box if the image has already been compressed or if you aren't sure whether compression has been applied. Checking this avoids the nasty results of applying double compression to an image.

- Quality **setting**: If you deselect the Use Imported JPEG data check box, you can apply your own compression settings. In fact, let's try it.

5. Make sure your compression setting is Photo (JPEG) and that you have deselected the Use Imported JPEG Data check box. Change the Quality value to 10% and click the Test button. The image in the Preview area, shown in Figure 2-52, is just plain awful. The good news is that the file size, at the bottom of the dialog box, is 1 KB.

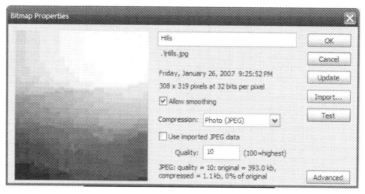

Figure 2-52. At 10% quality, the image is terrible.

6. Change the Quality setting to 50% and click the Test button. Things are a little better, but the sky in the upper-left corner looks pixelated, and the file size has gone up to 2.4 KB.

7. Change the Quality value to the normal 80% value used by imaging applications and click the Test button. The sky issue is resolved but the file size, as shown in Figure 2-53, has risen to 6.4 KB. As you are seeing, there is an intimate relationship between the Quality setting and file size.

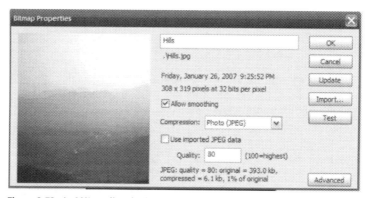

Figure 2-53. At 80% quality, the image is much better.

8. Knowing the quality between 50% and 80% is a vast improvement, let's see if we can maintain quality but reduce the file size. Set the Quality value to 65% and click the Test button. The difference between 65% and 80% is minimal, but the file size has reduced to 3 KB. Click OK to apply this setting and close the dialog box.

9. Save the movie and press Ctrl+Enter (PC) or Cmd+Return (Mac) to test the movie. This will create the SWF you need. Minimize Flash and the SWF window and navigate to your Exercise folder. The results are, to say the least, dramatic. The file size, as you see in Figure 2-54, has reduced to 4 KB from 69 KB. Save and close the open movie.

Figure 2-54. Applying compression in Flash can result in seriously smaller and more efficient SWF files.

Using GIF files in Flash CS3

There was point a few years back where many web and Flash designers were preparing to celebrate the death of the GIF image and the GIF animation. The reason was simple: in a universe where bandwidth is plentiful and every computer on the planet is able to display 16-bit color, the limited color range and small file size of a GIF image that made the format so important became irrelevant. GIF images were developed for an era of limited color depth—monitors that could only display 256 colors—and dial-up modems. Then a funny thing happened on the way to the wake: they arose from their death bed. The reason was banner advertising.

Ad agencies and their clients were discovering the Web really was a viable advertising medium and that Flash was a great interactive tool for ads. The problem was, standards for banner advertising appeared on the scene, and the agencies discovered they were handed a file size limit of 30 KB. This tended to go against the grain, and as they grappled with the requirement for small files, they rediscovered the GIF image and the GIF animation.

This isn't to say you should use the GIF format only in banner ads. It can be used in quite a few situations where size is a prime consideration. Here's how to use GIF images and GIF animations in Flash:

1. Open the GIF.fla file in your Chapter 2 Exercise folder. When the file opens, open the library. There are two GIF files in the library.

2. Drag the Figurines image from the library to the stage. Notice how you can see the stage color behind the image. This image is a transparent GIF. When it comes to GIF transparency, you have to understand it is an absolute. It is either on or off. There are no shades of opacity with this format. GIFs may contain up to 256 colors, and one of those colors may be transparent.

3. Drag the FigurinesNoTrans image to the stage and position it beneath the image already there. This image is a GIF image with no transparency applied.

4. Select the image you just dragged onto the stage and press the Ctrl+B (PC) or Cmd+B (Mac) combination to break the image apart. Hold on, that isn't right. Only the figurines in the image break apart (see Figure 2-55). That is an expected behavior. Remember what we said in the previous step? The background in a GIF image is either on or off. If it is on, it can't be removed in Flash.

Figure 2-55. Transparent and regular GIFs are treated differently in Flash.

When you break apart an image like this, here's what's really going on. That image is simply translated into a shape with a bitmap fill. It is the same thing as drawing a shape and filling it with that bitmap. This is why file size is identical between the white and transparent versions of this image. The GIF is the same in all respects—except that a slot in one file's color table is white and in the other file's color table is transparent. But both GIFs have the same number of colors and weigh the same.

To "get rid of" the white background, you can drag in the edges of the shape that contains the white version, just like the star shape from the earlier bitmap fill example. Obviously, this would be nearly impossible by hand with an image of this complexity, but any portion of the bitmap fill can be hidden by changing the shape that contains it.

5. Close the file and don't save the changes.

Animated GIFs are a bit different. They are a collection of static images—think of a flip book—that play one after the other, all stored inside a single GIF file. The "pages" of this flip book can be imported either directly into the main timeline (not a good idea) or into a separate movieclip. Here's how:

1. Open a new Flash document and create a new movieclip named Counterforce. The Symbol Editor will open.

2. Select File ➤ Import ➤ Import to Stage, and when the Open dialog box appears, locate the Counterforce.gif file, select it, and click the Open button.

3. When the import is finished, you will see that each frame of the animation has its own Flash frame and each image in the animation, as shown in Figure 2-56, has its own image in the library.

Figure 2-56. Importing GIF animations into a movieclip

4. Press the Enter key to test the animation or click the Scene 1 link to return to the main timeline, add the movieclip to the stage, and test the movie.

> *A good habit to develop is to place the images in the library in a folder.*

Importing Fireworks CS3 documents into Flash CS3

When Macromedia was acquired by Adobe in 2006, the betting in the Macromedia community was that Fireworks, Macromedia's web imaging application, would simply not make the cut. The reason was that the market regarded Fireworks as a competitor to Photoshop—it wasn't—and, as such, the application was doomed to extinction.

What the Macromedia community failed to comprehend was that Adobe, prior to the acquisition, had quietly announced it was no longer supporting ImageReady, which was the web imaging application for Photoshop. When the acquisition was settled, Fireworks did indeed make the cut, and in fact, Adobe had decided to reposition Fireworks CS3 as a rapid prototyping application for web designers. Along the way, Adobe improved how Fireworks PNG files integrate with Flash CS3 along with Illustrator CS3, Flex Builder 2, and Photoshop CS3, and the movement of files from Photoshop and Illustrator into Fireworks. The end result is Flash designers now have a tool that will seriously improve their workflow.

We will be showing you elsewhere in this book techniques in which Fireworks integration will be a huge timesaver. For now, though, let's concentrate on getting a PNG image—the native file format used by Fireworks—into Flash.

As you can see in Figure 2-57, the Fireworks file we will be working with is composed of one layer, Background, and three sublayers. When you import this PNG image into Flash, you will see these layers carry over, intact, into the movie.

Figure 2-57. We start with a Fireworks CS3 PNG image.

To import the PNG image, follow these steps:

1. Open the Fireworks.fla file. When it opens, you will see the stage is blank and is set to the dimensions of the Fireworks image.

2. Select File ➤ Import to Stage and navigate to the Clouds.png image in the Chapter 2 Exercise folder.

3. When you click the Open button, the dialog box will close and the Fireworks PNG Import Settings dialog box, shown in Figure 2-58, will open.

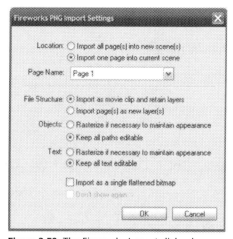

Figure 2-58. The Fireworks Import dialog box

Let's review the options:

- Location: The important aspect of this is not the scene but the fact you are being asked to import pages. This feature is new to Flash CS3. Because it is a rapid prototyping application, Fireworks CS3 is able to create multipage documents for websites. If the PNG file contains multiple pages, you can select the page to be imported from the drop-down menu.

- File Structure: **Select** Import as movieclip and retain layers so all of the layers in the image are placed into separate layers in the movieclip. When this occurs, Flash creates a new folder in the library named Fireworks Objects and places the movieclip in this folder. The second choice allows you to add the selected page as a new layer on the main timeline.

- Objects: The choices are to flatten everything on the Fireworks layer or keep each object editable.

- Text: Same choices as objects. We tend to keep text editable just in case there is a typo.

- Import as a single flattened bitmap: This option flattens all of the layers into a bitmap.

4. Go with the default values for this example. Click OK to import the image into Flash.

5. When the import finishes, you will see the Fireworks Objects folder in the library. Open it, and you will see that Flash has created a folder for the page just imported, and if you open that folder, you will see the movieclip and a flattened bitmap of the file.

6. Double-click the movieclip to open it. Compare the Flash file (shown in Figure 2-59) to the Fireworks file in Figure 2-57. You can now either save the file or close it without saving the changes.

Figure 2-59. The Flash movieclip layers match those in the Fireworks PNG image.

Importing Illustrator CS3 documents into Flash CS3

Prior to this version of Flash, the movement of Illustrator documents into Flash was, understandably, difficult. The products came from different companies, and Flash designers, realizing this, took the path of least resistance and simply copied and pasted their Illustrator drawings into Flash movieclips. This has all changed.

Flash lets you import Illustrator AI files directly into Flash and generally allows you to edit each piece of the artwork when it is in Flash. The new Illustrator File Importer also provides you with a great degree of control in determining how your Illustrator artwork is imported into Flash. For example, you can now specify which layers and paths in the Illustrator document will be imported into Flash and even have the Illustrator file be converted to a Flash movieclip.

The Flash Illustrator File Importer provides the following key features:

- Preserves editability of the most commonly used Illustrator effects such as the Flash filters and blend modes that Flash and Illustrator have in common.
- Preserves the fidelity and editability of gradient fills.
- Imports Illustrator symbols as Flash symbols.

- Preserves the number and position of Bezier control points; the fidelity of clip masks, pattern strokes, and fills; and object transparency.

- Provides an improved copy-and-paste workflow between Illustrator and Flash. A copy-and-paste dialog box provides settings to apply to AI files being pasted onto the Flash stage.

To many Flash designers, that list is "nirvana," but there are two critical aspects of the Flash-to-Illustrator workflow that must be kept in mind:

- Flash only supports the RGB color space. If the Illustrator image is a CMYK image, do the CMYK-to-RGB conversion in Illustrator before importing the file into Flash.

- To preserve drop shadow, inner glow, outer glow, and Gaussian blur in Flash CS3, import the object to which these filters are applied as a Flash movieclip. In Flash, these filters can be applied only to movieclips.

Let's import an Illustrator CS3 drawing to see what is causing all of the joy. The file we will be using, x-factor.ai, contains a number of Illustrator layers and paths (see Figure 2-60). One path—in the star layer—contains a drop shadow.

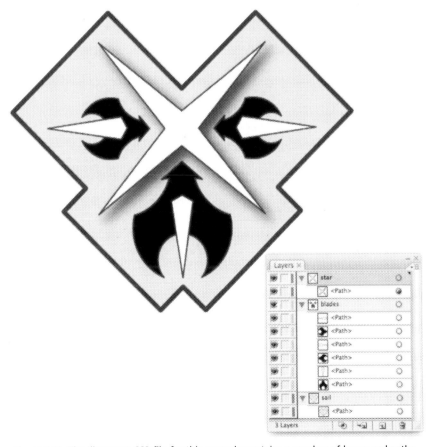

Figure 2-60. The Illustrator CS3 file for this example contains a number of layers and paths.

The authors would like to thank Bruce Hartman for the use of the x-factor.ai *file. His original design, built from this file, won the Best Bowed Kite in the Adult Division at the 35th Annual Smithsonian Kite Festival in 2001 and the Grand Master award at the Old Dominion Sport Kite Championships in the same year. Bruce likes to get his hands dirty in all sorts of artistic endeavors, many of which he recounts on his blog,* www.brucehartman.net/.

Follow these steps to import an Illustrator CS3 document into Flash CS3:

1. Open a new Flash document and import the x-factor.ai file into the Flash library.

2. The Import dialog box, shown in Figure 2-61, will appear. Keep in mind the Star layer contains a Drop Shadow filter and must be imported into Flash as a movieclip in order to retain the drop shadow.

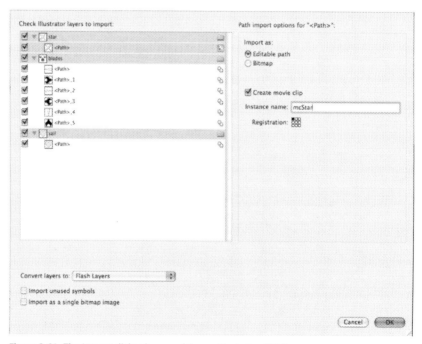

Figure 2-61. The Import dialog box used for an Illustrator CS3 image

3. Click the <Path> in the Star layer and select Create movie clip. Give the movieclip the instance name of Star. Select the remaining layers, not the paths, and select Create movie clip. Name the movieclips blades and sail. Click OK.

The Convert layers to drop-down menu allows you to convert your Illustrator layers to Flash layers or to a series of Flash keyframes (this is handy if they are animated), or to put the whole image into one Flash layer. You are also given the opportunity to import unused symbols created in Illustrator or to flatten the image and bring it in as a bitmap.

4. Click OK, and when the import process finishes, open the library, as shown in Figure 2-62. The image has been brought into Flash as a graphic symbol, but each of the layers has its own folder containing the movieclip you created in the Import dialog box.

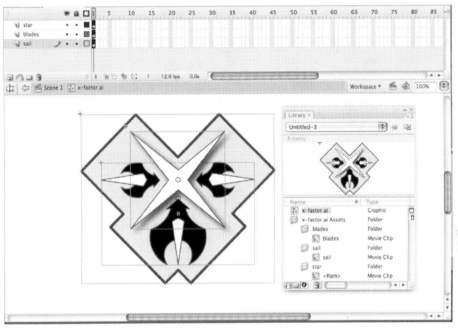

Figure 2-62. The Illustrator image in the Flash library. Note the drop shadow on the star.

At the top of this section, we mentioned how developers would simply copy Illustrator documents and paste them into Flash to avoid "issues." This can still be done, but when you paste the drawing into Flash CS3, the dialog box shown in Figure 2-63 appears. This dialog box is fairly self-explanatory, though you may be wondering about the AI File Importer preferences choice.

Figure 2-63. Pasting a drawing from Illustrator to Flash will bring up this dialog box.

The preferences can be found in Edit ➤ Preferences (PC) or Flash ➤ Preferences (Mac). When the Preferences dialog box opens, click the AI File Importer selection at the bottom of the Category list. This will open the AI File Importer preferences as shown in Figure 2-64. As you can see, many of the choices are also available in the Import dialog box.

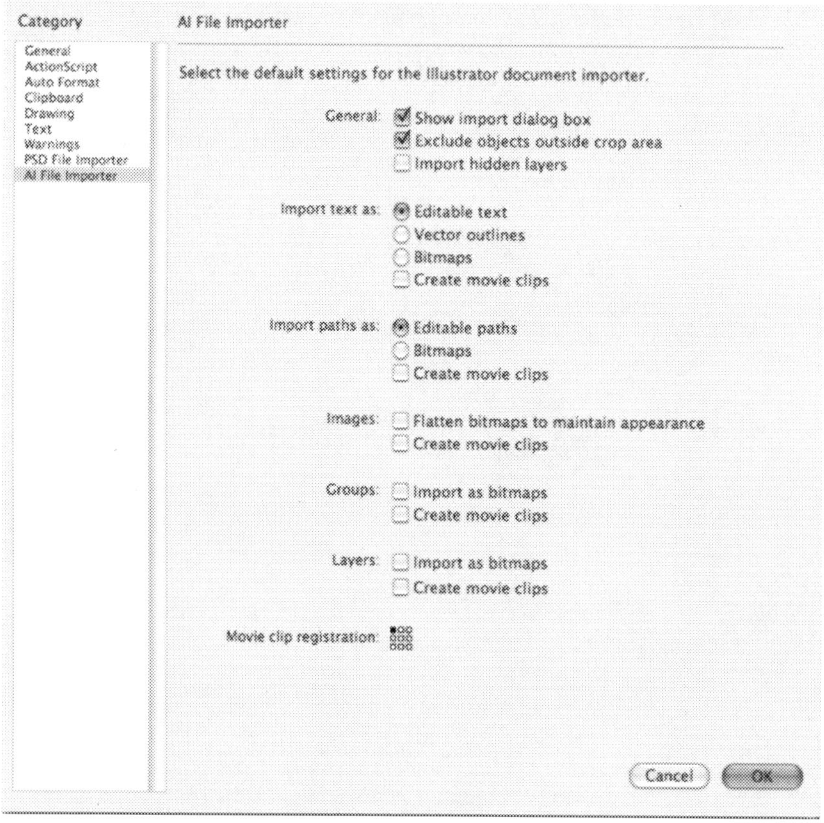

Figure 2-64. The AI File Importer preferences

Importing Photoshop CS3 documents into Flash CS3

We wind up this overview of Flash's drawing features with the import of Photoshop CS3 images into Flash. As you saw with Illustrator CS3, the process has been streamlined, and you are in for a rather pleasant surprise. Even so, there are some important gotchas you need to be aware of, and we will review them after the end of this exercise in the section "Notes from the PSD File Import front."

Follow these steps to import a Photoshop document into Flash:

1. Open a new Flash document. When the document opens, select File ➤ Import ➤ Import to Stage and navigate to the banner.psd document. Click Open to launch the new PSD File Importer shown in Figure 2-65.

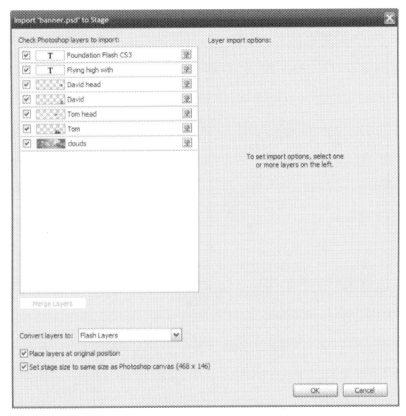

Figure 2-65. The PSD File Importer

2. The dialog box looks similar to its Illustrator counterpart. Still, there are a couple of major differences. The inclusion of a Place layers at original position check box option ensures the contents of the PSD file retain the exact position that they had in Photoshop. For example, if an object was positioned at X = 100, Y = 35 in Photoshop, it will be placed at those coordinates on the Flash stage. If this option is not selected, the imported Photoshop layers are centered on the stage.

The other check box option, Set stage to same size as Photoshop canvas, is a real godsend. In the case of this image, the canvas size is not the default Flash size—500 by 400—but 468 by 146. When the file imports, the Flash stage will be resized to the dimensions of the Photoshop document.

The manner in which PSD files are imported into Flash is set in the Preferences *dialog box. You can reach them by selecting* Edit ➤ Preferences *(PC) or* Flash ➤ Preferences *(Mac) and selecting* PSD File Importer *in the* Category *listing.*

3. Hold down the Shift key and click the first two layers to select them. The Merge Layers button lights up. This means you can combine the selected layers into one layer. This works for selected adjacent layers only. Deselect the layers.

4. Click the check box beside the first layer. What you have just done is to tell Flash to ignore importing that layer. Reselect the check box.

5. Click the name of the first layer. The import options, as shown in Figure 2-66, appear on the right side of the dialog box. The first thing you should notice is the Importer has figured out you clicked a text layer. You have three choices as to how the text will be handled, and if you wish, you can put the selection in its own movieclip. Select the Editable text import option.

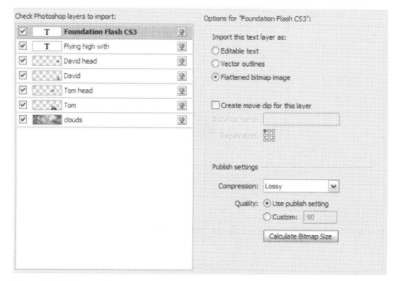

Figure 2-66. The text import options

If the text in the PSD file is PostScript or TrueType, always select Editable text. *If you select the other two options, typos move, cemented, into Flash.*

6. With the layer still selected, click the Create movie clip for this layer check box option and enter Headline as the instance name. Notice the placement of a movieclip icon on the layer strip.

7. Click the David layer. Pay attention to how, as shown in Figure 2-67, the import options change to reflect the selection of a bitmap. You can choose to put the layer in a movieclip—Bitmap image with editable layer styles—or import a flattened bitmap image. It makes sense with this image to choose the first option to maintain the layer transparency.

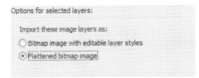

Figure 2-67. The text import options for a bitmap image

Hold on, does this mean you have to repeat this step with the remaining four layers? No. Shift-click each layer to select all of them and click the first option. A movieclip icon, as shown in Figure 2-68, will appear beside each layer.

Figure 2-68. How to import a series of bitmap layers as movieclips

8. Click OK to import the image. The layers are placed on the main timeline, and the movieclips requested appear in the library, as shown in Figure 2-69. Save the file as BannerEx.fla.

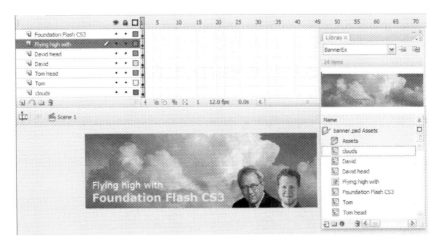

Figure 2-69. The Photoshop file is imported and placed on the Flash stage and in the library.

Notes from the Photoshop File Importer front

We took some time to dig into the Photoshop File Importer feature. The files we used have the potential to demonstrate some pretty useful gotchas.

In wheat_grass_01.psd, note that the buttons, shown in Figure 2-70, are masked vectors of the Photoshop variety with filters applied. The filters make an important difference. As this file stands, you may choose on import to Import this shape layer as and specify either Editable paths and layer styles or Flattened bitmap image. Because of the filters, both choices pretty much amount to the same thing: namely, a bitmap asset in Flash wrapped in an object, wrapped in an enigma. If you clear the filters in Photoshop—not hide, but actually clear them—and then reimport the PSD, you'll see an interesting thing. This time, if you choose editable paths, you get a masked bitmap in Flash. This has potentially dangerous consequences, as the bitmap is much larger than it needs to be. It's simply a huge (big as the stage) bitmap, masked to the size of the button. In this case, it happens three times. Not the sort of overlap a good designer would do by hand.

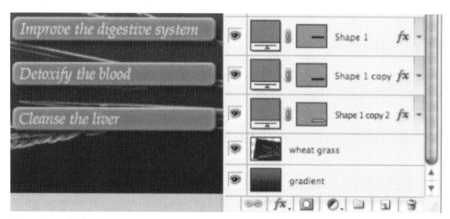

Figure 2-70. The buttons are masked vectors.

In wheat_grass_02.psd, those buttons have been rasterized in Photoshop, but each is still on its own layer, as Figure 2-71 shows. In this case, you don't get the unnecessarily large bitmap, but this approach still produces three identical button images in the library when the ideal would be a single, reusable asset. Although it's possible, in theory, for Flash to recognize that each button is identical, that isn't what happens here.

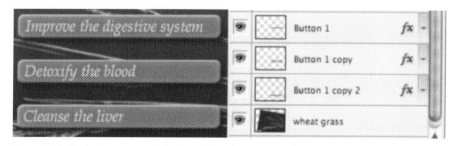

Figure 2-71. The buttons are rasterized and placed on separate layers.

Finally, in `wheat_grass_03.psd`, the buttons have been merged into a single layer, as shown in Figure 2-72. Be advised that the layer comes in as a single asset. In this case, we believe Flash is doing the only possible thing it can do. There is no way to second guess the designer's intent: a layer is a layer, and Flash doesn't have the AI of, say, C3PO to make quality guesses on how to optimize the designer's assumed intent. Just keep in mind that if one layer in Photoshop contains merely 2 pixels—one on opposite corners—a PNG will be imported that is as large as the stage itself. Unless separate objects are close together, put them on their own layers in the PSD.

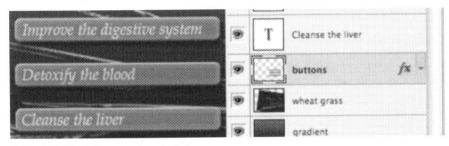

Figure 2-72. The buttons are in a single layer.

Why bring up these points?

While this import feature is amazing and facilitates a significant workflow improvement, it's important you make sure to keep yourself at the helm. You're the Flash designer. Baby-sit the process and be prepared to override the results with your own best judgment. Since the button text can be overlaid in separate text layers, the button image itself need only be imported once. The background gradient should by no means be imported: the effect can easily be reproduced with a vector gradient in Flash.

Here are a few more noteworthy issues. When importing a layer as a bitmap image with editable layer styles, you'll find that Photoshop filters are imported into Flash whether or not they're visible in the original PSD. So hiding them temporarily isn't enough. If you want them gone, clear them—or import the layer as a flattened bitmap image. None of the filters actually carry over as editable effects. They're imported as PNGs, even though Flash now supports many of them. This is different from filters imported from Illustrator files.

Naturally, there are pros and cons to everything: on the plus side, imported PSDs can be published as pre–Player 8 SWFs just fine (because they don't rely on the relatively new Flash filters); on the minus side, any changes to the filters means that the affected PSD must be reimported. Plus, the bitmapped filters are bulkier than their native filter counterparts.

Text with filters in Photoshop may be imported as text fields in Flash, but if that's your choice, filters don't come along for the ride. You'll have to reapply text field filters by hand after the import. Speaking of text fields, check out `text_fields_01.psd`. This is a mixed bag, but mostly good.

As Figure 2-73 shows, vertical text in Photoshop converts into a proper vertical Flash text field. Left, center, and right align convert. Warped text does not, but that's no surprise. Left-, center-, and right-aligned multiline text correctly convert. Left-, center-, and right-justified text become only left justified in Flash. To be fair, the Property inspector only features left justification. Italic and bold convert fine, and faux italic and bold become their nonfaux cousins. All good stuff to know.

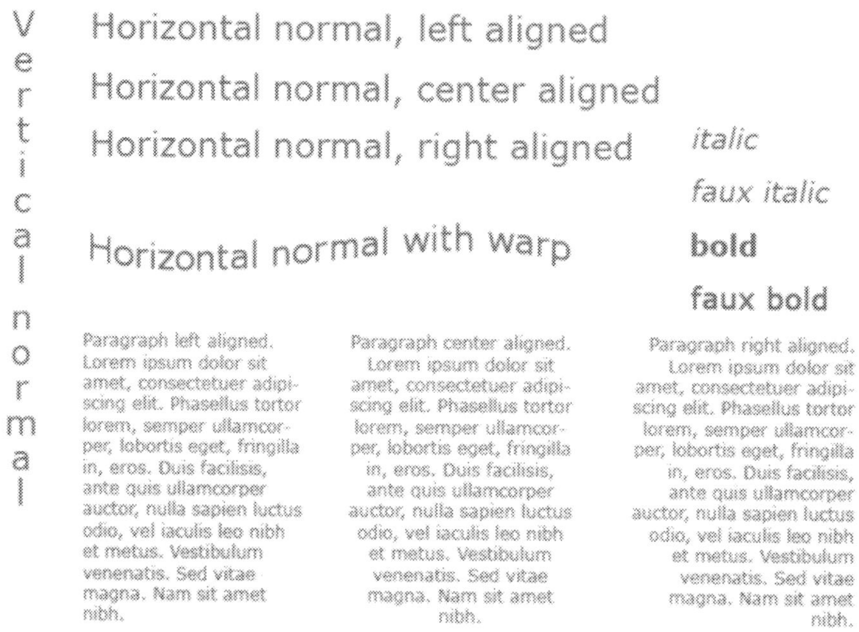

Vertical normal

Horizontal normal, left aligned

Horizontal normal, center aligned

Horizontal normal, right aligned

italic

faux italic

Horizontal normal with warp

bold

faux bold

Paragraph left aligned. Lorem ipsum dolor sit amet, consectetuer adipiscing elit. Phasellus tortor lorem, semper ullamcorper, lobortis eget, fringilla in, eros. Duis facilisis, ante quis ullamcorper auctor, nulla sapien luctus odio, vel iaculis leo nibh et metus. Vestibulum venenatis. Sed vitae magna. Nam sit amet nibh.

Paragraph center aligned. Lorem ipsum dolor sit amet, consectetuer adipiscing elit. Phasellus tortor lorem, semper ullamcorper, lobortis eget, fringilla in, eros. Duis facilisis, ante quis ullamcorper auctor, nulla sapien luctus odio, vel iaculis leo nibh et metus. Vestibulum venenatis. Sed vitae magna. Nam sit amet nibh.

Paragraph right aligned. Lorem ipsum dolor sit amet, consectetuer adipiscing elit. Phasellus tortor lorem, semper ullamcorper, lobortis eget, fringilla in, eros. Duis facilisis, ante quis ullamcorper auctor, nulla sapien luctus odio, vel iaculis leo nibh et metus. Vestibulum venenatis. Sed vitae magna. Nam sit amet nibh.

Figure 2-73. Text effects can be problematic.

Note in text_fields_02.psd, as shown in Figure 2-74, that a single paragraph with several different fonts, colors, and styles (italic, faux italic, bold, faux bold) comes out more or less as you'd expect, following the same caveats as previously discussed. It even accounts for extended leading. This is a good thing.

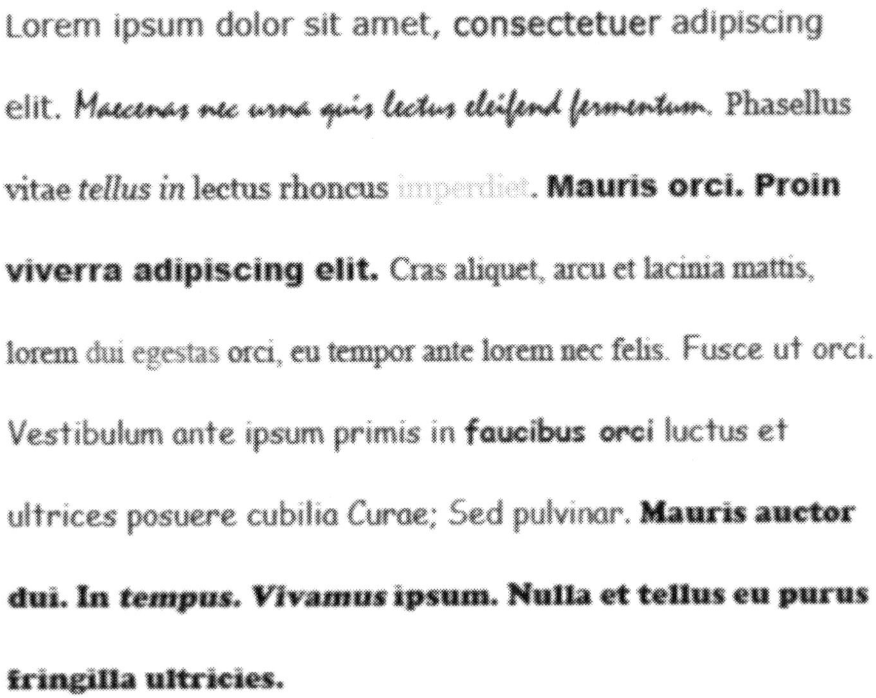

Lorem ipsum dolor sit amet, **consectetuer** adipiscing

elit. *Maecenas nec urna quis lectus eleifend fermentum.* Phasellus

vitae *tellus in* lectus rhoncus imperdiet. **Mauris orci. Proin**

viverra adipiscing elit. Cras aliquet, arcu et lacinia mattis,

lorem dui egestas orci, eu tempor ante lorem nec felis. Fusce ut orci.

Vestibulum ante ipsum primis in **faucibus orci** luctus et

ultrices posuere cubilia Curae; Sed pulvinar. **Mauris auctor**

dui. In *tempus*. *Vivamus* ipsum. Nulla et tellus eu purus

fringilla ultricies.

Figure 2-74. Single paragraphs with multiple styles will import into Flash.

Creating a banner ad

This has been a long chapter, and we have covered a lot of topics that have a direct effect upon your future as a Flash designer. At this point of the chapter, you may be feeling a bit overwhelmed. Recognizing this, we are going to give you a break. Instead of asking you to complete an exercise that pulls together this chapter, we are going to dissect one.

As you may have gathered, Flash designers live in a world of small and fast. They live there because they intimately understand their audience. Think of a site you may have encountered where it took maybe 20 seconds to load. We are willing to bet that after 5 seconds you were getting impatient, and that 5 seconds later you moved on. In the early days of the Internet when modems were even slower than the 56K dial-up standard today, a site that loaded in 20 seconds was regarded as blazingly fast. In an Internet awash in bandwidth and high-speed access, the situation has become reversed.

In this dissection, we are going to look at a banner ad, `banner.fla`, and explain to you how the SWF, `banner.swf`, comes in under 24 KB. We employed a lot of the techniques presented in this chapter to accomplish this feat because we have learned, in the words of one of the most important Flash designers on the planet, Hillman Curtis, to "keep an eye on the pipe."

If you double-click the SWF file to run the movie, you will see it uses the same assets and stage size as the Photoshop import exercise. It even includes the kite used in the Illustrator import exercise. The difference is how the images were created. We didn't simply import an entire Photoshop image and put it into motion. Each image in that presentation was individually created and compressed to be the smallest file size possible with the best quality possible.

That is a fundamental truth of imaging. Reducing file size reduces quality, so the trade-off for you will be to find the balance between low file size and acceptable image quality. Let's see how we reached that balance.

1. Open the `banner.fla` file and open the library. When you look at the assets in the library, as shown in Figure 2-75, you will see that the images are, on the whole, GIF images. One of the things you can do with a GIF image is to reduce the number of colors in the color palette used for the image. This reduces the file size. If you double-click the `david.gif` file in the library, you will see the original image in the Bitmap Preview dialog box is about is about 3 KB in size. With compression, it reduces to about 1.5 KB.

Figure 2-75. GIF images are really small.

2. How did we get the file size so small but still retain a quality standard? Each image started out as a 4×5 high-resolution image. Each one was opened in Photoshop, and the head was tightly cropped and reduced to a physical size of around 50 by 50 pixels. This change in physical size also reduced the file size by a rather massive percentage. The images were then converted to GIF images. The conversion to a GIF image reduced the file size even further to 3.0 KB.

3. The kite image was treated a bit differently. It was imported into the library at the original size of 381×324. We could do this because it is composed of vectors, and as you now know, resizing a vector has no impact upon the resolution of the image or upon its file size. By placing the kite into a symbol, we could bring the kite onto the stage and resize it using the Free Transform tool.

4. The beams that shoot out of our heads, starting in Frame 220, are nothing more than a shape drawn into a graphic symbol. Double-click the library symbol and click the edge with the Subselection tool. The shape has no stroke, and if you switch to the Selection tool and click the fill, you will see the fill in the Property inspector is nothing more than a solid color whose opacity was reduced to 35% in the Color Picker. By drawing the shape using the Flash Tools panel, we knew it would be extremely small and be painted to the screen rather rapidly when the movie played.

5. From there, the project was simply assembled on the stage, and the tweens added between the keyframes.

What you've learned

- How to use the drawing tools in the Tools panel
- The process of creating and customizing gradients
- How to create custom strokes and fills
- The various color features in Flash and how to create and save a custom color
- How to trace a bitmap in Flash
- The process of importing and optimizing graphics in Flash
- The use of the new Illustrator and Photoshop File Importers in Flash CS3

We aren't going to deny this has been a pretty intense chapter. Even so, all of the topics covered here will ripple through the remainder of this book. Most important of all, you have learned how graphic content is created, added to Flash, and optimized in Flash. The next step is making that content reusable in Flash movies or available to different Flash movies. That is the subject of the next chapter. See you there.

3 SYMBOLS AND LIBRARIES

To this point in the book you have been briefly introduced to symbols in Flash. This chapter is designed to show that symbols are one of the most powerful features of the application because they allow you to create reusable content. What we mean by this (and this is something you may have already discovered) is that you only need one copy of a symbol. Once it is on the stage, that symbol can then be manipulated in any number of ways without those changes affecting the original piece of content.

What we'll cover in this chapter:

- Creating and using symbols
- Creating, using, and sharing libraries
- Adding filters and blends to symbols
- Grouping and nesting symbols
- Using rulers, stacking, and alignment to manage content on the Flash stage
- Creating masks
- Creating soft masks

Files used in this chapter:

- GraphicSymbol.fla (Chapter03/ExerciseFiles_CH03/GraphicSymbol.fla)
- ButtonSymbol.fla (Chapter03/ExerciseFiles_CH03/ButtonSymbol.fla)
- MovieClip.swf (Chapter03/ExerciseFiles_CH03/MovieClip.swf)
- MovieClip.fla (Chapter03/ExerciseFiles_CH03/MovieClip.fla)
- 9Slice.fla (Chapter03/ExerciseFiles_CH03/9Slice.fla)
- PeterPan.fla (Chapter03/ExerciseFiles_CH03/PeterPan.fla)
- 9Slice2.swf (Chapter03/ExerciseFiles_CH03/9Slice2.swf)
- MoonOverLakeNanagook.fla (Chapter03/ExerciseFiles_CH03/MoonOverLakeNanagook.fla)
- Filter.fla (Chapter03/ExerciseFiles_CH03/Filter.fla)
- Blends.fla (Chapter03/ExerciseFiles_CH03/Blends.fla)
- NuttyProfessor.fla (Chapter03/ExerciseFiles_CH03/NuttyProfessor.fla)
- Stacks.fla (Chapter03/ExerciseFiles_CH03/Stacks.fla)
- AlignPanel.fla (Chapter03/ExerciseFiles_CH03/AlignPanel.fla)
- SimpleMask.fla (Chapter03/ExerciseFiles_CH03/SimpleMask.fla)
- Windows.fla (Chapter03/ExerciseFiles_CH03/Windows.fla)
- Places.fla (Chapter03/ExerciseFiles_CH03/Places.fla)
- background.jpg (Chapter03/ExerciseFiles_CH03/background.jpg)
- Softmask2.fla (Chapter03/ExerciseFiles_CH03/SoftMask2.fla)

Symbols are also the building blocks of everything you will do in Flash. They are inevitably created when you come to the realization that the piece of content you are looking at will be used several times throughout a movie. In fact, the same content may appear in a number of a number of movies, or even have a single use, such as a movieclip that plays a particular video or sound. Finally, the most important aspect of symbols is they keep the file size of a SWF manageable. The end result of a small SWF is fast load times and users that aren't drumming their fingers on a desk waiting for your movie to start.

Symbol essentials

Reduced to its basics, a symbol is something you can use and reuse. It could be an image, an animation, a button, or even a movie used within the main movie. When a symbol is created, it is placed in the library, and any copy of that symbol on the stage at any point in the movie is said to be an **instance** of that symbol. Let's create a symbol and start examining how these things work. Follow these steps:

Figure 3-1. Creating a symbol

1. Launch Flash, and when a new document opens, select the Rectangle tool and draw a rectangle on the stage.

2. Right-click (PC) or Ctrl-click (Mac) on the shape and select Convert to Symbol from the context menu (as shown in Figure 3-1). You can also select the object on the stage and press the F8 key, or select the object and choose Modify ➤ Convert to Symbol.

3. When the Convert to Symbol dialog box opens, name the symbol Box and select Movie clip as its Type (see Figure 3-2). The dialog box will close and the new symbol will appear in the library.

If you are new to Flash, you may notice a button named Advanced in the Convert to Symbol dialog box. When you click it, a number of extra options will open. Let's look at each element in the dialog box:

- Name: The name you enter here will be the name for the symbol as it appears in the library.

- Type: You select the symbol type here. These were explained in Chapter 1 when you created the MoonOverLakeNanagook project, and will be explained in even greater depth later on in this chapter.

- Registration: Each of the nine dots represents a possible location for the symbol's registration point. The registration point is used for alignment with other objects on the stage and for movement along a motion guide.

- Linkage: You can use ActionScript to pull symbols out of the library and either put them on the stage or use them for another purpose, such as playing audio. To do this, you need to assign a name, called a **linkage class**, for ActionScript to be able to find it in the library. The Linkage check boxes allow the symbol to be used by ActionScript, to be shared by other Flash movies, and to load the symbol into the first frame of the movie when the movie plays.

- Source: This area allows you to identify external content in a shared library to be used as a symbol. This comes into play in cases where you've dragged an asset from one FLA into another. For example, a Flash animator might build a character's body parts in one FLA, save it, and then use that external library in a completely different series of movies. If the color of a shirt changes in the original library from blue to red, the shirt can be configured to change in the current movie as well. Note that you can check Always update before publishing, which makes the change in each linked FLA occur automatically.

- Enable guides for 9-slice scaling: Select this and the guides for this special scaling will appear. We'll get deeper into this in the next section.

Figure 3-2. The Convert to Symbol dialog box

4. Click OK. If you look at the box on the stage, you will see it now surrounded by a thin blue line. This tells you that the object just selected is a symbol. The Property inspector will also change to show that you have, indeed, selected a symbol.

5. Open the library and drag another copy of the symbol to the stage. Click the symbol to select it. Select the Free Transform tool and scale and rotate the object. As you can see, changing one instance of a symbol does not affect any other instance of that same symbol on the stage. Close the movie without saving it.

Symbol types

As you have seen, there are three basic symbol types to choose from: graphic, button, and movieclip. Each one has specific capabilities, and the type you choose will be based upon the goals of what needs to be done. For instance, say you have a logo that will be used in several places throughout a movie. In this case, the graphic symbol would be your choice. If the need is for a racing car zooming across the screen with the engine sounds blasting out of the user's speakers, then the movieclip symbol is your choice. Let's briefly review each symbol type.

Graphic symbols are used primarily for static images or content used in a project. They can be used as the building blocks for elaborate animations, and though we say they are primarily static, they can be put into motion on the main timeline and the timelines of other symbols. It is important to understand that graphic symbols, unlike their movieclip cousins, do not play independently of the timeline they're in. They also need a matching number of frames on the containing timeline for each frame to be visible in the symbol. For example, if a graphic symbol has a length of 80 frames, and you want it to be on the main timeline for half of its life, then you would need to allocate 40 frames on the main timeline for this task. That may sound a little convoluted. We agree, and have provided a small movie that shows you what we mean:

1. Open the GraphicSymbol.fla file. When it opens, you will see a gray box on the stage that has a duration of 10 frames on the main timeline. Scrub across the timeline, and the box will move a short distance.

2. Double-click the graphic symbol in the library, and when the Symbol Editor opens, you'll see that the animation has a length of 85 frames.

3. Click the Scene 1 link to return to the main timeline.

4. Select frame 85 on the main timeline and add a frame. Scrub across the timeline. This time, the box moves right off the right side of the stage at frame 85 and pops back to the left side of the screen in the new frame. It does this because the graphic symbol, having reached the end of its timeline, pops back to frame 1 of its timeline.

5. Close the file without saving the changes.

> *If you want a graphic symbol to repeat or loop on the main timeline, you will need to add a another series of frames on the main timeline to match the length of the graphic symbol for each loop. This sort of explains why, unless there is a really good reason for it, graphic symbols are rarely animated in the Symbol Editor. If you want to see a really good reason, keep your eyes peeled for Chapter 7, which touches on complex character animation.*

Button symbols are rather interesting in that they are able to do a lot more than you may think. Button symbols have a four-frame timeline in which each frame is the state of the button (up, over, down, and hit), as shown in Figure 3-3. The button states can be created using graphic symbols or movieclips, or drawn directly into the frame using the tools. Let's look at a typical button:

1. Open the ButtonSymbol.fla file and select Control ➤ Enable Simple Buttons. If you roll over the button and click it, you will see that the button changes in relation to whether it has been clicked or rolled over, and whether the mouse is off of the button.

If you use the Enable Simple Buttons *menu item, do your sanity a favor and deselect it after you have tested the button. This menu item puts the button into its "live" state, meaning that you can't move it to another location on the stage.*

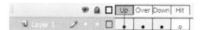

Figure 3-3. The button symbol timeline

2. Double-click the button symbol in the library. When the Symbol Editor opens, you will see that each state of the button is in its own keyframe. Select the Hit keyframe.

3. Select the Rectangle tool and draw a large square or rectangle that covers most of the stage.

4. Click the Scene 1 link, turn on Enable Simple Buttons, and drag the mouse across the stage. The over state will appear even though the mouse pointer is not over the button. This is the hit state coming into play. The area of the shape determines the active area for an event. This should tell you that you can have a button composed only of a hit state. If you do, what you have created is a **hotspot**, sometimes referred to as an invisible button, on the stage.

You can add layers to a button symbol. A common use of this feature is adding a sound to a button. For example, you could have something explode only when the mouse is over a button. Drag the BlowUp *button to the stage and try it out. The explosion sound is on the* Audio *layer of the symbol, and is only triggered when the mouse is over the button on the stage.*

Movieclip symbols can be thought of as movies within movies. These symbols, unlike their graphic counterparts, actually run independent of the timeline. They can contain code, other symbols, and audio tracks. As well, movieclips can be placed inside other movieclips—the term for this is **nesting**—and they have become so ubiquitous and useful among Flash designers that they are, in many cases, replacing graphic and button symbols on the stage.

Movieclips continue to play even if the timeline is stopped, which explains why they are traditionally placed in a single frame on the main timeline. In cases where, for example, a movieclip fades in over a period of time, it may extend across a number of frames to accommodate this effect—but generally, movieclips need only a single frame on the timeline that contains them. The other major feature of movieclips is that they automatically loop. This means the animation will play as many times as you wish without your having to add an inordinate number of extra frames to the main timeline. Let's see how all of that works:

1. Double-click the MovieClip.swf file to launch Flash Player. You will see a sports car come roaring onto the screen and drive off the right edge of the stage. Close the SWF, and let's look at how this was put together.

2. Open the MovieClip.fla file. If you look at the timeline, you will see that the car starts moving in frame 6 and is off the stage by frame 18.

3. Open the library, and you will see that the car is actually composed of three movieclips. The Car movieclip doesn't contain a rear wheel. The Rear movieclip contains the wheel. Double-click the Race movieclip to open the Symbol Editor. You will see that the car is composed of two layers, and each layer contains a movieclip. This is what is meant by "nesting." Movieclips can be placed inside of other movieclips.

4. Click the Scene 1 link to return to the main timeline. If you select the car on the stage, you will see that the Racer movieclip is used for the animation.

5. Scrub the playhead across the timeline. You'll see that the car gets larger and smaller, thanks to a tween. The key aspect of this is that movieclip properties can be changed, and in the case of nested movieclips, this change is reflected throughout the entire symbol, including the movieclips nested inside the main movieclip.

Yes, we agree this is not exactly a well-designed piece. In fact, one of the authors saw it and said, "Dude, what's with that?" Sometimes the technique is more important than the actual content that answers the author's question. This is an important concept for those of you who are new to Flash: get it to work, understand why it works, and then start playing with it. Everything you will do in Flash starts with a basic concept, and everything else in the movie builds upon that concept. For example, Joshua Davis, one of the more influential characters in the Flash community, started one project by simply watching how a series of gray squares rotated on the Flash stage. Once he got the squares to rotate in a manner that worked for him, he simply swapped out the squares for shapes he had drawn in Illustrator.

Editing symbols

There will be occasions where you will want to edit a symbol. This is where the Symbol Editor becomes an invaluable tool. There are two ways of opening the Symbol Editor:

- Double-click the symbol in the library. The Symbol Editor will open. Click the Scene 1 link in the Layers panel to return to the main timeline.

- Double-click the symbol you resized and rotated on the stage. This will also open the Symbol Editor, but, as you may have noticed, the other instance of the symbol on the stage is visible. If you try to select that instance, you will notice you can't. This technique, called **editing in place**, allows you to see how the change to a symbol or instance affects, or works with, the rest of the content on the stage, without your being able to access anything but the selected symbol. The other thing that is important with this technique is that even though you are in the Symbol Editor, the resizing and rotation of the selected object won't change.

Once in the Symbol Editor, you can make changes to the symbol. Click the symbol to select it and, in the Tools panel, change the fill color to a different color. When you do this, both instances of the symbol will change color.

What you can gather from this is that instances of symbols can be changed without affecting the original symbol in the library. Change the symbol in the Symbol Editor, however, and that change is applied to every instance of the symbol in the movie.

Symbols and 9-slice scaling

Until the release of Flash 8, Flash designers essentially had to put up with a rather nasty design problem. Scaling objects with rounded or oddly shaped corners was, to put it mildly, driving them up a wall across the ceiling and down the other wall. No matter what they tried to do, scaling introduced distortions to the object. The release of Flash 8 and the inclusion of 9-slice scaling solved that issue. To be fair, there are still a few issues—but it was so welcome in Flash that this feature is now appearing in Fireworks and Illustrator CS3. The best part of this addition to those two applications is that symbols created in these applications that are destined for Flash can have 9-slice scaling applied to them that carries over into Flash as well.

What the heck is 9-slice scaling?

That question is not as dumb as it may sound because it is a hard subject to understand. What happens is that the symbol in question—in Flash it can only be a movieclip—is overlaid with a 3 by 3 grid. This grid divides the movieclip into nine sections, and allows the clip to be scaled in such a way that the corners, edges, and strokes retain their shape.

Figure 3-4 shows the actual grid that Flash places over the object. The object is broken into the nine areas. The eight areas surrounding the center area—the area with the 5—will scale either horizontally or vertically. The area in the middle—area 5 itself—will scale on both axes. The really interesting aspect of this feature is that each section of the grid is scaled independently of the other eight sections.

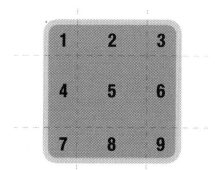

Figure 3-4. The 9-slice scaling grid

The best way of understanding how all of this works is to actually see it in action.

1. Open the 9Slice.fla file. When it opens, you will see two movieclips on the stage. The upper movieclip doesn't have 9-slice scaling applied; the lower one does (see Figure 3-5). The key to both of these objects is that they are the identical in size and the stroke width around both shapes is also identical.

2. Click the upper movieclip, open the Transform panel, and change the Horizontal scaling value to 300%. When you press the Enter/Return key, the shape scales along the horizontal axis, but as you can see, the corners flatten out and distort, and the stroke gets fatter.

3. Click the lower movieclip, open the Transform panel, and change the Horizontal scaling value to 300%. When you press the Enter/Return key, the shape scales along the horizontal axis, and the corners don't distort (as shown in Figure 3-6). You can see why by looking at Figure 3-4. The areas numbered 2, 5, and 8 are scaled horizontally, and the corner areas are unaffected.

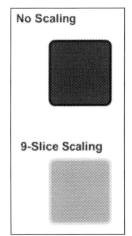

Figure 3-5. You start with two movieclips on the stage.

3

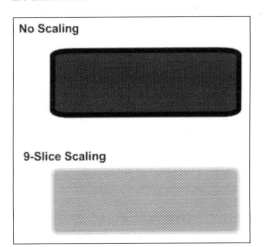

Figure 3-6. Both movieclips are scaled at 300% along the horizontal axis; the movieclip without 9-slice scaling is distorted.

As we pointed out in the "Symbol essentials" section of this chapter, 9-slice scaling is applied to movieclips in the Convert to Symbol dialog box. If you create a movieclip and then decide at a later date to apply the scaling, select the movieclip in the library and open the Library Options menu. Select Properties, and add 9-slice scaling by selecting this option at the bottom of the Symbol Properties dialog box.

> *Movieclips with 9-slice scaling applied to them will show the grid in the library's preview window.*

Finally, the guides are adjustable. They can be moved, which allows you to control how the scaling will be applied. Here's how:

1. Double-click the 9Scale movieclip in the library to open the Symbol Editor. You will see the grid.

2. Roll the cursor over one of the slice guides, and it will change to include a small arrow pointing to the right if you are over a vertical guide, or pointing downward if you are over a horizontal guide (see Figure 3-7).

3. Click and drag the selected guide to its new position. When you release the mouse and return to the main timeline, you will see the change in the library's preview window.

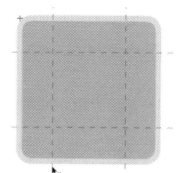

Figure 3-7. The guides can be repositioned.

So far, so good. You have applied the slice guides to a geometric object. OK, we hear you. You are probably muttering, "Not exactly a real-world project." We thought about that, and agree with you. What about occasions where the corners are irregular? Let's go visit Peter Pan in Never Land to give you some "real-world" experience with that issue.

Randy Constan has gained quite a bit of fame by portraying himself as Peter Pan on his site, at www.pixyland.org. This hasn't gone unnoticed, and he has appeared on TechTV, "Late Night with Conan O'Brien," and other outlets. When we approached this exercise, the question was, "What could we put in a picture frame that would be memorable?" Flowers and other images are interesting, but really don't make the point. Then one of the authors said, "How about a picture of Peter Pan?" The reply was, "Disney would never go for it." To which the author who made the original suggestion said, "No. No. No. There is a guy that has a whole site of pictures of himself as Peter Pan. Everyone would recognize him. Maybe we can use those?" So we contacted Randy, and the end result was this exercise.

1. Open PeterPan.fla. When the file opens, you will notice that the images of Peter Pan don't exactly fit their frames (see Figure 3-8). Let's fix that.

http://peterpan.pixyland.org

Figure 3-8. The picture frames don't fit the images.

2. Select the Frame movieclip in the library and enable 9-slice scaling. Open the movieclip in the Symbol Editor and adjust the guides to match those shown in Figure 3-9. Note that the top guide, in area 1, is positioned low enough to encompass the full extent of the feather.

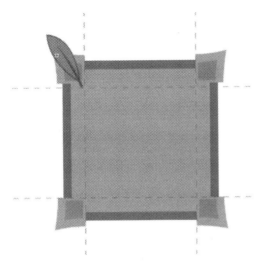

Figure 3-9. Applying 9-slice scaling and adjusting the guides

3. Click the Scene 1 link to return to the main timeline.

4. Select the Free Transform tool and adjust the picture frames to fit the image, as shown in Figure 3-10. Even though each photo has its own width, the same symbol can now be used to neatly frame these different dimensions.

Figure 3-10. 9-slice scaling allows Peter Pan to fly.

Now that you have seen how 9-slice scaling works, how it is applied, and how to use it, don't get lulled into thinking it is especially easy to use. That is a real danger with books of this sort, where everything appears rosy, wonderful, and trouble-free. In many cases, it is. In this one, it isn't. When we started working on Peter Pan's picture frame, we felt like we had walked into an uncharted minefield. The corner images started blowing up and distorting when they shouldn't have. This caused us to halt the process and really dig into this particular feature. The next section gives you the un-rosy, "it ain't all that wonderful and easy to use" rundown regarding what we discovered about 9-slice scaling. Thankfully, our pointers should help you steer clear of the mines. Pixie dust to the rescue!

The 9-slice "gotchas"

You need to know that there are a handful of interesting "gotchas" involved with 9-slice scaling.

The first concerns the area in the middle of the 9-slice grid, which scales across both the horizontal and the vertical axes. If you have content in the center area of the grid (area 5), such as a gradient or image, it will distort if the scaling is uneven. Take a look for yourself.

Open the 9Slice2.swf file and drag out a corner. Notice how the flower distorts. This is because the frame and the flower are both in the area 5 slice (see Figure 3-11). Depending on your needs, this makes 9-slice symbols useful only as background borders, layered behind content that simply must not be distorted. In the PeterPan.fla file, the photos are on layers of their own.

Figure 3-11. The center area of a symbol containing 9-slice scaling scales on two axes. The area in the middle will distort.

The second involves maintaining the integrity of any drawings or objects used in the corners. Shapes, drawing objects, primitives, or graphic symbols can be used. Movieclips or rotated graphic symbols can't be used. That would be easy enough to remember, but an interesting quirk rears its head with graphic symbols: if you use graphic symbols that are rotated, they will not display correctly as specially scaled 9-slice elements in the Flash interface. Rest assured, they work just fine in the SWF—you just can't see that they're working until you test your movie. If this annoys you, bear in mind that Flash 8 didn't show 9-slice scaling in the authoring environment at all, so this is an improvement!

You can see what we are talking about in Figures 3-12 and 3-13. We started with nothing more than a box with a circle. The circle was converted to a specific object and, in one instance, the graphic symbol was rotated 45 degrees.

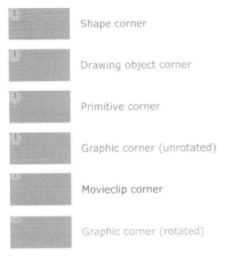

Figure 3-12. We start with a simple object.

When the objects were stretched along the horizontal axis using the Free Transform tool, the object in the upper-left corner was fine in all versions except the movieclip and rotated graphic symbol versions, which were distorted (see Figure 3-13). Remember, however, that the rotated graphic symbol works fine in a published SWF. We obtained the same results by stretching along the vertical axis.

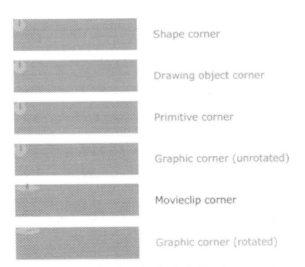

Figure 3-13. Note the distortion in the bottom two examples.

Joseph Balderson, a Community MX colleague, has reported that 9-slice movieclips can go batty when edited in place—that is, when a given instance is double-clicked on the stage, rather than edited directly from the library. We were able to reproduce his experience intermittently. Interestingly enough, in cases where the 9-slice movieclip broke, it would fix itself again when we closed the FLA and reopened it or used File ➤ Save and Compact. Such Twilight Zone occurrences tended to get worse when we used imported graphics files inside any of the allowable object types, whether simply as images or bitmap gradients.

The bottom line is, use 9-slice with care. The idea is a good one, but don't go nuts with it. Keep it simple! Avoid nesting symbols in the corners and sides. If you insist on using bitmaps, bear in mind that they'll stretch in ways that may not be predictable. We encourage you to experiment on your own, but by all accounts, the simpler, the better.

Sharing symbols

One of the really useful features of symbols in a library is that they are available to files other than the current movie. Symbols in a Flash library can be shared with other Flash movies. This is extremely helpful if you are working on a number of movies and need to use the same symbol or symbols in numerous Flash documents.

Animators make extensive use of this feature. An animator will, for example, create a character composed of a number of symbols—eyes, arms, legs, and hands, for instance—that are used to put the character in motion. As the animations are built in a given movie, the animator will use symbols that were created in a separate character library movie instead of redrawing them. Here's how to use symbols from another movie:

1. Create a new Flash document and open the new document's library. As you can see, it is empty.

2. Select File ➤ Import ➤ Open External Library (Ctrl+Shift+O [PC] or Cmd+Shift+O [Mac]), as shown in Figure 3-14. When the Open dialog box appears, navigate to the Chapter 3 Exercise folder and open MoonOverLakeNanagook.fla.

Figure 3-14. Importing a library into from one Flash document into another

3. The library for the selected movie will open, but there are a couple of things missing from that library. There is no drop-down menu, the pushpin is missing, and the Open New Library buttons are missing. As well, the library looks grayed out. All of these are visual clues that the MoonOverLakeNanagook.fla file isn't open, only its library is.

4. Drag the Trees symbol to the empty library. When you release the mouse, the symbol will appear in the empty library and become available for use in the movie (see Figure 3-15).

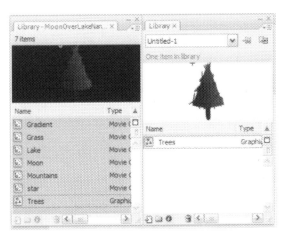

Figure 3-15. Drag a symbol from the imported library to the empty library.

> *You can also share font symbols between movies. We'll get into that subject in Chapter 6.*

Sharing libraries

Since the introduction of Flash 5, Flash designers and developers have had the ability to link symbols, sounds, animations, bitmaps, and other library symbols within external SWF files to other Flash movies. These external SWF files are called **shared libraries**, and what you must know about this feature is that a shared library is different from a SWF in that the shared library is really nothing more than a library where each symbol has a unique class identifier.

Why would you want to create a shared library? The reason is that it only needs to be downloaded once, even though several other Flash movies may need to access the same symbol. For example, you may be creating a character animation that uses the same image background in ten of the movies that comprise the animation. Rather than adding it in each of the ten movies that use it—not a good idea because the file size of the image will be added to the final SWF for each movie—you can have that symbol reside in a shared library SWF file. This way, the file is only loaded once, but used by several movies.

The other thing that sets a shared library SWF apart from a regular SWF is that it doesn't load into a movieclip. Instead you create the library as you would any other library, but none of the content in that library is put on the Flash stage. Then, each item in the library is given a class identifier, which allows ActionScript to access that item. The file is saved and the SWF is published.

The key is the **linkage class**. When you select an item in the library and select Linkage in the Library Options menu, you will see the Linkage Properties dialog box (shown in Figure 3-16). If a library is to be shared at runtime, then you must select Export for runtime sharing, and enter the location of the shared library. In the case of Figure 3-16, the URL indicates that the shared library SWF will be located in the same folder as the other SWFs that use it. If the shared library were in a different location, you would enter a full path, such as http://www.myMostExcellentSite.com/excellentMovie/SharedLibrary.swf.

Figure 3-16. Adding items to a shared library using the Linkage Properties dialog box

Items in shared libraries can also be created when the symbol is created (see Figure 3-17), or by selecting Properties from the Library drop-down menu.

Figure 3-17. Symbols can be added to shared libraries when they are created.

Obviously, things will rarely remain the same in your workflow. Things change and, more often than not, these changes ripple through a number of movies. Let's assume, for example, you need to add or remove something from the background image used in a number of animations in the movie. This is quite easily accomplished.

The first step is to open the FLA containing the background and make the change in the Symbol Editor. When you finish, save and publish the document, and close the FLA. With the change made, open a Flash document that uses the shared asset and open its library. Select the symbol that was changed, and select Update from the Library drop-down menu or, alternatively, right-click (PC) or Ctrl-click (Mac) on the item and select Update from the context menu. This will open the Update Library Items dialog box (shown in Figure 13-18). Select the check box next to the item's name and click the Update button.

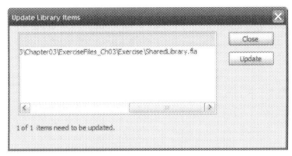

Figure 3-18. Symbols that have changed in a shared library can quickly be updated wherever they are used.

If you have been carefully going through the chapter to this point, you are probably thinking, "Man, there is a lot of serious stuff that I have to know." We can't deny that, but once you understand the serious stuff, you can then start having fun with symbols. In fact, let's start.

A word from the bunnies

Jennifer Shiman has created what is arguably one of the funniest sites on the Web (www.angryalien.com/). On a regular basis, she releases a Flash movie that uses the following premise: the movie is a 30-second synopsis of a popular film and the actors are bunnies. Drawing and animating each bunny would be a daunting task. Jennifer's solution is the use of a shared library containing all of the "bunny bits" needed to create the animations (see Figure 3-19). This is what Jennifer says about how she does it:

> **"***This is my library of "bunny bits," which I incorporate into each of my 30-Second Bunnies Theatre cartoons. I've compiled a bunch of the symbols I use most commonly in animating the bunnies, and I grouped them into folders. For instance, within the "bun mouths" folder are subfolders of different mouth shapes for lip sync; mouths smiling and frowning; mouths in color and black and white; mouths of differing line thickness. The "bkgds" folder contains background symbols I frequently use, such as standardized clouds, grass, and trees. At the beginning of production, I'll open the bunny bits library and drag the folders into the library of my current cartoon file. Then I import the additional artwork specifically pertaining to that cartoon.*

During the course of production, if I create new bunny-related artwork I want to use in future files (such as a new version of a bunny mouth shape or a bunny arm position I'll use often), I drag those symbols into the bunny bits library file. It saves time to have one central location for these types of reusable elements. **"**

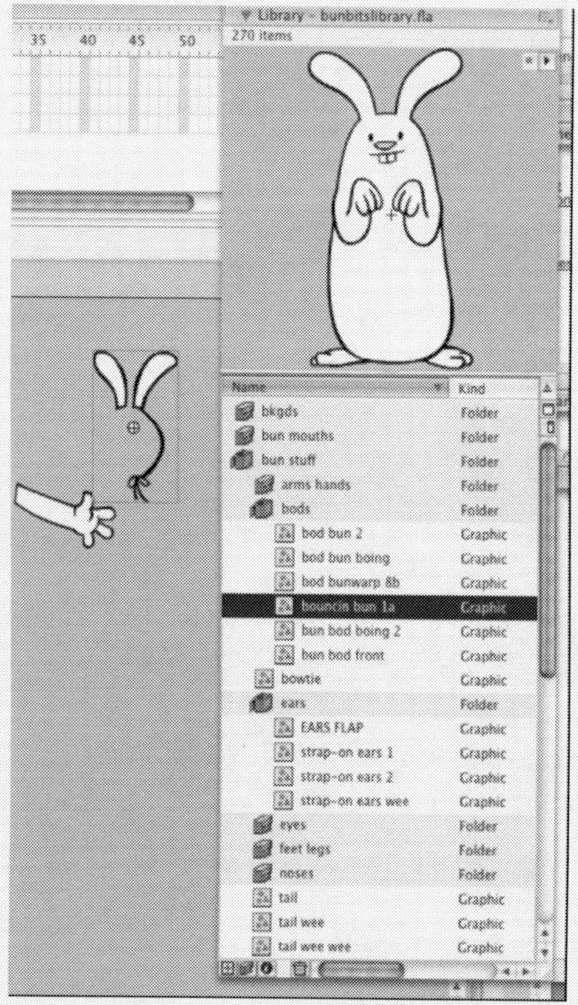

Figure 3-19. Shared libraries help Jennifer manage complex animations.

Filters and blend modes

Flash 8 was a "designer's release." The versions prior to that saw a lot of improvements and features added to the application that directly benefited the Flash coders, resulting in an increasing chorus from the Flash designers as they asked, "Hey, what about us?"

One of the many responses to this question was the introduction of filters and blend modes to Flash. Flash designers were quite comfortable using the Photoshop filters or Fireworks Live Effects, but if a change needed to be made to an image, it meant leaving Flash and opening an imaging application where blurs, drop shadows, and glows could be applied. These same filters are now a part of Flash. Although, in many cases, filters should be applied in the originating application, the ability to use these filters directly in the Flash authoring environment has handed you a quick and easy method to create some fascinating visual effects. The filters that are available in Flash are as follows:

- **Drop Shadow**: Places a colored shadow beneath an object, which gives it the appearance of floating over the background
- **Blur**: Takes the subject out of focus, making it look smudged or out of the depth of field
- **Glow**: Creates a faint glowing outline around an object by following its curves
- **Bevel**: Gives an object a 3D look by creating shadows and highlights on opposite edges of the object
- **Gradient Glow**: Quite similar to the Glow filter, except that the glow follows a gradient of colors from the inside to the outside edges of the object
- **Gradient Bevel**: Similar to the Bevel filter, except that a gradient is applied to the shadow and the highlights of the bevel
- **Adjust Color**: Allows you to adjust the brightness, contrast, hue, and saturation of an object

> *There are also three filters that can be applied only through the use of ActionScript: Color Matrix, Displacement Map, and Convolution. Their use is out of the scope of this book, but check out the ActionScript 3.0 Language and Components Reference in the Help menu for explanations and demonstrations of how to use these filters.*

The blend modes operate quite differently from the filters. If you are a Fireworks or Photoshop user, you may already be familiar with the concept. In applications like those, such modes are commonly used to manipulate the colors of pixels to create new colors based on combinations with underlying pixels. How this works is that the pixel color values are considered from two separate layers of an image and mathematically manipulated by the mode to create the effect. An excellent example of this manipulation is the Multiply mode. This mode will multiply the color values of a pixel in the source layer with the color values of the pixel directly below it in the destination layer. The result is divided by 256, and is always a darker shade of the color. In Flash, these calculations are performed on overlapping movieclips or buttons on the stage.

When applying a blend mode in Flash, keep in mind that it is not the same task as it is in Photoshop or Fireworks. Flash lets you place multiple objects in a layer. When a blend mode is applied to a movieclip or button in Flash, it is the object (which could be a photo) directly under the movieclip or button that will supply the color for the change in the movieclip or the button.

The blend modes in Flash are as follows:

- Normal
- Layer
- Darken
- Multiply
- Lighten
- Screen
- Overlay

- Hard Light
- Add
- Subtract
- Difference
- Invert
- Alpha
- Erase

Let's start with using the filters, and then we'll start playing with the blend modes.

Applying a Drop Shadow filter

The first thing you need to know about this or any other filter is that it can't be applied to everything. Filters can only be applied to movieclips, buttons, or text. This makes sense because the bulk of the movieclips receiving a Drop Shadow or other filter will either arrive in Flash as PNG or PSD images from Photoshop or Fireworks, or as line art from Illustrator. When you import these images into Flash, you will most likely import them as movieclip symbols; and for filters, a movieclip is your best bet. If an imported image has transparent areas, the shadow, when applied to the symbol that contains the image, will be applied to the opaque edges of the image.

In Flash, you can apply filters using a couple of methods. The most common, and the one used in this exercise, is to select the object on the stage and then click the Filters tab on the Property inspector. Filters can also be applied through ActionScript, but we don't get into that in this book. Here's how to get creative with the Drop Shadow filter:

1. Open the Filter.fla file. You will see that a cartoon of one of the authors has been placed over an image of a walkway in the Beijing Zoo (see Figure 3-20). The cartoon is a Photoshop image that was imported into the library as a movieclip.

The authors would like to thank Chris Flick of Community MX and CSFGraphics (www.csf-graphics.blogspot.com/) for allowing us to use this caricature of Tom. Chris is a colleague at Community MX, where he produces the weekly strip CMX Suite every Tuesday at www.communitymx.com/.

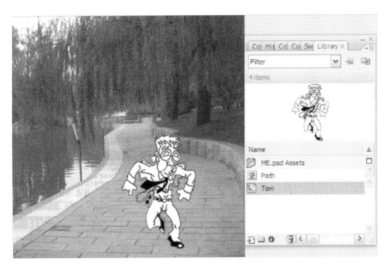

Figure 3-20. We start with a Photoshop image imported into Flash.

2. Select the character on the stage and click the Filters tab in the Property inspector. The blue + sign tells you a filter can be applied to the selection. Click the + sign to open the Filters drop-down menu, and select Drop Shadow.

3. The Property inspector will change to show the various options for this filter and the selection on the stage will also develop a drop shadow using the current default values for the Drop Shadow filter.

4. Change the Blur X and the Blur Y values to 8 to make the shadow a little bigger. Also change the Quality setting to High. The shadow should now look a lot better (see Figure 3-21).

Figure 3-21. The filter is applied to the selection.

> *The lock joining the* Blur X *and* Blur Y *values ensures that the two values remain equal. Click the lock if you want the* Blur X *and* Blur Y *values to be different.*
>
> *The first rule of "Flash physics" states: For every action, there is an equally opposite and ugly implication. Selecting a* Quality *setting of* High *results in a great-looking shadow. The ugly implication is that this setting requires more processing power to apply. This is not a terrible thing if the image is static. For objects in motion, however, keep the setting at* Low.

Not bad, but we can do a lot better than that.

5. Select the object on the stage and click the - sign to remove the Drop Shadow filter. With the object selected on the stage, copy it to the clipboard.

6. Add a new layer, give it a name, and with the new layer selected, select Edit ➤ Paste in Place. A copy of the character is pasted into the new layer. Turn off the layer's visibility.

> *You also have the ability to copy the contents of a particular frame in the timeline. Right-click (PC) or Ctrl-click (Mac) the frame or sequence of frames and select* Copy Frames *from the context menu. Select the frame where the content on the clipboard is to be placed. You can then select the frame where the content is to be placed, open the context menu again, and select* Paste Frames.

What we are going to do is to make this effect look a little more realistic. Applying the Drop Shadow in the previous steps resulted in a character that looks flat. In this exercise, you are going to add perspective. Follow these steps:

1. Select the character on the stage and apply a Drop Shadow filter. Use these settings:

- Blur X: 6
- Blur Y: 5
- Strength: 40% (this is an opacity value)
- Quality: High
- Hide Object: Selected

What you should see is nothing more than a somewhat transparent shadow on the sidewalk due to your selecting Hide Object (see Figure 3-22). This opens you up to some rather creative applications. For example, just a shadow appearing over something adds a bit of a sinister feeling to a scene.

2. To add the perspective, select the object with the Free Transform tool and scale and skew the selection.

3. Turn on the visibility of the hidden layer. Select the shadow on the stage and, using the arrow keys, move the shadow to align with the foot that is on the ground.

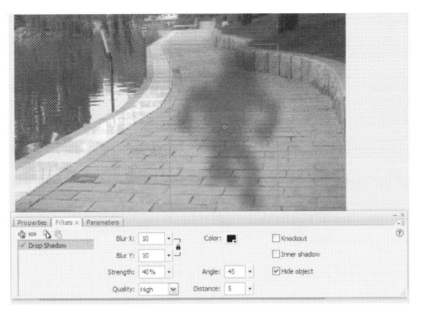

Figure 3-22. Hiding the object allows you to only show the shadow.

4. Select the copy on the stage and apply the Drop Shadow. This time leave the values alone, but select High as the Quality setting, and select Inner shadow. The character takes on a bit of a 3D look to go with the shadow he is casting, as shown in Figure 3-23.

Figure 3-23. Apply an inner shadow to add some depth.

Before we move on to applying a blend, here are a few things you should know about adding and using filters:

- You can apply multiple filters to an object. The character can, for example, have the Drop Shadow, Glow, and Bevel filters applied to it. If you need to remove one, select the filter name and click the - sign in the Filters area.

- You cannot apply multiple instances of a filter to an object. You saw this in this exercise. Each movieclip has a single Drop Shadow filter applied to it.

- Filters do take a hit on the user's processor. Use them judiciously.

- Filters applied to layers in Photoshop will be visible in Flash, but will not be editable in Flash when the image is imported into the Flash library or to the stage.

- Alpha channel video in a movieclip can have filters applied to it.

Playing with blends

Blends are extremely powerful creative tools in the hands of a Flash artist. Though they can only be applied to movieclips and buttons, applied judiciously, the blend modes can provide some rather stunning visual effects. To apply a blend mode, you simply select the movieclip to which it is to be applied and select the mode from the Blend drop-down menu in the Property inspector. Let's look at a few of the blend modes and learn some blend fundamentals along the way.

1. Open the Blends.fla file. When the file opens, you will see we have put two movieclips on the stage (see Figure 3-24). The movieclips are also in separate layers named Source and Destination. Those layers have been given those names for a reason: *blending modes are applied in a top-down manner*. This means that the effect will do the manipulation using the source layer's pixels and apply the result to the movieclip on the destination layer. In fact, anything under the source (including the stage) and visible will be affected by the transformation.

Figure 3-24. The pixels in the Source layer—the graffiti wall—are used to create the effect with the pixels in the Destination layer.

2. Select the image in the Source layer—the graffiti wall—and in the Blend area of the Property inspector, select Normal from the drop-down menu, as shown in Figure 3-25. The Normal mode does not mix, combine, or otherwise play with the color values.

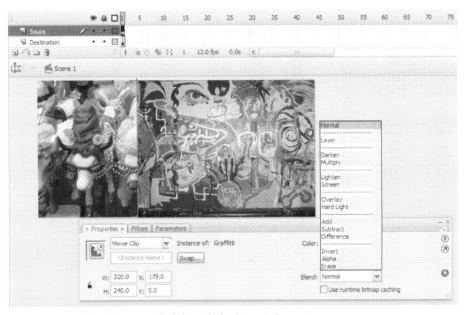

Figure 3-25. Blend modes are applied through the Property inspector.

3. With the image still selected, apply the Multiply mode. As shown in Figure 3-26, the colors have mixed and the darker colors make the Source image darker. The important thing to notice here is how the medium gray of the stage is also being used where the Source image overlaps only the stage. If you return the mode to Normal, select the image in the Destination layer and apply the Multiply mode—the image will darken due to the color of the stage. Nothing happens to the image in the Source layer.

Figure 3-26. The Multiply mode

4. Set the blend mode of the Destination layer to Normal. Select the image in the Source layer, set its x and y coordinates to 0 in the Property inspector, and apply the Lighten mode. In this example (shown in Figure 3-27), the lighter color of both the Source and Destination images is chosen. As you can see, the lighter pixels in the Destination image are replacing the darker pixels in the Source image.

Figure 3-27. The Lighten mode

5. Finally, select the image in the Source layer and apply the Difference mode. This mode is always a surprise. This one works by determining which color is the darkest in the Source and Destination images, and then subtracting the darker of the two from the lighter color. The result, shown in Figure 3-28, is always a vibrant image with saturated colors.

Figure 3-28. The Difference mode

Managing content on the stage

Now that you have had some fun, playtime is over. It is now time to get back to the serious issue of managing content. Though we have talked about using folders in layers and in the library, we really haven't addressed the issue of managing the content on the stage.

As we have been telling and showing you to this point, you can determine the location of objects on the stage by dragging them around. We look upon that practice in many respects as attempting to light your barbecue with an atom bomb. You will light the barbecue, but taking out the neighborhood is a lot less precise than striking a match and lighting a burner. This why we have been doing it by the numbers. We enter actual values into the Property inspector or use menus to precisely place items on the stage, and resize and otherwise manipulate content.

We'll start by showing you how to group content:

1. Open the NuttyProfessor.fla file, and open the Professor movieclip from the library. Click the Professor layer, and you will see that the drawing is composed of quite a few bits and pieces (see Figure 3-29). If you wanted to move that drawing over a couple of pixels, you would have to select each element to be moved. There is an easier method.

Figure 3-29. Line art, in many cases, is the sum of its parts.

2. Select Modify ➤ Group or, if you are a keyboard junkie, press Ctrl+G (PC) or Cmd+G (Mac). The pieces become one unit, as indicated by the square surrounding them. Deselect the group by clicking the stage, and then click the image of the professor on the stage. Again, you will again see the box indicating that the selection is grouped, and you will also be given the same information in the Property inspector, as shown in Figure 3-30.

Figure 3-30. A group is indicated both on the stage and in the Property inspector.

3. To ungroup the selection, select Modify ➤ Ungroup, or press Ctrl+Shift+G (PC) or Cmd+Shift+G (Mac).

4. Close the file without saving the changes.

Aligning objects on the stage

Now that you know how to make your life a little easier by grouping objects, let's turn our attention to how objects can be aligned with each other on the stage. Reopen the NuttyProfessor.fla file and click the Scene 1 link to return to the main timeline. You will see the movieclip and some text on the stage.

The first technique is the use of Snap Align. You can switch on this very handy feature by selecting View ➤ Snapping ➤ Snap Align. When Snap Align is switched on, dragging one object close to another object will show you a dotted line. This line shows you the alignment with the stationary object.

Click the words on the stage and slowly drag them toward the bottom-left corner of the movieclip. You will see the Snap Align indicator line (see Figure 3-31) telling you that the left edge of the text is aligned with the left edge of the movieclip. By dragging the text up and down the indicator line, you can align objects at a distance. Release the mouse and the text will snap to that line.

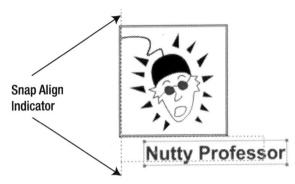

Figure 3-31. Using Snap Align

You can also align objects on the stage through the use of a grid. This is a handy way of precisely positioning objects on the stage. You can turn on the grid by selecting View ➤ Grid ➤ Show Grid. When you release the mouse, a grid will appear on the stage. This grid is what we call an "authortime" feature. That means that the grid won't appear when you publish the SWF and put it up on a web page.

You can also edit the grid by selecting View ➤ Grid ➤ Edit Grid. The Grid dialog box, shown in Figure 3-32, will appear. Here you can change the color of the grid lines, determine if items snap to the grid, and change the size of the squares in the grid. The Snap accuracy drop-down menu lets you choose how snapping to the grid lines will be managed by Flash.

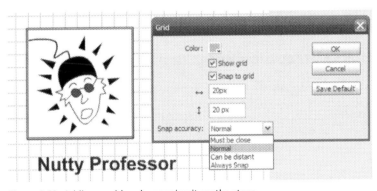

Figure 3-32. Adding a grid and managing it on the stage

Another method of aligning objects or placing them in precise locations on the stage is to use guides. You can add guides by dragging them off of either a horizontal or a vertical ruler. The ruler isn't shown by default in Flash; to turn it on, select View ➤ Rulers. At 100% view, the rulers are divided into 5-pixel units. If you need even more precise placement, zooming in to 2,000% view allows you to work in units of .5 pixels. To add a guide, drag it off of either the horizontal or vertical ruler and, when it is in position, release the mouse. To remove a guide, drag it back onto the ruler.

Once a guide is in place, you can then edit it by selecting View ➤ Guides ➤ Edit Guides. This will open the Guides dialog box (see Figure 3-33), which is quite similar to the Grid dialog box. The Snap accuracy drop-down menu allows you to determine how close an object needs to be to a guide before it snaps to the guide. You can also choose to lock the guides in place. Locking guides once they are in position is a good habit to develop. This way, you won't accidentally move them. If you need to turn off the guides, select View ➤ Guide ➤ Show Guides; reselect it to turn them on again. If you no longer need the guides, you can remove them with a single click of the mouse by selecting View ➤ Guides ➤ Clear Guides.

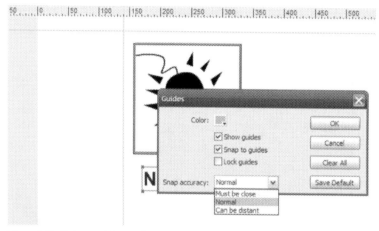

Figure 3-33. Rulers, guides, and the Guide dialog box

Stacking order and using the Align panel

Layers are effective tools for managing content, but there is another related concept you need to be aware of: **stacking**. When multiple objects are in a layer, the objects also have a front-to-back relationship with each other, appearing to be placed on top of each other, which is called the **stacking order**.

Symbols, drawing objects, primitives, text fields, and grouped objects can be stacked. Everything else essentially falls to the bottom of the pile in the layer. To accomplish this, each new symbol or group added to a layer is given a position in the stack, which determines how far up from the bottom it will be placed. This position is assigned in the order in which the symbols or objects are added to the stage. This means that each symbol added to the stage sits in front, or above, the symbols or objects already on the stage. Let's look at this concept:

1. Open the Stacks.fla file. You will see four objects on the stage.

2. Drag the objects on top of each other and you will see a stack; the location of each object in this stack is a visual clue regarding when it was placed on the stage (see Figure 3-34).

Stacking order is not fixed. For example, suppose you wanted to move the circle to the top of the stack and move the yellow pentagon under the Pac-Man shape. Here's how:

3. Select the circle on the stage and select Modify ➤ Arrange ➤ Bring to Front. The circle moves to the top of the stack. This tells you that the Bring to Front and Send to Back menu items are used to move selected objects to the top or the bottom of a stack.

4. Select the pentagon and select Modify ➤ Arrange ➤ Send Backward, as shown in Figure 3-35. The pentagon moves under the Pac-Man symbol. This tells you that the Bring Forward or Send Backward menu items can be used to move objects in front of or behind each other.

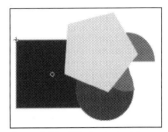

Figure 3-34. Objects stacked in a layer

3

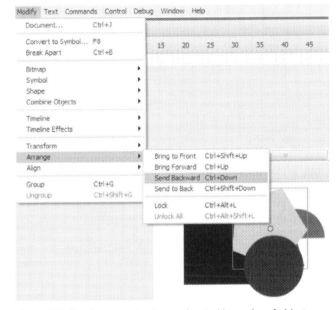

Figure 3-35. Use the menu to change the stacking order of objects.

Throughout this book, we have been talking about the use of layers to manage content. Obviously, stacking objects on top of each other flies in the face of what we have said. Not so fast. There is an incredibly useful menu item that actually allows you to bring a bit of order to the chaos.

1. Select all the items on the stage.

2. Select Modify ➤ Timeline ➤ Distribute to Layers. When you release the mouse, the order of the objects in relation to each other doesn't change, but each object is now on its own named layer, as shown in Figure 3-36.

3. Close the file and don't save the changes.

Now that you see what you can do with this powerful menu item, you also need to understand some rules regarding its use:

- Symbols, text fields, and grouped objects will be placed on their own individual layers.

- Primitives or drawing objects, if they touch each other, will be regarded as one object and placed on the same layer if Object Drawing mode is not selected in the Tools panel.

- Layer names are based upon either the instance name in the Property inspector or the symbol name in the library. If you are a stickler for precision, instance names take precedence over symbol names.

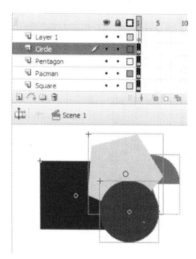

Figure 3-36. Distribute to Layers places each selected object on its own layer.

The final method for aligning objects with each other on the stage uses the Align panel. This panel allows you to line up and center objects, and otherwise bring order to chaos with a click or two of the mouse.

You can access the Align panel either by selecting Window ➤ Align or pressing Ctrl+K (PC) or Cmd+K (Mac). You can also access this panel by clicking the Align button on the main toolbar, as shown in Figure 3-37. When the panel opens, you are presented with a number of alignment options—there are 17 options available. You can align selected objects with each other, or align them to the stage with the To stage button.

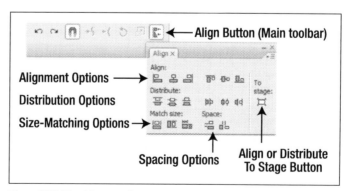

Figure 3-37. The Align panel

So much for the overview—let's see how all of this works:

1. Open the `AlignPanel.fla` file. As you can see, the file consists of a number of buttons scattered across the stage. Open the Align panel.

2. Select all the buttons, and click the Left Align button in the panel. The buttons all line up along their left edges.

3. Click the Vertical Spacing button in the Spacing options, and the buttons will be spaced evenly on the vertical axis (see Figure 3-38).

Figure 3-38. Aligning objects vertically using the Align panel.

Now let's use the panel to create a button bar across the top of the stage.

1. Click the To stage: button on the Align panel.

2. Select all the buttons and click the Align Top Edge button. The buttons will all pile on top of each other at the top of the stage.

3. With the buttons still selected, click the Distribute Horizontal Center button. The buttons spread out along the top of the stage, as shown in Figure 3-39. Not bad . . . two clicks and you have a button bar.

Figure 3-39. Two clicks is all it takes to create a button bar.

Masks and masking

Before we turn you loose on a project, the final subject we will be examining is the issue of masking in Flash. As you know, masks are used to selectively show and hide objects on the Flash stage. The value of a mask is, in many respects, not clearly understood by Flash

143

designers. They tend to regard masking as a way to hide stuff. They see it as an overly complicated method of doing something that could be more easily done in an imaging application. This is not exactly incorrect, but what they tend to miss is the fact that masks in Flash can be animated and can even react to events on the stage. For example, one of the authors connects a webcam to his computer, and using Flash, is able to broadcast himself peering out of billboards in Times Square, waving at people walking by in Piccadilly Circus in London, or looking out of the porthole of a sensory deprivation tank. When the camera is not connected, the images used revert to their normal states.

In this final section of the chapter, you will be doing the following:

- Creating a simple mask
- Creating an masked animation
- Discovering how text can be used as a mask

A simple mask

In this exercise, we are going to show you the basic steps involved in a creating a mask in Flash. Once you have the fundamentals under your belt, you can then apply what you have learned in a rather creative manner. Let's start:

1. Open the SimpleMask.fla file.

2. Add a new layer named Mask and draw a circle on the new layer.

3. Right-click (PC) or Ctrl-click (Mac) on the Mask layer to open the Layer context menu. Select Mask. When you release the mouse, the image of the motorcyclist will look like it is circular. You should also notice that the appearance of the layers has changed, and that they are locked (see Figure 3-40). The icon beside the Mask layer name (the rectangle with a cutout) indicates that the layer is a mask, and the indent for the Cycle layer name indicates that it is the object being masked.

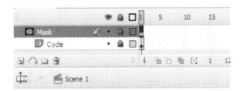

Figure 3-40. Applying a mask

What you are looking at is the image showing through the circle in the Mask layer, with the stage color visible. One thing you need to know about masks is that you can't drag layers under them. Do that, and they too will be masked. The following steps explain what we're getting at:

4. Add a new layer above the mask and name it Square. Select the Rectangle tool and draw a rectangle on this new layer.

5. Drag the Square layer under the Cycle layer. When you release the mouse, the circle and the square are visible. Click the Lock icon in the Square layer, and it will disappear because it is under the photograph.

The locks turn the masks on and off and allow you to edit or manipulate the content in the layers, including the masks. When you finish making your changes, click the locks to reapply the mask. When all layers are locked (the masked layers and the mask), the mask goes into a preview mode.

6. Unlock the Square layer and drag it back above the Mask layer. This time, drag the Mask layer above the Square layer. When you release the mouse, you will see that both the Mask and Cycle layers have moved above the Square layer, and that the shape in the layer is visible, as shown in Figure 3-41.

7. Close the file without saving the changes.

Figure 3-41. Masking layers can be moved around.

Now that you understand the fundamentals, let's get a little more complex.

The art of Flash is, in many respects, the art of illusion. In this exercise, you'll create the illusion of a couple of people—the authors—suddenly appearing in the windows of a building. The problem to contend with is the fact the windows are large and each window is broken into eight pieces of glass, each of which is separated by a thin wooden frame. How do you get the authors to appear in the window but behind a frame?

You think a bit differently.

The effect you want to create is shown in Figure 3-42. Instead of using the windows as the mask, you only need to use the bottom four panes of glass as the mask. The following steps show you how to accomplish this.

Figure 3-42. The authors under glass

1. Open the Windows.fla file. All of the items you will need for this exercise are located in the library.

2. Drag the Building movieclip to the stage and, in the Property inspector, set its x and y coordinates to 0. Name this layer Building and lock the layer.

3. Add a new layer named Mask. Select the Magnifying Glass tool and zoom in on the bottom four panes of glass.

4. Select the Rectangle tool and draw a rectangle over each of the four panes. Holding down the Shift key, select each of the rectangles you have just drawn, and convert the selection to a movieclip named Mask.

5. Open the Mask movieclip in the Symbol Editor. Change Layer 1's name to Windows, and add a new layer named Guys to the timeline. Drag the Guys layer under the Windows layer.

6. Select frame 1 of the Guys layer and drag a copy of the Authors movieclip to the stage. Place the movieclip just under the rectangles in the Windows layer, as shown in Figure 3-43.

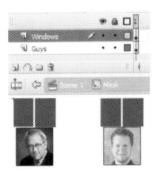

Figure 3-43. The assets are in place, and you can now move on to creating the movie.

With the assets in place, you can now concentrate on creating the animation. The plan is to have the pictures rise up in the window and then sink back down out of view. Here's how you do that:

1. Select frame 20 of the Windows layer and insert a frame.

2. Select frame 20 of the Guys layer and add a keyframe. Select frame 10 of the Guys layer and add another keyframe.

3. Click the Authors movieclip in frame 10 to select it and, using the arrow keys on your keyboard, move the movieclip to the top edge of the window shapes.

4. With the Authors movieclip selected in frame 10, reduce its alpha in the Property inspector to 50%. Select the movieclip in frames 1 and 20, and reduce its opacity to 10%. Reducing the opacity will allow the glass pane to faintly show through the images in the final animation.

5. Add motion tweens between the keyframes in the Guys layer by right-clicking (PC) or Ctrl-clicking (Mac) between the keyframes and selecting Create Motion Tween from the context menu.

6. Select the Windows layer and turn it into a Mask layer. If you scrub across the timeline, you will see the images fade in and back out as they move up and down (see Figure 3-44).

> *Why are the authors images in a movieclip? The opacity reduction is the reason. Another point to keep in mind is that you can't put both images in motion in a mask unless they are either in a movieclip or, if the images have been dragged from the library to the stage, are grouped. If the images aren't grouped, the first one to hit the stage will be masked, and the other image will essentially be ignored by Flash. This doesn't apply if each object has been tweened on its own layer.*
>
> *The one thing you need to take away from this part of the exercise is that animations can be masked.*

Figure 3-44. The animation and the mask

7. Click the Scene 1 link to return to the main timeline. The Mask movieclip just created is the white dot in the corner of the window.

8. Save the movie and test it.

Using text as a mask

Though we are going to fully explore the use of text in Flash in Chapter 6, we can't overlook the power of using text as a mask. If you are going to be using text for this purpose, use a font that has a separate bold version, such as Arial Black, or another font that has the words *Heavy*, *Black*, *Bold*, or *Demi* in its name. These fonts are traditionally used as headline fonts, which makes them ideal for use as a mask.

Let's have some fun with a text mask and create an intro screen for a site named Places.

1. Open the Places.fla file. Add a new layer and name it Text.

2. Select the Text layer, and then select the Text tool. Click in the Text layer and enter the word Places. Select the word with the Text tool.

3. In the Property inspector, change the font to a strong sans serif—we chose Arial Black—and set the point size for the text to 125, as shown in Figure 3-45. The font size slider in the Property inspector only goes up to a value of 96, so double-click the value and enter 125 from the keyboard.

Figure 3-45. Use a strong font as the mask.

4. Select the Text layer and turn it into a mask layer. The mountains will appear through the characters in the text.

Now let's add a bit of motion to this movie. To start, turn off the mask in the Text layer and unlock both layers.

5. Add a frame in frame 60 of the Text layer and add a keyframe to frame 60 of the image layer.

6. Select the image in frame 60 and, using the arrow keys, move the image downward until the top of the letter *P* touches the top of the image, as shown in Figure 3-46. Add a motion tween between the keyframes and reapply the mask. If you press the Return/Enter key, the image moves through the letters.

Figure 3-46. The image is animated in the mask.

You can also add a bit of graphic interest to the mask by applying a filter to the text. If you intend to go this route, though, keep in mind that filters can't be applied to text that's being used as a mask. Instead, the filter needs to be applied to a copy of the text and its layer moved under the mask to give the illusion that a filter has been applied. Here's how:

1. Add a new layer named Filter to the timeline, and add a frame at frame 60.

2. Unlock the Text layer, select the text on the stage, and copy the text to the clipboard.

3. Relock the Text layer to apply the mask. Select frame 1 of the Filter layer, and select Edit ➤ Paste in Place to position the text directly over the mask.

4. Select the text in the Filter layer and apply the Gradient Glow filter using the following settings in the Property inspector (see Figure 3-47):

- Blur X: 7
- Blur Y: 7
- Strength: **100%**
- Quality: High
- Angle: 295
- Distance: 6
- Knockout: Selected (this will turn the text transparent and apply the glow to the edges)
- Type: Outer
- Start Color: #FFFFFF (white)
- End Color: #999900

5. Drag the Text layer above the Filter layer. The effect gives the mask a bit of a 3D look.

Figure 3-47. Filters can add a bit of zing to mask effects.

Your turn: Creating a soft mask in Flash

You may have gone through the masking section and thought, "Gosh, the masks all have a hard edge. Is there a way to create a mask that fades the image out along the edges of the mask?" Great question. Prior to the release of Flash 8, it could be done, but the process was rather complex and, we might add, time-consuming. With the release of the filters and blend modes in Flash Professional 8, this task has become quick and painless.

In this exercise you are going to create a soft mask. Here's how:

1. Open a new Flash document.

2. Select File ➤ Import ➤ Import to Stage, and import the background.jpg image to the stage. When the image appears on the stage, select it and convert it to a movieclip named softmask.

3. There is obviously a lot more stage than there is image. Click the stage, and in the Property inspector, click the Size button to open the Document Properties dialog box. Click the Contents radio button to shrink the stage to the size of the image, and click OK.

> *If you are designing Flash movies and the stage is larger than the stuff on it, get into the habit of reducing the stage size. Wasted space, in the Flash universe, translates into increased download times. Remember, when you think Flash, think small.*

4. Add a new layer to the timeline.

5. Select the Oval tool in the toolbox. Turn off the stroke and pick a fill color in the Tools panel.

6. Make sure you are not in Object Drawing mode, and draw an Oval on the new layer, large enough to cover a lot of the image (see Figure 3-48). This shape will be used to create the mask.

7. Select the Oval and convert it to a movieclip named Mask. You can now delete Layer 2, which was only needed for creating an appropriately sized oval.

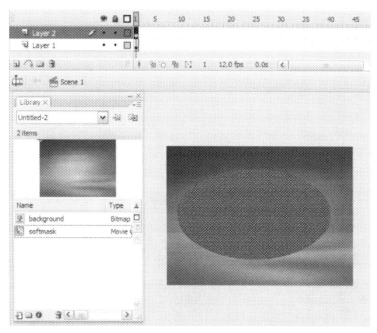

Figure 3-48. The stage is set for a soft mask.

Creating the cutout for the mask

With the objects created and converted to movieclips, you can turn your attention to the creation of the effect. What you need to do first is create the mask by manipulating the Mask movieclip:

1. Double-click the Mask movieclip to open it in the Symbol Editor.

2. Add a new layer below the current layer.

3. Select the Rectangle tool and draw a large rectangle that goes well beyond the edges of the oval. Before you draw the rectangle, be sure to choose a contrasting fill color, and ensure that you are not in Object Drawing mode.

4. Select the oval on the stage and select Edit ➤ Cut to place the oval on the clipboard.

5. Select the bottom layer containing the rectangle, and select Edit ➤ Paste in Place to paste the oval into the rectangle. Deselect the oval.

6. Select the oval and press the Delete key to cut a hole in the rectangle (see Figure 3-49). If it doesn't look like it worked, change the stage color, and you'll see the oval showing through the hole in the rectangle.

> *Why not just do the delete thing when the oval is pasted onto the rectangle? When you pasted the oval, it was actually floating over the rectangle. Deselecting the object drops it onto the rectangle and makes it a part of that shape.*

3

7. Delete the empty layer and save your project.

Figure 3-49. Poking a hole through an object creates a cutout that can be used as a mask.

A mask without a mask layer

It should be obvious that this effect is going to involve the background image showing through the hole you just created in the rectangle. Through the clever use of filters and blend modes, you are going to remove the solid color around the hole and feather the edges of the oval to create the soft mask effect. Here's how:

1. Open the Softmask2.fla file. When the file opens, open the library, and open the softmask movieclip in the Symbol Editor. Add a new layer named Mask.

2. Select the Mask movieclip and drag it to the new layer. Move it into position in order to have the background image appear through the oval.

3. Select the movieclip in the Mask layer, and click the Filters tab of the Property inspector. When the filters appear, click the + sign and select the Blur filter.

4. When the Blur filter properties appear, use these settings:

- Blur X: 15
- Blur Y: 15
- Quality: High

The outside edges of the rectangle and the inside edges of the cutout, as shown in Figure 3-50, will have a blur applied to them.

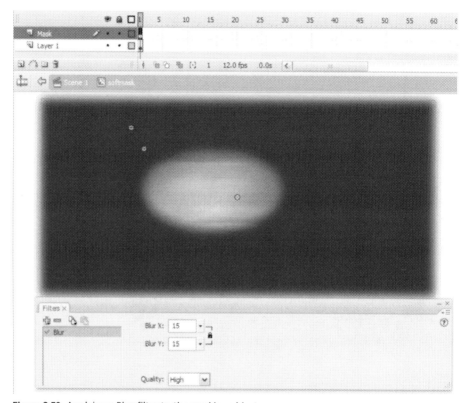

Figure 3-50. Applying a Blur filter to the masking object

5. Select the mask shape, and in the Property inspector, select the Erase blend mode. The whole shape disappears . . . or does it?

The Erase mode removes the base color from the pixels of the movieclip to which it is attached. It also removes anything behind it. In this case, the content will show through the hole. Also, as we pointed out in an earlier masking exercise, content on a mask layer can't have a filter applied to it. The blend modes allow filters, which means that the content showing through the hole will gradually fade out.

6. To complete the effect, return to the main timeline by clicking the Scene 1 link. Click the movieclip on the stage to select it.

7. With the movieclip selected, apply the Layer blend mode in the Property inspector. The mask effect now becomes apparent, as shown in Figure 3-51.

8. Save the movie.

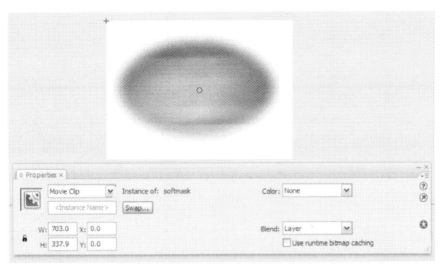

Figure 3-51. Apply the Layer blend mode to the movieclip on the stage to create the effect.

What happened? There are 11 blend modes in Flash, and 2 of them—Alpha and Erase—require that a Layer blend mode be applied to the parent movieclip or object. In the case of this exercise, the softmask movie clip is the parent of the Mask movieclip. The parent is required because of the hierarchy that Flash uses for managing content on the stage, which is different from Photoshop CS3 or Fireworks CS3. This is why the Alpha and Erase modes require that an additional movieclip be set to the Layer blend mode.

Flash treats this movieclip as an entirely different canvas. In this specific case, the embedded blending modes are first calculated, and then the parent—softmask—is redrawn using the Normal mode. This is needed because you can't have an invisible stage on the main timeline. This is awfully techie, but you now know how to use the Erase and the Alpha blends to create a soft mask effect.

What you've learned

- How to create and use symbols in Flash animations and movies
- How to create and share libraries among Flash movies
- The power of filters and blends
- A variety of methods for managing onstage content
- How to create and use a mask
- A rather new Otechnique for creating soft masks

In the next chapter, you. will be exposed to ActionScript 3.0, the latest version of Flash's programming language.

4 ACTIONSCRIPT BASICS

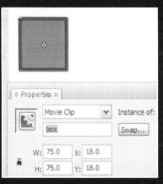  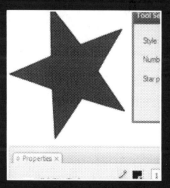

Programming is a discipline all its own. In fact, Flash has grown so much over the ten years of its existence that people are actually earning fairly decent incomes as ActionScript programmers, or as they are known in the industry, Flash developers. This is not to say our intention is to turn you into a programmer, but an understanding of the ActionScript 3.0 language and the fundamentals of its use will make your day-to-day life easier.

What we'll cover in this chapter:

- Using the Actions panel
- The fundamentals of objects
- Commenting code
- Creating and using variables
- Data types, operators, and conditionals
- Getting help

Files used in this chapter:

- Box1.fla (Chapter04/ExerciseFiles_CH04/Box1.fla)
- Box2.fla (Chapter04/ExerciseFiles_CH04/Box2.fla)
- Box3.fla (Chapter04/ExerciseFiles_CH04/Box3.fla)
- Box4.fla (Chapter04/ExerciseFiles_CH04/Box4.fla)
- Box5.fla (Chapter04/ExerciseFiles_CH04/Box5.fla)
- DragStar.fla (Chapter04/ExerciseFiles_CH04/DragStar.fla)
- DatatypeError.fla (Chapter04/ExerciseFiles_CH04/DatatypeError.fla)
- PauseTimeline.fla (Chapter04/ExerciseFiles_CH04/PauseTimeline.fla)
- LoopTimeline.fla (Chapter04/ExerciseFiles_CH04/LoopTimeline.fla)

Using ActionScript is a lot like owning a car. Our hunch is that most of you either own one, or have at least thought about owning one. We also suspect that some of you (including one of the authors) find the mechanics of a car so mystifying that you prefer to let a mechanic handle routine maintenance. Others of you won't be happy unless the hood is up and you're covered in grease up to your elbows.

Whichever way you lean, it's hard to argue against acquiring at least the basic skills necessary to change the oil and maybe fix a flat tire. You never know when you'll be stuck on the side of the road without a cell phone! This chapter gives you an introduction to programming as it relates to Flash CS3. We trust the following information will guide you past the first few mile markers.

> *If you find yourself inspired, we encourage you to pursue ActionScript further with Foundation ActionScript 3.0 with Flash CS3 and Flex 2, by Steve Webster and Sean McSharry.*

Before we move forward, it is important that you understand the reasoning behind a decision the authors made before we started writing this book: every code example and snippet presented from this point forward will use the new ActionScript 3.0 language, even though Flash CS3 is perfectly capable of using ActionScript 2.0. Here's why:

- Trying to present two totally different ways of doing the same thing is a waste of space and time, and can be terribly confusing to you.

- The language is not really new. Adobe used the Labs section of its site for over a year to allow the Flash community to test drive the prototype (to stay with the car metaphor). The consensus of those who have taken it for a spin is, "Wow, I can hardly wait."

- ActionScript 1.0, the first iteration, is on its last legs, and ActionScript 2.0 is heading for that status as well. The adoption of ActionScript 3.0 will be more rapid than in the past due to the introduction of Flex and the fact that the Flash developer community was exposed to the language so far in advance of the introduction of Flash CS3.

- If you are new to Flash, then it makes sense to use the current version of the language. If you are currently a Flash developer or designer, it will only be a matter of months before you switch to ActionScript 3.0, so now would be a good time to figure out what all of the fuss is about.

4

The power of ActionScript

When Flash first appeared on the scene as FutureSplash, and then Flash, web designers were quite content to populate sites with small movies that moved things from here to there, which resulted in the rise of the infamous "Skip Intro" screen. This was a natural evolution, but once ActionScript was introduced into the mix, Flash started its march forward.

Today, Flash is a mature application, and Adobe now refers to the use of Flash CS3 as part of the Flash Platform. What that means is that SWF files are no longer the exclusive property of the Flash authoring environment. Flex Builder 2 also produces SWFs. They're fundamentally the same as SWFs built in Flash—they all run in the same Flash Player—but Flex is geared toward programmers who normally work in applications like Microsoft Visual Studio or Borland JBuilder. Not at all the domain of artsy types! Flash can still be used, as you have seen in the preceding chapters, to move things from here to there. On the one hand, you have an animation tool for building scalable, lightweight motion graphics that renders animated GIFs extinct, and many Flash designers are using the application to create broadcast quality cartoons for display on the Web and television.

On the other hand, even without Flex Builder 2, Flash developers get to spread their wings. They use the platform for everything from building online banking applications to fully realized clones of Super Mario Bros. In between is a cornucopia of content ranging from interactive banner ads to MP3 players, from viral e-cards to video-enhanced corporate multimedia presentations. How far you go, and the directions you take, are up to you—that's an exciting prospect! These are all possible thanks to ActionScript.

Put simply, ActionScript brings your movies to life. No matter how impressive your sense of graphic design, the net result of your artistry gets "baked," as is, into a published SWF. What's done is done—unless you introduce programming to the picture. With ActionScript, your opportunities extend beyond the bounds of the Flash interface. You can program movies to respond to user input in orderly or completely random ways.

ActionScript also has a pragmatic side. You can reduce SWF file size and initial download time by programming movies to load images, audio, and video from external, rather than embedded, files. You can even make things easier for yourself by loading these files based on information stored in XML documents and styled with CSS. (These topics are covered in later chapters.)

ActionScript 3.0 is the latest and most mature incarnation of the programming language used by Flash. As a point of interest, it was supported a full year before Flash CS3 came to market by two related, but distinct, Adobe products: Flex Builder 2 and Flash Player 9. This is an all-time first in the history of Flash, and the decision to do so was a wise one on the part of Adobe. What it means is that the Flash developers have already become familiar with the new features and improvements of ActionScript 3.0. If you're in an academic or office setting, chances are better than ever that a kind and wise soul has already forged ahead and cleared the path. Numerous tutorials and articles on ActionScript 3.0 are already available online at the Adobe Developer Center (www.adobe.com/devnet/).

So where did ActionScript come from? Macromedia, now Adobe, looked at the programming languages used for web interactivity and realized JavaScript was predominant. Rather than add yet another language, the decision was made in Flash 5 to stay within the parameters of something called the ECMA-262 specification. This makes ActionScript a close cousin of JavaScript, so if you're already comfortable with that, you may find ActionScript encouragingly familiar.

> *Ecma International (formerly the European Computer Manufacturers Association) is an industry standards association that governs a number of specifications for data storage, character sets, and programming languages, including specs for C++ and C#. It's something like the W3C (World Wide Web Consortium), which manages the specifications for HTML, XML, and CSS.*

So much for history. Let's roll up our sleeves and get covered in electrons up to our elbows by getting to know the interface with ActionScript: the Actions panel.

The Actions panel

The Actions panel is your portal into the powerful realm of ActionScript. Other entryways do exist, but they are geared toward hardcore programming, in which ActionScript code is stored in external text files. These entryways include the Script window—a full-screen version of the Actions panel that temporarily locks out access to other panels—third-party script editors, such as SE|PY (www.sephiroth.it/python/sepy.php) and PrimalScript (www.primalscript.com/), and even Adobe Flex Builder 2 (www.adobe.com/products/flex/). In advanced scenarios, in which ActionScript does most of the legwork in a published SWF, such alternative coding environments are a good idea. But that's not our focus in this book. We're more interested in using basic ActionScript to assist the techniques discussed so far—to boost what's possible with the Flash interface alone. At the end of the chapter, we'll take a brief look at external ActionScript files.

Of the script editors mentioned, the Actions panel has been around the longest. It has evolved through significant changes since its introduction in Flash 4, and even reveals a handful of new features since Flash 8. Let's take a look.

Create a new Flash ActionScript 3.0 document. When Flash opens, select Window ➤ Actions to open the Actions panel (shown in Figure 4-1).

You can use the keyboard to access this panel. On the PC, press the F9 key. The Mac is a little bit different, as the F9 key is reserved for Exposé. If you're a Mac user, press Option+F9 to open the Actions panel.

Actions Toolbox

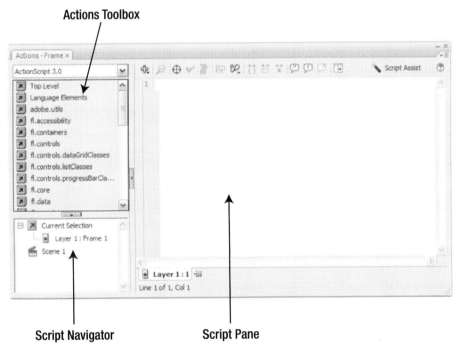

Script Navigator   **Script Pane**

Figure 4-1. The Actions panel

There are three distinct zones in the Actions panel. Starting from the upper left, moving clockwise, we have the following:

- **The** Actions **toolbox**: This provides a kind of "card catalog" for the available scripting functionality in Flash. Those little book icons with arrows are clickable. Clicking one opens that book to reveal either more books—in an extensive, cascading organization of categories—or a circle icon that lets you add that particular bit of ActionScript to your code. You may do this by double-clicking the desired circle icon or by dragging it to the Script pane at right. In theory, this gives you a helpful point-and-click mechanism for building complex expressions without having to memorize the whole language. In practice, however, this is like using alphabet magnets to compose sonnets on the refrigerator. It's much easier and quicker to simply type the code you need by hand. ActionScript 3.0 is significantly larger in scope than previous versions of the language, and no one has the full API memorized.

- **The** Script **pane**: This is the high-traffic zone, because it's where you type your code. There are a number of icons along the top designed to make your life easier (as shown in Figure 4-2). They are as follows:

  - Add a New Item to the Script: Functionally equivalent to the Actions toolbox.

  - Find: Lets you find and replace text in your scripts.

  - Insert a Target Path: Helps you build dot notation reference paths to objects.

  - Check Syntax: Provides a quick "thumbs up" or "thumbs down" on whether or not your code is well formed. Note that if you relied on this feature in Flash 8, be prepared for a bit of disappointment. This button behaves very differently for ActionScript 3.0 documents, though it still works the same for ActionScript 2.0 documents. For details, see the "Checking syntax" section later in this chapter.

  - Auto Format: Sweeps through your code to correct its posture, based on your own formatting preferences.

  - Show Code Hint: Summons a tooltip that suggests what you might want to type next.

  - Debug Options: Lets you set and remove breakpoints, which are used to help debug ActionScript.

  - Collapse Between Braces, Collapse Selection, **and** Expand All: Allow you to "fold up" long stretches of code to reduce clutter, and then open them again.

  - Apply Block Comment, Apply Line Comment, **and** Remove Comment: Allow you to add code comments in two different ways, and then remove them again.

  - Show/Hide Toolbox: Opens and closes the books.

  - Script Assist: Puts the Actions panel into a special line-by-line mode that provides programming hand-holding.

  - Help: Opens the ActionScript Help panel.

- **The** Script **navigator**: ActionScript may be placed in any frame on any timeline. This area shows which frames have script, and allows you to quickly jump to the desired code. Selected scripts may be "pinned" beneath the Script pane. Each pinned script is displayed as a new tab, which provides an alternative navigation method.

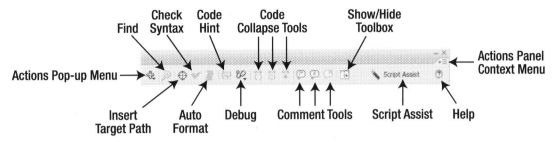

Figure 4-2. The Script pane buttons

One final important area, the Actions panel's context menu, shown in Figure 4-3, resides in the upper-right corner. Note that many of its choices repeat functionality already discussed—Pin Script, Auto Format, and Check Syntax—but a good handful of choices show features unavailable anywhere else. These include the ability to import in, export out, and print script from the Actions panel; show and hide hidden characters and line numbers; and wrap text.

Figure 4-3. The Actions panel context menu

A really good habit to develop is to keep Line Numbers *selected in the context menu. Code can get very long, and if there is a mistake, Flash usually tells you the line number where the mistake can be found.*

ActionScript vs. behaviors

If you're an existing Flash designer or developer, you may already be familiar with the Behaviors panel. This panel allows you to select an object with the mouse, such as a button symbol, and apply a prewritten script—a behavior—to it. **Behaviors** include such common functionality as pausing and playing embedded video, sending the playhead to a particular frame, dragging a movieclip, and so on. This panel is still available in Flash CS3—under Window ➤ Behaviors—but it is not compatible with ActionScript 3.0 documents.

That's right. If you're using ActionScript 3.0, you have to write your own code. The reason for this is partly that the on() and onClipEvent() functions, which allowed earlier ActionScript to be attached directly to objects, are no longer part of the language. Is this a big loss? Not really. The truth of the matter is that code written through the Behaviors panel is of the canned, one-size-fits-all variety. This means that it is often more compli-cated than it needs to be, which can make your code harder to maintain or customize. In fact, many Flash developers avoid behaviors because, as they rightly claim, it produces "bloated code." By that they mean that a behavior may need six lines to accomplish what could otherwise be done using one or two lines.

Are behaviors a bad thing? No, but they frequently give you a false sense of freedom. As soon as you find yourself in a position where you "just need this one part to act a bit dif-ferently," you're stuck, because you haven't the foggiest idea where to begin. Why? The reason is simple: it isn't the Behaviors panel's job. Its purpose is to write the code for you, not tell you what it is doing.

It is a lot like buying coffee from a vending machine in the office. Coffee from a vending machine might seem convenient at first, but it is never as good as a pot you have attentively brewed on your own. When you finish this chapter, you'll be well equipped to explore ActionScript on your own and use much more of it than the Behaviors panel offers.

Before you start entering code in the Actions panel, let's step back and understand exactly what it is you are working with when you enter code. It is called an object.

Everything is an object

Your first step, and possibly the most important, is to think in terms of objects. This con-cept is fundamental to an object-oriented environment like ActionScript and ties the whole language to an elegant, unifying metaphor. So, what is an object? Well, that's just it: you already know what an object is! An object is a thing—something you can look at, pick up, and manipulate.

The Flash interface allows you to "physically" manipulate certain objects—movieclips, text fields, and so on—by means of the Transform tool, the Property inspector, and other tools or panels. But that's only the tip of the iceberg, and merely one way of looking at the "reality" of the parts of a Flash movie.

In ActionScript, objects aren't physical things, but if you place yourself mentally into Flash territory, you'll find it helpful to imagine them that way. With programming, you're dealing with a non-concrete world. In this world, objects "live" in the parallel universe determined by the binary information stored in a SWF. That information may be governed by tools and panels or by ActionScript—or both.

Every movieclip in a SWF is an object. So is every text field and button. In fact, every content element, interactive or not, is an object. For visual elements, this is generally an easy concept to grasp—you can see them on the stage—but it goes further. Even things you might not think of as objects, such as the characteristics of the Glow effect, or changes in font settings, can be described in terms of objects. Even nonvisual notions, such as math functions, today's date, and the formula used to move an object from here to there are objects. Thinking of these last examples in this way may seem disorienting at first, but the concept should ultimately empower you, because it means you can manipulate everything of functional value in a SWF as if it were a tangible thing. The best part is, all objects are determined by something called a **class**. In many respects, classes provide a kind of owner's manual for any object you encounter.

Before we move on to the owner's manual, let's look at two objects: David and Tom.

The authors of this book, in object terms, are human beings. Let's say our class is Male. You can look at either one of us and say, with certainty, "Yep, those are two guys." We both have the male chromosome and so on. But drill deeper and you'll discover that even though we are of the same class, we are also quite different . . . which is where the owner's manual comes into play.

Classes define objects

Think of a class as a sort of blueprint or recipe for a given object. If you're a fan of pizza, all you need is a single pizza recipe and you're good to go. As long as you follow the recipe, every pizza you make will be as good as the one that came before it. Some pizzas will be larger than others—some will be square, some round, and the toppings will certainly change—but there's no mistaking what's on your plate. It's the same with objects. A movieclip symbol is defined by the MovieClip class. Any given movieclip will have its own width and height, and it might have a longer or shorter individual timeline, but all movieclips *have* dimensions, and all movieclips *have* a timeline.

Along the same lines, every type of object in ActionScript has its own unique qualities. These are generally defined by some combination of three facets:

- Characteristics the object has
- Things the object can do
- Things the object can react to

In programming terms, these facets are known respectively as **properties**, **methods**, and **events**. Collectively, these are called **members of a class**. This also explains why even though David and Tom fit into the class Male, we are also different. We feature the same properties across the board—height, fishing rod, Moose Lodge membership, and, say, hair—but each has his own unique values for those properties. For example, Tom's Moose Lodge membership expires next year, but David's has only begun. Someday, one of us might have the value bald for his hair property. It's the same with methods and events.

Both of us can throw a football, and because our married properties are set to true, both of us respond to the wife-is-calling event.

Properties

Properties might be the easiest members to conceptualize, because they seem the most concrete. For example, David and Tom both have hair, but the value of our hair property is different. David's is red. Tom's is black. Now wrap your mind around a movieclip on the Flash stage. That movieclip symbol clearly exists at a particular position on the stage. Its position is apparent during authoring because you establish it yourself, perhaps by dragging the movieclip by hand or by setting its coordinates with the Property inspector.

To access these same properties with ActionScript, you'll need to be able to call the movieclip by name, so to speak. This is the purpose of the Instance Name field of the Property inspector. As you learned in Chapter 3, you may drag as many instances of a symbol to the stage as you please. In order that each instance is set apart from the others—at least in terms of ActionScript—each instance needs a unique instance name, just as the two authors are unique instances of the Male class. You tell us apart by giving each of us a name. Once a movieclip has this name, you can access its MovieClip class members in terms of that particular movieclip. Here's how:

1. Create a new Flash document and save it as Box1.fla. Rename Layer 1 to content and add a new layer named scripts. Use the Rectangle tool to draw a square approximately 75 by 75 pixels into the content layer.

   > *A standard practice in Flash development is to put scripts in a separate layer named* scripts, actions, *or some other meaningful description. This way, all the code is in one place.*

2. Convert the square to a movieclip symbol. Give it the name square so that it appears in the library by that name. Select the movieclip on the stage and give it the instance name box in the Property inspector (as shown in Figure 4-4).

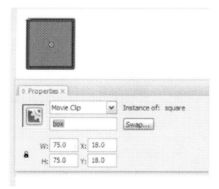

Figure 4-4. Instance names are added in the Property inspector.

3. Use the Selection tool to drag the box instance to the upper-left corner of the stage—not flush with the corner, just in the vicinity. Note its x and y coordinates as indicated by the Property inspector. You're about to see ActionScript tell you these same figures.

4. Open the Actions panel by selecting Window ➤ Actions. Select frame 1 in the scripts layer. This directs the Actions panel to that frame—this is where your script will be stored. Type the following ActionScript into the Script pane:

```
trace(box.x, box.y);
```

5. Close the Actions panel and test your movie.

After the SWF has been created, locate the Output tab of the Property inspector (also known as the Output panel). Select the Output tab, and you'll see two numbers (as shown in Figure 4-5). These numbers are the result of the trace() function you just typed, and those numbers are the horizontal and vertical coordinates—the MovieClip.x and MovieClip.y properties—of the box MovieClip instance. In fact, they match the x and y coordinates in the Property inspector.

4

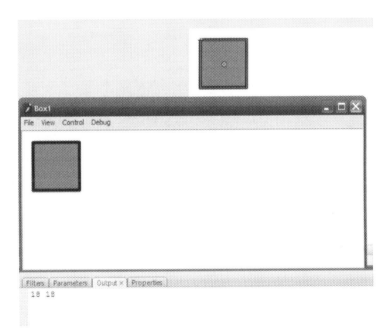

Figure 4-5. The box movieclip on the stage shows its coordinates in the Property inspector. In the SWF, it shows its coordinates in the Output tab, thanks to the trace() function.

How does this work? The trace() function accepts something called parameters, and these parameters affect the way the trace() function acts. The values—called expressions—you place between its parentheses (separated by a comma) are displayed in the Output panel. In this case, the two expressions are box.x and box.y. We'll show you some additional examples of functions later in the chapter.

> You'll find the `trace()` *function to be a useful tool in experimenting with ActionScript. Its sole purpose is to display information normally under wraps, such as the value of an object property, an expression, or a variable. In actual practice, you might use a movieclip's position, or the value of a property of an object, to determine the outcome of some goal. For example, you might want a movieclip to stop being draggable after it has been dragged to a certain location on the stage. You wouldn't need the* `trace()` *function to accomplish such a task, but it could certainly help you test your code along the way.*

In addition to being retrieved, or read, in this manner, many properties (but not all) can also be set via ActionScript. Here's how:

1. Save your current file as Box2.fla.

2. Select frame 1 of the scripts layer, if it isn't already selected, and return to the Actions panel. Delete the existing line of ActionScript. Enter the following new lines and test your movie again:

```
box.x = 300;
box.y = -50;
```

> *If you are familiar with ActionScript 2.0, you may be thinking, "Guys, isn't there something missing?" There is. In the former version of ActionScript, the x property contained an underscore, like this:* _x. *This underscore has been removed in ActionScript 3.0.*

This time, you'll see the box instance positioned at 300 pixels in from the left and 50 pixels past the top of the stage, just as if you had placed it there yourself. Want to adjust something else? How about width?

1. Save your current file as Box3.fla.

2. Replace the existing ActionScript to make it look like the following code, and then test your movie:

```
box.x = 200;
box.y = 100;
box.width = 300;
```

See what happens? Not only does the movieclip change position—this time to 200 pixels in from the left and 100 pixels down from the top—but it also stretches to a new width of 300 pixels.

> *Changing the code and then testing it to this point may seem a bit mundane. There is a very good reason why we are doing this. What you have been doing is changing the code and adding to it. ActionScript can get pretty complex. This is why now would be a good time to get into the habit of "Do a bit. Test it." This way, if there is a problem or an unexpected result you can easily fix it because you know exactly where the change was made.*

There are literally dozens of MovieClip properties, and we mentioned that not all are settable. One example is the MovieClip.totalFrames property, which indicates the number of frames in a movieclip's timeline. Another is MovieClip.mouseX, which indicates the horizontal position of the mouse in reference to a given movieclip. Some things simply are what they are. The Help panel tells you at a glance what the full set of an object's properties is, and which ones are read-only. Later in the chapter, we'll discuss how to best approach the Help panel, and the ActionScript 3.0 Language and Components Reference in particular, but for now, let's keep rolling.

Methods

Methods are the "verbs" of an object—things the object can do. Staying with Tom and David, both of us can walk, but David walks faster than Tom. As with properties, each unique object type has its own set of methods. The TextField class, for example, provides for the selection of text in various ways. These methods are absent in the MovieClip class, which makes perfect sense. The Loader class provides for the loading of files and data from outside a SWF. It makes equally good sense that its methods are unique to instances of Loader, and that neither text fields nor loader objects can send the playhead to the frame of a movieclip's timeline.

ActionScript 3.0 is much better organized in this regard than previous versions of the language. In ActionScript 1.0 and 2.0, movieclips were responsible for loading external SWFs and images. There was also a class called MovieClipLoader that did the same thing, but in a more useful way. Thanks to the new virtual machine in Flash Player 9, ActionScript 3.0 slices through such legacy ambiguity.

Let's keep exploring our MovieClip instance, because movieclips are arguably the most important object in Flash to learn. Why? It is because the main timeline itself is a MovieClip instance, which means SWF files are functionally equivalent to movieclip symbols. If you're interested in controlling the main timeline, you'll want to know where to look for the necessary methods, and those are found in the MovieClip class.

As you've already learned, movieclips have timelines, and timelines have frames. By default, the playhead runs along timelines, displaying whatever their frames specify. In other words, the natural tendency of a movie is to move, rather than stand still. As you'll see, the MovieClip class provides methods to stop the playhead, send it to a specified frame (skipping frames in between) and play from there, plus plenty more.

1. Save your current file as Box4.fla.

2. Delete the existing three lines of ActionScript and close the Actions panel for now.

3. Click frame 50 of the content layer. Select Insert ➤ Timeline ➤ Keyframe to add a keyframe. Use the Selection tool to reposition the box instance at frame 50. Move it to the right side of the stage and use the Free Transform tool to increase its size.

4. Select the span of frames between frame 1 and 50. Select Motion from the Tween drop-down menu in the Property inspector to apply a motion tween. Test your movie.

You should see the box instance move from the left side of the stage to the right, increasing in size as it goes. So far, nothing new. This is the same sort of tweening done in Chapter 1. In the previous section, we referred to the box instance to access its MovieClip properties. We could access its methods in essentially the same way—and we will in the "Events" section—but for the time being, let's refer to the main timeline instead.

Ah, but wait a moment! The main timeline doesn't have an instance name. How is this going to work? Enter, the keyword this. Since your ActionScript is in a keyframe of the main timeline, the this keyword—in this context—refers to the main timeline.

> The this keyword is one of a small selection of special statements in ActionScript that stand apart from all the classes that make up the language's objects. When you see this in code, recognize it as a reference to the timeline in which it appears or to the object in which it appears.

1. Click in frame 1 of the scripts layer and open the Actions panel.

2. Type the following ActionScript and test your movie:

```
trace(this);
```

The movie will animate as before, but this time you'll see a new message in the Output panel: [object MainTimeline]. Bingo! As the movie naturally loops, the message will repeat itself whenever the playhead enters frame 1. So, you have your reference to a MovieClip instance (the stage). Now, you simply need to follow it with a dot and refer to the desired method.

3. Replace the existing code with the following ActionScript, and then test your movie:

```
this.stop();
```

This time, the movie stays put at frame 1. Visually, that's pretty boring, but the fact is, you just used ActionScript to direct the course of a SWF! Let's do something a little more interesting.

4. Comment out the existing ActionScript by putting two forward slashes at the beginning of line 1. You may either type them yourself or use the Actions panel's Apply line comment button. To use this button, either position your cursor at the beginning of the line or highlight the entire line, and then click the button. If code coloring is active, you'll see your ActionScript change color.

```
//this.stop();
```

> Code coloring? Certain words, phrases and other terms that ActionScript recognizes will be colored blue, green, or gray. The words this and stop are words reserved for ActionScript, and are traditionally blue. Gray indicates that the code is commented and is nonfunctional. Keep an eye on the code color. If the word stop, for instance, is not blue, you have a problem.

170

5. Click frame 50 of the scripts layer and add a keyframe. Select this keyframe and note that the Actions panel goes blank. That's because no code yet exists on this frame. You're about to add some. Type the following ActionScript into this frame, and then test your movie:

```
this.gotoAndPlay(25);
```

Because the ActionScript in frame 1 is commented out, it's ignored. The playhead breezes right on past frame 1. When it reaches frame 50, the MovieClip.gotoAndPlay() method is invoked on the main timeline, and the movie jumps to frame 25, where it eventually continues again to 50. At frame 50, it will again be invoked and send the playhead to frame 25, and the cycle will repeat—sort of like a dog chasing its tail. The only difference between ActionScript and a dog is that a dog will eventually stop. The only way to stop this movie is to quit Flash Player.

What makes the playhead jump to frame 25? That's determined by the number inside the method's parentheses. Like the trace() function mentioned earlier, some methods accept parameters, and MovieClip.gotoAndPlay() is one of them. If you think about it, the idea is reasonably intuitive. A method like MovieClip.stop() doesn't require further input—stop just means "stop"—but gotoAndPlay() wouldn't be complete without an answer to the question "go where?"

To be fair, it isn't always obvious when parameters are accepted. In fact, in many cases, when parameters are accepted, they are optional. What's the best place to find out for sure? The answer, once again, is the Help panel. Seriously, it is your quickest source for definitive answers to questions about class members. We'll cover a number of Help panel tips near the end of the chapter.

Events

Events are things an object can react to. Yell at David and he will turn his head in your direction. Push Tom to the right and, if he is walking, he will veer in that direction. It is no different in ActionScript. Events represent an occurrence, triggered either by user input such as mouse clicks and key presses, or Flash Player itself. In the case of Flash Player, most events are time-based, such as internal timers and the passing of timeline frames. Because of this dependence on outside factors, the response to events—called event handling—requires an additional object.

It is just like physics: for every action (event), there is a reaction (event handling). You may want to roll up your pant legs at this point, because we're going to wade a little deeper here. Not a lot deeper, but a little.

Event handling in ActionScript 3.0 requires an instance of the Event class or one of its many derivatives, including MouseEvent, ScrollEvent, TimerEvent, and others listed in the Event class entry of the ActionScript 3.0 Language and Components Reference. The actual handling is managed by a custom function, written to perform whatever you want to happen when the event occurs. Before this begins to sound too complex, let's return to our MovieClip instance:

4

1. Save your current file as Box5.fla.

2. Double-click the box instance on the stage to open the Symbol Editor. Select frame 2 and select Insert ➤ Timeline ➤ Blank Keyframe to add a blank keyframe. Use the Oval tool to draw a circle that is approximately 75 by 75 pixels in frame 2. If you like, use the Property inspector to adjust these dimensions precisely and to position the shape at coordinates (0, 0).

Test the movie and you will see the box instance animate from left to right, increasing in size as before. This time, however, that second frame in the box instance's own timeline causes the symbol to naturally loop, fluttering between the square and circle—something like an abstract artist's impression of a butterfly. Neat effect, but let's harness that and make it act in response to the mouse instead.

3. Click the Scene 1 link to return to the main timeline. Select frame 1 of the scripts layer and open the Actions panel. After the existing commented line, type the following ActionScript:

```
box.stop();
```

4. Test your movie and you will see that the fluttering has stopped and only the box is visible on the stage. This happened because you invoked the MovieClip.stop() method on the box instance, essentially telling the timeline of that movieclip to stay put. Now let's use the mouse to manage the events.

5. Open the Actions panel and click once at the end of line 2 of the code. Press the Enter/Return key and add the following lines of code:

```
box.addEventListener(MouseEvent.CLICK, clickHandler);
box.addEventListener(MouseEvent.MOUSE_OVER, mouseOverHandler);
box.addEventListener(MouseEvent.MOUSE_OUT, mouseOutHandler);

box.buttonMode = true;

function clickHandler(evt:Object):void {
  trace("You just clicked me!");
}

function mouseOverHandler(evt:Object):void {
  box.gotoAndStop(2);
}

function mouseOutHandler(evt:Object):void {
  box.gotoAndStop(1);
}
```

That may seem like an awful lot of complicated code but it really isn't. What you are doing is essentially telling Flash to listen for a series of mouse events and do something in response. In Flash, when you want it to react to an event, you have to tell it what event to listen for. The events happen, regardless. It's your call when you want to handle the event. The first three lines do just that. Let's dissect the first line, which will cause the other two to make a bit of sense.

In plain English, the line says, "When the mouse is clicked (MouseEvent.CLICK) over the thing on the stage named box, do the thing called clickHandler." It's a lot like visiting the local fire station.

Let's assume you are in a fire station and this is the first time you have ever been there. Suddenly there is a bell sound and the firemen slide down a pole, jump into their suits, and pile onto the truck. The truck, with the firemen aboard, goes roaring out of the front door of the fire station. This is all new to you and you just stand there and watch. The firemen, trained to react to the bell, did something completely opposite from what you did.

The difference is that the firemen knew what to do when the bell rang. You did not. The fireman knew (addEventListener()) what to listen for (an event)—a bell, not the phone—and what to do when that event occurs (an event handler). What you are doing with this movie is telling Flash how to behave when the bell rings (clickHandler), when the phone rings (mouseOverHandler), or when the ice cream truck arrives (mouseOutHandler).

The fourth line

```
box.buttonMode = true;
```

essentially tells Flash to treat the box like a button. This means that the user is given a visual clue—the cursor changes to the pointing finger shown in Figure 4-6—that the box on the stage can be clicked. The remaining functions tell Flash to put some text in the Output panel if the box is clicked, to go to frame 2 of that movieclip and show the circle if the mouse is over the box, and to go to frame 1 of that movieclip and show the box again if the mouse rolls off that object.

If you get errors or the code doesn't work, don't worry. Open the Box5.fla file or double-click the Box5.swf file in the Exercise folder. We'll talk about checking for coding mistakes a little later in the chapter.

6. Test the movie, and the cursor should now control the action. In fact, just place the cursor in the path of the box moving across the stage and watch what happens.

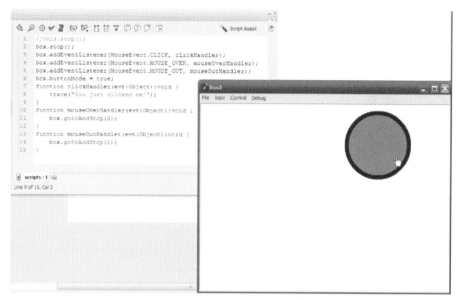

Figure 4-6. The mouseOverHandler function is what changes the box into the circle.

Syntax

Just like English, ActionScript has a set of grammatical rules that governs its use. In English, for example, sentences begin with a capital letter and end with a period, exclamation point, or question mark. Of course, it gets much more complicated than that, but we assume you know most of the important stuff, even if you don't have an English degree. ActionScript's grammar is called syntax, and it's easier than you might think. For starters, here are two major rules when working with ActionScript. The first rule of grammar is: *Capitalization matters.*

ActionScript 3.0 is a case-sensitive language. If you want to know what frame a movieclip is currently on, you must reference its MovieClip.currentFrame property, spelled just like that—not currentframe, or any other combination of upper- and lowercase letters. If the thought of memorizing arbitrary capitalization has you worried, have no fear. ActionScript follows a manageably small set of conventions. As a general rule of thumb, just imagine a camel. Those humps will remind you of something called **camel case**, a practice in which spaces are removed from a group of words, and each letter that begins a new word is capitalized. So "current frame" becomes currentFrame, "track as menu" becomes trackAsMenu, and so on.

Add to this the observation that class names begin with a capital letter. The class that defines text fields is TextField, the class that defines movieclips is MovieClip, and the class that defines the stage display state is StageDisplayState. Still camel case, but with an initial cap.

*The only oddball is something called a **constant**, which you won't use nearly as often. Constants are properties, but can't be changed. They appear in full uppercase, with underscores where the spaces should be. For example, in the* StageDisplayState *class just mentioned, the constant that refers to "full screen" is* FULL_SCREEN—*note the underscore between the two words—and the constant that refers to "normal" is* NORMAL. *You've already seen a few examples in the* MouseEvent *events of the previous exercise.*

In any case, the Actions panel provides a convenient clue when you get it right. Correctly typed ActionScript is displayed in color, as opposed to plain old black and white. In fact, different categories of ActionScript are colored in different ways. You may configure these colors as you please, or turn them off completely, under the ActionScript user preferences (either by choosing Edit ➤ Preferences and going to the ActionScript category, or by selecting the Preferences choice under the Actions panel's context menu).

The second major rule is: Semicolons mark the end of a line.

As you've already seen, every line of ActionScript code terminates with a semicolon (;). Adding semicolons is optional, but if you omit them, Flash will make the decision on your behalf as to when a given statement has ended. Better to place them yourself.

What, only two rules of syntax? Truthfully, no. It can get as complex as you like, but this is a "basics" chapter, and these two rules will help you ward off some of the most common beginner errors. Offshoots of the syntax concept are spelled out in greater detail in the following sections.

Commenting code

Now that you are aware of the two major grammar rules, you should also be aware of a coding best practice: **commenting**.

In the previous exercise, we asked you to enter a lot of code. We are willing to bet that when you first looked at it on the page, your first reactions was, "What the hell does this stuff do?" A major use of commenting is to answer that question. Flash developers heavily comment their code in order to let others know what the code does and to make it easy to find all of the functions in the code.

A single-line comment always starts with a double forward slash: //. The Flash developer can then add comments after it to tell you what the code does. If we had added comments to the earlier code, you wouldn't have had to wonder what was going on when you looked at it. For example, this should make your life easier:

```
// Tell the box what events to listen for and what to do
// when an event is detected

box.addEventListener(MouseEvent.CLICK, clickHandler);
box.addEventListener(MouseEvent.MOUSE_OVER, mouseOverHandler);
box.addEventListener(MouseEvent.MOUSE_OUT, mouseOutHandler);
```

```
// Treat the box as though it were a button to let user know it is live

box.buttonMode = true;

// Put a message in the Output panel when the object is clicked

function clickHandler(evt:Object):void {
  trace("You just clicked me!");
}

// Go to frame two and show the ball movieclip
// when the mouse is over the box

function mouseOverHandler(evt:Object):void {
  box.gotoAndStop(2);
}

// Go to frame one and show the square
// when the mouse is outside of the object

function mouseOutHandler(evt:Object):void {
  box.gotoAndStop(1);
}
```

You can even put the two slashes at the end of line, if you like:

```
someObject.someProperty = 400; // These words will be ignored by Flash
```

You can also use a comment to temporarily "undo" or "hold back" a line of ActionScript. For example, you might want to experiment with a variety of possible values for a property. Single-line comments make it easy to switch back and forth. Just copy and paste your test values, commenting each one, and remove the slashes for the desired value of the moment.

```
//someObject.someProperty = 400;
someObject.someProperty = 800;
//someObject.someProperty = 1600;
```

You can comment whole blocks of ActionScript by using a block comment. Rather than two slashes, sandwich the desired code or personal notes between the special combination of /* and */ characters.

```
/*someObject.someProperty = 400;
someObject.someProperty = 800;
someObject.someProperty = 1600;*/
```

Dot notation

Objects can be placed inside other objects, just like those Russian stacking dolls, *matryoshki*. Actually, that analogy gives the impression that each object can only hold one other object, which isn't true. A better comparison might be folders on your hard drive, any of which might hold countless files and even other folders. On Windows and Macintosh systems, folders are usually distinguished from one another by slashes. In ActionScript, object hierarchies are distinguished by dots. As you have already seen, class members can be referenced by a parent object followed by a dot, followed by the desired member.

Nested movieclips can be referenced in the same way, because after all, movieclips are just objects. All you need is a movieclip that has its own instance name.

Junk food is a great example of this concept. Imagine a nested set of movieclips in the main timeline that, combined, represent the Hostess Twinkie in Figure 4-7. The outermost movieclip is made to look like the plastic wrapper. Inside that is another movieclip that looks like the yellow pastry. Finally, the innermost movieclip represents the creamy filling.

Figure 4-7. Real-world dot notation

If each movieclip is given an instance name that describes what it looks like, the innermost clip would be accessed like this from a keyframe of the main timeline:

```
plasticWrapper.yellowCookie.creamyFilling
```

Note the camel case. Because creamyFilling is a MovieClip instance, it contains all the functionality defined by the MovieClip class. If the innermost movieclip—creamyFilling—has a number of frames in its own timeline, and you want to send the playhead to frame 5, you would simply reference the whole path, include another dot, and then reference a relevant MovieClip method, like this:

```
plasticWrapper.yellowCookie.creamyFilling.gotoAndPlay(5);
```

This linked series of objects is known as a **path**. The extent of a path depends on the "point of view" of the ActionScript that refers to it. In Flash, this point of view depends on where the ActionScript itself is written. In this case, it's written inside a keyframe of the main timeline, and you're aiming for the innermost object; therefore, the full path is required. If ActionScript is written inside a keyframe of the innermost movieclip's timeline—then the this keyword would suffice. The creamyFilling instance would simply be referring to itself.

```
this.gotoAndPlay(5);
```

It wouldn't make sense to mention yellowCookie or plasticWrapper in this case unless you needed something in those movieclips. From the point of view of creamyFilling, you could reference yellowCookie via the Movieclip.parent property, like this:

```
this.parent;
```

But bear in mind that it's usually best to keep your point of view in the main timeline. Why? Well, when all of your code is on one place—in the same layer or even in the same frame—it's much easier to find six months from now, when you have to frantically update your movie.

The most important thing to realize is that you're the one in control of what you build. If it's easier for you to drop a quick MovieClip.stop() method into some keyframe of a deeply nested movieclip—as opposed to "drilling down" to it with a lengthy dot-notated path—then do that. Just keep in mind that paths are fundamentally important, because they serve as the connection between objects.

If you want to actually see how movieclips are nested using dot notation, open twinkie.fla. We have constructed the image on the stage as a series of movieclips from the library. The code in the scripts layer

```
trace(plasticWrapper.yellowCookie.creamyFilling);
```

essentially asks, "What are these things?" If you test the movie, the Output panel will tell you the object is a MovieClip.

Variables

Variables are often described as buckets. It's not a bad analogy. Like buckets, variables are containers that temporarily hold things. Like buckets, variables come in specific shapes and sizes, and these configurations determine what sorts of things, and how many of them, a given variable can hold. In fact, variables are practically the same as properties, but the difference is, variables are not associated with a given class.

A great way of understanding the concept of a variable is going to the supermarket. You pay for a bunch of tomatoes, a can of soup, a box of Twinkies, a head of lettuce, and paper toweling. The clerk puts them in a bag, and you pay for them, pick up the bag, and walk out of the store. If somebody were to ask you what you were carrying, the answer would be "groceries." The word describes all of the objects you have purchased, but it doesn't describe each one.

Variables are essentially properties that aren't associated with a particular class, which means you can create a variable in any timeline and access it from that timeline without having to refer to an object first. The formal term for creating a variable is **declaring a variable**. This is done using the var keyword, like this:

```
var myFavoriteActor:String = "Buster Keaton";
```

or like this:

```
var groceries:Array = new Array("tomatoes", "soup", "twinkies",➥
"lettuce", "toweling");
```

From that point forward, the variable myFavoriteActor is a stand-in, or placeholder, for the phrase "Buster Keaton," the deadpan comedian of early silent film. The variable groceries is a placeholder for an instance of the Array class, which lets you store lists of things.

To summarize, the var keyword dictates, "All right, folks, time for a variable," and the word myFavoriteActor is an arbitrary name provided by you, used to set and retrieve the contents of the variable. The :String part is interesting. While not strictly necessary, its presence declares the variable as efficiently and succinctly as possible. The reason for this is explained in the next section, "Data types." Finally, the assignment operator (=) sets the value of the variable to a string, delimited by quotation marks.

> *One of the authors, in order to get his students to understand variable naming, tells them they can use any name they wish, and then creates a variable named scumSuckingPig. A few years back, Macromedia asked for a videotape of one of his lessons, and not even thinking while the camera was rolling, he wrote "scumSuckingPig" on the whiteboard, pointed to it, and asked the class, "What is this?" Thirty voices answered, "A variable." To this day, those Macromedia people who saw the tape never forget to mention this to him.*

Shock value aside, it isn't entirely true that a variable can be named absolutely anything. You can't, for example, name your own variable after an existing keyword in ActionScript, and that makes sense. How is Flash supposed to know the difference between a variable named trace and the trace() function? A full list of the words you can't use is provided in the Help panel. Search the phrase *keywords and reserved words*, and, as shown in Figure 4-8, you'll find this list. Also, your variable names may only contain letters, numbers, dollar signs ($), and underscores (_). If you decide to use numbers, you may not use a number as the first character.

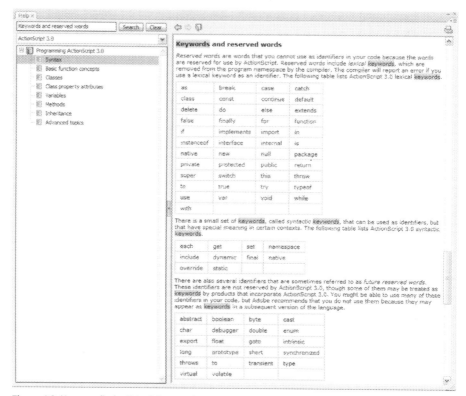

Figure 4-8. You can find a list of the words you can't use for variable names in the Help menu.

Data types

Arguably, data types are just another way to describe classes. When used with variable declarations, however, they provide a useful service. Specifying a variable's data type not only helps you avoid code errors, in ActionScript 3.0 it can also reduce memory usage, which is always a good thing. Many of the people who have been test driving ActionScript 3.0 have discovered that this also is a factor in the speed of playback of presentations in Flash Player 9. Adobe is not shy of claiming speed boosts of up to 75 percent, and we aren't disputing that claim.

Another important result of using data types is that you avoid coding errors. The more Flash knows about your intentions, the better it is able to hold you accountable for them. If a variable is supposed to hold a number—the phrase used for this is "strict (or strong) data typing"—and you accidentally set it to a bit of text, Flash will let you know about it. Mistakes like that happen more often than you might think and, to be honest, it will happen to you. Let's make a mistake and see what happens:

1. Create a new Flash ActionScript 3.0 document and save it as DatatypeError.fla. Rename Layer 1 to text field. Use the Text tool to draw a text field somewhere on the stage. Select the text field and use the Property inspector to set its type to Input Text (as shown in Figure 4-9). Give it the instance name input.

Figure 4-9. Setting the text field to Input Text

2. Create a new layer and name it scripts. Select frame 1 and open the Actions panel. Type the following ActionScript into the Script pane:

```
var num:Number = 0;
num = input.text;
```

Another way of writing the first line would be as follows:

```
var num:Number = new Number(0);
```

The keyword new is normally used when creating new instances of complex data types, such as a Sound object or NetStream used to play a video. Less complex data types, including simple stuff like numbers and strings, really don't require the new keyword for them to be instantiated.

3. Test the SWF and keep your eye on the Compiler Errors tab in the Property inspector group. You'll see a helpful error warning that lets you know that the num variable, a Number data type, doesn't like the idea of being fed a String data type, which is what the TextField.text property provides (see Figure 4-10).

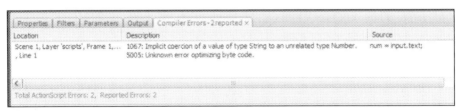

Figure 4-10. Trying to set a numerical variable to a string results in an error, thanks to data typing.

> Note that you can double-click on the error in the Compiler Errors *tab, and it will take you to the exact line in the* Actions *panel that contains the error. This is new in Flash 9, and is a welcome feature.*

4. For extra credit, use the Number() function to convert the String to a Number on the fly.

```
var num:Number = 0;
num = Number(input.text);
```

Thanks to the way Flash Player 9 has been constructed, strongly typed variables in ActionScript 3.0 can reduce memory usage because they allow variables to be only as big as they need to be. When a variable is created, the computer is asked to set aside a certain amount of memory (RAM) to hold whatever information needs to be stored in the variable. Some data types require more memory than others, and when ActionScript knows what type you intend to use, it requests the minimum amount of memory necessary.

Besides indicating the sort of variable something is, data typing can also specify the return value of functions and methods. If a function returns a string, for example, it can (and should) be typed like this:

```
function showMeTheMoney():String {
  return "$$$";
}
trace(showMeTheMoney());
```

Many functions don't return anything, which means they get to use :void.

```
function manipulateAMovieclipSomewhere():void {
  // movieclip manipulation code here
  // notice the function doesn't return anything
}
manipulateAMovieclipSomewhere();
```

For further detail on available data types, search the topic *Data type descriptions* in the Programming ActionScript 3.0 book of the Help panel.

Operators

Whether you are a casual ActionScript programmer making things move from here to there or a hardcore coder, you will use operators. These things can't be avoided.

In ActionScript, operators are special characters—usually punctuation, but sometimes words—that evaluate or change the value of an expression. Some of the most commonly used operators look and act just like mathematical symbols. For example, the addition operator, +, adds numbers together; and the subtraction operator, -, subtracts them. The multiplication and division operators, * and /, multiply and divide numbers, respectively. Let's use our old friend trace() to see these in action:

1. Create a new Flash ActionScript 3.0 document and open the Actions panel.

2. Type the following ActionScript into the Script pane and test your movie to see the results of these simple math problems:

```
trace(5 + 5);
trace(7 - 2);
trace(5 * 5);
trace(7 / 2);
```

The Output panel shows 10, 5, 25, and 3.5, as you would expect.

The thing about operators is they deal with complexity in a very different manner than they deal with simplicity. For example, consider this calculation:

```
trace(5 + 5 / 2 * 3 - 1);
```

Now, what would that produce? If you answered 14, you are wrong. The answer is 11.5, and it is vitally important to your sanity that you understand how Flash arrives at this answer. The result depends on something called **operator precedence**.

Generally speaking, expressions are evaluated from left to right. The thing is, certain calculations take priority over others. This is the concept of precedence.

The rule is simple: *multiplication and division take priority over addition and subtraction.* A good way to remember this is to think of how multiplication and division problems quickly reach higher (or lower) numbers than addition and subtraction do. Let's slowly walk through that calculation to help you grasp the precedence concept.

Here's another way of wrapping your mind around precedence, which our tech editor, Adam Thomas, uses. When he was in high school, he used the acronym PEDMAS to remember the order of operations:

P: Parentheses

E: Exponents

D: Division

M: Multiplication (D and M in the order they appear)

A: Addition

S: Subtraction (A and S in the order they appear)

In the preceding expression, various pairings are considered in the order in which they appear, and operator precedence determines which pairings are evaluated in what order. For example, the first pairing is 5 + 5, and, sliding over one "slot," the next pairing is 5 / 2. Between those two, the division operation wins. Under the hood, the division is done before the addition, and the "new" expression reads as follows:

```
5 + 2.5 * 3 - 1
```

Now the process starts again. The first two pairings at this point are 5 + 2.5 and 2.5 * 3. Which one wins? Multiplication. The process continues, with the newest expression now reading:

```
5 + 7.5 - 1
```

Here, the pairings have been simplified—there are only two left—to 5 + 7.5 and 7.5 - 1. Neither trumps the other. Each pair is calculated, in the order in which it appears. In this case, 5 is added to 7.5, resulting in 12.5; and 12.5 has 1 removed, which leaves 11.5.

```
5 + 7.5 - 1
12.5 - 1
11.5
```

As you can see, precedence can be quite complex. Thankfully, there happens to be a way to override the natural precedence of operators. Unless you aim to specialize in operators (and there's nothing wrong with that), we recommend you use parentheses to group expressions:

```
3 + 5 * 4 is 23, because 5 * 4 takes priority and evaluates to 20,
then 3 + 20 is 23

(3 + 5) * 4 is 32, because (3 + 5) now takes prority
and evaluates to 8, then 8 * 4 is 32
```

The addition operator also works for text, by the way, in which case it is called *concatenation*, which is a fancy word for joining things. For example, the concatenation of the strings Twin and kie is the complete word Twinkie, as illustrated here:

```
trace("Twin" + "kie"); // outputs the value Twinkie, which is a string
```

Numbers concatenated with text become text, so be careful of your data types!

```
trace(5 + 5); // outputs the value 10, which is a number
trace(5 + "5"); // outputs the value 55, which is a string
```

Another operator that you will use practically every time you fire up the Actions panel is the assignment operator (=). In fact, you have used it several times already in this chapter. The assignment operator assigns a value to a variable or property. It is an active thing because it changes the value. In the following lines, the value of the looseChange variable is updated repeatedly:

```
var looseChange:Number = 5;
looseChange = 15;
looseChange = 99;
```

or

```
var author:String = "David";
author = "Chris";
author = "Tom";
```

In plain English, the assignment operator could be described as "equals," as in "looseChange now equals 99" (hey, that's almost a dollar!) or "author now equals Tom."

Contrast this with the equality operator (==), which is used for checking the value of a variable and making sure it is only that value. Don't confuse the assignment and equality operators! When you see something like this:

```
if (looseChange == 67) {
  // buy a twinkie
}
```

you are not changing the value of that variable. You are checking to see if looseChange has the value 67. If you want to check for any number but 67, use the inequality operator (!=), as in:

```
if (looseChange != 67) {
  // look for something else
}
```

What if you do not know the exact value you're looking for? The equality operator seeks a very specific value—not a range. The inequality operator, if you really think about it, only seeks a very specific value too, just from the opposite angle. As often as not, you'll find yourself in a position to make decisions on whole sets of numbers.

Think of this concept in terms of those restriction signs at a theme park: "You must be at least 42 inches tall to ride this roller coaster." They're not looking for people exactly 3.5 feet tall, they're looking for people greater than or equal to that number. ActionScript offers quite a few ways to compare values in this manner; the symbols used are called relational operators. These include the following:

- **Less than**: <
- **Greater than**: >
- **Less than or equal to**: <=
- **Greater than or equal to**: >=

In the next section, we'll see some of these in action. Before we do, just be aware that there are plenty more operators than we've touched on here. To see the full list, search the term *operators* in the Help panel.

Conditional statements

One of the cornerstones of programming is the ability to have your code make decisions. Think about it. You make decisions every day. For example, if you want to visit the authors of this book, you have a decision to make: do I go to Canada to visit Tom or to the United States to visit David?

ActionScript provides a handful of ways to make this determination, and the most basic is the if statement. An if statement is structured like this:

```
if (condition is true) {
  do something
}
```

Thus, in ActionScript terms, the decision to visit an author would look somewhat like this:

```
if (visitTom == true) {
  bookflightToCanada();
}
```

The condition between the parentheses can be relatively simple. One could be

```
if (fruit == "apple")
```

which might mean something like "if the fruit is an apple" (hand it over to Snow White). On the other hand, it might be a little more complex, such as the following:

```
if (beverage == "coffee" && dairy == "milk" || dairy == "cream")
```

which may seem to mean "if the beverage is coffee and the dairy is either milk or cream," but actually means something quite different. In the preceding expression, && and || represent "and" and "or," respectively. Because of the way precedence works, the expression hinges on the ||: we're checking if the beverage is coffee and the dairy is milk . . . or simply if the dairy is cream, regardless what the beverage is (if there even is a beverage). Contrast that with this:

```
if (beverage == "coffee" && (dairy == "milk" || dairy == "cream"))
```

As you may have guessed, the only decision an if statement ever makes is whether something is true or false. Let's just jump in and take a look at this concept.

In the following example, you're going to make a draggable star that dims when it's moved too close to the moon. The determination will be made by an if statement. Here's how:

1. Start a new Flash document. Change the name of Layer 1 to sky stuff.

2. Select the Polystar tool—it's under the same button as the Rectangle and Oval tools—to draw a polygon or star.

3. Click the Options button in the Property inspector to open the Tool Settings dialog box (see Figure 4-11).

4. In the Style drop-down menu, select star and click OK. Click and drag to create the star shape. Convert this shape into a movieclip and give it the instance name star. Position it on the left side of the stage.

Figure 4-11. Click the Options button on the Property inspector to draw a star.

5. Use the Oval tool to draw a circle. Convert it into a movieclip and, in the Property inspector, give it the instance name moon. Position it on the right side of the stage.

6. Create a new layer and name it scripts. Select frame 1 of the scripts layer, open the Actions panel, and type the following ActionScript:

```
star.addEventListener(MouseEvent.MOUSE_DOWN, mouseDownHandler);
star.addEventListener(MouseEvent.MOUSE_UP, mouseUpHandler);

star.buttonMode = true;

function mouseDownHandler(evt:Object):void {
  star.startDrag();
  star.addEventListener(MouseEvent.MOUSE_MOVE, mouseMoveHandler);
}

function mouseUpHandler(evt:Object):void {
  star.stopDrag();
  star.removeEventListener(MouseEvent.MOUSE_MOVE, mouseMoveHandler);
}

function mouseMoveHandler(evt:Object):void {
  if (star.x > moon.x) {
    star.alpha = 0.4;
  } else {
    star.alpha = 1;
  }
}
```

OK, that may look like a lot of code, but there really isn't a whole lot new. Just as you saw in the "Events" section, you are calling the star instance by name and assigning a couple event listeners, one for when the mouse is down (when the user presses the mouse button) and one for when the mouse is up (when the user releases the mouse button). Once again, buttonMode supplies the visual clue that star is clickable.

The function that handles the MouseEvent.MOUSE_DOWN event does an interesting thing. First, it invokes the Sprite.startDrag() method on the star instance. Sprite? What's that? The MovieClip class picks up much of its functionality from the Sprite class, thanks to a principle called **inheritance**. This allows the star to follow the mouse. Second, it adds a new event listener to the star instance—this time on an event that occurs while the mouse is moving. Just as you have seen with the other event handlers, this one has its own function, and that's where the if statement is found. The MouseEvent.MOUSE_UP event handler stops the dragging and tells star to stop listening for the MouseEvent.MOUSE_MOVE event. So, pressing the mouse button starts the dragging, and letting go stops it. Pretty straightforward. Let's look closer at that third event handler.

Here's where the decision-making occurs. An if statement evaluates the expression star.x > moon.x by asking if star's horizontal position is greater than moon's horizontal position. The answer, as you know, can only be true or false.

This question is asked every time you move the mouse. When the star instance moves beyond the right side of the moon instance, based on the registration point of each movieclip, the expression evaluates to true. In this case, the DisplayObject.alpha property or transparency of the star instance is set to 0.4 (40%), which makes it see-through. When the expression is false, the star is to the left of or behind the moon and the alpha is set back to 1 (100%). DisplayObject.alpha is another example of inheritance. When you're studying class members in the documentation, make sure to click the Show Inherited Public Properties hyperlink—you'll also see one for methods and events—to see the full list of features for each class.

7. Test your movie. When the SWF opens, drag the star and see it turn semitransparent when you drag it to the right of the moon, as shown in Figure 4-12.

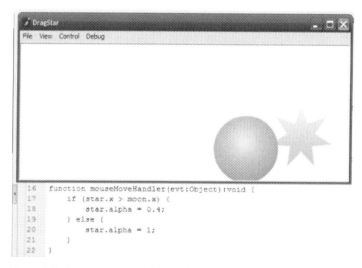

Figure 4-12. An opaque star and the code that handles the opacity based on the star's position relative to the moon's position on the stage

There's more to if statements than just the word *if*.

When the need arises, you may want to provide an else clause (which says, essentially, "Do this other thing if a condition is not met"), as in the preceding code. If the else portion had been left off, the opacity of star would be reduced the first time its path crossed that of moon, but once dimmed, it would never go back.

In cases where you want to test several conditions in a row, you may want to consider a switch statement. From a practical standpoint, switch and if do the same thing, so it's really up to you, but compare the two to see which you think looks cleaner or more compact. We are not saying one is more correct to use than the other. We just want to point out the options available to you.

```
var favoriteColor:String = "deep purple";
if (favoriteColor == "red") {
  // do something reddish
} else if (favoriteColor == "blue") {
  // do something blueish
} else if (favoriteColor == "green") {
  // do something greenish
} else {
  // do something else, because no one guessed
}

var favoriteColor:String = "deep purple";
switch(favoriteColor) {
  case "red":
    // do something reddish
    break;
  case "blue":
    // do something blueish
    break;
  case "green":
    // do something greenish
    break;
  default:
    // do something else, because no one guessed
    break;
}
```

What is the purpose of all those break *statements? In the context of* switch *statements,* break *tells ActionScript to ignore the rest of the list as soon as it matches a* case.

4

189

Class files

With all of this talk of objects and classes, you may be wondering if it is possible to create classes of your own. The answer is yes, and is squarely in the realm of "advanced ActionScript not covered in this book." Still, be aware that ActionScript allows you to come up with completely new objects of your own design. If you wish to start spreading your ActionScript wings, Steve Webster and Sean McSharry's *Foundation ActionScript 3.0 with Flash CS3 and Flex 2* is an excellent resource.

In Flash, classes are stored in external text files and imported dynamically for use in movies. There are many benefits to writing code in this way, not the least of which is that classes allow you to separate your visual design from your programming design. An experienced programmer might, for example, program a game in a series of classes—a SpaceShip class, a LaserBeam class, and so on—which would allow new laser beam objects to be created as needed, regardless of what library assets might be used to visually portray those lasers. Artwork could be given to a designer and later "married" with the code with relative ease, because external class files aren't spread among dozens of keyframes. It is, in fact, entirely possible to produce a heavily coded SWF without any ActionScript touching the FLA at all. This is accomplished via something called the Document class.

Document class

Click somewhere on the stage or work area to put the Property inspector into "stage" mode. When you do that, you will see a field in the lower-right corner of the Property inspector that reads Document class (as shown in Figure 4-13). This field allows you to associate a class file with the Flash document itself—think of it as being a main script that creates all the other ActionScript objects necessary to do the developer's bidding. In earlier editions of Flash, and even in Flash CS3 in anything other than ActionScript 3.0, this sort of association isn't possible. Developers could get close, by typing a line or two of ActionScript into frame 1 to import the main class, and perhaps calling an initialization method to set everything in motion—but ActionScript 3.0's Document class concept allows a fully programmed FLA file to literally be code-free.

No, we are not going to talk about custom class files in this book. When one of the authors mentioned doing a section on these things to the other, he fell on the ground in a dead faint and started babbling incoherently.

Figure 4-13. Document class files are accessed through the Property inspector.

Migrating to ActionScript 3.0: The pain and the joy

Kristin Henry is president and lead developer at GalaxyGoo (www.galaxygoo.org/), a nonprofit organization dedicated to increasing science literacy. She specializes in developing educational applications and interactive visualizations of scientific data using Flash. She has also contributed to Flash books and has presented at both industry and academic conferences including Flashforward and the Gordon Research Conference on Visualization in Science and Education.

To the authors of this book, it was a no-brainer to ask such an accomplished developer for an "in the trenches" glimpse at what it's like to migrate from ActionScript 2.0 to 3.0. We're grateful to Kristin for sharing a few of her impressions.

"*Learning AS3, after years of working with Flash, was both exciting and frustrating for me. At first, I was going back and forth between the versions. That didn't work well for me. So I jumped in with both feet and started coding everything in AS3. Once I'd gone through deep immersion in the new language, it was easier for me to go back and forth to earlier versions when needed.*

The syntax is very similar to previous versions of ActionScript, but subtle differences took some getting used to. For a while, my fingers twitched into habitually typing an underscore for properties like this._x. *In AS3, most of these properties have lost the underscore and are now* this.x.

In my projects, I use XML to format external data all the time. The way AS3 handles XML is fantastic! It's so much simpler to work with, and it's wonderful for searching and moving through an XML structure. [Note: This is covered in chapter 11 of this book.]

One of my favorite things about AS3 is the display list concept. Instead of attaching a movieclip to the stage and then building up its content, you can now prepare your movieclip first, building up any content and computational graphics, assign property values, and then add it to the display list, by way of the addChild() *method, when you're ready. [Note: This is true not only of movieclips, but any class that extends the* DisplayObjectContainer *class, including dynamic text fields. You can see an example in Chapter 6.]*

I'm a bit of a foodie, and to me this is a lot like preparing mise en place before firing up the pots and pans. Get everything ready first, then add it. It can be much more elegant and clean to code in that style. After coding with AS3 for a while now, I'm not sure how I got by without it for so long."

4

How to read the ActionScript 3.0 Language and Components Reference

Have you ever had to give a presentation in front of a room full of people? If you're not used to that, it can be pretty nerve-wracking. In spite of hours of preparation, presenters have been known to draw a complete blank. The authors have seen many newcomers to Flash react in the same way to the Help panel, especially when faced with the ActionScript 3.0 Language and Components Reference. You may have been following along just fine in this chapter—nodding your head, because things seem to make sense—but then, when you find yourself sitting in front of an empty Flash document . . . gosh, where to begin?

The Help panel isn't especially larger than the other panels you've seen, but it contains immeasurably more information. You may be feeling a sense of the old "dictionary catch-22"—how are you supposed to look up a word to find out how it's spelled . . . if you don't know how it's spelled?

Let's get you past Help panel stage fright.

There are several places where you can access this panel. If you are working in the Flash interface, select Help ➤ Flash Help. If you have the Actions panel open, simply open the panel's context menu and select Help.

If you really need help in a hurry, press the F1 key.

If you really need help in a hurry regarding a specific term in the code, highlight the term in the Script pane and press the F1 key. The Help panel will display information pertinent to the selection.

The Help panel behaves something like a browser. You have a search field, history navigation (back and forward buttons), a print button, and a few more odds and ends. The interface (shown in Figure 4-14) is actually quite sparse for the incredible volume of information this panel holds.

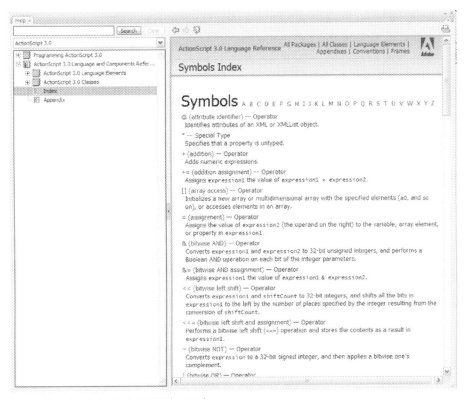

Figure 4-14. The ActionScript 3.0 Help panel

Search tactics

Browsing the ActionScript 3.0 Language and Components Reference is a good thing. We heartily encourage the practice. Flip open a section, even at random, and dig in—there's always plenty to learn, even for the expert. That said, busy schedules often mean that spare moments come at a premium. The Help panel's Search field can be a speedy assistant when your manager is breathing down your neck.

Your number one strategy at all times is to reduce the number of places you need to look.

First things first: Use the Book Category list box to filter the books in which you're interested (see Figure 4-15). If you're not looking for ActionScript-related information, select Features. If you're tracking down programming information, select ActionScript 3.0. What this does is keep the Search field from even looking at books you don't need.

Figure 4-15. The Book Category list box in the Help panel

This keeps you from having to wade through unnecessary search results, including results that might steer you down a very wrong path. Remember, if your movie's publish settings are configured for ActionScript 3.0, you can't put code from any other version of ActionScript into the mix. For the last several versions of Flash, advanced developers have had access to something called the Flash JavaScript API, also known as JSFL. This special language is different from ActionScript altogether, because it allows the Flash interface itself to be manipulated programmatically. For example, you can automate repetitive tasks with JSFL or even build new drawing tools from scratch. But this language can only be used with Flash itself and Flash documents—not SWF files. The last thing you want to do is discover some exciting new "feature" in JSFL and spend hours trying to figure out why it doesn't work in your movie.

Take the time to learn two important descriptive ActionScript terms: conditionals and operators. Write them on a sticky note, if you like, and keep it taped to your monitor. You won't get anywhere searching the word *if*, for example, because although if is an important ActionScript statement, it's also a common word in everyday speech. If you want to see the entry on if, if..else, and the like, look up the sort of ActionScript an if statement is—which is a conditional. Here's a helpful two-item cheat sheet:

- **Conditionals**: if, if..else, and switch
- **Operators**: <, >, +, -, and other symbols practically impossible to find otherwise

Perhaps the biggest tip we can give you is this: *think in terms of objects*. Sounds familiar, right? We hit that topic pretty hard early in the chapter, so why is it coming up again here? To recap, objects are defined by classes, and classes are comprised of all the little owner's manuals you will need. If you're dealing with a movieclip instance, think to yourself, "What class would define this object?" Nine times out of ten, the answer is a class of the same name. Search *MovieClip* in the Help panel, filtered for the ActionScript 3.0 books, and you'll very quickly be brought to the MovieClip class entry.

As you have already learned, a class entry will show you the properties, methods, and events relevant to any instance of this class. No more hunt and peck! If you're dealing with a text field and stumble across a question, search *TextField*. If you're having trouble with audio, look up the Sound class. If your problem is with any of the UI components, look up the class for that component. The only common object whose class name isn't the same as what it's called is the button symbol. In ActionScript 3.0, button symbols are instances of the SimpleButton class. (There's always an exception, right? But at least they're usually rare.)

Once you get to a class entry, use the hyperlinks in the upper-right corner to quickly jump to the class member category you need. Remember, properties are an object's characteristics, methods are things the object can do, and events are things it can react to. When you get to the desired category, make sure to show the inherited members in that category.

What is this "inherited" business? Let's think back to Tom and David as instances of the Male object. Sure, they're both males, but it gets more specific than that, doesn't it? Tom is a professor and David is a unicyclist. It also gets more general than that, because both of the authors are humans. From general to specific, each object builds on what came before it. A human can be either male or female, but males and females alike are both humans. (Yes, we realize they could actually be chimpanzees, but roll with us on this admittedly superficial analogy.) When we're dealing with people, it can be said that their base class is Human. A more specific class of human is Male, which "inherits" all the functionality of Human, but adds to it in various ways to make it more exclusive. From there, it gets even more selective, as the "class members" that describe professors differ from those that describe unicyclists—even though David and Tom both share all the properties, methods, and events of the Male class, which in turn shares all the properties, methods, and events of the Human class.

In a similar fashion, MovieClip instances are more specific versions of a class called Sprite. MovieClip extends the Sprite class, which means it inherits all of the Sprite class's members. In turn, Sprite extends the DisplayObjectContainer class, and so on, all the way back to the base Object class, the mother of them all. By showing inherited members, you'll get a better idea of the full functionality of a given object. From dealing with movieclips in the Flash interface, you already know they support alpha blending (transparency) and blend modes. As it happens, these two properties are actually defined by the DisplayObjectContainer class, so don't panic if you don't see them right away in the MovieClip class—just study its family tree.

Edgar Allen Poe once mentioned something about a "dream within a dream." It was actually a pretty tormented poem about not being able to hold onto life, or perhaps time. Fortunately for you, it's not so bad with Flash. The Help panel provides a search within a search that actually saves you time. Click in the upper-right corner to access the Help panel's context menu. You'll find access to a Find dialog, which searches the currently open page.

The other neat thing about the Help panel is that it's loaded with code examples that show you how to use what you are exploring. For example, you may want to use a preloader and need to know how to tell Flash to look for the number of frames that have been loaded. Here's how you would do that:

1. Open the Help panel and select the ActionScript 3.0 Language and Components Reference book.

2. Enter framesLoaded into the Search box and press the Enter/Return key. The result appears, giving an example of how it can be used (as shown in Figure 4-16).

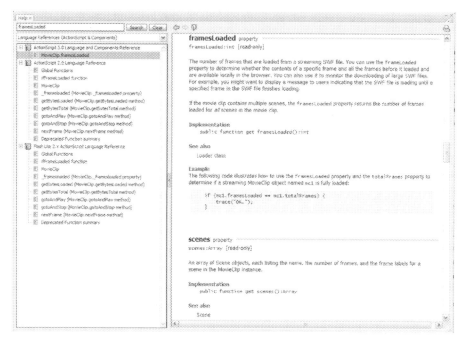

Figure 4-16. The Help file also shows you how the result can be used.

Checking syntax

In Flash 8, and even earlier, the Check syntax button of the Actions panel was a little friendlier than it is today. Even in Flash CS3, if you set the document's publish settings to ActionScript 2.0 (File ➤ Publish Settings, Flash tab), you can get a taste of the "good old days"—but ActionScript 3.0 documents represent a new era, where all is not as it seems and that many of you may feel is frustrating. Here's a look at what we mean:

1. Create a new Flash File (ActionScript 2.0) document—not 3.0!—and save it as AS2Syntax.fla in the Exercise folder for this chapter. Rename Layer 1 to scripts. Open the Actions panel and type the following ActionScript into frame 1:

   var str:String = 5;

2. Click the Check syntax button at the top of the Script pane. Behold! You get a useful error message, as shown in Figure 4-17. An alert box tells you to check the Compiler Errors panel, which in turn tells you about a "type mismatch" error: Flash was looking for a string value in the str variable, but you gave it a number instead.

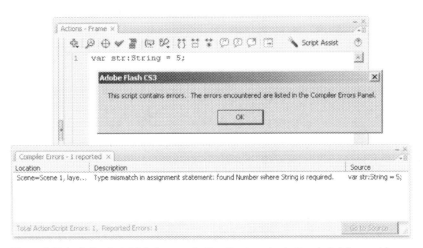

Figure 4-17. In ActionScript 2.0 documents, the Check syntax button helpfully provides even the most basic syntax checking.

3. Click OK, then save and close the document. Bearing in mind what you just saw, create a new Flash File (ActionScript 3.0) document—yes, 3.0—and save it as AS3Syntax.fla in the Exercise folder for this chapter. You're about to perform the same experiment, so rename Layer 1 to scripts. Open the Actions panel and type the following identical ActionScript into frame 1:

```
var str:String = 5;
```

Syntax doesn't necessarily carry over so easily from one version of the language to another, but in this case, the variable declaration in question is indeed the same in both ActionScript 2.0 and 3.0.

4. Click the Check syntax button. You'll see an alert box as before, but this time it tells a fib, as shown in Figure 4-18.

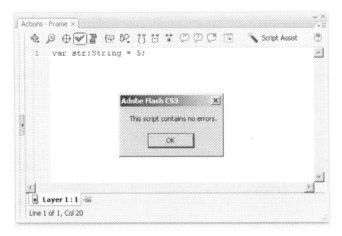

Figure 4-18. In ActionScript 3.0 documents, the Check syntax button doesn't always tell the truth.

197

5. As you saw in the "Data types" section, Flash does check syntax during a compile—that is, when you actually test the movie. To prove it here again, click OK, then test the movie and keep an eye on the Compiler Errors panel. Sure enough, you get the expected "type mismatch" error (see Figure 4-19).

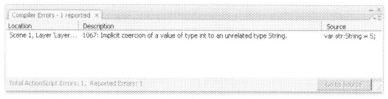

Figure 4-19. Thankfully, syntax is checked when a movie is tested.

The trouble with testing a movie in order to proof your syntax becomes clear as soon as your movie takes on any complexity. There will be times you simply want to "check your bearings" in place, without having to go to the trouble of generating a SWF file. Does this mean the Check syntax button is useless in ActionScript 3.0 documents? Well, the word *useless* might be a little harsh. Might be. To be fair, the Check syntax button does report on certain kinds of errors . . . it's just that they're hard to find.

You have two documents handy, so let's tag-team between them and look at a few more examples. We recommend you keep both AS2Syntax.fla and AS3Syntax.fla open, and flip back and forth as you test the following code.

1. Delete the existing code in your ActionScript 3.0 document and type the following into the Actions panel in frame 1:

```
var d:Date = new Date();
d.setMillennium(3);
```

As you do, you'll see some code hinting when you get to line 2. Thanks to the strongly typed variable d in line 1—the strong typing is provided by the :Date suffix—Flash knows that d is an instance of the Date class. As a courtesy, the Actions panel gives you a context-sensitive drop-down menu as soon as you type the dot after the variable. The drop-down menu suggests Date class members, as seen in Figure 4-20.

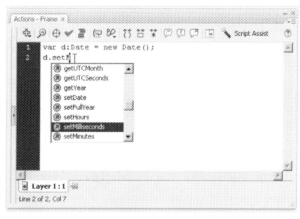

Figure 4-20. Using strongly typed variables gives you useful code hinting.

198

Type "s" and the drop-down menu jumps to class members that start with "s," such as setDate, setFullYear, and so on. Type as far as "setM" and you'll see setMilliseconds. At this point, you're going to be a rebel. Rather than go with any of the suggestions, type "setMillennium(3)," to complete line 2 of the code shown previously. As you can see from the drop-down menu, the Date class features no such method. Does the Check syntax button agree?

2. Click the Check syntax button to find out. In the ActionScript 3.0 document, the alert box will put on a shady poker face: *This script contains no errors*. Tut, tut! We know better than that ourselves. Click OK to close the alert box.

3. Repeat the same steps in the ActionScript 2.0 document. Once you've replaced the existing code with the 2-line Date-related ActionScript—complete with the made-up setMillennium() method—click the Check syntax button. Here, the alert sends you to the Compiler Errors panel, which slams you with the hard truth: *There is no method with the name 'setMillennium'*. Hey, even if the truth hurts, it's good to know.

4. Return one last time to the ActionScript 3.0 document. Delete the last two characters in your code, so that it looks like this:

```
var d:Date = new Date();
d.setMillennium(2000
```

Now click the Check syntax button. Are you holding your breath? Go ahead and exhale. Ahhh, finally, we get a useful error message. The alert box leads us to the Compiler Errors panel, which reads:

```
1084: Syntax error: expecting rightparen before end of program.
```

Sure, it sounds a little stilted, as if intoned by the red-eyed, Cyclopic HAL of Stanley Kubrick's *2001: A Space Odyssey*—but it's an error message, and that's a good thing. Click OK to close the alert box.

5. For good measure, make a final visit to the ActionScript 2.0 document and remove the closing); characters there, too. Click the Check syntax button. What do you get? You get an alert box that tells you to check out the error message in the Compiler Errors panel: *')' or ',' expected*. More or less the same message, just stated more succinctly. Click OK to close the alert box.

What can you learn from this? In ActionScript 3.0 documents, the Actions panel's Check syntax button reports on gross structural problems. If you have a missing parenthesis or bracket, such as in the expression

```
if ((2 + 2) == 4) {
   trace("Yes, 2 + 2 is 4.");
} else
   trace("Oddly, it isn't.");
}
```

you'll be warned about it. In the preceding code, the else clause is missing a bracket ({) to its right. This sort of error reporting, even if it's all you get, is a positive asset. In the words of our mothers, "Be thankful for what you have." To that, we add this: If you need a bit of something to lean on in your programming, use the resources at hand, which include the ActionScript 3.0 Language and Components Reference and code hinting. Even

4

the Script Assist feature of the Actions panel, which will step you through code writing line by line, only catches the sort of errors found by the Check syntax button in ActionScript 3.0 documents.

So . . . tuck your feet, pretzel-like, beneath you and then up again over your legs. This is the lotus position. It encourages breathing and good posture—and is said to facilitate meditation. Don't lose heart! The very best syntax checker is sitting closer than you think: it's right there between your shoulders.

Your turn: Using ActionScript

You are going to be using ActionScript throughout the rest of the book. Hopefully, if you have made it to this point of the chapter, you should feel pretty confident about facing it. In fact, once you have coded a few projects, you will actually be able to read code. Once you arrive at that point, you are on your way to mastering the application.

Flash has come a long way from its vector animation roots and has improved significantly with ActionScript 3.0. It's a more powerful language than ever. The really neat thing about ActionScript is it is relatively accessible for navigational programming of the sort used in presentations, banner ads, and other interactive projects you may undertake.

Here's a recap of our recommendations:

- Get into the habit of creating a Scripts or Actions layer in the main timeline and movieclip timelines, if you choose to add code to nested symbols. When everything has its place, it's easier to find, which means it's easier to update.

- Take a pragmatic approach. Hardcore programmers may insist that you put all your code in a single frame, or better, in external files. In complex situations, that may be the best way to go. When you're ready to undertake complex coding and the circumstances require it, go for it. In the meantime, don't lose any sleep over doing this the old-fashioned way in Flash, which amounts to little snippets of code among many keyframes. Remember, *nobody cares how it was done. They only care that it works.*

- Strongly type your variables.

- Use comments to leave footnotes through your code. Even if you are the only one working on your files, you'll appreciate your efforts later, when the client asks for a change. Comments help you get your bearings quickly.

- Use the `trace( )` function to help yourself see where you are in a published SWF.

> *ActionScript has matured to the point where there are a lot of people making a very good living from writing ActionScript code. If code isn't your thing, learn it anyway. The odds are almost 100% that you will eventually work with an ActionScript programmer, and being able to speak the language will make your design efforts even smoother.*

With the advice out of the way, let's look at two practical uses for ActionScript by applying it to two very popular requests on the Adobe support forums.

People often want to know how to pause the main timeline for a certain amount of time before moving on, and they often want to know how to loop a movie a certain number of times before stopping at the end. Let's wire them up.

Pausing the main timeline

The key to this project is understanding Flash's wrist watch. If you have an analog wrist watch, the minutes are marked around the dial and the second hand ticks around the dial. Flash doesn't have a second hand, it has a millisecond hand; and the watch face is not divided into minutes or seconds—there are 1,000 little division marks.

Instead of a millisecond, think about a mouse click. There are actually two things involved in that event. There is the event in which the mouse button is down and the event in which the mouse button is up. How fast that happens is dependent on the amount of time you use to press and release the button. In Flash, we can capture that small amount of time and turn it into an eternity if we so choose. Same thing when you let go of the button. When it comes to working with time in Flash, the unit of measure is the millisecond, and we can turn a millisecond into an eternity (which, incidentally, is not a good idea).

In this exercise, you are simply going to tell Flash, "When you hit this point on the timeline, hang around for two seconds before moving on to the next millisecond and doing what needs to be done." Here's how:

1. Open the PauseTimeline.fla file. If you scrub the playhead across the timeline, the box, thanks to the tween, gets bigger.

2. Add a keyframe to frame 15 of the scripts layer. Select the keyframe and open the Actions panel.

3. Enter the following code into the Script pane:

```
this.stop();
```

This is the line that stops the playhead from moving forward, and it is also the line of code that can turn a millisecond into an eternity. If you stop the playhead, have a solid plan in place to get it back in motion.

4. Press the Enter/Return key, and enter the following code:

```
var timelinePause:Timer = new Timer(2000, 1);
timelinePause.addEventListener(TimerEvent.TIMER, timerHandler);
timelinePause.start();
```

The first line tells Flash to create a Timer object. In ActionScript, when you use the class name followed by parentheses, you are creating what is called a **constructor**, which is a fancy term for an instance of a class. The numbers between the parentheses tell Flash the duration of the timer (2,000 milliseconds, or 2 seconds) and how often to wait around for that 2 seconds. The 1 means "only wait for it once."

> There are two ways to create object instances. If it is a movieclip, button, or text field, it can be created on the stage or dragged onto the stage from the library by hand. Programmatic instances need to use a constructor.

The next line tells Flash what to do when the two seconds are up; which is to execute a function named timerHandler. The final line tells Flash to reset the timer, and start the timer if it isn't already running.

5. Press the Enter/Return key and enter the following code:

```
function timerHandler(evt:Object):void {
  this.play();
}
```

As you may have guessed, this is what happens when Flash waits around for the 2 seconds. The play() method simply tells the timeline to start playing again (see Figure 4-21).

6. Save and test the movie. The box will grow, stop growing for 2 seconds, and then continue to grow.

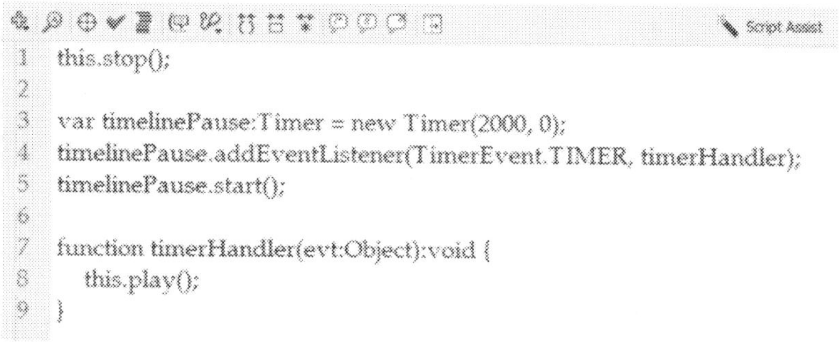

```
1   this.stop();
2
3   var timelinePause:Timer = new Timer(2000, 0);
4   timelinePause.addEventListener(TimerEvent.TIMER, timerHandler);
5   timelinePause.start();
6
7   function timerHandler(evt:Object):void {
8     this.play();
9   }
```

Figure 4-21. Pausing the Flash timeline

Looping the timeline

We have all seen those banner ads that play two or three times and are replaced by another version of the ad. To loop the main timeline three times—this is a popular number for banner ads—declare a loop variable in frame 1 and initialize it to 0. Here's how they do it:

1. Open the LoopTimeline.fla file. When it opens, you will see, as you scrub the playhead across the frames, that the box grows.

2. Add a keyframe in frame 1 and frame 30 of the scripts layer, select the keyframe in frame 1, and open the Actions panel.

3. Enter the following code into the Script pane:

```
var loop:Number = 0;
```

Nothing new here—you create a variable named `loop` and give it a number value of 0. In many respects, what you are doing here is setting the initial value, because all of the action in this example takes place between frames 2 and 30.

4. Select the keyframe in frame 30 and add the following code:

```
loop = loop + 1;
if (loop < 3) {
  this.gotoAndPlay(2);
} else {
  this.stop();
}
```

Let's take a look at what you have done. The first line adds 1 to the value of the variable you named `loop` in the first frame. The next four lines are the conditional statement that essentially says, "If the value of `loop` is 1 or 2 (if `loop < 3`), then scoot the playhead back to frame 2 (`this.gotoAndPlay(2)`). If it is already 3—`else`—then stay put on frame 30."

The first time the playhead hits frame 30, the value of `loop` is 1, and the playhead scoots back to frame 2. (The reason it goes to frame 2 is because frame 1 would set the value of `loop` to 0 again.) The next time it hits frame 30, the value of `loop` is changed to 2 and, again, the playhead scoots back to frame 2 and plays the animation. This time, when the playhead hits frame 30, the value of `loop` is changed to 3, and the playhead stays put on frame 30.

5. Save and test the movie.

What you've learned

- The basics of ActionScript
- Why objects are so important
- The difference between a property, a method, and an event
- What a class is and why it is so important in ActionScript 3.0
- How to use the ActionScript 3.0 Language and Components Reference in the Help panel

A lot of ground has been covered in this chapter. Hopefully, you are eager to start learning how to use ActionScript in your everyday workflow. In fact, every chapter from this one to the end of the book will use it, so feel free to keep returning here to refresh your knowledge. In Chapter 1, we told you we would get you deep into using audio in Flash. With the basics under your wing, let's see what we can do with audio in Flash and how ActionScript and audio are the ideal pairing.

4

5 AUDIO IN FLASH CS3

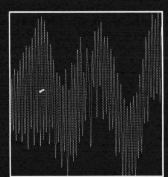

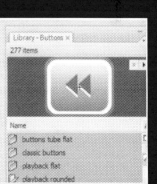

If you're one of those who treat audio in Flash as an afterthought . . . think again. In many respects, audio is a major medium for communicating your message. In this chapter, we dig into audio in Flash: where it comes from, what formats are used, and how to use it in Flash. Regardless of whether you are new to Flash or an old hand, you are about discover the rules regarding audio in Flash have changed . . . for the better.

What we'll cover in this chapter:

- Audio file formats used in Flash
- Adding and previewing audio in Flash
- Playing audio from the library
- Playing remote audio files
- Using ActionScript 3.0 to control audio
- Playing and controlling multiple audio files

Files used in this chapter:

- Number6.aif (Chapter05/ExerciseFiles_CH05/Exercise/Number6.aif)
- Frog.fla (Chapter05/ExerciseFiles_CH05/Exercise/Frog.fla)
- Chill.mp3 (Chapter05/ExerciseFiles_CH05/Exercise/Chill.mp3)
- FrogMC.fla (Chapter05/ExerciseFiles_CH05/Exercise/FrogMC.fla)
- Remote.fla (Chapter05/ExerciseFiles_CH05/Exercise/Remote.fla)
- Remote2.fla (Chapter05/ExerciseFiles_CH05/Exercise/Remote2.fla)
- Player.fla (Chapter05/ExerciseFiles_CH05/Exercise/MP3Player/Player.fla)
- alternative.mp3 (Chapter05/ExerciseFiles_CH05/Exercise/ MP3Player/alternative.mp3)
- rockfunk.mp3 (Chapter05/ExerciseFiles_CH05/Exercise/ MP3Player/rockfunk.mp3)
- chill.mp3 (Chapter05/ExerciseFiles_CH05/Exercise/ MP3Player/chill.mp3)

The authors would like to express their deep appreciation and thanks to Claudio Capellari out of Geneva, Switzerland, and Ryan Longo (www.asylumsound.ca), a young sound engineer in Toronto, Canada, for supplying us with a number of audio tracks and giving us permission to use them in this chapter.

Flash and the audio formats

When it comes to sound, Flash is a robust application in that it can handle many of the major audio formats available . . . including the more common formats listed here:

- **MP3 (Moving Pictures Expert Group Level-2 Layer-3 Audio)**: This cross-platform format is a standard for web and portable audio files. In many respects the growth of this format is tied to the popularity of iPods and audio players on cell phones. Though you can output these files in stereo, you'll want to pay close attention to bandwidth settings for your MP3s.

- **WAV**: If you use a PC to record a voiceover or other sound, you are familiar with the WAV format. WAV files have sample rates ranging from 8 kilohertz (the quality of your phone) up to 48 kilohertz (DAT tapes) and beyond. These files are also available with bit depths ranging from 8 bits right up to 32 bits. Just keep in mind that a file with a sample rate of 48 kilohertz and a 32 bit depth will result in a massive file size that simply shouldn't be used with Flash.

- **QuickTime**: These files have extensions of `.qta` or `.mov` and can contain audio in many formats. If you do create a QuickTime audio file, you need to make the movie self-contained in QuickTime Pro.

- **AIFF (Audio Interchange File Format)**: AIFF is the standard for the Macintosh and offers the same sample rates and bit depths as a WAV file. Many purists will argue that the AIFF format is better than the WAV format. This may indeed be true, but to the average person the difference between this format and WAV is almost inaudible.

> *Take this obscure fact to a trivia contest, and you will clean up. AIFF also has a sample rate of 22,254.54 kilohertz. Why the odd sample rate? This was the original Macintosh sample rate and was based on the horizontal scan rate of the monitor in a 128 KB Mac.*

Bit depth and sample rates

We traditionally visualize sound as a sine wave—when the wave rises above the vertical, the sound gets "higher;" where it runs below the vertical, the sound gets "lower." These waves, shown in Figure 5-1, are called the **waveform**. The horizontal line is silence, and the audio is "measured" from the top of one "blip" to the top of the next one along the waveform. These blips are called **peaks**, and the sampling is done from peak to peak.

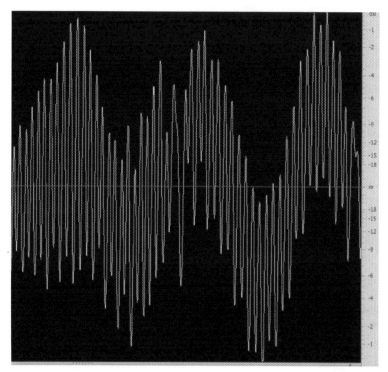

Figure 5-1. A typical waveform

For any sound to be digitized, like a color image in Fireworks or Photoshop, the wave needs to be sampled. A **sample** is nothing more than a snapshot of a waveform at any given time. This snapshot is a digital number representing where on the waveform this snapshot was taken. How often the waveform is sampled is called the **sample rate**.

Bit depth is the resolution of the sample. "8 bits" means the snapshot is represented as a number ranging from –128 to 127. "16 bits" means that the number is between –32,768 to 32,767. If you do the math, you see that an 8-bit snapshot has 256 potential samples, whereas its 16-bit counterpart has just over 65,000 potential samples. The greater the number of potential samples of a wave, the more accurate the sound. The downside to this is, of course, the more samples on the wave, the larger the file size. These numbers represent where each sample is located on the waveform. When the numbers are played back in the order in which they were sampled and at the frequency they were sampled, they represent a sound's waveform. Obviously, a larger bit depth and higher sample rate means that the waveform is played back with greater accuracy because more snapshots are taken of the waveform, which results in a more accurate representation of the waveform. This explains why the songs from an album have such massive file sizes. They are sampled at the highest possible bit depth.

One wave cycle in 1 second is known as a **hertz**, which can't be heard by the human ear, except possibly as a series of clicks. Audible sound uses thousands of these waves, and they are crammed into a 1-second time span and measured in that span. A thousand waveform cycles in 1 second is called a **kilohertz** (KHz), and if you listen to an audio CD, the audio rate is sampled at the frequency of 44 thousand waves per second, which is traditionally identified as 44 KHz. These waves are also commonly referred to as the sample rate.

The inference you can draw from this is that the more samples per wave and the more accurate the samples, the larger the file size. Toss a stereo sound into the mix, and you have essentially doubled the file size. Obviously, the potential for huge sound files is there, which is not a good situation when dealing with Flash. Large files take an awfully long time to load into a browser, which means your user is in for a painful experience. One way of dealing with this is to reduce the sample rate or number of waves per second.

The three most common sample rates used are 11 KHz, 22 KHz, and 44 KHz. If you reduce the sample rate from 44 KHz to 22 KHz, you achieve a significant reduction, roughly 50%, in file size. You obtain an even more significant reduction, another 50%, if the rate is reduced to 11 KHz. The problem is, reducing the sample rate reduces audio quality. Listening to your Beethoven's Ninth Symphony at 11 KHz results in the music sounding as if it were playing from the inside of a tin can.

As a Flash designer or developer, your prime objective is to obtain the best quality sound at the smallest file size. Though many Flash developers tell you that 16-bit, 44 KHz stereo is the way to go, you'll quickly realize this is not necessarily true. For example, a 16-bit, 44 KHz stereo sound of a mouse click or a sound lasting less than a couple of seconds—such as a whoosh as an object zips across the screen—is a waste of bandwidth. The duration is so short that average users won't realize it if you've made your click an 8-bit, 22 KHz mono sound. They hear the click and move on. The same holds true for music files. The average user is most likely listening to the cheap speakers that were tossed in as an inducement against the sale of the PC. In this case, a 16-bit, 22 KHz soundtrack will sound as good as its CD-quality rich cousin.

Flash and MP3

The two most common sound formats used in Flash are WAV and AIFF. Both formats share a common starting point—they are both based on the "Interchange File Format" proposal written in 1985 by Electronic Arts to help standardize transfer issues on the Commodore Amiga. Like video, sound contains a huge amount of data and must be compressed before it is used. This is the purpose of a codec. **Codec** is an acronym for **enCODer/DECoder**, and the format used by Flash to output audio is the MP3 format, regardless of the format(s) of imported files.

From your perspective, the need to compress audio for web delivery makes the use of AIFF or WAV files redundant. The MP3 format is the standard, which explains why WAV and AIFF files are converted to MP3 files on playback. If you are working with an audio production facility, you will often be handed an AIFF or WAV file. Even if they give you the option of receiving an MP3, you are better off with the AIFF or WAV file for the same reason that you wouldn't want to recompress a JPG file: they are both lossy compression schemes. An obvious question is this: Why are MP3 files so small but still sound so good? The answer lies in the fact that the MP3 standard uses perceptual encoding.

All Internet audio formats toss a ton of audio information into the trash. When information gets tossed, there is a corresponding decrease in file size. What gets tossed when an

5

MP3 file is created are sound frequencies your dog may be able to hear, but you can't. In short, you hear only the sound a human can perceive, and this sort of explains why animals aren't huge fans of iPods.

All perceptual encoders allow you to choose how much audio is unimportant. Most encoders produce excellent quality files using no more than 16 Kbps to create voice recordings. When you create an MP3, you have to pay attention to the bandwidth. The format is fine, but if the bandwidth is not optimized for its intended use, your results will be unacceptable, which is why applications that create MP3 files ask you to set the bandwidth along with the sample rate.

So much for theory, let's get practical.

Adding audio to Flash

Knowing that you can bring all of these formats into Flash and that MP3 is the output format for Flash is all well and good. But how do they *get* into Flash, and, more importantly, how does an AIFF or WAV file get converted to an MP3 file when it plays in Flash? Let's do that right now starting with an import:

1. Open a new Flash document. When the document opens, import Number6.AIF in your Exercise folder to the library. This is a standard practice in the industry. Audio files are rarely, if ever, imported to the timeline. In fact, audio files, due to the unique manner in which they are added to a Flash movie, simply can't be imported to the stage.

> *If you select* Import to Stage *when importing an audio file, it won't be placed on the stage. Instead, it will be placed directly into the Flash library.*

2. When you open the Flash library and select the file, you will see the file's waveform, shown in Figure 5-2, in the Preview area.

Figure 5-2. Select an audio file in the library, and its waveform appears in the Preview area.

3. Double-click the audio file in the Flash library to open the file's Sound Properties dialog box, shown in Figure 5-3. Click the Test button to preview the sound file. Click the Stop button to stop the sound playback.

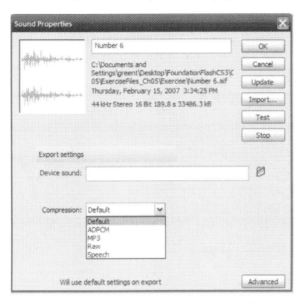

Figure 5-3. The Sound Properties dialog box is opened when you double-click an audio file in the library.

> There is another way to preview audio without a trip to the Sound Properties *dialog box. Click the* Play *button that is located above the waveform in the Preview area of the library (refer back to Figure 5-2).*

This dialog box is a really useful tool. As you have discovered, you can use it to preview and stop an audio file. The Update button is really handy. If an audio file has been edited after being placed into Flash, you can click the Update button to replace the file in Flash with the edited version.

Also, notice the audio information under the path and the date information. This file, at 32 MB and over 3 minutes in duration—189.8 seconds—is massive.

The Export Settings area is where you choose the sound type chosen and add compression. Don't worry about device sounds. They are used in PDAs and other devices that employ Flash Lite. From our perspective, the Compression drop-down list is of major importance.

In this drop-down, you are asked to pick a codec. In Flash, the default is to export all sound in the MP3 format. Still, the ability to individually compress each sound in the library is an option that shouldn't be disregarded. Your choices are as follows:

- ADPCM: This type of sound file is best suited for very short clips and looped sound. This format was the original sound output format in older versions of Flash. If, for example, you are outputting for use in Flash Player 2 or 3, ADPCM is required.

- MP3: Use this for Flash Player versions 4 or higher. This format is not compatible with Flash Player 4 for Pocket PC. It is, however, compatible with the Flash Lite player, which is used in devices such as cell phones and PDAs. MP3s are also not suited for looping sounds because the end of a file is often padded.

- Raw: No compression is applied, and it is somewhat useless if sound is being delivered over the Web. If you are creating Flash Player for use on a DVD or CD or a Flash movie for incorporation into a video, this format is acceptable.

- Speech: Introduced in Flash MX, this codec (originally licensed by Macromedia from Nellymoser) is ideal for voiceover narrations.

If you select a codec, additional compression settings will appear.

4. Select MP3 from the Compression drop-down menu, and the settings change as shown in Figure 5-4. Click the Test button and listen to the sound. What you may notice is how flat the audio is compared to the original version. If you take a look at the Bit rate and Quality settings, you will see why. That 34 MB file is now sitting at about 1% of its original size, or 379 KB.

Figure 5-4. Setting MP3 compression

5. Change the bit rate to 48 kbps and select Best in the Quality drop-down menu. Also make sure that Convert stereo to mono is checked. If you click the Test button, you will hear a marked improvement in the audio quality.

Asking you to compare the audio quality to the original in the previous two steps is a bit disingenuous on our part. Our intention was to let you "hear" the quality differences . . . not compare them with the original audio. In the final analysis, comparing compressed audio against the original version is a "fool's game." The user never hears the original file, so what does he or she have as a basis for comparison? When listening to the compressed version, listen to it in its own right and ask yourself whether it meets your quality standard.

No, you can't "super size" an audio file. If an MP3 being used has a bit rate of 48 Kbps in the original file imported into Flash, you never increase the bit rate above that level in Flash. "Up-sampling" audio will more often than not decrease, not increase, the audio quality.

Unless your audio includes specialized panning or there is some other compelling reason for using stereo, feel free to convert the stereo sound to mono. The user won't miss it, and the audio file size will plummet. Flash even allows mono sounds to be panned.

There is one other place where the sound output format can be set: the Publish Settings panel.

6. Close the Sound Properties dialog box. Select File ➤ Publish Settings. When the Publish Settings panel opens, click the Flash tab.

At the bottom of this panel, shown in Figure 5-5, are Audio stream and Audio event settings. We'll get into these two in the next section, but the important thing to note for now is the Override sound settings check box.

Figure 5-5. The audio options in the Publish Settings panel

If you select this check box, the audio settings shown for the Audio stream and Audio event areas will override any settings applied in the Sound Properties dialog box. Think of this as the ability to apply a global setting to every sound in your movie. Unless there is a compelling reason to select this choice, we suggest you avoid it.

If you do have a compelling reason to use it, click either Set button, and you will be presented with the same options in the Sound Properties dialog box.

7. Click Cancel to close the Publish Settings dialog box. Close the movie without saving the changes.

5

Using audio in Flash

In Chapter 1, you added an audio file containing crickets and wolves howling to enhance the ambience of your Lake Nanagook movie. We asked you to do a couple of things in that chapter, but we didn't tell why you were doing them. The purpose was to get you hooked on Flash, and it obviously worked because you are now at this point of the book. The time has arrived give you the answers to the "Why?" questions.

There are two types of sound in Flash:

- **Event sound**: This tells Flash to load the sound completely before playing it. Once loaded, the audio continues to play even if the movie's playhead stops, which means event sounds are not locked to the timeline. (Audio can be forced to stop, but that takes specific action on your part.) If the Number6.aif file, used in the previous section, is being played back on a slower machine than yours, the odds are really good the audio will not conclude on the frame you expected. In other words, event sounds are not reliable in terms of synchronizing with visuals on the stage. Also, a movie in this situation would take a very long time to start playing, because Flash has to load the sound fully before playback can begin. Event sound is ideal for pops, clicks, and other very short sounds or in situations where the audio will be played more than once or looped.

- **Stream sound**: This is a sound that can begin playing before it has loaded. The thing is, it must be loaded every time you want to play it. This sound type is ideal for longer background soundtracks that only play once. Because it is locked in step with the timeline, stream sound is the only realistic option for cartoon lip-synching.

Now that you know what to expect, let's work with both types so you can get a "feel" for what we are talking about:

1. Open the Frog.fla file. When it opens, you will see we have included the Frog.mp3 audio file in the library.

2. Rename the layer in the timeline to Audio and drag the Frog.mp3 file from the library onto the stage. Audio files are added to the Flash timeline by dropping them on the stage—where they seemingly vanish—not onto the timeline. When you release the mouse, you may see a line running through the middle of frame 1 in the timeline. This line is the start of the waveform.

3. Insert a frame in frame 7 of the timeline. You can now see the entire waveform on the timeline.

4. Right-click (PC) or Ctrl-click (Mac) on the layer name and select Properties from the context menu. When the Layer Properties dialog box opens, as shown in Figure 5-6, select 300% from the Layer height drop-down menu and click OK. When you release the mouse, the layer view is three times larger, and you can see the full waveform.

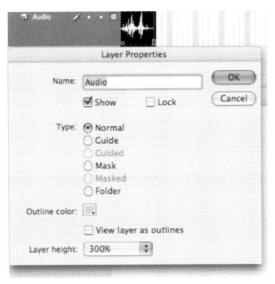

Figure 5-6. Use the layer properties to "zoom in" on the timeline.

> *Being able to see the waveform on the timeline is a huge advantage to you because you can now use the waveform's peaks or valleys to time animation of other events to the audio file in Stream mode.*

5. Click in the waveform on the timeline anywhere but frame 1, and in the Sync area of the Property inspector, select Event from the drop-down menu. Press Enter (PC) or Return (Mac). The playback head moves, but the sound doesn't play. Drag the playback head to frame 1 or frame 7 and press Enter (PC) or Return (Mac). What you have just heard is a fundamental truth of an event sound: you can only preview event sounds by playing them in their entirety.

> *Being the nice guys we are, you can thank us for not using the Number6.aif audio file. If it were an event sound, you would be sitting here listening to the full 3 minutes of the file. Event sounds play for their entire duration, and you can't stop playback by pressing Enter (PC) or Return (Mac). All that does is to start playing another copy of the sound over the one that is currently playing.*

6. Change the Sync setting to Stream as shown in Figure 5-7. This time drag the playback head across the timeline. Notice you can hear the sound as you scrub across it. Drag the playback head to frame 2 and press Enter (PC) or Return (Mac). The sound plays from that point and, for longer audio files, pressing the Enter or Return key stops playback. The downside is, the playback is only for the frame span on the timeline. For example, the Number6.aif file would require about 2,100 frames on the timeline to play the entire track. If the span were only 50 frames, you would only be able to play about 4 seconds of the file, assuming your frame rate is set to 12 frames per second.

Figure 5-7. Using stream or event sound in the Property inspector

> *You may notice there are Stop and Start choices in the Sync drop-down menu. Stop is almost the same as the Event option, except that it won't allow more than one version of the sound file to play at the same time. Start essentially won't play the sound until the sound that is currently playing has finished.*

7. Let's get this out of the way, right now. Audio files can't be deleted from the timeline. Hold down the Shift key and select frames 1 and 7 on the timeline to select the audio file. Press the Delete key. Nothing happens. To remove an audio file from the timeline, select a frame in the audio waveform and, in the Property inspector, select None from the Sound drop-down menu. The sound is removed. To put the Frog.mp3 audio file back on the timeline, open the Sound drop-down menu and select Frog.mp3. If you have a number of audio files in your library, they will all be listed in this drop-down menu, and you can use it to add or change audio files without deleting them or dragging them onto the timeline.

A note from a master

Dave Shroeder is regarded by many in this industry as being a master when it comes to the use of audio in Flash. He has spoken at a number of very important industry conferences and his company, Pilotvibe (www.pilotvibe.com), has developed a solid international reputation for supplying the industry with high-quality sound loops and effects for use in Flash. In fact, his home page, shown in Figure 5-8, can be regarded as a master class in the effective use of audio to set the "mood" in a Flash movie.

Who better to talk to you about the use of audio in Flash than the guy who is setting the standard:

"Once you start to play around with adding sound to Flash files, you'll probably realize that it can add an incredible dimension to your project. Sound can really tie an experience together.

It can bring an animation to life. It can create a mood, or suggest characteristics that reinforce your message. It can be entertaining, or informative, or both.

If sound is an option for your project, start with some simple planning. First determine why adding sound makes sense. What purpose does it serve? Does voiceover communicate a story? Do button sounds make the site easier to navigate? Do sound effects make a game more fun, or easier to play? Does music give it a cool character? Use answers to these questions to generate a short 'sonic mission statement' that outlines why and how you plan to use sound. Do this early in project planning, not after the Flash work is done.

Sourcing sounds is easier, and cheaper than ever before, thanks to the Internet. There are many websites that will allow you to search and download files for reasonable fees. Once you've found sounds, use audio editing software to adjust them to have similar sonic qualities. You want them to sound like they're in the same room, or in the same canyon, or the same secret underground lair, and so on. Adjust their volumes and equalization (EQ) to achieve this. Use your ears, listen, you'll do fine. Do they sound close or far, light or heavy, fast or slow? Also, trim the heads and tails of the sound files to be as short as possible without cutting the sound off. The shorter the file, the better it syncs, and the smaller the file size.

When you're picking music, try to find a piece that fits the mood or reinforces the story. Don't just use death metal because you like death metal, or techno for techno's sake. Music has emotional power that transcends genre, and you want to leverage it to make your project as engaging as possible. If you're working with loops, try to use as long a loop as possible given your file size considerations. Anything under 10 seconds gets old pretty fast unless it's something minimal like a drumbeat. Look into layering loops to create the illusion of a longer track with more variation.

A sound on/off button is a courtesy I always recommend. Compress your sounds so they sound good. A little bit bigger file is worth it if it means people will listen to it. A tiny file that sounds lousy is worse than no sound. Also, compress each sound so it sounds good by itself, and in relation to the other sounds. A combination of hi-fi and lo-fi sounds wrecks the illusion of the sounds existing together."

Thanks Dave, and also thank you for supplying our readers with the Pilotvibe clips in the Exercise folder.

Figure 5-8. The PilotVibe home page is a Master Class in the effective use of sound in Flash.

Your turn: Adding sound to a button

Now you'll put what you have learned to practical use. It has been decided that the frog sound should play when a button is clicked on the stage. Follow these steps to accomplish this task:

1. Open a new Flash document and import the Frog.mp3 sound into the library.

2. Select Window ➤ Common Libraries ➤ Buttons to open a collection of button symbols that are included when you installed Flash CS3.

3. Scroll down to the playback flat folder in the Buttons library, open it, and drag a copy of the flat blue Play button to the stage.

4. Double-click the button on the stage to open it in the Symbol Editor.

5. Add a new layer named Audio and add a keyframe to the Down area of the timeline.

6. With the keyframe selected, drag a copy of the Frog.mp3 audio file to the stage. Your timeline should now resemble that shown in Figure 5-9.

Figure 5-9. You can add sound to buttons.

7. Click in the waveform, and in the Property inspector select Event in the Sync drop-down menu.

8. Click the Scene 1 link to return to the main timeline.

9. Select Control ➤ Enable Simple Buttons. Click the button on the stage, and you will hear the frog croak.

10. Save the file as SimpleButton.fla and publish the SWF file. When the SWF file is created, double-click it to open Flash Player, and click the button. You will hear the frog croak every time you click the button.

Be careful with this technique, because when you create a SWF file that contains audio, the audio files in the library are embedded into the SWF file. The result, depending upon the audio files and their length, could be an extremely large SWF file that will take a long time to load.

Now that you understand how audio files can be used in Flash, let's take that knowledge to the next level and actually control sound using ActionScript. This is where the full power of audio in Flash is handed to you.

Controlling audio with ActionScript 3.0

Before we start, let's really get clear on the following: you aren't going to be fully exploring the nuances and features of audio controlled by code. We are going to give you the basics in this section:

- Playing a sound in the library without adding it to the timeline
- Using movieclips and buttons to turn audio on and off
- Using movieclips and buttons to load sound dynamically—from your HTTP server—into your Flash movie

Still, if you are familiar with controlling sound through ActionScript 2.0, you need to know there have been some renovations. For example, the Sound.attachSound() method is no longer around, and even familiar things like creating linkage identifiers have fundamentally changed. Just keep in mind, change is a good thing. It just takes a bit of getting used to.

Playing a sound from the library

This technique is ideal for sounds that need to play in the background. Be aware that any sound played through ActionScript is treated as a streaming sound.

1. Open a new Flash document and import the Chill.mp3 file into the library. The plan is to have this sound play, almost as background audio, when the movie starts.

2. Select the Chill.mp3 file in the library. Right-click (PC) or Ctrl-click (Mac) the audio file and select Linkage to open the Linkage Properties dialog box shown in Figure 5-10. If you are going to play audio files contained in the library and control them through ActionScript, they must be given a special label to let ActionScript find them in the library.

Figure 5-10. Establishing a linkage identifier

In ActionScript 2.0, "linkage" was accomplished with a linkage identifier. In fact, you'll see a disabled Identifier field in the dialog box. What gives? In ActionScript 3.0, the rules are different. You need to create a custom class that extends the native Sound class. Fortunately, Flash handles the entire process for you, though advanced developers may, if they wish, go to the expense of writing the actual external text file normally needed.

3. Select Export for ActionScript and enter the text Tune into the Class area of the dialog box. Click OK to close the dialog box. You will get a warning telling you there is no such thing as a Tune class. Click OK to close it. By clicking OK, you are telling Flash to go ahead and create this class on your behalf. The name Tune, by the way, is arbitrary . . . but as our audio file is a song, Tune makes good sense.

4. Rename Layer 1 as Actions, select the first frame in the layer, and press F9 (PC) or Option-F9 (Mac) to open the Actions panel.

5. Click in Line 1 of the Script pane and enter the following code:

```
var audio:Tune = new Tune();
audio.play();
```

The first line of the code creates a variable named audio and uses the Tune class—from the Linkage Properties dialog box—as its data type. The rest of the line creates a new Tune object. In English this line would read, "Create a new Tune object named audio and make sure it is an instance of the Tune class." Flash is smart enough, by the way, to recognize that Tune is an audio file because the Linkage Properties dialog specifies the Sound class—flash.media.Sound—as the base class that defines Tune. Thanks to object-oriented inheritance, Tune literally is a Sound object—with all the properties, methods, and events defined by the Sound class—it's just a very specific example of one.

The second line simply uses the Sound class's play() method to play the audio file.

6. Save the file as attachSound.fla and test the movie by pressing Ctrl+Enter (PC) or Cmd+Return (Mac) on the keyboard. When the SWF opens in Flash Player, the sound will play.

> *If you are used to using the* attachSound() *method, understand that it doesn't apply in ActionScript 3.0. All you need to do now is extend the Sound class in the Linkage Properties dialog box, then use the subclass's name.*

Using a movieclip to play a sound

In the previous section, you added the frog sound directly to the timeline of the button symbol. This time, you are going to use a movieclip—though you can just as easily use a button—and, instead of embedding the frog sound in the movieclip, you are going to have the sound play from the library. Follow these steps:

1. Open the FrogMC.fla file. If you open the library, you will see we have added a movieclip and the Frog.mp3 audio file to the library.

2. Select the Frog.mp3 audio file in the library and specify Frog as the class in the Linkage Properties dialog box.

3. Click the movieclip on the stage and give it the instance name of mc. Remember, movieclips controlled by ActionScript need an instance name.

4. Add a new layer named Actions to the timeline, select the first frame, and open the Actions panel.

5. Click in the Script pane and enter the following code:

```
var audio:Frog = new Frog();

mc.buttonMode = true;
mc.addEventListener(
  MouseEvent.MOUSE_UP,
  function():void {
    audio.play();
  }
);
```

The first line is familiar, so turn your attention to the next two statements.

The first of those—mc.buttonMode = true;—is how a movieclip is treated as a button in ActionScript 3.0. If this line weren't there, the arrow cursor would not change to the finger cursor at runtime, and the user wouldn't have a clue the movieclip can be clicked. It would *be* clickable, but wouldn't look like it.

The next statement is how things now get "clicked" in ActionScript 3.0. The onPress and onRelease events that were common in ActionScript 2.0 are now gone. Their replacement, though it looks more complex, is actually more efficient. This mechanism tells Flash what to listen for and what to do when that something occurs. These are provided as two parameters to the addEventListener() method, which is part of the EventDispatcher class in ActionScript 3.0 that is inherited by countless other classes, including Button and MovieClip.

In the case of this statement, Flash is adding the mc movieclip as a listener for a particular event—the MOUSE_UP event, which corresponds to the old onRelease. That's the first parameter. The second parameter, spread over three lines of its own, is the function to be triggered when the event occurs. This could be a custom named function, such as playMySound(), or a function literal. Here, you're using a function literal: this function simply tells the Frog instance to call the play() method it inherits from the Sound class. If your brain is buzzing, don't worry. Figure 5-11 gives you a quick diagram.

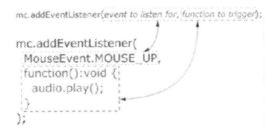

Figure 5-11. How the code works

Now would be a good time to get you used to using the code hinting tooltips. When you enter

```
mc.addEventListener(
```

the tooltip shown in Figure 5-12 appears.

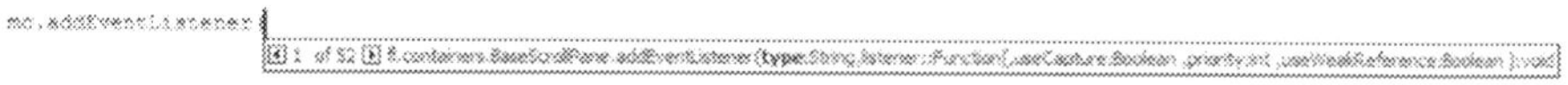

Figure 5-12. An ActionScript tooltip

The first time you see one of these, you may feel a bit disoriented. Instead, simply take your hands off of the keyboard and read the information required. The tiny left and right arrows tell you the addEventListener() method is supported by quite a few objects. Click those arrows with the mouse—or press Control+Left Arrow or Control+Right Arrow—to scroll to the flash.display.MovieClip entry. In this case, the first bit of information required is the type, and it must be a string. This string—the type of event being listened for—is provided as a result of the static MouseEvent.MOUSE_UP property. Enter that text and press the comma key. Notice how the next area of the tooltip lights up? You are being asked to specify a listener, and it must be a function. In this case, you're entering the word function() right there, rather than creating a function elsewhere and stating its name in this slot. The void at the end simply says, "This function does not return a value; it simply does what it does and doesn't report back." Finally, the ActionScript inside the curly braces, {}, defines what this function does. The tooltip will disappear when you press Enter (PC) or Return (Mac).

6. Save the file and test the movie. When you click the movieclip on the stage, the frog sound plays.

Playing a sound from outside of Flash

You know that embedding sound into a SWF file adds to its file size. Is there a way to play a sound that isn't inside the SWF file? The answer is absolutely. Here's how:

1. Open the Remote.fla file. When it opens, you will see we have placed a movieclip on the stage and given it the instance name of Play_mc.

2. Select the first frame in the Actions layer, open the Actions panel, and enter the following code:

```
var audio:Sound = new Sound();
audio.load(new URLRequest("Chill.mp3"));

Play_mc.buttonMode = true;
Play_mc.addEventListener(MouseEvent.MOUSE_UP, function():void {
  audio.play();
 }
);
```

The only thing that is "new" here is the second statement. In ActionScript 3.0, you can't simply tell Flash, "There's an audio file in this folder that you need to play." Instead, you need to use the load() method of the Sound class to load an external sound. An **external sound** is one sitting in a folder and not embedded in the SWF file. To accomplish this, you use the new URLRequest class to specify the location of the file to be loaded into the Sound object that is created in the first line of the code. If you have used ActionScript 2.0, this new way of doing things may remind you of the getURL() function, used to grab external files and toss them into a Flash movie. In ActionScript 3.0, most things brought into a Flash movie—audio, images, even SWF files—need to be "called in" through a URLRequest object. One notable exception is video files. More on that in Chapter 8.

Finally, if you have an audio file located in a folder on the site, the syntax would be

```
audio.load(new URLRequest("http://www.mysite.com/AudioFiles/➥
Chill.mp3"));
```

3. Did you notice the variation in line breaks for the addEventListener() method? As long as the required parameters are present, line breaks aren't especially fussy. Close the Actions panel and test the movie. When you click the button, the sound plays.

Turning a remote sound on and off

In this exercise, you will code up two buttons: one button will play the sound, and the other will turn it off.

1. Open the Remote2.fla file. Again, we have provided you with the raw material as shown in Figure 5-13. The Start button with the instance name Play_mc will be used to turn the sound on. The Stop button, Stop_mc, will be used to turn the sound off.

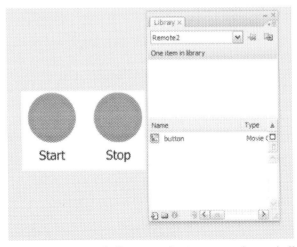

Figure 5-13. Two movieclips are used to turn a sound on and off.

> *The choice of instance names is deliberate. Many Flash designers try to use contractions that tell the coder what type of object is being used. This explains why you may see code elsewhere and the instance names somehow contain an indication of exactly what object is being used. For example, Play_mc could also be written as mcPlay. The key is the letters mc, which indicate it is a movieclip. The suffix form (e.g., _mc) actually helps trigger code hints.*

The plan for this project is to have the user click the Start button to have the audio file play and then click the Stop button to turn off the audio.

2. Click the first frame in the Scripts layer and open the Actions panel. When the Script pane opens, enter the following code:

```
var audio:Sound = new Sound();

audio.load(new URLRequest("Chill.mp3"));

var channel:SoundChannel = new SoundChannel();

Play_mc.buttonMode = true;
Play_mc.addEventListener(MouseEvent.MOUSE_UP,function():void {
    channel = audio.play();
  }
);

Stop_mc.buttonMode = true;
Stop_mc.addEventListener( MouseEvent.MOUSE_UP,function():void {
  channel.stop();
  }
);
```

The only major difference between this code and that used in the previous example is the addition of a SoundChannel object. The SoundChannel class controls a sound in an application. Each sound playing in a Flash movie now has its own sound channel, which means you can have up to 32 concurrent sound channels playing different audio files that can be mixed together. The SoundChannel class contains a stop() method for turning sound off.

In this case, the Play button, when clicked, associates the remote sound represented by the audio object (a Sound instance) with the SoundChannel object named channel. The Stop button, when clicked, will use the stop() method to stop playing the sound in the channel.

3. Save and test the movie.

Your turn: Building an MP3 player

One of the more common requests, when people get around to working with audio in Flash, is, "Can I make my own MP3 player?" You can, and that is exactly what you are going to do in this exercise. There is going to be a lot going on here, so we suggest you set aside sufficient time to carefully follow along. The reason is that this is a somewhat complex project, and you are about to be introduced to several new and fundamental concepts that will require your attention. Among them are the following:

- Creating a jog control that allows you to move through an audio selection
- Creating a volume control that allows the user to adjust the audio volume
- Creating buttons that go to the previous or the next audio track
- Displaying an audio track's ID3 information

The key to this exercise is understanding technique. Though there will be a lot going on, you will discover everything presented here builds upon what you have learned to this point in the chapter. This exercise also follows standard workflow, which is to assemble the assets and then "wire them up" using ActionScript. Let's get busy:

1. Open the Player.fla file found in the MP3Player folder of your Chapter 5 Exercise folder. If you open the library, you will see we have given you the bits and pieces needed to assemble the project. Of particular note are the buttons that will control the audio. When you installed Flash CS3, you also installed a Common Library, and in that folder are quite a few button symbols. They can be found by selecting Window ➤ Common Libraries ➤ Buttons. The ones used in this project, shown in Figure 5-14, are found in the playback rounded folder. We felt the "rounded grey" series fit the design quite nicely.

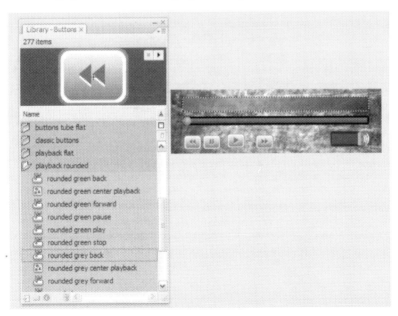

Figure 5-14. Why reinvent the wheel and build your own buttons when the Buttons library has a great selection of "prerolled" buttons?

2. The buttons are obviously misaligned. Here's a quick way of aligning and properly spacing them. Hold down the Shift key and click each of the four buttons on the stage. Open the Align panel by either clicking its tab in the panel strip or selecting Window ➤ Align. In the Align area of the panel, click the Align top edge button, and the buttons all move into place. With the buttons still selected, click the Distribute horizontal center button, shown in Figure 5-15, in the Distribute area of the panel. The buttons all spread out, equidistant from each other.

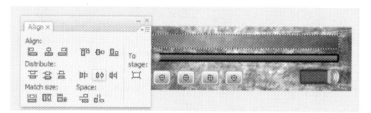

Figure 5-15. Use the Align panel to quickly align and distribute selected objects on the Flash stage.

3. The final step is to select each button on the stage and give it an instance name in the Property inspector. Use these names:

- Rounded grey back: btnPrev

- Rounded grey pause: btnPause

- Rounded grey play: btnPlay

- Rounded grey forward: btnNext

4. Save the file.

With the assets in place, you can start working on the ActionScript, but before you do, let's take a break so you first clearly understand how the volume and seek controls work.

The seek bar will allow you to drag the knob in the seek knob layer to the right and the left. When you do this, you will move forward or backward in the audio file. Also, when the song is playing, the knob will move across the bar on its own in the seek slider layer.

When you are constructing these things, you have to look at them not only as graphics, but also as graphical representations of an object. For example, the seek bar is indeed a graphic with a gradient, but it is also a graphical representation of the length of the audio file. The position of the knob, while the movie plays, is a graphical representation of a point in time. In this case, that representation will be a percentage of the audio file played so far.

The bar's length is 300 pixels, but it also represents 100% of the duration of the audio file. If the audio file is 1 minute long and the knob is at the 150-pixel mark of the seek bar, it will also be at the 30-second mark of the audio file. If the user drags the knob to the 225-pixel mark of the bar and releases the mouse, the audio file will start playing at the 45-second mark of the audio file.

The other important aspect of the knob is that is can only be moved horizontally, and it can't be moved off of the right or left edges of the bar. To ensure this doesn't happen, ActionScript will keep an eye on the center point of the knob, and when it touches the right or left edge of the seek bar, ActionScript will jump in and essentially say, "Whoa, that's far enough." At the same time it is doing this, it is also keeping track of where the knob is, expressed as a percentage, along the bar. The really neat thing about numbers is they are just that, numbers. This means ActionScript will not only figure out that the knob is at the 50% position of the bar's length, but also use that same number—50%—to determine where the audio should be. This means you could change the width of the seek bar's "track," and the knob would still move along it correctly.

The volume control works in exactly the same manner, but in this case the length of the bar in the volume slider layer is being used as a graphical representation of the volume level of the sound. The left edge is 0% volume—it is silent—and the right edge is 100% volume, which means people are yelling at you to turn it down.

One last thing before you start coding . . .

The user needs to know what song is playing and the name of the composer/artist. That is the purpose of the dynamic text box in the status layer. If you click it, you will see it has the instance name of songInfo and the Property inspector will show you the text formatting (see Figure 5-16). We are going to get deeper into text and dynamic text boxes in the next chapter, but here we'll give a brief overview so you understand exactly what a dynamic text box does.

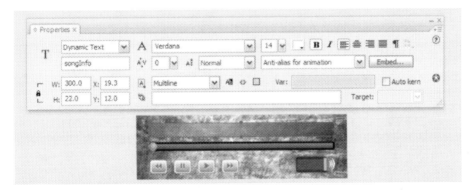

Figure 5-16. A dynamic text box can be formatted and given an instance name.

Each MP3 file you will be using contains some metadata—if you have wondered about this term, think of it as being the data about the data—that contains the name of the song and the composer. When the song is accessed, the plan is to pull this data out of the MP3 file and present it to the user. You have three songs, which means the data will be constantly changing. To show constantly changing data as text, you need to use a dynamic text box.

This metadata in MP3 files is contained in ID3 tags. If you have an iPod or other MP3 player, you have seen these, as the device shows you the title and artist while the song is playing. ActionScript can also access this data, which allows you to create some pretty sophisticated audio applications in Flash. Even so, keep in mind that not all MP3 files contain ID3 tags. So how does an id3 tag get "read" by ActionScript? Providing the data is there, when an MP3 file is loaded into a Sound object, that file's ID3 tags can be read by accessing the Sound object's id3 property. Some of the more common ID3 tags you can access are TALB (album), TRCK (track), TPE1 (artist), and TYER (year of the recording).

Now, let's start coding the MP3 player:

5. Select the first frame of the Actions layer, open the Actions panel, and enter the following code:

```
var songList:Array = new Array("alternative.mp3", "rockfunk.mp3",➥
"chill.mp3");
var isPlaying:Boolean = false;
var currentSong:Number = 0;
var song:Sound;
var channel:SoundChannel = new SoundChannel();
var xform:SoundTransform = new SoundTransform();
```

First, you start with a handful of variables to help make your programming easier. It is a common coding "best practice" to list variables right at the start of the code block. This way, they are all in one location and not scattered all over the code.

All of these variables are arbitrarily named, but of course it only makes sense to name variables descriptively, because that provides a reminder of what they're for. Speaking of which:

- songList is an instance of the Array class, which means songList stores an "array" of things—you can think of it as a list. There are three songs this MP3 player cares about, and they're the ones shown in quotes. If you want more songs or other songs, change the array's elements.

- isPlaying keeps track of whether or not audio is currently playing. At the beginning, no audio is playing, so this Boolean variable is set to false. Boolean values are really neat because they only have two possible values: true or false.

- currentSong keeps track of the number of the currently playing song. Remember, your songs are being stored in an array of three elements. Arrays start counting from zero, so a currentSong value of 0 refers to the first song("alternative.mp3").

- The last three variables each store an instance to one of three sound-related classes you'll need for this MP3 player: Sound, SoundChannel, and SoundTransform. The song variable is declared, but not instantiated, because the decision for which song to specify comes later; the other two are declared and instantiated.

6. Press Enter (PC) or Return (Mac) twice and add the following code:

```
seekKnob.buttonMode = true;
seekKnob.addEventListener(MouseEvent.MOUSE_DOWN, seekStartDrag);
btnPrev.addEventListener(MouseEvent.CLICK, prevHandler);
btnPause.addEventListener(MouseEvent.CLICK, pauseHandler);
btnPlay.addEventListener(MouseEvent.CLICK, playHandler);
btnNext.addEventListener(MouseEvent.CLICK, nextHandler);
volumeKnob.buttonMode = true;
volumeKnob.addEventListener(MouseEvent.MOUSE_DOWN, volumeStartDrag);
```

What you just did was to set up most (but not all) of the event handling you need. You have two draggable sliders in this project, and they are the movieclips shown in Figure 5-17. In order to make them "feel" like buttons—that is, to make the finger cursor show when the mouse rolls over them—you set their buttonMode properties to true. This happens with the seekKnob and volumeKnob instances. There are four additional button symbols—the buttons from the common library—used for pausing and playing, and then going backward and forward in the song list. Because those are button symbols, they don't need buttonMode properties set to true; in fact, as instances of the SimpleButton class, they don't even have buttonMode properties.

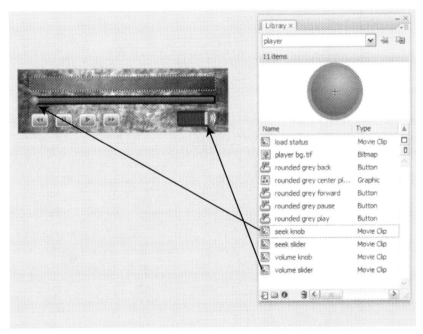

Figure 5-17. Two movieclips in the library will act as draggable buttons.

The slider knobs listen for a MOUSE_DOWN event, which triggers their respective drag functions, seekStartDrag and volumeStartDrag. But wait a minute, shouldn't you handle MOUSE_UP events, while you're at it? Don't you want to stop dragging when the user releases the mouse? Sure you do, but you only care about those events after the dragging has begun. Those are set inside the respective startDrag functions themselves, and you'll see those in a moment.

The buttons listen for MouseEvent.CLICK events and trigger respective functions, which will be the next block of code you will write.

7. Press Enter (PC) or Return (Mac) twice and enter following functions for the four buttons:

```
function prevHandler(evt:MouseEvent):void {
  prevSong();
}

function pauseHandler(evt:MouseEvent):void {
  pauseSong();
}

function playHandler(evt:MouseEvent):void {
  playSong(channel.position);
}

function nextHandler(evt:MouseEvent):void {
  nextSong();
}
```

These are the buttons' CLICK event handlers, which in turn simply call custom functions to be written later. Why the intermediate functions? Why not assign prevSong, pauseSong, and the rest, directly? Well, in the case of the playSong() function, you need to pass in a parameter that tells the application what position in the audio to play from, based on the position of the seekKnob movieclip on its track. These CLICK event handlers each carry with them a MouseEvent object, which automatically becomes the parameter to these functions. In this case, none of these functions really needs a parameter except for playSong()—and for that one, you're passing in your own parameter. So these basically filter the static out of the line. The inclusion of the event object parameter—here, evt:MouseEvent—is only necessary when you're using named functions like these. Function literals, in earlier samples in this chapter, omit them.

The playSong() parameter references a property of the SoundChannel class, which you instantiated as the variable channel. SoundChannel.position states how far along a sound has played. Used here, the Play button tells the song to play from the position it was when the music stopped. (Pause runs the pauseSong() function, and Play runs the playSong() function.)

A few more event handlers to go.

8. Press Enter (PC) or Return (Mac) and finish off the event handlers:

```
function id3Handler(evt:Event):void {
  songInfo.text = song.id3.artist + ": " + song.id3.songName;
}

function soundCompleteHandler(evt:Event):void {
  pauseSong();
  nextSong();
}
```

The Event.ID3 event raises an alert—evt:Event—when an MP3 file's ID3 tags are encountered. These are the metatags in MP3 files that store the song's name, the artist's name, and so on. When the Event.ID3 event is dispatched, we want to handle it and route the Sound.id3.artist and Sound.id3.songName properties to the dynamic text field shown in Figure 5-18.

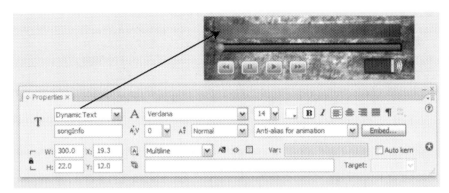

Figure 5-18. The ID3 tags will appear in the dynamic text box.

The next function tells Flash what to do when the end of a song is reached. In this case, the song that is playing is paused, and the next song is launched.

9. Press Enter (PC) or Return (Mac) twice and enter the following code:

```
loadSong(songList[currentSong]);

function loadSong(thisSong:String):void {
    song = new Sound();
    song.load(new URLRequest(thisSong));
    song.addEventListener(Event.ID3, id3Handler);
    playSong(0);
}
```

The first line calls the loadSong() function and checks the list in the songList variable to see which song in that list should play. In this case, the expression songList[currentSong] pulls song 0 (the first song, "alternative.mp3") from the songList array. The array contains three strings, remember, and the first of those is passed into the function, where it is received by the reference thisSong.

The function now tells Flash what to do with that song. The first thing it needs to do is point the song variable (declared earlier) to an instance of the Sound class. If you didn't do this, Flash wouldn't have a clue about what to do with the audio track. The next step is to actually load the audio track from the folder, tell Flash to listen for the ID3 tags, and if they are encountered, shoot the text into that dynamic text box. The final line tells Flash to actually play the song. Which, incidentally, is the next function that needs to be written.

5

Are you seeing a pattern here? The authors are firm believers in the axiom Deal with complexity from a position of simplicity. *To this point, we have identified the variables, given the buttons something to do, put the ID3 tags to work, and dealt with the first part of the audio process—what to do when told to load a song. Each of these code blocks are discreet "chunks" that all reference each other but follow a logical progress through the process of actually playing an audio file. The other thing to keep in mind here is a lot of what we are showing you, and are about to show you, has practical uses elsewhere in this book and and in other projects you may encounter.*

10. Save the movie, press Enter (PC) or Return (Mac) twice, and enter the following code:

```
function playSong(position:Number):void {
  if (!isPlaying) {
    isPlaying = true;
    channel = song.play(position);
    channel.soundTransform = xform;
    channel.addEventListener(Event.SOUND_COMPLETE,➥
soundCompleteHandler);
    seekKnob.addEventListener(Event.ENTER_FRAME, seekKnobUpdate);
  }
}
```

This function checks to see whether the song is already playing—that's your isPlaying variable. If it's not already playing (!isPlaying), you set the isPlaying variable to true, assign the song to a SoundChannel instance (which allows you to stop it again), set the soundTransform property (which lets you adjust the volume), add a SOUND_COMPLETE handler, and add an ENTER_FRAME handler to the seek knob, which will start to track across as the song plays.

There are a couple of new concepts here, so let's review them before we deal with how a sound is paused. The parameter for the playSong function—position:Number—might strike you as being a bit odd. In actual fact, it is dead on. Remember, the seekKnob movieclip is going to be moving along in time with the audio. When audio plays, there is a sort of playhead that moves along the audio track, meaning the position value will be the point in time that is currently playing in the audio track, and that value is what will be moving the seekKnob.

The next concept that may look a bit odd is !isPlaying. What is the purpose of the exclamation mark? Take your cue from the next line, which sets isPlaying to true. The exclamation mark is the logical NOT operator, which reverses a Boolean value. In plain English, if isPlaying is not actually true, the expression !isPlaying *is true.*

The final concept is the ENTER_FRAME event. When you think of Flash, you can imagine a playhead moving along the timeline, and when it hits the end of the movie's timeline, it stops. Even when it stops, the "engine is still running," and that running engine is expressed as an ENTER_FRAME event. This movie is only one frame long, so the playhead has nowhere to move. Regardless, an ENTER_FRAME event is dispatched 12 times a second, or 24 times a second, or whatever the movie's frame rate is set to.

Imagine a room with two doors. One is marked Enter, and the other is marked Exit. The room is the frame. The playhead comes in through the Enter door, passes through the room doing what it is supposed to do, and when it goes out the Exit door, it comes right back through the Enter door. This is called a **frame loop**. The last line of code, therefore, tells Flash that when the playhead comes through the Enter door, it must check to see where the playhead on the audio track is located and move the seekKnob movieclip.

Let's now concentrate on pausing an audio track.

When we first think of pausing audio, we instinctively know that the audio is stopped. Really? Actually, it is a bit more complicated than that. When you pause audio in this project, you need to stop the audio playing in its channel and also stop the seekHead movieclip from moving at the same time. Here's how:

11. Press Enter (PC) or Return (Mac) twice and enter the following code:

```
function pauseSong():void {
    seekKnob.removeEventListener(Event.ENTER_FRAME, seekKnobUpdate);
    channel.stop();
    isPlaying = false;
}
```

As you can see, to pause a song, you remove the seek knob's ENTER_FRAME handler (so that it stops tracking), invoke SoundChannel.stop() on the channel instance, and set isPlaying to false.

Now you'll turn your attention to the next two buttons: Previous and Next. When these buttons are clicked, Flash is going to check which song in the array is playing and either switch to the one before it or the one after it. Follow this step to code these two buttons:

12. Press Enter (PC) or Return (Mac) twice and enter the following functions:

```
function prevSong():void {
  if (currentSong > 0) {
    currentSong--;
    pauseSong();
    loadSong(songList[currentSong]);
  }
}

function nextSong():void {
  if (currentSong < songList.length - 1) {
    currentSong++;
    pauseSong();
    loadSong(songList[currentSong]);
  }
}
```

The prevSong() and nextSong() functions are similar. In the case of prevSong(), you check whether the current song is greater than 0. In your list of three songs, 0 represents the first element in the list, so you're essentially checking here whether the current song is anything but the first. If it is (if it's the second or third song), you reduce the value of currentSong by one—that's what the -- operator does—pause the song, and load the previous one. In the case of nextSong, you do the opposite. You check whether the current song is less than the total number of songs minus one. Why minus one? Again, arrays start at 0. The last song out of three is element 2. The number of elements in this array is 3 (from 0 through 2). So three minus one is the magic number.

With buttons all wired up, the time has arrived to write the code that manages the volume and seek sliders. You start with the seek slider.

13. Save the movie, press Enter (PC) or Return (Mac) twice, and enter the following code:

```
function seekStartDrag(evt:MouseEvent):void {
  pauseSong();
  seekKnob.startDrag(true, new Rectangle(seekSlider.x,➥
seekSlider.y + seekSlider.height/2, seekSlider.width, 0));
  stage.addEventListener(MouseEvent.MOUSE_UP, seekStopDrag);
}

function seekStopDrag(evt:MouseEvent):void {
  seekKnob.stopDrag();
  playSong(song.length * (seekKnob.x - seekSlider.x) /➥
seekSlider.width);
  stage.removeEventListener(MouseEvent.MOUSE_UP, seekStopDrag);
}

function seekKnobUpdate(evt:Event):void {
  var pos:Number = seekSlider.width * channel.position / song.length;
  if (!isNaN(pos)) {
   seekKnob.x = seekSlider.x + pos;
  } else {
    seekKnob.x = seekSlider.x;
  }
}
```

Let's carefully walk through the first function. Someone has just clicked the seek knob in order to drag it.

First, you pause the song. Next, you invoke the Sprite.startDrag() method. Why Sprite? Aren't these movieclips? You betcha they are, and in ActionScript 3.0, all movieclips inherit the Sprite class. Now, what are all those crazy parameters? The first simply sets the lockcenter parameter to true. This means the center point of the knob will snap to the mouse when you drag it to the right or to the left. The second is a Rectangle instance that specifies the position of where the dragging should be constrained. Here, you're constraining to the position of the seekSlider movieclip (that's the track on which the knob is perched), to seekSlider's width, and to a height of 0. This is how a slider can be made to move in only a horizontal direction.

At this point, as mentioned earlier, you're going to add a MOUSE_UP event. Interestingly, this event isn't handled for the knob, but for the stage itself.

Why? In ActionScript 2.0, movieclips and buttons featured an onReleaseOutside event. For dragging, this came in handy. You would program a dragging function for the onPress event (comparable to MOUSE_DOWN), and then add a stop dragging function for the onRelease event (comparable to MOUSE_UP), but that wasn't enough. You would then assign the onReleaseOutside event to the same function as onRelease. Why? Glad you asked.

Attend one of our classes or seminars, and one of the messages that will come roaring across the room at you is *Fall in love with the user, not the technology*. Users do weird things. For example, when a user starts dragging a knob, the mouse wanders a bit. The mouse may not actually be over the knob when the user decides to let go. When the mouse is over the knob (or whatever object) and the user lets go of the mouse, that counts as an onRelease. However, when the mouse is *not* over the knob and the user lets go, that does not count as an onRelease, so the dragging would continue. It counts as an onReleaseOutside, which ActionScript 3.0 simply doesn't have.

The remedy is to listen for a MOUSE_UP event for the whole stage—for everywhere on the stage, knob or not—that the user decides to release the mouse. You only need that event handled here, so it's only assigned here, rather than earlier on in the application. (A MOUSE_UP event from the stage's point of few would register every time the user releases the mouse, even over the Pause and Play buttons, and you only want it for the knob.)

The seekStopDrag() function is easier to understand after the preceding explanation. You simply invoke Sprite.stopDrag(), run the playSong() function—with a parameter that uses the knob's position to determine where to start the song—and remove the MOUSE_UP event handler from the stage, since you no longer need it.

The seekKnobUpdate() function positions the knob along the seek track according to how far along the song has played. This function is triggered via an ENTER_FRAME event, so its smoothness depends on the movie's frame rate. You set a local variable, pos, to an expression that evaluates the seekSlider instance's width (that's the knob's track) multiplied by the song's position divided by the song's length (its duration).

There are times when this calculation results in a weird number that makes absolutely no sense such as at the very beginning of the sound, while it's loading, so you check to make sure that pos actually counts as a number. If the isNaN() function (the term isNaN means "is Not a Number") comes back as true, you're in trouble. You want a number, so you need the opposite (!isNaN()). When pos is indeed a number, you set the knob's x position, seekSlider.x, to the track's x position plus pos; otherwise, you simply set it to the track's x position, which means the knob will sit on the left side of the track.

The final bit of code deals with the volume slider. It really isn't much different from this chunk.

14. Save the file and enter the following code:

```
function volumeStartDrag(evt:MouseEvent):void {
  volumeKnob.startDrag(true, new Rectangle(volumeSlider.x,➥
volumeSlider.y + volumeSlider.height/2, volumeSlider.width, 0));
  volumeKnob.addEventListener(MouseEvent.MOUSE_MOVE, volumeUpdate);
  stage.addEventListener(MouseEvent.MOUSE_UP, volumeStopDrag);
}

function volumeStopDrag(evt:MouseEvent):void {
  volumeKnob.removeEventListener(MouseEvent.MOUSE_MOVE, volumeUpdate);
  volumeKnob.stopDrag();
  stage.removeEventListener(MouseEvent.MOUSE_UP, volumeStopDrag);
}

function volumeUpdate(evt:MouseEvent):void {
  xform.volume = (volumeKnob.x - volumeSlider.x) / volumeSlider.width;
  channel.soundTransform = xform;
}
```

Much of the same thing happens with the volume slider. The same Sprite.startDrag() and stopDrag() methods are invoked, using the same Rectangle constraint. The only real difference here is that you assign a MOUSE_MOVE event to a custom volumeUpdate() function, which means the volume will be updated while the mouse moves (while it's dragging the knob).

Changing the volume of an audio file, regardless of whether you use a slider or a button, requires the use of the SoundTransform class. One of the properties in this class is volume, and the value for volume can range between 0 (silent) and 1 (full volume). To achieve that number, you subtract the volumeSlider's x position from the volumeKnob's x position and divide that result by the width of the volumeSlider. Let's assume the following:

- volumeKnob x position = 100
- volumeSlider x position = 0 (It is tucked right up against the left edge of the stage.)
- volumeSlider width = 300 pixels

If you do the math—(100 – 0)/300—the calculation yields a value of .3. The SoundTransform class translates that number into 30% volume.

15. Save the file and test it. The audio plays, the name of the song currently playing appears in the dynamic text box (see Figure 5-19), and the buttons and sliders do what you tell them to do.

Figure 5-19. The final product

What you've learned

- How to add audio to Flash
- The difference between an event and a streaming sound
- How to set the preferences for sound output in Flash CS3
- Various approaches to playing a sound in the Flash library and one located outside of Flash
- The various classes, properties, and methods ActionScript 3.0 uses to control and manage sound in Flash
- A variety of methods ranging from buttons to sliders to control audio in Flash
- A method of accessing the ID3 tags in an MP3 file and putting them to work

As you have discovered, there is a lot more to audio in Flash than simply tossing in some sort of electronica beat and becoming a "cool kid." Audio in Flash is a powerful communications tool, and savvy Flash designers and developers who realize this are leveraging audio in Flash to its full potential. Speaking of communications tools, text is no longer that gray stuff that goes around your animations. To find out more, turn the page, because text is the focus of the next chapter.

5

> Letterforms that honor and elucidate what humans see and say deserve to be honored in their turn. Well-chosen words deserve well-chosen letters; these in their turn deserve to be set with affection, intelligence, knowledge and skill. Typography is a link, and it ought, as a matter of honor, courtesy and pure delight, to be as strong as the others in the chain.

> *Robert Bringhurst*

This quote from Bringhurst's master work, *The Elements of Typographic Style, Second Edition* (Hartley and Marks, 2002), sums up the essence of type in Flash. The words we put on the stage and subsequently put into motion are usually well chosen. They have to be because they are the communication messengers, providing the user with access to understanding the message you are trying to communicate. In this chapter, we focus on using type to do just that.

The introduction of the CS3 product line from Adobe has put some powerful typographic tools in your hands, and with such applications as Adobe After Effects nudging closer to a confluence point with Flash, the field of motion graphics on the Web is about to move into territory that has yet to be explored. To start that exploration, you need to understand what type is in Flash and, just as importantly, what you can do with it to honor the communication.

What we'll cover in this chapter:

- The basics of type
- Using static, dynamic, and input text fields
- Putting type in motion
- Creating, formatting, and using dynamic text in Flash CS3
- Using ActionScript to create, format, and present text
- How to use HTML formatting with ActionScript
- Creating hyperlinks
- Using the spell checker

Files used in this chapter:

- Static1.fla (Chapter06/ExerciseFiles_CH06/Exercise/Static1.fla)
- Static2.fla (Chapter06/ExerciseFiles_CH06/Exercise/Static2.fla)
- Static3.fla (Chapter06/ExerciseFiles_CH06/Exercise/Static3.fla)
- HTML.fla (Chapter06/ExerciseFiles_CH06/Exercise/HTML.fla)
- EmbedButton.fla (Chapter06/ExerciseFiles_CH06/Exercise/EmbedButton.fla)
- SpellItOut.txt (Chapter06/ExerciseFiles_CH06/Exercise/SpellItOut.txt)
- StaticTriggerAS.fla (Chapter06/ExerciseFiles_CH06/Exercise/StaticTriggerAS.fla)
- DynamicTriggerAS.fla (Chapter06/ExerciseFiles_CH06/Exercise/DynamicTriggerAS.fla)

- ScrollComponent.fla (Chapter06/ExerciseFiles_CH06/Exercise/ScrollComponent.fla)
- scrollingAS.fla (Chapter06/ExerciseFiles_CH06/Exercise/scrollingAS.fla)

Fonts and typefaces

Before we answer what is a font and what is a typeface, let's get really clear on one point: type is not that gray stuff that flits around your "whizzy" Flash animations. It is your primary communications tool.

Reading is hard-wired into us. If it wasn't, you wouldn't be looking at this sentence and assimilating it in your brain. You have a need for information, and the printed word is how you get it. The thing is, the choice of font and how you present the text not only affects the message . . . it also affects the information. You can see this in Figure 6-1. The phrase "Flash rocks" takes on a different meaning in each instance of the phrase. Using the same Times font, but the bold and italic versions of it, the message "changes" depending on the style applied.

Figure 6-1. It is all about the message.

You can take this out to the next level and see how choice of typeface also has an effect upon the message. Figure 6-2 shows five examples of the same information presented using different fonts. You can see how the mood changes, based upon typeface.

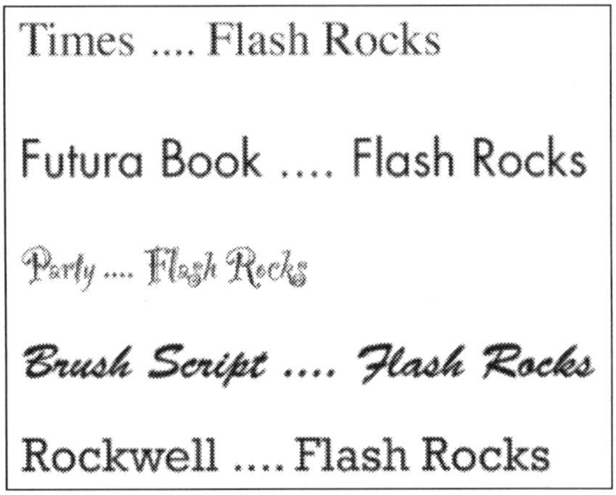

Times .... Flash Rocks

Futura Book .... Flash Rocks

Party .... Flash Rocks

Brush Script .... Flash Rocks

Rockwell .... Flash Rocks

Figure 6-2. It is all about the message and the font chosen.

When choosing your fonts, you also have to be aware of their impact upon readability and legibility. Both are achieved by an acute awareness of the qualities and attributes that make type readable. These attributes would include the typeface, the size, the color, and so on.

To illustrate this point, take a look at a small exercise one of the authors uses in his classes. What word is shown in Figure 6-3? Don't be too hasty to say "legibility." What are the 6th, 7th, 8th, and 9th characters? What letters are the first and second letters? Suddenly things become a bit disorienting.

Figure 6-3. What word is this?

This disorientation is important for you to understand. Our visual clue to legibility and readability, as shown in Figure 6-4, is the flow along the tops of the letters. This is why text that consists of all capital letters is so hard to read.

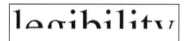

Figure 6-4. We get our clues to letterforms from the tops of the letters.

We include this exercise because there is a huge temptation on the part of people new to Flash to prove they are one of the "cool kids" and use font and color combinations that make otherwise legible and readable text impossible to read. A good example of this is Figure 6-5. The word is set in a medium gray color on a dark gray background, and the size for the text is 10 pixels. The text is very difficult to read, and yet somehow the "cool kids" think this is really cool. Wrong! They just killed all access to the information contained in the text.

Figure 6-5. It is all about the message and the font chosen.

What is a typeface, and what is a font? Technically speaking, a **typeface** is an organized collection of glyphs (usually letters, numbers, and punctuation) that shares stylistic consistency. A **font** is one particular size or variety of a typeface. So Arial 10 and Arial 12 represent two distinct fonts but belong to the same typeface. Same goes for Arial and Arial Bold or the fonts—Times, Times Italic, Times Bold, Times Bold Italic—used in Figure 6-1: separate fonts that belong to the same font family. In everyday talk, for better or worse, most people simply use the word "font" for all of the preceding.

We're not here to argue the point one way or the other, but we would like to mention an advantage to Flash when it comes to typography: while HTML is only capable of displaying fonts that are installed on the viewer's computer, Flash can display whatever font you like. Want to use some zany dingbat characters or an extravagant cursive font you designed yourself? Have at it. Even input text fields, the sort typed into by the user, can be displayed in whatever font suits your fancy. Flash text fields even support the filters encountered in Chapter 3.

Does this sound too good to be true? Well, everything has a price. Fonts can add to a SWF's file size—the more ornate, the greater the penalty. Take a moment to consider what fonts are, and you'll see that this makes sense. Most fonts store a mathematical description of the lines and curves that define each glyph. Simple shapes require less description than complex shapes.

> *Does that sound oddly familiar? It should, because most fonts today are drawn in a PostScript drawing application. In fact, Illustrator CS3 is rapidly becoming the tool of choice among the type design community.*
>
> *Flash CS3 supports the following font formats: TrueType, OpenType, PostScript Type 1, bit (Macintosh), and device fonts.*

Staying with PostScript, you know the more complex the shape—that is, shapes with a lot of points—the larger the file size. To prove it, head over to www.lipsum.org, a terrific site for generating placeholder text, and copy a paragraph of "Lorem ipsum" to the clipboard.

1. Select the Text tool. In the Property inspector, choose a simple sans-serif font, like Arial, and confirm that the type of text is Static Text. Click in the upper-left corner of the stage, and, with the mouse still clicked, drag to the other side of the stage and let go.

2. Paste the "Lorem ipsum" text into this text field.

3. Test your movie and select View ➤ Bandwidth Profiler to see file size information. Your SWF should be in the neighborhood of 4 to 8 KB.

4. Close the SWF and change your text field's font to something more elaborate, such as Blackadder ITC, Brush Script, or whatever decorative typeface catches your fancy. Test again and compare file sizes. Your mileage will vary, of course, but experiment a bit and see how different fonts carry different weights.

> *Where did "Lorem ipsum" originate? Being a wealth of absolutely useless information, we are glad to oblige you with an answer. The earliest known example of its use is from an unknown type specimen produced in the 1500s. A printer jumbled up the text from Cicero's* de Finibus Bonorum et Malorum, Liber Primus, *sections* 1.10.32 *and* 1.10.33, *and used it to show off his fonts. It stuck and has been used ever since.*

By the end of this chapter, you'll know what your options are and will be equipped to make informed text field choices. For starters, let's look at how to dial back the font size to zero.

Working with device fonts

If you want, you certainly can go with fonts that are installed on the user's machine, just like HTML does. The benefit is that your SWF's weight will be completely unaffected by text content. The drawback is that you have to count on your audience having the same font(s) installed as you do (not a good idea) or choose among three very generic font categories: _sans (sans-serif), _serif, and _typewriter (monospace). These are the device fonts, and they are ideal for use on mobile devices.

Take a look at the Property inspector again and look at your font choices in the font drop-down list. The top three, shown in Figure 6-6, are preceded by an underscore. That's the tip-off. If you select one of these fonts, Flash will choose on your behalf whatever it thinks is the closest fit on the viewer's computer. _sans will probably be Arial or Helvetica, _serif will probably be Times New Roman or Times, and _typewriter will probably be Courier New or Courier—but who knows for sure?

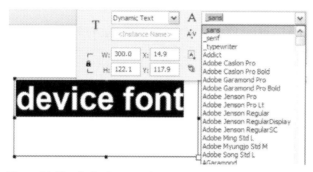

Figure 6-6. The device fonts work everywhere but have limitations.

Another place where you can use device fonts is in those situations where you choose a font, say Helvetica, and you aren't sure whether the user has the font. As shown in Figure 6-7, you can select Use device fonts in the Font rendering method pop-down menu, and the fonts will be substituted at runtime.

Figure 6-7. Device fonts can be used to override the fonts in the movie at runtime.

When you choose to use a device font, be aware of the following:

- Flash can't treat device fonts as graphics. Tweening stuff containing a device font is going to be unpredictable.
- Device font is a "weasel word" for "pick the closest approximation." This means you lose all control over the spacing and length of the text on the screen at runtime. Depending on the font chosen by the user's machine, you may wind up having the user view your work through a font that has a bigger x-height than your font. If you need an exact match, device fonts aren't the way to go.

X-height? What's that? It is the height of the letter x in the font, and this proportional characteristic can vary widely in different typefaces of the same size. Tall x-heights are two-thirds the height of a capital letter and short when they are one half the height of a capital letter. In the example shown in Figure 6-8, the font size chosen for the lowercase x is 30 points, and the fonts are Helvetica on the left and Times on the right.

Staying with our useless information theme, the trend to the larger x-height in the sans category was sparked by Adrian Frutiger in the last century when he released Univers 55.

Figure 6-8. X-height can affect design.

Types of text fields

The Property inspector indicates three ways to classify text on the stage: **static**, **dynamic**, and **input**. Truth be told, dynamic and input are actually the same thing, but that only matters in terms of ActionScript. In relation to the Property inspector, static text fields contain text that won't be edited after the SWF is published, dynamic text fields contain text that will (or can), and input text fields contain text that is entered by the user. Each classification carries its own characteristics, much of which is shared among all three. Let's get to our penmanship!

Static text

Static text is the less powerful sort of text in Flash, but don't let its humble nature fool you. If you're into speed, it's also true that horses run slower than cheetahs, but why split hairs?

As with most other tools in the Tools panel, the Property inspector, shown in Figure 6-9, controls text field properties in a big way, so let's take a look at each configurable item.

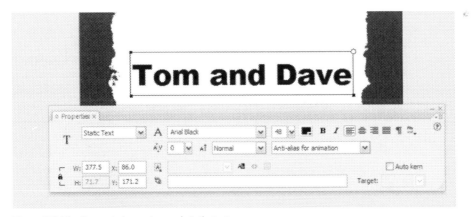

Figure 6-9. The Property inspector and static text

- **Text Type:** This determines whether the selected text field is static, dynamic, or input.

- **Font:** This lets you select from the list of fonts installed on your computer. With static text, in most cases, font outlines are included with the SWF. For that reason, it doesn't matter whether your audience has the same font installed or not. The only exception is when you use the first three device fonts—the ones with the underscores. This setting marks the first of many that may be applied more than once, and in various ways, in the same text field.

  To see this in action, start a new Flash document, select the Text tool, and click somewhere on the stage. Type your name. Select the second letter of your name by dragging the mouse from one side of the letter to the other. Change the font. Select the third letter, and change the font again.

> *Notice that the text field automatically widens as you type. The indicator for this is the little white circle in the upper-right corner of the text field, as you can see in Figure 6-9. If you keep typing, the text field will eventually extend past the stage and off into the wild blue yonder. To set a specific width, which causes text to wrap, hover over that white circle until you see the double-headed arrow cursor. Click and drag to the desired width. The white circle turns into a square. To switch back to auto-widen mode, double-click that square.*

- **Font Size:** This sets the selected font's size, in points. Multiple font sizes are allowed within the same text field. The slider ranges from 8 points to 96 points, but you may type in other values directly, anywhere from zero (invisibly small text) to 2,500 (jaw-droppingly way huge), including noninteger values, such as 12.75. Between 1,800 points and 2,000 points, the glyphs of most fonts "jump outside" the bounding box of their text fields, but this doesn't seem to affect text rendering—it merely makes the text field harder to select.

- **Text Color:** Want fuchsia text? Here's where to make that statement. Multiple colors are allowed within the same text field.

- **Bold, Italic:** These buttons toggle bold and italic styling. To apply either style to the whole text field, choose the Selection tool, click the text field, and then toggle one or both buttons. To apply either style to individual words or characters, use the Text tool to select the text field, highlight the desired glyphs, and then toggle one or both buttons. Bold and italic versions of the chosen font must exist on your computer for this styling to occur.

- **Align Left, Align Center, Align Right, Align Justify:** These only make practical sense when applied to fixed-width text fields. In cases where your words wrap, this determines how they do it. Align Left means the left edge of your lines of text will be even. Align Center means your lines will be centered inside the text field. Align Right means the right edge will be even. Align Justify means both the left and right edges will be even. Different alignments may be applied to each line of text in a text field.

- **Edit Format Options:** This button brings up a small Format Options dialog box that allows you to specify Indent, Line spacing (leading), Left margin, and Right margin settings for any line of text.

- Change Orientation of Text: Some writing systems, like Japanese, proceed vertically down (or up) the page. This setting changes the orientation of text in a given text field. In the case of Vertical, Left to Right or Vertical, Right to Left, an additional button appears, Rotation, that determines the rotation of vertical text.

- Letter Spacing: This determines the uniform distribution of space between glyphs, also known as **tracking**. The higher the number, the wider apart the characters—and vice versa. If you want, you can even squish letters together by using a negative number. Typographers have a term for this—**crashing text**. Multiple letter spacing settings may be applied to the same text field.

- Character Position: Want to put something in superscript or subscript? Here's the place. Can be applied to text fields as a whole or to individual glyphs.

- Font Rendering Method: The previous version of Flash Player (version 8) introduced a number of terrific new visual effects, and one of those was improved text rendering. This enhancement lives on in Flash Player 9, the Player that corresponds to the default publish settings for Flash CS3. There are five choices for font rendering:

  - Use device fonts: This relies on the user having your chosen font installed. Unlike the three device fonts mentioned earlier (_sans, _serif, and _typewriter), this setting uses exactly the font you specify—provided it is available on the computer playing the SWF file. If not, Flash makes the choice.

  - Bitmap text: This provides no anti-aliasing, which means characters will have jagged edges.

  - Anti-alias for animation: This provides normal text anti-aliasing. Glyphs appear smooth (no jaggies) and may be applied to text fields in earlier versions of Flash Player.

  - Anti-alias for reading: New since Flash 8, this format improves readability of small- and regular-sized fonts. Text animates smoothly because alignment and anti-aliasing are not applied while the text animates (it is reapplied when animation stops). This advanced anti-aliasing is not supported in Flash Player 7 or earlier SWFs, skewed or flipped text (rotated is okay), printed, or exported as PNG. Under these circumstances, the normal anti-aliasing (Anti-alias for animation) is applied.

  - Custom anti-alias: Also considered advanced anti-aliasing, this choice brings up a Custom Anti-Aliasing dialog box that allows you to specify your own Thickness and Sharpness settings.

- Line Type: Not available for static text. Text fields automatically widen as you type, or you can set a text field's width by dragging the white circle in its upper-right corner. Doing so causes text to wrap, period. Other types of text fields may be set to single-line or multiline text, but static text fields essentially take care of themselves.

- Selectable: Determines whether the text is selectable with the mouse in the published SWF. Even rotated, flipped, and skewed text may be set as selectable.

- Render Text as HTML: Not available for static text. Note that in spite of this feature for static text, hyperlinking is still supported (see the URL Link, Target entry in this list).

- Show Border Around Text: Not available for static text.

6

- Auto kern: Toggles auto-kerning. What is **kerning**? This is in the same ballpark as Letter Spacing discussed previously, except kerning refers to individualized spacing between glyphs. Consider the capital letters *A* and *V*: the bottom of the *A*'s right side extends out, which fits neatly under the "pulled-in" bottom of the *V*. Kerning reduces the space between glyphs that "fit together" in this way, which tends to provide greater visual balance.

- URL Link, Target: This allows you to create hyperlinks inside text fields. Either select the whole text or use the mouse to select individual glyphs or words, and then type a URL into the URL Link field (e.g., http://www.VisitMe.com/). Entering anything at all into the URL Link field activates the Target field next to it, which gives you the same four choices available to HTML anchor tags (<a>), namely:

  - _blank: Opens URL in a new browser window.

  - _parent: Opens URL in the parent frameset of an HTML frameset (this assumes the SWF is embedded in an HTML page that appears in multiple framesets).

  - _self: Opens URL in the same window or frame as the current HTML document that holds this SWF. This is the default behavior.

  - _top: Opens URL in the topmost window of a frameset, replacing the frameset with the new URL.

> *Hyperlinks in the* URL Link *field do not change the appearance of the text in any way, even though a dashed line appears under hyperlinked text during authoring. This differs from HTML hyperlinks, which are traditionally differentiated by an underline and a change in color. Although the Property inspector supports bold and italic, there is no way to add underlines to text without ActionScript (see the section "HTML formatting" later in this chapter). Flash hyperlinks are primarily meant for loading HTML documents, which may or may not contain additional Flash content. As a general rule, this is not the place to load external SWFs into the current movie, though it is possible to trigger ActionScript with the* URL Link *field. More on that in the section "Hyperlinks and Flash text" later on in the chapter.*

Note that selecting an individual static text field adds four more properties to the Property inspector: W (width), H (height), X, and Y. The height property is disabled because the height of static text fields is always determined by the amount of text they contain; that is, when width is taken out of its default widen-as-you-type mode. Setting width in the Property inspector is equivalent to dragging the white circle as described earlier.

Now that you know what all of that stuff in the Property inspector does, let's take that knowledge for a test drive.

Your turn: Playing with static text

There is a ton of stuff you can do with static text on the page, and the three exercises in this section will give you an idea of the creative possibilities open to you. In this first exercise, you will discover how to apply a filter to text and how to tween text to which a filter has been applied.

1. Open the Static1.fla file. Select the Text tool or press the T key, select the Text layer, click the stage, and enter your name. Use a bold sans serif font and a size ranging from 30 to 48 points depending upon the font chosen.

Points? Pixels? Which to choose? On computer screens, they're both the same, so the terms are interchangeable. Here's how that came about. Traditionally, 72-point type was actually 72.27 points, which is a hair over 1 inch. When computers took over print production and typesetting in the 1980s, purists using Apple computers who pointed out this discrepancy to Apple were essentially told, "Our screen resolution is 72 pixels per inch. We don't do .27 pixels." Thus a standard was born, and over 300 years of typesetting standards were changed.

2. Switch over to the Selection tool or press the V key, and select the text block.

3. Click the Filters tab, click the +, and select Drop Shadow from the Filter list. When the Drop Shadow filter panel appears, specify these settings:

- Blur X: 14
- Blur Y: 14
- Strength: 100%
- Quality: High

As you can see in Figure 6-10, you can apply a filter to text.

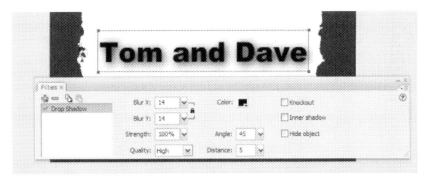

Figure 6-10. Text, buttons, and movieclips are the only Flash objects to which filters can be applied.

4. Add a keyframe to frame 15 of the Text layer, select the text on the stage, and remove the drop shadow from the text in frame 15.

5. Right-click (PC) or Ctrl-click (Mac) between the two keyframes and select Create Motion Tween from the context menu. The "tween arrow" appears between the two keyframes, but if you scrub between them, nothing happens. Let's fix that.

6. Remove the keyframe and the motion tween. You'll also notice a new Tween 1 symbol in your library, which was put there as a result of Create Motion Tween. Delete that symbol.

There's an interesting difference between Create Motion Tween and the application of a motion tween from the Property inspector. If you need to tween a filter effect, the text must be in a movieclip. Let's try it:

7. Add keyframes to the Text layer in frames 15 and 30, move the playhead to frame 15, and select the text on the stage. Remove the Drop Shadow filter at frame 15, as before. This time, click the span of frames in the Text layer anywhere between frames 1 and 15. Choose Motion from the drop-down menu next to the word Tween in the Property inspector. Do the same for the frames between 15 and 30. Press the Enter (PC) or Return (Mac) key. The shadow gradually appears and disappears (see Figure 6-11). You can save the file if you choose. This alternate approach to motion tweens is covered in greater detail in Chapter 7.

Figure 6-11. A motion tween applied to a Drop Shadow filter

In this next exercise, you are going "explode" some text. Along the way, you are going to learn how to convert text to letters and then to art. You are also going to learn a handy way of putting the individual pieces of a grouped object into motion. Let's get started:

1. Open the Static2.fla file in your Chapter 6 Exercise folder. When the file opens, create a new movieclip named myName, and enter your name when the Symbol Editor opens. We'll leave the font, style, and size to you. When you finish, set the text's X coordinate to 88 and the Y coordinate to 170 in the Property inspector. This odd positioning is chosen because we want the text to go flying out from the middle of the stage.

One of the themes that percolates through this book is *Let the software do the work*. In this case, you have a number of letters that will need to fly off of the screen. Trying to enter each one manually and then spending the time to ensure they are perfectly aligned with each other is both tedious and a waste of billable hours. There is an easier way.

2. Select the text on the stage and press Ctrl+B (PC) or Cmd+B (Mac). Each letter, as shown in Figure 6-12, is separated into its own piece of text. You could keep pressing those keys until the text looks pixelated. When that happens, the text is changed from text to shapes.

   The command you just issued by keyboard shortcut—Ctrl+B (PC) or Cmd+B (Mac)—is Break Apart (Modify ➤ Break Apart), and it is a great way of separating complex artwork into its basic pieces. Continually applying this command reduces text to nothing more than PostScript outlines, meaning the text is now a graphic and can't be edited as text. If you are an Illustrator CS3 or Fireworks CS3 user, this is quite similar to the Create Outlines command used to convert text to art in those applications.

Figure 6-12. Break text apart if you want to animate or manipulate the individual letters.

3. Now that the text has been broken apart into individual letters, let's get each letter into a layer so it can be animated. Select all of the text on the stage and select Modify ➤ Timeline ➤ Distribute to Layers. As soon as you do this, each letter is moved to its own layer, as shown in Figure 6-13, and the letters don't change their position on the stage. Another great example of letting the software do the work.

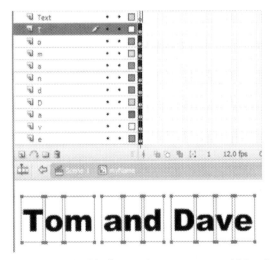

Figure 6-13. Use Distribute to Layers to move multiple selections to individual layers.

4. Delete the empty layer. Click in frame 30 of the top layer, hold down the Shift key, and click in frame 30 of the bottom layer. With the layers selected, right-click (PC) or Ctrl-click (Mac) to open the context menu. Add a keyframe. You have now prepared each letter to be animated. Repeat this step for frame 5.

5. Select a letter in frame 30, use the Selection tool to move the letter to a new location, and use the Free Transform tool to resize, rotate, or otherwise distort the letter. Do this for all remaining letters.

6. Add motion tweens on the timeline as shown in Figure 6-14.

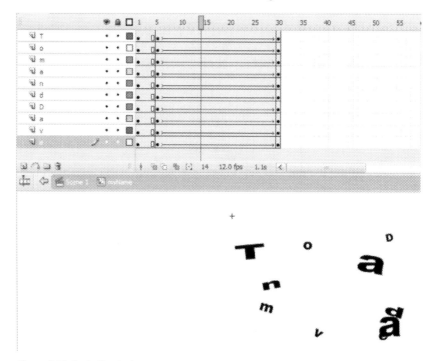

Figure 6-14. Exploding text

7. Click the Scene 1 link to return to the main timeline.

8. Select the Text layer and drag a copy of the myName movieclip to the stage.

9. Select the Actions layer, click the keyframe in frame 1 to select it, and press F9 (PC) or Option+F9 (Mac) to open the Actions panel. When it opens, enter the following code and close the panel:

```
stop();
```

If you didn't add this action, your movie would consist of your name blinking, not exploding, on the stage. The action stops the playhead dead in frame 1 of the main timeline, which allows the movieclip to play.

10. Close the Actions panel, save the movie, and test it. Your name explodes (see Figure 6-15).

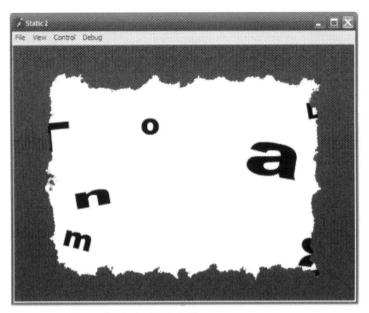

Figure 6-15. The movie playing in Flash Player

So far you have discovered that static text can be manipulated. It can have filters applied and tweened. You have also discovered how to turn the text into individual graphics and put them in motion. In this final exercise, you are going to explore how text can be manipulated using a blend mode from the Property inspector and how to change its color using the Property inspector. These are useful skills to know if you need to tween color changes or have the text interact with the content under it in the Timeline panel.

1. Open the Static3.fla file. When it opens, as shown in Figure 6-16, you will see we have added a background image to the stage and supplied you with some text in a movieclip.

2. Click the movieclip on the stage. If you look at the Property inspector, you will see the Color and the Blend areas are respectively set to None and Normal.

3. To really change the color of the text in the movieclip, click the Color drop-down button and select Advanced. When you see the Settings button on the Property inspector, click it.

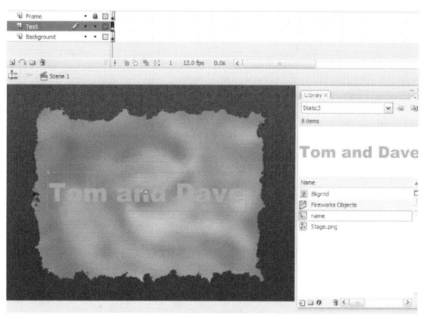

Figure 6-16. We start with text in a movieclip.

4. Clicking the Settings button opens the Advanced Effect dialog box shown in Figure 6-17. This dialog box allows you to adjust both the tint and the alpha values of the selected object. The controls on the left reduce the tint and alpha values for each of the RGB colors, whereas the controls on the right decrease or increase the color and alpha values by a constant amount. What happens when you change a value is that the current color values of the selection are multiplied by the numbers on the left and then added to the values on the right. To see how all of this works, use the following settings:

- Red: 30%
- Green: 70%
- Blue: 20%
- Alpha: 100%

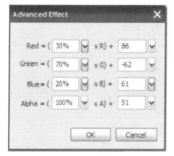

Figure 6-17. The Advanced Effect dialog box can be used to change the colors of selected objects.

The text changes color from the neutral gray to green, which is understandable considering it is now the predominant color. Make the following changes on the right side:

- x R) +: 86
- x G) +: -62
- x B) +: 61
- x A) +: 51

The color changes to a purple because we have increased the red and blue values and reduced the green value.

> Remember, even though we are using text in a movieclip, this effect can be applied to any graphical symbol you may make.

5. Now that you have changed the color, let's make it interact with the color in the image behind it. Select the movieclip and select Hard Light from the Blend drop-down menu. The text changes color because this effect mimics the shining of a very bright light through the selection. Change the Blend setting to Overlay. This time the text interacts with all of the colors behind it (see Figure 6-18). Overlay multiplies or screens the colors based upon the color of the selected object.

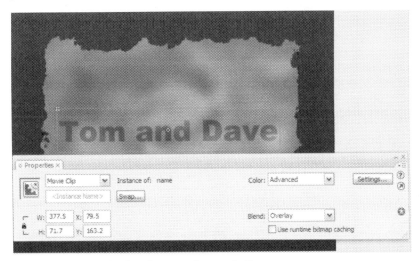

Figure 6-18. Using a blend mode on text in a movieclip

6. Close the file and don't save the changes.

> Yes, you can apply the blend modes using ActionScript. No, we aren't going to get into it.

Dynamic text

What makes dynamic text fields different from their static counterparts? From the point of view of the Property inspector, surprisingly little. Change the Text Type setting to Dynamic Text, and you'll only see three new properties appear. In addition, three previously disabled properties become available, and one becomes unavailable. The rest is the same.

- Change Orientation of Text: This property dims out because it's not available for dynamic or input text fields.

- Instance Name: A text field's instance name allows it to be "spoken to" by ActionScript, the same as an instance name for a movieclip, button, or any other object.

- Line Type: Options you can set for the selected text field are Single line, Multiline, and Multiline no wrap. If you're typing by hand, or cutting and pasting text from another document, Single means no line breaks are possible, even if the text field is tall enough to accommodate them. In fixed-width text fields, Multiline allows text to wrap when it reaches the right side, in addition to breaking along carriage returns. Multiline no wrap breaks on carriage returns only.

- Render Text as HTML: This setting is a godsend for quick-and-simple formatting such as bold and italic, and it's the only way to underline text in Flash. HTML formatting is covered in detail in its own section later in this chapter.

- Show Border Around Text: This toggles a solid black stroke around the text field. Border color can be changed with ActionScript, as long as the border is showing.

- Var: This setting, while visible for dynamic text fields, is not supported in ActionScript 3.0, so it's disabled. This particular feature is a historical throwback to Flash 4, when the way to set the content of a text field was to associate it with a variable. As recently as Flash 8, this approach was still in wide use. In fact, it's still possible in Flash CS3 if you change your publish settings for something earlier than ActionScript 3.0. Generally speaking, though, it's better to separate form from function. Let variables be variables and use the `TextField.text` property to set the display content of a dynamic text field. More on that in just a moment.

- Embed: This button allows you to specify what glyphs are included in the SWF. This happens automatically for static text fields unless you choose device fonts. With dynamic text, you get much more choice.

Is there more to it than that? There is, and most of it occurs in ActionScript. Before we look at a few examples, though, take note of one important change.

While formatting may be applied partially and more than once in a single static text field, the rules are different for dynamic and input text fields. In nonstatic text fields, when the text properties are set in the Property inspector, it's an "all-or-nothing" proposition. Change the color of one letter, and you've changed the color of the whole text field. Same goes for font. Same goes for bold, italic, and so on. The only way to apply varied formatting within the same dynamic or input text field is to use ActionScript. Bear that in mind as we continue. First, we'll start with the basics and add text to an existing dynamic text field. Next, we'll add line breaks and formatting, and finally create a text field from scratch.

1. Open a new Flash document, and use the Text tool to draw a text field approximately 300 pixels wide. Use the Property inspector, as shown in Figure 6-19, to ensure the Text Type is set to Dynamic Text. Choose whatever font you like, but keep it small, say, 12 points. Set the Line Type to Single line. Select Anti-alias for animation from the Font Rendering Method drop-down menu and click the Auto kern box to select it.

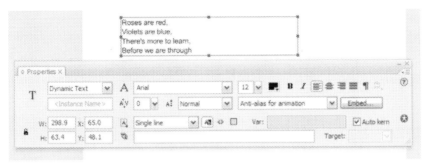

Figure 6-19. Applying dynamic text properties

2. Double-click the text field to enter its bounding box. Type in the following heart-rending poem, and press Enter (PC) or Return (Mac) after each line.

   Roses are red,

   Violets are blue.

   There's more to learn

   Before we're through.

3. Test the movie and confirm that the whole poem is collapsed into the single line shown in Figure 6-20. Why? Because the Line Type option is set to Single line. Change that property to Multiline and test again. This time, the poem appears in all its Bardian glory. Change to Mutliline no wrap and test a third time. No difference, right? That's because none of those lines hits the edge of the text field.

Figure 6-20. What happens when you select the Single line type

4. Double-click the text field to enter it. Hover over the right-edge drag handle until the cursor becomes a double-headed arrow. Drag the right edge over to the left until the text starts to wrap. Still using the Multiline no wrap setting, test the movie again. Each line breaks at the carriage return, but doesn't wrap. Switch to Multiline, and test one last time to compare. Now you understand Line Type.

6

5. Widen the text field again, and give it the instance name poetry in the Property inspector. Enter the text field, select the existing text, and delete it. Create a new layer in the main timeline and name it scripts. Click in frame 1 of the scripts layer, open the Actions panel, and enter

```
poetry.text = "Roses are red,";
```

Now, remember the discussion of classes from Chapter 4? Dynamic and input text fields are instances of the TextField class, which features a text property. In this line of ActionScript, we're referencing the TextField.text property by way of the poetry instance name. Test your movie and you'll see the first line of the poem, as shown in Figure 6-21, including the comma. But what about line breaks?

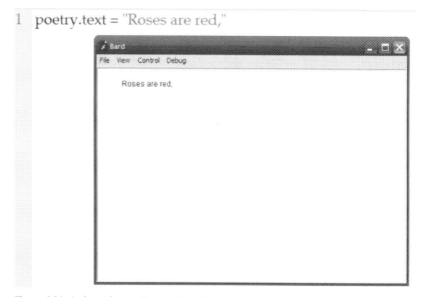

Figure 6-21. Actionscript can be used to add text to a dynamic text field.

ActionScript supports a widespread convention of **escape sequences** to represent carriage returns, tabs, special characters, and more. What are escape sequences?

They are arbitrary characters preceded by a backslash (\), like \n, \r, and \t. What is "escaping" good for? In escape sequences, it provides an encoded way to manipulate text or represent special characters. It can also be a way to tell ActionScript to accept a character at face value, rather than interpret it as a part of the programming. Here's a practical example.

As you've seen, the TextField.text property accepts a string value. Strings are denoted by a pair of double or single quotes. The quotation mark character (") tells ActionScript when a string begins and when it ends. But what if your string *contains* quotation marks, such as dialogue? You have to either nest your quotes carefully or escape them. This sentence gets it wrong:

```
var shortStory:String = "Mary, said Fred. Mary, I'm pregnant.";
```

Since the preceding is a conversation, Fred's words should actually be in quotes. To accommodate double quotes in this string, you could wrap the whole thing in single quotes, like this:

```
var shortStory:String = '"Mary," said Fred. "Mary, I'm pregnant."';
```

But whoops! There's still a problem. Can you spot it? Pardon the pun, but the contraction "I am"—"I'm"—itself contains a single quote! That means ActionScript considers the string ended immediately after the capital *I*, which makes the "m pregnant" fragment programmatic gibberish. This sort of situation happens so easily, and is so easy to overlook, we prefer instead to escape quotation marks. In this revision, the string is once again denoted by double quotes, and the interior double quotes are escaped.

```
var shortStory:String = "\"Mary,\" said Fred. \"Mary, I'm pregnant.\"";
```

> *Note that only the double quotes need to be escaped in this scenario. If the string had been wrapped in single quotes, only the apostrophe in "I'm" would have to be escaped. How? Just put a slash in front of it.*

So what about escape sequences? We're glad you asked. A handful of characters actually perform a task when you escape them, such as \n, the newline escape sequence, and \t for tabs. Let's take a look at both.

We're going to update the existing ActionScript to add a line break. You can either put everything within one line . . .

```
poetry.text = "Roses are red,\nViolets are blue";
```

. . . or break the ActionScript over as many lines in the Actions panel as you like, which is often easier on the eyes. In this case, you will want to use the TextField.appendText() method, which appends text to existing content, rather than replacing it.

```
poetry.text = "Roses are red,\n";
poetry.appendText("Violets are blue.\n");
poetry.appendText("There's more to learn\n");
poetry.appendText("Before we're through.");
```

You may also use the addition assignment operator to build a string first, and then assign that to the text field's text property:

```
var poem:String = "Roses are red,\n";
poem += "Violets are blue.\n";
poem += "There's more to learn\n";
poem += "Before we're through.";
poetry.text = poem;
```

> *Want to be a rebel? Select the poem text field and change its* Line Type *property back to* Single line. *Test your movie. In spite of that "single lines only, please" setting, the* \n *escape sequence succeeds loud and clear.*

What about those tabs we mentioned earlier? Use the \t escape sequence. Note that several tabs can be used in succession, which is also true for newlines. The following ActionScript pushes each text field line farther to the right:

```
var poem:String = "Roses are red,\n";
poem += "\tViolets are blue.\n";
poem += "\t\tThere's more to learn\n";
poem += "\t\t\tBefore we're through.";
poetry.text = poem;
```

Is it possible to set tab stops? Sure thing. For this, you'll need an instance of the TextFormat class. Set the TextFormat.tabStops property to an array of pixel values, and then apply the formatting object to your text field.

```
// First, the string
var poem:String = "Roses are red,\n";
poem += "\tViolets are blue.\n";
poem += "\t\tThere's more to learn\n";
poem += "\t\t\tBefore we're through.";

// Then, the formatting
var format:TextFormat = new TextFormat();
format.tabStops = new Array(20, 40, 60, 80);

// Finally, apply the string and the formatting
// to the text field
poetry.text = poem;
poetry.setTextFormat(format);
```

That puts four tab stops at 20-pixel intervals.

While we're on the subject, the TextFormat class provides a whole lot more. For a full list of functionality, we invite you to consult the TextFormat class entry of the ActionScript 3.0 Language Reference, but here are a few common properties you may want to set:

```
var format:TextFormat = new TextFormat();
format.font = "Verdana";
format.size = "24";
format.color = 0x3355CC;
format.bold = true;
format.italic = true;
existingTextField.text = "Lorem ipsum dolor sit amet.";
existingTextField.setTextFormat(format);
```

The TextField.setTextFormat() method accepts two optional parameters after the first, and those dictate where to start and stop. Let's say you have an overall style in mind for the whole text field. Aside from that, you want to apply special formatting to two different words and another set of formatting to a third word. Let's try it:

1. Open a new Flash document and add a new dynamic text field with instance name of existingTextField to the stage.

2. Add a new layer named Actions, open the Actions panel, and enter the following code:

```
var overallStyle:TextFormat = new TextFormat();
overallStyle.font = "Verdana";
overallStyle.size = 12;

var boldBlue:TextFormat = new TextFormat();
boldBlue.color = 0x0000FF;
boldBlue.bold = true;

var italicRed:TextFormat = new TextFormat();
italicRed.color = 0xFF0000;
italicRed.italic = true;

existingTextField.text = "Lorem ipsum dolor sit amet.";
existingTextField.setTextFormat(overallStyle);
existingTextField.setTextFormat(boldBlue, 0, 5);
existingTextField.setTextFormat(boldBlue, 12, 17);
existingTextField.setTextFormat(italicRed, 22, 26);
```

What's going on here? Think of the styling as a special brush—actually, three brushes. The first brush gives the text field an overall formatting of 12-point Verdana. Next, you switch to a brush that makes things blue and bold. You set your brush down at position 0, where first letter starts (see Figure 6-22), pull it across the first word, and then lift up at position 5, which is the beginning of the sixth character (the first space).

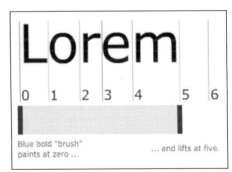

Figure 6-22. ActionScript can be used to selectively format a dynamic text field.

3. Test the movie. When the SWF opens, you will see the text Lorem and dolor colored blue and amet colored red. Don't save the document.

Want to create a text field completely with ActionScript? It's pretty straightforward. The TextField class is instantiated like any other. In this case, the instance name becomes the variable you use to refer to the instance. As always, consult the TextField class entry of the ActionScript 3.0 Language Reference to see the full set of properties, but here are a few in common use:

- autoSize: This property is only slightly tricky, because it expects a separate class just to provide its value. The static TextFieldAutoSize.LEFT property instructs the new TextField instance to be left-aligned and widen automatically (toward the right) to accommodate any text it is given. The available TextFieldAutoSize properties are LEFT, RIGHT, CENTER, and NONE. The first three allow the text field to widen as necessary and align the text to the left, right, or centered. The last keeps the text field from widening, in which case a width and height must be specified.

- selectable: This is equivalent to the Property inspector setting by the same name.

- x, y: These are interesting because they may not appear in the properties summary of the TextField class entry for you by default. It's fairly easy to guess what they refer to—the position of the text field on the stage—but where do they come from? This is where our ActionScript basics really come into play. Notice the "Inheritance" heading near the top of the TextField class entry: this class extends the InteractiveObject class, which in turn extends the DisplayObject class (and it goes further). DisplayObject is the source of the x and y properties. Thanks to the principle of inheritance, it is absolutely correct to say that text fields have their own sense of x and y, it's just that these properties originated elsewhere. To see them in the TextField class entry itself, click the Show Inherited Public Properties hyperlink beneath the "Public Properties" heading.

- text: Ah, we're already familiar with this one.

Let's try adding a text field with ActionScript:

1. Open a new Flash document and don't add anything to the stage.

2. Add a new layer named Actions, open the Actions panel, and enter the following code:

```
var benFranklinQuote:TextField = new TextField();

benFranklinQuote.autoSize = TextFieldAutoSize.LEFT;
benFranklinQuote.selectable = false;
benFranklinQuote.x = 50;
benFranklinQuote.y = 30;
benFranklinQuote.text = "Energy and persistence conquer all things.";

var format:TextFormat = new TextFormat();
format.font = "Courier";
format.size = 14;

benFranklinQuote.setTextFormat(format);
addChild(benFranklinQuote);
```

What's that addChild() business at the end? Until that final line, the previous ActionScript has gone to the effort of creating a TextField instance—and a TextFormat instance to style it—but hasn't actually displayed anything. ActionScript 3.0 introduces the concept of **display lists**, which gives you much more control over what actually gets displayed to the screen. By adding the benFranklinQuote object (the TextField instance) to the display list, you're effectively "lifting the curtain" to let the show begin.

3. Test the movie. When the SWF opens, you will see the quote, as shown in Figure 6-23. Don't save the document.

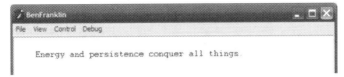

Figure 6-23. A text field added through the use of code

Input text

Input and dynamic text fields are practically identical. From the point of view of the Property inspector, only four things change. Three properties go away, and a new one appears:

- Selectable: This property becomes disabled, which makes good sense: by definition, input text is something the user types into the field. In order for typing to work, the text field must be selectable—so it is, and you can't make it otherwise.

- URL Link: This property disappears altogether. You may prepopulate an input text field with text; you may even format it, but you can't give it a hyperlink—without ActionScript. More on this in the section "Hyperlinks and Flash text."

- Target: Without a hyperlink, there's really no use for the Target property.

- Maximum Characters: This is the new one. It lets you specify the maximum number of characters the user may type in. Prepopulated text may override this setting, but the user will have to delete what's there in order to add new text—at which point the maximum value holds.

Although not required, it makes good sense to use the Show Border Around Text property, as shown in Figure 6-24, for input text fields, so the user can see where to type. If not, you may certainly position prettier artwork of your own behind the text field. To set the color of this border, use ActionScript:

```
textFieldInstanceName.borderColor = 0xFFFF00;
```

Figure 6-24. Adding a border to input text

The TextField.text property works the same way with input text. If you want to know what the user has typed, check the instance name of that text field and look at its text value.

HTML formatting

Although Flash only supports a small subset of the HTML language—and it's a very small subset—the ability to use familiar formatting tags for text is a very cool thing. In addition, most people find it less complicated, in many respects, than the TextFormat class discussed earlier. HTML formatting is only supported for dynamic and input text fields, and tags must be written and applied with ActionScript. We'll discuss the tags first, and then we'll show you how to use them.

- **Anchor tag (<a>)**: If you want to make a hyperlink without using the Property inspector, this is your tag. This tag supports three attributes:

  - href: An absolute or relative URL, up to 128 characters in length. This attribute corresponds to the URL Link setting of the Property inspector and is required if you want the hyperlink to actually do something. If you're opening a web document, use the http: or https: protocol. If you want to trigger ActionScript instead, use the event: protocol. More on this in the section "Hyperlinks and Flash text."

  - event: When a hyperlink is set to trigger ActionScript, this attribute provides one way to effectively pass a parameter along with the triggered function. More on this in the section "Hyperlinks and Flash text."

  - target: One of four values that correspond to the Target setting of the Property inspector: _blank (opens URL in a new browser window), _parent (opens URL in the parent frameset of an HTML frameset), _self (opens URL in the same window or frame as the current HTML document that holds this SWF; this is the default behavior), and _top (opens the URL in the topmost window of a frameset, replacing the frameset with the new URL).

- **Bold tag (<b>)**: Makes text bold, if the current font supports it.

- **Break tag (<br>)**: Represents a line break.

- **Font tag (<font>)**: Provides three ways to format the styling of text, by way of the following attributes:

  - color: A hex value representing a color.

  - face: The name of a font.

  - size: The size of the font in pixels. You may also use relative sizes, such as +2 or –1.

- **Image tag (<img>)**: Displays a graphic file, movieclip, or SWF inside a text field. Supported graphics are JPG, GIF, and PNG. This tag may be configured by way of quite a few attributes:

  - src: This, the only required attribute, specifies the URL of an external image or SWF, or the linkage class for a movieclip symbol in the library. External files do not appear until they are fully loaded, so depending on your needs, you may want to embed content in the SWF itself.

  - id: If you want to control the content of your image tag with ActionScript, you'll need to know the instance name of the movieclip that contains that content. This is where you provide that instance name.

- width, height: These specify the width and height of the image, SWF, or movieclip in pixels. If you like, you may scale content along the x-axis and y-axis by setting these attributes arbitrarily.

- align: This determines how text will flow around the image, SWF, or movieclip. The default value is left, and you may also specify right.

- hspace, vspace: Just as with HTML, these values determine how much "padding" appears around the image, SWF, or movieclip. Horizontal space is controlled by hspace, vertical by vspace. The default is 8 pixels. A value of 0 gets rid of the padding, and negative numbers bring in the edges, pulling adjacent content in with them.

- checkPolicyFile: This instructs Flash Player to check for a cross-domain policy file on the server associated with the image's or SWF's domain.

- **Italic tag (<i>)**: Makes text italicized, if the current font supports it.

- **List item tag (<li>)**: Indents text and precedes it with a round bullet. In the case of normal HTML, <li> tags may be further managed by parent list tags. The bullets of unordered lists (<ul>), for example, may be specified as circle, disk, or square. The bullets of ordered lists (<ol>) may be specified as numbers, Roman numerals, or letters. This is not the case in the microcosm of Flash HTML list items. Lists require neither a <ul> nor an <ol> tag, are unordered only, and feature only round bullets.

- **Paragraph tag (<p>)**: Our good, old-fashioned paragraph tag. Paragraphs come with a built-in line break, and you get two attributes with this tag:

  - align: This affects the text alignment. Valid settings are left, right, center, and justified, just like you get in the Property inspector.

  - class: Specifies the name of a Cascading Style Sheets (CSS) class selector, which can be used to stylize content.

- **Span tag (<span>)**: This tag doesn't do anything on its own, but it accepts a class attribute that supports Cascading Style Sheets (CSS) styling.

- **Text format tag (<textformat>)**: In many ways, this is the HTML version of the TextFormat class. Use the following parameters to stylize text content:

  - blockindent: Determines block indentation.

  - indent: Determines indentation of first line only and accepts both positive and negative values.

  - leading: Affects line spacing. Accepts both positive and negative values.

  - leftmargin, rightmargin: Determines the left and right margins of the text.

  - tabstops: Specifies tab stops.

- **Underline tag (<u>)**: Makes text underlined. This tag is the only way to underline text in Flash, unless you use CSS (covered in Chapter 10).

What? No tables? Yeah, that's been a pretty significant exclusion over the years. Is there a way, then, to easily display tabular data in Flash? There is. It may not seem as straightforward as the more familiar HTML table structure, but it works. In fact, you've already seen an example of it in this chapter. The answer is tab stops. Since we already used the TextFormat class, let's do it again with HTML.

1. Open the HTML.fla document. When it opens, you will see we have already added a dynamic text box and given it the instance name of output.

2. Click the first frame of the scripts layer, open the Actions panel, and enter the following code:

```
var htmlContent:String = "";
htmlContent += "<textformat tabstops='50,100,150'>➡
<b>One\tTwo\tThree</b></textformat><br>";
htmlContent += "<textformat tabstops='50,100,150'>➡
Eins\tZwei\tDrei</textformat><br>";
htmlContent += "<textformat tabstops='50,100,150'>➡
Un\tDeux\tTrois</textformat><br>";
htmlContent += "<textformat tabstops='50,100,150'>➡
Uno\tDos\tTres</textformat>";

output.htmlText = htmlContent;
```

> Looks a bit awkward to use the \t (tab) escape sequence mixed in with the HTML, but there it is.

3. Test the movie. The text is all lined up in columns, as shown in Figure 6-25, just like an HTML table.

Figure 6-25. HTML formatting applied to text

> For good measure, check out the html-tags.fla file in the Complete exercise folder for this chapter to see most of the tags and their attributes illustrated in one place. We left out CSS stuff for Chapter 10.

Hyperlinks and Flash text

Every type of text in Flash—static, dynamic, and input—supports hyperlinks. The big difference between static and nonstatic text fields is, unless ActionScript enters the picture, only static text fields allow for partial hyperlinking—for example, one word linked while the rest of the sentence is unlinked—or for more than one URL to be applied to the same field. All it takes for static text fields is to type in your text, select a few words, as shown in Figure 6-26, and enter the desired URL, with optional target, into the Property inspector.

Figure 6-26. Applying a hyperlink to text

If you do happen to want the whole text field hyperlinked, use the Selection tool to select the text field itself, and then use the URL Link and Target properties in the same way.

As easy as this approach is, nothing in the published SWF gives any indication that a hyperlink exists, unless the user just happens to move the mouse over the right spot. The cursor changes from the arrow cursor to the finger cursor, but nothing compels the user to put the mouse over a hyperlink in the first place. Pretty odd omission, if you ask us.

To work around it, take advantage of the non-ActionScripted ability of static text fields to display multiple formatting. After you associate a few words with hyperlinks, change the color of those words as well, or make them bold. Give the user a reason to distinguish the hyperlinked text from normal content.

Hyperlinks may be absolute, such as `http://www.SuperSite.com/thisPageHere.html`, or relative, such as `../thisOtherPage.html`, in which case—and this is important—the path will be determined not from the point of view of the SWF, but from the HTML file that contains it. For example, you may choose to keep all your HTML files in the root of your website. Because you're an organized developer, you may choose to put all your image files in their own subfolder of the root, and you may just do the same with your Flash content. From the SWFs' point of view, the relative path to all HTML files requires stepping back one folder, so if a SWF links to one of those pages, you might be tempted to put precede the destination's file name with `../`—but don't! The HTML file that contains the SWF in question is already in the same folder as the destination page, and it's the containing HTML file's point of view that matters.

Using HTML for hyperlinks

The URL Link setting in the Property inspector works for dynamic text fields, but remember, with nonstatic text, styling and hyperlinks are one-size-fits-all: either the whole text field links somewhere—even if you only apply the URL to one letter—or it doesn't link somewhere. That is, unless you use HTML tags. Which means . . . unless you use ActionScript.

You've already seen how HTML tags can be applied to a dynamic or input text field. All you need to do is use the anchor tag (`<a>`) with its `href` attribute, and you're set.

```
myTextField.htmlText = ➠
"<a href='http://www.domain.com/some-page.html'>click me</a>";
```

Note the single quotes around the href attribute's value. The single quotes keep Flash from getting confused regarding where your string starts and stops. This is the same issue we covered in our escape sequence discussion, and if you prefer to use double quotes around your attribute values, you may—but you'll have to escape them.

Ah, but wait! As with static text hyperlinks, the preceding example still doesn't give the user any indication that a portion of the text is clickable. To mimic the traditional underline that appears in HTML hyperlinks, consider using the underline tag (<u>) to set off the link. For example:

```
myTextField.htmlText = "<a href='http://www.domain.com/➠
some-page.html'><u>click me</u></a>";
```

Don't forget the optional target attribute if you want to control the target window of the specified URL. The default value for target is _self, which opens the destination URL in the same window the user is already in. If that window fills the browser window, the new page will also fill the browser window. If that window only fills one frame of an HTML frameset, only that frame will be replaced.

```
myTextField.htmlText = "<a href='http://www.domain.com/➠
some-page.html' target='_self'><u>click me</u></a>";
```

To "break out" of a frameset, use the _top target:

```
myTextField.htmlText = "<a href='http://www.domain.com/➠
some-page.html' target='_top'><u>click me</u></a>";
```

To open a new window altogether, use _blank:

```
myTextField.htmlText = "<a href='http://www.domain.com/➠
some-page.html' target='_blank'><u>click me</u></a>";
```

You may use as many anchor tags in a given text field as you like. Just surround whatever content you like with its own <a> tag, and do your audience a favor by emphasizing the hyperlink with an underline, bold, or italic style.

Using hyperlinks to trigger ActionScript

It's important to realize that hyperlinks are generally used for linking to a new HTML document. This is not the way to load image files or SWFs into the current Flash movie. (Loading is covered in Chapter 13, which discusses optimizing.) Fortunately, it is possible to trigger ActionScript with hyperlinks, so if you want to get fancy, you can use the humble anchor tag to perform whatever programming feat you desire. The trick is knowing how to listen for hyperlink clicks.

In ActionScript 3.0, hyperlinks dispatch a TextEvent.LINK event. This is different from the ActionScript 2.0 asfunction protocol, which called a custom function directly. To handle the LINK event in Flash CS3, you need two things. First, get rid of the http: protocol in your href attribute and replace it with event:. This tells ActionScript to forget about the browser and instead trigger a TextEvent.LINK event. Second, write an event handler. The result would look like this:

```
myTextField.htmlText = "<a href='event:'><u>click me</u></a>";
myTextField.addEventHandler(
  TextEvent.LINK,
  function():void {
    trace("Someone clicked the hyperlink!");
  }
);
```

Pretty neat so far, but not especially useful. You might have any number of hyperlinks in the text field or in other text fields currently showing, so here's one way to tell them apart. Add an arbitrary value after that event: inside the href attribute. This effectively becomes a parameter passed to the function that handles your event in the addEventHandler() method. For example:

```
myTextField.htmlText = "<a href='event:apples'><u>click me</u></a>";
myTextField.addEventHandler(
  TextEvent.LINK,
  function(evt:TextEvent):void {
    trace(evt.text);
  }
);
```

The dispatched LINK event object contains a text property that may be specified by you. The receiving function may reference that property in its parameter—in the preceding sample, we're naming the incoming event object evt, which makes evt.text the property that gives us back the message sent by the hyperlink.

Embedding font outlines

You saw at the beginning of this chapter that static text fields automatically embed font outlines as needed. For this reason, static text can be rotated, skewed, and otherwise distorted, as well as set to a semitransparent color without any problem. Dynamic and input text fields are different. The moment you do anything to the text that isn't perfectly "square," the text in nonstatic text fields simply vanishes. Rotate even one degree, and poof!

Why? The reason is simple: unless font outlines are included, Flash relies on fonts that exist on the user's computer. They're not *in* the SWF, so the SWF has no real control over them. But embed them in the movie . . . that's another matter. Keep in mind that adding font information to a movie increases its file size. There are trade-offs to everything. Okay, warning made. How is it done?

There are a couple ways to embed font outlines. The approach you use will probably depend on the amount of text your movie contains. On the one hand, each individual text

6

field can have its embedding handled separately. If you care to embed font outlines for a few text fields, that might be the quickest.

1. In a new Flash document, use the Text tool to draw a text field. Make it dynamic and enter a bit of text into it (standard "Lorem ipsum dolor sit amet" is fine).

2. With the text field selected, click the Embed button in the Property inspector. The Character Embedding dialog box shown in Figure 6-27 will open.

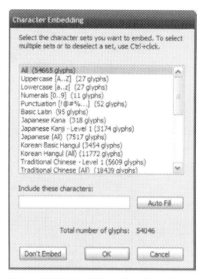

Figure 6-27. Embedding a font into the SWF

The choices are pretty clear-cut. As a general rule of thumb, we recommend you embed only the characters you're sure to need. No reason to use the All choice, for example, if the Basic Latin character set will do.

> *Basic Latin is generally good for English, but does not include accented characters, so please, no résumés.*

3. To see the kind of difference various character sets can make, select All and test your movie. In the window that contains the SWF, go to View ➤ Bandwidth Profiler to see how much the SWF weighs. Close that window, choose Basic Latin, and test again. Quite a difference!

If this text field requires only lowercase letters, choose the appropriate selection. To select more than one at the same time, hold down Ctrl (PC) or Cmd (Mac) while you click. The Auto Fill button is pretty neat: it includes one of each character currently in the text field, without repeats. If you change your mind and don't want to embed a character, click the Don't Embed button. What happens if you fail to embed a character the text field ends up needing? That particular character won't show, even while the others do.

Remember the very first topic at the beginning of this chapter, about what actually constitutes a font? Stylistic variations, such as bold and italic, are counted as distinct. Embedding roman (or normal) font outlines for a given character set *does not include* the corresponding bold or italic fonts, even for the exact same characters. To prove this point, open the EmbedButton.fla and test the movie.

Out of the four existing text fields, only the upper-left field, shown in Figure 6-28, will show in the SWF. Why? Only that text field has had font outlines included. Even though the one below it contains the same letters and features the same font family, that field's particular font is bold.

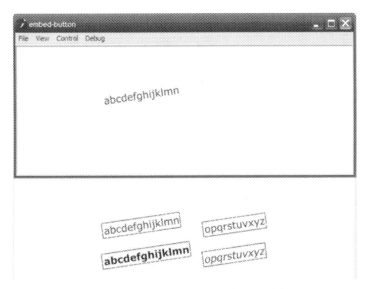

Figure 6-28. Only one of the text blocks uses an embedded font.

> **4.** Deselect the bold styling and test again. Now both text fields show. Select bold for the bottom-left text field again, and this time click the Embed button and embed lowercase letters. Again, both text fields show.

Here's another interesting point. The upper-left text field is set to embed lowercase letters. Odd that the upper-right text field, which is also comprised of lowercase letters (merely different ones), doesn't show. Have lowercase font outlines been embedded, or haven't they? We suspect this is a minor bug in Flash.

> **5.** Test your file and take note of the current file size. Close the SWF window and use the Embed button to embed lowercase font outlines for the upper-right text field. Test again. As expected, the upper-right field now shows, yet the SWF file size does not increase. This is good news: Flash isn't embedding the fonts more than once.

> **6.** The other way to embed fonts is to use a font symbol. Open EmbedFontSymbol.fla to see what we mean.

At first appearance, this file isn't any different from `EmbedButton.fla`, but there's a key distinction: take a look in the library. See that capital *A*? That's a font symbol. That library asset represents the font outlines for the Verdana font. Its presence does an interesting thing to the Font drop-down list in the Property inspector. A new "font" appears, by the name of VerdanaNormal, followed by an asterisk.

How did that font symbol get into the library? It's easy enough. Either right-click (PC) or Ctrl-click (Mac) somewhere inside the library that isn't the Preview area or an existing asset—or click the upper-right corner under the x—and you'll see a context menu that contains the choice New Font. That's the one you want. It opens a Font Symbol Properties dialog box, which allows you to specify an arbitrary custom name (such as VerdanaNormal), an actual font to embed, optional bold and italic styles, optional bitmap text, and size.

Bitmap text produces non–anti-aliased text, so it will look jagged. If you choose this option, you must specify the particular font size you're after. If you do not select it, font size doesn't matter, because the font outlines will be vectors. As explained previously, bold and italic are separate font outlines, so if you want normal text with the occasional italic words for emphasis, you'll have to include two font symbols.

The final step is to export your font symbol for ActionScript. Right-click (PC) or Ctrl-click (Mac) the font symbol in the library and choose Linkage. Put a checkmark in Export for ActionScript and Export in First Frame, and you're set. The class is automatically named for you based on the font's label (the class name may not contain spaces). The base class must be `flash.text.Font`.

As seen in `EmbedFontSymbol.fla`, both the upper-left and upper-right text fields show in the published SWF, even though neither embeds fonts by way of the Embed button. Instead, each text field has an instance name, and the scripts layer specifies a value of `true` for the `TextField.embedFonts` property for each instance. The lower-left and lower-right text fields do not show in the published SWF, because neither bold nor italic fonts have been brought into the library.

To prove that VerdanaNormal really is a "custom font," right-click (PC) or Ctrl-click (Mac) the font symbol and choose Properties. Change the Font entry to a visually different font, such as Courier. Test your movie. Even with a name like "VerdanaNormal," the font outlines look like the new replacement font.

> *Change the embedding option from lowercase to a single character in the* Include these characters *field. It can be any character, even a space. Test the movie, and you'll see that the upper-right text field still shows! Flash apparently needs to be nudged into "embed mode" for every single text field, but the decision of which characters to embed only needs to be made once. In ActionScript, this is accomplished via the* `TextField.embedFonts` *property.*

Checking spelling

Let's admit it: if we enter text, we will inevitably use the wrong spelling for a word or two. Flash CS3 contains a spell-checking tool that checks the spelling of all of the text in a document. You don't have heartless editors peering over your shoulders like we do, so spell checking your work before sending it to the Web is a really good idea. It should therefore not come as too much of a surprise to discover the spell-checking feature of Flash is quite robust. It allows you to check not only the spelling of the text in your text fields, but also the spelling in your layer names. Let's bring in some text—with typos—and check the spelling.

1. Open a new Flash document and open the Spelling Setup dialog box shown in Figure 6-29 by selecting Text ➤ Spelling Setup.

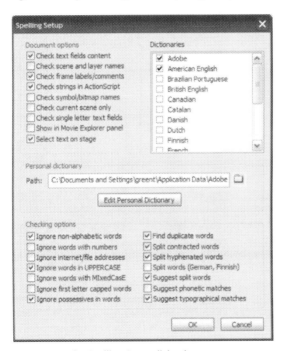

Figure 6-29. The Spelling Setup dialog box

If you have never used the spelling features of Flash CS3, you need to do this before you undertake your first spell check. The Document options area sets up what spelling is to be checked including any strings you may use in ActionScript. You can choose from a number of dictionaries and even create your own for commonly used words not found in a dictionary. The Checking options area permits you to decide what words or groups of words will be included or omitted from any spell checks.

It is heartening for one of the authors to see a Canadian dictionary and a British English dictionary. Canadian and British English are understandably similar, but writing for publishers based in the U.S. can be a bit disorienting. For example, one word—color—that is used extensively throughout this book is not correct in the U.K. or Canada, where it is spelled colour. Another word used in the American English dictionary is the word check. This important method of payment is spelled cheque using the Queen's English.

No, there is not a language known as Adobian. This dictionary is full of terms exclusively used by all of the Adobe products. A great example of the Adobian language would be ActionScript. It wouldn't be caught by the Adobe checker but will be flagged by all of the others.

2. Open the `SpellItOut.txt` document in a word processor, select the text, and copy it to the clipboard. Large amounts of text are pasted into Flash, as there is no ability in the application to import text into the library. Close the word processor.

3. Return to Flash, select the Text tool, and click the stage. Select Edit ➤ Paste to add the text to the stage.

4. Select Text ➤ Check Spelling and the Check Spelling dialog box shown in Figure 6-30 will appear. If the word is not recognized, the checker will provide you with a suggestion, which you can choose to either change or ignore. In the case of words like *check*, you can simply select the text in the Change to area of the dialog box and enter it.

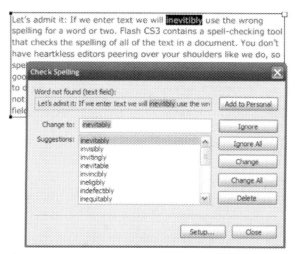

Figure 6-30. Using the Check Spelling dialog box

5. When you complete your spell check, click the Close button.

Your turn: A visit to the pond

We've perused quite a bit of theory. Now let's take a few text fields and actually do something with them. We'll start by looking at two ways to use hyperlinks to trigger the ActionScript that will make a frog disappear. We told you how it works earlier in the chapter, now it is time for you to try it. Though we are heavily into disappearing frogs, in this exercise you can use what you will learn to make images, movieclips, and other items on the stage disappear at the click of a mouse.

1. Open the `StaticTriggerAS.fla` file. When the file opens, you will see the image of a frog on the stage and two empty layers named Text and Actions. If you open the library, you will see the frog is in a movieclip named, well, frog, and if you click the image on the stage, you will see we have given it an instance name as well.

2. Click the Text layer and select the Text tool or press the T key.

3. Click the stage and enter Show the frog, hide the frog. Specify these text settings in the Property inspector:

   - Type: Static Text
   - Font: Arial
   - Size: 14
   - Color: #000000 (black)

4. Select the text Show and hide, and in the Property inspector, change their color to #0099FF (bright blue).

5. Using the Text tool, select the text Show and enter event:show into the URL Link area of the Property inspector as shown in Figure 6-31. The text you entered is the TextEvent:Link event you will be using when you write the code. Select the text hide and enter event:hide into the URL Link area of the Property inspector.

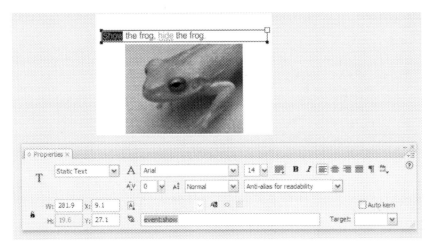

Figure 6-31. Use the URL Link area to trigger ActionScript text events.

6. Select the first frame in the Actions layer, open the Actions panel, and enter the following ActionScript:

```
addEventListener(TextEvent.LINK, linkHandler);
function linkHandler(evt:TextEvent):void {
  if(evt.text == "show") {
    frog.visible = true;
  } else {
    frog.visible = false;
  }
}
```

The first line of the code creates the listener, and tells Flash what to listen for (textEvent:Link) and what to do (execute the function named linkHandler) when it "hears" the event. The function checks to see which of the two hyperlinks were clicked. If it was the word *Show* and the event's text property is "show" (see Figure 6-31), the frog movieclip has its visible property set to true, which means the frog movieclip appears. The else simply says if it isn't the word *Show*, hide the frog movieclip by setting the movieclip's visible property to false.

7. Save and test the movie.

Now that you know how to control events using static text, let's try it out using a dynamic text field.

1. Open the DynamicTriggerAS.fla file. It is the same file as the previous exercise, and all we are going to ask you to do is to write the code.

2. Select the first frame in the Actions layer, open the Actions panel, click once in the Script pane, and enter the following:

```
changeTheFrog.htmlText = "<p><u><a href='event:show'>Show</a></u> ➡
the frog, <u><a href='event:hide'>hide</a></u> the frog.</p>";

changeTheFrog.addEventListener(TextEvent.LINK, linkHandler);

function linkHandler(evt:TextEvent):void {
  if(evt.text == "show") {
    frog.visible = true;
  } else {
    frog.visible = false;
  }
}
```

The first line is the major difference between this and the previous exercise. The text field on the stage has an instance name of changeTheFrog. This line tells Flash the text field is to be filled with HTML text and uses HTML tags instead of the Property inspector to add the text and enter the URL link.

3. Save the movie and test it. As you can see in Figure 6-32, the major change is the loss of the colored text. Instead the links, as expected in HTML, are underlined.

Figure 6-32. The links are formatted through the use of HTML tags.

Scrolling text

The final two exercises in the chapter deal with one of the more frequently asked questions regarding text: "How do I scroll a large amount of text?" In fact, there are two ways of approaching this one. The first is to use the UIScrollBar component, which, to quote a friend of ours, is "easy peasy." The second is to "roll your own" scroller using ActionScript.

Before you start, let's get clear on the fact that the text field must be dynamic, and Flash needs to know it is scrollable. This is done in one of three ways:

- Hold down the Shift key and double-click the circular handle of the text block. The circle will turn into the black square shown in Figure 6-33.
- Using the Selection tool, click the text block and select Text ➤ Scrollable.
- With the text block selected, right-click (PC) or Ctrl-click (Mac) the text box and select Scrollable from the context menu.

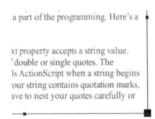

Figure 6-33. Your visual clue that a text field is scrollable

Let's start using the "easy peasy" method:

1. Open the ScrollComponent.fla file. When it opens, you will see we have put some text on the stage in a dynamic text box.

2. Switch to the Selection tool, click the text field, and select Text ➤ Scrollable. The hollow circle turns to a black box. Drag the bottom of the field to a point between the second and third paragraphs.

3. Select Window ➤ Components. When the Components panel appears, open the User Interface components and drag a copy of the UIScrollBar component, shown in Figure 6-34, onto the text.

Figure 6-34. The UIScrollBar component is found in the User Interface components.

4. Depending on which side of the text field you chose, the component will spring to the closest side of the text field. Switch to the Selection tool and move it to the opposite side of the field. Now move it back to the right side of the field and release the mouse.

5. Save and test the movie. The component, shown in Figure 6-35, will change, and you can scroll the text up and down.

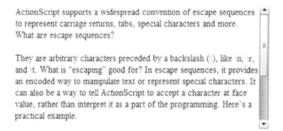

Figure 6-35. The UIScrollBar component in action

In this final exercise of the chapter, we are going to let you "wire up" a scroller using ActionScript. Just keep in mind there are several hundred ways of doing this, and the one we are creating is a very basic example of scroll buttons. In this example, we use two very simple button symbols as the scrollers, whereas other approaches may use movieclips. We use opacity to indicate when the scroll button is no longer active. Others may use different colors or even different shapes to indicate the same thing or when the mouse is pressed. This example moves the text up or down a short distance (one line) with each mouse press. Others may have the text move up or down until the mouse is released. Regardless, the text is scrolling, which is the point of this exercise. Let's get busy:

1. Open the `scrollingAS.fla` file. When the file opens you will see we have added the text field and the buttons to the stage. The text field has been given the instance name of output, and the buttons have the instance names of scrollUp and scrollDown.

2. Select the first frame of the Actions layer, open the Actions panel, and you will see we have provided you with the text.

3. Click in line 4 of the Script pane and enter the following code:

```
scrollUp.addEventListener(
  MouseEvent.MOUSE_UP,
  function():void {
    output.scrollV--;
    updateButtons();
  }
);

scrollDown.addEventListener(
  MouseEvent.MOUSE_UP,
  function():void {
    output.scrollV++;
    updateButtons();
  }
);
```

These two functions are how the text moves. The TextField.scrollV property moves the text up one line—scrollV--—or down one line—scrollV++—depending upon which button is clicked. The next step in the process is to add the opacity change when the button is clicked and to make sure the finger cursor no longer shows when the start or the end of the text block is reached. That is the purpose of the updateButtons() function.

> *This may seem like a lot of effort—and programming often is—but in this case, you're lucky. Text automatically stops scrolling up when the scrollV property is at 1 (same goes for the bottom end, vice versa), so you don't have to actually program the text field to stop scrolling when an end is encountered. Flash takes care of that for you. But it is a courtesy to hide the finger cursor by temporarily disabling the relevant button as necessary.*

6

4. Press Enter (PC) or Return (Mac) twice and enter the following code:

```
function updateButtons():void {
  if (output.scrollV == 1) {
    scrollUp.alpha = 0.5;
    scrollUp.enabled = false;
  } else {
    scrollUp.alpha = 1;
    scrollUp.enabled = true;
  }
  if (output.scrollV == output.maxScrollV) {
    scrollDown.alpha = 0.5;
    scrollDown.enabled = false;
  } else {
    scrollDown.alpha = 1;
    scrollDown.enabled = true;
  }
}

updateButtons();
```

As you can see, the scrollUp and scrollDown buttons additionally call a custom updateButtons() function.

This function examines the current value of scrollV against a couple of numbers to determine how to manipulate the scrollUp and scrollDown buttons. When the text is fully scrolled up, its scrollV value is 1, in which case alpha is reduced to half and enabled is set to false; otherwise, alpha is set to 1—in ActionScript 3.0 alpha values are a number between 0 and 1—and enabled with true. When text is fully scrolled down, scrollV will be the same value as that text field's maxScrollV value. The same procedure is practiced for that button.

The last line, updateButtons();, actually executes the function as declared in the preceding code, to update the buttons before they're pressed.

5. Close the Actions panel, and test the movie. The up button, shown in Figure 6-36, is grayed out (actually, its opacity is 50%) because it is at the top of the text block and the scrollV value is equal to 1. Notice how it turns dark when the down button is clicked. This is because the scrollV value is now greater than 1.

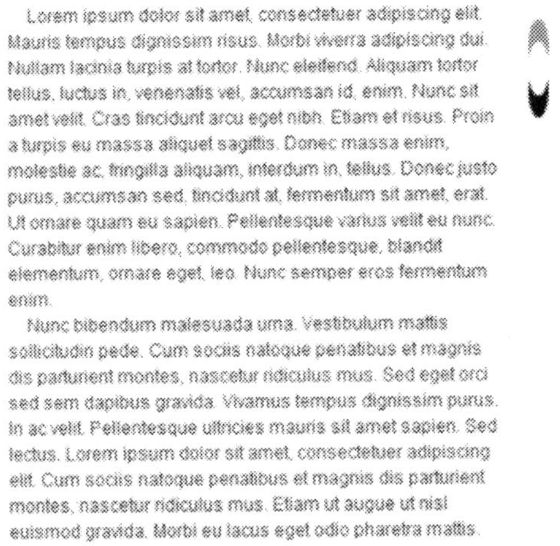

Lorem ipsum dolor sit amet, consectetuer adipiscing elit. Mauris tempus dignissim risus. Morbi viverra adipiscing dui. Nullam lacinia turpis at tortor. Nunc eleifend. Aliquam tortor tellus, luctus in, venenatis vel, accumsan id, enim. Nunc sit amet velit. Cras tincidunt arcu eget nibh. Etiam et risus. Proin a turpis eu massa aliquet sagittis. Donec massa enim, molestie ac, fringilla aliquam, interdum in, tellus. Donec justo purus, accumsan sed, tincidunt at, fermentum sit amet, erat. Ut ornare quam eu sapien. Pellentesque varius velit eu nunc. Curabitur enim libero, commodo pellentesque, blandit elementum, ornare eget, leo. Nunc semper eros fermentum enim.

Nunc bibendum malesuada urna. Vestibulum mattis sollicitudin pede. Cum sociis natoque penatibus et magnis dis parturient montes, nascetur ridiculus mus. Sed eget orci sed sem dapibus gravida. Vivamus tempus dignissim purus. In ac velit. Pellentesque ultricies mauris sit amet sapien. Sed lectus. Lorem ipsum dolor sit amet, consectetuer adipiscing elit. Cum sociis natoque penatibus et magnis dis parturient montes, nascetur ridiculus mus. Etiam ut augue ut nisl euismod gravida. Morbi eu lacus eget odio pharetra mattis.

Figure 6-36. A custom scrollbar

What you've learned

- How to add text to Flash
- The various text formatting features available to you in Flash CS3
- How to choose and work with static, dynamic, and input text fields
- How to put text in motion and manipulate many of its properties
- The ActionScript necessary to create, format, and provide interactivity through the use of text
- When to embed font outlines into a SWF and how to accomplish that task
- How to create scrolling text in Flash

We suspect you are more than a little confounded at the possibilities open to you when it comes to using text in Flash. If you are one of those who saw text as the gray stuff around animations, we hope you have seen the error of your ways. And, if you are one of those who want to get going and turn out really cool motion graphics pieces, we hope you paid close attention to what Bringhurst was saying in the quote that opened the chapter. Regardless of which camp you fall into, we know that you are now aware that adding text to a Flash CS3 animation doesn't stop with a click of the Text tool and the tapping of a few keys on the keyboard. Now that you know how to work with text and put it in motion, the time has arrived to put objects in motion. Animation in Flash is covered in the next chapter, and to find out more, turn the page.

7 ANIMATION IN FLASH CS3

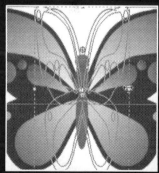

Ahh, animation! Where would we be without the likes of Disney, Warner Bros., Walter Lanz, Hanna-Barbera, and dozens more like them? For many people, animation is *the reason* to get involved with Flash as a creative outlet. This makes perfect sense, because Flash began life a full decade ago as an animation tool. Supplemental features like ActionScript, XML parsing, and video integration—every one a tremendous addition—all followed. What hasn't changed in all these years is Flash's ability to produce quality, scalable animation for the Web, and increasingly for television.

You caught the faintest whiff of tweening in Chapters 1, 2, and 3. It gets considerably more complex (read *considerably more fun!*), and because this chapter has a lot of moving parts, let's stop with the talking already and jump directly into the fray.

What we'll cover in this chapter:

- Shape tweening
- Shape hinting
- Motion tweening
- Easing
- Using the Custom Ease In/Ease Out editor
- Animating symbols
- Combining timelines
- Motion tween effects

Files used in this chapter:

- PepperShape.fla (Chapter07/ExerciseFiles_CH07/Exercise/PepperShape.fla)
- StarStar.fla (Chapter07/ExerciseFiles_CH07/Exercise/StarStar.fla)
- StarCircle.fla (Chapter07/ExerciseFiles_CH07/Exercise/StarCircle.fla)
- Ant.fla (Chapter07/ExerciseFiles_CH07/Exercise/Ant.fla)
- LogoMorphNoHints.fla (Chapter07/Exercise Files_CH07/Exercise/LogoMorphNoHints.fla)
- LogoMorph.fla (Chapter07/ExerciseFiles_CH07/Exercise/LogoMorph.fla)
- FlowerWeed.fla (Chapter07/ExerciseFiles_CH07/Exercise/FlowerWeed.fla)
- GradientTween1.fla (Chapter07/ExerciseFiles_CH07/Exercise/GradientTween1.fla)
- GradientTween2.fla (Chapter07/ExerciseFiles_CH07/Exercise/GradientTween2.fla)
- BitmapFillTween.fla (Chapter07/ExerciseFiles_CH07/Exercise/BitmapFillTween.fla)
- PepperSymbol.fla (Chapter07/ExerciseFiles_CH07/Exercise/PepperSymbol.fla)
- MalletNoEasing.fla (Chapter07/ExerciseFiles_CH07/Exercise/MalletNoEasing.fla)

- MalletCustomEasing.fla (Chapter07/ExerciseFiles_CH07/
  Exercise/MalletCustomEasing.fla)

- CustomEasingComparison.fla (Chapter07/ExerciseFiles_CH07/
  Exercise/CustomEasingComparison.fla)

- CustomEasingMultiple.fla (Chapter07/ExerciseFiles_CH07/
  Exercise/CustomEasingMultiple.fla)

- YawningParrot.fla (Chapter07/ExerciseFiles_CH07/
  Exercise/YawningParrot.fla)

- SyncPropertyGraphic.fla (Chapter07/ExerciseFiles_CH07/
  Exercise/SyncPropertyGraphic.fla)

- EditMultipleFrames.fla (Chapter07/ExerciseFiles_CH07/
  Exercise/EditMultipleFrames.fla)

- TimelineCombine.fla (Chapter07/ExerciseFiles_CH07/
  Exercise/TimelineCombine.fla)

- Grotto.fla (Chapter07/ExerciseFiles_CH07/Exercise/Grotto.fla)

- tronguy.png (Chapter07/ExerciseFiles_CH07/Exercise/tronguy.png)

- TronGuyGlow.fla (Chapter07/ExerciseFiles_CH07/
  Exercise/TronGuyGlow.fla)

- FadingParrot.fla (Chapter07/ExerciseFiles_CH07/
  Exercise/FadingParrot.fla)

- MotionGuide.fla (Chapter07/Exercise Files_CH07/Exercise/MotionGuide.fla)

- TweenMask.fla (Chapter07/ExerciseFiles_CH07/Exercise/TweenMask.fla)

- TweenMaskMotionGuide.fla (Chapter07/ExerciseFiles_CH07/
  Exercise/TweenMaskMotionGuide.fla)

- AnimatedButton.fla (Chapter07/ExerciseFiles_CH07/
  Exercise/AnimatedButton.fla)

- Zap.mp3 (Chapter07/ExerciseFiles_CH07/Exercise/Zap.mp3)

- CreateMotionAS3.fla (Chapter07/ExerciseFiles_CH07/
  Exercise/CreateMotionAS3.fla)

7

Shape tweening

As useful as symbols are, both in organizing artwork and reducing SWF file size, they shouldn't overshadow the importance of shapes. After all, unless a symbol is the result of text or an imported image file, chances are good it was constructed from one or more of Flash's most basic of visual entities: the shape.

Shapes differ significantly from symbols, though many of their features overlap. Like symbols, shapes are tweened on keyframes. Tweening may be finessed by something called easing, and can affect things like position, scale, distortion, color, and transparency. The difference comes in how these changes are achieved. In addition, shapes can do something symbols can't: they can actually morph from one set of contours to another!

Scaling and stretching

Let's start with the basics:

1. Open the `PepperShape.fla` file found in the `Chapter 7 Exercise` folder. You'll notice there's nothing in the library—this is because the hot pepper on the stage is composed entirely of shapes. Select Insert ➤ Timeline ➤ Keyframe to insert a keyframe at frame 10. This effectively produces a copy of the artwork from frame 1 in frame 10, and makes the copy available for manipulation. Any changes you make to frame 10 will not affect the shapes in frame 1, so you can always remove that second keyframe (Modify ➤ Timeline ➤ Clear Keyframe) and start again from scratch if you need to.

> *If you prefer, you can insert a blank keyframe at frame 10 (Insert ➤ Timelines ➤ Blank Keyframe), and then copy and paste the artwork from frame 1. It makes no practical difference, but clearly the first approach requires less effort. You may even draw completely new shapes into frame 10, and Flash will do its best to accommodate—but that's skipping ahead. More on that in the "Altering shapes" section.*

2. With frame 10 selected, choose the Free Transform tool and drag the right side of the pepper's bounding box to the right. As you do this, you'll see an outline preview of the shapes in their new stretched size, as shown in Figure 7-1.

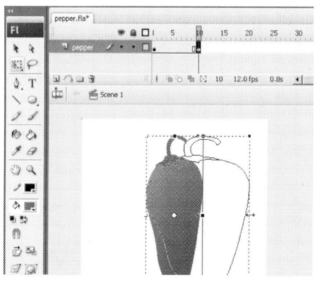

Figure 7-1. Changing a shape's shape in preparation for a shape tween

You might find that you have accidentally selected either only the pepper or only its cap. The Free Transform *tool's bounding box will let you know at a glance which shape you have selected, because it will either encompass the full surface area of the artwork or it won't. To ensure you've grabbed all the shapes, either use the* Selection *tool to first draw a marquee around the whole pepper or, even simpler, click the keyframe at frame 10, which selects everything on that layer in that keyframe.*

3. Select Edit ➤ Undo Scale to undo. This time, hold down the Alt (PC) or Option (Mac) key while dragging to the right. Notice how the artwork now scales out from the center. This feature often comes in handy, but it's important to understand what's really going on. When the Alt/Option key is used, it's not the center of the artwork that becomes the pivot, but rather the **transformation point**, as indicated by a small white circle. You can drag this circle where you like, even outside the confines of the shape's bounding box. With or without the Alt/Option key, the transformation point acts as the fulcrum of your modifications.

Because you're dealing with shapes, you can even use the Free Transform tool's Distort and Envelope options (shown in Figure 7-2). If you do, just be aware that things can quickly fall apart with such transformations unless you use shape hints (covered later in the chapter).

7

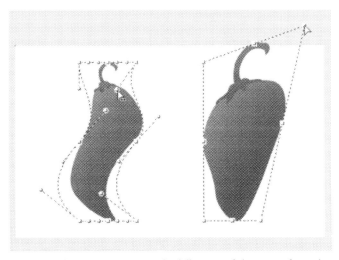

Figure 7-2. Shape tweens support the full gamut of shape transformations.

4. Now that you have two keyframes prepared, it's time for the magic. Click anywhere in the span of frames between both keyframes, and then select Shape from the Tween property in the Property inspector (see Figure 7-3). Two things will happen:

- The span of frames will turn green, which indicates a shape tween. They will also gain an arrow pointing to the right, which tells you that the tween was successful.

- The pepper will visually update to reflect a state between the artwork in either keyframe, depending on where the playhead is positioned.

Drag the playhead back and forth to watch the pepper seem to breathe.

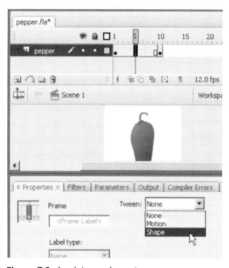

Figure 7-3. Applying a shape tween

If you applied the tween while in frame 1—a perfectly legal choice, by the way—you wouldn't immediately see the pepper change. Why? Because the tweening is applied between the two keyframes, and frame 1 still represents the artwork as it was before tweening was applied. Drag the playhead back and forth, and you'll see the tween.

What if the tweened frames don't turn green? By default, they will, but you may have experimented with your Timeline panel settings. Click in the panel's upper-right corner, just below the x, and ensure that Tinted Frames is selected in the context menu.

---

5. Select anywhere between the two keyframes and choose None as the Tween property setting. The tween goes away.

6. Let's purposefully make a mistake. This time, choose Motion as the Tween property. Motion tweening is not supported for shapes, and Flash gives you an unmistakable sign that you've gone wrong if you try to use it. Instead of green, the span of frames will become purple—the indication of motion tweens. More importantly, the arrow is now the broken line shown in Figure 7-4. Time to either undo or change the Tween property in the Property inspector.

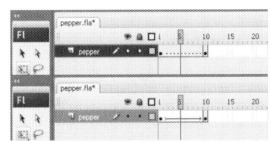

Figure 7-4. Erroneous tweens (top) are indicated by a broken line, while successful tweens (bottom) are indicated by a solid arrow.

7. Change the Tween property back to Shape. Select frame 10 and choose the Free Transform tool once again. Drag one of the bounding box corners to change both the horizontal and vertical scale. If you like, hold down Shift to constrain the aspect ratio, and Alt/Option to apply changes from the center of the transformation point. Make the pepper a good bit bigger than the original size. This shows that it's possible to adjust keyframes even after they're already part of a tween.

> *If you right-click (PC) or Ctrl-click (Mac) between any two keyframes, you'll see a* Create Shape Tween *choice in the context menu. This is new to Flash CS3 and is an alternate approach to applying a shape tween. This mechanism happens to be smart enough to avoid mistakes, so if you try to apply a shape tween to something that doesn't support shape tweens, it will simply ignore your attempt. If you open this context menu on an already shape-tweened span, you'll see a choice of* Remove Tween.

Shape tween modifiers

There are a couple ways to refine a shape tween once it's applied. These are shown in the Property inspector when you click in a tweened span of frames: Ease and Blend. We'll cover easing in greater detail in the "Motion tweening" section, but for now, here's the punch line: easing tends to make tweens look more lifelike because it gradually varies the amount of distance traveled between each frame.

If an astronaut throws a golf ball in outer space, the ball flies at a constant rate until . . . well, until it hits something. That's not how it works on a planet with gravity. The ball flies faster at first, and then gradually slows down. This deceleration is called **easing out**. A ball dropped from a tall building begins its descent slowly, and then gradually increases speed. This acceleration is called **easing in**. Adjust the Ease slider in the Property inspector to see how easing affects the shape tween applied to the pepper in the previous exercise. Supported values range from 100 (strong ease out), through 0 (no easing), to −100 (strong ease in). As shown in Figure 7-5, easing can have a profound effect upon an object in motion.

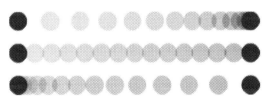

Figure 7-5. Examples of easing; from top to bottom: easing in, no easing, and easing out

289

Blend is a much subtler matter.

There are two blend settings: Distributive and Angular. According to Adobe, Distributive "creates an animation in which the intermediate shapes are smoother and more irregular," while Angular "creates an animation that preserves apparent corners and straight lines in the intermediate shapes." In actual practice, the authors find this distinction negligible, at best. In short, don't worry yourself over this setting. Use it or not, but we're willing to bet our hats that you won't be able to tell one from the other.

OK, so far, so good. These tweens have been pretty straightforward. In fact, as you'll find later in the chapter, everything you've seen to this point can be accomplished just as easily with motion tweens. This raises a good question: What makes shape tweens so special? Why not just use motion tweens?

The answer comes in two parts: gradients and shape. Let's tackle shape first, because it has the potential to set your teeth on edge if you aren't prepared for it.

Altering shapes

The compelling reason to use shape tweens is for their ability to manipulate the actual form of the artwork itself, beyond scaling and stretching. Let's keep playing:

1. Continuing with PepperShape.fla, use the Free Transform tool at frame 10 to rotate the pepper about 90 degrees in either direction.
2. You should still have a shape tween applied—if not, add one—and then drag the playhead back and forth to see a result that may surprise you. Rather than rotating, the pepper temporarily deforms itself as it changes from one keyframe to another (see Figure 7-6).

Figure 7-6. Sometimes shape tweens perform unexpected transformations.

What on earth is going on here? Though it may look like an absolute mess, what you are seeing is the key distinction between shape tweening and motion tweening. Believe it or not, this behavior can be a very useful thing. We'll see an example in just a moment. First, let's take a quick field trip to frame 10 in order to illustrate a point.

> *In case you're worried, we'll put your mind at ease without further ado: it is entirely possible to rotate artwork with tweens in Flash. In fact, it's easy. In contrast to shape tweens, motion tweens always maintain a strict marriage between one keyframe's anchor points and the next. We'll show you why later in the chapter. When you understand what each approach does best, you'll know which one to use for the task at hand.*

3. Choose the Subselection tool and click in frame 10 of the PepperShape.fla file. You'll see dozens of tiny squares that act as anchor points among the various lines and curves that make up the pepper's shape. All those points exist in frame 1 as well, of course, but they're in different positions relative to one another.

With shape tweens, Flash does not think of artwork in terms of a whole; instead, it manipulates each anchor point separately. What seems like a rotation to you is, to a shape tween, nothing more than a rearrangement of anchor points—sometimes a chaotic one, at that!

Think of it like a square dance. If a particular point happens to be in the upper-left corner on frame 1, it has no idea that its corresponding point may be in the upper-right corner on frame 10. It simply changes a partner—do-si-do!—and moves to a new spot during the tween. Like square dancing, there are sophisticated rules at play, and movement across the dance floor may appear unpredictable. It's possible, for example, that two keyframes may even present a completely different number of anchor points. Let's look at that next.

1. Open the StarStar.fla file from the exercise files for this chapter, and take note of the 22-point star in frame 1. Use the Subselection tool, if you like, to see the individual anchor points (there are 44). Click in frame 20 to see a 7-point star (14 anchor points). Note that a shape tween has already been applied between these two keyframes. Drag the playhead back and forth to watch the promenade (shown in Figure 7-7). Flash handles the reduction in anchor points in a neat, organized way. In this case, by the way, the star in the second keyframe was drawn as new artwork into frame 20.

Figure 7-7. The 44 anchor points artfully become 14.

2. Open the StarCircle.fla file and run through the same steps to see a 22-point star become an 8-point circle. These are some nifty transformations that are simply not possible with motion tweens.

This opens up a whole avenue of vector-morphing possibilities, from sunshine gleams to water ripples to waving hair and the antennae shown in Figure 7-8. For anything where you need the actual *shape* of an item to change—where anchor points themselves need to be rearranged—shape tweens are the way to go. Keep in mind that tweens happen on a keyframe basis, and timeline layers are distinct. If you have a complex set of shapes and you only wish to tween some of them, move those shapes to a separate layer. In fact, you may want to put every to-be-tweened shape on its own layer because that reduces the number of anchor points under consideration for each keyframe. Let's try it by setting some antennae in motion:

1. Open Ant.fla and insert a keyframe in frame 21 of the antenna2 layer.

2. Select the Subselection tool and change the shape of the antenna in the layer.

3. Add a shape tween between the keyframes and scrub through the timeline. The antennae move around (see Figure 7-8).

Figure 7-8. Need to change the shape of those antennae? Shape tweens to the rescue!

As we've seen, Flash can make some fairly stylish choices of its own in regard to the repositioning of anchor points. Well, most of the time. The earlier pepper rotation demonstrates that Flash's choices aren't always what you might expect. Fortunately, Flash provides a way to let you take control of shape tweens gone awry. The solution is something called shape hints.

Shape hints

What are shape hints? Though often overlooked and misunderstood, these useful contraptions allow you to specify a partnership between a region of your choosing from one keyframe to the next. They are a means by which you can guide an anchor point, curve, or line toward the destination you've determined is the right one. Let's take a look.

1. Open the LogoMorphNoHints.fla file from the samples for this chapter. Take a look at frame 1 to see a lowercase *i* that has been broken apart from a text field into two shapes. In frame 55, you'll see an abstract shape that represents a hypothetical logo. The aim here is to morph between the shapes in an appealing way, but something has gone horribly wrong (see Figure 7-9). Drag the playhead along the timeline and note the atrocities committed between frames 20 and 35.

Figure 7-9. Something has gone horribly wrong.

This looks as bad as (if not worse than) the hot pepper rotation . . . but why? On the face of it, this should be a basic shape tween. Seemingly, the letter and logo shapes aren't especially intricate, and yet . . . the timeline doesn't lie.

> At this point, the authors look deftly side to side, and with a sly, "Hey, pssst," invite you to step with them into a small, dimly lit alley. (Don't worry, we're here to help.) "The thing is," begins the first, "honestly, there's often a bit of voodoo involved with shape tweens, and that's the truth." "That's right," chimes in the other, lowering his voice. "To be frank, if I may"—you nod—"we don't know why these anchor points sometimes go kablooey. It's just a thing, and you have to roll with it." There is a slight pause, and suddenly a cappuccino machine splooshes in the distance. The first author draws a finger across his nose. "Keep that in mind as we continue," he says. Another pause. "You wanna see the shape hints?" You nod again.

2. Click in frame 20, and select Modify ➤ Shape ➤ Add Shape Hint (see Figure 7-10). This puts a small red circle with the letter *a* in the center of your artwork. Meet your first shape hint.

7

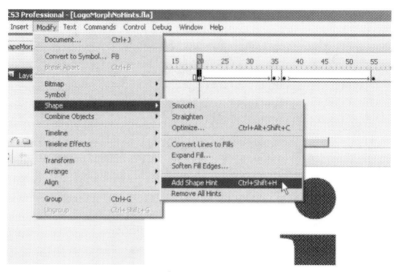

Figure 7-10. Inserting a shape hint

3. Make sure object snapping is on, either by selecting Snap to Objects in the Tools panel or ensuring that a check mark is present under View ➤ Snapping ➤ Snap to Objects. Snapping significantly helps the placement of shape hints. Drag and snap the a circle to the lower-left corner of the letter's upper serif, as shown in Figure 7-11.

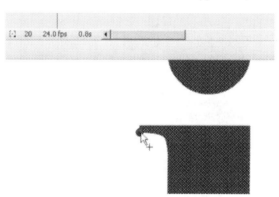

Figure 7-11. Positioning a shape hint

4. This next point is important: what you've done is placed *one half* of a shape hint *pair*. The other half—the partner—is on the next keyframe, frame 35. Drag the playhead to this frame and position the second a circle on the corresponding serif on this keyframe's shape, as shown in Figure 7-12.

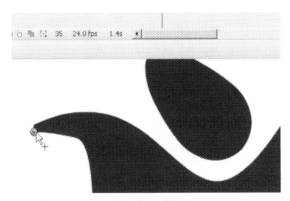

Figure 7-12. Positioning the shape hint's partner

5. When this partner snaps into place, it will turn green. Return to frame 20 and notice that the original shape hint has turned yellow. It may be that shape hints have a thing for stoplights (not that there's anything wrong with that), but the point is that the color change indicates something. It tells you that this shape hint pair has entered into a relationship. You have now indicated to Flash your intention that these paired regions correspond.

6. Slide the playhead along the timeline again, and you'll see a remarkable improvement (as shown in Figure 7-13). So remarkable, in fact, that the authors look deftly side to side, wink, and silently mouth the word *voodoo*. To be frank, if we may, the placement of shape hints often makes a noticeable difference, but the decision on placement is something of a dark art. We encourage you to reposition your first shape hint pair at other corners to see how the remaining trouble spots ripple to other areas.

Figure 7-13. A dramatic improvement, but there are still a few trouble spots

7. You should get the idea by now that shape hints are a bit like cloves (you know, the star-shaped things you poke into your ham during the holidays)—a little goes a long way. Let's add a few more, but do so sparingly. To get rid of the kink in the upper curve, add a new shape hint to the upper-right corner of the i on frame 20. This time, you'll see a small b in a red circle. Snap its b partner to the upper-right corner of the logo at frame 35, and drag the playhead again to see your progress.

8. Add shape hints c and d to the lower-left and right corners, and you should see a very smooth morph along this span of frames. The only thing remaining, if you're a perfectionist, is a slight wrinkle along the bottom of the "egg" between keyframes 37 and 55. Remedy this by adding a new shape at frame 37—it will start again at a, because this is a new pair of keyframes—and snap it in place to the corresponding curve at frame 55.

295

Compare your work with the LogoMorph.fla file, if you like. When you open a file that already contains shape hints, you'll need to take one small step to make them show, as they like to hide by default. To toggle shapes hints on and off, select View ➤ Show Shape Hints.

Even with the benefit of shape hints, we caution you to keep simplicity in mind. Certain collections of shapes are simply too intricate to handle gracefully. It is entirely possible to choke Flash through the use of an overwhelming number of anchor points, as shown in Figure 7-14.

1. Open the FlowerWeed.fla file and drag the playhead along the timeline. The morph isn't especially polished, but it certainly doesn't count as a complete eyesore.

2. Test the SWF (Control ➤ Test Movie), and you'll see that playback slows nearly to a halt as the tweening progresses. No amount of shape hinting can fix that.

Figure 7-14. Moderation in all things! While this transformation doesn't look awful, it nearly chokes Flash Player.

Altering gradients

If you want to animate gradients, shape tweens are the only way to do it. You may not immediately think of gradients as shapes, but when you select the Gradient Transform tool and click into a gradient, what do you see? You see the handles and points shown in Figure 7-15.

That center point, to Flash, is not much different from an anchor point. The resize, radius, and rotate handles are not much different from Bezier control point handles. In effect, you are manipulating a shape—just a special kind. When animating a gradient, you simply change these gradient-specific features from keyframe to keyframe, rather than a shape's corners, lines, and curves.

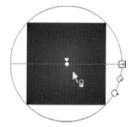

Figure 7-15. Gradients, like anything else, can be edited on keyframes, and those keyframes are tweenable.

1. Open the GradientTween1.fla file and drag the playhead along the timeline to see an example in action. Frame 1 contains a solid red fill. Frame 10 contains the built-in rainbow gradient, which is rotated 90 degrees in frame 20.

Frames 20 through 30 provide a bit of interest because they spell out a limitation of gradient shape tweens: it is not possible to tween one type of gradient to another. Well, we take that back. You certainly can, but the results are unpredictable. Flash tries its best to convert a linear gradient into a radial one, but between frames 29 and 30, the gradient pops from one type to the other.

2. Open the GradientTween2.fla file. This example shows a combination of gradient and shape change at the same time. Not only does the gradient fill transform, but anchor points move, and even stroke color (and thickness!) changes from keyframe to keyframe.

3. Experiment with solid colors as well as the Color panel's Alpha property. When you finish, close the file without saving the changes.

4. Even bitmap fills are tweenable, which, as shown in Figure 7-16, makes for some interesting visual possibilities. Open the BitmapFillTween.fla file and press the Enter/Return key. As with other types of gradients, use the Gradient Transform tool to manipulate gradient control handles at each keyframe, and then let the shape tween handle the rest. Easing works the same way.

Figure 7-16. Shape tween your bitmap fill transformations for some real zing!

Motion tweening

When we left that hapless hot pepper hanging, it had been hoping to rotate. It didn't, and instead found its molecules tumbling in a frenzied jumble. We told you there was a much easier way to handle that rotation, and motion tweening is it. Shape tweens are for rearranging anchor points and animating gradients; motion tweens are for everything else, from enlivening text and imported photos to animating vector artwork drawn directly in Flash or imported from another application like Illustrator CS3 or Fireworks CS3.

In contrast to shape tweens, motion tweens require self-contained entities. These include symbols, primitives, drawing objects, and grouped elements, which many designers find easier to work with than raw shapes. Open PepperSymbol.fla, for example, and you'll see that it's easier to select the whole pepper without accidentally omitting the cap.

Be aware that primitives and drawing objects blur the lines somewhat between what constitutes a shape and what constitutes a symbol. It is possible to apply both shape tweens and motion tweens to primitives and drawing objects, but many properties such as color, alpha, and the like—and in primitives, shape—are only properly animated with shape tweens. These "gotchas" tend to steer the authors toward a path of least resistance: use shapes for shape tweens and symbols for motion tweens. Within those symbols, use whatever elements you like.

One fundamental point: When it comes to motion tweens, always put each tweened symbol on its own layer. If you apply a motion tween to keyframes that contain more than one symbol, Flash will try to oblige—but will fail. It's a simple rule, so abide by it and you'll be happy.

Rotation

Let's pick up with that rotation, shall we?

1. Open the `PepperSymbol.fla` file. This time, you'll see a pepper symbol in the library because the shapes from the earlier `PepperShape.fla` have been placed inside a graphic symbol. Add a keyframe in frame 10. Select the Free Transform tool and rotate the artwork 90 degrees in either direction on that second keyframe. Sounds familiar, right? Here comes the difference.

2. Select Motion from the Tween property in the Property inspector. There it is! Drag the playhead back and forth to see a nice, clean rotation of the pepper. As you saw with shape tweens, the span of frames between the two keyframes changes color—this time, as shown in Figure 7-17, to purple—and a solid arrow appears within the span to indicate a successful tween.

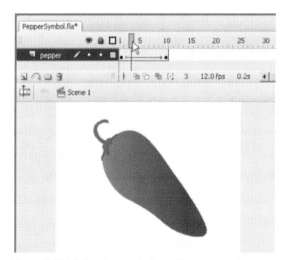

Figure 7-17. Motion tweens, indicated by an arrow between the keyframes, make rotations a snap.

3. Change the Tween property to Shape and the span of frames turns green, the color of shape tweens—but the solid arrow becomes a dashed line, indicating a failed tween. Change the Tween back to Motion and everything's right with the world.

4. Now, let's think about *real* rotation; topsy-turvy; a full 360 degree spin. How would you do it? (Hint: This is something of a trick question.) In a full spin, the pepper ends up in the same position at frame 10 as it starts with in frame 1, so there's not really a transformation to tween. Enter the Rotate drop-down menu in the Property inspector.

Figure 7-18. The Rotate property makes quick work of rotations.

Notice that the Rotate setting is currently Auto. This is because you have already rotated the pepper somewhat by hand. Click the pepper in frame 10 and select Modify ➤ Transform ➤ Remove Transform to reset the symbol's rotation. In the Rotate drop-down menu, change the setting to CW (clockwise), as shown in Figure 7-18, and drag the playhead back and forth. Pretty neat! CCW (counterclockwise) rotates the tweened symbol in the opposite direction, and the text field immediately to the right specifies how many times to perform the rotation.

Motion tween properties

While we're looking at the Property inspector, let's go through the other settings. Here's a quick overview of motion tween properties:

- Tween: This one should already be familiar. The choices are None, Motion, and Shape.

- Scale: If a check mark is present, tweening for the current span of frames will include a transformation in scale (size), *if such a transformation exists*. If you haven't scaled anything, it doesn't matter what state the check mark is in. If scaling and other transformations are combined in a given tween, only the other transformations will show if the check mark is vacant.

- Ease **and** Edit: These settings apply a range of easing to the tween. The Edit button allows for advanced, custom easing. More on this in the "Easing" section of this chapter.

- Rotate**, [number of]** times**, and** Orient to path: These settings control the type of rotation and the number of times the rotation occurs. Only CW and CCW support the [number of] times setting. The Orient to path setting only applies to tweens along a motion guide (discussed later in the chapter).

- Sync: In our experience, most people don't even realize this property exists, but it can be a real time saver when you're dealing with graphic symbols. Unlike movie clips, which have their own independent timelines, graphic symbols are synchronized with the timeline in which they reside. Even so, there is a bit of flexibility: graphics can be looped, played through once, or instructed to rest on a specified frame of their own timeline. If a particular graphic symbol has been tweened numerous times in a layer, the presence of the Sync check mark means you can update these timeline options for all keyframes in that layer simply by making changes to the first graphic symbol in the sequence. In addition, Sync allows you to swap one graphic symbol for another and have that change ripple through all the synced keyframes in that layer.

- Snap: This option helps position a symbol along its motion guide (motion guides are discussed later in the chapter).

299

Scaling, stretching, and deforming

We visited this topic in the "Shape tweening" section, and honestly, there's not a whole lot different for motion tweens. The key thing to realize is that scaling, stretching, and deforming a symbol is like doing the same to a T-shirt with artwork printed on it. Even if the artwork looks different after all the tugging and twisting, it hasn't actually changed. Shake it out, and it's still the same picture. Shape tweening, in contrast, is like rearranging the tiles in a mosaic. For this reason, the Free Transform tool disables the Distort and Envelope options for symbols. These can't be performed on symbols and therefore can't be motion-tweened. Let's take a quick look at the other options:

1. Return to the PepperSymbol.fla file and set the Rotation setting for the tween to None. Use the Free Transform tool to perform a shear transformation at frame 10. Shear? What's that? Something you do with sheep, right? Well, yes, but in Flash, shearing is also called skewing, which can be described as tilting. With the Free Transform tool active, click the Rotate and Skew option, and then hover over one of the side transform handles (not the corners) until the cursor becomes an opposing double-arrow icon. Click and drag to transform the pepper (see Figure 7-19).

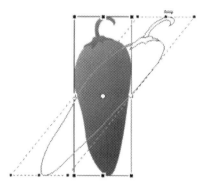

Figure 7-19. Motion tweening a symbol transformation

The outline preview gives you an idea what the symbol will look like before you let go of the mouse. Note that the skew occurs in relation to the transformation point, indicated by the small white circle. Drag this white circle around inside or even outside the bounding box of the pepper and skew again to see how its placement affects the transformation. Hold down Alt while skewing to temporarily ignore the transformation point and skew in relation to the symbol's opposite edge.

2. We've been using the Free Transform tool quite a bit, so let's try something different. Open the Transform panel (Window ➤ Transform) and note its current settings. You'll see the skew summarized near the bottom and, interestingly, the change in scale summarized near the top (see Figure 7-20).

From this, it becomes clear that skewing affects scale when applied with the Free Transform tool. To see the difference, select Modify ➤ Transform ➤ Remove Transform to reset the symbol. The scale area of the Transform panel returns to 100% horizontal and 100% vertical. Click the Skew radio button and type 38 into either one (but only one) of the skew input fields. Press Enter/Return to apply the change. Now enter 200 into the scale input fields at the top (the Constrain check mark means you only have to enter this number into one of them), and again press Enter/Return to apply the change. Slide the playhead back and forth to see two transformations tweened at once.

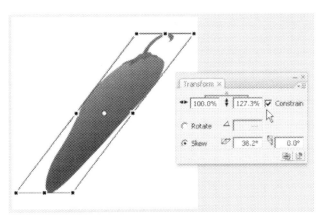

Figure 7-20. The Transform panel provides access to precision measurements.

Easing

Here's where motion tweening begins to pull ahead of shape tweening. Easing is much more powerful for motion tweens, thanks to the Custom Ease In/Ease Out editor. Before we delve into that, though, let's look at a sample use of the standard easing controls for a motion tween, so you can see how much easier things are with the custom variety.

1. Open the MalletNoEasing.fla file. You'll see a hammer graphic symbol in the library and an instance of that symbol on the stage. Select the hammer and note that the transformation point—the white dot in the handle—is located in the center of the symbol.

We're going to make this hammer swing to the left, so select the Free Transform tool. Selecting this tool makes the transformation point selectable. Click and drag that point to the bottom center of the mallet (see Figure 7-21).

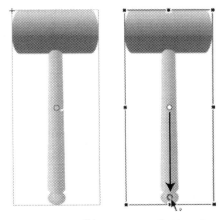

Figure 7-21. You'll have to move that transformation point to make the movement realistic.

7

301

2. Insert a keyframe at frame 10 (Insert ➤ Timeline ➤ Keyframe), and rotate the mallet at frame 10 to the left by 90 degrees. Apply a motion tween to the span of frames between 1 and 10, and scrub the timeline to see the effect. Not bad, but not especially realistic. How about some easing and bounce-back?

3. Drag the Ease slider all the way down to supply an ease of –100 (full ease in) to the tween, as shown in Figure 7-22.

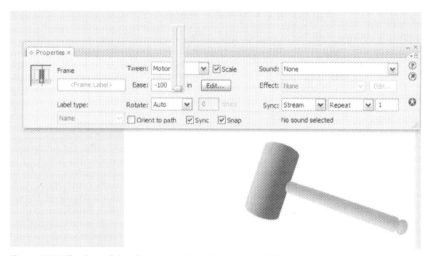

Figure 7-22. The Ease slider determines how the hammer falls.

This means that the hammer falls slowly as it begins to tip and increases speed as it continues to fall (see Figure 7-23).

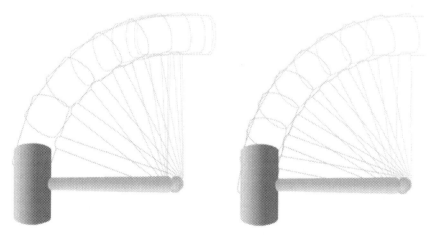

Figure 7-23. Ease in (left) vs. no easing (right). On the left, the hammer falls in a more natural manner.

4. This is a good start. To push the realism further, let's embellish the animation. Add new keyframes at frames 15, 20, 23, and 25. We're going to provide some tweening that makes the hammer rebound on impact and bounce a few times. At frame 15, use the Free Transform tool or the Transform panel to rotate the hammer to approximately northeast; in the Transform panel, this could be something like –55 in the Rotate area. At frame 23, set the rotation to roughly east-northeast (something like –80 in the Transform panel). A storyboard version of the sequence might look like Figure 7-24.

Figure 7-24. Using several keyframes to make the hammer bounce.

> The fading image trails—visual echoes of the mallet—are the result of something called onion skinning—very helpful in animation work. It's used here for illustrative purposes and is covered later in the chapter.

5. Now that the mallet has been positioned, it just needs to be tweened and eased. You can either click separately into each span of frames and apply a motion tween, or click and drag across as many spans as you need (as shown in Figure 7-25). That way you can apply the tweens all in one swoop.

Figure 7-25. Tweens can be applied to more than one frame span at a time.

6. Finally, click into each span of frames to apply easing, for the final touch. Span 1 to 10 already has –100. Apply the following easing to the remaining spans:

- **Span 10 to 15**: 100 (full ease out)
- **Span 15 to 20**: –100 (full ease in)
- **Span 20 to 23**: 100
- **Span 23 to 25**: –100

Drag the playhead back and forth to preview the action, and then test the movie to see the final presentation. If you like, compare your work with MalletNormalEase.fla. This exercise wasn't especially hard, but wouldn't it be even cooler if you could perform all of the above with a single motion tween?

7

Custom easing

Introduced in Flash 8, the Custom Ease In/Ease Out dialog box unleashes considerably more power than traditional easing. Not only does it provide a combined ease in/out—where animation gradually speeds up *and* gradually slows down, or vice versa—it supports multiple varied settings for various kinds of easing, all within the same tween. Let's take a look.

To perform custom easing, you have to first open the Custom Ease In/East Out dialog box. To get to the dialog box, select a span of motion-tweened frames, and then click the Edit button in the Property inspector. The result is a graph with time in frames along the horizontal axis and percentage of change along the vertical axis (shown in Figure 7-26).

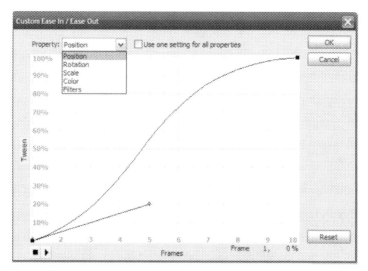

Figure 7-26. The Custom Ease In/Ease Out dialog box

Here's a quick rundown of the various areas of the dialog box:

- Property: By default, this is disabled until you deselect the check mark next to it. If the check mark is present, custom easing—as specified by you on the grid—applies to all aspects of the tween symbol. If the check mark is absent, this drop-down menu lets you distinguish among Position, Rotation, Scale, Color, and Filters.

- Use one setting for all properties: When checked, this allows multiple properties to be eased individually.

- Grid: The Bezier curves on this grid determine the visual result of the custom easing applied.

- Preview: Click the two buttons in this area to play and stop a preview of the custom easing.

- OK, Cancel, **and** Reset: The OK and Cancel buttons apply and discard any custom easing. Reset reverts the Bezier curves to a straight line (no easing) between the grid's opposite corners.

So, how does the grid work? Let's look at a traditional ease in to see how the Custom Ease In/Ease Out dialog box interprets it.

1. Open CustomEasingComparison.fla and set the Ease property to –100 (a normal full ease in) for the tween in the top layer. Scrub the timeline to confirm that the upper symbol starts its tween more slowly than the lower one, but speeds up near the end. The lower symbol, in contrast, should advance the same distance each frame (see Figure 7-27).

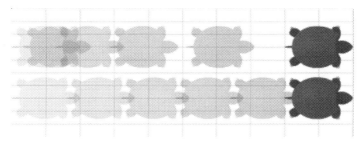

Figure 7-27. An ease in causes the upper symbol to start slower and speed up.

2. Click the Edit button to see what an ease out looks like on the grid. The curve climbs the vertical axis (percentage of change) rather slowly, and then speeds its ascent near the end of the horizontal axis (time in frames). Hey, that makes sense! Click Cancel, apply a full ease out (100), and then check the grid again . . . bingo, the opposite curve.

3. It follows that a combination of these would produce either a custom ease in/out (slow, fast, slow) or a custom ease out/in (fast, slow, fast). Let's do the first of those two. Click the upper-right black square in the grid to make its control handle appear. Drag it up to the top of the grid and about two-thirds across to the left, as shown in Figure 7-28.

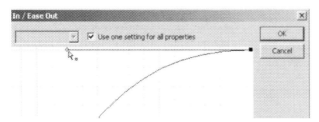

Figure 7-28. Dragging a control handle to create a custom ease

305

4. Click the bottom-left black square and drag its control handle two-thirds across to the right. The resulting curve—vaguely an *S* shape—effectively combines the curves you saw for ease in and ease out (see Figure 7-29).

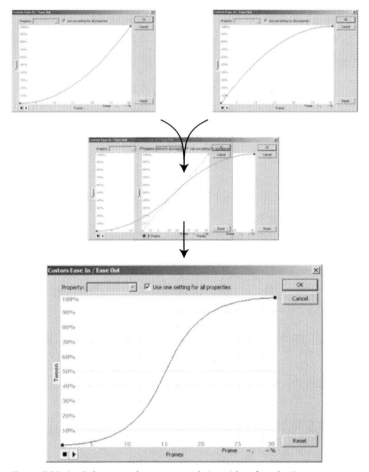

Figure 7-29. An *S* shape produces an ease in/out (slow-fast-slow) tween.

5. Click OK to accept this setting, and scrub the timeline or test the movie to see the results.

6. Let's inverse this easing for the lower symbol. Select the lower span of frames and click the Edit button. This time, drag the lower-left control handle two-thirds up the left side. Drag the upper-right control handle two-thirds down the right side to create the inverted *S* curve shown in Figure 7-30. Click OK and compare the two tweens.

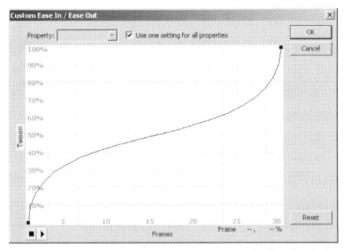

Figure 7-30. An inverted *S* shape produces an ease out/in (fast-slow-fast) tween.

Think this is cool? We're just getting started! By clicking anywhere along the Bezier curve, you can add new anchor points. This is where you can actually save yourself a bit of work.

7

1. Open `MalletNoEasing.fla` again. If you saved your work earlier, remove the tween and delete all frames except for frame 1. Use the mouse to click and drag from frame 2 to the right until you've selected them all, and then use Edit ➤ Timeline ➤ Remove Frames. Confirm that the mallet's transformation point is positioned at the bottom center of its wooden handle. Now add a new keyframe at frame 25 and apply a motion tween to the span of frames between 1 and 25.

2. Using the Free Transform tool at frame 25, rotate the mallet 90 degrees to the left. This may seem like déjà vu, but things are about to change. Because a tween is already applied, you can preview the falling mallet by scrubbing the timeline. Click in the tweened span of frames and click the Edit button in the Property inspector. We're going to emulate the same bounce-back tween we did earlier, but this time we're going to do it all in one custom ease.

3. When the Custom Ease In/Ease Out dialog box opens, click the Bezier curve near the middle and you'll see a new anchor point with control handles. Hold down Shift and click that new anchor point—it disappears. Add it again and straighten the control handles so that they're horizontal (as shown in Figure 7-31).

4. Repeat this process three more times, up the hill, as shown in Figure 7-32. This prepares the way for the sawtooth shape you'll create in the next step.

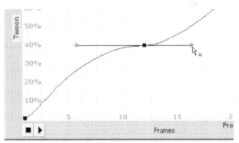

Figure 7-31. Starting a more complex custom ease

307

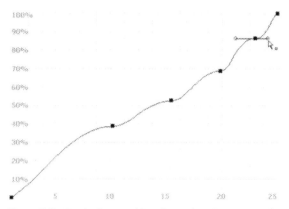

Figure 7-32. Continuing to add anchor points for a sawtooth curve

5. Leave the corner anchor points where they are. Position the four new anchor points as follows:

- 100%, 10
- 100%, 20
- 60%, 15
- 85%, 23

> *You'll notice that the anchor points gently snap to the grid while you drag. To temporarily suppress this snapping, hold down the X key.*

6. You've probably heard of certain procedures described as more of an art than a science . . . well, we've come to that point in this step. Here's the basic idea, but it's up to you to tweak these settings until they feel right to you. To achieve the sawtooth curve we're after—it looks very much like the series of shark fins shown in Figure 7-33—click each anchor point in turn and perform the following adjustment:

- If it has a left control handle, drag that handle in toward the anchor point.
- If it has a right control handle, drag that handle out a couple of squares to the right.

You should get something like the shape shown in Figure 7-33.

7. Click the Preview play button to test your custom ease. It should look similar to the original series of mallet bounce-back tweens, only now you've saved yourself a handful of keyframes. How does this work? As depicted in the grid, and following the horizontal axis, you have an ease-in curve from frames 0 to 10, an ease-out curve from 10 to 15, an ease-in curve from 15 to 20, and so on—just like your series of keyframes from earlier in the chapter. The mallet moves from its upright position to its leaned-over position in the very first curve. From frames 10 to 15, the vertical axis goes from 100% down to 60%, which means that the mallet actually rotates clockwise again toward its original orientation, but not all the way. With each new curve, the hammer falls again to the left, and then raises again, but never as high. Compare your work with MalletCustomEasing.fla.

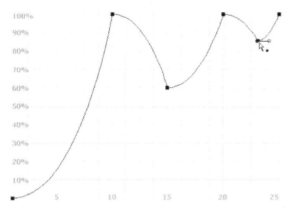

Figure 7-33. Shark fins produce a bounce-back effect.

On the final leg of our custom easing expedition, let's pull out all the stops and examine a tween that updates multiple symbol properties at once. You'll be familiar with most of what you're about to see, and the new parts will be easy to pick up.

1. Open the `CustomEasingMultiple.fla` file. Select frame 1 and note that a movieclip symbol appears in the upper-left corner of the stage. It is solid green. Select frame 55 and note the changes. At this point, the apple is positioned in the center of the stage, much larger, more naturally colored, and has a drop shadow (see Figure 7-34).

   From this, we can surmise that color and filters are tweenable—that's the new part—and in fact, they are. In frame 1, select the apple symbol itself to see that a Tint has been applied in the Property inspector, which is replaced by None in the other keyframe. Likewise, select the Filters tab at frame 55 and click the apple to see that a drop shadow has been applied that is not present in frame 1. These properties are no different from position and scale as far as tweens are concerned.

Figure 7-34. You are about to discover that it isn't only rotation that can be tweened.

2. Click into the span of tweened frames and note that a CW (clockwise) rotation has been specified for Rotation. The Tween type is Motion, and Scale is enabled (without it, the apple wouldn't gradually increase in size). The Ease property reads ---, which means custom easing has been applied. That's what we're after. Click the Edit button.

3. Thanks to the empty Use one setting for all properties check box, the Property drop-down menu is now available. Use the drop-down menu to look at the grid curve for each of five properties, all of which are depicted in the tween: Position, Rotation, Scale, Color, and Filters. Each curve has its own distinct curve, which translates into five individual custom ease settings for their respective properties (see Figure 7-35).

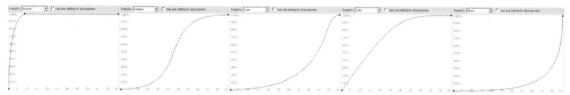

Figure 7-35. The Custom Ease In/Ease Out dialog box lets you specify distinct easing for five different tweenable properties.

Click the check box to disable the drop-down menu. Ack! Have you lost your custom settings? Thankfully, no. Flash remembers them for you, even though they're hiding. Click the Preview play button to preview the tween with no easing (the default lower-left to upper-right curve). Click the check box again to see that the custom ease settings are still intact. Preview the tween again, if you like.

Using animation

To this point, we've shown you a hefty animation toolbox. We've opened it up and pulled out a number of powerful tools to show you how they work. In doing so, we've covered quite a bit of ground, but there are still a handful of useful features and general workflow practices to help bring it all together. Let's roll up our sleeves, then, shall we?

A closer look at the Timeline panel

Whether you use shape or motion tweens, the Timeline panel gives you a pint-sized but important dashboard to take advantage of while you work. Don't let its small size fool you. This strip (shown in Figure 7-36) along the bottom of the timeline lets you quickly find your bearings, gives you at-a-glance detail on where you are, and even lets you time travel to see where you've been—into both the past and the future.

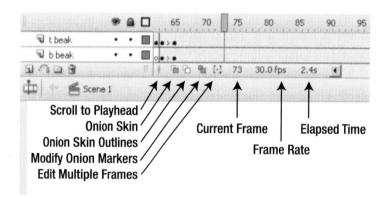

Figure 7-36. The bottom edge of the timeline provides a collection of useful tools.

"OK, guys," you may be thinking, "Time travel? Explain that one." We will, but first let's take an inventory of this useful, if small, real estate.

- Scroll to Playhead: In timelines that are long enough to scroll, this button centers the timeline on the playhead.

- Onion Skin **and** Onion Skin Outlines: These toggle two different kinds of onion skinning, which give you a "time machine" view of your work.

- Modify Onion Markers: Click this and you get a drop-down menu that controls the functionality of the onion skin buttons.

- Edit Multiple Frames: This allows you to select more than one keyframe at the same time, in order to edit many frames in one swoop.

- Current Frame: This indicates the current location of the playhead.

- Frame Rate: This indicates the movie's frame rate. Double-click this setting to change it.

- Elapsed Time: Given the current frame and the movie's frame rate, this indicates the duration in seconds of the playhead's position. For example, in a movie with a frame rate of 24 fps, this area will say 1.0s at frame 24.

Onion skinning

Traditional animators—the people who brought us the Mickey Mouse and Bugs Bunny cartoons we all grew up on—often drew their artwork on very thin paper over illuminated surfaces called lightboxes. This "onion skin" paper allowed them to see through the current drawing to what had gone on in the previous frames. In this way, they could make more informed choices on how far to move someone's head . . . or the anvil about to fall on it.

Flash offers you the same benefit, but with much more flexibility. In Flash, you can choose to see through as many frames as you like—backward and even forward—in solids or in outlines.

1. Open the YawningParrot.fla file that accompanies this chapter. Note that the movie's frame rate is 30 fps. Drag the playhead to frame 15, just as the bird begins to lower its head, and confirm that the Elapsed Time indicator reads 0.5s (see Figure 7-37). This makes sense: 15 divided by 30 is 0.5. Double-click the Frame Rate indicator to open the Document Properties dialog box. Change the movie's frame rate to 60 fps and click OK. Note that the elapsed time is 0.2 seconds (still good: 15 divided by 60 is 0.2—if you don't round up). One last observation: Change the frame rate to 15 fps and check the Elapsed Time indicator. You were probably expecting 1.0s, but the answer is a very close 0.9s. Why the discrepancy? We aren't sure, but it is close enough to the original value to satisfy us. Change back to the original 30 fps.

7

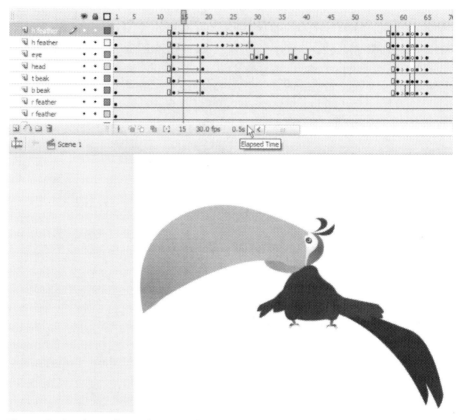

Figure 7-37. Another really good reason this is called the timeline

2. Drag the playhead to the right far enough that the timeline starts to scroll a bit, and then leave the playhead where it is. Use the timeline's scrollbar to scroll back to the left, which hides the playhead. To quickly bring it back, click the Scroll to Playhead button, which centers the timeline on the current frame. This is a good "you are here" panic button that's useful for especially long timelines.

3. Position the playhead at frame 125 and click the Modify Onion Markers button. Choose Onion 5 from the drop-down menu. This positions two new markers on either side of the playhead, as shown in Figure 7-38.

Figure 7-38.
Onion skinning adds two markers on either side of the playhead.

These markers extend five frames back and forward from the current position, which explains the name of the Onion 5 setting. What they show are semitransparent views of those frames fading as they get farther from the playhead—just like artwork on thin paper! Not only do they let you see back in time at previous frames, they also show artwork on future frames, which provides practical sequential context for any moment in time. In this case, you're seeing 11 "sheets"; the one under the playhead (which is the darkest), and then five ahead and behind.

4. Click Modify Onion Markers again and choose Onion 2, as shown in Figure 7-39. This reduces your view to five "sheets." Drag the playhead slowly to frame 170 and back. Notice that the onion markers move with you.

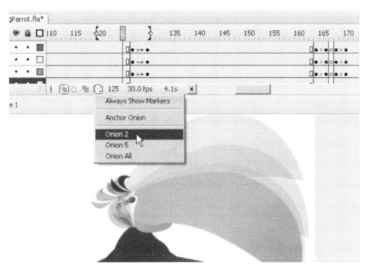

Figure 7-39. Various onion skin settings

5. What are the other onion modifiers? Onion All spreads the onion markers along the whole timeline. Try it with this file—the result is overwhelming (and also makes it hard to drag the playhead around), but with timelines of little movement, it probably has its place. If you want some setting besides 2, 5, or All, drag the markers along the timeline yourself. If you like, you can look eight frames back and two frames forward—or any combination that suits your animation.

The top two choices work like this: Always Show Markers keeps the onion markers visible, even if you toggle the Onion Skin button off; and Anchor Onion keeps the onion markers from following the playhead.

6. Choose Onion 5 and drag the playhead to frame 15. Click the Onion Skin Outlines button. Note that the same sort of onion skinning occurs, but that the tweened areas are shown in wireframe format (see Figure 7-40). This makes it even clearer to see what's moving and what isn't.

7

313

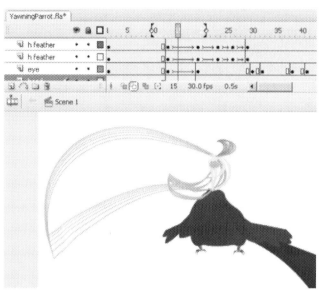

Figure 7-40. Onion skin outlines show tweened artwork in a wireframe format.

Remember, onion skinning is just as relevant to shape tweens as it is to motion tweens.

Editing multiple frames

Timeline animation can be painstaking work, no doubt about it. Even if you're using onion skinning, chances are good that you're focused on only a handful of frames at a time. There's nothing wrong with that—as long as you remember to keep your eye on the big picture, too. Sooner or later, it happens to everyone: artwork is replaced, your manager changes her mind, or you find that you've simply painted yourself into a corner and need to revise multiple keyframes—maybe hundreds—in as few moves as possible.

Fortunately, the timeline has a button called Edit Multiple Frames, which allows you to do just what it describes. That's the obvious answer, of course, and we'll cover that in just a moment, but it's worth noting that the concept of mass editing in Flash extends into other avenues.

Due to the nature of symbols, for example, you can edit a library asset and benefit from an immediate change throughout the movie, even if individual instances of that symbol have been stretched, scaled, rotated, and manipulated in other ways. If an imported graphic file, such as a BMP, has been revised outside of Flash, right-click (PC) or Ctrl-click (Mac) the asset in the library and, from the context menu, select either Update (if the location of the external image hasn't changed) or Properties, and then click the Import button to reimport the image or import another one.

Sometimes it's not that easy. Sometimes you will have finished three days of meticulous keyframing only to learn that the symbol you've tweened isn't supposed to be *that* symbol at all. Time to throw in the towel? Well, maybe time to roll the towel into a whip. But even here, there's hope . . . if you're using graphic symbols. It's easy enough to swap out symbols of any type for any other type at a given keyframe, but the swap only applies to the frames leading up to the next keyframe. With graphic symbols, it's possible to apply a swap across keyframes, but you have to know the secret handshake.

1. Open SyncPropertyGraphic.fla and note that a cube has been motion-tweened for you along a clockwise rectangular path. Use your imagination to picture the rectangular path as something more spectacular. Now, revel in that moment, because in this hypothetical world, you did that—and it's really cool. Here comes the drama: the boss eases into your cubical, apologetic at first, but steadily annoyed at having to elbow past your high-fiving buddies. Something is wrong, says the boss. Something is dreadfully wrong. The client wanted the pyramid, not the cube.

2. Select the cube at frame 1 and press the Swap button. (Remember, the boss is watching.) Select the pyramid symbol and press OK. Scrub the playhead a bit to confirm that the tween movement has picked up the new symbol. Smile as the boss leaves.

3. Now scrub to frame 80 and beyond. Look quickly over your shoulder. Good, the boss is still walking away. Why didn't the swap (shown in Figure 7-41) take? The answer rests on a tween property called Sync, which you can see in the Property inspector when you click anywhere in the span of frames that comprises a motion tween. The Sync property sets up a relationship between keyframes that locks their symbol in an unbreakable chain—well, unbreakable until you choose to remove the check mark from the Sync setting.

7

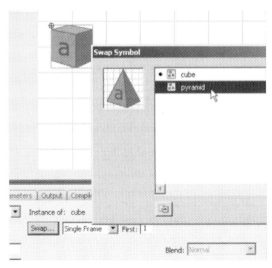

Figure 7-41. Swapping symbols can sometimes produce unexpected results.

4. Select the span of frames between each pair of keyframes, and click Sync to enable it (see Figure 7-42). As you do this, note that the small vertical line to the left of each keyframe disappears. This indicates the synchronized relationship. Note also that the pyramid swap occurs.

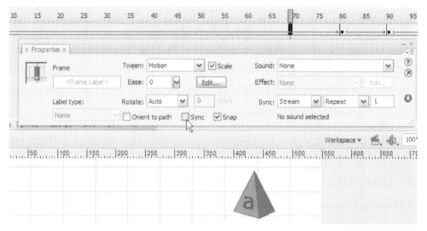

Figure 7-42. Tweens that are absent of Sync are "segregated" by a vertical line to the left of each keyframe in the timeline.

5. Now that all of the keyframes are synchronized, select any keyframe after frame 1 and use the Swap button to change the symbol back to the cube. You'll find that you can't. The Sync option prevents changes to any keyframe but the first in the chain.

6. Select the first keyframe and use the Swap button to change the symbol back to the cube. Scrub the timeline and verify that the swap has occurred across the board.

> There are actually two ways to apply a motion tween, and we've purposefully been steering you toward one of them so far in this chapter. Why? Because the other way has an interesting, but not at all obvious, side effect that is omitted by the Property inspector approach. As with shape tweens, you can right-click (PC) or Ctrl-click (Mac) between any two keyframes and select Create Motion Tween from the context menu. Applying the tween from this location automatically puts check marks in the Sync and Snap properties every time. This does not happen when a motion tween is applied via the Property inspector. With the Property inspector approach, Flash remembers whether Sync and Snap have already been chosen, and sets their check marks accordingly.
>
> In addition to this, Create Motion Tween has the potential to create new library assets on your behalf, which you may not want. This happens when you use this approach to apply a motion tween to non-symbols, such as a shape, a primitive, or grouped elements. Try it and you'll see: Flash will attempt to make the motion tween work even though you've applied it to the wrong sort of object. You'll find two new symbols, Tween 1 and Tween 2, in the library—more, if you do it repeatedly—and Flash will apply motion tweens to those symbols instead.

So much for updating content by swapping out symbols. You may be perfectly happy with the artwork as is—it may be the *placement* of content that's out of whack. This is where the Edit Multiple Frames button makes its entrance. Using this button requires a bit of prep work, so let's step through that:

1. First, you've got to decide on a range of possibly editable frames. This range extends both horizontally and vertically. Do you want to edit one layer only, multiple layers, or all layers? The easiest way to keep from editing the wrong layer is to temporarily lock it. Open EditMultipleFrames.fla and click the Lock icon in the Pyramid layer. This makes the Cube layer the exclusive focus of your attention. Next, make your horizontal decision. The extent of your onion skin markers determines the lateral range. Use the Modify Onion Markers drop-down menu to select Onion All.

2. Click the Edit Multiple Frames button. At this point, you've chosen a valid range of editable frames and have activated the possibility to select them.

3. Now . . . to do it. Select Edit ➤ Select All and drag the upper-left cube down so that it rests on the pyramid's peak, as shown in Figure 7-43. Thanks to the Edit Multiple Frames button, all four keyframes of this animation are moved at the same time in relation to each other.

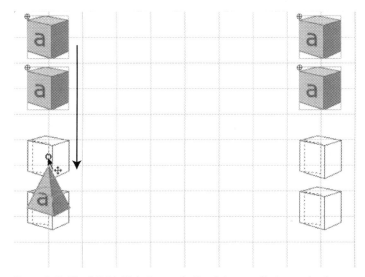

Figure 7-43. The Edit Multiple Frames button lets you adjust many keyframes at the same time.

Test your movie to confirm that the cube now rests on the pyramid for the full duration of the animation. By following this procedure, you can edit not only the position, but also the scale, rotation, and any other property available to the element at hand, whether shape or symbol.

> *In complex movies, you may find it tedious to temporarily lock a great number of layers. Instead of using Select All, you can simply select the desired layer by single-clicking its name. Hold Shift while clicking to select multiple adjacent layers and Ctrl/Cmd while clicking to select multiple non-adjacent layers.*

7

Combining timelines

Pat your head. Good! Now rub your tummy. Excellent. Now . . . do those both at the same time. Until the undertaking snaps into place, it might seem an impossible feat, but once you manage to pull it off, you know you've done something pretty snazzy. Flash animations get interesting in the same way when you combine techniques and timelines. This is where the distinction between graphic symbols and movieclip symbols really comes into play. Both types of symbols have timelines, but each behaves in a different way. Understanding this paves the way toward good decision-making in your animations.

Movieclips operate independently of the timelines they sit in. You can create a 500-frame animation on the main timeline, and then transfer all those frames into a movieclip symbol, and everything will run the same—even if that movieclip only occupies a single frame on the main timeline. Not so with graphic symbols. Graphic symbols are synchronized with the timelines that contain them, so if you transfer all those frames into a graphic symbol, that symbol will have to span out a length of 500 frames in the main timeline in order for its own timeline to fully play.

While movieclips can be instructed with ActionScript to stop, play, and jump to various frames, graphics can only be told to hold their current position, play through once, or loop. This instruction comes not from ActionScript, but by Property inspector settings. ActionScript within the timelines of graphic symbols is not performed by a containing timeline. Sound in graphic symbols is also ignored by parent timelines.

1. Open TimelineCombine.fla and select the symbol at frame 1. Look in the Property inspector and you'll see that the Options for graphics drop-down menu, next to the Swap button, is set to Single Frame, and that the single frame shown is frame 1. The frame in question belongs to the timeline of this graphic symbol. Change this number to 5 and press Enter/Return. Depending how you left things in an earlier exercise, you'll either see a cube or a pyramid—but in both cases, you'll see the graphic's text content, a lowercase a, become a lowercase b, as shown in Figure 7-44.

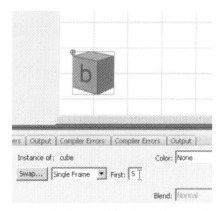

Figure 7-44. Changing the displayed frame of a graphic symbol

2. Double-click the cube or pyramid asset in the library and you'll see why. Both symbols have a timeline, and the text layer in each changes every five frames.

3. Select the symbol again in the main timeline. Change the Single Frame setting to Play Once, and change the First input field to 10. This updates the displayed letter to c and instructs the graphic symbol to play through the end of its timeline once. Drag the playhead slowly to the right to see the letters d, e, and so on, displayed through j while the symbol moves across the stage. At j, the symbol continues to move, but no longer updates its text. The reason for this is that the symbol's timeline has reached its end, but does not repeat.

4. Change the Play Once setting to Loop, and change First to 1. Scrub again and you'll see the letters start from a and repeat again from a after j is reached.

Designer and animator Chris Georgenes (www.mudbubble.com) has lent his talents to numerous cartoons on television and the Web, including *Dr. Katz, Professional Therapist*, Adult Swim's *Home Movies*, and, well, more online animation than either of us could shake a stick at. One of the giants in the field, Chris uses combined timelines to great effect in practically all of this Flash work. From walk cycles to lip-synching, Chris builds up elaborate animated sequences by organizing relatively simple movement into symbols nested within symbols. The orchestrated result often leaves viewers thinking, "Wow, how did he do that?!" Luckily for us, Chris was kind enough to share one of his character sketches, which provides a simplified example.

1. Open the Grotto.fla file from the examples folder for this chapter. Note that the main timeline only has one frame and only one symbol in that frame (see Figure 7-45). This base symbol is a movieclip, because Chris wanted a slight drop shadow effect on the friendly monster, and graphic symbols don't support filters.

7

Figure 7-45. Nested symbols allow you to take the most useful features of each symbol type.

2. Double-click this movieclip to enter its timeline.

Even with a basic example like this one, you may be surprised by the number of layers inside. Try not to feel overwhelmed! The layers, as shown in Figure 7-46, are neatly labeled. (Now that you see how a pro does it, start labeling your layers as well.) Also, although there are many of them, they all have a purpose. If you like, hide a number of layers by clicking in the eye column of each to see how each adds to the complete picture. What we're interested in is the mouth.

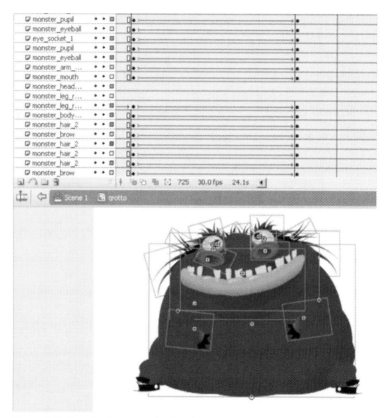

Figure 7-46. Complex images and animations are built up from simple pieces.

3. Double-click the mouth symbol to enter its timeline. Here too there is a handful of layers, comprising the lips, teeth, and a few shadows of this monster. There are 115 frames of animation here—mostly motion tweens, but also a shape tween at the bottom—and if you scrub the timeline, you'll see the mouth gently move up and down . . . this is Grotto breathing (see Figure 7-47).

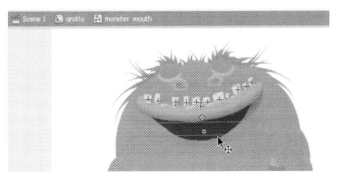

Figure 7-47. Nesting timelines is a way to compartmentalize complexity.

Because the mouth symbol itself is a graphic symbol, its movement can be made to scrub along with the timeline of its parent.

4. Return to the grotto timeline by clicking the grotto movieclip icon in the bread-crumbs area at the bottom of the Timeline panel.

Drag the playhead to a keyframe, such as 11, and click the mouth symbol. Note that it's set to Loop in the Property inspector and starts at frame 11. Because the mouth symbol loops, the mouth itself can be tweened to various locations and rotations during the course of the grotto symbol's timeline. The complexity of the mouth's inner movement is neatly tucked away into the mouth symbol.

At any point, you can pause this breathing movement by adding a keyframe in the grotto symbol's timeline and changing the mouth symbol's behavior setting from Loop to Single Frame.

The phenomenon you've just seen can be nested as deeply as you like. Even limited nesting, like that in Grotto.fla, can, for example, be used to animate a bicycle—the wheels rotate in their own timeline while traveling along the parent timeline—or twinkling stars. Just keep in mind, if a given graphic symbol's timeline is, say, 100 frames long, and you want *all* of those frames to show, the symbol will have to span that many frames in the timeline that contains it. Of course, you may purposefully want to show only a few frames. Let's look at that parrot again for an example:

1. Open YawningParrot.fla and drag the playhead slowly back and forth between frames 60 and 65. As the head turns, the beak moves from left to right. A bit of motion tweening squashes the beak as it nears the crossover, and the shape changes completely in the middle at frame 62.

2. Select the upper beak at frame 61. Open the Transform panel (Window ➤ Transform) and note that the width of this symbol has been reduced to half. In the Property inspector, note that this symbol is an instance of the beak top asset in the library. It is set to Single Frame at frame 1.

7

3. Select the upper beak at frame 62. This symbol is still the beak top asset and is still set to Single Frame, but this time its First property is set to 2 (see Figure 7-48). All it takes is one quick frame to complete the illusion of a head turn!

Figure 7-48. Graphic symbols can be used as mini-libraries to keep the real library from overcrowding.

This is a perfect example of how a graphic symbol's timeline can be used to reduce clutter in the library. It's not hard to imagine how handy this would be for swapping out mouth shapes in the case of an animated character that speaks. Sure, you can use the Swap button to replace any symbol with another at any keyframe, but it is much less hassle to update the First field in the Property inspector for graphic symbols. This technique is one of those hidden gems that becomes a favorite once you realize it, and we thank Chris for sharing such a useful trick.

> For more information on character design, advanced tweening, and lip-synching techniques, search "Chris Georgenes" on the Adobe website (www.adobe.com/) to see a number of Chris's articles and Macrochats (Flash-based recordings of live tutorial presentations).

Motion tween effects

A common question on the Adobe support forums is how to fade in an imported photo, and then fade it out again. People are comfortable enough importing a BMP or PNG, but when they drag it to the stage, there doesn't seem to be a way to adjust its transparency at all, much less over time. The trick here is to convert the photo into a symbol. The type of symbol depends on what effects you want to apply. Both graphics and movieclips support color effects such as Brightness, Tint, Alpha, and Advanced, but only movieclips support filters. Let's try it:

1. Create a new Flash document and save it as TronGuy.fla. Using the Property inspector, set the document's dimensions to 550 × 400 and its background color to black.

2. Select File ➤ Import to Stage to import the tronguy.png graphic file from the exercises folder for this chapter. Use the Align panel (Window ➤ Align) to center the image.

> *Who is this debonair futuristic fellow? Ladies and gentleman, we present to you Jay Maynard, better known on the Internet as Tron Guy (www.tronguy.net/). Jay has made numerous appearances on "Jimmy Kimmel Live" in his homemade costume inspired by the 1982 Disney film Tron and was good enough to let us use his likeness for this book.*

There is doubtless no better way to demonstrate a tweened Glow filter than to apply it to Tron Guy—but first, let's tween an alpha transition.

3. Select the imported PNG and note the absence of color styling properties. With the PNG selected, go to Modify ➤ Convert to Symbol and choose Graphic, as shown in Figure 7-49. Name the symbol tron guy and click OK. Select the symbol and note the Color drop-down menu.

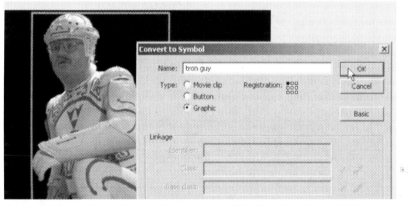

Figure 7-49. Converting an imported image to a symbol allows for color and alpha tweens.

4. Insert a keyframe at frame 10. Select frame 1 and choose Alpha from the Color drop-down menu. A slider will appear. Drag this down to zero, and then apply a motion tween between the two keyframes. Suddenly Tron Guy's entrance is visually more interesting.

5. To make it even more dramatic, choose the Advanced option, which makes a Settings button appear. Select the symbol at frame 10 and click the Settings button. In the Advanced Effect dialog box, drag the right-hand red and green sliders down to −225, and then click OK. Select the symbol at frame 1 and click the Settings button again. Drag the left-hand Alpha slider up to 100%. Drag the right-hand red, green, and blue sliders down to −225. Click OK and scrub the timeline to see the results.

7

6. For the final touch, let's add some glow to Tron Guy's costume. Open the TronGuyGlow.fla file for this one, because we've outlined some of his circuits for you. Insert a keyframe in the costume layer at frame 20. Select the costume symbol at this frame and flip the Property inspector to the Filters tab. Add a Glow filter with the following settings:

- Color: #0099FF
- Blur X: 8
- Blur Y: 8
- Strength: 330%

7. Insert a keyframe in the circuits layer at frame 20 and add a Glow filter to the symbol on that layer. Use the same settings, except make the color #FFFFFF (white). Apply a motion tween between the keyframes in both layers. A single line of ActionScript in the scripts layer—gotoAndPlay(10)—loops the movie between frames 10 and 20. Test the movie to see your handiwork (see Figure 7-50).

Figure 7-50. Say, that looks just like the movie!

The reason the costume layer's glow follows the contours of the costume is because this image is a PNG with a transparent background. If the photo had a solid background, the glow would outline a rectangle around the photo itself.

If you motion tween the alpha property of nested vector art, you may be in for a surprise. Semitransparent graphic and movieclip symbols that are made up of other symbols don't fade out cleanly as a whole. Instead, each piece fades individually, as shown in Figure 7-51.

Figure 7-51. Unintentional X-ray effect caused by alpha reduction to nested symbol

There are two ways to avoid this phenomenon. On solid backgrounds, replace the alpha tween with a tint tween set to the same color as the background. In the case of movieclips, you may alternatively leave the alpha tween as is, but set the blend mode to Layer. These solutions are demonstrated in the FadingParrot.fla file.

Motion guides

Tweening in a straight line is effortless, and we've shown how easing can make such movement more realistic. But what if you want to tween along a curve? Wouldn't it be great if we could tell you that's only marginally more difficult? Well, we can, and we'll even show you. The trick is to use something called a motion guide.

1. Open the MotionGuide.fla file that accompanies this chapter. You'll see a butterfly graphic symbol in one layer and a curvy squiggle in another. If you scrub the timeline at this point, you'll see the butterfly tween in a straight line with a slight rotation between frames 240 and 275. Butterflies don't really fly like that, so let's fix the flight pattern.

2. Right-click (PC) or Ctrl-click (Mac) the flutter by layer and choose Guide from the context menu, as shown in Figure 7-52. Its icon turns from a folded page to a hammer.

Figure 7-52. Changing a normal layer into a guide layer

   This changes that layer into a guide layer, which means anything you put into it can be used as a visual reference to help position objects in other layers. Depending on your snap settings (View ➤ Snapping), you can even snap objects to drawings in a guide layer. Artwork in guide layers is not included in the published SWF and does not add to the SWF's file size. In this exercise, the squiggle is your guide—but setting its layer as a guide layer isn't enough. It must be a motion guide, as shown in Figure 7-53. To make this happen, gently drag the butterfly layer up and to the right. The hammer icon will change back to the folded paper icon, and when you let go, it will change again into what looks like a shooting comet.

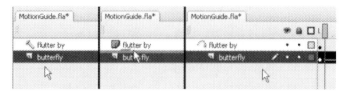

Figure 7-53. Changing a guide layer into a motion guide layer

The other way to create a motion guide layer is make it from scratch by selecting the layer you want to guide, and then pressing the Add Motion Guide button on lower left of the timeline.

> Motion guides must have a clear beginning and end point, as does the squiggle shown. Guides that cross over each other may cause unexpected results, so take care not to confuse Flash. Also, make sure your motion guide line extends the full length between two keyframes.

3. Thanks to the Snap setting in the tweened frames (see the Property inspector while clicking anywhere inside the tween), the butterfly should already be snapped to the closer end point at the last keyframe. Scrub to make sure. The butterfly should follow the squiggle along its tween (as shown in Figure 7-54). If it doesn't, make sure to snap the butterfly to the squiggle's left end in frame 1 and right end in frame 240. Imagine tweening that by hand!

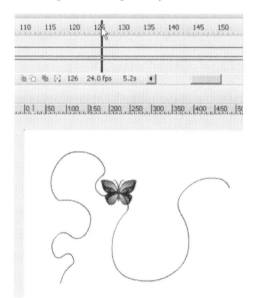

Figure 7-54. A motion guide affects the tweened path of a symbol.

4. Click anywhere inside the tween and put a check mark in the Orient to Path check box in the Property inspector. Scrub the timeline to see how this affects the butterfly's movement. The butterfly now points in the direction described by the squiggle.

5. To add even more realism, let's add some complexity, as described earlier in the "Combining timelines" section. Double-click the butterfly asset in the library to enter the Symbol Editor. Add a keyframe to the upper wings and lower wings layers in frames 5 and 10. In the body layer, click in frame 10 and extend the frames to that point (Insert ➤ Timeline ➤ Frame). Select both wings symbols at frame 5, and use the Free Transform tool to reduce their width by about two-thirds. Use the Alt/Option key to keep the transformation centered.

6. Motion tween the wings layers as shown in Figure 7-55, and test your movie to see the combined effect.

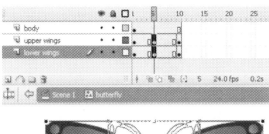

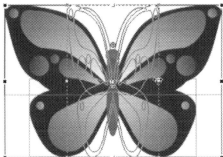

Figure 7-55. Tweening a timeline inside the butterfly graphic symbol

Tweening a mask

In Chapter 3, you used text to create a mask. In this chapter, you'll use a shape, and you'll apply a shape tween to it to produce an iris wipe transition, like in the old movies. Animating masks is no more difficult than animating normal shapes or symbols. In fact, the only difference is the status of the layer that contains the mask itself.

1. Open the TweenMask.fla file that accompanies this chapter. You'll see three layers: a photo of one of the authors as a young boy, a text layer to provide some background texture, and a small yellow dot. Insert a keyframe at frame 30 in the dot layer. Use the Transform panel (Window ➤ Transform) to increase the size of the dot in frame 30 to 800%. This makes the dot much easier to manipulate.

2. Use the Free Transform tool to increase the size of the dot yet further, so that it matches the width and height of the photo. Because the dot is a shape, apply a shape tween between the keyframes in the dot layer. Scrub the timeline to see the result (shown in Figure 7-56). Easy as pie!

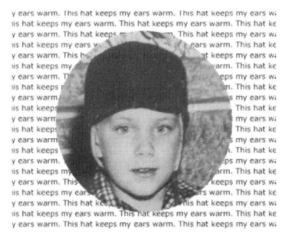

Figure 7-56. Masks can be tweened just as easily as regular shapes or symbols.

Often, once new designers get comfortable with motion guides and masks, they come to the realization that a layer can either be converted to a guide or mask layer, but not both. Naturally, the question arises, "Is it possible to tween a mask along a motion guide?" The answer is yes, and yet again, combined timelines come to the rescue.

1. Open the TweenMaskMotionGuide.fla file. The setup is very similar to the TweenMask.fla file, except that the dot layer is now named guide mask. Double-click the guide mask symbol to enter its timeline.

2. Confirm that a dot symbol is motion tweened in association with a motion guide. Return to the main timeline.

3. Right-click (PC) or Cmd-click (Mac) the guide mask layer and select Mask from the context menu. This nested combination gives you a motion-guided mask!

Your turn: Making an animated button

By now, you should get the idea that combined timelines are useful things. Here's a quick look at a very popular effect for the over state of a button symbol. Even a little bit of motion can add just the right touch to liven up an otherwise simple button.

1. Open the `AnimatedButton.fla` file that accompanies this chapter. Test the movie to see how the buttons currently work. It's certainly not bad looking, but plain vanilla nonetheless. We're going to add some animated glint to the Over frame.

2. Double-click the glint asset in the library to enter its timeline. There are three things to notice here:

   - A scripts layer tells the timeline to only play once (`stop()` in frame 5).

   - A mask layer constrains the animation to the shape of the button only.

   - A shape-tweened layer, named glint, moves a rounded rectangle from above to below the mask.

3. Double-click the button symbol to enter its timeline. Add a new layer above the bg (background) layer. Name the new layer glint. Insert a keyframe in the glint layer at the Over frame.

4. Drag the glint movieclip to the stage in the Over keyframe. Use the Property inspector to position the glint symbol at x: 0 and y: –30. Insert a blank keyframe (Insert ➤ Timeline ➤ Blank Keyframe) in the Down frame of the glint layer. This keeps the animation from occurring while the mouse clicks the button; it will only show when the mouse hovers over the button and when the mouse releases from a clicked state, both of which lead to an over state.

An even cooler animated button

This technique goes right back to the roots of Flash and the first efforts aimed at getting video to play in Flash. You will be dealing with it in greater depth in the next chapter, but here is a rather interesting technique that doesn't put objects in motion, but instead treats motion as a sort of flip book. Here's how:

1. Open a new Flash document, change the stage dimensions to 94 pixels wide by 44 pixels high, and set the frame rate to 24 fps. Name the Flash file Circuit and save it to the Circuit folder in your Exercise folder.

Inside the Circuit folder are a QuickTime movie named Circuits and a folder named Images, which contains 50 sequentially numbered JPG images. These images were created by opening the QuickTime movie in QuickTime Pro—you can do this with any video editor that has QuickTime output capability—and exporting the movie as an image sequence (as shown in Figure 7-57). This technique, called **rotoscoping**, breaks a video into a series of images (which in this case, we then saved to the Images folder).

2. Create a movieclip named Circuit, and when the Symbol Editor opens, select File ➤ Import ➤ Import to Stage.

7

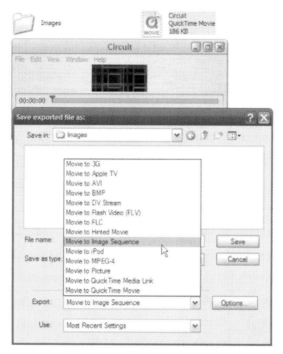

Figure 7-57. We start with a rotoscoped video.

3. When the Import dialog box opens, navigate to the Images folder and select the first image in the sequence (Image01), and click Open. Flash will grab the image, notice that there is a number after it, and think, "Hmmm, this seems to be part of a sequence." This is why Flash asks you, as shown in Figure 7-58, if you want to import the entire sequence. Click Yes. You will see a progress bar appear; when it is finished, each image will appear in the timeline. The neat thing about this is that all the images are in exactly the same position in each frame, and they are also placed in the library.

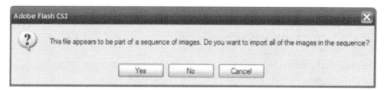

Figure 7-58. Flash, seeing a sequence of images, asks if it can import the entire sequence.

4. Import the Zap.mp3 file into the library.

5. Create a new button symbol named btnCircuit. Drag the Image01 file from the library to the stage and, using the Property inspector, set its x and y coordinates to (0, 0).

6. Add a keyframe to the Over frame of the button symbol, and drag the Circuit movieclip to the stage. Set its x and y position to (0, 0) using the Property inspector.

7. Insert a blank keyframe in the Down frame.

8. Insert a keyframe in the Hit frame, draw a box that is 94 pixels wide by 44 pixels high, and position it at (0, 0). The content in the Hit frame won't be visible. Hit frames are used by Flash to determine the hotspot for a button.

9. Add a new layer named Audio to the button timeline, and insert a keyframe in the Over frame of the Audio layer. Drag the Zap file from the library to the stage. Click the sound in the Over frame and set its property to Event. When the button is rolled over, sound in the Over frame will play, and the sequence of images in the movieclip will also start to play (see Figure 7-59).

10. Click the Scene 1 link to return to the main timeline and test the file.

Figure 7-59. Couple audio with rotoscoping to add a bit of zing to an animated button.

Copy motion as ActionScript 3.0

You may have noticed a distinct lack of ActionScript in this chapter. The reason is that the subject of programmatic motion simply can't be covered with any degree of thoroughness in one chapter. If you are really interested in the subject, then *Foundation ActionScript 3.0 Animation: Making Things Move!* by Keith Peters or *Foundation ActionScript 3.0 with Flash CS3 and Flex 2,* by Steve Webster and Sean McSharry (the companion volume to this book) are two excellent starting points. Still, we'd like to mention a really neat addition to Flash Professional CS3 that fits this chapter like a glove.

The feature is copy motion as ActionScript 3.0. Here's how it works:

1. Open the CreateMotionAS3.fla file. When the file opens, you will see we have added an animated ball and a parrot to the stage, as well as an Actions layer (see Figure 7-60).

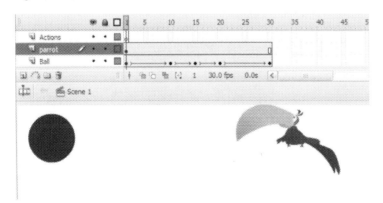

Figure 7-60. We start with a ball and one slightly worried parrot on the stage.

2. Scrub the playback head across the timeline. You will see the ball fall to the bottom of the stage, squash, stretch, and bounce back up to the top of the stage. Let's apply that animation to the slightly worried parrot.

3. Select the parrot on the stage and, in the Property inspector, give it the instance name of Parrot.

4. Select the first frame of the Ball layer, press the Shift key, and select the last frame of the layer. This selects all of the frames.

5. With the frames selected, either select Edit ➤ Timeline ➤ Copy Motion as ActionScript 3.0, as shown in Figure 7-61, or right-click (PC) or Ctrl-click (Mac) and select Copy Motion as ActionScript 3.0 from the context menu.

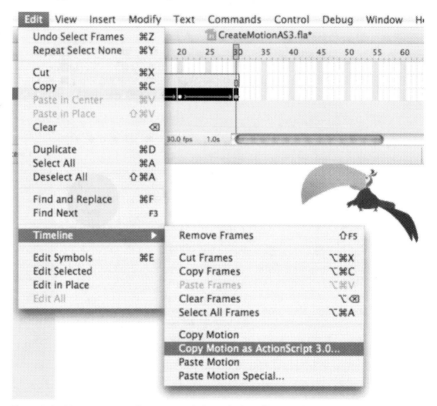

Figure 7-61. You can access the command through the Edit menu item or the context menu.

6. When you select that menu item, a dialog box will open asking you for the name of the symbol to which the motion will be applied (see Figure 7-62). Enter Parrot and click OK.

What you have done is ask Flash to translate the motion of the ball into ActionScript and apply that same motion to the parrot. This all happens in the background, and when the motion is translated into ActionScript, the code is placed on the clipboard.

Figure 7-62. You must identify the instance to which the ActionScript will be applied.

7. Select the first frame of the Actions layer and open the ActionScript Editor. Click in the Script pane and select Edit ➤ Paste. The code will be pasted into the Script pane.

8. Close the ActionScript Editor to return to the main timeline. Save and test the movie. The parrot takes on the animation and distortion of the ball in the SWF (see Figure 7-63).

Figure 7-63. Being squashed sort of explains why the parrot looks worried.

Now that you know how this works, there are obviously some rules. The first one is that the motion must be a motion tween using a symbol, and the second is the code can only be applied to a movieclip on the stage. The great thing about this new feature is that the motion tween can contain the following properties (many of which we've talked about in this chapter):

- Position
- Scale
- Skew
- Rotation
- Transformation points
- Color
- Blend modes
- Orientation to path
- Cache as bitmap
- Frame labels
- Motion guides
- Custom easing
- Filters

The bottom line is that you can create some pretty amazing animation effects without writing a single line of ActionScript.

Noggin nuggets of gold from a visionary rascal

Back in high school, one of the authors fancied himself a poet. As often happens in those formative years, the subject was introduced in terms of rhyme schemes. To be sure, there's nothing essentially wrong with that. The usual Romantic role models—Byron, Wordsworth, Keats, Longfellow, Emerson—wallowed in rhyme. It's a long-standing custom in many artistic disciplines to "study the masters" first, and for good reason. The masters figured out where all the pebbles were, which toughened their feet. Walk in their shoes, and you benefit in the same way.

Of course, once traditions are in place, the path is cleared for visionaries: inventive weirdos who see things differently, who dash off into the brush and break the rules. People who find new pebbles. Think e.e. cummings. What we've shown you in this chapter are a number of well-worn trails. Shape tweening and shape hints, motion tweening and easing . . . these are familiar corridors for many a Flash master. We encourage you to tramp along these paths until your shoes are good and comfortable (and then be at the ready to kick off your shoes and sprint with the visionaries).

If you can keep up with him, you'll want to chase the flapping longfellows of John Kricfalusi (http://johnkstuff.blogspot.com/), creator of the "The Ren & Stimpy Show" and pioneer of the Flash-animated cartoon series. A full decade ago, John broke new ground with the "The Goddamn George Liquor Program," which had cartoon fans laughing until . . . well, until milk spurted from their noses. For Flash cartooning, that was an Internet first. What's John's rhyme scheme? Enjoy Flash for the useful tool it is, but pile up most of your eggs in that basket called your brain.

> *"David asked me to write up some tips about how to creatively use Flash. I guess my best advice is to lean on it as little as possible, to not use it as a creative crutch. Flash isn't inherently a creative tool. It's not like a pencil or a brush or talent.*
>
> *I use it mainly as an exposure sheet to quickly test my drawings and animation to see if they work. Your best Flash tool is your drawing skill. You will always creatively be limited by your ability to make interesting drawings and move-ment. I see many animators using Flash mainly for its in-betweens, or "tweens" as they are now called. This little tool makes every movement look smooth. But if you want to compete against the best animators, whether in Flash or in tradi-tional animation, you will be competing with drawings, acting, and real motion (see the following illustration). Real motion has non-mathematical in-between-ing. Every in-between looks different and conveys information that mere tweening can't. Tweening just moves the same drawing from one place to another, and it's completely obvious when you watch most Flash cartoons that you are watching tricks, not animation.*

No amount of tweening can accomplish such joyous hand clapping: those are frame-by-frame drawings.

Since I started using Flash back in caveman times, I've been trying to find ways to make it not look like Flash, to try to undermine all its computery tricks. I've tried different approaches. It's hard for me to draw my key poses directly on the computer, so I usually draw them in pencil and scan them in. Once they are in, I time them in the timeline to musical beats. When I'm satisfied with the rough timing, I then draw breakdown poses directly on a Cintiq (www.wacom.com/cintiq/) in the timeline. I constantly roll across the animation to see if the motion is smooth. If I'm animating to a dialogue track, I draw the mouth positions in Flash and, again, roll back and forth to see if the animation is working.

I am always trying new ways to beat Flash's limitations and don't have a perfect solution. The best thing about Flash, to me, is that you can instantly see if your animation works, because you can play it back right after you do it. But Flash isn't doing the creative part. The drawings are. My best advice for how to be good at Flash is to learn as much about drawing and traditional animation as you can. That'll put you ahead of every Flash animator who just drags around some simple primitive pictures. More and more real animators are starting to use Flash, so the competition is going to get tougher for those who are lacking in drawing skills. **"**

7

What you've learned

- The difference between a shape tween and a motion tween
- Various methods of using easing to add reality to your animations
- How to use the timeline and the Property inspector to manage animations
- The creation and use of motion guides in animation
- How to translate an animation into ActionScript

This has been a busy chapter. The path led from tweening shapes to turning animations into ActionScript that can be used to animate movieclips on the stage. In many respects, this is an important chapter, because whether you care to admit it or not, Flash is quite widely regarded as an animation program first—all that other cool stuff it does is secondary. Many of the techniques and principles presented in this chapter are the fundamentals of animation in Flash. If there is one message you should get from this chapter, it is pay attention to how things move.

It is the attention to detail that separates the pros like Chris Georgenes (and now you) from the rest of the crowd. Whether it is a ball landing on the floor, a parrot turning its head, or a mallet striking a nail, a passion for detail will be the difference between a great animation and one that is so-so.

Now that you know how to move stuff around the stage, let's look at one of the rising stars of Flash: Flash video. Things have really changed in Flash CS3, and to find out how, all you have to do is to turn the page.

8 VIDEO IN FLASH

When Macromedia, now Adobe, launched Flash 8 Professional and included the Flash Video (FLV) Encoder and the FLVPlayback component with the application, a valid argument could be made that this marked the final acceptance of Flash as a viable web video medium. As more and more sites started featuring Flash video, there was a corresponding decline in sites that used the web video solutions provided by QuickTime, Windows Media, and Real Player.

The reason has more to do with cunning than market acceptance. Flash Player by that point in time could be found on well over 90% of all computers on the planet. The thing is, most people didn't see Flash as a media player. They thought of it as being this "cute thing" that played animations. When they suddenly realized they could stream audio (Chapter 5) and video through Flash Player without excessive wait times or downloading a plug-in, it was basically "game-set-match" for the others.

What we'll cover in this chapter:

- Streaming video
- Encoding an FLV
- Using the FLVPlayback component and a video object to play video
- Using the FLVPlayback control components
- Playing full-screen video
- Adding captions to Flash video
- Adding filters and blend effects to video

Files used in this chapter:

- DisgruntledDan.mov (Chapter08/ExerciseFiles_CH08/ Exercise/DisgruntledDan.mov)
- DisgruntledDan.flv (Chapter08/ExerciseFiles_CH08/ Exercise/DisgruntledDan.flv)
- ThroughAdoor.flv (Chapter08/ExerciseFiles_CH08/Exercise/ThroughAdoor.flv)
- Control.fla (Chapter08/ExerciseFiles_CH08/Exercise/Control.fla)
- Captions.flv (Chapter08/ExerciseFiles_CH08/Exercise/ CaptioningVideo/Captions.flv)
- captionsFLV.xml (Chapter08/ExerciseFiles_CH08/Exercise/ CaptioningVideo/captionsFLV.xml)
- Alpha.mov (Chapter08/ExerciseFiles_CH08/Exercise/Alpha.mov)
- DisgruntledDan.flv (Chapter08/ExerciseFiles_CH08/Exercise/ FullScreenSkin/DisgruntledDan.flv)
- Apparition.flv (Chapter08/ExerciseFiles_CH08/Exercise/Apparition.flv)
- RainFall.fla (Chapter08/ExerciseFiles_CH08/Exercise/Rain.fla)

- Rain.flv (Chapter08/ExerciseFiles_CH08/Exercise/Rain.flv)
- BlobEffect.fla (Chapter08/ExerciseFiles_CH08/Exercise/BlobEffect.fla)
- CuePoints.xml (Chapter08/ExerciseFiles_CH08/Exercise/
  YourTurn/CuePoints.xml)
- VideoJam.fla (Chapter08/ExerciseFiles_CH08/Exercise/
  YourTurn/VideoJam.fla)

The authors would like to take this time to thank William Hanna, Dean of the School of Media Studies, at the Humber Institute of Technology and Advanced Learning in Toronto, and Robert O'Meara, a faculty member with the Film and Television Arts program at Humber, for permission to use the videos in this chapter. The videos were produced by students of the Interactive Multimedia and Film and Television programs at Humber.

Video on the Web

Before we turn you loose with creating and playing Flash video, it is critically important that you understand how it gets from the server to the user's machine.

The Flash video format uses the .flv extension. It can't be played anywhere else other than in Flash or through the use of a third-party Flash video player such as Riva FLV Player (www.rivavx.com/index.php?id=422&L=3), Fluffy (www.nothing.ch/research/applications/43), or one offered by long-time Flash developer Martijn de Visser (www.download.com/FLV-Player/3000-2139_4-10467081.html) that will play FLV files on your desktop. The key thing about this format is that the data is sent to the user's computer from the server where it is played by Flash Player. To help you understand this process, let's go visit the Hoover Dam in the United States.

The Hoover Dam was built in the 1930s to control the Colorado River. When the dam was completed, the water behind it backed up to form Lake Mead. This means the water flows along the Colorado River into Lake Mead, and the dam releases the water in the small lake directly behind it, in a controlled manner, back into the Colorado River. The thing is, if the water rushes to the dam and overwhelms it or the dam operator releases too much water, the people downstream from the dam are in for a really bad day.

Streaming video is no different from the water flow to the Hoover Dam and beyond.

The data in the FLV is sent, at a data rate established when the video was encoded, from the server to Flash Player, where it is held in a buffer and released, in a controlled manner, by Flash Player to the browser. If the flow is too fast—the data rate is too high for the connection—the browser is overwhelmed, and the result is video that jerkily stops and starts. This is due to the buffer constantly emptying and having to be refilled. In many respects, your job is no different from that of the crew that manages the flow of water from the buffer behind the Hoover Dam back into the Colorado River. When you create the FLV, the decisions you make will determine whether or not your users are in for a really bad experience (see Figure 8-1).

8

Figure 8-1. When it comes to Flash video, you control the Hoover Dam.

Encoding an FLV

The first step in the process of creating the FLV file that will be used in the Flash movie is to convert an existing video to the FLV format. This means you will be working with digital videos that use the following formats:

- **AVI (Audio Video Interleave)**: A Windows format that supports a number of compression schemes but also allows for no compression
- **DV**: The format used when video moves directly from a video camera to the computer
- **MPG/MPEG (Motion Pictures Experts Group)**: A lossy standard for video that is quite similar to the lossy JPG/JPEG standard for images
- **MOV**: The QuickTime format

Do yourself and your user a favor and check out the compression used to create the video. If a lossy compressor was used, you are going to have a serious quality issue. The compressors used to create FLV files are also lossy, meaning you will be compressing an already-compressed video. You can check to see which compressor was used in either Windows Media or QuickTime by selecting File ➤ Properties in the Windows Media Player or Window ➤ Show Info in the QuickTime player. The resulting dialog box, shown in Figure 8-2, will indicate the compressor used.

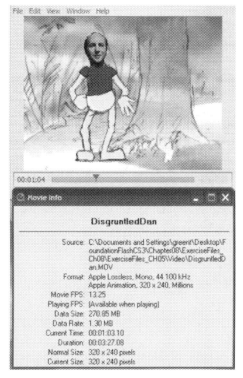

Figure 8-2. Apple Lossless animation compressor is used.

Surprisingly, the first step in the conversion process has absolutely nothing to do with Flash. Instead, open the video in your player of choice and watch the video twice. The first time is to get the entertainment/coolness factor out of your system. The second time you watch it, ask yourself a few questions:

- Is there a lot of movement in this video?
- Is the audio of major importance?
- Is there a lot of color in the piece?
- Is the video in focus, or are there areas where the image becomes pixelated?

The answers to these questions will determine your approach to encoding the video. The file you will be encoding is DisgruntledDan.mov. Go ahead, open it up in QuickTime and watch it twice.

8

Yes, the file is huge—277 MB. There is a reason. When creating Flash video, you need every bit of information contained in the video when you do the conversion. Uncompressed video is about as big as it gets. When you finish converting the video into an FLV, you will be in for a rather pleasant surprise.

1. Open the Adobe Flash Video Encoder found in C:\Program Files\Adobe\Adobe Flash Video Encoder on a PC or Macintosh HD\Applications\Adobe Flash Video Encoder on a Mac. When the Encoder opens, as shown in Figure 8-3, drag a copy of the DisgruntledDan.mov file into the render queue. Alternatively, you could click the Add button or select File ➤ Add and, using the Open dialog box, navigate to your Exercise folder, select the video, and click the Open button to add the video to the FLV Encoder.

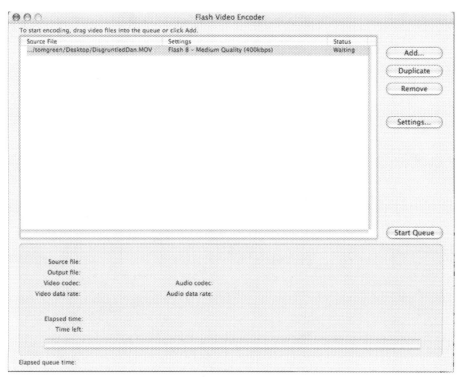

Figure 8-3. A file is in the render queue waiting to be encoded.

2. Click the Settings button to open the Encoding Settings window shown in Figure 8-3. As you can see, this window is broken into two areas. At the top is a Preview area. Under this window is the current time indicator. It displays time in the format hours:minutes:seconds:milliseconds. The triangle at the top of the line is the jog controller. If you drag it back and forth, the video will follow along. Underneath the jog controller are two other triangles. The one on the left is the in point, and the one on the right is the out point. You can use these to trim the video. For example, assume there are 2 seconds of black screen and no audio at the end of the video. If you drag the out point to the start of the stuff you don't need, it will be removed when you create the FLV.

Here's a neat little trick: the preview controls are very precise, and reaching a precise point in time can be an exercise in tediousness. Assume you want the current video to last 3 minutes and 27 seconds instead of 03:27:266. Select the out point and press and hold the left arrow key. When the key is down, the milliseconds measure will reduce. When you are close to the 000 milliseconds point, release the key and then press it in slow succession. The millisecond number will reduce in 1-millisecond increments.

As shown in Figure 8-4, the bottom half of the window consists of a series of tabs that allow you to choose a preset encoding profile (not a good idea, and more on that later on), set the video compression and the audio compression, add cue points that can be accessed by ActionScript, and crop and resize the video.

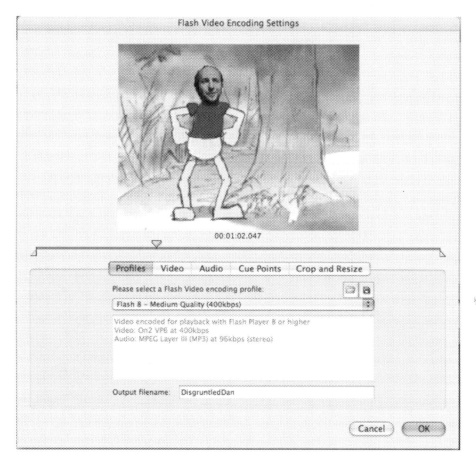

Figure 8-4. The Encoding Settings dialog box allows you to choose a preset encoding profile and to set the in and out points for the video.

3. Click in the Output filename input box and enter DisgruntledDan.

If you have used the Flash Video Encoder prior to this release, you may notice the addition of a couple of buttons above the Encoding Profile drop-down menu. New to Flash CS3 is the ability to save your custom settings as a profile and also to load that custom profile and use it. The other major change is the video and audio portion of the FLV Encoder have been given separate panels.

4. Click the Video tab to open the Encode Video panel shown in Figure 8-5. This is where you set the all-important video data rate. The various areas of the panel are as follows:

- Video codec: You have two choices: On2 VP6 and Sorenson Spark. If your target Flash Player is Flash Player 7 or lower, your only choice is the Sorenson Spark codec.

- Encode alpha channel: If your video contains an alpha channel, select this. Alpha channel video can only be encoded using the On2 VP6 codec.

- Deinterlace: If your source video was prepared for television broadcast, the odds are almost 100% it was interlaced. Select this option to remove it.

*Interlacing? Huh? Your TV screen shows alternate lines of the signal when it is playing. They appear so fast, the human eye is tricked into seeing them as a solid screen. The technique of splitting a video into alternating lines for TV broadcast is called **interlacing**. In many respects, the Encoder is not the place to do this. If you are receiving a file prepared for TV broadcast, ask the supplier to provide you with a deinterlaced, uncompressed version of the video.*

- Frame rate: This determines how often the video updates. The measurement is frames per second (fps). If you are unsure of which frame rate to use, a good rule of thumb is to choose a rate that is half that of the original file. If the original was prepared using the NTSC standard of 30 fps, select 15 fps. If the PAL standard was used, rates of 12 or 15 fps are acceptable.

- Quality: Choose a preset from this drop-down to set the data rate for the video track. You can also select Custom to enter your own value.

- Max data rate: You can choose the rate to be used. If you change the value, the Quality setting will change to Custom.

Be very, very careful when choosing a quality setting. For example, don't think you can "super size" the quality and set the data rate to, say, 1000 kilobits per second. Do that, and you can guarantee that residents downstream from the Hoover Dam are in for a really, really bad day. Also, you need to know the Max data rate setting is a bit misleading. That rate is for the video portion only. The data rate for an FLV is the sum of the audio and the video data rates. So what to choose? Until you become comfortable with creating FLV files, consider a combined audio and video data rate of around 350 kilobits per second as being a fair target.

- Key frame placement: This is one of those areas where, unless you have mastered video, it is best to let the software do the work.

- Key frame interval: Enter a value here, and the Key frame placement selection will change to Custom.

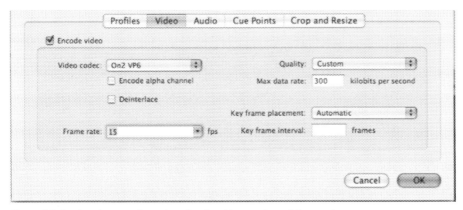

Figure 8-5. Setting the encoding values for the video portion of the movie

Remember that first question you were to ask—Is there a lot of movement?—at the start of the chapter? The answer determines key frame placement. If you are recording paint drying, having a keyframe every 300 frames of the video would work. If you are encoding a video of a Formula One race from trackside, you will want the keyframes to be a lot closer to each other, such as every 30 frames or so.

5. Specify the following values in the Video pane. When you finish, click the Audio tab, not the OK button, to open the Audio settings pane.

- Video codec: On2 VP6

- Quality: Custom

- Max data rate: 300

- Key frame placement: Automatic

- Frame rate: 15

6. The Audio pane, shown in Figure 8-6, is where you manage the audio quality. You have to make two decisions:

- Stereo or mono?

- What will be the data rate?

  Select 64 kbps (mono) from the Data rate drop-down menu. In fact, your two choices should be 48 kbps or 64 kbps. Anything lower results in an increasing degradation of audio quality. Still, 32 kbps is a good choice if the soundtrack is nothing more than a voiceover, and 16 kbps is ideal if the soundtrack is composed of intermittent sounds such as the frogs and wolves used in the Lake Nanagook project that started this book.

8

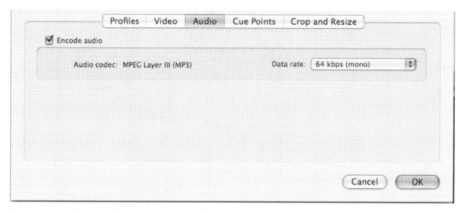

Figure 8-6. Setting the data rate for the audio portion of the movie

Unless there is a compelling reason—you are encoding a band's video, for instance—staying with a mono setting should be your first choice. Outputting stereo will only serve to increase the final file size of the FLV.

Don't think you can improve the audio track by outputting it as a stereo track if it was originally recorded in mono. Sure, you can change mono to stereo in these settings, but all you get are two identical mono tracks. It's wasted bandwidth. Also, as we pointed out in Chapter 5, the default format for all audio in Flash is MP3. This explains why you only have that one choice in the Audio pane.

7. Click the Crop and Resize tab. You aren't going to do anything here, but there is an aspect of this pane that you need to know about. When you click the tab, the Crop and Resize pane opens, and you can see the pane is split into three areas: Crop, Resize, and Trim. We aren't concerned with the Crop and Trim areas. The Resize area, shown in Figure 8-7, is critical to your survival.

When digital video is created for your television, it is created at a 4:3 ratio. This ratio is called the video's **aspect ratio** and fits most computer monitors. Other common examples would be widescreen TV video, which has an aspect ratio of 6:5, and HDTV, which uses a 16:9 aspect ratio.

For example, the video you are encoding has a physical size of 320 pixels wide by 240 pixels high. The width is easily divisible by 4, and the height is divisible by 3. If you need to resize a video, be sure to select Maintain aspect ratio. This way you avoid introducing artifacts (blocky shapes and other nastiness) into the video when it is resized.

While we are on the subject of resizing video, never increase the physical size of the video. If you need to change the size, use this area to reduce, not increase, the width and height values. Increasing the physical dimensions of the video from 320 by 240 to 640 by 480 will only make the pixels larger, just as it does in Photoshop and Fireworks. The result is pixelated video, and it will also place an increasing strain on the bandwidth.

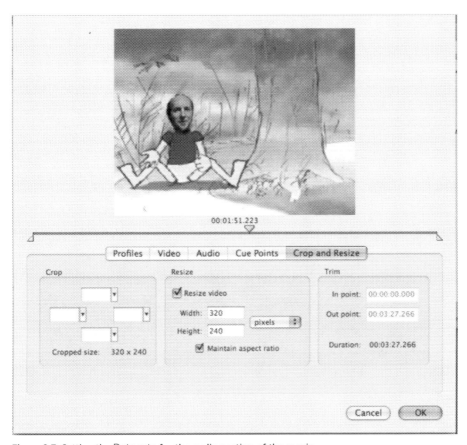

Figure 8-7. Setting the Data rate for the audio portion of the movie

In spite of our having said to never increase the size of a video, Flash Player 9 now permits full-screen video playback. We'll review this feature later on in the chapter.

8. Click OK to return to the render queue. Click the Start Queue button to start the process.

You will see the progress bar move across the screen as the video is being rendered, and you will also see the video being rendered in the Preview area shown in Figure 8-8. If you click the Stop Queue button, you will see a dialog box asking you whether you wish to stop the process or finish the render. If you have a number of videos in the queue, clicking the No button in the dialog box will stop the process, and an Errors dialog box will appear telling you that you stopped the render process. If you want to make changes to the settings or restart the render process, select the video—its status will be set to Skip in the Status area—and select Edit ➤ Reset Status.

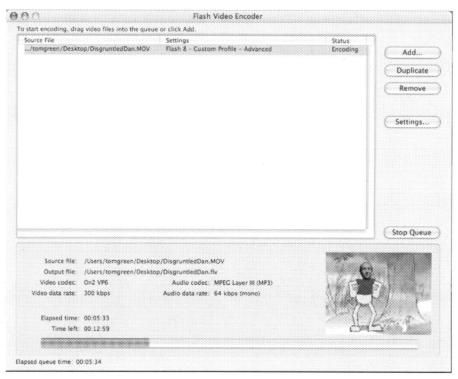

Figure 8-8. Rendering an FLV

Here's an unknown technique that will make your life much less stressful. Selecting a video in the render queue and clicking the Remove button will remove it from the render queue. What if you have a made a mistake and need to make a simple change to the video or audio settings? If the video is still in the render queue and its status is set to either Skip or Completed, you can select the video and select Edit ➤ Reset Status to put it back into the render queue, and clicking the Settings button will return you to the original video and audio settings. This is really handy in situations where you have messed up a cue point or two. For this to work, though, you can't move the video from its original folder.

9. When the encoding is complete, a green check mark will appear in the Status area. Close the FLV Encoder and open the Chapter 8 Exercise folder. If this is the first time you have used the FLV Encoder, you had better sit down. You will notice the FLV and the QuickTime movie are in the same folder. Check out the file size of the FLV. The size, as you see in Figure 8-9, has plummeted from 277 MB to 9.7 MB. Don't panic, this is common with the FLV Encoder. Remember, the On2 VP6 codec is lossy, and it really spreads out the keyframes. Both of these combine to create significant file-size reductions. This also explains why it is so important that the source video not be encoded using a lossy codec.

Figure 8-9. It is not uncommon to have an FLV shrink to 10% or less of the original file size.

Playing an FLV in Flash CS3

Having encoded the video, the time has arrived to have it play in Flash. There are three ways to accomplish this task, listed here, and we are going to show you each method:

- Let the Import Video wizard do it for you.
- Use the FLVPlayback component.
- Use a video object.

The first two are actually variations on the same theme. Both will result in the use of the FLVPlayback component. The difference is the workflow. They each approach the task from opposite angles. The final method is the most versatile but involves the use of ActionScript. Regardless of which method you may choose, the end result is the same: you are in the video game.

Using the Import Video wizard

This example covers the steps involved in actually adding video to Flash. If you have never used Flash video, this is a great place to start. Let's get going:

1. Open a new Flash document and select File ➤ Import ➤ Import Video. This will open the Import Video wizard.

2. The first step in the process is to tell the wizard where your file is located. Click the Browse button and navigate to the folder where you placed the FLV created in the last exercise, or use the DisgruntledDan.flv file in your Chapter 8 Exercise folder. When the path is established, click the Next button to open the Deployment screen.

   There are only two possible locations for a video: your computer or a web server. If the file is located on your computer, the Browse button allows you to navigate to the file, and when you select it, the path to the file will appear, as shown in Figure 8-10, in the File Path area. This rather long path will be trimmed, by Flash, to a relative path when you create the SWF that plays the video. The second choice requires you to add an absolute path to the file. If you have a lot of videos, you may have them located in a folder on your website. In this case, the path to DisgruntledDan.flv would be http://www.mySite.com/FLVfile/DisgruntledDan.flv. The path to the Flash Video Streaming Service or Flash Media Server would be a bit different. You would add a path that looks something like this: rtmp://myHost.com/Dan.

8

351

We won't be getting into the use of Flash Video Streaming Service or Flash Media Server in this book. All videos will be played back either locally or through an HTTP site.

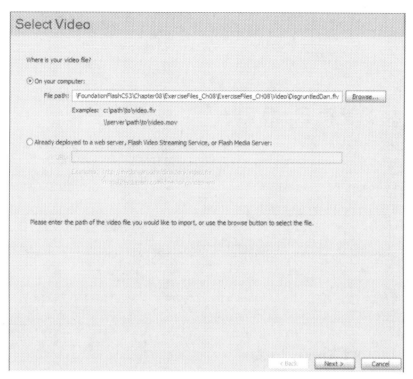

Figure 8-10. Setting the path to an FLV using the Import Video wizard

3. The Deployment screen, shown in Figure 8-11, tells Flash how the video will be streamed into Flash Player and ultimately through the browser. Select Progressive download and click the Next button to open the Skinning pane.

As you can see, there are six deployment options. Here's what they mean:

- Progressive download from a web server: This option is one of the most common video delivery methods on the Web. In fact, it is the method used by YouTube to deliver video. A progressive download means Flash Player is constantly checking how much of the video has arrived, and if there is enough to start playing the video, the video starts to play. Though you might have inferred from this that there will be an inordinate wait time, this is simply not true. Usually only about one-half second of the video has to load before the video starts to play.

  Although this is the most common option out there, it is also the least secure. The FLV file is downloaded into the browser cache, and if you are smart, you can copy it and use elsewhere. This is why such companies as recording studios, television networks, and movie studios have some sort of jihad against this format, because once the FLV arrives in the user's cache, they potentially lose control of the file's usage. If your client is adamant that the content rights must be protected, this option is not the one for you.

- Stream from Flash Video Streaming Service: There are a number of companies that will host and stream your video for you using Flash Media Server technology. It is quite secure—nothing arrives in the browser cache—and the network of servers used by these companies ensures your content is played on demand. You can find out more about this solution at www.adobe.com/products/flashmediaserver/fvss/.

- Stream from Flash Media Server: You either own your own server or use the services of an ISP to set up a media server account. Two companies that we have been exposed to are NI Solutions in Toronto (www.nisolutions.ca) and Influxis located in Los Angeles (www.influxis.com). You can also try this out for yourself and learn how to use it by visiting the Flash Media Server Development Center on the Adobe site (www.adobe.com/devnet/flashmediaserver/).

- As mobile device video bundled in SWF: This option essentially embeds the entire video into the Flash timeline in Flash Lite 2.0 and 2.1 Players used by cell phones and other mobile devices. This option is grayed out because you are targeting Flash 9 Player. We'll deal with mobile features in greater depth in Chapter 12.

- Embed video in SWF and play in the timeline: Not a good idea with this video, but a great idea if you have clips that are 1 or 2 seconds in duration.

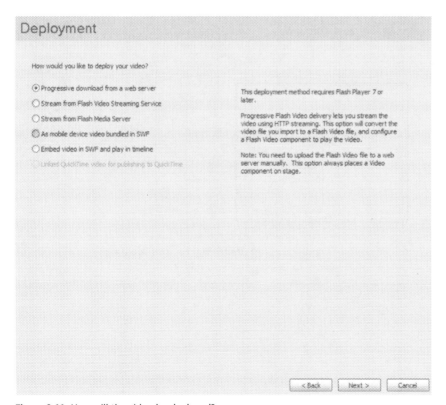

Figure 8-11. How will the video be deployed?

4. Click the Skin drop-down menu to see the choices available to you. Click a skin style and the Preview area, shown in Figure 8-12, will change to show you the skin chosen. Click the color chip to open the Color Picker, choose a color, and the skin will change to that color. Select SkinUnderAllNoCaption.swf and pick a color.

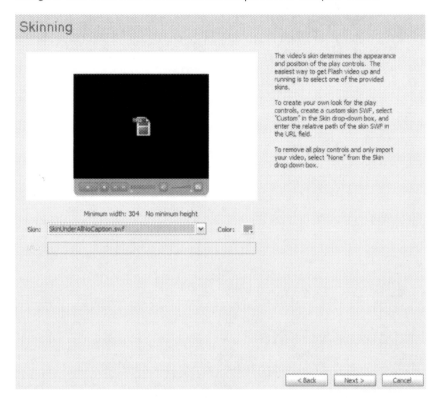

Figure 8-12. What skin or control style will be used?

Skin? Think of it as a techie word for video controls.

Selecting None in the Skin drop-down means there will be no skin associated with the video. Choose this option if you are going to create your own custom controls or use the components in the Video area of the Components panel.

Pay close attention to the minimum width for each skin. For example, selecting SkinUnderAll.swf requires a video that is at least 330 pixels wide. Considering our video is 320 pixels wide, the skin is going to hang off of the sides of the video. You can see this in the preview.

This is a big change from the previous versions of Flash. You are essentially presented with two major skin groupings: **Over** and **Under**. Controls containing the word *Over* will place the control over the video, and the controls will be visible, if this option is chosen, when the user places the cursor over the video. Controls containing the word *Under* place the controls below the video, and they are always visible.

The URL input area lights up if you select Custom Skin URL in the Skin drop-down menu. If you have created a custom skin such as one containing a client's branding, you would enter the path or the HTTP address to the skin's location.

The ability to add a custom color to a skin is also a major improvement. This way you can, for example, use a client's corporate color in the controls . . . something unavailable to you without a lot of work in previous versions of Flash. You can even make the color semi-transparent—extremely useful in an Over skin—by setting the alpha to less than 100%.

5. Click the Next button to be taken to the Finish Video Import screen. This screen simply tells what will happen when you click the Finish button at the bottom of the pane.

The most important thing that will happen is you will be prompted to save the FLA file to the same folder as the FLV you linked to. The FLVPlayback component needs this path to ensure playback of the video. When the Save As dialog box opens, make sure you navigate to the folder containing your FLV. Name the file, and click the Save button to return to the Finish Import pane. Click the Finish button.

You will see a progress bar showing you the progress of the video being added to the Flash stage. When it finishes, the FLVPlayback component, shown in Figure 8-13, will be placed on the Flash stage.

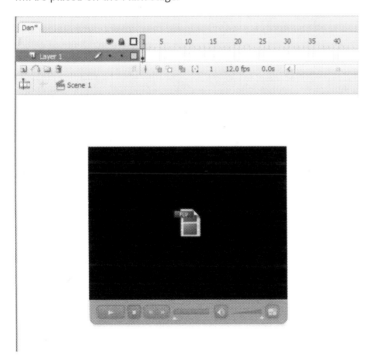

Figure 8-13. The video is "good to go."

6. Click the video on the stage, and in the Property inspector, set its x and y coordinates to 0. Save the movie and test it. The video will start playing, as you see in Figure 8-14, in Flash Player. Feel free to try out the controls. Congratulations, you are in the video game.

Figure 8-14. Welcome to the video game.

7. Close the video in the SWF to return to the Flash movie. Select Modify ➤ Document and, when the Document Properties dialog box opens, click the contents radio button to shrink the stage to the video and click OK to close the dialog box. Select the component on the stage and press the left or right arrow key a few times. Holy smokes! The controls, shown in Figure 8-15, are hanging off the stage. If the controls are hanging off of the stage, the odds are good, depending upon the embedding options in the HTML, they won't be visible on the web page. What's with that?

The simple answer is *This is a "gotcha," applicable only to the Under skins, that you need to be aware of.* When you use the FLVPlayback component, only the component is seen when you shrink the stage. The controls, which are a separate SWF added at runtime, aren't. If you are shrinking the stage and the only content on the stage is the FLVPlayback component, do yourself and your sanity a favor and manually change the stage dimensions. The width can be set to the width of the FLV, but add about 45 pixels to the height of the stage to accommodate the skin.

Figure 8-15. The two SWF files and the FLA must be
in the same directory if you are uploading to a web page.

8. Change the stage dimensions to 320 by 285. Save the movie and test it.

9. There is one last thing you need to know before we move on. Open the Chapter 8 Exercise folder, which contains the FLV. As you see in Figure 8-15, it contains a number of files: the FLA, the SWF, another SWF containing the name of the skin, and the FLV. If you are going to be embedding this particular project into a web page, you must move the two SWFs and the FLV to the same directory on your website. If they are not in the same folder, the video will either not play or the controls won't be available. Why? Because we haven't concerned ourselves with the complexities of file paths in this exercise. Putting these files in the same folder equates to the least amount of hassle.

Using the FLVPlayback component

In the previous exercise, you used the Import Video wizard to connect an FLV to the FLVPlayback component. In this exercise, you'll be doing the process manually. Once you are comfortable with it, you will discover this method to be a lot quicker than the previous one. Follow these steps:

1. Open a new Flash document and save it to your Chapter 8 Exercise folder. Remember, the FLA needs to be in the same folder as the FLV.

2. If it isn't open, open the Components panel by selecting Window ➤ Components. When the panel opens, click the Video category. Drag a copy of the FLVPlayback component, shown in Figure 8-16, onto the stage. When you do this, the first thing you will notice is the component has the same skin color from the previous exercise. This is normal. Also, if you open the library, you will see a copy of the component has been added to the library. This is a handy feature because you can use the library, not the Components panel, to add subsequent copies of the FLVPlayback component to the movie.

Figure 8-16. The FLVPlayback component is found in the Video section of the Components panel.

3. Click the component on the stage and click the Parameters tab of the Property inspector. The parameters, listed here, allow you to determine how the component will function:

- align: The choices in this drop-down menu have nothing to do with the physical placement of the component on the Flash stage. The choices you make here will determine the position of the FLV in the playback area of the component if the component is resized.

- autoPlay: Choose true, the default, and the video plays automatically. Select false, and the user will have to click the Play button in the component to start the video. In either case, the FLV file itself starts downloading to the user's computer, so keep this in mind if you put several FLV-enhanced SWFs in a single HTML document.

- cuePoints: If cue points are embedded in the FLV, they will appear in this area.

- preview: This feature is new to the component. If you select this, and an FLV is connected to the component, you can see the video without having to test the movie.

- scaleMode: Leave this at the default value—maintainAspectRatio—if video is to be scaled.

- skin: Select this, and the Select Skin dialog box will appear.

- skinAutoHide: Choose true, and the user will have to place the mouse over the video for the skin to appear. This only applies to skins that appear over the video.

- skinBackgroundAlpha: Your choices are any two-place decimal number from 0 to 1. 0 means the background is totally transparent and 1 means there is no transparency. 0.5 is semitransparent by 50%.

- skinBackgroundAlpha: Select this, and the Flash color chips appear.

- source: Click the Magnifying Glass icon, and the Content Path dialog box opens. From here you can either set a relative path to the FLV or enter an HTTP or RTMP address path to the FLV.

- volume: The number you enter—any two-place decimal number between 0 and 1—will be the starting volume for the video.

There is another place to see these parameters. Select Window ➤ Component Inspector and the Component Inspector panel, shown in Figure 8-17, will appear. Click the Parameters tab to bring up the FLVPlayback component parameters. We will be using this panel to show you the parameters for the component. The reason is that this panel, unlike the Parameters area of the Property inspector, shows you all of the parameters without scrolling. This makes things easier for you to follow.

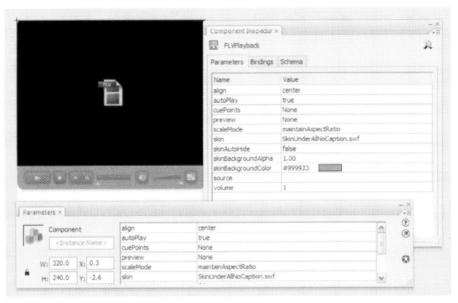

Figure 8-17. The FLVPlayback component uses parameters that can be set either in the Property inspector or the Component Inspector panel to determine its look and functionality.

4. With the component selected on the stage, use the following parameter values:

- autoPlay: false
- skinBackgroundColor: #999999 (medium gray)
- source: ThroughAdoor.flv

When you click the source parameter, be sure to click the Magnifying Glass icon to open the Content Path dialog box shown in Figure 8-18. Click the Navigate button—the File Folder icon—which opens the Browse for FLV file dialog box. Navigate to the Chapter 8 Exercise folder, select the video, and click the Open button to close the dialog box. The relative path to the FLV will appear in the Content Path dialog box. Also be sure to select the Match source FLV dimensions check box. Selecting this will size the component to the exact dimensions of the FLV file.

5. Save and test the movie in Flash Player. Click the Play button to start playing the video. When you have finished, close the SWF to return to the Flash stage.

8

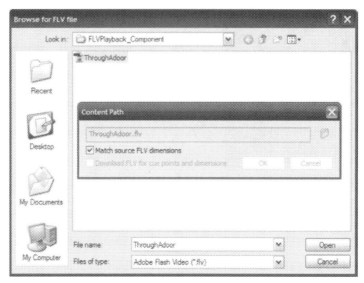

Figure 8-18. Setting the content path to the FLV to be played in the component

6. Select the component on the stage and click the Parameters tab in the Property inspector.

7. Click the preview parameter and click the Magnifying Glass icon to open the Select Preview Frame dialog box (see Figure 8-19). Here you can watch a live preview of the video. Click Cancel to close the dialog box.

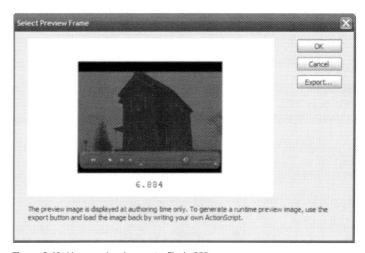

Figure 8-19. Live preview is new to Flash CS3.

This isn't the only purpose of the preview. The FLV controls in the dialog box are live, meaning you can scrub to a frame of the video. If you click OK, the frame will appear in the component, and the time of the frame will appear beside the preview parameter. This image is there only to show you how the video will appear in the component. This preview is only used at authoring time—think of it as a position-only graphic—and won't appear in the final SWF. To use the image as a poster frame or a graphic, click the Export button. The Export Image dialog box will appear, and you can save the image as a Fireworks PNG file and use it with ActionScript or import it into the library.

Why would you want to export a frame of the video? Frames can be used as movieclips or buttons to launch a video or as navigation elements to move the timeline, or even the web page, to where the video is located.

Playing video using ActionScript

In the previous two exercises, you have seen different ways of getting an FLV file to play through the FLVPlayback component. In this exercise, you won't be using the component; instead, you'll let ActionScript handle the duties. It is a lot like connecting your new TV to the cable in an empty room. There are essentially three steps involved:

- Connect
- Stream
- Play

When you walk into the room where you are about to hook up the TV to the cable, the TV is sitting on a shelf, and there is a spool of coaxial cable sitting on the floor. When you screw the cable into the wall outlet, you are establishing a connection between the cable company and your home. When you screw the other end of the cable into the TV, the TV is now connected to the cable company. When you turn on the TV, the show that is flowing from the cable company to your TV starts to play. Let's connect our TV to an FLV. Here's how:

1. Open a new Flash document, and then open the Flash library. If you don't have the library in your panel group, select Window ➤ Library to open the library.

2. Click the library drop-down menu in the upper-right corner of the panel and select New Video. The Video Properties dialog box will open (see Figure 8-20). Make sure the Video (ActionScript-controlled) radio button is selected, and click OK to close the dialog box. If you open the library, you will see there is a little video camera named Video 1 sitting in your library. This camera is called a **video object**, and it will be your TV.

8

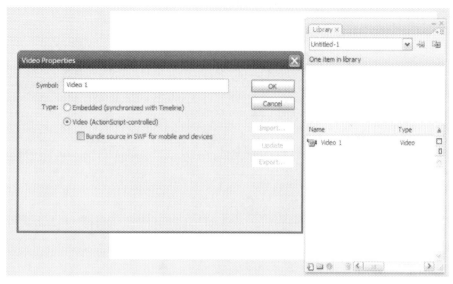

Figure 8-20. Creating a video object that will play an FLV

3. Drag your video object from the library to the stage. When you release the mouse, it will look like a box with a big X through it. After a bit of ActionScript, it will display video, as shown in Figure 8-21. Click the video object and specify these values in the Property inspector:

- Instance name: myVideo
- Width: 320
- Height: 240
- X: 0
- Y: 0

When you have finished, save this file to the Chapter 8 Exercise folder.

Figure 8-21. Eight simple lines of ActionScript code drive the playback of this video.

4. Add a new layer named Actions. Select the first frame of the Actions layer, open the Actions panel, and enter the following code:

```
var nc:NetConnection = new NetConnection();
nc.connect(null);

var ns:NetStream = new NetStream(nc);
myVideo.attachNetStream(ns);
```

The first line establishes the NetConnection between the player and the server. The second line tells the player it is an HTTP connection, not an RTMP connection. The third line establishes the stream and, finally, the fourth line connects the video object named myVideo to the stream that is connected to the server.

5. Press Enter (PC) or Return (Mac) twice and enter the following code:

```
var listener:Object = new Object();
listener.onMetaData = function(md:Object):void {};

ns.client = listener;
```

If you don't have this listener in the code, you are going to have very mysterious compiler errors coming out of your ears. The reason is that most FLV files have metadata contained in them. For example, the duration or length of the file is often contained in the FLV metadata. ActionScript 3.0, and for that matter Flash Player 9, are trained to look for that metadata, and if they don't find it, they get a little frantic and fill your output panel with this sort of error message:

```
Error #2044: Unhandled AsyncErrorEvent:. text=Error #2095:
flash.net.NetStream was unable to invoke callback onMetaData.

error=ReferenceError: Error #1069: Property onMetaData not found ➥
on flash.net.NetStream and there is no default value.
   at DanCode_fla::MainTimeline/ThroughAdoorfla::frame1()
```

The listener object and the onMetaData handler function team up to "chill out" ActionScript because you don't need to actually "do" anything with the event handler. You can if you want, but all you *have* to do to avoid errors is handle the event.

By setting the client property of the NetStream instance to the listener object, you have effectively told Flash CS3 to ignore the metadata in the FLV. This is the purpose of the last line.

6. Press Enter (PC) or Return (Mac) twice and enter the following code:

```
ns.play("ThroughAdoor.flv");
```

This line uses the NetStream.play() method to actually stream the FLV file into the video object on the stage. The important thing to note here is that the name of the video is a string because it is between quotation marks and the .flv extension is added to the name of the video.

To recap:

8

If you want to play video using ActionScript, here is all of the code you will need to get yourself started:

```
var nc:NetConnection = new NetConnection();
nc.connect(null);
var ns:NetStream = new NetStream(nc);
myVideo.attachNetStream(ns);

var listener:Object = new Object();
listener.onMetaData = function(md:Object):void {};
ns.client = listener;

ns.play("ThroughAdoor.flv");
```

The only thing you will ever need to do to reuse this code is to make sure the video object's instance name matches the one in line 4 and change the name of the FLV file in the last line.

7. Save and test the movie. When Flash Player opens, the video, as shown in Figure 8-21, starts to play.

You are probably thinking, "Hey, I have the FLVPlayback component. Why do I need code? The answer can be summed up in one word: size. The size of a code-driven SWF is about 1 KB, and its FLVPlayback counterpart weighs in at over 30 KB. The difference is due to the various control components—take a look in your library—that are added into the SWF. The increasing use of video in banner advertising is forcing developers to think small, because the maximum size of a Flash SWF that can be used in a banner ad is often no more than 30 KB. Obviously, the component is simply too "heavy" for use in banner ads. The other reason, which we won't be getting into in this book, is that there is going to come a point in your life when the FLVPlayback component simply isn't going to "cut it" any longer. When you reach this point, you will be creating your own ActionScript-driven controllers, and this will require the use of a video object. The real payback for you will come when you discover you can create your own custom controllers that weigh in under 10 KB.

Using the FLVPlayback control components

In the Video components area of the Components panel, there are a bunch of individual buttons and bars. They are there for those situations when you look at the skin options available to you and think, "That's overkill. All I want to give the user is a play button and maybe another one to turn off the sound." This is not as far-fetched at it may seem. There are a lot of websites out there that use custom players that are nothing more than a series of the individual controls. In this exercise you will build a custom video controller using these controls. Let's get started:

1. Open the Control.fla document. When it opens, you will see that the only thing on the stage is a beveled box with a bit of branding on it. If you wish, feel to change the text in the Text layer to your name.

2. Select the Video layer and drag an FLVPlayback component to the stage. Click the Parameters tab in the Property inspector and set skin to none and source to ThroughAdoor.flv.

3. In the Property inspector, set the X and Y locations of the FLVPlayback component to 0.

4. Select the Controls layer and drag the following components to the stage:

- BackButton
- PlayPauseButton
- SeekBar
- VolumeBar

5. Hold down the Shift key and select each of the controls on the stage. Open the Align panel, and, being sure To stage is not selected, click the Center Align button. When you finish, your stage should resemble that shown in Figure 8-22.

If you open the library, you won't see the PlayPauseButton. You will see separate Play and Pause buttons. Don't panic. The PlayPauseButton is actually a combination of both of them.

Figure 8-22. The video control components, when added to the stage, are also added to the library.

This is the point in this exercise where what you have done is about to shift from "interesting" to "way too cool." With all of those components on the stage, you are probably preparing yourself, especially if you used them in Flash 8, to start writing a whack of code. Not any more. As long as the components are in the same frame as the FLVPlayback component, they become fully functional. Think about it . . . you have just created a custom video controller in a "code-free zone." Don't believe us? Check it out yourself:

6. Save and test the movie. Drag the Seek control, shown in Figure 8-23, to the right and left. See . . . we told you.

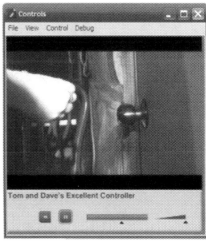

Figure 8-23. A custom video control created in a code-free zone

365

Using the FLVPlaybackCaptioning component

A couple of years ago, one of the authors had written a piece about Flash video and how easy it was to get video onto a website. The thrust of the article was that this was a wondrous technology and that video was about to sweep the Web. The reaction to the article was strongly positive, and the author was feeling pretty good about himself—that is, until he received the following e-mail:

> 'Love your books and tutorials! They are very well explained. I have a question. Have you done any tutorials on how to add captions to videos? For example, there is a CC button in your "Talking Head" video box. I would love to learn how to write CC for that. I am deaf and would strongly advocate for all websites that have videos to have captions, but that won't happen right away due to $ and timing. I will be making a small "Talking Head" video introducing myself in sign language, but I want to have captions for hearing people to know what I am saying :-)'

In our zeal to get video out there, we tend to forget that accessibility is a major factor in our business. As well, accessibility is now the law around the world, and up until Flash CS3, video was somewhat or totally inaccessible to those with hearing impairments.

This isn't to say captions couldn't be added to video in Flash 8. They could, but it required quite a bit of work on the designer's or developer's part to get them to work properly. It usually involved XML, cue points in the FLV, and an understanding of how to use XML in Flash and to write the proper ActionScript to make it all work. Flash CS3 streamlines this process with the inclusion of the FLVPlaybackCaptioning component.

Before we get going, it is important you understand this is not a point-and-click workflow. Entering cue points by hand into the Video Import dialog box in Flash is tedious business. For all but the shortest of video clips, it makes best sense to use a special XML document to make it all work—easier to edit later, too—and then you need to "connect" that document to the FLVPlaybackCaptioning component.

Timed text XML for captions

The FLVPlaybackCaptioning component allows for the display of captions in the FLVPlayback component through the use of a **Timed Text (TT) XML** document. If you open the captions.xml document you will see, as shown here, the Timed Text XML code used in this exercise:

```
<?xml version="1.0" encoding="UTF-8"?>
<tt xml:lang="en" xmlns=http://www.w3.org/2006/04/ttaf1 ➡
xmlns:tts="http://www.w3.org/2006/04/ttaf1#styling">

  <head>
    <styling>
      <style id="1" tts:textAlign="right"/>
      <style id="2" tts:color="transparent"/>
      <style id="3" style="2" tts:backgroundColor="white"/>
      <style id="4" style="2 3" tts:fontSize="20"/>
    </styling>
  </head>
```

```
    <body>
      <div xml:lang="en">

    <p begin="00:00:00.25" dur="00:00:03.25">Dreamweaver users ➡
now have access to Flash Video. Didn't have it before.</p>

    <p begin="00:00:04.20"dur="00:00:03.07">And if you were to ➡
talk to a Dreamweaver user about three or four years ago</p>

    <p begin="00:00:08.03" dur="00:00:01.04">and ask, "You want ➡
to put video on a web page?"</p>

    <p begin="00:00:09.11" dur="00:00:04.00">They would look at ➡
you and go "Yeah.Dude.Yeah.Right.Uh Huh. Next."</p>

      </div>
    </body>
  </tt>
```

You may notice the format is a bit different from that you may be used to when writing an XML document. This is because Timed Text is a specification used for captioning set by the World Wide Web Consortium, and the XML document prepared for use with the FLVPlaybackCaptioning component must follow that standard.

If you really want to dig into the specification, it can be found at www.w3.org/AudioVideo/TT/.

You will notice that you can set the styling for the text, and that each caption needs to have a start and an end point. This means each caption must have a begin attribute, which determines when the caption should appear. If the caption does not have a dur or end attribute, the caption disappears when the next caption appears or when the FLV file ends. The begin attribute means "This is where the caption becomes visible." The dur attribute means "This is how long the caption remains visible." Alternatively—and this is really a matter of taste—you can omit dur and replace it with end, which means "This is where the caption stops being visible."

Where do you get those numbers? You can use the time code in the FLV Encoder to find them, or you can use the time code displayed in the QuickTime or Windows Media Player interfaces. Another place would be in the video editing software used to create the video in the first place.

Follow these steps to apply the captions in the preceding XML example to a video:

1. Open a new Flash document and save it to the CaptioningVideo folder in your Chapter 8 Exercise folder.

2. Drag an FLVPlayback component to the stage and set its source to Captions.flv and the skin parameter to SkinUnderPlayCaption.swf. Name the layer video.

3. Add a new layer named Captions. Drag a copy of the FLVPlaybackCaptioning component to this new layer.

8

4. Select the FLVPlaybackCaptioning component and click the Parameters tab. As shown in Figure 8-24, the parameters you see are

- autoLayout: A value of true lets the FLVPlayback component determine the size of the captioning area.

- captionTargetName: This parameter identifies the movieclip or text field instance where the captions can be placed. The default is auto, which means the component will make that decision.

- flvPlaybackname: This is the instance name for the FLVPlayback component, which is set in the Property inspector. If there is only one instance of the component, leave the value at the default of auto.

- showCaptions: If set to false, the captions will not display.

- simpleFormatting: If you have no formatting instructions in the XML document, set this to true. Otherwise, leave it at the default value of false.

- source: The location of the Timed Text XML document used to supply the captions.

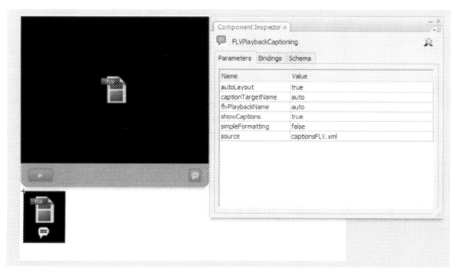

Figure 8-24. The FLVPlaybackCaptioning component and its parameters

5. Click the source parameter and enter captionsFLV.xml as the value for the parameter, and change the showCaptions setting to true.

6. Save and play the video. The captions, as shown in Figure 8-25, will appear.

Figure 8-25. The captions will appear over the video.

Be careful with this feature. The example shown assumes the controls will appear under the video. If your controls or skins are to appear over the video, they will hide the captions. To nix this, add a dynamic text field to the stage under the video, give it an instance name, and link the captions to it using the captionTargetName parameter for the FLVPlaybackCaptioning component. Finally, set the autoLayout parameter to false; otherwise, Flash puts the new text field right back inside the video.

Preparing and using alpha channel video

There will be times when you need a talking head video or you want to artificially move the subject of the video from the studio to another location. These are the instances where an alpha channel video fits the bill.

If you watch the weather on your local TV station, you are seeing this in action. The weatherman stands in front of a green wall and starts pointing to fronts and cloud formations. The thing is, the stuff he is pointing at isn't on the wall. The weatherman is pulled out of the green background and superimposed on the radar image or whatever else he is pointing at. The type of video where a green or blue background is removed, or "keyed," is called **alpha channel video**. If you are a Photoshop CS3 user, you are quite familiar with the concept of an alpha channel or masking channel. The only difference between those created in Photoshop CS3 and those created in a video editing application such as After Effects is the channel or mask is in motion.

The ability to use this type of video was introduced in Flash 8 Professional. To use this feature in Flash CS3, you need to use the On2 VP6 codec in the Flash Video Encoder. This means that if your target Flash Player is Flash Player 7 or lower, you can't use alpha channel video.

In this exercise, you are going to encode a small clip of a young adult who has just been informed by his friend that he is dead as the result of being hit by a bus. You are going to encode the video and place it over an image in Flash. Let's get started:

8

369

1. Open the Flash Video Encoder and import the Alpha.mov file into the render queue.

2. Click the Settings button and name the file Alpha in the Output filename area. Click the Video tab.

3. Select the On2 VP6 codec from the Video codec drop-down menu and select the Encode alpha channel option shown in Figure 8-26. If you fail to select this check box option, you will lose all transparency in the background.

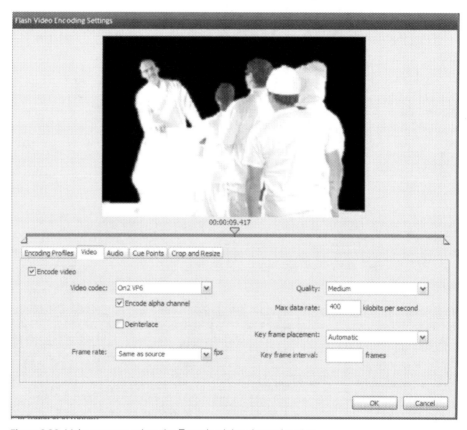

Figure 8-26. Make sure you select the Encode alpha channel option.

How do you know you have been handed a video containing an alpha channel? Open it in the QuickTime player and check the movie information. If the codec used to prepare the video is Animation and the number of colors is Millions +, the channel is there.

4. Reduce the Max data rate setting to 300 kilobits per second and change the frame rate to 15 fps. Click OK to return to the render queue. Click the Start Queue button. When the render process is finished, quit the Flash Video Encoder.

5. Open the AlphaEx.fla file in Flash. When it opens, you will see we have tossed an image of a store into the Background layer.

6. Select the Video layer and drag an FLVPlayback component to the stage. Click the Parameters tab in the Property inspector and set source parameter to your alpha channel video, and set the skin parameter to None. With the component selected, set its X and Y location in the Property inspector to 0.

7. Save and test the movie. The video, as shown in Figure 8-27, appears over the background image.

Figure 8-27. Alpha channel video in action

Going full screen with video

In the autumn of 2006, Adobe quietly announced that full-screen Flash video was no longer a dream. They released it as a part of the Adobe Flash Player 9 beta, and even though it was well received, many felt the process was a bit too convoluted. Guess what happened on the way to Flash CS3? Depending on how you wish to approach the application of full-screen video, it can be either dead simple to achieve or require a bit of poking around with ActionScript and in the web page's HTML. In this exercise, you are going to explore both methods. Here's how:

1. Open a new Flash movie and save it to the FullScreenSkin folder in your Chapter 8 Exercise folder.

2. Set the stage size to 400 by 300 pixels and set the stage color to #006633 (dark green).

3. Drag an FLVPlayback component to the stage and specify the following parameters:

- skin: SkinOverAllNoCaption.swf
- skinAutoHide: true
- skinBackGroundColor: #999999 (medium gray)
- source: DisgruntledDan.flv

4. Save the file as `FullScreenSkin.fla`.

5. Select File ➤ Publish Settings to open the Publish Settings dialog box shown in Figure 8-28.

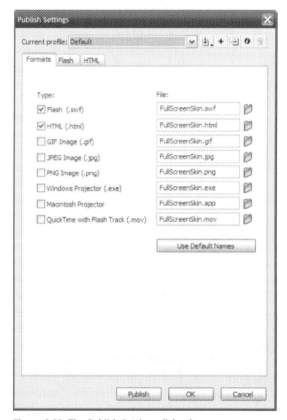

Figure 8-28. The Publish Settings dialog box

6. Make sure the Flash and HTML options are selected. Click the Use Default Names button to trim off the path, if there is one, and click the Publish button. When the progress bar finishes and closes, click the OK button to close the dialog box. When you return to Flash, save the file.

You have completed the first part of the process. The skin chosen contains a Full Screen button in the bottom-right corner. The next step is to let the browser know that the video is to be played full screen.

To start, minimize Flash and navigate to the folder where you saved the SWF and the HTML files. When you published the HTML file you actually created two files: the first is the HTML file that contains the SWF, and the second is a file named AC_OETags.js which, as shown in Figure 8-29, is a JavaScript file. This file is what allows the SWF to play in

Internet Explorer 7 or later without alerting the user to "Click to activate and use this control." That browser by default blocks active content, such as a SWF file, in a web page, and this JavaScript file does the "unblocking" chores.

Figure 8-29. The only file that doesn't get uploaded is the FLA file.

All of these files must be in the same root directory if you plan to upload the project to a web server.

If you are a Dreamweaver CS3 user, you can skip the HTML step in the Publish Settings dialog box. When you place a SWF into a Dreamweaver page, Dreamweaver will handle the active content unblocking chore automatically.

7. Open the HTML file in either your favorite HTML editor such as Dreamweaver CS3 or in a word processing application.

8. Locate the `<script language = "javascript">` tag inside the `<body>` tag (not the `<head>` tag). Click at the end of the line `'salign', ''` and add a comma. The line now looks like this:

   `'salign', '',`

   Now press Enter (PC) or Return (Mac). Enter the following code:

   `'allowFullScreen','true'`

What you have just done is to make the Full Screen button functional. This tells the browser it really is OK to allow for full-screen playback of the video.

9. Scroll down to the `<noscript>` area of the HTML where the `<object>` and `<embed>` tags can be found. Click at the end of the `<object classid...>` tag and enter the following line (see Figure 8-30):

   `<param name="allowFullScreen" value="true" />`

10. Scroll down to the `<embed src...>` area and click once between `align="middle"` and `allowScriptAccess = "sameDomain"`. Enter the following:

    `allowFullScreen="true"`

11. Save the HTML file and open it in a browser. When the video starts, click the Full Screen button in the bottom-right corner of the controller. The video fills the screen. You can either press the Esc key or click the Full Screen button in the controller, as shown in Figure 8-31, to reduce the video to actual size.

8

373

```
34            'movie', 'FullScreenSkin.swf',
35            'salign', '',
36            'allowFullScreen', 'true'                          Line 1
37          ); //end AC code
38      }
39  </script>
40  <noscript>
41      <object classid="clsid:d27cdb6e-ae6d-11cf-96b8-444553540000" codebase=
    "http://download.macromedia.com/pub/shockwave/cabs/flash/swflash.cab#version=9,0,0,0" width="320" height="270" id="FullScreenToggle"
    align="middle">
42          <param name="allowFullScreen" value="true" />              Line 2
43          <param name="allowScriptAccess" value="sameDomain" />
44          <param name="movie" value="FullScreenSkin.swf" />
45          <param name="loop" value="false" />
46          <param name="quality" value="high" />
47          <param name="bgcolor" value="#006633" />
48          <embed src="FullScreenSkin.swf" loop="false" quality="high" bgcolor="#006633" width="320" height="270" name="FullScreenToggle"
    align="middle" allowFullScreen="true" allowScriptAccess="sameDomain" type="application/x-shockwave-flash" pluginspage=
    "http://www.macromedia.com/go/getflashplayer" />
49      </object>
```

Line 3

Figure 8-30. Add a line to the JavaScript parameters and to the object and embed tags in the HTML to get the full-screen playback working.

Figure 8-31. Full-screen video is a reality with Flash CS3.

The choice of an OverAll controller is deliberate. This controller becomes visible when the user rolls over the video. If the user clicks the Full Screen button, the video will expand to full screen without the controller interfering in the screen area.

When video is not video

To this point in the chapter, we have treated video as video content. This is great, but there are going to be occasions where video becomes content and does not require a player, captions, or even full-screen capability. In this case, video can be imported directly into a Flash movieclip and becomes fully accessible to Flash as content on the stage.

Before we start, we want you to be real clear on a fact of "video life:" video files are large, and importing any of the files you have worked with to this point in the chapter directly onto the Flash timeline would be a major error. When considering working with video content on the Flash timeline, think short—loops of about 2 seconds—and think small—the physical size of the video should match precisely the area of the stage where it will be used.

The FLV files used in this exercise were all created in Adobe After Effects 7 Professional. The creation of the videos used is beyond the scope of this book but is covered in some depth in *From After Effects to Flash: Poetry in Motion Graphics* by Tom Green and Tiago Dias (friends of ED, 2006).

Try a couple of exercises to see what we are talking about:

1. Open a new Flash document and change the stage size to 468 pixels wide by 60 pixels high, which is a common banner ad size.

2. Select File ➤ Import ➤ Import Video. When the Select Video dialog box opens, navigate to the Apparition.flv file in your Chapter 8 Exercise folder. Click the Next button to open the Deployment window.

3. In the Deployment window, select Embed video in SWF and play in timeline. Though you are going to see a missive on the right side of the dialog box warning you of the evils of this technique, the file isn't that big. Click the Next button to open the Embedding window.

4. In the Embedding window, select Embedded video from the Symbol type drop-down menu. Also be sure the check boxes for Place instance on stage, Expand timeline if needed, and Embed the entire video are selected as shown in Figure 8-32. Click the Next button to open the Finish Video Import window. Click the Finish button to return to the Flash stage.

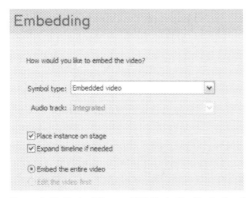

Figure 8-32. Embedding an FLV file in the Flash timeline

8

5. You will see a progress bar, and when it finishes, the video will be on the stage, and the timeline will expand to accommodate the number of frames in the video. Select the video, and in the Property inspector, set its X and Y coordinates to 0. If you open the library, you will also see the video is in a video object.

6. Add a new layer to the timeline and enter your name. Save and test the movie. The weird ghostlike apparitions, shown in Figure 8-33, move around behind your name.

Figure 8-33. Embedded video can be used as content.

In this next exercise, you are going to create a rainy day in the mountains of Southern California. In this technique, you will discover the power of matching Flash's blend modes with video. Here's how:

1. Open the Rainfall.fla file in your Chapter 8 Exercise folder. When it opens, you will see we have placed an image of the mountains on the stage.

2. Click the first frame of the Video layer. Select File ➤ Import to stage. When the Import dialog box opens, select the Rain.flv file and click Open.

3. This will launch the Import Video wizard. Embed the video in the timeline, but this time, when you reach the Embedding window shown in Figure 8-34, select Movie clip as the symbol type. This is a good way to go, because it routes all the necessary timeline frames into a movieclip timeline, rather than expanding the main timeline off a mile to the right.

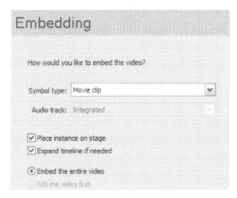

Figure 8-34. Embedded video can be turned into a Flash movieclip.

4. Drag the movieclip from the library to the first frame of the Video layer, and using the Property inspector, set its X and Y coordinates to 0. Obviously a big, black movieclip that hides the mountains isn't doing the job. Let's fix that.

5. Select the movieclip on the stage, and in the Property inspector, set the movieclip's blend mode to Add. The rain, as shown in Figure 8-35, becomes visible.

Figure 8-35. Use the Add blend mode to remove the black background in the FLV.

6. Save and test the movie.

So far you have discovered how video content can interact with Flash content. In this final exercise, you are going in the opposite direction: Flash content interacting with video content.

1. Open the BlobEffect.fla file. You will see we have already placed an embedded video on the timeline. The video is a blobs effect. To see it, open the Blobs movieclip in the library, and when the Symbol Editor opens press Enter (PC) or Return (Mac). As you can see in Figure 8-36, green blobs ooze from the top of the window and coalesce into a giant blob, which then splits apart into smaller blobs.

Figure 8-36. We start with some green blobs, which is an FLV file embedded into a movieclip.

2. Click in the Text layer, select the Text tool (or press T), and enter your name. Use a font and size of your choosing, but change the color of the text in the Property inspector to #FFFF00 (bright yellow).

3. With the text selected, convert the text to a movieclip symbol named Name.

4. With the Name movieclip symbol selected, select Overlay from the Blend drop-down menu. The text will disappear. This is because the overlay mode either multiplies or screens the colors, depending on the destination color, which is the color immediately under the text. In this case, the yellow text is against a black background, meaning you can't see the effect.

5. Save and play the movie. Notice how the text, as shown in Figure 8-37, changes and becomes visble as the blobs pass under it.

Figure 8-37. A classic example of Flash content interacting with video content

8

Your turn: XML captions for video

In the exercise in the section "Timed text XML for captions," you used the Timed Text XML standard for adding captions to a video. In this exercise, you will be adding captions using a completely different "flavor" of XML and method of getting the captions and their respective cue points into the FLV file.

There are four ways of adding cue points to an FLV file:

- Add them when you create the FLV file in the Flash Video Encoder.
- Add them using the FLVPlayback component's parameters.
- Add them using the addASCuePoint() method in ActionScript.
- Add them using an XML document.

The first two methods are what we call "destructive." Once you add a cue point using those two methods, it can't be removed. This means if your timing is off, the video will have to be reencoded and new cue points added.

Here's some self-defense if you go this route. Don't remove the video from the render queue until the video is approved for play. In this circumstance, and it only works for cue points added in the Flash Video Encoder, you select the video in the render queue and select Reset Status in the Edit menu. When you return to the Cue Points tab, they will all be there and can be removed and changed.

The last two ways are the most flexible because, if the timing is off, you simply open the code and change a number.

This exercise concentrates on using an XML document to insert the cue points. Before we dig into the XML, it is important you understand that in Flash video, there are two flavors of cue points. The first type of cue point is called a navigation cue point. Navigation cue points do exactly what the name implies: they are used to navigate, or seek, to keyframes in the video itself. If you create a navigation cue point, Flash will actually insert a keyframe at that point in the video. Event cue points are the most common. They tell Flash and/or ActionScript to do something when they are encountered. This is why the cue points you will create are event cue points. They will be used to tell Flash to display a caption.

Though we think Timed Text XML is the way to go when using XML to insert captions, you may just decide to use "plain old" XML to do it. If you do, there is a very specific format you must follow. Let's look at it:

1. Open the CuePoints.xml document in your YourTurn folder. You can use Dreamweaver CS3 or even a word processor for this purpose. When the document opens, the first "chunk" of code you will encounter is the following:

```
<?xml version="1.0" encoding="UTF-8" standalone="no" ?>
<FLVCoreCuePoints>
 <CuePoint>
    <Time>9000</Time>
    <Type>event</Type>
    <Name>fl.video.caption.2.0.0</Name>
```

```
      <Parameters>
       <Parameter>
        <Name>text</Name>
        <Value><![CDATA[<font face="Arial, Helvetica, _sans" ➥
  size="12">Look ... up in the sky ... look...</font>]]></Value>
       </Parameter>
       <Parameter>
        <Name>endTime</Name>
        <Value>11.0</Value>
       </Parameter>
      </Parameters>
    </CuePoint>
  </FLVCoreCuePoints>
```

This is the syntax that must be used. Deviate from it at your own peril. The first line declares the doctype, and the second line tells Flash that anything between the FLVCoreCuePoints tags is to be used within a cue point.

Each cue point you will add must be enclosed between <CuePoint> and </CuePoint> tags. The <Time> tag is the start of the cue point, and this number must be expressed in milliseconds. The next tag, <Type>, tells Flash that the cue point is to be an event cue point, and the tag following it, <Name>, is the name of the cue point.

The rules regarding naming are rigid. The <Name> tag must be fl.video.caption.2.0 followed by a series of sequential numbers to guarantee uniqueness. In our sample XML, it goes fl.video.caption.2.0.0, fl.video.caption.2.0.1, and so on.

The parameters contain the styling data for the text that will appear in the caption and an end time for the caption. Notice how we used the <i> tag to identify who is speaking by setting the person's name in italics. HTML tags may be used only if they're supported by Flash; a list of these may be found in the "HTML formatting" section of Chapter 6. The endTime property, which must be expressed in seconds, will be the time when the caption disappears from the screen. This number can either be an integer (no decimals) or can contain up to three decimal places.

Finally, you may optionally contend with using color in captions, and there are a couple of rules involving this as well. If you scroll down to caption 2.0.7, you will see the text in the caption uses #FF0000, which is a bright red. A couple of lines later the backgroundColor parameter changes the background color of the caption to 0x01016D, which is a dark blue.

The key here is how the colors are identified. Colors are specified by hexadecimal values, but the *indication* that the color is in hex—# or 0x—depends on where it's being stated. The first change to the red uses the pound sign, #, as traditionally used in HTML. Why? Because it appears within HTML-formatted content. The second change—to the dark blue—uses the format for specifying hexadecimal notation in ActionScript, 0x. If you do change the background color of a caption, that color will "stick." This means all subsequent captions will use this background color. If you only need a single change, like our example, change the backgroundColor parameter back in the next cue point. In our case, we changed it to black again (0x000000), as seen in caption 2.0.8.

8

Do your sanity a favor and separate each caption with an empty line or two in the XML. This makes them easier to read and locate. The space, called **whitespace**, will be ignored by Flash.

So what does all of this have to do with cue points and FLV files? You are about to find out. First, though, you need to download a cartoon.

In the 1940s, the original Superman cartoons were produced by a gentleman named Max Fleischer. Though we aren't going to get into the details, a small number of these cartoons have entered the public domain—that means they are free for you to download and use. One of them, "Superman: the Mechanical Monsters," is the cartoon you will be captioning. In order to remain purer than pure, we aren't including the cartoon in the Exercise downloads. We would respectfully ask that you head over to www.archive.org/details/ superman_the_mechanical_monsters. The file on the left side of the page can be downloaded. In theory, it doesn't matter which file you download—many exist, at different compressions and file sizes—but we used the 256 KB MPEG4 (27MB) version.

As an aside, we find it rather fascinating that the copy of the video that plays on the page is Flash Video. A low quality one . . . but Flash Video all the same.

2. Now that you have downloaded the movie, open the Flash Video Encoder and drag the video from its location into the render queue.

3. In the Encoding Profiles window, enter Superman as the Output filename. Click the Video tab.

4. When the Video settings open, ensure you are using the On2 VP6 codec, change the Max data rate value to 275 and specify a frame rate of 15 fps. Click the Audio tab.

5. When the Audio settings open, change the Data rate setting to 64 kbps(mono). Click the Cue Points tab.

6. As shown in Figure 8-38, this is where all of the pain, sweat, and aggravation that went into creating the XML document comes into play. The care and diligence you put into ensuring all of the tags in the XML document are correct are about to pay off. How so? Manually add the first cue point to give you a taste of manually adding cue points. Scrub the playback head of the FLV to the 00:00:09.500 mark of the video.

7. Click the + sign, which is the Add Cue Point button. Enter fl.video.caption.2.0.0 as the name of the cue point. Notice how the default value for Type is Event.

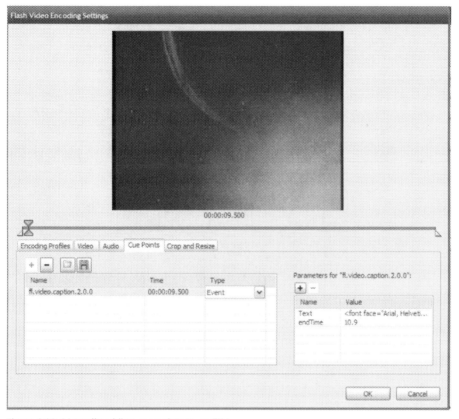

Figure 8-38. Manually adding cue points to an FLV

8. Click the Add Parameter button and enter Text into the name area. Click in the Value area and enter <font face="Arial, Helvetica, _sans" size="12">Up in the sky, look!</font>.

9. Click the Add Parameter button and enter endTime as the name and 10.9 as the value.

Now repeat steps 7 and 8 about 30 more times to add the remaining cue points. (Yeah, we are kidding.)

Obviously, going the manual route is tedious at best. Surely there must be an easier method. There is: embed the CuePoints.xml document right into the FLV file. If you have used Flash 8, this method might seem a bit unfamiliar. It is. The ability to embed an XML document into an FLV file is new to Flash CS3. Here's how:

8

1. Select the cue point and click the Remove Cue Point button (the – sign) to remove the cue point just added.

2. Click the Navigate button—it looks like a file folder—in the Cue Points window. This will open the Load Cue Points File dialog box. Navigate to the YourTurn folder, select the CuePoints.xml file, and click the Open button.

3. When you return to the Cue Points window, you will notice all of the cue points in the XML document have been added. If you select the first one, as shown in Figure 8-39, you will also see that the parameters have also been added.

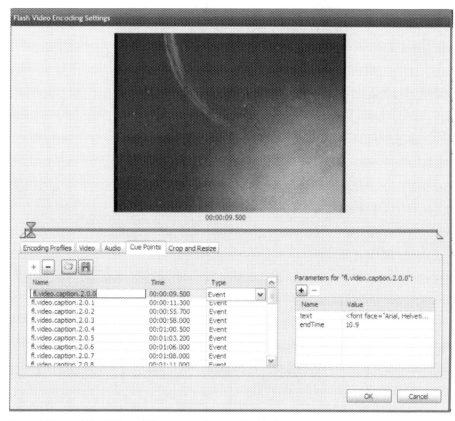

Figure 8-39. Load the XML, and the cue points are added in less than one second.

4. Click the OK button to return to the render queue, and click the Start Queue button to encode the cartoon.

5. Open Flash CS3 and create a new document. Save this document to the YourTurn folder.

6. Drag an FLVPlayback component to the stage, add a skin (we used SkinUnderAllNoFullScreen.swf), and set the source to the FLV file just created.

7. Drag a copy of the FLVPlaybackCaptioning component onto the pasteboard. This component only needs to be in the SWF (not necessarily the stage) for it to work. If you put it on the pasteboard, it won't be mistaken as a piece of content.

You will notice you don't have to add the CuePoints.xml document as a parameter in the FLVPlaybackCaptioning component. You only need to do this when using Timed Text captions.

8. Save and test the movie. Notice how the captions automatically appear (see Figure 8-40).

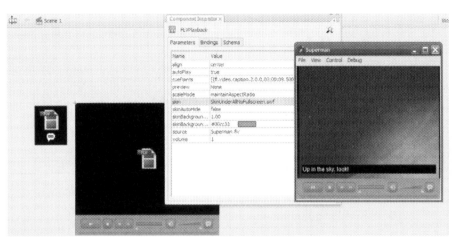

Figure 8-40. The FLVPlaybackCaptioning component only need to be in the SWF. . . not on the stage.

If you think this exercise is nothing more than mildly interesting, you would be making a profound error in judgment. One of the reasons Flash video rarely appears on government or other publicly funded/subsidized websites is because video was, for all intents and purposes, inaccessible. The ability to easily add captioned video and to turn the captions on and off has opened up a market that was otherwise closed to Flash designers and developers.

Playing with alpha channel video

In this final exercise in this chapter, we introduce you to a couple of new concepts. The first is that video doesn't necessarily have to use the FLVPlayback component and reside on the main timeline for it to work. The second concept is that just because it is video is no reason for not having fun with it. Let's start jamming with video:

1. Open the VideoJam.fla file in the Chapter 8 Exercise folder. You will notice we have provided the background image.

2. Create a new movieclip symbol and name it Video.

3. In the Symbol Editor, open the library and select New Video from the library drop-down menu. Just click OK when the Video Properties dialog box opens.

4. Drag the video object from the library onto the stage, and in the Property inspector, give it the instance name of myVideo, set its X and Y position to 0, and change its width and height values to 320 and 214.

5. Add a new layer to the movieclip and name it Actions. Select the first frame of the Actions layer, open the ActionScript Editor, and enter the following code:

```
var nc:NetConnection = new NetConnection();
nc.connect(null);
var ns:NetStream = new NetStream(nc);
myVideo.attachNetStream(ns);

var listener:Object = new Object();
listener.onMetaData = function(md:Object):void {};
ns.client = listener;

ns.play("Alpha.flv");
```

6. Return to the main timeline, select the Video layer, and drag your new movieclip symbol to the stage. Save and test the movie.

What you have just discovered is video can be put into a movieclip and will still play on the main timeline. This is an important concept for two reasons:

- The resulting SWF is under 30 KB, meaning you can use it in banner ads. In fact, if you want it to be even smaller, remove the image, and the file size drops to 1 KB.
- Objects contained in movieclips are open to creative manipulation

Let's check that last point out:

1. Select the movieclip on the stage and click the Filters tab. Click the + sign to open the Filters drop-down menu and select Drop Shadow.

2. In the Drop Shadow filter options of the Filters panel, apply these values:

- BlurX: 15
- BlurY: 15
- Strength: 75%
- Quality: High
- Distance: 10

3. Test the movie. The people in the video, as shown in Figure 8-41, have all developed shadows. This is because the video, like a box drawn in a Flash file, a Fireworks CS3 PNG, or a Photoshop CS3 image, contains an alpha channel. In the case of video, this channel moves, and Flash applies the drop shadow to the channel.

4. This looks OK, but how about we give the subjects a bit of depth? Select the movieclip on the stage, click the Filters tab, and add a Bevel filter to the video.

Figure 8-41. Filters can be applied to video contained in a movieclip.

5. In the Bevel filter options of the Filters panel, specify these values:

- BlurX: 6
- BlurY: 6
- Quality: High
- Distance: 3

6. Save and test the movie. The subjects, shown in Figure 8-42, take on a bit of depth, and you have also added a hint of backlighting. Don't get aggressive with filters; subtlety counts.

8

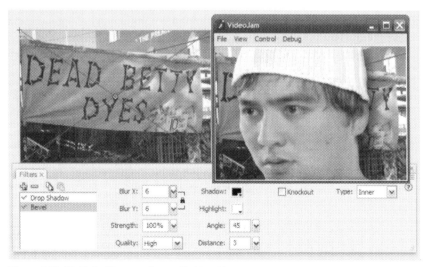

Figure 8-42. Multiple filters can be applied to video.

Hang on, these guys are ghosts. Can you turn them into ghosts? You bet.

1. In the Filters panel, select the Drop Shadow filter and select Knockout, Inner Shadow and Hide Object.

2. Test the movie. You have a 3D ghost.

Interesting, but can you do better. Of course.

3. In the Filters panel, select the Drop Shadow filter and deselect Knockout, Inner Shadow and Hide Object.

4. Click the Properties tab in the Property inspector.

5. Select the video on the stage and select Overlay from the Blend drop-down menu. Test the video. The subjects take on a "ghost-like" appearance, as shown in Figure 8-43.

Figure 8-43. Don't be afraid to use the blend modes to create some interesting effects.

What you've learned

- How video can be streamed from your web server
- How to use the Flash Video Encoder
- How to encode video containing an alpha channel
- Several methods of embedding and streaming video without the use of the FLVPlayback component

- How to add Timed Text captions to a video and how to use the FLVPlaybackCaptioning component
- A method of creating captioned video through the technique of embedding a video into the FLV file
- The power of the creative use of filters and blend effects that can be applied to video

This has been quite the chapter, and we suspect you are just as excited about the possibilities of Flash video as we are. The key to the use of Flash video is really quite simple: keep an eye on the pipe. The Flash Video Encoder is one of the most powerful tools in the Flash Video arsenal, and mastering it is the key to Flash video success. From there, as we showed you in several exercises, the only limit to what you can do with Flash video is the one you put on your creativity.

As you started working with the Flash video components, we just know you were wondering, "How do those UI components work?" Great question, and we answer it in the next chapter.

8

9 USING THE FLASH UI COMPONENTS TO BUILD INTERFACES

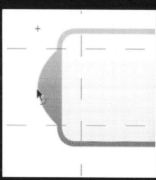

Since early in its life, Flash has proven itself the leader in web animation. In recent years, that dominance has nudged into the realm of online applications as well. For user-facing applications, you need user interface (UI) elements, plain and simple—something to receive input from the person viewing your content or to display information in a specific way, such as in a grid or selection box. Sure, you've already seen how button symbols work, and you're aware that input text fields accept hand-typed content. Those make a good start, but they're also nothing more than the tip of the iceberg.

The UI components that ship with Flash CS3 are an improvement over the Flash 8 set in a number of ways: size (much smaller), performance (faster, better) and ease of customization.

As a bonus, Flash CS3 even gives you the previous set, known as the v2 components, but those only work with ActionScript 2.0. That's an important point! They're for publishing older movies if you have to. Choosing the Flash document type or changing your publish settings between ActionScript 3.0 and 2.0 automatically updates the Components *panel to offer the correct set. You cannot mix and match components designed for different versions of ActionScript. In ActionScript 1, you lose the UI components altogether.*

What we'll cover in this chapter:

- Using the Flash CS3 UI components
- Using ActionScript 3.0 to control components
- Changing component skins

Files used in this chapter:

- Button01.fla (Chapter02/ExerciseFiles_CH09/Exercise/Button01.fla)
- Button02.fla (Chapter02/ExerciseFiles_CH09/Exercise/Button02.fla)
- Button03.fla (Chapter02/ExerciseFiles_CH09/Exercise/Button03.fla)
- Button04.fla (Chapter02/ExerciseFiles_CH09/Exercise/Button04.fla)
- CheckBox.fla (Chapter02/ExerciseFiles_CH09/Exercise/CheckBox.fla)
- ColorPicker.fla (Chapter02/ExerciseFiles_CH09/Exercise/ColorPicker.fla)
- ComboBox.fla (Chapter02/ExerciseFiles_CH09/Exercise/ComboBox.fla)
- DataGrid.fla (Chapter02/ExerciseFiles_CH09/Exercise/DataGrid.fla)
- Label.fla (Chapter02/ExerciseFiles_CH09/Exercise/Label.fla)
- List.fla (Chapter02/ExerciseFiles_CH09/Exercise/List.fla)
- Mug01.jpg (Chapter02/ExerciseFiles_CH09/Exercise/Mug01.jpg)
- Mug02.jpg (Chapter02/ExerciseFiles_CH09/Exercise/Mug02.jpg)
- Mug03.jpg (Chapter02/ExerciseFiles_CH09/Exercise/Mug03.jpg)
- Mug04.jpg (Chapter02/ExerciseFiles_CH09/Exercise/Mug04.jpg)
- Mug05.jpg (Chapter02/ExerciseFiles_CH09/Exercise/Mug05.jpg)

- Mug06.jpg (Chapter02/ExerciseFiles_CH09/Exercise/Mug06.jpg)
- Mug07.jpg (Chapter02/ExerciseFiles_CH09/Exercise/Mug07.jpg)
- Mug08.jpg (Chapter02/ExerciseFiles_CH09/Exercise/Mug08.jpg)
- NumericStepper.fla (Chapter02/ExerciseFiles_CH09/
  Exercise/NumericStepper.fla)
- Onion.jpg (Chapter02/ExerciseFiles_CH09/Exercise/Onion.jpg)
- ProgressBar.fla (Chapter02/ExerciseFiles_CH09/Exercise/ProgressBar.fla)
- RadioButton.fla (Chapter02/ExerciseFiles_CH09/Exercise/RadioButton.fla)
- ScrollPane.fla (Chapter02/ExerciseFiles_CH09/Exercise/ScrollPane.fla)
- Slider.fla (Chapter02/ExerciseFiles_CH09/Exercise/Slider.fla)
- TextArea.fla (Chapter02/ExerciseFiles_CH09/Exercise/TextArea.fla)
- TextInput.fla (Chapter02/ExerciseFiles_CH09/Exercise/TextInput.fla)
- TileList.fla (Chapter02/ExerciseFiles_CH09/Exercise/TileList.fla)
- UILoader.fla (Chapter02/ExerciseFiles_CH09/Exercise/UILoader.fla)

Anyone familiar with HTML development knows how easy it is to add a check box, radio button, or other form element into a document. These are usually used in "contact us" pages, online surveys, and other application scenarios. Flash components provide you the same set of "widgets," but you also get a whole lot more, including components not possible in a browser alone. A smidgen of ActionScript is required to wire them together, but for the most part, these are drag-and-drop convenient. In any case, this chapter will help you make sense of it all.

Out of the box, the Flash UI components are styled in a modest, attractive manner that comfortably fits a broad range of designs. Of course, Flash being what it is—free from the relative constraints of HTML—you may want to customize their appearance, and you can. Designers and developers familiar with Flash 8 might warn you with a shudder that you're in for a barrel of headaches. Tell the old-timers they can breathe easy. Things have improved considerably in Flash CS3.

We'll start our exploration with the Button component and spend a bit more time with it than the others, simply because once you "get it," you get it. To be sure, certain components are more complex than others, and we certainly won't skimp as we visit each one—but if you're a complete newcomer, you may want to read through the "Button component" section first, and then breeze the other headings until you find components of interest to you.

Button component

At first glance, the Button component is just another button symbol, but the two shouldn't be confused. As discussed in Chapter 3, button symbols have a specialized timeline, made of Up, Over, Down, and Hit frames. As such, button symbols are very malleable: Over artwork can be made to spill over the button's Up shape, paving the way for quick-and-dirty tooltips and other tricks. Hit artwork can make the button invisible—but still clickable—if

9

it is the only frame with content. In contrast, the Button component has no discernible timeline. It's a self-contained component (as shown in Figure 9-1) and is much more conservative (at first glance) than its wild, partying cousin.

> *Using one or more instances of the Button component in your movie will add 15 KB to the SWF if no other components share the load.*

Poke My Belly **Figure 9-1.** The Button component. Pretty conservative, even without the tie.

Using the Button component

What makes the Button component so special? In two words, *consistency* and *toggleability*. The first of those, consistency, will be evident in each of the components we visit. If you accept the default skin for every component, you'll get a reliable uniformity among your UI widgets. The second word—well, we admit it, *toggleability* isn't a word—but what it means is that you get a button that optionally stays pressed after you click it, and releases again when you click it a second time. This useful feature is possible without a lick of ActionScript knowledge. Let's see how:

1. Start a new Flash document and open the Components panel (Window ➤ Components). In the Components panel, open the User Interface branch by clicking the + button or double-clicking the words User Interface. When this branch is open, the + button becomes a -, and you'll see the list of available UI components. Drag an instance of the Button component to the stage, as shown in Figure 9-2.

Figure 9-2. Adding a UI component to the stage is as easy as dragging and dropping.

Doing this drops a copy of the Button component and a folder named Component Assets into your library. You can ignore the Component Assets folder for the time being. Any time you want additional Button instances, drag them from your library.

2. The first thing to do is give your button an instance name. Select the button by clicking it once, and then type button into the Instance Name field of the Property inspector, as shown in Figure 9-3.

It is also possible to provide the instance name via the Parameters *tab.*

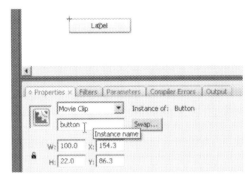

Figure 9-3. Always give your component instances an instance name.

Under normal circumstances, you should make your instance name something more meaningful than the generic *button*, but for now, this will do. If you like, use the Free Transform tool to change the dimensions of the button. Note that it resizes much like any symbol, but its text label stays the same size.

Skewing or rotating the button makes its label disappear because font outlines are not embedded on their own.

3. By default, the button's label is the self-descriptive term *Label*. Let's change that. Click the Parameters tab (shown in Figure 9-4), and double-click the right column in the label row. Change the word Label to Activate. When this button becomes a toggle, you'll make it actually activate something. For now, leave the toggle parameter at its default setting of false.

Another useful tool for changing a component's parameters is the aptly named Component Inspector panel, found in the Window *menu. Open this and all of a component's parameters are available in one screen, meaning you don't have to scroll tediously through parameters in the Property inspector. Which method is best? Whatever works for you.*

9

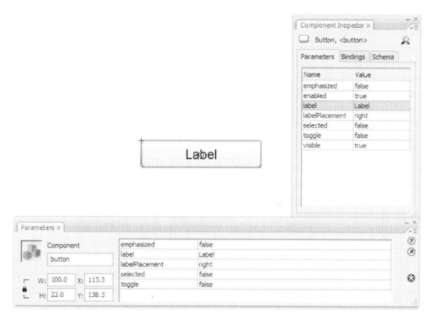

Figure 9-4. The label parameter determines the text used in the button.

4. Rename your button's layer from Layer 1 to button, and create a new layer. Name the new layer scripts and click inside frame 1 of the scripts layer. Open the Actions panel and enter the following ActionScript:

```
button.addEventListener(
  MouseEvent.CLICK,
  function(evt:MouseEvent):void {
    trace("By George, I've been clicked!");
  }
);
```

5. Test your movie (Control ➤ Test Movie) to verify that a button click sends the message "By George, I've been clicked!" to the Output panel.

> *For an explanation of how this ActionScript works, be sure to read Chapter 4.*

6. To make this button a toggle, return to the Parameters tab and change the toggle parameter to true. Test the movie again, if you like, to confirm that the button now stays in when you click it and pops out again when you click it a second time. Compare your work with Button01.fla in the Exercise folder for this chapter.

To actually make use of this toggled/untoggled state, you will need to use the BaseButton.selected property of the Button component instance on the stage. Many button-like components, including Button, CheckBox, and RadioButton, inherit from the BaseButton class family tree, which means that they support a selected property like their ancestor does. The button's instance name lets you access this property easily.

1. Open the Button02.fla file that accompanies this chapter. This file picks up where we left off in the previous exercise. The only difference is a movieclip containing a PNG image has been added to the library. You're going to make this movieclip draggable, but only when the button is pressed. Create a new layer and name it mystical dude. Select the new layer and drag an instance of the movieclip dude to the stage. Give this movieclip the instance name dude.

2. In the scripts layer, select frame 1 and add the following new ActionScript beneath the existing code:

```
dude.addEventListener(
  MouseEvent.MOUSE_DOWN,
  function(evt:MouseEvent):void {
    if (button.selected == true) {
      dude.startDrag();
    }
  }
);
dude.addEventListener(
  MouseEvent.MOUSE_UP,
  function(evt:MouseEvent):void {
    dude.stopDrag();
  }
);
```

The key here is the if statement in the MouseEvent.MOUSE_DOWN handler. The if evaluates the button's selected property as described previously. When it's set to true, dragging commences, as shown in Figure 9-5; otherwise, dragging is ignored.

Figure 9-5. Checking the button's selected property allows you to perform actions only when the button is clicked.

9

> *To see the full list of events available to the* Button *component, look up the* Button *class in the ActionScript 3.0 Language and Components Reference. Don't forget to select the* Show Inherited Styles *hyperlink beneath the* Events *heading!*

One final note before we start playing with the looks of this component. Unlike normal library assets, UI components add to the weight of your movie whether or not they're used in the timeline. This is why seasoned Flash developers regard these things in much the same way Dracula regards garlic. The reason for this is that components are set to export for ActionScript. Right-click (PC) or Ctrl-click (Mac) any component in your library and choose Linkage to see for yourself.

The first UI component in your movie usually adds the most weight, proportionately speaking, to the SWF. Some components weigh more than others, but all of them rely on a base framework that provides functionality for the whole set. For this reason, your first instance of Button will add 15 KB. The second and third instances won't add anything. Your first CheckBox instance, on its own, will add 15 KB, and additional CheckBox instances will add nothing. However, if you *already have* a Button instance in the movie and *then* add a CheckBox, the combined total of both components is only 16 KB.

> *To remove the weight of these components, in case you change your mind and decide to omit them from your design, delete the component(s) and* Component Assets *folder from the library.*

Changing the Button component's appearance

What you're about to see can be achieved with most of the UI components, not just Button. (Some components have few or no visual elements, so there are exceptions.) This is good news, because it means you'll get the basic gist right off the bat. There are two ways to alter a UI component's appearance: skinning and styling. The first generally deals with the material *substance* of the component—the shape of the clickable surface of a button, the drag handle of a scrollbar—and the second generally deals with text, dressing, and padding.

Skinning

Before Flash CS3, the practice of skinning UI components was an exercise in alchemy. Only the wisest and purest of wizards would trust themselves to toss mysterious ingredients into the frothing cauldron. All of that has changed. In fact, it couldn't get much easier.

1. Create a new Flash document and drag an instance of the Button component to the stage. Double-click the button and you'll see a convenient "buffet table" of the various visual states available to the button, as shown in Figure 9-6.

Figure 9-6. Skinning UI components is just way easy.

2. The up skin is the button's default appearance. Double-click that and you'll come to the symbol that represents the up skin for this component, complete with 9-slice scaling (as shown in Figure 9-7).

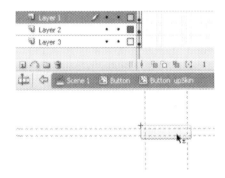

Figure 9-7. A mere two levels in, and you're ready to change the apperance of the button.

3. This skin happens to be made of three layers, but it really doesn't matter. Other skins may be different, in this component or another. Select an area in one of these layers and change the button's appearance, perhaps like Figure 9-8—but the choice is yours.

Make sure that the existing shapes, or any new ones, align to the upper left (0, 0) of the symbol's registration point. Adjust the 9-slice guides as necessary. See Button03.fla for an example with minor changes to the up and over skins.

9

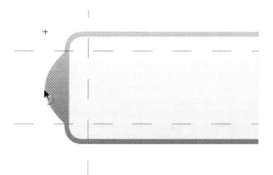

Figure 9-8. Adjust the existing shapes or create new ones.

4. Select Edit ➤ Edit Document to return to the main timeline. What the . . . ? In the authoring environment, your button hasn't changed. Folks, this is a fact of life with skins in Flash: there is no preview mode for skinning. Test your movie to see that your alteration appears as the new up skin in the published SWF. Hover over the button to verify that the other skins function as before.

> To reskin a component completely, every skin symbol must be edited or replaced.

Styling components

As you've seen, components are easy enough to customize, even if a complete job takes a while. You may have noticed an important omission, however, while poking around the skin symbols. Even though the Button component features a text label, none of the skins contains a text field. What if you want a different font in there, or at least a different color? ActionScript to the rescue.

Each component has its own list of styled elements. Many overlap, but you can see the definitive list for each in the class entry for that component. For example, filter the Help panel for ActionScript 3.0 (as shown in Figure 9-9), search the word *Button* to find the Button class entry, and then browse the Styles heading. Don't forget to click the Show Inherited Styles hyperlink to see the full listing.

Components that include text elements, such as the Button component, support the inherited UIComponent.textFormat style, which lets you make changes to the button's label. Other button styles include the inherited LabelButton.icon, which lets you specify an optional image for the button in addition to text.

Figure 9-9. UI component styles are listed under the class entry for each component in the Help panel.

For this sort of styling, ActionScript allows you to affect the following:

- All components in a document
- All components of a certain type (for example, all Button components)
- Individual component instances

Let's see it in action:

1. Open the Button04.fla file that accompanies this chapter. You'll see three instances of the Button component and one of the CheckBox component (as shown in Figure 9-10). Note that each has its own label.

Figure 9-10. Styling is about to change these components.

2. Open the Actions panel (Window ➤ Actions) and type the following ActionScript into frame 1 of the scripts layer:

```
import fl.managers.StyleManager;
import fl.controls.Button;
```

9

399

```
this.stop();

var fmt1:TextFormat = new TextFormat();
fmt1.bold = true;
fmt1.color = 0xFF0000;

var fmt2:TextFormat = new TextFormat();
fmt2.color = 0x0000FF;
fmt2.bold = false;

StyleManager.setStyle("textFormat", fmt1);
StyleManager.setComponentStyle(Button, "textFormat", fmt2);

btn2.setStyle("icon", "star");
```

Test the movie and note the following changes:

- The check box's label is red and bold.
- The buttons' labels are blue and not bold.
- The second button contains an icon.

Chapter 6 discusses the TextFormat class in detail, but there are a few twists here that deserve some clarification.

First up are the opening two lines, which make use of the import statement. We've been sidestepping this one so far because the import statement isn't often necessary in timeline code. In ActionScript 3.0 class files—that is, code written outside of Flash altogether—the import statement is not only more prevalent, it's actually *required* at the opening of each class to let the compiler know which other classes you intend to use. In contrast, Flash takes care of this for you—for the most part—with keyframe scripts. This just happens to be an exception. Without those first two lines, Flash will get confused about what you mean later when you mention StyleManager and Button directly.

> *These hierarchical class arrangements are called packages. To find the package for other components so that you can carry the preceding styling knowledge to other scenarios, look up the component's class in the ActionScript 3.0 Language and Components Reference. The package is always listed first.*

Two variables, fmt1 and fmt2, are declared and set to instances of the TextFormat class, each with its own styling. Here's where it gets interesting. The StyleManager class has two methods you can use to apply styling to components. Both methods are static, which means they're invoked on the class itself, rather than an instance. The first of these, StyleManager.setStyle(), applies formatting to all components. In this case, we're setting the textFormat style of all components that have a textFormat property to the fmt1 TextFormat instance. We programmed this style to make text red (0xFF0000) and bold, and it is indeed applied to all three buttons and the check box. You can specify any style you like, but the textFormat style is common to many.

"Wait a minute, guys," you may be saying. "Only the check box is red!" This is true. The reason for this is the other method, StyleManager.setComponentStyle(). That one applies styling to all components of a certain type, which explains the fact that it accepts three parameters. Here, we've specified Button, and then set the textFormat style of all Button instances to fmt2. This overrides the red, bold formatting of fmt1 applied in the previous line. Comment out the second StyleManager line and test your movie again to prove it.

A good way to tell which style will take effect is to remember this: the more specific the style—for example, Button components vs. all components—the higher priority it has.

Finally, the UIComponent.setStyle() method is invoked specifically on the Button instance whose instance name is btn. It works just like StyleManager.setStyle() in that it accepts two parameters: the style to change and the setting to change it to. Here, the LabelButton.icon style, which Button inherits, is set to "star", which is the linkage class of the star asset in the library. Right-click (PC) or Ctrl-click (Mac) the star asset and choose Linkage to verify.

And now you've had a quick tour of the lobby and one of the rooms here at the UI Component Hotel. There are other rooms, of course, some more elaborate than others, but the layout for each is basically the same.

We're pleased in a big way about the current UI component set, but even Paradise has its trouble. Some components—specifically List, ComboBox, TileList, and DataGrid—only obey certain styles, such as textFormat, when they're set for all components by way of StyleManager.setStyle(). For component-specific and per-instance formatting, these four culprits require something called a custom cell renderer, which gets into the sort of programming not covered by this book. You have two workarounds: either set textFormat for all, then tweak other components' styles individually, or—for List, TileList, and DataGrid only—specify the instance name and use setRendererStyle() instead.

9

CheckBox component

You met CheckBox briefly in the "Button component" section, but let's take a closer look. This component is essentially a toggle button with its label on the side. Click the box or its label, and the box gets a check mark (as shown in Figure 9-11); click again, and the check mark goes away.

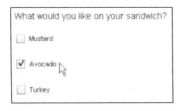

Figure 9-11. The CheckBox component is essentially a toggle button with its label on the side.

The Parameters tab of the Property inspector is fairly light for CheckBox: label sets the text label (left, right, top, or bottom), labelPlacement determines the position of the label, and selected lets you show an instance with the check mark by default. Double-click any CheckBox instance to change the skinning for all. Styling works as described in the "Button component" section.

> *Using one or more instances of the* CheckBox *component in your movie will add 15 KB to the SWF if no other components share the load.*

Let's take a look at how to interact with check boxes via ActionScript:

1. Open the CheckBox.fla file that accompanies this chapter. Note that each CheckBox instance has its own label and instance name.

2. Open the Actions panel (Window ➤ Actions) and enter the following ActionScript into frame 1 of the scripts layer:

```
addEventListener(Event.CHANGE, changeHandler);

function changeHandler(evt:Event):void {
var str:String = "";
  if (cb1.selected == true) {
    str += cb1.label + "\n";
  }
  if (cb2.selected == true) {
    str += cb2.label + "\n";
  }
  if (cb3.selected == true) {
    str += cb3.label;
  }
  output.text = str;
}
```

This assigns an event handler to the main timeline, listening for Event.CHANGE events. This event handler could have been attached to each CheckBox instance individually, but by doing it this way, the events of all three can be handled at the same time. When any of the three CheckBox instances is changed by clicking, each member of the group is checked in turn to see if it is selected. If so, the value of its label is added to a string that is ultimately sent to a text field beneath the check boxes.

ColorPicker component

ColorPicker is a fun component, because nothing like it exists in the realm of HTML—at least, not without a swarm of complicated JavaScript!—but it's common enough in applications like Microsoft Word, Adobe Photoshop, and even Flash itself. In a nutshell, the ColorPicker component is a clickable color chip that reveals an assortment of colors when pressed (as shown in Figure 9-12). It allows the user to choose one of the presented colors or optionally to type in a hex value, at which point the chosen color is available for use.

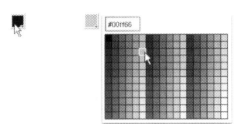

Figure 9-12. The ColorPicker component lets users choose from a range of colors.

Double-clicking a ColorPicker instance inside the authoring environment makes its skins editable, and styling works the same as it does for the Button component. The palette of colors displayed by this component is also editable, but requires just a bit of ActionScript, as shown in the following code.

> Using one or more instances of the ColorPicker *component in your movie will* *add 19 KB to the SWF if no other components share the load.*

The ColorPicker.fla file that accompanies this chapter shows this component in action.

1. Open the ColorPicker.fla file and note that the component itself has the instance name cp. The dynamic text field next to it has the instance name poem. Click into frame 1 of the scripts layer and open the Actions panel (Window ➤ Actions) to see the following ActionScript:

```
var fmt:TextFormat = new TextFormat();

cp.addEventListener(
  Event.CHANGE,
  function changeHandler(evt:Event):void {
    fmt.color = cp.selectedColor;
    poem.setTextFormat(fmt);
  }
);
```

Here, a variable, fmt, is declared and set to an instance of the TextFormat class. An Event.CHANGE event listener is assigned to the ColorPicker instance, cp—it does two things. First, it sets the TextFormat.color property of the fmt instance to the selected color of the cp instance. Second, it applies that format to the poem text field.

> *See Chapter 6 for more information on the* TextFormat *class.*

9

2. Now let's determine what colors to display. Update the existing ActionScript to look like this:

```
var fmt:TextFormat = new TextFormat();

cp.colors = new Array(
  0x6E1E46,
  0xA12F1C,
  0xD47565,
  0x557A40,
  0x79A11C
);
cp.selectedColor = cp.colors[0];

cp.addEventListener(
  Event.CHANGE,
  function changeHandler(evt:Event):void {
    fmt.color = cp.selectedColor;
    poem.setTextFormat(fmt);
  }
);
```

Specifying your own color palette couldn't be easier. Just provide the desired hexadecimal values (up to 1,024 individual colors!) as array elements to the ColorPicker.colors property of your component instance. To configure the color chip's initial display color, set the ColorPicker.selectedColor property. (Here, it's set to the first element in the colors array.)

3. Drag the ColorPicker instance to the lower-right corner of the stage. Test the movie to see that the pop-up color palette is smart enough to position itself to the upper left of the color chip. Note that in the Parameters tab of the Property inspector, the color palette's text field can be hidden by setting the showTextField parameter to false. You'll also see an alternate way to set the component's selectedColor.

ComboBox component

The ComboBox component is very much like the <select> element in HTML; specifically, the <select> element without its optional size and multiple attributes. It gives users the ability to make one selection at a time from a drop-down list (see Figure 9-13). In addition, the component can be made editable, which lets the user manually type in a custom selection.

Figure 9-13. ComboBox allows users to make one selection at a time from a drop-down list.

ComboBox skinning is a little more complicated than Button component skinning, but the basic approach is the same. The reason for the complexity is the ComboBox combines two other components, List and TextInput, which are described later in this chapter. Adding a ComboBox instance to your movie puts three components into your library—ComboBox, List, and TextInput—plus the Component Assets folder used by all UI components. Double-clicking a ComboBox instance in the authoring environment opens the first tier of skins (see the left image in Figure 9-14). Double-clicking the List element in this tier opens up the skins for the embedded List component (the right image in Figure 9-14).

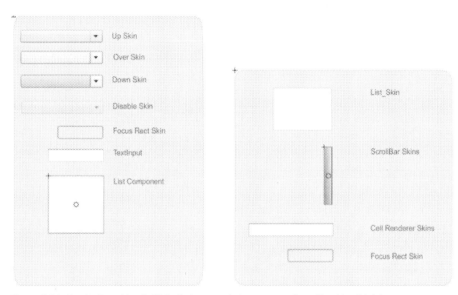

Figure 9-14. ComboBox skins (left) include nested elements, such as List skins (right).

In turn, the skins for List include a third tier for scrollbars. In spite of this nesting, individual skins are nothing more than symbols, usually with 9-slice guides, such as the up and over skins for the Button component. Styling works the same as it does for the Button component. The textFormat style, in particular, can only be set for all instances of the ComboBox component by way of the StyleManager.setStyle() method.

> *Using one or more instances of the* ComboBox *component in your movie will add 35 KB to the SWF if no other components, other than the automatically included* List *and* TextInput, *share the load.*

9

1. Open the ComboBox.fla file that accompanies this chapter and select the ComboBox instance on the stage by clicking it once. Note that in the Parameters tab of the Property inspector some information has already been entered into the dataProvider parameter shown in Figure 9-15. This is an array of objects, each of which represents the visible portion of a drop-down choice (label) and the hidden value each label contains (data).

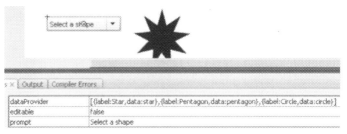

Figure 9-15. An array of objects defines the labels and data that populate a ComboBox.

2. Double-click the right column of the dataProvider row to open the Values dialog box shown in Figure 9-16.

3. Click the + button in the Values dialog box to create a new entry, which will appear below the existing Circle entry. Double-click the right column of the label row and change the existing stand-in label to Square. Double-click the right column of the data row and enter the value square. Pay attention to the capitalization. Test your movie to verify that the combo box now includes a Square choice that changes the shape to its right.

Figure 9-16. The Values dialog box lets you specify the content and order of a ComboBox instance.

How does this work? Let's take a look. The shapes symbol in the library contains a series of shapes drawn every few frames of its own timeline. Frame labels are provided for each shape, and it is these frame labels that are represented by the data row in the Values dialog box. Click into frame 1 of the scripts layer to see the ActionScript that pulls this off:

```
cbx.addEventListener(
  Event.CHANGE,
  function(evt:Event):void {
    shapes.gotoAndStop(cbx.selectedItem.data);
  }
);
```

The combo box is referenced by its instance name, cbx. An Event.CHANGE event triggers a function that tells the shapes instance to stop at the frame label determined by the selected item's data property of the cbx instance.

4. To populate the combo box by way of ActionScript, add the following line before or after the existing code:

```
cbx.addItem({label:"Triangle", data:"triangle"});
```

Pretty straightforward! The other parameters in the Parameters tab are just as intuitive: editable determines whether the user can type in a custom selection (if so, check for this value by referencing the combo box's instance name, and then the text property), prompt determines the default text (in this example, the phrase "Select a shape"), and rowCount determines how many selections to show in the drop-down list (if there are 15 selections and the value of rowCount is 5, only five will show, but the rest will be available via scrollbar).

DataGrid component

The DataGrid is the most complex component in the UI arsenal. Its purpose falls almost entirely in the realm of übergeek interface programmers, but we're going to give you a cursory look, including a basic sample file. In short, the DataGrid component gives you a spreadsheet-like, sortable display for tabular data, as shown in Figure 9-17.

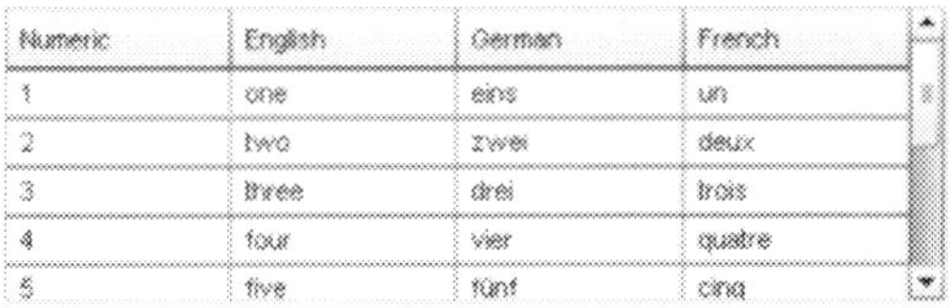

Numeric	English	German	French
1	one	eins	un
2	two	zwei	deux
3	three	drei	trois
4	four	vier	quatre
5	five	fünf	cinq

Figure 9-17. DataGrid displays scrollable, sortable tabular data.

9

> *Using one or more instances of the DataGrid component in your movie will add 40 KB to the SWF if no other components share the load.*

See the DataGrid.fla file that accompanies this chapter for a working demonstration. Click into frame 1 of the scripts layer to see the ActionScript. Here's a bird's eye view of that code:

```
dg.addColumn("num");
dg.addColumn("eng");
dg.addColumn("ger");
dg.addColumn("fre");
```

These first lines reference the DataGrid component's instance name, dg, and instructs the component to add four columns. These column names are arbitrary and, here, represent a column for numbers, and then their English, German, and French equivalents.

```
dg.addItem({num:1, eng:"one", fre:"un", ger:"eins"});
dg.addItem({num:2, eng:"two", fre:"deux", ger:"zwei"});
dg.addItem({num:3, eng:"three", fre:"trois", ger:"drei"});
```

```
dg.addItem({num:4, eng:"four", fre:"quatre", ger:"vier"});
dg.addItem({num:5, eng:"five", fre:"cinq", ger:"fünf"});
dg.addItem({num:6, eng:"six", fre:"six", ger:"sechs"});
dg.addItem({num:7, eng:"seven", fre:"sept", ger:"sieben"});
dg.addItem({num:8, eng:"eight", fre:"huit", ger:"acht"});
dg.addItem({num:9, eng:"nine", fre:"neuf", ger:"neun"});
dg.addItem({num:10, eng:"ten", fre:"dix", ger:"zehn"});
```

There is not a way to populate DataGrid instances from the Parameters tab of the Property inspector, and we're sure you can see why. It's much easier to type in the data in the relatively spacious environs of the Actions panel.

```
dg.getColumnAt(0).headerText = "Numeric";
dg.getColumnAt(1).headerText = "English";
dg.getColumnAt(2).headerText = "German";
dg.getColumnAt(3).headerText = "French";
```

These lines make the header text a bit more "friendly" to the eye. Test the movie at this point to see how it all comes together. Click the headers to sort each column. When you sort the Numeric column, you'll see something odd. By default, sorting is alphabetical, which puts the numbers 1 and 10 right next to each other. To fix that for columns that contain numerical data, remove the comment (//) from the final line of ActionScript so that it looks like this:

```
dg.getColumnAt(0).sortOptions = Array.NUMERIC;
```

This is great for displaying data, but what about retrieving what cell has been selected? Yeah, we thought that was a good question, too. The selectedItem property for this component returns the contents of the whole row you click, not just the clicked cell. It is possible to return the selected cell, but it requires something called the CellRenderer class and more ActionScript, and frankly, it rockets way out of the atmosphere that makes this book breathable.

Label component

Label is something of an oddball in the UI components collection. Unless you're an avid programmer, we're almost certain you'll want to forego Label in favor of a simple dynamic text field. Why? Practically speaking, from a designer's point of view, Label doesn't really *do* anything that a text field can't—and besides, by using a text field, you'll save the 14 KB that an instance of Label would have brought to the table.

Labels don't really have skins, and double-clicking an instance will tell you as much. Styling works the same as for Button, but again, trust us on this one . . . just use a dynamic text field. If you still want to see a Label component in action, check out Label.fla in the exercise files.

> *See Chapter 6 for a full discussion on text fields in Flash.*

List component

The List component is akin to the <select> element in HTML when its optional size and multiple attributes are specified. This component is basically a combo box without the drop-down aspect—it's always dropped down—and it allows multiple selections, as shown in Figure 9-18.

Like ComboBox, the List component has nested skins, so when you double-click an instance in the authoring environment, the skins become available for editing in tiers. Styling is handled the same way as described in the "Button component" section; however, the textFormat style must be set using the SelectableList.setRendererStyle() method, as in myList.setRendererStyle("textFormat", fmt).

Figure 9-18. The List component optionally allows multiple selections.

> *Using one or more instances of the List component in your movie will add 29 KB to the SWF if no other components share the load.*

The Parameters tab in the Property inspector is relatively hefty for the List component, and the Component Inspector panel comes in handy for looking over this component's settings. Most of the choices pertain to scrolling (the distance to scroll horizontally and vertically, whether scrolling should be automatic or constant, etc.), but the important parameters are allowMultipleSelection and dataProvider (see Figure 9-19).

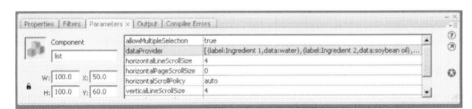

Figure 9-19. The important parameters for the List component are allowMultipleSelection and dataProvider.

To populate your user's choices in a given List instance, double-click the right column of the dataProvider row and use the Values dialog box as described in the "ComboBox component" section. Setting showMultipleSelection to true (the default is false) lets your users hold down Ctrl (PC) or Cmd (Mac) while they click in order to select more than one of the listed choices. (just like the multiple option in HTML).

1. Open the List.fla file that accompanies this chapter. Note that the instance name for the List instance is list, which only works because ActionScript is a case-sensitive language—you couldn't call it List, because that's the name of the class that defines this object. In your own work, you'll want to use an instance name that describes the list's use (in this case, that might be the word *ingredients*). Note that the dynamic text field, next to the List instance, has the instance name output.

9

2. Click into frame 1 of the scripts layer and type the following ActionScript:

```
list.addEventListener(
  Event.CHANGE,
  function(evt:Event):void {
    var str:String = "The secret ingredient(s): ";
    for (var i:uint = 0; i < list.selectedItems.length; i++) {
      str += list.selectedItems[i].data;
      if (i < list.selectedItems.length - 1) {
        str += ", ";
      } else {
        str += ".";
      }
    }
    output.text = str;
  }
);
```

This one may look more complicated than it actually is, so let's break it down. As always, we're using addEventListener() to associate a function with an event. In this case, the event is Event.CHANGE and the function does three things.

First, the variable str holds the phrase "The secret ingredient(s): ".

```
var str:String = "The secret ingredient(s): ";
```

Next, a for loop repeats a particular set of actions. The duration of the loop depends on the number of selected items, based on the Array.length property of the selectedItems property, which is an array. The variable i starts at zero and increments at each "lap" around the loop, so that the line

```
str += list.selectedItems[i].data;
```

refers to the first selected item (item 0), and then the second selected item (item 1), and so on, of the List instance. The reason there's a .data tacked onto the end is because List items are made up of two parts: label and data, which are—bingo!—the elements that comprise the dataProvider parameter described previously.

An if statement adds a comma between items in the middle and a period after the item at the end. Finally, the str variable, which has continuously been updated by this process, is set to the TextField.text property of the output instance.

The net result is that List selections populate a dynamic text field with the ingredients of Kraft Cucumber Ranch dressing.

> *For extra credit, add the line* list.addItem({label:"Ingredient 11", data:"natural flavor"}); *after the existing ActionScript to show that it's also possible to populate a* List *instance programmatically.*

NumericStepper component

NumericStepper is a compact little gadget that lets the user specify a numeric value, either by typing it in or by clicking up and down arrow buttons (see Figure 9-20). You, as a designer, can specify your own desired minimum and maximum values, as well as the size of each increment (count by ones, by twos, by tens, etc.), which can be set via the Parameters tab of the Property inspector.

Figure 9-20. The NumericStepper component

NumericStepper's skins can be edited by double-clicking an instance, and styling can be applied as described in the "Button component" section. This component carries with it the TextInput component, so you'll see both in your library if you add NumericStepper to your movie.

> *Using one or more instances of the* NumericStepper *component in your movie will add 18 KB to the SWF if no other components (other than the automatically included* TextInput*) share the load.*

1. Open the NumericStepper.fla file that accompanies this chapter. Note that the NumericStepper instance has the instance name ns and that the thermometer movieclip has the instance name thermometer. Double-click that movieclip to enter its timeline, and you'll see a red rectangle (masked by a green shape) with the instance name mercury (see Figure 9-21). You're going to set the height of this nested movieclip based on the value property of the NumericStepper instance.

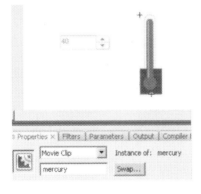

Figure 9-21. The mercury will rise and fall in response to NumericStepper clicks.

2. Select Edit ➤ Edit Document to return to the main timeline. Click into frame 1 of the scripts layer and type the following ActionScript:

```
ns.addEventListener(
  Event.CHANGE,
  function(evt:Event):void {
    thermometer.mercury.height = ns.value;
  }
);
```

3. Test your movie and click the up and down arrow buttons to see it in action.

ProgressBar component

Used often for preloading, the ProgressBar component (shown in Figure 9-22) gives you a rising thermometer–style animation to display load progress when loading files of known size, and a barber pole–style animation to indicate that the user must wait (e.g., for files of unknown size to load or for processes to finish).

Figure 9-22. The ProgressBar component indicates load progress (top), and also presents a "waiting" animation (bottom).

This component doesn't have a whole lot to skin, but you can access what's there by double-clicking a ProgressBar instance. Styling works as it does for the Button component, but ProgressBar doesn't even have text, so your styling choices are fairly slim. (Yes, Figure 9-22 shows text, but that's an example of the Label component.)

> *Using one or more instances of the ProgressBar component in your movie will add 16 KB to the SWF if no other components share the load—that means 16 KB of non-preloadable content (the preloader itself!), so don't put much else into the frame that contains the ProgressBar instance.*

1. Open the ProgressBar.fla file that accompanies this chapter. Note that a ProgressBar instance exists in frame 1 with the instance name pb, as well as a text field with the instance name output. In frame 5, you'll find a fairly heavy image of a homegrown onion, snapped years ago by one of the authors. In the scripts layer, there's a stop() action in frames 1 and 5.

2. Click into frame 1 of the scripts layer and type the following ActionScript:

```
root.loaderInfo.addEventListener(
  Event.COMPLETE,
  function(evt:Event):void {
    play();
  }
);
```

```
pb.source = root.loaderInfo;
```

So far, here's what's going on. An Event.COMPLETE event kicks the playhead back into gear. In other words, when the root (the movie itself) has completed loading, the playhead will play until frame 5 stops it again, revealing the onion.

The ProgressBar part is practically magic. Simply set the ProgressBar.source property to the root's loaderInfo property. It couldn't be simpler. In Chapter 13, you'll see additional loading examples, including one that uses the Loader class. In a case like that, you would set the source property of your ProgressBar instance to the Loader.contentLoaderInfo property of the Loader instance. Later in this chapter, you'll see an example using the UILoader component, in which case it is sufficient merely to point to the UILoader instance itself.

3. Now, if you also want to display a text message indicating a percent loaded, you could do something like the following. Add a few more lines below the existing code:

```
pb.addEventListener(
  ProgressEvent.PROGRESS,
  function(evt:ProgressEvent):void {
    output.text = Math.floor(pb.percentComplete).toString() + "%";
  }
);
```

The ProgressBar component features a percentComplete property, which we're using here. The addEventListener() method is invoked against the pb instance, and the function it performs sets the output text field's text property to a rounded-down string version of the progress percentage—with the percent sign tacked onto the end for good measure.

RadioButton component

Radio buttons are social creatures. They belong in groups, and courteously defer to each other as each takes the spotlight. What are we talking about? We're talking about a component identical in functionality to radio buttons in HTML. Groups of these are used to let the user make a single selection from a multiple-choice set (see Figure 9-23).

Figure 9-23. The RadioButton component lets the user make a single selection from a multiple-choice set.

Double-clicking a RadioButton instance provides access to its skins, which you can edit as described in the "Button component" section. Styling works the same way.

> *Using one or more instances of the* RadioButton *component in your movie will add 16 KB to the SWF if no other components share the load.*

1. Open the RadioButton.fla file that accompanies this chapter. Because radio buttons work in groups, the Parameters tab of the Property inspector has a "group think" parameter we haven't seen with other components: groupName. Select each of the three radio buttons in turn and verify that each belongs to the same group, stooges, even though each has its own distinct label: Moe, Curly, and Larry (see Figure 9-24). Note also the empty dynamic text field whose instance name it output. You're about to wire up the radio buttons to that text field.

9

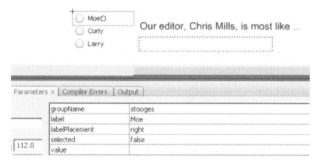

Figure 9-24. RadioButton instances must be associated with a group name.

2. Click into frame 1 of the scripts layer and type the following very condensed but interesting ActionScript:

```
rb1.group.addEventListener(
  Event.CHANGE,
  function(evt:Event):void {
    output.text = rb1.group.selection.label;
  }
);
```

What makes this interesting? In most of the event-handling samples in this book, you've invoked the addEventListener() method on an object that you personally gave an instance name. Here, that might have been rb1—but that's not the focal point in this case. You're not adding an event listener to a particular radio button, but rather to the *group* these buttons belong to. The RadioButton class provides a group property, which means that each instance knows what group it belongs to. It's the group dispatching the Event.CHANGE event, which occurs when any one of these radio buttons is clicked.

It doesn't matter which radio button's group property you use, because all of them point to the same RadioButtonGroup instance. The associated function updates the output text field by sending it the selected button in this group—in particular, that button's label property, which is either Moe, Curly, or Larry.

Note that the Parameters *tab gives you the option to supply a value for each radio button. This allows you to say one thing and do another, just as in the* List *example—except that the* List *choices were* label *and* data; *here, they're* label *and* value, *and the data type of* value *is* Object *(not* String). *The text field wants a string, so you would change that line of ActionScript to* output.text = rb1.group.selection.value.toString();.

ScrollPane component

The ScrollPane component lets you have eyes bigger than your stomach. If you want to display a super-large image—so large that you'll need scrollbars—ScrollPane is your component; Figure 9-25 shows it in action.

Figure 9-25. ScrollPane provides optional scrollbars to accommodate oversized content.

ScrollPane has nested skins because of its scrollbars, so double-clicking an instance during authoring will open up its skin elements in tiers. Styling works the same as described in the "Button component" section, though with no text elements, most of your customization work will probably center around skins.

> *Using one or more instances of the* ScrollPane *component in your movie will add 21 KB to the SWF if no other components share the load.*

1. In this example, there's no need for ActionScript. Open the ScrollPane.fla file that accompanies this chapter. Select the ScrollPane instance and click the Parameters tab of the Property inspector.

2. In the Parameters tab, double-click the right column of the source row. Type Onion.jpg and test the movie. Pretty slick! The source parameter can be pointed to any file format that Flash can load dynamically, including GIFs, PNGs, and other SWFs.

Slider component

The Slider component is conceptually the same thing as NumericStepper, except that instead of clicking buttons to advance from one number to the next, the user drags a knob along a slider, as shown in Figure 9-26. You, as designer, are responsible for setting the minimum and maximum values, and this component lets you specify whether sliding is smooth or snaps to increments specified by you.

Figure 9-26. Slider lets the user drag a handle back and forth to specify a value.

Slider has no text elements, so styling is fairly light. What's there works as it does for the Button component. Skinning also works as it does for Button: double-click a Slider instance in the authoring environment to change the knob and track skins.

> Using one or more instances of the Slider component in your movie will add 17 KB to the SWF if no other components share the load.

1. Open the Slider.fla file that accompanies this chapter. Note that the instance name for the Slider instance is slider, which only works because ActionScript is a case-sensitive language—you couldn't call it Slider, because that's the name of the class that defines this object. Note, also, the instance names circle1 and circle2 on the two circles. You're about to wire up the Slider component to adjust their width and height.

2. Click into frame 1 of the scripts layer and type the following ActionScript:

```
slider.addEventListener(
  Event.CHANGE,
  function(evt:Event):void {
    circle1.scaleX = slider.value / 100;
    circle2.scaleY = slider.value / 100;
  }
);
```

When the Event.CHANGE event is dispatched—this happens as the knob moves along the track—the slider's value property is used to update scaling properties of the circle movieclips. Why divide by 100? In movieclip scaling, 0% is 0 and 100% is 1. Because the Slider instance happens to have its maximum parameter set to 100, the division puts value into the desired range, as shown in Figure 9-27.

Be sure to experiment with the parameters in the Property inspector's Parameters tab. Most of them are intuitive, but liveDragging probably isn't. The liveDragging parameter tells Slider how often to update its value property. Change it to false and test again to see the circles resize less smoothly.

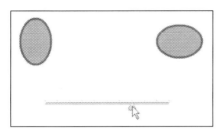

Figure 9-27. A single Slider instance can adjust many objects. Hey, that looks like a face!

You may be surprised to find a direction *parameter (its values are* horizontal *and* vertical*). Why not just use the* Free Transform *tool to rotate this slider? Well, try it. We'll wait . . . Kinda weird, right? It doesn't work. Components are a sophisticated phenomenon, even though they look so simple. What if you want a slanted slider, not horizontal or vertical? Here's a trick: select the* Slider *instance, convert it to a movieclip* (Modify ➤ Convert to Symbol)*, and give that movieclip an instance name. When both the movieclip (here,* sliderClip*) and its nested* Slider *have instance names, you're set.*

```
sliderClip.slider.addEventListener(
  Event.CHANGE,
  function(evt:Event):void {
    circle1.scaleX = sliderClip.slider.value / 100;
    circle2.scaleY = sliderClip.slider.value / 100;
  }
);
```

9

TextArea component

Chapter 6 introduced you to text fields. Consider the TextArea component a text field in a tux. It has an attractive, slightly beveled border, lets you limit how many characters can be typed into it (like input text fields), and is optionally scrollable (see Figure 9-28). This component is akin to the <textarea> element in HTML.

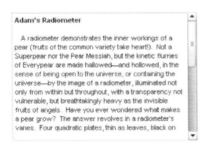

Figure 9-28. TextArea is the James Bond of text fields.

417

TextArea is skinnable, but its parts are few. You'll see a nested skin for the scrollbars when you double-click an instance in the authoring environment. More likely, you'll want to style its text contents, which works as described in the "Button component" section.

> *Using one or more instances of the* TextArea *component in your movie will add 21 KB to the SWF if no other components (other than the automatically included* UIScrollBar*) share the load.*

See the TextArea.fla file that accompanies this chapter for an example of populating a TextArea instance with text. (We figured it would be cruel to make you type in a lengthy bit of sample text on your own.) Note that the TextArea component can display HTML text, as shown in the sample file, or plain text. Use the htmlText or text property accordingly. Note that the Parameters tab of the Property inspector only shows a text parameter for supplying text. We can't imagine anyone using that tiny space to enter more than a sentence.

TextInput component

The TextInput component is the single-line kid brother to TextArea. For this reason, to trump it up, we'll show it displaying one of the shortest short stories in the world, attributed to Ernest Hemingway (see Figure 9-29).

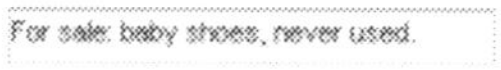

For sale: baby shoes, never used.

Figure 9-29. TextInput features
a slightly beveled look.

TextInput is primarily used to collect typed user input, such as happens in HTML-based "contact us" forms, and can even be set to display password characters as asterisks. The component is skinnable—just double-click an instance in the authoring environment—but there's not much to skin. Styling works as described in the "Button component" section.

> *Using one or more instances of the* TextInput *component in your movie will add 15 KB to the SWF if no other components share the load.*

1. Open the TextInput.fla file that accompanies this chapter. Note the two TextInput instances, with instance names input (top) and output (bottom). Select each component in turn and look at the Parameters tab as you do. For the top TextInput instance, the displayAsPassword and editable parameters are set to true. For the bottom, both of those parameters are set to false. You're about to make the upper component reveal its password to the lower one.

2. Click into frame 1 of the scripts layer and type the following ActionScript:

```
input.addEventListener(
  Event.CHANGE,
  function(evt:Event):void {
    output.text = input.text;
  }
);
```

As text is typed into the upper TextInput instance, the Event.CHANGE event updates the lower instance's text content with that of the other. Because of the parameter settings, the text content is hidden above, but clearly displayed below.

TileList component

TileList is not unlike the ScrollPane component. Both load files for display, optionally with scollbars, but TileList displays numerous files—JPGs, SWFs, and so on—in the tiled arrangement shown in Figure 9-30.

Figure 9-30. TileList displays a tiled arrangement of content, optionally scrolling as necessary.

Double-click a TileList instance to edit its skins. You'll see a second tier of skins for the scrollbars. Styling may be accomplished as described in the "Button component" section; however, the textFormat style must be set using the SelectableList.setRendererStyle() method, as in myTileList.setRendererStyle("textFormat", fmt).

> *Using one or more instances of the* TileList *component in your movie will add 32 KB to the SWF if no other components share the load.*

There are quite a few parameters listed in the Parameters tab of the Property inspector for this component, but they're all easy to grasp. For example, there are settings for the width and number of columns, height and number of rows, direction or orientation (horizontal

9

or vertical), and scrolling settings (on, off, and auto, which makes scrollbars show as necessary). The dataProvider parameter is the most important, because that's where you define the content to show. It works the same as the dataProvider for ComboBox, except that instead of label and data properties, TileList expects label and source.

If you find the Parameters tab a bit confining, you can always use ActionScript to add items to TileList instances.

1. Open the TileList.fla file that accompanies this chapter. Note that the TileList instance has the instance name tl, and the dynamic text field below it has the instance name output.

2. Click into frame 1 of the scripts layer and type the following ActionScript:

```
tl.addItem({label:"Mug 6", source:"Mug06.jpg"});
tl.addItem({label:"Mug 7", source:"Mug07.jpg"});
tl.addItem({label:"Mug 8", source:"Mug08.jpg"});

tl.addEventListener(
  Event.CHANGE,
  function(evt:Event):void {
    output.text = tl.selectedItem.label;
  }
);
```

The first three lines use practically the same approach we used in adding an additional item to the ComboBox instance in that section of the chapter. Here, they give us a few more mug shots (heh, mug shots—we love that joke). In the event handler, the function updates the output text field's text property with the label value of the tile list's selected item.

> TileList *also supports multiple selections, like the* List *component. The sample code in the "List component" section provides the same basic mechanism you would use here, except instead of targeting the* data *property, you'll probably want to target* label, *as shown in the preceding single-selection sample.*

UILoader component

If the Flash CS3 UI components all went to a Halloween party, UILoader would show up as the Invisible Man (see Figure 9-31).

Figure 9-31. Practically speaking, UILoader has no visual elements (and yes, this figure is empty; it tickled us to include it).

So what's the point? Ah, but UILoader is such a selfless, *giving* component! Its purpose is to load and display content other than itself. This keeps you from having to use the Loader class (described in Chapter 13)—in case the thought of ActionScript makes you feel like you just found half a worm in your apple. Simply enter a file name into the source parameter of the Property inspector's Parameters tab, and you're set (see Figure 9-32).

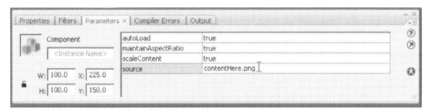

Figure 9-32. Just enter in the name of a supported file format, and Flash will load it.

Using one or more instances of the UILoader component in your movie will add 15 KB to the SWF if no other components share the load.

1. Open the UILoader.fla file that accompanies this chapter. Double-click the UILoader instance if you like; you'll see message that no skins are available. Since we aren't speaking to this component with ActionScript—yet—it doesn't need an instance name. In the Parameters tab of the Property inspector, enter the file name Onion.jpg into the right column of the source row. This references a JPG file in the same folder as your FLA. Test your movie, and you'll see the onion load into its UILoader container.

2. In the Parameters tab, change the maintainAspectRatio parameter to false and test again. This time, the onion loads a bit squished. Our personal preference is usually to maintain aspect ratio. The scaleContent parameter determines whether the loaded content is scaled or cropped in its container.

9

3. Our friend ProgressBar is about to make a cameo appearance. Drag an instance of the ProgessBar component to the stage below the UILoader instance, and give the UILoader instance the instance name loader (see Figure 9-33).

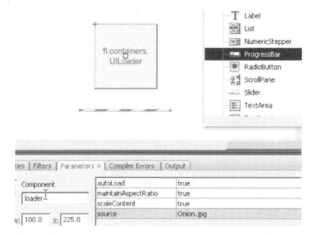

Figure 9-33. It's very easy to show the load progess of a UILoader instance.

4. Select the progress bar, and in the Parameters tab, set its source parameter to loader—that's the instance name you just gave the UILoader instance. You're associating the two. Test your movie, and then in the SWF window that opens, select View ➤ Simulate Download to see some super-easy preloading action.

5. To wrap up, let's add a teensy bit of ActionScript. (Don't worry, that half a worm we mentioned earlier was just a centipede—half a centipede.) To make sure ActionScript talks to the ProgressBar instance, give it an instance name. We're using pb. Click into frame 1 of the scripts layer and type the following ActionScript:

```
pb.addEventListener(
  Event.COMPLETE,
  function(evt:Event):void {
    removeChild(pb);
  }
);
```

What does that do? That makes the progress bar disappear when loading is complete.

UIScroller component

If you read any other sections of this chapter, you've probably already been introduced to the UIScroller component. This component is a humble but useful member of the team, as it allows things to have scrollbars. UIScroller is skinnable when you double-click any instance of it in the authoring environment. Styling doesn't make much sense, but it is possible as described in the "Button component" section.

Using one or more instances of the UIScroller *component in your movie will add 18 KB to the SWF if no other components share the load.*

So as to avoid repeating ourselves, we'll direct your attention to Chapter 6's "Scrolling Text" section to see this component in action.

What you've learned

- How to use the various Flash CS3 UI components
- How to write the ActionScript that controls components
- How to skin a component
- How to manage components in a Flash movie

In the next chapter, we'll show you how to use CSS to format text in a Flash movie. It isn't as dry as it sounds because you can do some pretty interesting things with CSS-formatted text in Flash CS3. What are they? Turn the page to find out.

9

Cascading Style Sheets (CSS) refers to a W3C (World Wide Web Consortium) specification that, in the W3C's own words, provides "a simple mechanism for adding style (e.g., fonts, colors, spacing) to Web documents (www.w3.org/Style/CSS/)." Simple concept, sure—but, as any web developer will tell you, CSS can be a Marlboro-smokin', tumbleweed-kickin' maverick cowboy when it comes to corralling HTML. In other words, CSS is rugged, powerful, and does a great job at making HTML behave. Obviously, this is a good thing. But CSS can also be a bit hard to work with, which makes sense when you're dealing with a stubbly, saddle-sore buckaroo.

In the world of HTML, this trouble is due to the wide variety of browsers (and versions of browsers) in use by the general public. Each browser supports CSS to a varying, and often buggy, degree. In Flash, you have a lot less to worry about, even though the use of CSS requires ActionScript. Why are things easier in a SWF? The answer is mainly that Flash supports only a very small subset of the full CSS specification. This means that there are only a few cows to wrangle. As a Flash designer, you're not worried about half a dozen browsers, but merely a single Flash Player plug-in. As an extra plus, the supported CSS subset hasn't really changed since the feature was introduced in Flash MX 2004 (Flash Player 7).

> "Wait a minute, varmints," you might be saying, "If CSS has been available since Flash Player 7, what you're really talking about are three Flash Players, versions 7 through 9. Don't try to pull a fast one on us!" Well, if we opened it up to ActionScript 2.0, you'd have a good point. Even so, the supported styles are pretty much the same; it's only the ActionScript nitty-gritty that's been updated. In any case, three plug-ins are nothing compared to a herd of browsers—and since we're only dealing with ActionScript 3.0 in this book, Flash Player 9 is the only one that counts. Yippee-ki-yay!

What we'll cover in this chapter

- A brief overview of CSS, including what makes it so useful
- Some of the limitations of CSS in Flash
- How to generate and apply CSS in ActionScript
- The difference between element selectors and class selectors
- Custom HTML tags
- Inheritance basics
- How to style anchor tag hyperlinks
- How to embed fonts for CSS
- How to load styles from an external CSS file

Files used in this chapter:

- Styling01.fla (Chapter10/ExerciseFiles_CH10/Exercise/Styling01.fla)
- Styling02.fla (Chapter10/ExerciseFiles_CH10/Exercise/Styling02.fla)
- Styling03.fla (Chapter10/ExerciseFiles_CH10/Exercise/Styling03.fla)
- Styling04.fla (Chapter10/ExerciseFiles_CH10/Exercise/Styling04.fla)

- ClassSelectors.fla (Chapter10/ExerciseFiles_CH10/ Exercise/ClassSelectors.fla)

- ElementSelectors.fla (Chapter10/ExerciseFiles_CH10/ Exercise/ElementSelectors.fla)

- Hyperlinks.fla (Chapter10/ExerciseFiles_CH10/ Exercise/Hyperlinks.fla)

- HyperlinksVaried.fla (Chapter10/ExerciseFiles_CH10/ Exercise/HyperlinksVaried.fla)

- Inheritance.fla (Chapter10/ExerciseFiles_CH10/Exercise/Inheritance.fla)

- styles.css (Chapter10/ExerciseFiles_CH10/Exercise/styles.css)

- StylingEmbeddedFonts01.fla (Chapter10/ExerciseFiles_CH10/ Exercise/StylingEmbeddedFonts01.fla)

- StylingEmbeddedFonts02.fla (Chapter10/ExerciseFiles_CH10/ Exercise/StylingEmbeddedFonts02.fla)

- StylingExternal.fla (Chapter10/ExerciseFiles_CH10/ Exercise/StylingExternal.fla)

The power of CSS

In a nutshell, the power of CSS is that it allows you to separate styling from informational content. In Flash, we're essentially talking about text. You'll wrap text content in HTML tags—that's one side of the coin—and you'll style those HTML tags with CSS—that's the other side. Flip that coin as you see fit: if you change your mind about how the text should look—regarding font, color, indentation, spacing, and the like—you can change the CSS without upsetting the text. The reverse is also true. Not only that, but styling can be applied to numerous text fields at once, and even managed from a convenient external file. As if that wasn't enough, this external style sheet can update a movie's styles without your having to recompile the SWF! Have we got your interest yet?

Here are the available style properties:

- color: This property determines the color of text, specified as a hexadecimal value preceded by the # sign, as in #FFFFFF, rather than the 0xFFFFFF you would use in ActionScript.

- display: This property determines how the styled object is displayed. Values include inline (displayed without a built-in line break), block (includes a built-in line break), and none (not displayed at all).

- fontFamly: This property allows you to specify fonts for text content—either a single font or comma-separated collection of fonts listed in order of desirability.

- fontSize: This property is used for specifying font size in pixels. Only number values are accepted (units such as pt or px are ignored).

- fontStyle: This property optionally displays text content in italics, if the font in use supports it. Values include normal and italic.

10

- fontWeight: This property optionally displays text content in bold, if the font in use supports it. Values include normal and bold.

- kerning: This property, if specified as true, allows embedded fonts to be rendered with kerning, if the fonts support it. **Kerning**, the removal of a bit of space between letters, is only applied in SWF files generated in the Windows version of Flash. Once the SWF is published, the kerning is visible both in Windows and Mac.

- leading: This property determines the amount of space between lines of text. Negative values, which are allowed, condense lines. Only number values are accepted (units such as pt or px are ignored).

- letterSpacing: Not to be confused with kerning, this property determines the amount of space distributed evenly between characters. Only number values are accepted (units such as pt or px are ignored).

- marginLeft **and** marginRight: These properties add marginal padding by the specified amount in pixels to the left and right. Only number values are accepted (units such as pt or px are ignored).

- textAlign: This property aligns text. Values include left, center, right, and justify.

- textDecoration: This property adds or removes underscoring by way of the underline and none values.

- textIndent: This property indents a text field by the specified amount in pixels—only number values are accepted (units such as pt or px are ignored).

Now let's roll up our sleeves and use some of these properties:

1. Open the Styling01.fla file that accompanies this chapter. There are a few things already in place for you. Note the two dynamic text fields, side by side, with instance names unstyled and styled. There's also a bit of ActionScript in frame 1 of the scripts layer, which does nothing more than build a string of HTML tags and apply that string to the TextField.htmlText property of the two text fields.

2. Test the movie to see two identical copies of the wasabi salmon recipe shown Figure 10-1 (yup, it's a real recipe).

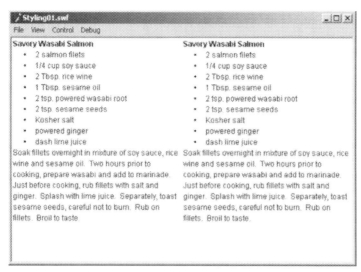

Figure 10-1. CSS is about to save you a lot of effort.

3. Click into frame 1 of the scripts layer and open the Actions panel. The first thing you need to do is import the StyleSheet class, otherwise none of this is going to work. Put your cursor in line 1, in front of the word var, and then press the Enter/Return key a couple times to make room. Type the following code in line 1 (see Figure 10-2):

```
import flash.text.StyleSheet;
```

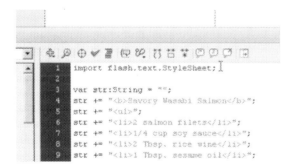

Figure 10-2. The StyleSheet class must be imported.

4. The thing about CSS in Flash is that styling must be applied to a text field before any text is added to it. We're going to leave the unstyled text field as is, in order to have a running comparison. The CSS that formats the styled text field will have to appear before the last line of ActionScript, because the last line actually provides the HTML text. Put your cursor in front of the last line of code and press Enter/Return three times. This is where the new ActionScript will go. Now, hold that thought.

How is this CSS thing going to work? That's a good question, and thankfully, the answer isn't especially hard, even though the process takes a few steps. First, you're going to create an instance of the StyleSheet class. Next, you'll decide on a handful of style properties. You'll repeatedly use the StyleSheet.setStyle() method to associate those properties with an HTML tag. Finally, you'll associate the StyleSheet instance itself with a given text field and add HTML content to that text field.

The crafty thing is that there are a number of ways to handle the setStyle() part. We're going to step you through a wordy approach first, because we think it best summarizes, on a conceptual level, what's going on. When you've seen that, we'll steer you toward a more compact approach, which will eventually lead toward an external CSS file, which is the most versatile way to handle styling in Flash.

5. OK, still holding the thought? Good. Put your cursor into the second of the three blank lines that precede the last line of code. Type the following ActionScript:

```
var css:StyleSheet = new StyleSheet();
var condensed:Object = new Object();

condensed.fontStyle = "italic";
condensed.color = "#A2A2A2";
condensed.leading = "-2";

css.setStyle("li", condensed);
styled.styleSheet = css;
```

Let's review what you've done so far. The first line declares a variable, css, that points to an instance of the StyleSheet class. The second line declares another variable, condensed, that points to an instance of the generic Object class—that's right, this is an Object object—and the next three lines set arbitrary properties of this new object; namely, fontStyle, color, and leading, each of which is set to a string value. The second-to-last line refers again to the css instance, using that instance to invoke StyleSheet.setStyle() with two parameters: an HTML tag to style and the object to style it with. Quite simply, this line says, "Any <li> tags in the house? If so, you're about to get comfy with the condensed object, whose instructions are to render you in italics, in the color #A2A2A2, and at a leading of -2." Finally, a text field whose instance name is styled has its styleSheet property set to the css instance.

6. Test the movie so far to see a change to all the <li> content, as shown in Figure 10-3. You can save and close the movie if you wish.

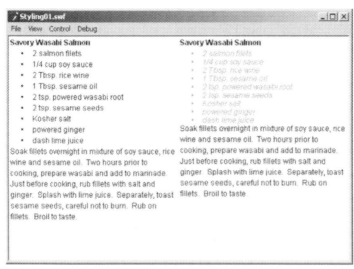

Figure 10-3. CSS styling applied to a series of <li> tags.

Pretty nifty! Now, in case you thought that ActionScript was a lot to type, keep in mind that what you've seen is the gabbiest of the styling approaches. It's possible to collapse five of those lines into one, which we'll do in just a moment. First, let's take a look at how this might have happened without CSS—because once you see that catastrophe, even this version will seem a welcome relief.

Taking just the first <li> tag's content, how would you apply italics? Easy enough; you'll remember from Chapter 6 that this happens with the <i> tag. So far, then, we've got one nested pair of tags:

```
<li><i>2 salmon filets</i></li>
```

What about the coloring? That's the <font> tag. Combined, that makes

```
<li><i><font color="#A2A2A2">2 salmon filets</font></i></li>
```

Almost done! The final style property is leading (the spacing between lines). In the HTML-only realm, that requires the Flash-specific <textformat> tag. This brings the combined total to the following example of spaghetti code:

```
<li><i><font color="#A2A2A2"><textformat leading="-2">2 salmon ➥
filets</textformat></font></i></li>
```

Multiply that by the nine bullet points in this recipe, and you've got carpal tunnel syndrome just waiting to happen! If you decide later to change the text color, you'll have to revisit all nine nested <font> tags and either edit or remove them. It's a mess. Definitely, the CSS styling mechanism is the nicer pick. All the more so if we can reduce the lines of ActionScript.

10

In order to accomplish that, we're going to rely on a shortcut in creating our Object instance, involving the use of the {} characters. Our setStyle() line will continue to use "li" as the first parameter, but the second parameter will be composed of a single shortcut object that holds all three styling properties at once, as shown in Figure 10-4.

```
var condensed:Object = new Object();

condensed.fontStyle = "italic";
condensed.color = "#A2A2A2";
condensed.leading = "-2";

css.setStyle("li", condensed);
```

Figure 10-4. These lines can be folded into a single object reference.

The actual ActionScript looks like this:

```
css.setStyle("li", {fontStyle: "italic", color: "#A2A2A2",➥
leading: "-2"});
```

This brings the full ActionScript styling portion to a mere three lines:

```
var css:StyleSheet = new StyleSheet();
css.setStyle("li", {fontStyle: "italic", color: "#A2A2A2",➥
leading: "-2"});
styled.styleSheet = css;
```

Following suit, let's style up a few more HTML tags:

1. Open the Styling02.fla file that accompanies this chapter. This file picks up where we left off. The same text fields are in place and some styling has already been applied (see the scripts layer). What's there uses the shortened code version we just looked at.

2. Next, you'll style all the <p> tags. Position your cursor after the setStyle() line and press Enter/Return to make room for the new code. Update your ActionScript so that it includes the following new code (shown in bold):

```
var css:StyleSheet = new StyleSheet();
css.setStyle("li", {fontStyle: "italic", color: "#A2A2A2",➥
leading: "-2"});
css.setStyle("p", {textAlign: "justify", leading: "6"});
styled.styleSheet = css;
```

3. Test your movie to see the new formatting—justified and with a taller line height—below the bullet points at the bottom right (see Figure 10-5).

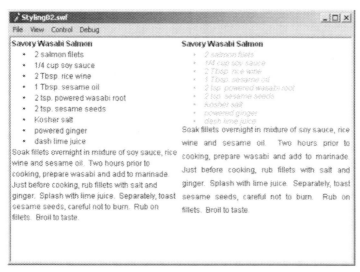

Figure 10-5. After the first style is in place, additional styles are a snap.

Say, this is encouraging! Let's keep right on going. There really isn't enough space between the bullet points and the text below them, so let's pad the bottom of the `<ul>` tag a bit. We'll also want the recipe's title to stand out more.

4. Enter the scripts layer again and update the styling ActionScript so that it includes the following new code (shown in bold):

```
var css:StyleSheet = new StyleSheet();
css.setStyle("li", {fontStyle: "italic", color: "#A2A2A2", ➥
leading: "-2"});
css.setStyle("p", {textAlign: "justify", leading: "6"});
css.setStyle("ul", {leading: "6"});
css.setStyle("b", {fontFamily: "Impact", fontSize: "14", ➥
color: "#339966"});
styled.styleSheet = css;
```

5. Test the movie to see the new styling . . . or part of it. Whoops. There's now space after the bullets—that's the additional 6 pixels of leading we wanted—but the title (the `<b>` content) hasn't changed at all! What's going on? It is a matter of selectors, which we'll deal with in the next section.

6. Feel free to save the file or close it without saving the changes.

> *We're going to go off on a sizable tangent here, but don't worry. It all eventually leads back to the salmon.*

10

Element selectors vs. class selectors

To this point, we've limited our view to something called **element selectors**. These refer to HTML tags—also called HTML elements—and they apply their styling, in one swoop, to all tags of a specified kind. Want to format all <p> content? Write a p element selector. Need to style a bunch of list items (<li>)? Write an li element selector. Pretty easy procedure. At the end of the previous section, though, we saw that it doesn't always work. This is one of the limitations of Flash CSS, and it's an important one to note.

In HTML documents, practically all HTML elements can be styled by way of an element selector. In Flash, the list is vastly reduced. According to the Flash CS3 documentation, the following tags comprise the meager list: <body>, <p>, <li>, and <a>. The interesting thing about this list is that <body> doesn't appear as one of the supported tags noted in the ActionScript 3.0 Language and Components Reference entry for TextField.htmlText. Then again, <ul> doesn't appear in that list either, and yet we saw that tag implement a leading style. So . . . is there a method to this madness? Is there some easy way to keep track of which tags can be styled with element selectors and which can't?

The authors spent a bit of time studying the tea leaves, and this is what we discovered: officially documented or not, the tags that support element selectors are all block elements, with the exception of the anchor tag (<a>). In other words, the rule of thumb is this: if the tag carries with it a built-in line break, then an element selector will do the trick. The special case is hyperlinks, which we'll cover in detail later in the chapter (hyperlinks are a special case in several ways).

For your reference, let's take a quick look at a "proof is in the pudding" sample file:

1. Open the ElementSelectors.fla file that accompanies this chapter. You'll find a text field with the instance name output. The ActionScript in the scripts layer shouldn't be any trouble for you by now: the StyleSheet class is imported, a string of HTML is created, element selectors are defined and then assigned to the StyleSheet instance, and finally, the HTML is supplied to the text field. Test the movie to see the result shown in Figure 10-6.

   The output may not look all that interesting, but it is, because it spells out a few additional "gotchas" while verifying the block element principle.

2. Click into frame 1 of the scripts layer and take a look at the ActionScript in the Actions panel. Each line of HTML ends in a break tag (<br />), just to keep things visually neat. The <a> tag is not a block element, so it does not display an additional, built-in line break as with later tags; but element, so it does not display an additional, built-in line break as with later tags; but

Figure 10-6. Only block elements—and one exception, anchor tags—support element selectors.

as the exception to the rule in question, it does pick up the blue color from its element selector. The <body> and <p> tag contents carry their own additional line breaks—these are block elements—and both display the expected element selector color styling. The <ul> and <li> tags' content is combined. These are also block elements and therefore display a combined pair of extra line breaks—and the expected element selector styling.

Comment out the body and li element selectors in the ActionScript by preceding those lines with double slashes (//), as shown in Figure 10-7.

```
16  var css:StyleSheet = new StyleSheet();
17  css.setStyle("a", {color: "#0000FF"});
18  css.setStyle("b", {color: "#00FF00"});
19  //css.setStyle("body", {color: "#0000FF"});
20  css.setStyle("img", {color: "#00FF00"});
21  css.setStyle("font", {color: "#0000FF"});
22  css.setStyle("i", {color: "#00FF00"});
23  css.setStyle("ul", {color: "#0000FF"});
24  //css.setStyle("li", {color: "#00FF00"});
25  css.setStyle("p", {color: "#0000FF"});
26  css.setStyle("span", {color: "#00FF00"});
27  css.setStyle("textformat", {color: "#0000FF"});
28  css.setStyle("u", {color: "#00FF00"});
```

Figure 10-7. Commenting out the body and li selectors leads to a line-spacing quirk and the idea of inheritance.

3. Test the movie again. It should come as no surprise that the <body> tag content is no longer styled. What may raise your eyebrows is that the extra line break is missing. This is a quirk involving only the <body> tag, and will raise its head again in the "Custom tags" section of this chapter, which follows. The other thing to notice is that the <ul>/<li> content has changed color. The reason for this is that a distinct color style was applied to each tag (green for <ul> and blue for <li>), and the blue won the wrestling match earlier because of a CSS concept called inheritance (covered in the "Style inheritance" section later in the chapter).

4. As a final test, uncomment the body element selector by removing the double slashes from that line. Instead, comment out the p element selector. Test the movie, and you'll see that the <p> content is still blue. Why? Again, this is an example of inheritance, but in a really twisted way. Under normal circumstances, HTML documents feature most of their content inside a <body> tag. If a style is applied to the body, it will "trickle down" to tags inside that body if those inner tags happen to support the style properties at hand. Here in this Flash file, the <p> content is clearly not inside the <body> content, and yet some phantom inheritance seems to still hold sway. Comment out the body element selector one last time, and the <p> content finally turns black.

5. Close the file without saving the changes.

Every development platform has its quirks, and these are a few of the ones that belong to Flash. Being aware of these, even if they aren't burned into your neurons, might just save your hide when something about CSS styling surprises you.

10

Now you've had some experience with block elements and the anchor tag, with the under-standing that anchor tags still hold a bit of mystery, yet to be unfolded. Meanwhile, what remains of the other supported HTML tags? What's the opposite of a block element, and how can one be styled?

In Flash, if it is not a block HTML element, it is an inline element. All that means is that you don't carry your own line break with you. Examples include the <b> and <i> tags, which apply their own innate formatting—bold and italic, respectively—without otherwise inter-rupting the flow of text. As you've seen, inline elements in Flash do not support element selectors. Is there another option, then? You bet your spurs, podner. But it only goes so far.

Not to be confused with the classes discussed in Chapter 4, CSS features **class selectors**, which differ from element selectors in a significant way. Rather than apply their style to all tags of a specified type, class selectors only look for tags that have a class attribute whose value is set to the name of the class in question. We'll see an example of this in just a moment. In HTML documents, just about any tag can be given a class attribute, but this isn't the case in Flash. Actually, nothing *stops* you from giving an HTML tag such an attrib-ute in Flash, but Flash only applies class selector styling to a few tags—and only one of those as an inline element.

Here's another "proof is in the pudding" sample file, which should make everything clear:

1. Open the ClassSelectors.fla file that accompanies this chapter. At first glance, this file may look identical to ElementSelectors.fla, but click into frame 1 of the scripts layer to lay eyes on a different hunk of code. To wit, every HTML tag now has a class attribute, set either to blue or green, and the number of selectors has been reduced to two—the selfsame blue and green styles. Now, how can you tell that these are class selectors and not element selectors? The giveaway, which is easy to miss if you aren't looking for it, is the dot (.) in front of the style names (see Figure 10-8).

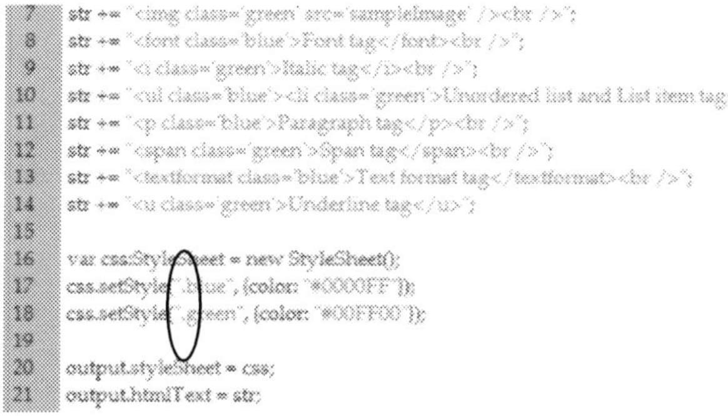

```
7    str += "<img class='green' src='sampleImage' /><br />";
8    str += "<font class='blue'>Font tag</font><br />";
9    str += "<i class='green'>Italic tag</i><br />";
10   str += "<ul class='blue'><li class='green'>Unordered list and List item tags</li></ul><br />";
11   str += "<p class='blue'>Paragraph tag</p><br />";
12   str += "<span class='green'>Span tag</span><br />";
13   str += "<textformat class='blue'>Text format tag</textformat><br />";
14   str += "<u class='green'>Underline tag</u>";
15
16   var css:StyleSheet = new StyleSheet();
17   css.setStyle(".blue", {color: "#0000FF"});
18   css.setStyle(".green", {color: "#00FF00"});
19
20   output.styleSheet = css;
21   output.htmlText = str;
```

Figure 10-8. Class selectors are much more selective than element selectors. You can spot them by their dot prefixes.

Those dots change everything, because at this point, CSS doesn't care what tag it's dealing with—it only cares if that tag has a class attribute set to blue, green, or whatever the style's name is.

> *Be careful where you put your dots! They only belong in the* setStyle() *method, never in the* class *attribute of any tag.*

2. Test the movie to see the result. Remember, in the "real world" outside of Flash, every one of these tags would be affected by the relevant style. In the SWF, only the following tags do anything: <a>, <li>, <p>, and <span>. Unfortunately, we haven't found as neat a way to memorize this list as the other, but if you can remember the block elements that go with element selectors, you need only swap the <body> tag for the <span> tag and drop <ul> to know the block and inline elements that go with class selectors. (Yeah, we agree, it's not especially intuitive.)

3. For the sake of completeness, comment out the .green class selector and test the movie to verify. The <ul>/<li> content turns black because class selectors don't apply to <ul> tags in Flash.

4. Close the movie without saving the changes.

Custom tags

Ready to head back to the wasabi salmon? When we abandoned it to venture out on our educational tangent, most of our styling had taken—all of it had, in fact, except the <b> content, and now we know why. The <b> tag is not a block element, which means it simply doesn't support element selectors. In any case, element selectors affect all tags of a given type, and for the sake of illustration, let's say we only want this recipe's title to stand out, not all content that happens to be set in bold. An obvious solution, then, based on your current knowledge, would be to swap the <b> tag for something that supports class selectors.

1. Open the Styling03.fla file to see an example of just that approach. The key changes in the ActionScript from Styling01.fla are shown in bold in the following code:

```
var str:String = "";
str += "<p class='heading'>Savory Wasabi Salmon</p>";
str += "<ul>";
...
css.setStyle("ul", {leading: "6"});
css.setStyle(".heading", {fontFamily: "Impact", fontSize: "14",➡
color: "#339966"});
styled.styleSheet = css;
```

This mix-and-match approach is perfectly valid. In fact, it's a good basic methodology: use element selectors to sweep through the styling for most tags, and then cover the exceptions with class selectors. Or, you can use custom tags, which provide a kind of hybrid mechanism. They save you from having to type class='someStyleName' throughout your HTML content, and the best part is, you can use familiar, genuine HTML tags from the "real world," if you like (think along the lines of <h1>, <h2>, <strong>, etc.). Flash happily accepts these as "custom" tags, because in its skimpy repertoire, they are.

10

437

2. Open the `Styling04.fla` file to see a custom tag in action. Once again, this file is virtually identical to the previous one, except for the parts shown in bold:

```
var str:String = "";
str += "<strong>Savory Wasabi Salmon</strong>";
str += "<ul>";
...
css.setStyle("ul", {leading: "6"});
css.setStyle("strong", {fontFamily: "Impact", fontSize: "14",➡
color: "#339966"});
styled.styleSheet = css;
```

Note the *absence* of a dot preceding the strong element selector: this is *not* a class selector! If you put 50 <strong> tags full of content in your SWF, all 50 occurrences will pick up the style from this setStyle() method. That said—and we can't stress this enough—please understand that this is not a magical, undocumented way to squeeze additional tags out of Flash's limited HTML support. Flash has no idea what a <strong> tag is, much less that most browsers treat it like a <b> tag. This is nothing more than a convenient hook for CSS, an excuse to dodge class selectors if you happen not to like them. In fact, to prove it, and to reveal a limitation of the custom tag approach, proceed to step 3.

3. Replace the <strong> tag in the highlighted ActionScript with the completely made-up <citrus> tag. There is no such tag in any of the W3C specifications (we looked). Your code will only change in three places:

```
var str:String = "";
str += "<citrus>Savory Wasabi Salmon</citrus>";
str += "<ul>";
...
css.setStyle("ul", {leading: "6"});
css.setStyle("citrus", {fontFamily: "Impact", fontSize: "14",➡
color: "#339966"});
styled.styleSheet = css;
```

4. In addition, find the word "lime" in the bulleted list and wrap it with this new <citrus> tag:

```
str += "<li>powered ginger</li>";
str += "<li>dash <citrus>lime</citrus> juice</li>";
str += "</ul>";
```

5. Now test the movie and take a look. You should see the styling shown in Figure 10-9.

Danger, Will Robinson! What do we learn from the broken dash lime juice line? A valuable lesson, that's what. The recipe's title is fine, but that's because it stands on its own. The lime line breaks because custom tags become block elements when styled. In this case, the word juice has even been pushed past the extra line height given earlier to the <ul> tag.

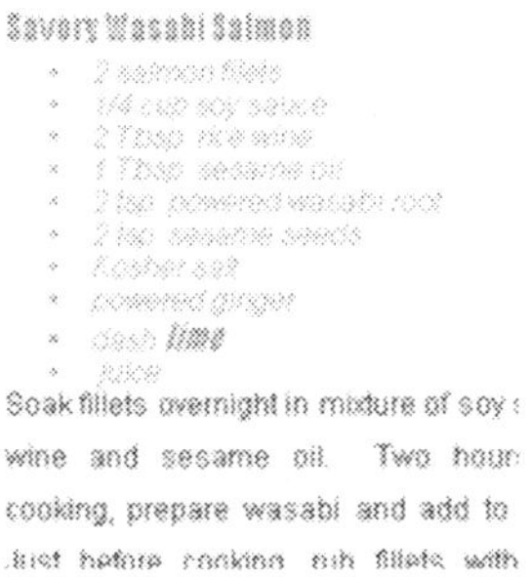

Figure 10-9. Whoops, something isn't right with the lime.

We've spent the last several miles mulling over some pretty arcane rules and even hazier exceptions to them. CSS was supposed to be easier in Flash, right? If your head is spinning, take a sip from the canteen and rest for a spell. While we wait, one of the authors will hum an old, lonely cowboy tune. The lyrics go something like this: "To get the biggest bang for your buck, use element selectors first, then custom tags for headings and other short or specific blocks, and finally class selectors for special cases." (Hey, no one said it had to rhyme, and the melody really is pretty.)

Style inheritance

In moving from Object instances to the object shortcut characters ({}) earlier in the chapter, we saw one way to trim CSS into a more compact form. There's another way to compact things even further, but it's more conceptual than syntactical. The concept is called **inheritance**, and it basically means that styles applied "up the creek" tend to eventually flow down to lower waters. A concrete example will spell this out quicker than an explanation.

1. Open the Inheritance.fla file that accompanies this chapter. You'll see a text field with the instance name output.

2. Click into frame 1 of the scripts layer to view the ActionScript. As with the other samples in this chapter, the code begins by building an HTML string. In this case, the structure of the HTML tags is important. Stripping out the text content, the tag hierarchy looks structurally like this:

```
<body>
  <p></p>
  <outer>
    <mid>
      <inner><span class='big'></span></inner>
    </mid>
  </outer>
</body>
```

Styling is applied to the <body> tag, which sets its font to Courier. The tags nested inside this tag, <p> through <mid>, gain the same font thanks to inheritance. The custom <inner> tag would also inherit Courier, except that this particular tag bucks the trend by specifying

10

439

its own font, Arial, which overrides the inherited Courier and sets up its own new inheritance. Note that the <span> tag within <inner> displays Arial, like its parent, as shown in Figure 10-10.

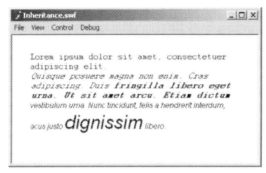

Figure 10-10. CSS inheritance at work

This sort of procedure can get fairly sophisticated. For example, the custom <outer> tag adds italics to the mix.

```
css.setStyle("outer", {fontStyle: "italic"});
```

Because the flow goes downhill, <mid>, <inner>, and <span> inherit not only the font of <outer>'s parent, but also its italics, while sibling tags (<p>) and parent tags (<body>) do not. And honestly, that makes good sense.

In the same vein, the custom <mid> tag introduces bold:

```
css.setStyle("mid", {fontWeight: "bold"});
```

Now, unopposed, <inner> and <span> would inherit that bold styling as well, but <inner> purposefully overrides that by setting fontWeight to normal in its own element selector:

```
css.setStyle("inner", {fontFamily: "Arial", fontWeight: "normal"});
```

In turn, this causes <span> to inherit the override, as it too ignores the bold. Note, however, that <span> does inherit the italics, which were not overridden by a parent tag.

Use this inheritance phenomenon to your advantage. It saves you keystrokes, for one—there's absolutely no need to specify font families for whole groups of related tags, for example—and in addition, it gives you the opportunity to make sweeping changes from relatively few locations.

Styling hyperlinks

Anchor tags are fun to style because of something called pseudo-classes. In CSS talk, a **pseudo-class** corresponds to various possible states of an HTML element and is indicated by a colon (:) prefix. In Flash, the only supported pseudo-classes are associated with the anchor tag (<a>) and correspond to the following states: :link (an anchor tag that specifically contains an href attribute), :hover (triggered by a mouse rollover), and :active (triggered by a mouse click). The long and short of this is that you have the tools you need to create different anchor tag styles that update as the mouse moves and clicks your hyperlinks. Note that Flash does not support the :visited pseudo-class, which in normal CSS indicates that a hyperlink has already been clicked.

Think of pseudo-classes as a second tier of styles, not separated by hierarchy, as shown in the "Style inheritance" section, but separated by time or events.

1. Open the Hyperlinks.fla file to see an example in action. The ActionScript begins, as always, by establishing an HTML string:

```
var str:String = "";
str += "<ul>";
str += "<li><a href='http://www.apress.com/'>Hyperlink 1</a></li>";
str += "<li><a href='event:someFunction'>Hyperlink 2</a></li>";
str += "<li><a href='http://www.friendsofed.com/'>➡
Hyperlink 3</a></li>";
str += "</ul>";
```

These anchor tags happen to be nested within list items, but they needn't be. The important part is that anchor tags exist that have href attributes actively in use. In these next three lines, the element selectors provide a style of anchor tags in any state—that's the first highlighted line—followed by distinct styles for the :hover and :active pseudo-classes.

```
var css:StyleSheet = new StyleSheet();
css.setStyle("li", {leading: "12"});
css.setStyle("a", {textDecoration: "none"});
css.setStyle("a:hover", {fontStyle: "italic"});
css.setStyle("a:active", {fontStyle: "italic",➡
text-decoration: "underline", color: "#FF0000"});
output.styleSheet = css;
```

2. Test this movie to verify that hovering over hyperlinks puts them temporarily in italics, and that clicking additionally displays an underline and new color. Note that the italic style isn't inherited by :active because :active is not a child of :hover; they have a sibling relationship.

What if you'd like more than one style for your hyperlinks? Answer: Use a class selector.

3. Open HyperlinksVaried.fla for an example. First, here's the new HTML:

```
var str:String = "";
str += "<ul>";
str += "<li><a href='http://www.apress.com/'>Hyperlink 1</a></li>";
str += "<li><a href='event:someFunction'>Hyperlink 2</a></li>";
str += "<li><a href='http://www.friendsofed.com/'>➡
Hyperlink 3</a></li>";
str += "</ul>";
str += "<ul>";
str += "<li><a class='oddball' href='http://www.apress.com/'>➡
Hyperlink 4</a></li>";
```

10

```
str += "<li><a class='oddball' href='event:someFunction'>➥
Hyperlink 5</a></li>";
str += "<li><a class='oddball' href='http://www.friendsofed.com/'>➥
Hyperlink 6</a></li>";
str += "</ul>";
```

Unfortunately, it isn't possible to create unique pseudo-classes for the oddball-specific anchor tags, but the following new class selector at least separates the new batch of hyperlinks in their default state:

```
var css:StyleSheet = new StyleSheet();
css.setStyle("li", {leading: "12"});
css.setStyle("a", {textDecoration: "none"});
css.setStyle("a:hover", {fontStyle: "italic"});
css.setStyle("a:active", {fontStyle: "italic",➥
textDecoration: "underline", color: "#FF0000"});
css.setStyle(".oddball", {color: "#00FF00"});
output.styleSheet = css;
```

4. Close the open files, and let's now look at embedding fonts.

Embedded fonts

Before we take what we've learned and nudge it all toward an external CSS file, let's make a quick stop at the Last Chance Saloon to talk about embedded fonts. CSS in Flash requires HTML, which in turn requires a dynamic text field. As you learned in Chapter 6, only static text fields embed font outlines by default. What this means is that unless you purposefully embed your fonts—and the choice is yours—CSS-enhanced SWFs tend to have that jagged, non-font-embedded look (shown in Figure 10-11).

Figure 10-11. Text can look a bit choppy if fonts aren't embedded.

Font symbols were introduced in Chapter 6, but there's a new twist in how they're used with CSS. To recap, the font embedding process is as follows:

1. Add a font symbol to the library and associate it with the desired font on your system.

2. Enable the font symbol's linkage by exporting the symbol for ActionScript.

3. Set the text field's embedFonts property to true.

4. Reference the font symbol's linkage class name—this has nothing to do with CSS class selectors; it's just coincidentally the same term—in place of the font's actual name in any relevant styles.

The trouble is that the process doesn't work as advertised. Here's how to fix it.

1. Open the StylingEmbeddedFonts01.fla file that accompanies this chapter. Test the movie and you'll see a blank SWF. This is odd because with the inclusion of the ActionScript, this movie should presumably work just fine.

2. Click into frame 1 of the scripts layer and note the following pertinent lines of code:

```
css.setStyle("strong", {fontFamily: "ImpactNormal", fontSize:➡
"14", color: "#339966"});

output.embedFonts = true;
```

In the first line, notice the reference to a font named ImpactNormal. This name refers to the linkage class name of a font symbol in the library, which we'll see in just a moment. The second line turns on font embedding for the output text field instance.

3. Right-click (PC) or Ctrl-click (Mac) the ImpactNormal font symbol in the library. Choose Linkage from the context menu and verify that the font is exported for ActionScript (see Figure 10-12), and has a Class name of ImpactNormal.

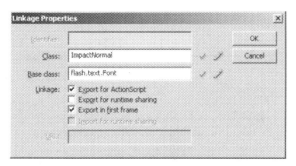

Figure 10-12. The font symbol has been given what at first glance appears to be valid linkage properties.

Flash simply doesn't like something in this file as it stands. The trouble—and this is a bona fide bug—is due to the arbitrary class name given to the font symbol. In the Chapter 6 sample file, this didn't matter because the text field's font was specified via the Property inspector rather than ActionScript. In an ideal world, the linkage class name provides the necessary "link" to this library asset, but in this case, we'll have to roll with Flash's whim.

4. Update the ActionScript to reference the font's actual name, as shown in the font list of the Property inspector:

```
css.setStyle("strong", {fontFamily: "Impact", fontSize: "14",➡
color: "#339966"});
```

Note that it makes no difference what the font symbol's library name or linkage class is. In this case, the library name is still ImpactNormal. Test your movie, and the text shown in Figure 10-13 magically appears. Hey, that's an improvement! Not only does the recipe's title show up, but the lettering is smooth. Now for the rest of the text.

10

443

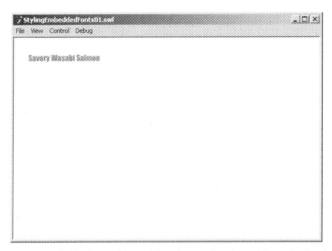

Figure 10-13. The ImpactNormal font is now showing, without the jaggies.

5. Even though it isn't explicitly done, this text field is being asked to display more than one font. Sure, the only font mentioned in the css instance is Impact, but the Property inspector happens to show Arial for the text field, which means the default font is Arial. The text field's embedFonts property has been set to true, which means only embedded fonts can be displayed. Two fonts are being summoned, so two fonts need to be embedded.

6. Using the technique described in Chapter 6, add an Arial font symbol to your library and name the symbol whatever you like. Make sure to export it for ActionScript. To prove that neither the library name nor linkage class name matters—because ActionScript does not reference this second font directly—compare your work with StylingEmbeddedFonts02.fla, whose embedded Arial is named HornyToads in the library. Test your movie (see Figure 10-14). Bingo! All of the text content shows.

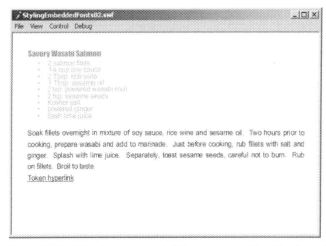

Figure 10-14. All the text is accounted for, and none of it suffers from the jaggies.

Loading external CSS

If we had to pick our favorite aspect of CSS in Flash, it would undoubtedly be the fact that CSS styling can be loaded from an external file. The existence of this feature brings the concept of separating style from informational content to its logical conclusion. Given all you've learned so far in this chapter, you'll be happy to find that loading external CSS is a piece of cake. There's really only one snare to be aware of: some of the style properties we showed you in the beginning of the chapter are spelled just a tad differently when they appear in an external file. Single-word properties, such as color or display, are identical. Multi-word properties, such as fontFamily or fontSize, are split into hyphenated parts: font-family, font-size, and so on.

1. Open the StylingExternal.fla file that accompanies this chapter. You'll see a single text file with the instance name output. Click into frame 1 of the scripts layer and take a quick look at the ActionScript. By now, the HTML portion will be old hat—it's a resurrection of the salmon recipe one last time, with a token hyperlink at the bottom. The new stuff is just below:

```
var css:StyleSheet = new StyleSheet();
var loader:URLLoader = new URLLoader();
loader.load(new URLRequest("styles.css"));
loader.addEventListener(
  Event.COMPLETE,
  function(evt:Event):void {
    css.parseCSS(URLLoader(evt.target).data);
    output.styleSheet = css;
    output.htmlText = str;
  }
);
```

The first line creates our familiar StyleSheet instance. The next . . . aha, that's the nifty one! A variable, loader, is declared and set to an instance of the URLLoader class. This differs from the Loader class (which you'll see in Chapter 13), which loads images or SWFs. What makes URLLoader different is that it not only loads files, but actually reads them, which is essential when the goal is to sift through external CSS.

The URLLoader.load() method is invoked on the loader instance with the expression new URLRequest("styles.css") as the parameter. This is a shortcut way of converting the raw string "styles.css" into the format needed. Finally, the Event.COMPLETE event is handled with a function that performs three straightforward tasks: parse the loaded CSS, set the text field's styleSheet property to the css instance, and set its htmlText property to the prepared HTML string. You already know how the last two work, so let's pick apart the first line of this function. The StyleSheet.parseCSS() method takes a single parameter, which in this case is the expression URLLoader(evt.target).data. That may look like a mouthful, but it's nothing more than a compact way of getting at the CSS styles themselves. The evt.target part refers to the file loaded by loader, and is wrapped in a URLLoader() function to make it presentable. Consider that its calling card, or that URLLoader() has run a comb through evt.target's hair. The data part refers to the data inside said file.

10

2. Open the `styles.css` file in Dreamweaver CS3 or any simple text editor such as NotePad on the PC or TextEdit on the Mac.

> *CSS files, though they serve a special styling purpose, are really just text files with a `.css` file extension).*

The contents should be easily recognizable to you:

```
li {
    font-style: italic; color: #A2A2A2; leading: -2;
}

p {
    text-align: justify; leading: 6;
}

ul {
    leading: 6;
}

strong {
    font-family: Impact; font-size: 14; color: #339966;
}

a {
    font-family: Courier; font-weight: bold;
}

a:hover {
    color: #FF00FF;
}
```

Besides the hyphenated style properties and a few minor syntactical differences, these selectors represent the same styling approach you've seen throughout this chapter. The syntax differences to look out for are as follows: in this version, neither property names nor values are wrapped in quotation marks, as they are in ActionScript (e.g., font-style: italic instead of fontStyle: "italic"); and properties are separated by semicolons rather than commas, like this:

```
li { fontStyle: italic; color: #A2A2A2; leading: -2; }
```

instead of this:

```
css.setStyle("li", { fontStyle: "italic", color: "#A2A2A2", ➥
leading: "-2" });
```

By the way, thanks to this punctuation, you have some leeway in how you arrange the properties, both in ActionScript and the CSS file; single-line or spread over several lines—it doesn't matter. As long as the required parts are present, Flash can figure out what you mean. So go ahead and suit your fancy. For example, this

```
li { fontStyle: italic, color: #A2A2A2, leading: -2 }
```

is the same as

```
li {
  fontStyle: italic;
  color: #A2A2A2;
  leading: -2;
}
```

3. And now we've arrived at the punch line. Test the movie to generate a SWF file, which should look something like Figure 10-15. Now close Flash. That's right, shut down the application. The rest is a matter between you, a SWF, and a CSS file.

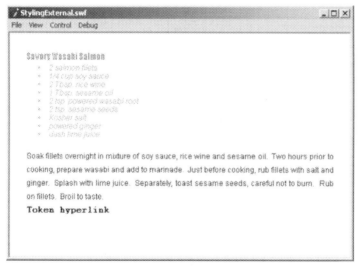

Figure 10-15. CSS styles pulled from an external CSS file

10

4. Double-click your newly created StylingExternal.swf file to give it one last look. This is a bit like making sure the magician has nothing up either sleeve. Now change a few of the style properties in styles.css. As a suggestion, update the p and strong styles as follows:

```
p {
  margin-left: 100; leading: 12;
}

strong {
  font-family: Impact; font-size: 40; color: #339966;
}
```

5. When you make your changes, save the document.

6. Close StylingExternal.swf and double-click it again to launch the SWF. Notice how you can change the look of a movie without having to change the code (see Figure 10-16).

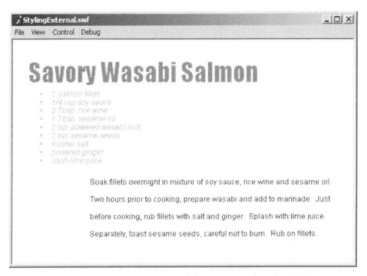

Figure 10-16. Look, Ma—style changes without re-creating the SWF!

Without republishing the SWF, you've updated its formatting! That's no small feat.

Hey, did you catch something missing? What happened to that hyperlink? The increased leading in the p style has pushed it off the stage! In fact, the phrase Broil to taste has also been shoved aside. No problem. Just readjust the leading property or decrease the strong style's font-size property until everything fits. This sort of tweaking is what CSS was made for.

> At the time this chapter was written, one of the authors had recently completed a Flash-based training presentation for a U.S. government agency that featured over 250 slides. At one point, the author needed to change the color of one of the heading styles to a slightly different orange. Guess who was happy that day because he had used CSS in his SWFs?

What you've learned

Apart from learning what to serve the authors at your next barbecue, you have discovered that the CSS techniques widely employed in the HTML universe are just as applicable to your Flash efforts. As you moved through this chapter, you learned the following:

- How to apply CSS styling through ActionScript
- The difference between an element selector and a class selector
- That you can create your own custom tags

- How to use the concept of inheritance to your advantage
- That there is a pesky bug—and a workaround—when it comes to using embedded fonts in the library
- How to use an external CSS style sheet in Flash

If there is one major theme running through this chapter, it is this: your CSS skills put a powerful tool in your arsenal. Speaking of powerful tools, XML's relationship with Flash just got a. power boost. Turn the page to find out.

10

11 DYNAMIC DATA (XML) AND FLASH

Flash is a social creature. Not only does it rub elbows with HTML, coexisting happily with text, JavaScript, images, audio, video, Cascading Style Sheets (CSS), and more, but it can also reach out past its own SWF boundaries to collaborate with data hosted on a server.

In the hands of an experienced programmer, Flash can interact with database applications by way of the URLLoader and URLVariables classes, perform web service and Flash remoting calls, and even slap a secret handshake with Ajax, thanks to the ExternalInterface class. All this from a browser plug-in that began its life as a way to improve on animated GIFs! It's easy to see why Flash has become a widespread phenomenon, and its versatility makes equally social creatures of the countless designers and developers who end up warming their diverse mitts around the same campfire because of it.

This book isn't here to make programmers out of artists. We don't have the page count to delve into most of the concepts just mentioned, but we are going to introduce you to a markup language called XML that, with a bit of help from ActionScript, can make your SWFs dynamic.

What we'll cover in this chapter:

- An overview of XML
- How to retrieve and filter XML data using E4X syntax
- How to build a dynamic slideshow driven by XML

Files used in this chapter:

- LoadXML.fla (Chapter11/ExerciseFiles_CH01/Exercise/LoadXML.fla)
- LoadXML-E4XFiltering.fla (Chapter11/ExerciseFiles_CH01/ Exercise/LoadXML-E4XFiltering.fla)
- LoadXML-E4XBonusRound.fla (Chapter11/ExerciseFiles_CH01/ Exercise/LoadXML-E4XBonusRound.fla)
- popeye.xml (Chapter11/ExerciseFiles_CH01/Exercise/popeye.xml)
- slideshow.xml (Chapter11/ExerciseFiles_CH01/Exercise/slideshow.xml)
- Slideshow.fla (Chapter11/ExerciseFiles_CH01/Exercise/Slideshow.fla)
- SlideshowXML.fla (Chapter11/ExerciseFiles_CH01/ Exercise/SlideshowXML.fla)
- geocache01.jpg (Chapter11/ExerciseFiles_CH01/Exercise/geocache01.jpg)
- geocache02.jpg (Chapter11/ExerciseFiles_CH01/Exercise/geocache02.jpg)
- geocache03.jpg (Chapter11/ExerciseFiles_CH01/Exercise/geocache03.jpg)
- geocache04.jpg (Chapter11/ExerciseFiles_CH01/Exercise/geocache04.jpg)
- geocache05.jpg (Chapter11/ExerciseFiles_CH01/Exercise/geocache05.jpg)
- geocache06.jpg (Chapter11/ExerciseFiles_CH01/Exercise/geocache06.jpg)

The power of XML

To start, let's take a quick survey of what XML is. If you haven't already worked with XML, well . . . we bet our next single malt Scotch you've at least heard of it. The letters stand for eXtensible Markup Language, and extensibility is almost certainly the reason XML has become a towering champ in data communication. Countless markup languages and file formats are based on XML, including SMIL, RSS, XAML, MXML, RDF, WAP, SVG, SOAP, WSDL, OpenDocument, XHTML, and truly more than would fit on this page. We'll leave the letter combinations to a Scrabble master.

"That's fine and dandy," you might be saying, "But guys—*what is XML*?" Fair enough. The remarkable thing about this language is that it can basically be whatever you want it to, provided you stick by its rules. The main purpose of XML is to expedite the sharing of data. In fact, XML is so flexible that newcomers are often baffled on where to even begin. On paper—or rather, on the screen—XML looks a lot like HTML, except instead of predetermined tags and attributes, you organize your content into descriptive tags of your own design. HTML formats data, and XML describes data. The combination of familiar, hierarchical format and completely custom tags generally makes XML content easy to read, both to computers and humans. By separating your data from the movie, you give yourself the opportunity to change content from the outside, affecting SWFs without having to republish them.

Writing XML

Let's say you've been tasked with organizing a collection of vintage Popeye cartoons. You've got five short films on your list: *I Yam What I Yam*; *Strong to the Finich*; *Beware of Barnacle Bill*; *Vim, Vigor, and Vitaliky*; and *Little Swee' Pea*. Each cartoon has its own release date, running time, and cast of characters. Where to begin? Let's take a look.

Every XML document must have at least one tag, which constitutes its **root element**. The root element should describe the document's contents. In this case, we're dealing with cartoons, so let's make that our root:

```
<cartoons></cartoons>
```

11

> *Looks kinda crazy, doesn't it? Almost like you're getting away with something. After all, a technology that facilitates stock market transactions and configures user preferences should be . . . somehow . . . serious—right? Hey, if you don't think Popeye is seriously funny, you haven't spent enough time with Descartes. I think, therefore I yam. (Thank you! We'll be here all week.)*

The rest of our elements will layer themselves inside this first one. Every cartoon is its own film, so we'll add five `<film>` elements:

```
<cartoons>
  <film></film>
  <film></film>
  <film></film>
  <film></film>
  <film></film>
</cartoons>
```

Each film has a title, so the next step seems obvious enough:

```
<cartoons>
  <film>
    <title>I Yam What I Yam</title>
  </film>
  <film>
    <title>Strong to the Finich</title>
  </film>
  <film>
    <title>Beware of Barnacle Bill</title>
  </film>
  <film>
    <title>Vim, Vigor, and Vitaliky</title>
  </film>
  <film>
    <title>Little Swee' Pea</title>
  </film>
</cartoons>
```

You get the idea. It doesn't take much effort to connect the rest of the dots. An excerpt of the completed document might look something like this:

```
<cartoons>
  <film>
    <title>I Yam What I Yam</title>
    <releaseDate>September 29, 1933</releaseDate>
    <runningTime>6 min</runningTime>
  </film>
    . . .
</cartoons>
```

Actually, that's isn't complete after all, is it? The cast of characters is missing. For that, another tier of elements is in order:

```
<cartoons>
  <film>
    <title>I Yam What I Yam</title>
    <releaseDate>September 29, 1933</releaseDate>
    <runningTime>6 min</runningTime>
```

```
      <cast>
        <character>Popeye</character>
        <character>Olive Oyl</character>
        <character>Wimpy</character>
        <character>Big Chief</character>
      </cast>
    </film>
    . . .
  </cartoons>
```

That would certainly do it. The tag names are meaningful, which is handy when it comes time to retrieve the data. The nested structure organizes each concept into a hierarchy that makes sense: characters belong to a cast, which is one aspect, along with title, release date, and running time, of a film. Nicely done—though in a sizable collection, this particular arrangement might come across as bulky. Is there a way to trim it down? Sure thing. Remember, XML allows you to create your own attributes, so you have the option of rearranging the furniture along these lines:

```
  <cartoons>
    <film title="I Yam What I Yam" releaseDate="September 29, 1933" ➥
  runningTime="6 min">
      <cast>
        <character name="Popeye" />
        <character name="Olive Oyl" />
        <character name="Wimpy" />
        <character name="Big Chief" />
      </cast>
    </film>
    . . .
  </cartoons>
```

The exact same information is conveyed. The only difference now is how it would be retrieved, which you'll see in the "E4X" section of this chapter. Which approach is better? Honestly, the choice is yours. It's not so much a question of better as it is what best matches your sense of orderliness. Ironically, this open-ended quality, which is one of XML's strongest assets, is the very thing that seems to scare off so many XML freshmen.

11

> *Working with and structuring an XML document follows the first principle of web development: "Nobody cares how you did it. They just care that it works." Find what works best for you, because in the final analysis, your client will never pick up the phone and say, "Dude, that was one sweetly structured XML document you put together."*

Folks, this is a bit like an artistic ceramics class. As long as you're careful around the kiln, nobody can tell you whose vase is art and whose isn't. Just work the clay between your fingers, let a number of shapes mull around your noggin, and then form what you've got into a structure that appeals to you. While you're at it, keep a few rules in mind:

- If you open a tag, close it (<tag></tag>).

- If a tag doesn't come in two parts—that is, if it only contains attributes, or nothing at all—make sure it closes itself (<tag />).

- Close nested tags in reciprocating order (<a><c /></a> is correct; <a><c /></a> lights your pants on fire).

- Wrap attribute values in quotation marks (<tag done="right" />, <tag done=wrong />).

The Popeye example just shown would be saved as a simple text file with the .xml file extension—for example, popeye.xml—and that's that.

Now that our introductions have been made, let's get social.

> *Feel free to use a text editor such as NotePad on the PC or TextEdit on the Mac. Just be sure you add the .xml extension to the file's name. If you have Dreamweaver CS3, that's even better, because it will offer code completion suggestions to speed up your workflow.*

Loading an XML file

The ActionScript required for loading an XML document isn't especially involved. You'll need an instance of the XML and URLLoader classes, and then, of course, an XML document. In our case, the document will always be an actual XML file, although XML documents can be built from scratch with ActionScript.

Open the LoadXML.fla file that accompanies this chapter. Click into frame 1 of the scripts layer and open the Actions panel to see the following code:

```
var xml:XML = new XML();
var loader:URLLoader = new URLLoader();
loader.load(new URLRequest("popeye.xml"));
loader.addEventListener(
  Event.COMPLETE,
  function(evt:Event):void {
    xml = XML(evt.target.data);
    trace(xml);
  }
);
```

Let's break it down. The first two lines declare a pair of variables, xml and loader, that point to instances of the XML and URLLoader classes, respectively.

Line 3 then invokes the URLLoader.load() method on the loader instance, specifying the expression new URLRequest("popeye.xml") as the parameter. In your own projects, you will of course replace popeye.xml with the name of your own XML files. This procedure starts the load process, but the data isn't available until the XML document has fully arrived from the server. For this reason, the final block attaches an Event.COMPLETE handler to the loader instance.

In response, the handler function sets the xml instance to the data property of the target of the evt parameter passed into the function. That's a mouthful, but it basically means that the xml instance is associated with the actual text content of the popeye.xml file. At this point, the text file's XML tags become a "living XML object" in the SWF, accessible via that xml variable. To prove it with this sample, a trace() function sends the full set of Popeye elements to the Output panel. Test the movie and compare the Output panel's content to the popeye.xml file itself, which you can open with Dreamweaver CS3 or any simple text editor.

The preceding sample code will serve as the basis for all loading for the rest of the chapter. It's really that simple. Even better, ActionScript 3.0 makes it just as easy to actually *use* XML, so let's jump right in.

E4X

In ActionScript 2.0, interacting with an XML class instance was a bit like groping in the dark for matching socks (and it's hard enough to sort laundry with the lights on!). The reason for this is because of the way XML elements used to be accessed once loaded, which wasn't by the practical tag names we supplied earlier in the chapter.

Until Flash CS3 arrived on the scene, XML in Flash was not up there on the list of "cool things I really need to do." In fact, many designers and developers (one of the authors among them) regarded the use of XML as being similar to the long walk to the principal's office in grade school. The walk was so painful because you just knew your parents were about to be involved and a world of grief was to be opened on you. Readers familiar with Flash XML prior to CS3 will doubtless groan to remember obtuse expressions such as, for example, xmlInstance.firstChild.firstChild.childNodes[2]. Flash developers used properties like firstChild and childNodes because they had to, not because it was fun. Then there was the "now defunct" XMLConnector component, which complicated our lives more than simplifying the process. ActionScript 3.0 does away with this groping, thanks to something called E4X. Hey, hear that whooshing noise? That's the sound of everyone dashing to meet this new kid in the neighborhood with the really cool bike.

What is E4X, and what makes it so good? Seemingly named after an extra from a George Lucas feature, those three characters form a cutesy abbreviation of ECMAScript for XML, a specification that provides a completely new, simplified way to access data in an XML instance. In E4X, elements are referenced by the name you give them. Paths to nested elements and attributes are easily expressed by a neatly compact syntax of dots (.) and *at* symbols (@), which closely matches the dot-notation pathing you're already familiar with from the Twinkie example in Chapter 4.

Here's how it works:

11

1. If you haven't already, open the LoadXML.fla file that accompanies this chapter. Click into frame 1 of the scripts layer and open the Actions panel to reveal the ActionScript. The trace() function at line 8 is about to illustrate a number of dynamite E4X features.

2. Testing the movie as it stands puts the full XML document's contents into the Output panel. So far, so good; but if you don't care about the root element, <cartoons>, and simply want to see the <film> elements, update the trace() line to read trace(xml.film);. Once you do that, test the movie again. This time, the <cartoons> tag doesn't show, because you're only accessing its children.

   To view <film> elements individually, use the array access operator, [ ], and specify the desired element, starting your count with 0 (zero):

   ```
   trace(xml.film[0]);
   // displays the first <film> element (I Yam What I Yam)
   // and its children

   trace(xml.film[1]);
   // displays the second <film> element (Strong to the Finich)
   // and its children
   ```

3. Now, what about attributes? To see those, just precede an attribute's name with the @ symbol as part of your dot-notation path reference. For example, if you want to see the title attribute of the first <film> element, type the following:

   ```
   trace(xml.film[0].@title);
   ```

   To see the second <film> element's title, substitute 0 with 1; to see the third, substitute 1 with 2; and so on. Based on this pattern, the last element's title attribute would be xml.film[4].@title—but we only know to use the number 4 because we're aware how many <film> elements there are. What if we don't know?

   In this case, it helps to understand exactly what you're getting back from these E4X results. What you're getting are instances of the XMLList class, which means you can invoke any of the methods that class provides on these expressions.

   For example, we've already seen that the expression xml.film returns a list of all the <film> elements. That expression *is* a bona fide XMLList instance, so by appending an XMLList method—say, length()—to the expression, you get something useful (in this case, the length of the list, which is 5). We know that in this context, counting starts with 0, so to see the title attribute of the last <film> element, put the following somewhat complex expression inside the array access operator ([ ]):

   ```
   trace(xml.film[xml.film.length() - 1].@title);
   ```

   It may look a little scary, but it isn't when you reduce it to its parts. The expression xml.film.length() - 1 evaluates to the number 4, so what you're seeing is as good as actually *using* the number 4.

   To see the title attribute of all <film> elements, drop the array access operator altogether:

   ```
   trace(xml.film.@title);
   ```

In the Output panel, you'll see that the combined results run together (as shown in Figure 11-1). The reason is because these attributes don't have any innate formatting; they aren't elements in a nested hierarchy, they are just individual strings. Let's fix that.

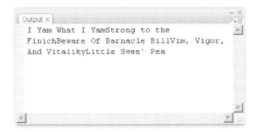

Figure 11-1. Unless they have their own line breaks, attributes will run together.

4. In this situation, another XMLList method can help you out. To make each title appear on its own line, append toXMLString() to the existing expression:

```
trace(xml.film.@title.toXMLString());
```

5. Swap title for releaseDate to see release dates instead, as shown in Figure 11-2:

```
trace(xml.film.@releaseDate.toXMLString());
```

```
Output ×
    September 29, 1933
    June 29, 1934
    25 January 1935
    January 03, 1936
    September 25, 1936
```

Figure 11-2. Any element's attributes can be retrieved.

6. What about looking at a list of the cast members? Viewing individual cast members is just as easy. Update the trace() function to look like this:

```
trace(xml.film[0].cast.character[1]);
```

That instructs Flash to look at the first <film> element's cast element and pull out the second of its character elements, which happens to be Olive Oyl. For fun, and to see how easy E4X makes things for you, contrast the preceding intuitive reference with its ActionScript 2.0 equivalent: xml.firstChild.firstChild.firstChild.childNodes[1]. Which would you rather use?

Moving back to the kinder, gentler world of ActionScript 3.0, update the trace() function as follows to see the whole cast of the third film:

```
trace(xml.film[2].cast.character);
```

Interesting—this time you get actual elements, complete with their tags, as shown in Figure 11-3.

11

Figure 11-3. Accessing elements selects the elements themselves, as well as their children.

This happens because of a characteristic of XML that isn't especially obvious. Once you know it, though, you're set. The characteristic goes like this: in the expression <character>Popeye</character>, you're not just looking at one element, you're *really* looking at two.

Both the tag (<character>) and its content (Popeye, in this case) are considered elements. In XML proper, these are also known as nodes, and there are a dozen node types. Flash only supports two of them, ELEMENT_NODE and TEXT_NODE, which is a relief—and knowing those two lets you easily pull out a tag's content. As before, an XMLList method, descendants(), comes to the rescue:

```
trace(xml.film[2].cast.character.descendants());
```

This gives you run-on results, because, like attributes, these text elements don't have any inherent formatting. All you need to do is just slap the toXMLString() method onto the end of the code line:

```
trace(xml.film[2].cast.character.descendants().toXMLString());
```

The result is exactly the sort of thing you might use to populate a text field (as shown in Figure 11-4).

Figure 11-4. Like attributes, text-only elements are nothing more than strings.

Remember, we are dealing with text in this example, so although the results may look rather plain, you can format and manipulate them in a number of ways, as outlined in Chapters 6 and 10.

7. All right, we'll give you one more illustration of E4X (we've saved the best for last). The popeye.xml file included with this chapter has slightly different runningTime attributes from those shown earlier in the chapter. Instead of a whole phrase, such as "6 min," these attributes show only numbers. Why? Because E4X allows you to make comparisons, which lets you filter content based on specific criteria.

Let's say you want to know which films have a running time longer than 6 minutes. Return again to our humble trace() function and update its parameter to the following:

```
trace(xml.film.(@runningTime > 6));
```

The result is a list of the <film> elements, and all their children whose runningTime attribute is greater than 6 (see Figure 11-5).

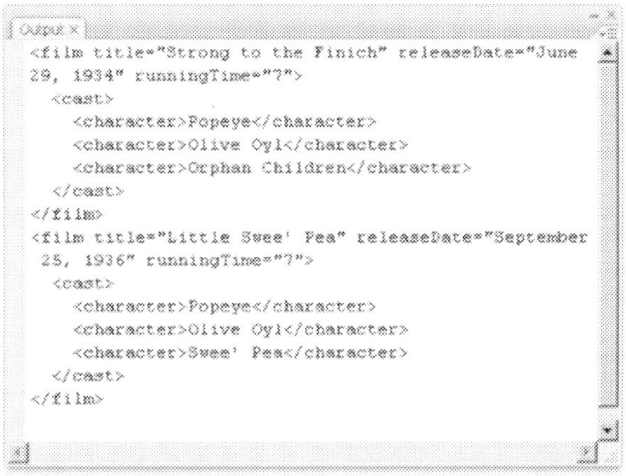

Figure 11-5. E4X allows filtering by way of comparison operators.

The parentheses tell Flash you're intending to filter the XMLList instance you get back. Inside the parentheses, the expression is a simple comparison, @runningTime > 6, which in plain English would be, "If you would be so kind, please tell us which <film> elements' runningTime attributes match this criterion." The reason Flash searches every <film> element in the bunch is because nothing appears between the word film and the dot that begins the next expression.

What if you want only the title of these films? Try this:

```
trace(xml.film.(@runningTime > 6).@title.toXMLString());
```

The trick, as always, is to break each expression into its parts. On its own, each concept is usually easy enough to understand. Concepts—expressions—are separated by dots. A blow-by-blow account of the preceding trace() goes like this:

trace(xml.film traces all <film> elements in the xml instance whose runningTime attribute is greater than the value 6—.(@runningTime > 6). This returns an XMLList instance that comprises a list of <film> elements, which the remaining expressions now reference. .@title shows the title attribute of <film> elements in the filtered XMLList instance, and .toXMLString() invokes the XMLList.toXMLString() method to clean up the results. Finally,); closes the trace() function.

11

> *See the* `LoadXML-E4XFiltering.fla` *file for a working example of the preceding E4X filtering.*

E4X bonus round

True, we already said "one more illustration of E4X," and that's the preceding one. If you're in a hurry to dispense with all this theory and jump head-first into a practical application, we doff our hats and invite you to make a beeline for the next section—but we figure at least a handful of you are wondering if it's possible to return film titles based on who appears in the cartoon. Let's pop open a can of spinach and take a gulp.

Open the `LoadXML-E4XBonusRound.fla` file that accompanies this chapter, and click into frame 1 of the scripts layer. Most of the ActionScript should look familiar. The important part appears in lines 9 through 11:

```
for each (var node:XML in xml.film.cast.character.➡
(descendants() == "Bluto")) {
  trace(node.parent().parent().@title);
}
```

Yup, this is new. The for each..in statement was introduced to ActionScript 3.0 thanks to the E4X specification. There has been a similar statement in ActionScript for quite some time, for..in, that works almost the same way, which is this: you point for..in at an object, and it loops through that object's properties, however many properties there happen to be. What it loops on, however, are the properties' *names*, rather than the properties themselves. This is either nifty or frustrating, depending on your needs. In contrast, the new for each..in statement loops on an object's actual properties, which is great for the need we have in this particular endeavor.

To understand the mechanism of this E4X filtering, let's start with a skeleton and slowly build up to the skin.

```
for each (someProperty in someObject) {
  // do something
}
```

The someObject in question is the hardest part of this equation, but based on what you've seen, it shouldn't be impenetrable. The object is an XMLList instance determined by the expression xml.film.cast.character.(descendants() == "Bluto"). Stepping through the subexpressions dot by dot, we get the following:

- xml.film: All <film> elements in the xml instance.
- .cast: All <cast> elements of those films (each <film> element happens to only have one).

- .character: All <character> elements of those cast elements (each film's cast happens to have its own particular number).

- .(descendants() == "Bluto"): A comparison of the TEXT_NODE descendants of each <character> element—these could arguably be called the *value* of each <character> element—against the string "Bluto", which returns the XMLList instance. It's this XMLList instance that is the "someObject" of our skeleton.

That gives us the following:

```
for each (someProperty in xml.film.cast.character.➥
(descendants() == "Bluto")) {
  // do something
}
```

The replacement for our stand-in "someProperty" is an XML instance, stored in an arbitrarily named variable, node.

```
for each (var node:XML in xml.film.cast.character.➥
(descendants() == "Bluto")) {
  // do something
}
```

All this means is that for each..in is going to update the value of node to the latest XML object it finds in the XMLList instance as it steps through that list. The node variable effectively *is* the XML object in question, which means that you can apply your recently acquired E4X magic to it. Remember, at this point you're dealing with a text element, Bluto, inside the <character> element of a <cast> element of some <film> element. The text element's parent is <character>, whose parent is <cast>, which puts our point of view inside a <film> element. This outermost element has a title attribute, and we reference that with the @ symbol:

```
for each (var node:XML in xml.film.cast.character.➥
(descendants() == "Bluto")) {
  trace(node.parent().parent().@title);
}
```

11

Your turn: Using XML to build a slideshow

The popularity of websites like Flickr and Photobucket prove that people like to share photos. Of course, this was true even before the Internet, but modern technology makes it easier than ever to whip out that tumbling, unfolding wallet and proudly show off all the kids, aunts, uncles, cousin Eds, and Fidos, not only to friends, but to every continent on the planet. At the rate most people take pictures, if you were to make a photo slideshow in Flash, you'd want to be sure it was easy to update. With XML, that goal is closer than you may think.

To start, we're going to walk you through a self-contained, "hard-wired" movie that displays a small collection of external JPGs and their captions. The number of JPGs, and the order in which they appear, are "baked into" the SWF, which means that the movie must be edited and republished to accommodate new images. This slideshow features a ComboBox and Button component to let people choose which JPGs they want to see, and it even uses the UILoader and ProgressBar components to load the images, so this will be something of a cumulative exercise.

Once the test model is complete, we'll free the photo-specific data from its dungeon and move it to an XML file, where it can leap free in the fields like a shorn sheep. Here we go!

1. Start a new Flash document and save it as Slideshow.fla in the Slides folder that contains the six JPGs accompanying this chapter. Set the movie's dimensions to 320×480 and set the background color to whatever you like (we chose #336699, which is light blue).

2. Create the following five layers: scripts, progress bar, loader, caption, and nav. Now it's time to populate this framework.

3. Open the Components panel (Window ➤ Components) and drag an instance of the ProgressBar component to the progress bar layer. Use the Property inspector to set its width to 150, height to 22, x position to 85, and y position to 200. Give it the instance name pb.

4. Drag an instance of the UILoader component to the loader layer. In the Property inspector, set its width to 300, height to 400, x position to 10, and y position to 10. Give it the instance name loader.

5. Captions will be displayed with a text field. Use the Text tool to create a dynamic text field in the caption layer. Switch to the Selection tool and set the text field's width to 300, height to 28, x position to 10, and y position to 416. Give this text field the instance name caption. Using the Property inspector, set the following values for the text box:

   - Font: _sans
   - Size: 18pt
   - Color: #FFFFFF (white), so that it shows over the blue background

6. Drag an instance of the ComboBox and Button components to the nav layer.

7. In the Property inspector, set the combo box's width to 220, height to 22, x position to 10, and y position to 450. Give it the instance name images. For the button, set its width to 70, height to 22, x position 240, and y position to 450. Give it the instance name next.

8. With the button selected, click the Parameters tab and set the button's Label parameter to Next. At this point, you have something like the scaffolding shown in Figure 11-6.

Figure 11-6. The parts are in place; time for the ActionScript.

Now it's time to bring these parts to life. For the most part, it's a matter of handling events for the components and populating the combo box. We only have a handful of steps, here, and we'll have something to test.

1. Click into frame 1 of the scripts layer and open the Actions panel (Window ➤ Actions). Here's the first chunk of code:

```
import fl.data.DataProvider;

// Set up image file info and captions
var imageData:Array = new Array(
  {label:"Geocaching Photo 1", data:"geocache01.jpg", caption:➥
"I have the GPS; you follow me."},
  {label:"Geocaching Photo 2", data:"geocache02.jpg", caption:➥
"This says three paces ahead."},
  {label:"Geocaching Photo 3", data:"geocache03.jpg", caption:➥
"Cool!  Fingerpuppet treasure!"},
  {label:"Geocaching Photo 4", data:"geocache04.jpg", caption:➥
"I found a pretty pony!"},
  {label:"Geocaching Photo 5", data:"geocache05.jpg", caption:➥
"Treasure hunting with my cousins."},
  {label:"Geocaching Photo 6", data:"geocache06.jpg", caption:➥
"May I have the stickers?"}
);
```

11

The first line imports the DataProvider class, which is needed later when it's time to populate the combo box. After that, an arbitrarily named variable, imageData, is set to an instance of the Array class. Arrays are lists of whatever you put in them. You can use the Array.push() method on an instance to add elements to that instance, but you can also pass in the whole collection at once, which we've done here. This array has six items, and each item is an instance of the generic Object class with three properties. What, no new Object() statement? How are these objects being created? The curly braces ({}) take care of that. It's a shortcut, and we're taking it. You'll remember from Chapter 9 that ComboBox instances can be supplied with label and data information, so that explains what those properties are. The caption property is a custom addition.

2. Press the Enter/Return key a couple times and type in the following:

```
// Keep track of current image
var currentImage:Number = 0;

// Picture changing function
function changePicture(pict:Number):void {
  pb.visible = true;
  caption.text = imageData[pict].caption;
  loader.load(new URLRequest(imageData[pict].data));
}
changePicture(0);
```

The first line after the comment declares a variable, currentImage, and sets it to 0. This number will keep track of which image is being looked at. The next several lines declare a custom function, changePicture(), that accepts a single parameter, pict. This function does the following three things:

- Makes the ProgressBar instance visible (yes, it's already visible at this point, but later code turns off its visibility when an image finishes loading).

- Makes the text field display the current caption. The incoming pict parameter determines which element to retrieve from the imageData array, and that element's caption property is consulted.

- Makes the UILoader instance load the current image. Here, again, the imageData array is consulted, but this time from the relevant item's data property.

Immediately after its declaration, the changePicture() function is called, with 0 as its parameter. Why start at 0? Because that's where arrays start counting. We're displaying the first image and its caption.

Now we just have to hook up the components.

3. Press Enter/Return a couple times, and type in the following:

```
// Wire up progress bar
pb.source = loader;

// Handle progress bar loading completion
```

```
pb.addEventListener(
  Event.COMPLETE,
  function(evt:Event):void {
    pb.visible = false;
  }
);
```

The first line after the comment associates the ProgressBar instance with the UILoader instance. As the UILoader component loads images, the progress bar will auto*magically* know what to do. The next little block makes the progress bar invisible when loading is complete.

4. Press Enter/Return a couple times, and type in the following:

```
// Wire up combo box data provider
images.dataProvider = new DataProvider(imageData);

// Handle combo box changes
images.addEventListener(
  Event.CHANGE,
  function(evt:Event):void {
    changePicture(images.selectedIndex);
  }
);
```

The first line after the comment populates the combo box by setting its dataProvider property to a new DataProvider instance (this is why we need the import statement at the top). All the DataProvider instance needs is an array whose elements have label and data properties, which is exactly what we have. The caption properties are extra, but they don't hurt anything. This one line—images.dataProvider = new DataProvider(imageData);—shoves the whole imageData array's content into the combo box in one swoop. Next, the Event.CHANGE event is handled for the combo box. The handler function calls the custom changePicture() function and feeds it a number determined by the combo box's current selection.

5. There's just one thing left—the button. Press Enter/Return a couple times and type in the following:

```
// Handle button clicks
next.addEventListener(
  MouseEvent.CLICK,
  function(evt:MouseEvent):void {
    currentImage++;
    if (currentImage == imageData.length) {
      currentImage = 0;
    }
    images.selectedIndex = currentImage;
    changePicture(currentImage);
  }
);
```

11

Here, the MouseEvent.CLICK event is handled for the button. The handler function does the following:

- Increments the currentImage variable by one.

- Checks to see if currentImage shares the same value as the expression imageData.length (the number of items in the imageData array). If so, it sets currentImage back to 0.

- Sets the combo box's current selection to currentImage.

- Calls the custom changePicture() function and passes it currrentImage as its parameter.

6. Test the movie. You'll be treated to a mini-geocaching excursion, led by a young enthusiast, as shown in Figure 11-7. Click the Next button to flip through the pictures in sequence, or use the combo box to skip around. To simulate image downloads, so you can see the progress bar in action, select View ➤ Simulate Download from the SWF window.

Figure 11-7. A few quick components and a bit of ActionScript, and you're off!

As it turns out, geocaching photos make a decent metaphor for this chapter, because after all this careful, plodding double-checking of coordinates, we're about to uncover some treasure—only a few more paces in a westerly direction.

1. Save your file to keep everything safe, and then select File ➤ Save As and save a copy as SlideshowXML.fla into the same folder.

2. Click back into frame 1 of the scripts layer to make a few changes. Here's the first chunk of code, with the revisions shown in bold:

```
import fl.data.DataProvider;

// Pull in image information from XML
var xml:XML = new XML();
var xmlLoader:URLLoader = new URLLoader();
xmlLoader.load(new URLRequest("slideshow.xml"));
xmlLoader.addEventListener(
  Event.COMPLETE,
  function(evt:Event):void {
    xml = XML(evt.target.data);
    images.dataProvider = new DataProvider(xml);
    changePicture(0);
  }
);

// Keep track of current image
var currentImage:Number = 0;
```

The imageData array is gone completely. In its place stands our trusty XML loading formula. The only difference here is that the instance name for the URLLoader instance has been changed to xmlLoader, because loader is already in use as the instance name for the UILoader component. This time, we're loading the file slideshow.xml, and that's where the former imageData content now resides. Translated into XML, it looks like this:

```
<slideshow>
  <slide label="Geocaching Photo 1" data="geocache01.jpg" ➡
caption="I have the GPS; you follow me." />
  <slide label="Geocaching Photo 2" data="geocache02.jpg" ➡
caption="This says three paces ahead." />
  <slide label="Geocaching Photo 3" data="geocache03.jpg" ➡
caption="Cool!  Fingerpuppet treasure!" />
  <slide label="Geocaching Photo 4" data="geocache04.jpg" ➡
caption="I found a pretty pony!" />
  <slide label="Geocaching Photo 5" data="geocache05.jpg" ➡
caption="Treasure hunting with my cousins." />
  <slide label="Geocaching Photo 6" data="geocache06.jpg" ➡
caption="May I have the stickers?" />
</slideshow>
```

As you can see, this XML document closely mirrors the original imageData array.

11

Let's take another look at the Event.COMPLETE event handler for the xmlLoader instance. The function runs as follows:

```
function(evt:Event):void {
  xml = XML(evt.target.data);
  images.dataProvider = new DataProvider(xml);
  changePicture(0);
}
```

There are a couple of important things to note. First, the DataProvider goings-on have been moved here from their former position next to the combo box Event.CHANGE handler. Why? Because under the circumstances, the combo box can't be populated until the XML has loaded. Next, the changePicture() call has been removed from its original place and relocated here. Why? Same reason—until the XML loads, the changePicture() function has no reference for what image to summon.

Two more paces!

3. At or near line 20, you'll find the changeFunction() declaration. You'll need to tweak two lines (the changed portions are shown in bold in the following code):

```
// Picture changing function
function changePicture(pict:Number):void {
  pb.visible = true;
  caption.text = xml.slide[pict].@caption;
  loader.load(new URLRequest(xml.slide[pict].@data));
}
```

> Note that the changePicture(0) line after this function has been removed. Instead of pulling from the old imageData array, the text field and UILoader component now draw their information from the xml instance, using the E4X syntax to specify the relevant <slide> element attributes. Here, the function's incoming pict parameter serves the same purpose it did before: it specifies which <slide> element to consult. Don't forget to delete what used to be the last line in this chunk—that changePicture(0); call is now inside the Event.COMPLETE event handler for the xmlLoader instance.

Treasure's in sight!

4. Here are the last touch-ups. First, delete the data provider line:

```
images.dataProvider = new DataProvider(imageData);
```

which has since been moved to the Event.COMPLETE handler. Finally, change one reference in the button's event handler:

```
// Handle button clicks
next.addEventListener(
  MouseEvent.CLICK,
  function(evt:MouseEvent):void {
    currentImage++;
```

```
    if (currentImage == xml.slide.length()) {
      currentImage = 0;
    }
    images.selectedIndex = currentImage;
    changePicture(currentImage);
  }
);
```

Since imageData is no more, the if() statement needs to look to the number of
<slide> elements, instead.

5. Test the movie and watch the show again.

If you think you missed a step, compare your work to the SlideshowXML.fla file in the
Complete folder. Now that the movie has become *XML-ified*, you can have some fun editing slideshow.xml and running the SWF to see the changes.

For example, delete the first three <slide> elements and test the movie again. Like magic,
only the three remaining slides and captions display. Change the wording of one of the
captions and run the SWF again. Change the order of the <slide> elements. Every time,
the SWF takes these changes effortlessly in stride.

What you've learned

In this chapter, we gave you the absolute basics of XML use in Flash. Though on the surface
it may not seem like much, what we have presented in this chapter forms the foundation
for complex Flash projects ranging from video pickers, MP3 players, and portfolio sites to
e-commerce applications. In this chapter, you have discovered

- The relationship between an XML document and Flash CS3

- How to retrieve and filter XML data using E4X syntax

- How to build a dynamic slideshow driven by XML

The most important point you need to take away from this chapter is the sheer flexibility
of XML in your Flash design and development efforts. You can make your movies expand
or contract effortlessly by simply adding to or subtracting from the XML document being
used by the movie. This is the true meaning of *dynamic*.

Speaking of dynamic, one of the hottest and most dynamic aspects of our industry is the
recent emergence of cell phones as yet another medium for our work. Turn the page to
discover how we can pull our Flash work off of the computer and make it mobile.

11

12 GOING MOBILE IN FLASH

The first thing you need to know about mobile is this: the question to be asked is not *if* you will develop a mobile Flash application but *when* you will develop a Flash mobile application. In this chapter, our intention is not to turn you into a mobile developer. Instead, it is to introduce you the tools you will use: Device Central and Flash CS3.

As you are reading this, Flash is rapidly becoming the de facto standard for content delivery through cell phones in Asia and Europe. Recent announcements regarding the North American market indicate this geographic region is also "getting in the game." In fact, things are happening so quickly in North America that the question we asked in the previous paragraph—When will you start developing mobile applications?—is one you will have to answer much sooner than you may think.

What we'll cover in this chapter:

- Navigating around Device Central
- Creating device sets
- Creating mobile Flash documents using Device Central
- Using Flash Lite 2, Flash, and Device Central to test a simple movie
- Using ActionScript 2.0 to control a mobile application

Files used in this chapter:

- OjaiAdventure.fla (Chapter12/ExerciseFiles_CH12/OjaiAdventure.fla)

Flash and devices

It should not be news to discover that Flash has gone mobile. The sheer number of wireless handsets and other wireless devices is driving a demand for rich content that makes the text-based solutions for cell phones and PDAs that were all the rage a couple of years ago look like charcoal scrawls on a cave wall. The reason is the mobile market discovered what Flash developers have known for years: Flash content results in small, fast-loading files.

It isn't only corporations that are driving the demand for mobile content. Educational institutions ranging from K-12 to postsecondary across North America are seriously examining how these devices can be used to deliver educational content and are developing courses that teach their students how to produce applications for these devices. Whether it is a Flash developer friend of ours using his cell phone to track his progress along the Pacific Coast Highway in California or pedestrians hooking into the traffic cameras in New York City, it is difficult for most to understand this technology is still in its infancy. To get a real sense of what you can do, start with this chapter, and then point your browser to the Adobe Mobile & Devices Developer Center at www.adobe.com/devnet/devices/.

We would be remiss in not mentioning that one of the best Flash mobile books out there is Foundation Flash Applications for Mobile Devices *by Richard Leggett et al. (friends of ED, 2006).*

The first thing you need to know about developing Flash applications for mobile devices is: *Not one thing you have learned about Flash CS3 and ActionScript 3.0 in this book applies to devices.* Everything you have done to this point in the book has relied on Flash Player 9. Flash mobile uses *Flash Lite 2.0,* which is roughly equivalent to Flash Player 7. This means that every scrap of ActionScript 3.0 code and every component, filter, or blend effect added to a new ActionScript 3.0 document simply can't be used in a device.

We tell you this not to scare you off but to make sure you enter this fascinating and emerging field with your eyes wide open. Other things you need to know include the following:

- **The phone is not a computer**: There is no mouse for user input. You are limited to the up, down, and select keys on a handset along with the number keys and * and # keys on the phone's keypad.

- **Forget about fonts**: You are dealing with a screen that could be around 170 pixels square. This means text must be both legible and readable. Though you can embed fonts, they add to file size.

- **Small is a very good thing**: If something has no purpose other than to add weight . . . throw it overboard. Flash content in devices is the only content you will deliver that people have to pay for. Data downloads are charged on the user's cell bill by having the user "pay by the K." For example, one of the authors has a plan that charges 3 cents per kilobyte downloaded. This can quickly add up. Keep the code to a minimum, and, if you must use bitmaps, use them at their final size and use compressed bitmaps. Avoid vectors if you can, and substitute them with JPG images. (Yes, this isn't what you would expect to hear while authoring Flash content—devices are different!)

- **Be aware of the device**: No two handsets are the same, and this includes screen real estate. Device Central will become your most important resource for this aspect of Flash development.

- **Test, test, test, test, test . . .** : Did we mention test everything? That includes testing both in the emulator in Device Central and on the actual handset.

12

Device Central CS3

New to the CS3 Studio is Device Central. Though aimed primarily at Flash designers and developers, direct access to Device Central is also available in Dreamweaver CS3, Illustrator CS3, and Photoshop CS3. In fact, when you launch the application, the Start page, shown in Figure 12-1, gives you the option of creating Illustrator, Photoshop, or Flash documents. Let's go wander around Device Central and get comfortable with it.

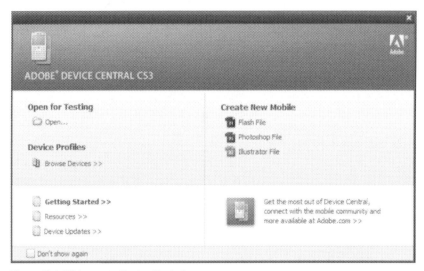

Figure 12-1. Welcome to Device Central.

1. Launch Device Central, and in the Start page, under Create New Mobile, select Flash File.

2. When Device Central opens, click the Flash Lite 2.0 32 240X320 device in the Device Sets area. If it isn't selected, click the Device Profiles tab. The Device Profile screen that opens will present you with a view of a generic phone (see Figure 12-2). Along with the phone you will be given a lot of information, ranging from generic properties such as Dimensions and Weight to the languages available in phones that use Flash Lite Player. Selecting the Flash, Bitmap, Video, and Web links will also give you extra information regarding what types of FSCommands can be used in Flash, the types of images you can prepare, the video formats that work on the device, and the coding languages you can use when developing web pages for the device. Now let's get more specific and actually choose a device.

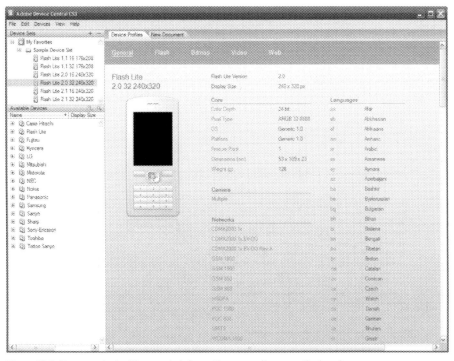

Figure 12-2. You can start with generic information regarding a particular player.

FSCommands? *These were quite common and quite mysterious in ActionScript 1.0 and Flash Player 3. These commands are used to allow Flash Lite Player to communicate with the device's operating system.*

3. Along the bottom-left side of Device Central is a listing of all the phones for which profiles are currently available in Device Central. As the next few months and years pass, we suspect this will become a rather crowded list. For now, click the + sign beside the Motorola link and select the Motorola RAZR V3m device. As soon as you do this, the image in the Device Profiles panel will change, as you see in Figure 12-3, as will the general information for the selected device.

12

477

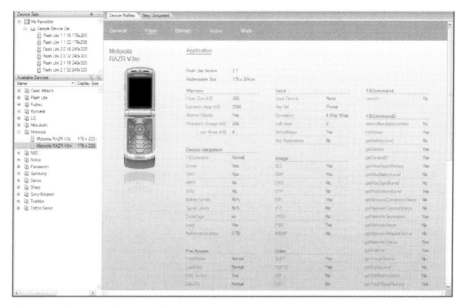

Figure 12-3. You can select a specific device.

4. There will also be occasions when you can't remember the name of a device, but you know who made it and you know what it looks like. To see all of the Nokia devices, for example, click Nokia. All of the Nokia phones in the category will appear along the top of the Device Profiles panel, and the various features of the phone will be listed under the phone's image. Twirl down the various sections, as shown in Figure 12-4, to obtain even more specific information regarding a specific model of handset.

5. What if you know the name or the model number but can't remember the manufacturer? Click the Search Devices icon on the Available Devices bar—it is the Magnifying Glass—to open the Search dialog box. Enter the number 6 in the Search For text input box, and all of the devices with that number in the model name will appear. Add a 0 to the search criteria, and the list is winnowed even further to all devices with 60 in the model name.

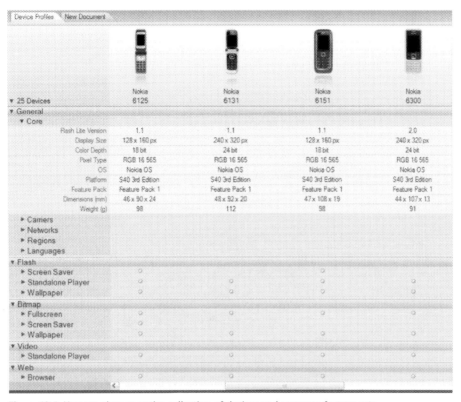

Figure 12-4. You can view an entire collection of devices and compare feature sets.

6. You can also do very specific searches. For example, say you are curious which devices use only Flash Lite 2.0 Player. Open the Search dialog box. Leave the Search For area empty, but click the Add Search Criteria button to the right of the Search For input box. When the menu expands, select Flash Lite Version from the drop-down menu on the left, select Exactly from the middle drop-down menu, and enter 2.0 into the input box as shown in Figure 12-5. You will see a list of the devices that use this player.

Figure 12-5. Device Central contains a blazingly fast search engine.

7. You don't always have to use the search engine to group the devices. Click the Group By button (the icon to the left of the Magnifying Glass) and select Flash Lite Version from the drop-down menu. The devices will all be grouped by version. If you open the Flash Lite 2.0 grouping, all of the devices that use this player will be listed.

8. Another scenario you might encounter is your constantly having to develop for the same various handsets. In this instance, click the + sign (New Device Sets button) in the Device Sets bar. Name the folder that appears as Test Set. Select the Nokia phones listed in the 2.0 listing of the Available Devices area and drag them to the folder. If you expand the Test Set folder, as in Figure 12-6, you will see you have created a test set of all the Nokia phones that use Flash Lite 2.0.

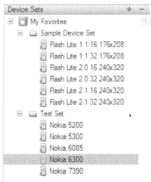

Figure 12-6. You can create custom groupings, called "sets," of the devices you will design for.

To remove a set, select its name in the Device Sets panel and press the Delete key.

Creating a new Flash document using Device Central

When you launch Flash CS3, you will notice one of the new document options in the Start page is Flash File (Mobile). Clicking this will launch Device Central, and the New Document tab will be selected. This is how you start creating Flash movies for mobile devices.

An interesting aspect of this path to Device Central is contained on the right side of the Flash Start page in the Create from Template area. If you click the Global Handsets selection, the New from Template dialog box opens and a preselected list of Flash Lite 2.0 templates will appear (see Figure 12-7). Click one of those choices, and Device Central will launch. The bottom line is it is irrelevant whether you start in Flash or start in Device Central because you are going to wind up in Device Central no matter which route you take. Now that you know how to get there, let's look at how to create a mobile document.

Figure 12-7. How to get to Device Central from Flash

A lesser-known path to Device Central is through Adobe Bridge. With Bridge open, you can either select an item and select File ➤ Test in Device Central, *or right-click (PC) or Ctrl-click (Mac) an item and select* Test in Device Central *from the context menu.*

---

1. Launch Device Central and select the Nokia 6300 device in your set or in the Available Devices area.

2. Click the New Document tab, and the phone and a Flash document icon will appear in the New Document panel.

3. Click the Test Set folder created in the previous section, and all of the devices and Flash page sizes will appear (see Figure 12-8). This is how you can select multiple devices. From this you can instantly determine that you may need to create two presentations, because the devices in the set have differing screen sizes. Let's not get complicated. Reselect the Nokia 6300 device.

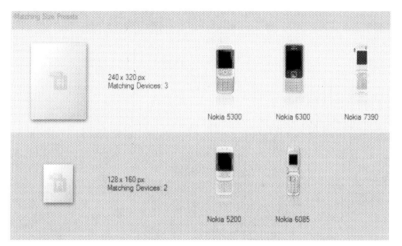

Figure 12-8. You can create content for a single device or for a device set.

4. In the New Document panel, select Flash Lite 2.0 in the Player Version drop-down menu and ActionScript 2.0 from the ActionScript Version drop-down menu. In the Content Type drop-down menu, shown in Figure 12-9, select Standalone Player.

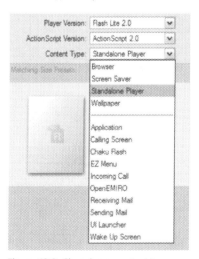

Figure 12-9. Choosing a content type

You are probably looking at that list in the Content Type drop-down menu and wondering "What the . . . ?" The good news is not all devices support everything in the list. If you were to select Calling Screen from the list, the device would disappear. This is a visual clue the Nokia 6300 doesn't support this content type.

Still, it is important that you at least have a vague understanding of the content types. Here's a brief description of each one:

- Browser: Uses the player to render Flash content embedded in a mobile web page and viewed in the device's browser.

- Screen Saver: Uses Flash Lite to show the device's screen saver.

- Standalone Player: Turns Flash Lite into a stand-alone application. This means the user can open the SWF anytime and view the movie without having to launch a browser.

- Wallpaper: Turns the Flash movie into the screen's wallpaper.

- Application: Defines the movie as a stand-alone Flash application.

- Calling Screen: Uses Flash Lite to play an animation when the user receives or makes a call.

- Chaku Flash: Uses the SWF as the ring tone.

- EZ Menu: Uses the SWF as the device's menu.

- OpenEMIRO: Plays the SWF while the device is waking up from standby mode.

- Receiving Mail: Plays the SWF animation when an e-mail is received.

- Sending Mail: Plays the SWF animation while the e-mail message is being sent.

- UI Launcher: Defines Flash Lite as the device's application launcher and to display the device's launcher application.

- Wake Up Screen: Plays the SWF as the phone is starting.

5. Click the Create button in the bottom-right corner of the New Document panel. This will launch Flash CS3 and, when the document opens, note the Flash Player chosen in Device Central—Flash Lite 2.0—appears in the Property inspector.

6. Add a new layer, and name Layer 1 as Text and Layer 2 as Ball.

7. Click the Ball layer to select and draw a circle on the stage. Convert the shape to a movieclip named Ball.

8. Move the movieclip to the bottom of the stage and add a keyframe in frame 20 of the Ball layer. Move the ball to the top of the stage and insert a motion tween.

9. Add a keyframe in frame 10 of the Text layer. Select the Text tool, click the stage, and enter Hello World. Use _sans as the font and set the size to 24 pixels.

10. Add a frame to frame 20 of the Text layer, as shown in Figure 12-10, and save the movie to your Exercise folder.

12

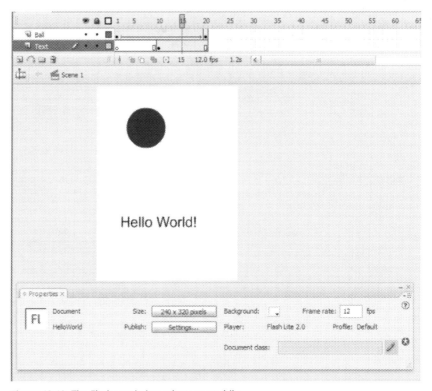

Figure 12-10. The Flash movie is ready to go mobile.

Testing a mobile movie

Normally your final instruction would be to test the movie. Not just yet. We want to save the best for last. Unlike what you have done to this point in the book, when you test a movie, you don't play the movie in Flash Player. When it comes to mobile, you test your movie in the device chosen. Here's how:

1. Test the movie. What happens next is Device Central opens and sprouts a new Emulator tab, and the movie starts playing in the device chosen as shown in Figure 12-11.

Figure 12-11. Welcome to the world of mobile Flash content.

There are some aspects of the emulator of which you need to be aware.

The first item you should notice is your Flash movie is now at the top of the device list, and you see the device being used to test the movie. The next thing to notice is a change to the icon beside Nokia 6300 under Test Set. This icon is telling you this is the device being used in the emulator. The Emulator panel, where the movie is actually playing, gives you some information regarding the phone, the screen size, and the player version being used. The three buttons allow you to play, stop, and rewind the movie. You can also zoom in or zoom out on the device. The button on the right is the Toggle Detached View button. This mode is designed for devices such as clamshell devices that don't allow you to view the content at 100% view.

The panels on the right side of the emulator are the "jewels" of Device Central. These are called the **testing panels** and, in many respects, can be regarded as the "Flash Bandwidth Profiler on Steroids." For example, many devices allow you to control screen brightness. What would be the effect of reducing the brightness on how the movie looks while it is playing? Let's find out:

2. Twirl down the Display panel and drag the Backlight, Gamma, and Contrast sliders to the right or left. Notice how the changes affect the "look" of the screen in the emulator.

12

3. What would the movie look like in the Nokia 7390? Double-click the device in the Test Set. The emulator will change, as shown in Figure 12-12, to the device chosen.

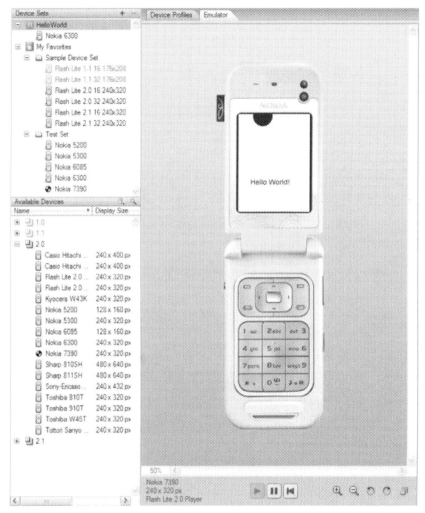

Figure 12-12. Switch devices by double-clicking the name of the new device.

Here's a little-known trick regarding Device Central. If you were to move the HelloWorld.fla file to a Mac and open it in Flash CS3, you will see it is a Flash Lite 2.0 device. If you test the movie, Device Central will open, and the movie will start playing in a Nokia 6300 emulator.

Publishing a mobile movie

You have done all of the emulator stuff and are happy with the movie. The final step in the process is actually publishing the SWF file for the Nokia 6300. Here's how you do that:

1. In Device Central, select File ➤ Return to Flash. Alternatively, you could press Ctrl+Shift+O (PC) or, as shown in Figure 12-13, press Cmd+Shift+O (Mac).

Figure 12-13. From Device Central back to Flash to publish the SWF

12

> *If you open a new Flash document in Device Central, the* Return to Flash *menu item will change to* Jump to Flash. *Select this, and Flash CS3 will launch.*

2. When you return to Flash, select File ➤ Publish Settings to open the Publish Settings dialog box. As this is a stand-alone player, HTML is not necessary. Deselect HTML in the Formats panel.

3. Click the Flash tab to open the Publish Settings dialog box. Notice, as you see in Figure 12-14, that Flash Lite 2.0 is the player version selected. Click the Publish button.

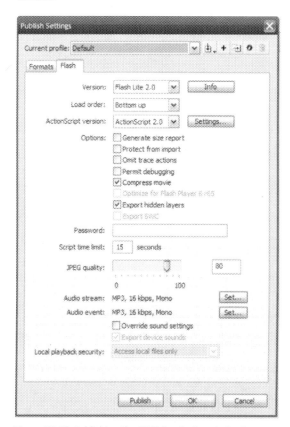

Figure 12-14. Publishing the SWF for device playback

At this point in the process, we step aside because how content moves from the PC to the device is dependent upon the software provided by the handset manufacturer. In the case of our test device, it would be the **Nokia PC Suite** software. Getting the SWF file from the desktop to the phone is as easy as dragging the file from the Chapter 12 Completed folder into the folder targeted in the Nokia software (see Figure 12-15). From this point on, you would test the software and make any changes needed.

Figure 12-15. It is as simple as a drag-and-drop operation to get the SWF from the computer into the phone.

Constructing a mobile application

In this exercise, you are going to construct a small application that presents a series of images from a recent trip to California. The purpose here is to get you sensitized to the fact that constructing mobile presentations is a lot different from building a web page in Dreamweaver CS3 or a Flash presentation in Flash Professional CS3.

The first thing you must understand is simply moving an HTML site onto a mobile site is somewhat similar to trying to stuff 10 pounds of leaves into a bag that only holds 5 pounds of leaves. You can put a lot of information into a space that has a resolution of 1440×900 pixels or more of screen real estate. When you try to present the same amount of information in a screen that is 320×240, the information hierarchy becomes paramount, and design, in many cases, takes a back seat. To understand what we are talking about, let's look at the entry to David Stiller's blog shown in Figure 12-16.

12

There is a lot of information on the page. There is the banner at the top, the text block, the search box, and links to all of David's postings on the right side of the page. For all of this information to move into the mobile space, David would have to redesign the page and actually make it a series of screens on a mobile device. For example, the banner at the top could be common to each screen, but the post would need to be scrolling text, as shown in Figure 12-17, and the right and left soft keys—they are the ones to the right and left of the navigation buttons in the center—would need to be coded to allow the user to press the keys to either go to the main blog screen or navigate to the links screen.

Figure 12-16. You can't simply "port" a site from the web space to the mobile space.

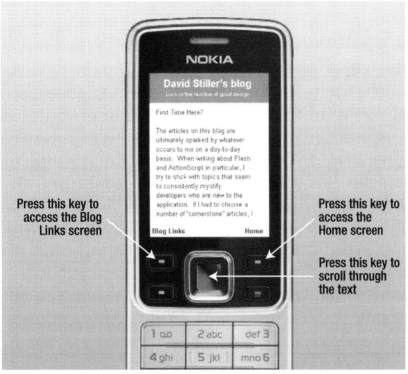

Press this key to access the Blog Links screen

Press this key to access the Home screen

Press this key to scroll through the text

Figure 12-17. There is no mouse in the mobile space. There are only soft keys.

As well, the up and down keys found in the four-directional pad would need to be coded to allow the user to scroll through the post.

Now that you are aware that developing for mobile requires you to "think differently," let's create an application:

1. Open the OjaiAdventure.fla file in the Chapter 12 Exercise folder. The bits and pieces needed to construct this application can be found in the library. Other than that, you are going to pull this project together and test it on the Nokia 6300 we have been using throughout this chapter.

What's with the fixation on the Nokia 6300? Nothing really. We want to be able to use ActionScript 2.0, which many of you are familiar with, and Flash Lite 2.0 Player. The device we are using simply looks "sexy" and makes for great screen shots.

12

2. Add seven layers to the movie and name them, from the top down, as follows:

- Labels
- Actions
- Images
- Thumbs
- Open
- NavButtons
- SoftKeyID
- Head

3. Add a frame at frame 25 for all of your layers.

> By the time this project is finished, you will look at the timeline and think, "Shoot, I could have done this in three frames." You would be quite correct with this statement, but we are using the extra frames to give you an opportunity to "see" how the various features of this presentation are constructed on the timeline.

4. Select the Head layer. Select the Text tool, click the stage, and enter Excellent Ojai Adventure. In the Property inspector, apply the following formatting:

- Text Type: Static Text
- Width: 205
- X: 18.9
- H: 9.4
- Font: Times **or** _serif
- Size: 30 pixels
- Color: #E6E1AF **(yellow)**
- Alignment: Centered
- Aliasing: Use device fonts

5. Select the keyframe in the Labels layer, and in the Property inspector, change the Frame label to Main.

6. Select the SoftKeyID layer. Select the Text tool, click the stage, and enter the word Main. Use the following settings:

- Text Type: Static Text
- X: 5
- Y: 300
- Font: _sans
- Size: 12
- Color: #E6E1AF **(yellow)**

7. Repeat Step 5 and enter the word Exit. The only difference will be the text will be placed at the X and Y coordinates of 198 and 300.

The text created is a major job to do. It will be used to inform the user which keys need to be pressed to get out of the presentation and to return to the main screen. In fact, you are going to have the Home button do double duty later on in the movie.

8. Select the NavButtons layer and open the InterfaceElements folder in the library.

9. Drag the Call movieclip to the stage and place it on the horizontal guide on the stage and between the two vertical guides. In the Property inspector, give it the instance name of Call_btn. As you may have guessed, this button will be a "speed-dial" button.

10. Drag the Photos movieclip to the stage and place it directly above the Call button on the NavButtons layer. Give this button the instance name of Photos_btn.

> *Yeah, yeah. We know. Why is one button a button symbol and the other a movieclip? Either symbol type can be used, so we decided to use one of each in this exercise. In fact, avoiding button symbols in mobile interfaces is a good thing in certain cases. Button symbols change when they are used, but that assumes a mouse action. In the mobile space, a button, if you decide it is necessary, will put a border around the object to give the user a visual clue that it is live. This explains why the button only has an up state.*

11. Select the Open layer and drag the OpenImage symbol from the library to the stage. Using the Property inspector, set its X and Y coordinates to 16.4 and 91. Save the project. As shown in Figure 12-18, you have created the opening screen of this movie.

Figure 12-18. The main screen has been assembled.

You could also test the app at this point to see how the interface looks in the device.

Adding the gallery

With the main screen in place, we can turn our attention to the gallery of images that will display. Follow these steps to put it in place:

1. Add a keyframe in frame 10 of the Labels layer. Name the label Gallery and insert a keyframe in frame 10 of the Thumbs layer.

2. You aren't going to need to see the buttons or the start image. To remove the image, add a blank keyframe to frame 2 of the Open layer and another blank keyframe to frame 9 of the NavButtons layer.

3. Open the InterfaceElements folder in the library and drag a copy of the Thumbs movieclip to frame 10 of the Thumbs layer.

   If you open the Thumbs movieclip in the Symbol Editor, as shown in Figure 12-19, you will see that each image is, in fact, a movieclip. Each movieclip is also given an instance name because the instance will be used to show a larger version of the image. The individual images can be found in the ThumbImages folder in the library.

Figure 12-19. The primary navigation tool will be a series of movieclips.

4. Add a blank keyframe to frame 11 of the Thumbs layer.

5. Add a keyframe to frame 20 of the Labels layer and name the label Images.

6. Add a keyframe to frame 20 of the Images layer and drag a copy of the ImageStrip movieclip to the stage. Line up this movieclip with the top of the stage and against the left guide. Give the movieclip the instance name of mcImages.

7. Finally, add a blank keyframe to frame 20 of the Head layer. Save the project.

Now would be a good time to review the rules regarding the use of bitmaps and vectors on mobile devices. The thing to keep in mind is you are dealing with a small screen area and a device whose computing power and memory are a fraction of those of a laptop computer. Though Flash Lite can render both types of graphics, there are a number of factors to consider when adding graphics to a movie destined for mobile playback.

Though Flash adores vectors and their use will reduce file size, they have their problems. Compared to bitmaps, vector graphics require more processing power to render, especially vector graphics that have many complex shapes and fills. Consequently, heavy use of vector shapes could slow things down. On the other hand, bitmap graphics do not require as much processing time to render as vector graphics and just might be a better choice for such things as a route map meant to be animated and scrolled on a mobile phone.

When authoring mobile presentations that use graphics, keep the following in the back of your mind:

- Avoid using outlines or strokes on vector shapes. Outlines have an inner and outer edge (fills have only one) and are twice the work to render.

- Corners are simpler to render than curves. When possible, use flat edges, especially with very small vector shapes.

- Optimization is especially helpful with small vector shapes such as icons. Complex icons may lose their details upon rendering, and the work of rendering the details is wasted.

- Import bitmap graphics at the correct size; don't import large graphics and scale them down in Flash, because this wastes file size and runtime memory. All of the graphics used in this exercise were created using the batch processing feature of Fireworks CS3 to allow us to import them into Flash size rather than scaling them.

- Flash Lite Player does not support bitmap smoothing. If a bitmap is scaled or rotated, it will pixelate. If it is necessary to scale or rotate a bitmap, consider using a vector graphic instead.

- Text is essentially just a shape. When text is needed, avoid animating it or placing it over an animation. Consider using text as a bitmap.

- Minimize, if not avoid altogether, the use of transparency in PNG files; Flash must calculate redraws even for the transparent portions of the bitmap. This will slow things down big time.

12

"Wiring it up" with ActionScript

With the assets in place, you can now turn your attention to writing the ActionScript that brings this presentation to life. As we said at the start of this exercise, you can only use ActionScript 2.0 with the Flash Lite Player version we are using. As well, we are going to need to use some specific code to ensure the soft keys return us to the main screen or quit the presentation.

1. Add a keyframe to frame 1 of the Actions layer. Open the ActionScript editor and enter the following code:

```
stop();

_focusrect = true;

fscommand2("SetSoftKeys", "Options", "Exit");
fscommand2("SetQuality", "high");
fscommand2("Fullscreen", "true");
```

There is a lot of new stuff here, so we'll explain it so you understand what you are doing. The first line stops the playback head on frame 1, and the remaining lines do some housekeeping.

When an object is selected on a device, a yellow border appears around it. This border is called the **focus rectangle** and is moved around the screen using the up or down keys on the four-directional pad on the device. The _focusrect property turns this rectangle on (true) or off (false). The default value is true.

The three fscommand2() functions are how your movie communicates with the device's operating system. The first function relabels the two soft keys to Options and Exit. This means when the key is pressed, the function associated with that key is executed. You added the two labels at the bottom because this movie will be displayed in full-screen mode. When you do this, you have to manually add the labels.

The next two functions set the rendering quality of Flash Player to high and forces the player to display the movie in the full screen.

2. Press Enter (PC) or Return (Mac) and add the following code:

```
if (selectedItem == null) {
  Selection.setFocus(Photos_btn);
}
else {
  Selection.setFocus(selectedItem)
}
```

This conditional statement makes sure something—the Photos_btn—is always selected on the stage. It is always a good idea to give your user a visual clue that something is selected on the stage.

3. Press Enter (PC) or Return (Mac) twice and enter the following:

```
Photos_btn.onPress = function() :Void {
  selectedItem = this;
  gotoAndStop("Gallery");
};

Call_btn.onPress = function():Void{
  selectedItem = this;
  getURL("tel: 4165552365");
};
```

These are the button functions. The first one scoots the playback head to the frame labeled "Gallery." The second one uses a getURL method to actually dial the phone. You can't just toss in a number. You must use the tel: protocol. Now you know how to add a speed-dial function to a mobile movie.

4. Press Enter (PC) or Return (Mac) and enter the following code, which creates the listeners for the soft key events:

```
Key.removeListener(myListener);

var myListener:Object = new Object();

myListener.onKeyDown = function() :Void {
  var keyCode = Key.getCode();
    if(keyCode == ExtendedKey.SOFT1) {
      gotoAndStop("Main");
    }
    else if(keyCode == ExtendedKey.SOFT2) {
      fscommand2("Quit");
    }
};

Key.addListener(myListener);
```

You first remove any listeners that may be in place and create the Listener object. When the user presses the left soft key, the playback head is sent to the frame labeled "main," and if the right soft key is pressed, the application is closed.

12

5. Check your syntax, and then save and test the movie. When Device Central opens, the Photos button is surrounded by a focus rectangle, and if you mouse over the keys, they will change color to show you they are active (see Figure 12-20).

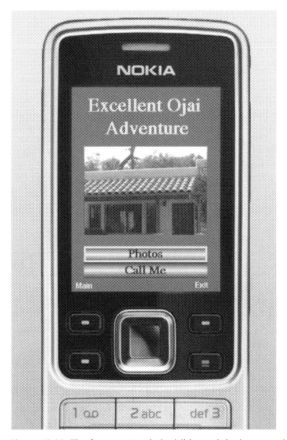

Figure 12-20. The focus rectangle is visible, and the keys are "hot."

6. The next bit of code makes the buttons in the Thumbs movieclip active. Add a keyframe in frame 10 of the Actions layer and open the ActionScript Editor. Enter the following code:

```
stop();

_focusrect = true;

fscommand2("SetSoftKeys", "Options", "Exit");
fscommand2("setquality", "high");
fscommand2("fullscreen", "true");
```

```
if (selectedItem == null) {
  Selection.setFocus(Photos_btn);
  }
    else {
  Selection.setFocus(selectedItem)
}

Photos_btn.onPress = function():Void {
  selectedItem = this;
  gotoAndStop("Gallery");
};

Call_btn.onPress = function() :Void {
  selectedItem = this;
  getURL("tel: 4165552365");
};

// remove any previously assigned listeners
Key.removeListener(myListener);

// create key listener object and assign onKeyDown handlers to it
var myListener:Object = new Object();

// listener actions
myListener.onKeyDown = function() :Void {
  var keyCode = Key.getCode();
  if(keyCode == ExtendedKey.SOFT1) {
    gotoAndStop("Main");
  }
    else if(keyCode == ExtendedKey.SOFT2) {
      fscommand2("Quit");
    }
};

Key.addListener(myListener);

function showImage(num:Number):Void {
  selectedItem = this;
  gotoAndStop("Images");
  mcImages.gotoAndStop(num);
}

for (var i:Number = 0; i < 10; i++) {
  mcImageSet["Button0" + i].onPress = function():Void {
  showImage(this._name.substr(7, 1));
  }
}
```

12

We know that was a lot of typing. In fact, you could have copied and pasted the code from frame 1 into this frame, and then entered the function at the end. It checks to see which movieclip has been selected and uses an array for the instance names of the clips that are the buttons to be clicked. The array access operator ([ ]) converts that string into an actual object reference.

The next code block makes use of the String.substr() method, which takes a given string and lets you give it a haircut. In this case, the this._name expression refers to the MovieClip._name property of the thumbnail movieclip "buttons." In a case-by-case basis, inside the for loop, this._name returns "Button01", "Button02", and so on, and these values are the actual instance names of the buttons. Applying the substr() method to that string, you're basically saying, "Go seven characters in and give me one character from that point." That snips out the final character, which is a number—and that number gets passed to the showImage() function.

The beauty of this approach is that instead of writing nine separate button functions, you bundle the button functions into one function.

Each button function tosses the focus rectangle around the selected button—selectedItem = this—and the rest of the function scoots the playback head to the Images frame and then to the frame where the image is located in the mcImages movieclip.

If you are "old school," then be our guest and write nine separate button functions. The first one would be

```
mcImageSet.Button01.onPress = function():Void {
    selectedItem = this;
    gotoAndStop("Images");
    mcImages.gotoAndStop(1);
}
```

All you need to do for the remaining eight buttons is to copy and paste this code into the Script pane and change the button number and the frame number in the last line.

---

7. Check your syntax to be sure there are no errors. If there are no errors, copy all of the code to line 41—Key.addListener(myListener);—to the clipboard.

8. Save and test the movie in Device Central. You will start in the main Screen, and the Photos button will be highlighted. Click the center button in the four-directional pad, and you will be taken to the Gallery frame. Press the right and left buttons on the four-directional pad, and each button in the interface will be given a focus rectangle as shown in Figure 12-21. Click the left soft key—Main—and you are returned to the main screen.

Figure 12-21. The keys on the keypad allow you to move around the interface and select the image to be viewed.

There is one last issue to address. Though the movie is fully functional, you may have noticed that when you pressed the Main soft key, you weren't taken back to the Gallery page. You went right back to the start. Obviously, this is not going to result in a good user experience. Let's fix that right now:

9. Add a keyframe in frame 20 of the Actions layer and open the ActionScript Editor. When it opens, paste the code on the clipboard into the Script pane. You are going to make one small change to the code.

10. Scroll down to the Listener object and change the word Main to Gallery. The Listener should now look as follows:

```
myListener.onKeyDown = function() {
  var keyCode = Key.getCode();
    if(keyCode == ExtendedKey.SOFT1) {
      gotoAndStop("Gallery");
    }
```

12

```
        else if(keyCode == ExtendedKey.SOFT2) {
          fscommand2("Quit");
      }

    };
```

11. The last thing to do is to change the key label from Main to Back. Add keyframes in frames 19 and 20 of the SoftKeyID layer. Select the word Main in frame 20 and change it to Back.

12. Save and test the movie. Click an image button, and as shown in Figure 12-22, the image appears and the soft key ID is changed to Back. Click the left soft key, and you will be returned to the gallery.

Figure 12-22. The project is complete.

What you've learned

- How to use Device Central
- The process used to create content for a mobile application
- The process for testing a mobile application in Flash CS3
- How to plan and execute a mobile application
- The basic ActionScript to control a mobile application

This chapter only scratched the surface of the mobile market that is rapidly opening up to Flash developers around the world. Device Central is "Ground Zero" if you are at all serious about mobile, and we think you can see how important it is to your efforts. Mobile is a totally different space from that which you use every day, and the one thing to keep in mind is that mobile content is the only content you will create that the user actually pays for through network access charges. This is why it is so vitally important that you squeeze out every extra bit and kilobyte from the application before it goes live.

Speaking of squeezing and small, the next chapter shows you how to turbo charge your Flash movies. See you there.

12

13 OPTIMIZING FLASH MOVIES

One of the most common user experiences, when it comes to Flash on the Web, is sitting around waiting for the movie to start. From your perspective, as the developer who designed the site, this is an odd situation to encounter because, when you tested the movie, it was seriously fast and played flawlessly. What happened? To be succinct: the Web happened. Your movie may indeed be cool, but you made a fundamental mistake: you fell in love with the technology, not the user.

What we'll cover in this chapter:

- How Flash movies are streamed to a web page
- Using the Bandwidth Profiler to turbo charge movies
- Optimizing Flash movies
- Creating a simple preloader
- Converting a Flash movie to a QuickTime video

Files used in this chapter:

- YawningParrot.fla (Chapter13/ExerciseFiles_CH13/ Exercise/YawningParrot.fla)
- BandwidthTest.fla (Chapter13/ExerciseFiles_CH13/ Exercise/BandwidthTest.fla)
- BandwidthTest1.fla (Chapter13/ExerciseFiles_CH13/ Exercise/BandwidthTest1.fla)
- Chill.mp3 (Chapter13/ExerciseFiles_CH13/Exercise/Chill.mp3)
- Loading.fla (Chapter13/ExerciseFiles_CH13/Exercise/Loading.fla)
- LoadingJPG.fla (Chapter13/ExerciseFiles_CH13/Complete/ Exercise/LoadingJPG.fla)
- LoadingSWF.fla (Chapter13/ExerciseFiles_CH13/Complete/ Exercise/LoadingSWF.fla)
- PreloadEX.fla (Chapter13/ExerciseFiles_CH13/Exercise/PreloadEX.fla)
- YawningParrotPreloader.fla (Chapter13/ExerciseFiles_CH13/ Exercise/YawningParrotPreloader.fla)
- BubblingLettersFinal.mov (Chapter13/ExerciseFiles_CH13/ Exercise/BubblingLettersFinal.mov)

Flash's "love-hate" Internet relationship

Back in the early days of Flash, when we really didn't know better, Flash designers would prepare these really "cool" intros to a site, which played while the rest of the site loaded. The problem was they were overly long, and in many cases the intro seemed to take almost as long to load as the site. The solution was the infamous Skip Intro button. A couple of seconds after the intro started playing, the Skip Intro button would appear, and users would click it only to discover the site hadn't quite loaded, so they would sit there drumming their fingers on their desk. It became so ludicrous, users would see the button not as a Skip Intro button but as a "Skip Site" warning. This resulted in Flash gaining a rather nasty reputation for "bloat," which it still hasn't shaken.

> *If you are interested, the Flash community does have quite a sense of humor, and one of the more popular Flash sites of the time was named "Skip Intro" (see Figure 13-1). You can still visit it at* www.skipintro.nl/skipintro/skipintro98.htm.

SKIPINTRO

Figure 13-1. Welcome to "Skip Intro" hell.

To deal with the bloat issue, it is critical that you comprehend the underlying technology behind your Flash movie. This means you need to understand what the Web really is and become familiar with many of the terms commonly used in the Flash designer and developer community.

This "Internet" thing

The Internet's roots go back to the U.S. Department of Defense's need to create a bullet-proof means of maintaining communications between computers. This involved such things as file transfers, messaging, and so on. At the time, computers were a virtual Tower of Babel, which meant different computer types and operating systems rarely, if ever, could talk to each other. As well, in battle conditions, the system needed would have to carry on even if a piece of it was knocked out, and it had to be accessible to everything from portable computers to the big, honking mainframes in "clean rooms" around the world.

13

The solution was an enabling technology called **Transmission Control Protocol/Internet Protocol**, though we know it by a far sexier name, **TCP/IP**. This is how data moves from your computer to our computers or from your web server to our computers, and, as you may have guessed, the slash indicates it comes in two parts.

Internet Protocol (IP) is how data gets from here to there by using an address called the **IP address**. This address is a unique number used to identify any computer currently on the Internet. What it does is to create little bundles of information, called **packets**, that can then be shot out through the Internet to your computer. Obviously the route is not a straight line. The packets pass through special computers called **routers**, and their job is to point those packets to your computer. Depending on the distance traveled, there could be any number of routers that check your packets and send them either directly to your computer or the next router along the line.

The **Transmission Control Protocol** (TCP) part of the process is the technology that verifies all the data packets got to your computer. The thing is, the IP portion of the trip couldn't care less if packet 10 arrives at your computer before packet 1, or that it even got there at all. This is where TCP comes in. Its job is to ensure that all of the packets get to where they are supposed to go.

Once all of the kinks got worked out, the military had quite the communications system on its hands.

Enter the World Wide Web

The Web is a network of networks. It came about because people realized straight data transmission was interesting, but once the cool factor wore out its welcome, they started wondering how it would be possible to use this communication network to access files containing images, audio, and video.

The solution was the World Wide Web, which is commonly seen as web pages and hyperlinks. A web page is a simple text file that uses HTML—a system of tags and text—to define how a page should look and behave. This is important because your Flash movies are always found in an HTML wrapper.

> *If you are a history buff, the concept of hyperlinks and hypertext was around long before the Internet. The gentleman who managed the atomic bomb project for the U.S. during World War II, Vannevar Bush, wrote an article for the* Atlantic Monthly *in July 1945 that proposed a system of linking all information with all other information. The article was entitled "As We May Think," and you can still read it at* www.theatlantic.com/doc/194507/bush.

An HTML page may only be a text file, but it can contain links to other assets such as your Flash SWF. These links take the form of a **Uniform Resource Locator** (URL) and specify the location of the assets. When Firefox or Internet Explorer translates the page, those addresses are used to load the assets and display them on the computer screen. Thus the Web is really composed of two parts: browsers and servers, which are the computers that hold the assets and shoot them to your computer when the browser asks for them.

As you can see, the movement of your SWF file from here to there is a rather uncomplicated process. Where your pain and heartache comes into play is through something called **bandwidth**.

Bandwidth

In the early days of Flash, around the year 1999, one of the authors read an article written by a New York Flash designer—Hillman Curtis—and one phrase leaped out of the article and has been glued to the front of his cerebral cortex ever since. The phrase? "Keep an eye on the pipe."

The "pipe" is bandwidth. Bandwidth is a measure of how much data will move along a given path at a given time or how much information can be downloaded through a modem and how fast. One of the authors, when speaking to this topic at conferences or in classes, uses a rather amusing graphic analogy that will help you to understand this topic. Imagine trying to push the amount of data contained in your favorite TV show through a modem that is connected to a phone. Trying to push that amount of data through a dial-up modem is no different from "trying to push a watermelon through a worm."

Bandwidth is measured in bits (usually kilobits) per second. A bit is either a 1 or a 0, so bandwidth is a measure of how many 1s and 0s can be fed through a modem each second. The higher the number, the greater the bandwidth, and the faster things get from here to there. The thing is, bandwidth is not constant. It requires more bandwidth to move a video from here to there than this page of text that you are reading. The issue is not "here to there." The issue is the modem's capacity to move the data. This is the "pipe." Users with 56K dial-up modems have a pipe that has the diameter of a garden hose. Users with cable modems have a pipe the diameter of a fire hose. Connect the garden hose to the fire hydrant in front of your house, and you will get a graphic demonstration of data flow and the "pipe" when you turn on the hydrant.

As we pointed out earlier, the data packets sent to your computer get there, eventually, and the route is never a straight line. Over time, the TCP/IP model nudges the transmission rate toward a relatively predictable rate, but this is technology we're dealing with here, and it is the prudent Flash designer who approaches technology with a dose of pragmatism and does not assume a constant flow. This has implications behind your design efforts, and we will get into those shortly.

You need to regard the pipe and data transmission in much the same manner you regard your local highway. It may have six lanes for traffic and a posted speed limit of 60 mph or 100 kph, but that all becomes irrelevant in rush hour. Traffic moves at the pace of the slowest car. It is no different with the Internet. Servers can become overloaded.

The best example of that is the infamous tragedy often referred to as 9/11. On that day, the Internet essentially ground to halt as, it seemed, every computer on the planet was attempting to get the latest information. What people overlooked on that day was that a server is only a computer and can only reply to requests for information at a set rate. If the browser can't get the information, it will eventually assume the assets are not there, and the requested page will either not be displayed or will be displayed with information missing. It got so bad on that day for CNN and the BBC, for example, they were forced to post a message that essentially told people "come back later." People lucky enough to get connected

13

experienced pauses in the download and disconnection, which are the hallmarks of an overloaded server.

What you need to take away from this "horror story" is that the time it takes to download and play your Flash movie is totally dependent on the contents of your Flash movie and traffic flow on the Internet. This means you need to concentrate on not only what is "in" your movie, but also who wants to access it. This is where you fall in love with the user and not the technology.

So who are these folks we call users?

The Flash community is an odd-ball collection of people ranging from those who ride skateboards for entertainment to the classic "nerd" working in a corporate cubicle farm. This disparity, which actually is the strength of the Flash community, has resulted in a bit of a split between those who use supercharged computers to develop their content and take a "sucks to be you" attitude if you can't revel in their work and the corporate types who work within the strict standard set by their IT department. This standard is usually in the form of the following Commandment: *Thou shalt develop to a Flash Player 7 standard, and may whatever god you worship have mercy upon your miserable soul if you step outside of this stricture.*

Which begs the question, What do you need to know before putting your work out there?

Here are some general guidelines:

- Small means fast. Studies show you have 15 seconds to hook the user. If nothing is happening or is appealing to the user, that user is gone. Small SWFs mean fast download. The days of eye candy at the start of a Flash movie are over. If the content users see within that 15-second window is not relevant to the site or the experience, they will be gone.

- If a bleeding edge Flash site isn't viewable on a two-year-old computer with a standard operating system and hardware, it is time to go back to the drawing board.

- For a commercial site, give yourself another year and go back three years. Corporations are relatively slow to upgrade because of the significant cost incurred to do so.

- If your target audience is urban and in a developed country, assume they have, at minimum, a cable connection.

- If your audience is the world, develop to the lowest common denominator, which is a dial-up modem.

Now that we have inundated you with "techie talk," let's look at how your Flash file gets from here to there. How that happens is through a concept we talked about in Chapter 8—*streaming*.

Streaming

As you have discovered by this point in the book, simply tossing a bunch of audio, images, and video into your movie is not a good thing. They take an inordinate amount of time to download. In fact, toss all of that content into frame 1, and you can kiss your "15-second window of opportunity" goodbye.

It is the prudent Flash designer or developer who realizes this and structures a movie in such a way that it starts playing before the content has finished loading. Like video, your Flash movie uses a progressive download process. This means when enough data has been downloaded to start something happening, that 15 seconds is a godsend.

Streaming doesn't make things faster. What it does is intelligently organize things to start the movie playing in very short order. Used wisely, streaming can ensure that everything in the Flash movie is downloaded before it is needed. The result is a Flash movie that seems to start playing almost immediately and plays "as smooth as the hair on a frog's back."

So what happens when a web page requests your movie? Two things are sent to the browser:

- The movie's timeline, including ActionScript and stuff not in the library, such as text and shapes that haven't been converted to symbols
- Library items, including audio, video, images, and symbols—if they appear in the timeline or are set to export for ActionScript

You need to clearly understand this: when your Flash movie is shot through the Internet to the user's browser, the movie is sent in frame order. If the movie is split into scenes, a relatively rare practice today, the scenes will be sent in the order in which they appear. The library is also sent, but the library items are not sent in the order in which they appear in the library. They are sent in the sequence in which they appear on the timeline. To reinforce what we have just said, let's take a look at a typical file:

1. Open the YawningParrot.fla file in your Chapter 13 Exercise folder.

   The timeline, shown in Figure 13-2, is linear, but you will notice there are a lot of layers. Your first reaction could be, "Man that is going to take a while to load." Not really.

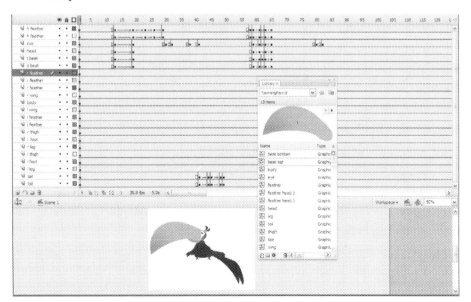

Figure 13-2. Streaming plays a movie in frame order and loads the content in the library in the order in which it appears on the timeline.

2. Open the library. You will notice there is a lot less content in the library than there are layers. This is because the symbols in the library are reused and repurposed. All of the feather layers use the feather symbol.

When this movie loads, the parrot is constructed, in frame 1, of all of the objects in the library. The thing about each of the library objects is they are physically small. This means they are also relatively small in file size, and the result is not a lot of bandwidth is required to load them and get the movie playing.

To visualize how this movie will stream, you will need to add an extra, imaginary playhead to the timeline. When the movie starts, they are both in frame 1, but the imaginary playhead—let's call it *streamhead*—moves ahead of the actual playhead. The streamhead's position on the timeline indicates how much of the movie has been downloaded. The playhead will stay put because its purpose is to indicate the frame currently playing.

Now let's assume that you toss in a movieclip containing a 3-second FLV file that has been embedded into its timeline, and this movieclip is added to frame 10. The odds are really good that the streamhead will stay put on frame 10 and the playhead will "catch up" to arrive at frame 10 and also stay put. What will happen is the movie will essentially stop until the movieclip's inner timeline, including the FLV, is loaded, at which point the streamhead restarts its journey along the timeline.

To avoid this nastiness, Flash designers and developers give the streamhead a head start by creating a **streaming buffer**. This could be in the form of a preloader (we'll get into this subject later) or any other technique that keeps the playhead behind in "second place" in order to let the streamhead do its job and load content.

Though you may be having difficulty visualizing two heads on the timeline, Flash has a tool that lets you see how these two heads work and how the pipe can affect the delivery of your Flash movie to the browser. Where is this tool? Let's go look at the Bandwidth Profiler.

The Bandwidth Profiler

In many respects, the Bandwidth Profiler is quite similar to what you see in Device Central when you test a mobile movie. The movie opens up in a device that emulates the performance of your movie in the chosen device. The Bandwidth Profiler emulates how your movie will behave when it downloads to the user's machine.

Though the Bandwidth Profiler is an extremely useful tool, keep in mind it is nothing more than an emulator. It won't mimic real life completely, mainly because it assumes a steady transfer rate into the browser, in contrast to an Internet universe that actually ebbs and pulses based on traffic.

Regardless, the Bandwidth Profiler can give you a good idea of where streaming bottlenecks are likely to occur. This can be an invaluable aid in relieving "data jam" and solving a problem before it becomes a major one. Let's take a look at the Bandwidth Profiler:

1. Open the BandwidthTest.fla file in Flash. When the movie opens, you will see we have placed an audio file on the timeline, embedded an FLV into a movieclip, and placed it in frame 1, and if you scrub over to frame 2, you will see we have added some text to the stage. If you open the library, you will see the text is actually a graphic symbol. Just by looking at the timeline, you can see that the movieclip with the FLV and the audio file will be the first pieces of content to load, and then the text will load.

2. Test the movie. This time when the SWF opens, select View ➤ Bandwidth Profiler. Take a look at the graph, shown in Figure 13-3, that suddenly appears above the movie.

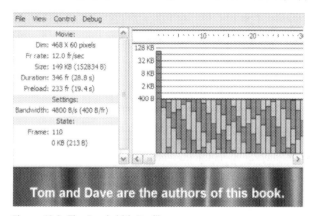

Figure 13-3. The Bandwidth Profiler

On the left side are three headings: Movie, Settings, and State. To the right is a frame-by-frame representation of the data downloading into each frame. Notice the spike in frame 1. This is understandable because the audio file and the FLV need to load in this frame. Under the settings, you will see something like Bandwidth:4800B/s(400 B/frame). Now look at where that red line is sitting. The values match. This red line is the **bandwidth limit**, which represents the maximum throughput a modem can handle. Bars under the line are handled quickly. Bars rising above the line indicate potential bottlenecks.

3. Select View ➤ Download Settings. The drop-down menu that appears (see Figure 13-4) allows you to choose a particular modem speed.

4. Select DSL (32.6 KB/s) from the drop-down menu and scroll back to the start of the movie. You will notice the bandwidth limit has increased from 400 bytes to 2.78 KB and that the markings on the graph have changed to reflect your selection.

5. You are most likely looking at that spike in the first frame and thinking, "Yeah, so? What's the deal?" Rather than having us explain it, we are going to let you experience it. Change back to the 56K modem choice and this time select View ➤ Simulate Download.

   Let's guess. You sat around for about 25 seconds waiting for the movie to start? What you have just experienced is the other, and most important, half of the Bandwidth Profiler. You just sat through what a person with a 56K modem will experience. Let's take a minute and talk about this.

13

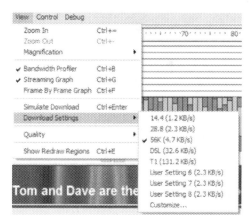

Figure 13-4. You can change the modem speed.

When you selected Simulate Download, you essentially emulated how the movie will load into a 56K modem. The other thing that happened is the Bandwidth Profiler developed a green bar at the top of the graph, which stayed put until the movie started to play (see Figure 13-5).

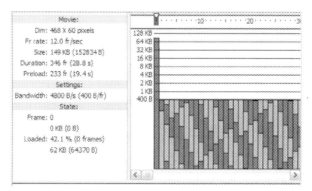

Figure 13-5. You can experience the issue with the first frame when you simulate the download.

The green bar is important. At the start of this section, we talked about two imaginary playheads. What you are seeing is what happens when the streamhead and the playhead catch up to each other. To visualize what is going on, think of the playhead as the playhead indicator at the top of the screen and the streamhead is the green bar. How long will they be stuck there?

On the left side of the Bandwidth Profiler is a value for the Preload setting, which in our example is 233 fr (frames) or 19.4 s (seconds). When you starting emulating the movie, the Settings area became active (you may have to increase the size of the Bandwidth Profiler window by dragging the bottom edge down). The size area will show you the activity, and you can see that it will take just over 19 seconds to load in all of the content in the first frame. What you should have seen, when everything loaded, was the green bar suddenly roaring off to the right, and the playhead moving across the frames as it follows the streamhead.

6. Change the download settings to DSL and select Simulate Download. You'll still experience a short delay, but there will also be a marked decrease in how long you have to wait. The Preload setting should show you 33 fr (2.8 s), which is a dramatic decrease from the almost 20 seconds you had to wait simulating a 56K modem.

As you can see, the Bandwidth Profiler is a rather powerful tool that you need to master. With it, you can tailor your movie to the bandwidth constraints of your user and ensure you meet that 15-second window of opportunity that will open to you. With the Download Settings option, not only do you get to see how bandwidth will affect your movie, you also actually get to experience it.

At this point, you may be thinking, "Shoot, I can cut back the preload by using ActionScript to play the sound because the sound is embedded into the library." Let's see if that works:

7. Open the BandwidthTest1.fla file. If you open the library, you will see the sound file is absent, and if you open the code in frame 3 of the Actions layer, you will see we have added the call to the sound.

8. Test the movie and select Simulate Download. The graph, as you see in Figure 13-6, has significantly changed, but the spike in frame 1 really hasn't. As well, the delay is still there. This tells you the issue really isn't the sound, but the FLV embedded into the movieclip. (The sound wasn't adding a lot up front because its Sync setting was set to Stream, which distributed its weight across many frames.) You have just discovered another use for the Bandwidth Profiler. Not only can it show you where the problem is, but it can also be used to isolate the content causing the delay.

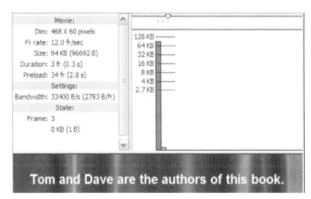

Figure 13-6. Use the Bandwidth Profiler to identify the content causing the delay.

How would we fix this? First off, there will always be that spike in frame 1 of any movie you will create. The goal is to get that spike as close to the red line as possible. To fix this, one approach would be to reduce the time of the curtains effect from its current 46 frames to 23 frames in the background *movieclip. Do this, and the preload time drops to 1.4 seconds.*

13

Optimizing and fine-tuning your Flash movies

As you saw in the previous example, a simple thing like reducing the number of frames in an FLV can have a dramatic impact on how the movie loads. What we plan to do in this section is to outline a few tips, tricks, and techniques you can use to make your Flash movies leaner, meaner, and faster. Surprisingly, the first mistake most people make is made even before a pixel is lit up. They forget to plan the movie.

Structure

That old adage—*Plan your work and work your plan*—is especially true when working with Flash. You can't make it up as you go along. You have to take the time before you start to think about what the user sees, and in what order, before you start firing content into the library and then onto the stage. For example, a video site that lets the user choose from a number of videos would involve the following:

- Preloader
- Intro screen
- The main movie screen where the videos are chosen and viewed
- A set of links to other video sites you may have created

This means when the user arrives at the site, he or she would most likely do the following:

- The user would see the preloader for a few seconds and then be taken to the intro frame.
- From there, the user would choose to read the information and then move to the video picker screen by clicking a button.
- The video frame would load up, and the user can click a series of buttons to view the videos associated with the buttons.
- The viewer can then choose to return to the intro screen or go to a frame that contains a series of interactive links.

Now that you have an idea of what will happen, you might even want to pull together a small flowchart that shows the purpose of each frame in the movie, As you can see in Figure 13-7, having one of these handy allows you to visualize how the user will move around the movie and provides a broad view of the content of each frame.

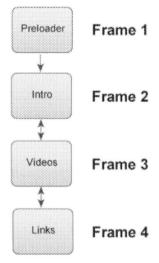

Figure 13-7. Map out your plan.

In fact, if you have arrived at Flash CS3 through the Adobe Web Premium Bundle, you have an ideal tool for this process at your disposal. Fireworks CS3 has been repositioned as a rapid prototyping tool. If you open the application and select Window ➤ Common Library, you will see a bunch of folders that contain symbols for a variety of rapid proto-typing tasks. The flow diagram symbols shown in Figure 13-8 are ideal for planning out a Flash or HTML project.

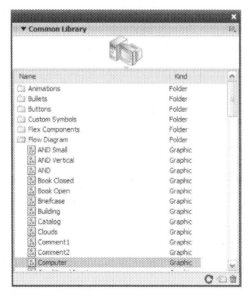

Figure 13-8. Use Fireworks CS3 as a planning aid.

13

By writing out what each frame does or using Fireworks CS3 to create a flow diagram, what you are doing is ordering the content on the timeline. By "falling in love with the user" and streaming the content into the movie in that order, your site will meet the needs of your users. If you randomly place the content on the timeline, you have no way of ensuring it will load in any meaningful manner. The result is a site that has to download in its entirety before the user can interact with it. Though many sites do this, it is not considered to be a best practice within the Flash design community.

Optimizing elements in the movie

Every chapter in this book has directly or indirectly made it clear that Flash loves "small." After your experiences with the Bandwidth Profiler, we think you now understand why we are so adamant on this point. A small file means a fast load. A fast load means short wait time. A short wait time puts you squarely in that 15-second window of opportunity. We have shown you several methods of keeping things small when it comes to images, fonts, sounds, video, and drawing. What about vectors?

We know Flash loves vectors. The thing is, vectors can be both small and large at the same time. Huh? The reason is every time Flash encounters a vector point, it has to load it into memory in order to draw the shape. If you create a vector with a large number of vector points, you may have a small file on your hands, but you have also increased the demand on memory to redraw the image. The result is the inevitable spike in the Bandwidth Profiler. Here's one way of addressing this issue:

1. Create a new Flash document. When Flash opens, add three more keyframes to Layer 1 in the Layers panel. You now have four keyframes on the timeline.

2. Select the Pencil tool, and in frame 1, draw a "curvy" shape like we have done in Figure 13-9.

Figure 13-9. Start by drawing a shape containing a lot of vector points.

3. Copy your shape to the clipboard. Select each of the remaining three keyframes in Layer 1 and select Edit ➤ Paste in Place (Ctrl+Shift+V on a PC or Cmd+Shift+V on a Mac).

4. Select the shape in frame 2 and select Modify ➤ Shape ➤ Smooth. Not a lot seems to happen.

5. Select the shape in frame 3 and select Modify ➤ Shape ➤ Straighten. A couple of the lines straighten out.

6. Select the shape in frame 4 and select Modify ➤ Shape ➤ Optimize. This time you are presented with the Optimize Curves dialog box. Move the slider all the way to the right and click OK. The dialog box will close and be replaced by an Alert dialog box, shown in Figure 13-10, telling you how many curves were found, how many were optimized, and the size of the reduction as a result of the optimization.

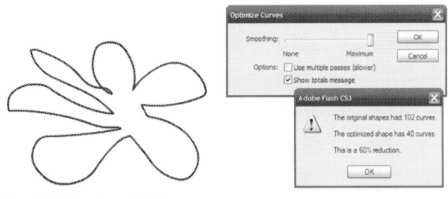

Figure 13-10. Using shape optimization

The image shown in Figure 13-10 is a composite image. We created it to show you the Alert *dialog box resulting from clicking* OK *in the* Optimize Curves *dialog box.*

7. Test the movie. As you see in Figure 13-11, the graph shows you the file size of the content in each frame and the effect modifying the shape has in each frame. The results are quite dramatic.

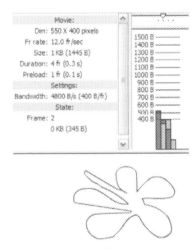

Figure 13-11. Smoothing, straightening, and optimizing curves can have a profound effect upon download times.

You are most likely looking at the graph and thinking, "Wow, I am going to start optimizing all of my vector shapes." Not so fast. Each of the three methods presented did a good thing and a bad thing. The good thing was they did indeed reduce the bandwidth load. The bad thing was they introduced distortions into the image. If you are happy with the distortions, fine. If you aren't, you might want to consider doing the optimization, selecting the shape with the Subselection tool, and manually manipulating the shape and the points.

So why was there such a drop in the graph between the object in frame 1 and its counterpart in frame 4? Remember, vector nodes require bandwidth. You removed a ton of them, as shown in Figure 13-12, using the Shape Optimization dialog box, which accounts for the drop in required bandwidth.

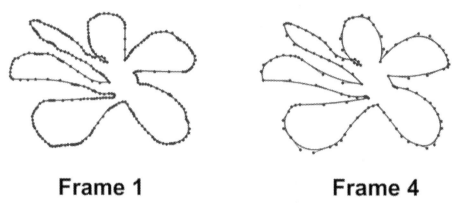

Frame 1   Frame 4

Figure 13-12. Each node on a shape requires a "piece" of bandwidth.

Using the Loader class to display images and SWFs

As you saw in the Bandwidth Profiler exercise, using ActionScript to load content into a movie can result in a performance boost because the content is not contained in the library. Instead the data is streamed into the SWF from your HTTP server. This technique can also be applied to images and SWF files as well. Just keep in mind that content still needs to be streamed into the SWF that calls the content, meaning there will still be a slight delay, but the performance boost comes in the form of reduced wait times.

All of this is accomplished through the use of the Loader class in ActionScript 3.0. The Loader class is used to load SWF files or image (JPEG, PNG, or GIF) files into a SWF through the use of the load() method. The loaded display object is added as a child of the Loader object. Here's how all of this works:

1. Open the Loading.fla file in the Exercise folder. When the file opens, you will see there is a single movieclip on the stage, and if you open the library, you will see this movieclip is the only object in the library. If you select the clip in the stage, you will also see we have given it the instance name of clip.

2. Select the first frame of the scripts layer, open the Actions panel, and add the following code:

```
var loader:Loader = new Loader();
addChild(loader);
//clip.addChild(loader);
```

```
loader.contentLoaderInfo.addEventListener(
  Event.COMPLETE,function(evt:Event):void {
    //clip.x = 50;
    //clip.y = 50;
  }
);
loader.contentLoaderInfo.addEventListener(
  ProgressEvent.PROGRESS, function(evt:ProgressEvent):void {
    trace(evt.bytesLoaded);
  }
);
//loader.load(new URLRequest("toBeLoaded.swf"));
loader.load(new URLRequest("toBeLoaded.png"));
```

The first line of the code creates the Loader object. The next two lines either load the content onto the stage—addChild(loader);—or into the movieclip itself. The two EventListeners tell the loader where to place the content and to let you see the progress by using the trace() function to display how many bytes have been loaded in the Output panel.

The final two lines are used to tell the SWF what content is to be loaded.

3. Test the movie.

4. Return to the Actions panel and comment out lines 2 and 17 of the code (//addChild(loader)) and delete the comment in lines 3, 8, 9, and 18.

5. Test the movie. This time the SWF is called in, added to the stand in movieclip, and placed 50 pixels out and down on the stage, as shown in Figure 13-13.

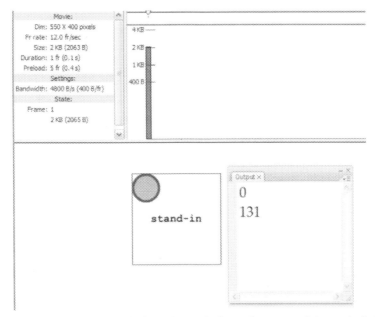

Figure 13-13. A SWF is loaded into the movieclip on the stage, and the movieclip is moved to a new location. Note as well the Output panel shows you the bytesLoaded value.

Final copies of these two movies—LoadingJPG.fla and LoadingSWF.fla—can be found in this chapter's Completed folder.

You may have noticed throughout this book that the layer where scripts are placed is either called Actions or scripts. What you are seeing is a clash of naming conventions. Ultimately, the name of the layer doesn't matter, as it has no practical effect on the functionality of the movie. This is not to involve you in a debate, but to make you aware that layer naming conventions need to be defined right at the start of a project. We aren't trying to be difficult by throwing two choices at you; we're following current industry best practice of giving layers a meaningful label—it's just that we didn't consult beforehand. Using one or the other is an acceptable best practice.

Your turn: Creating a preloader

We have been talking about preloaders, and the time has arrived to create one of your own. In this exercise, you will not only create a preloader, but also use the bytesLoaded values to give the user some feedback regarding the loading of the file. Preloaders can range from the simple, such as the one you'll create here, to the incredibly complex, involving clever animation and even sound effects. Regardless of the approach taken, the purpose of a preloader is to get something happening within that 15-second window of opportunity and have the user become engaged in the site almost immediately. To do this, you will be using assets from the YawningParrot.fla file as the preloader for the file used in the Bandwidth Profiler exercise. Here's how:

1. Open the PreloadEX.fla file in your Exercise folder. Scrub through the timeline, and you will see the familiar yawning parrot and then be taken right into a clone of the heavy BandwidthTest1.fla file used earlier in this chapter.

2. Open the library and double-click the parrot movieclip to open it in the Symbol Editor. You will notice that we have added a dynamic text box with the instance name of percentage under the parrot. This text box, shown in Figure 13-14, will be used to display the percentage value of how much of the file has loaded.

3. Click the Scene 1 link to return to the main timeline. Add a keyframe to frames 1 and 5 of the scripts layer. Select the keyframe in frame 1 of the scripts layer and open the Actions panel.

4. Click in the Script pane and add the following code:

```
root.loaderInfo.addEventListener(
  Event.COMPLETE,
  function(evt:Event):void {
    if (currentFrame == 5) {
      play();
    } else {
      gotoAndPlay(10);
    }
  }
);
```

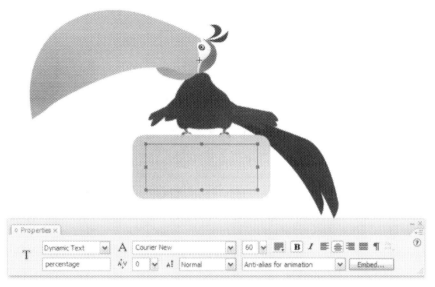

Figure 13-14. A yawning parrot and a dynamic text box are the key elements used in this preloader.

Let's take a moment and figure out what is going on. First off, this movie actually preloads itself. There is no external content being used. The "trick" therefore is to determine where to target the events used by ActionScript.

The first line of the code targets the `loaderInfo` property of the main timeline—root. Where does `loaderInfo` come from? This property hails from the `DisplayObject` class, which is in the inheritance chain for `Sprite` and ultimately the `MovieClip` class.

In frame 1, you "wire up" a `COMPLETE` event. A `COMPLETE` event is fired when the movie data has loaded successfully. In this case, you are saying, "If the data hasn't loaded, keep moving forward." If the current frame is 5, that means all of the content hasn't loaded, and the parrot is yawning away. Instead of looping back to frame 1, you tell the playhead to keep going to frame 5 and `play()` from there. If not, because the user has already visited the page that contains this movie, it means that the content has loaded after all. In that case, you use the `gotoAndPlay(10)` method to bypass the parrot.

5. Click the keyframe in frame 5 of the scripts layer and add the following code:

```
stop();

root.loaderInfo.addEventListener(
  ProgressEvent.PROGRESS,
  function(evt:ProgressEvent):void {
    var percent:Number = Math.floor(evt.bytesLoaded /➡
evt.bytesTotal * 100);
    parrot.percentage.text = percent + "%";
  }
);
```

You know what the `stop()` method does, so let's concentrate on the listener and the function.

13

The first line tells the main timeline to listen for something that just happens to be the loaderInfo property of the main timeline. The next line uses the ProgressEvent class to keep an eye on when the load operation has started. A ProgressEvent is usually triggered when SWF files, images, or data are loaded into Flash Player. In the case of this movie, you are going to keep an eye on the data part of the equation because all of the stuff in the movie is in the library. One of the properties of the ProgressEvent class is bytesLoaded. This is great because Flash knows how many bytes there are in the movie, and as you saw in the previous exercise, it keeps track of how many bytes have been loaded at any point in time. Knowing this, you can then do the math to compare how many bytes have been loaded as a percentage of the total bytes in the movie. These calculations inevitably wind up with copious numbers after the decimal, so you strip them off using the Math.floor() method. One of the easiest ways to get a handle on this sort of thing is to actually do the math. Let's assume there are 275 bytes in the movie (bytesTotal), and you have loaded in 71 of them (bytesLoaded). Let's follow the numbers:

```
var percent:Number = Math.floor(71 / 265 * 100);
```

The result of 71 / 265 * 100 is 26.792, which you round down (Math.floor()) to a value of 26 for your var percent:Number.

Now that you have a number, you can use it. In this case, you take the number and use it in the dynamic text box with the instance name of parrot under the yawning parrot. As more data loads, this number will not only change, but also appear as a percentage to the user because you told ActionScript to tack a % sign after the number.

6. Close the Actions panel. Save the movie and test it.

7. When the SWF opens, change the download setting to 56K and select Simulate Download. The parrot fades in and yawns as it waits for the rest of the movie to load. While the parrot is yawning, you also see the percentage of the content that has loaded, as shown in Figure 13-15.

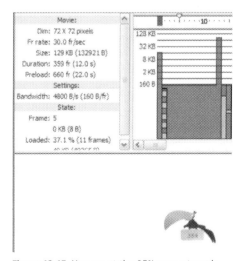

Figure 13-15. You are at the 35% percent mark.

What about those cases where content is loading from an external source? This could be the loading of a SWF or a JPEG image that is not embedded into a SWF. Here is how you do that:

1. Open the `YawningParrotPreloader.fla` file in your Chapter 13 Exercise folder. You will notice our bored friend is back, but this time in the library there is a blank movieclip named photo. In this exercise, you are going use the preloader to monitor the progress of a JPEG on another website loading into the photo movieclip. Not only that, but the photo loading from the other website will fade in.

2. Add keyframes to frames 15 and 30 of the scripts layer.

3. Select the keyframe in frame 15 of the scripts layer, open the Actions panel, and enter the following code:

```
stop();

var loader:Loader = new Loader();

loader.contentLoaderInfo.addEventListener(
  Event.COMPLETE,
  function(evt:Event):void {
    play();
  }
);

loader.contentLoaderInfo.addEventListener(
  ProgressEvent.PROGRESS,
  function(evt:ProgressEvent):void {
    var percent:Number = Math.floor(evt.bytesLoaded /➡
evt.bytesTotal * 100);
    parrot.percentage.text = percent + "%";
  }
);

loader.load(new➡
URLRequest("http://www.FoundationFlashCS3.com/rocket.jpg"));
```

There are three major differences between this code and the code entered into frame 5 of the previous example. The first is the playback head is told to stay put and not go anywhere until the image has loaded.

The next change is the use of the contentLoaderInfo() property. This property kicks out a LoaderInfo object, which is used to supply the loading progress information that is used in the dynamic text box under the parrot. The neat thing about that LoaderInfo object is that it comes into play before the content is fully loaded so the eventListener is being used to monitor the progress of the download.

The final difference is the last line of the code. So far, you have used the load() method to bring in content that is in the same folder as the SWF. In this case, you are going to an external URL to grab the image and load it into the photo movieclip. If you have a lot of

13

images or SWFs to be loaded, this is a great way of having them all stay in one folder but still be accessible to your SWF.

4. Even though the photo of the rocket has been loaded, Flash doesn't have a clue where the photo is supposed to go. Let's deal with that. Add a keyframe in frame 30 of the scripts layer, open the Actions panel, and add this line of code:

```
photo.addChild(loader);
```

You used the addChild() method to tell Flash to add the content just loaded to the display list of the movieclip on the stage whose instance name is photo. The tween between frames 30 and 35 simply fades the image in from 0% alpha to 100%.

5. Save and test the movie. The parrot will tell you how much of the rocket has loaded, and then the rocket engine, as shown in Figure 13-16, fades in.

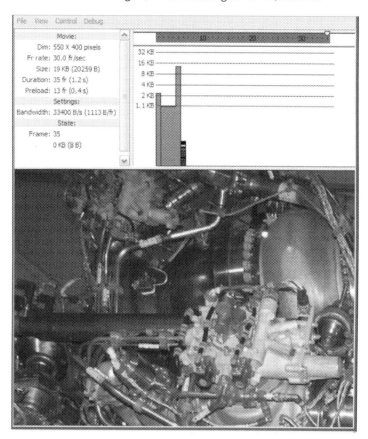

Figure 13-16. Loading external content into a movieclip

Optimizing Flash content for use in video

As you may have surmised when reading the heading for this exercise, you are not going to be thinking "outside the box" but thinking outside of the room where the box is located.

This may come as a bit of a surprise, but Flash is often used to create animated cartoons that are shown on television and animations used in commercials. The process has historically been, to say the least, convoluted, but it could be done. The problem was, even though Flash could output to QuickTime, only the main timeline could be exported. Library content, ActionScript-driven animation, and even nested movieclips were not exported. When you consider the fact that the maximum length for the Flash timeline is just over 16,000 frames, the achievement of a short 10-minute cartoon was not possible unless the movie was broken into pieces and stitched together in a video editing program.

Flash CS3 contains a really cool feature that allows you to not only export the content on the timeline, but also create animations that are solely driven by ActionScript as QuickTime movies and then use them as motion graphics in such applications as Adobe After Effects CS3. In fact, in this exercise, the stage is blank. All of the letters that appear in this animation will be randomly generated, colored, and put in motion using ActionScript. Follow these steps to create a QuickTime movie in Flash:

1. Open a new Flash document and set the stage color to black.

2. Rename Layer 1 as scripts.

3. Select the keyframe in the scripts layer and open the ActionScript Editor.

4. Enter the following code:

```
var t:Timer = new Timer(50, 0);
t.addEventListener(TimerEvent.TIMER, createLetter);
t.start();

function createLetter(evt:Event):void {
  var f:TextFormat = new TextFormat();
  f.size = randomBetween(80, 120);
  f.color = Math.floor(Math.random() * 16777216);
  var mc:MovieClip = new MovieClip();
  var t:TextField = new TextField();
  t.autoSize = "center";
  t.text = String.fromCharCode(randomBetween(97, 122));
  t.setTextFormat(f);
  mc.addChild(t);
  mc.x = (Math.random() * stage.stageWidth);
  mc.y = stage.stageHeight;
  mc.ang = 0;
  mc.range = randomBetween(4, 20);
  addChild(mc);
  mc.addEventListener(Event.ENTER_FRAME, shimmy);
}
```

13

The first line of code creates a timer that tells Flash to create a new Timer object—new Timer(50, 0)—which will wait 50 milliseconds before adding another letter, and that the sequence repeats forever. The next line creates the listener that will "listen" for this virtual "beep" every 50 milliseconds, and when it hears the beep, it will create a random letter. The third line—t.start();—is the method of the Timer class that starts the clock running.

The createLetter() function is how the letters arrive in the movie. The first variable creates a TextFormat object, which is used to format text fields.

Now that you have the object, you need to give it the formatting information. The size of the text is set by using a custom function, randomBetween(), that determines the maximum and minimum size of the letters. The color is set by picking a random value between 0 and 1 and then multiplying that result by 16,777,216 and rounding the answer down to the nearest integer. Where did that number come from? That's how many colors you can find in the 24-bit color space.

You then create a movieclip and a text field. The text field is centered, the letters are added to it, and formatting is applied.

The line t.text = String.fromCharCode(randomBetween(97, 122)), which determines which letter appears in the text field, looks rather complex, but it isn't really. You needed random values, so you used the fromCharCode() method of the String class to return a string derived from integers that represent ASCII values for the desired letters (the lowercase alphabet, as it happens). To ensure they are all different, you use that custom randomBetween() function again and tell Flash, in plain English, "You go pick an ASCII value between 97 and 122. When you have it, add the letter of the alphabet that value represents to the text field." The next two lines tell Flash the size and color of the text formatting (f) and add the text field to the display list of the movieclip (mc.addChild(t)).

The remainder of the code tells Flash where to put the movieclip, adds the movieclip to the display list of the stage, and puts the movieclip in motion using a custom shimmy() function. Now you'll write that function.

5. Press Enter (PC) or Return (Mac) twice and enter the following code that will put the letters in motion:

```
function shimmy(evt:Event):void {
  var mc:MovieClip = MovieClip(evt.target);
  mc.y -= randomBetween(6, 10);
  mc.x += (mc.range * Math.cos(mc.ang += 0.4));
  mc.scaleY -= 0.02;
  if (mc.scaleY <= 0) {
    mc.removeEventListener(Event.ENTER_FRAME, shimmy);
    removeChild(mc);
  }
}
```

Before we start explaining this code, remember, all motion in Flash is either across the stage on the x axis or up and down the stage on the y axis. Objects moving from the top to the bottom of the stage have increasing y values, and all objects moving from left to right have increasing x values . . . and vice versa.

This code block determines the stage movement of the movieclip containing the letter from the previous code block. Each one is randomly placed on the y axis, and the cosine method—Math.cos()—of the Math class is used to add a left-to-right shimmy, which really is the movement along a cosine wave, as the letters move upward.

As the letters move up the stage along the y axis, they are scaled down by 2%—mc.scaleY -= 0.02;—every time the timer "beeps." The last three lines essentially tell Flash, "Look, this thing is going to eventually scale down to a value of 0. When you hear that, get rid of the movieclip."

There's that randomBetween() function again. Next, you'll write that to finish off this code.

6. Press Enter (PC) or Return (Mac) twice and enter the following:

```
function randomBetween (min:Number, max:Number):Number {
  return (Math.random() * (max - min)) + min;
}
```

This function picks a random number based on the parameters provided within the parentheses. The return statement does a bit of math and spits back a number. Let's see how this works in regard to setting the size of the letters. The line that does that is

```
f.size = randomBetween(80, 120);
```

This means the calculation would be

```
return (Math.random() * (120 - 80)) + 80;
```

Let's assume the Math.random() value is .35. The calculation would be

```
return (.35 * (120 - 80)) + 80;
```

Here, the result of (.35 * (120 – 80)) + 80 is 93.6, so the size of this letter would be 93.6 pixels.

> *Aren't pixels integers? You betcha. Then how can Flash display something at a height of 93.6 pixels? Ultimately, the end result will be 94, but Flash stores an internal representation of coordinates down to the 1/20th of a pixel, a unit known as a **twip**.*

13

7. Save and test the movie. You should see letters, as shown in Figure 13-17, moving up the stage in a wavy motion. They get smaller as they move upward and eventually disappear.

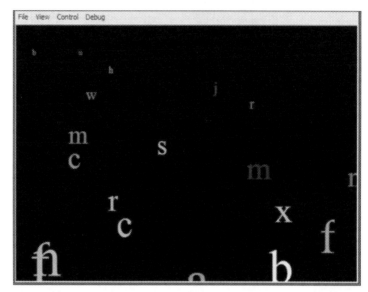

Figure 13-17. Letters randomly generated, formatted, and put into motion using ActionScript

8. Select File ➤ Export ➤ Export Movie. When the Export Movie dialog box opens, navigate to the folder where you want to save the file and select QuickTime (*.mov) from the Save as type drop-down menu shown in Figure 13-18. Click OK to open the QuickTime Export Settings dialog box.

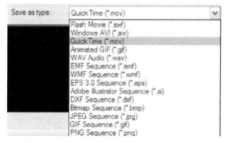

Figure 13-18. Exporting a Flash file as a QuickTime movie

9. Select Ignore stage color (generate alpha channel) as shown in Figure 13-19 and change the After time elapsed value to 10. Click the Export button.

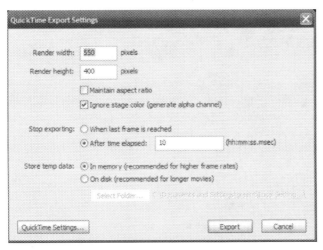

Figure 13-19. The QuickTime Export Settings dialog box

Let's quickly review this dialog box. The Render width and Render height values match the current stage size and will be the physical dimensions of the video. You can change these values. The Maintain aspect ratio selection, when checked, ensures distortion is not added to the video if you resize the video. The Ignore stage color (generate alpha channel) selection essentially turns the stage color invisible, which makes this ideal if you want this animation to play over content in After Effects CS3 or some other video editor.

The Stop exporting area gives Flash an idea of when to stop the process. The first choice, When last frame is reached, should be used if you have content on the timeline. The second one, After time elapsed, is ideal for situations such as this exercise where content is generated by ActionScript. In this case, you are producing a clip with a duration of 10 seconds.

The Store temp data options come into play during the render process. You can choose to either store the temp data in memory for short movies or create a temporary file on the desktop or some other location. The QuickTime Settings button opens the QuickTime Settings dialog box where you can change the codec and audio settings for the final movie.

When you click the Export button, a progress bar will appear as well as an alert telling you where the export log can be found.

10. Click OK and quit Flash. Open your new QuickTime movie and check it out—pretty neat!

As we said earlier, you can export these things as animations for use in other applications. For example, one of the authors dropped the file into an After Effects CS3 project, as shown in Figure 13-20, and then created the QuickTime movie named BubblingLettersFinal.mov that is found in your Chapter 13 Exercise folder.

13

Figure 13-20. The video is used in After Effects CS3.

What you've learned

- How Flash movies are streamed to a web page
- A couple of ways of turning the Bandwidth Profiler into your new best friend
- Tips and tricks for optimizing content for fast download
- One method of creating preloader in Flash
- How to convert a Flash movie into a QuickTime video for use in a video editing application

There wasn't a lot of "geeky" or cool stuff in this chapter. Instead the focus of this chapter was on how to optimize your Flash movies for web playback. We examined how the data in your Flash movie gets from "here to there" and in what order. We reviewed several ways of using the Bandwidth Profiler from identifying content bottlenecks to actually emulating the download of a bloated Flash movie into a dial-up modem. It wasn't pleasant, but we then showed you a number of ways to fine-tune your Flash movies in order to let you maximize that 15-second window of opportunity you get when a user hits your site. The chapter wrapped up by showing you a couple of ways to create preloaders for your site, how to load remote content into a movieclip, and ended by moving into the "uber-cool" zone as we showed you how to convert a Flash movie into a QuickTime video.

Now that you know how to prepare files for streaming, let's look at the end game . . . preparing the SWF file. Turn the page, and we'll see you in the next chapter.

14 PUBLISHING FLASH MOVIES

If there is one fundamental fact regarding publishing your Flash movie to the Web, it is this: *The SWF isn't a web document.* Nothing drives us crazier than somebody telling us, "Dudes, check out my Flash site," only to have that individual double-click a SWF on his or her computer's desktop. Flash SWFs should only appear on the Web if they are embedded into an HTML page. Thus a "Flash site," to be precise, is composed of an HTML page that points to the SWF and any media—audio, video, images, text—that the SWF may need from external sources.

What we'll cover in this chapter:

- The web formats used by Flash
- Publishing a SWF for web playback
- Dealing with remote content

Files used in this chapter:

- YawningParrot.fla (Chapter14/ExerciseFiles_CH14/Exercise/ YawningParrot.fla)
- ParrotFW.gif (Chapter14/ExerciseFiles_CH14/Exercise/ParrotFW.gif)
- MoonOverLakeNanagook.fla (Chapter14/ExerciseFiles_CH14/Exercise/ MoonOverLakeNanagook.fla)
- MoonOverLakeNanagook.fla (Chapter14/ExerciseFiles_CH14/Exercise/ Nanagook/MoonOverLakeNanagook.fla)
- Player.fla (Chapter14/ExerciseFiles_CH14/Exercise/Player.fla)

Web formats

Creating the SWF is a bit more complicated than selecting File ➤ Publish Preview and merrily clicking away in the Publish panel. As we pointed out in the previous chapter, you need a grounding in what's under the hood before you create the car.

If there is one theme have been stressing since page 1 of this book, it is *Keep it small!* This is the reason for Flash's broad acceptance on the Web and where an understanding of the publishing process is invaluable. Up to this point, we have essentially created a bunch of FLA files and asked you to test them. The time has arrived to get off of the test track and put the vehicle on the street. When you publish your movie, Flash compresses the file, removes the redundant information in the FLA, and what you are left with—especially if you took the last chapter to heart—is one sleek, mean web presentation. The default output file format—yes, there is more than one—is the SWF (pronounced *swiff*). The SWF is wrapped in HTML through the use of <object> and/or <embed> tags, plus extra information on how the browser should play the SWF.

> *Yes, you can link directly to a SWF without that bothersome HTML. Just be aware that the SWF will expand to the full size of the browser window, meaning all of the content on the stage will also enlarge. In many respects, linking directly to the SWF is "Rookie Error #1."*

Before we move into actually publishing a movie, let's look at some of the more common file types used on the Web, listed here:

- Flash (.swf)
- HTML (.htm or .html)
- GIFs (.gif)
- QuickTime (.mov)

Flash

Before there was Flash, there was Director. Though used primarily for interactive CDs, DVDs, and kiosks, it was at one time the main method employed to get animations to play on the Web. The technology developed by Macromedia to accomplish this was named **Shockwave**, and the file extension used was .dcr. Flash also made use of this technology, and in order to differentiate between them, it became known as **Shockwave for Flash**. Flash Player is the technology that allows the SWF to play through a user's browser. Through a series of clever moves, Flash Player has become ubiquitous on the Web. In fact, Adobe can rightfully claim that Flash Player, regardless of version, can be found on 98% of all Internet-enabled computers on the planet. This means, in theory, you can assume your movies are readily available to anyone who wishes to watch them. But the reality gets a bit more complicated.

> For you trivia buffs, the first couple of iterations of Shockwave for Director used a small application named Afterburner to create the .dcr files. When a Director developer prepared a presentation for the Web, he or she didn't create the .dcr. The movie was "shocked." One of the authors happened to be around the night Macromedia quietly released Shockwave and Afterburner to the Director community, and he still remembers the excitement generated by members of the group as they posted circles that moved across the page, and the "oohs" and "aahs" that followed as the circles moved up and down.

Each new Flash Player brings with it new functionality. Flash Player 8 introduced filter effects and blend modes, which can't be played in Flash Player 7. FLV video can't be played in Flash Player 5. Any movie you prepare using ActionScript 3.0 can only be played in Flash Player 9 or higher. Though you may initially regard this as a nonissue, you would be making a gross miscalculation. Corporations, through their IT departments, have strict policies regarding the addition or installation of software to corporate-owned computers. We personally know of one organization that isn't budging, and its Flash Player policy is Flash Player 6 or lower. The upshot is, it is the shrewd Flash designer who actually asks a potential client to let him or her know what versions of Flash Player are to be targeted for the project. The last thing you need is to find yourself rewriting every line of code and reworking the project when you assumed the target was Flash Player 9 but corporate policy dictates Flash Player 7 or lower.

14

> *Flash Player 9 follows a tradition that each successive version of Flash Player will play content faster than its predecessors. Adobe is claiming that there is a 75% speed increase of Flash Player 9 over Flash Player 8. This sort of increase is usually enough for most users to install the new version. Even so, in many instances, actually down-loading and installing the plug-in is becoming a thing of the past. Flash Player has the ability to download and install in the background, but, as one of the authors is quick to point out: "It takes a programmer to make it work."*

HTML

HTML is short for **HyperText Markup Language**. Where HTML and ActionScript part company is that HTML is a formatting language, whereas ActionScript is a scripting language. This means HTML is composed of a set of specific instructions that tell the browser where content is placed on a web page and what it looks like. ActionScript has nothing to do with the browser. It tells Flash how the movie is to work.

The HTML instructions, or tags, are both its strength and its weakness. HTML was originally developed to allow the presentation of text and simple graphics. As the Web matured, HTML found itself hard pressed to stay current with a community that was becoming bored with static content on pages.

The real problems with HTML start when you try to drop multimedia or interactive media into a web page. HTML simply wasn't designed for this sort of "heavy lifting," which explains why JavaScript (a language that shares roots with ActionScript) is now so widely used.

For a Flash designer, knowledge of how HTML works is critical, because it is the technology that enables your movies to be played on the Web. Of course, this isn't as difficult as it once was. Today, through the use of Dreamweaver CS3 and even Flash, it involves nothing more than a couple of mouse clicks to create the HTML that makes this possible. You will still need to play with the HTML—you saw this in Chapter 7 when you had to dig into the JavaScript code to enable full-screen playback of a Flash video—because your HTML document can do things that Flash can't. This would include such features as ALT attributes for screen readers and key words used to attract search engines.

> *Dreamweaver CS3 is what is called a **WYSIWYG editor**. The acronym is short for "what you see is what you get." In many cases this is true, but more often than not, these pages, when viewed in a browser, don't look the same way they did in Dreamweaver CS3. Maybe it should be called a WYSINNWYG editor—what you see is not necessarily what you get.*

The other thing to stick in the back of your mind is that Flash web pages aren't as common as they once were. Web pages consisting solely of one SWF are still around, but Flash is also becoming a medium of choice for the delivery of banner ads, videos, and other inter-active content that are elements of an HTML web page. To see an example of this, you need look no further than our beloved publisher. If you hit the friends of ED home page at www.friendsofEd.com (see Figure 14-1), you will see a Flash banner at the top of the home page, while the rest of the page is composed of HTML.

Figure 14-1. A typical Flash/HTML hybrid page

Animated GIFs

Before there was Shockwave, there was the infamous animated GIF file. These files were the original web animations, and you can export your Flash movie as an animated GIF. Why would you want to do this if Flash Player is so ubiquitous? The reason is users don't need to install the Flash plug-in to view them. In fact, it is a two-way street: you can import a GIF animation into a Flash movie, and you can export a Flash movie as an animated GIF. Here's how:

1. Open the YawningParrot.fla file. This is the file to be exported out as an animated GIF. How this works is Flash will convert each frame of the movie to a GIF image. There are 355 frames in this animation, meaning you really should prepare yourself to create 355 separate GIF images.

> OK web heads, settle down. Creating an animated GIF consisting of 355 frames is, as our editor, Chris Mills, would say, "Simply not done, old chap." We know that, but if you understand what happens . . . in a big way . . . you'll be more cautious in your efforts. Anyway, the parrot is pretty cool and makes for a rather interesting workout for Fireworks CS3.

14

2. Select File ➤ Export ➤ Export Movie (press Ctrl+Alt+Shift+S on the PC or Cmd+Option+Shift+S on the Mac) to open the Export dialog box. Navigate to the Parrot folder in the Chapter 14 Exercise folder and select GIF Sequence (*.gif) in the Save as type drop-down menu (see Figure 14-2).

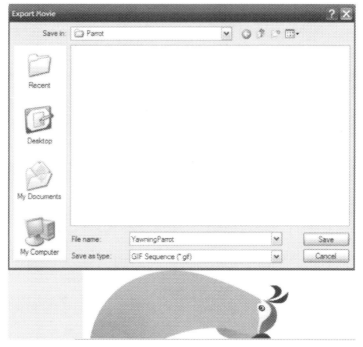

Figure 14-2. Select GIF Sequence (*.gif) as the image type.

3. Click Save to open the Export GIF dialog box shown in Figure 14-3. Specify these settings:

● Dimensions: 113 X 109

● Colors: 256

● Smooth: **Selected**

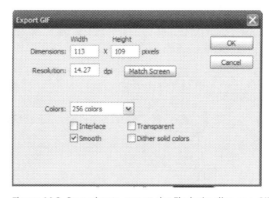

Figure 14-3. Preparing to export the Flash timeline as a GIF animation

You should have noticed that when you changed the Dimensions settings, there was a corresponding reduction in the Resolution value. If you click the Match Screen button, you will be returned to the original settings for this image. The physical reduction of each frame and its corresponding reduction in resolution have the net effect of creating a rather small GIF image.

4. Click the OK button, and a progress bar will appear showing you the progress of the export. This is a fairly quick process and should take less than 10 or 15 seconds. When it finishes, the progress bar will disappear, and you will be returned to the Flash stage. At this point, you are now the proud owner of the 355 GIF images that will be used to create the animation.

We aren't going to get into the nitty-gritty of creating the GIF animation in Fireworks CS3. The process is fairly simple. Launch Fireworks CS3, click the Open button on the Start screen, and navigate to the folder containing your GIF images. Select all of them in the Open dialog box, as shown in Figure 14-4, and select Open as animation. When you click the Open button, Fireworks will create the animated GIF by putting each image in a frame. You can then do what you need to do and export the file out of Fireworks CS3 as an animated GIF.

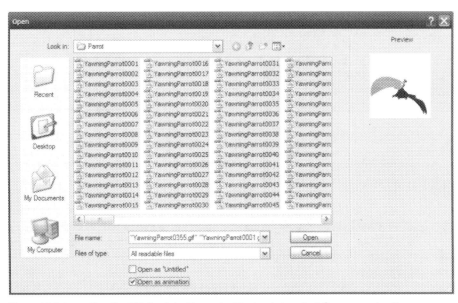

Figure 14-4. Importing the GIF files into Fireworks. The key is to select Open as animation.

> *Only the main timeline is considered when Flash content is converted to an animated GIF. Nested movieclip timelines do not make it through the translation process. The simple rule of thumb is, if you can see it move while you manually scrub the timeline, the GIF can too. If you can't, it won't show.*

14

Now that you know how to create a GIF animation in Flash, let's look at the reverse process: importing a GIF animation into Flash.

1. Open a new Flash CS3 document and select File ➤ Import ➤ Import to Library.

2. Navigate to the ParrotFW.gif file in your Chapter 14 Exercise folder and click Open.

3. When the process finishes, you will see that each image in the animation, along with a movieclip, has been added to the library.

4. Drag the movieclip to the stage and test the movie. You have a low-res version of the yawning parrot, as shown in Figure 14-5.

Figure 14-5. A yawning parrot in the GIF format

Yes, the earlier export exercise was partly mischievous. If you select File ➤ Export ➤ Export Movie, *you can bypass the need to restitch the GIF sequence in Fireworks by choosing* Animated GIF *from the* Export Movie *dialog box. Still, it's good to know your options!*

QuickTime

QuickTime is Apple's Internet steaming video technology. As we have pointed out throughout this book, QuickTime is losing its grip as the premiere web video technology. What you should have learned from the BubblingLetters.fla exercise in the "Optimizing Flash content for use in video" section of the previous chapter is this: *The reports of its death are premature.*

Flash is gaining ground as a broadcast animation technology, and no matter how you slice it, QuickTime is the way to go with digital video. Up until this release of Flash, QuickTime and Flash have had a rather uneasy relationship. It was extremely difficult to get Flash animations into QuickTime for editing in a video editing application. This impediment has been removed, and publishing a Flash document as a QuickTime movie is easier than it ever has been.

Which begs the question: How do you publish a Flash movie?

It's showtime!

Everything works as it should. You have sweated buckets to optimize the movie, and the client has finally signed off on the project. It is showtime. The Flash movie is ready to hit the Web and dazzle the audience. Though you may think publishing a Flash movie involves nothing more than selecting Publish in the File menu, you would be seriously mistaken. The process is as follows:

- Open the Publish Settings window to determine how the movie will be published.
- Publish the movie and preview the SWF.
- Upload the SWF and any support files to your web server.

Let's publish a movie. Here's how:

1. Open MoonOverLakeNanagook.fla. Seeing as how this is the last chapter, let's finish the book by working with the file you created when you started the book.

2. Select File ➤ Publish Settings (Ctrl+Shift+F12 on a PC or Option+Shift+F12 on a Mac) to open the Publish Settings dialog box shown in Figure 14-6.

Figure 14-6. The Publish Settings dialog box

You can also click the Settings *button on the Property inspector to launch the* Publish Settings *dialog box. The one thing you don't want to do, unless you have a lot of Flash experience under your belt, is to select* File ➤ Publish. *Selecting this will publish the movie using whatever default settings are in place.*

As you can see, this dialog box is divided into three distinct sections: Format, Flash, and HTML. In fact, that last tab (or tabs) will change depending on the format chosen. We'll get to that in a minute. The five buttons along the top are the Profile buttons. These allow you to "tweak" your settings and then save them for future use.

The file types are as follows:

- Flash (.swf): Select this, and you will create a SWF that uses the name in the File area unless you specify otherwise.
- HTML (.html): The default publishing setting is that the Flash and HTML settings are both selected. This does not mean your SWF will be converted to an HTML document. What it means is Flash will generate the HTML wrapper for the SWF.

If you are a Dreamweaver CS3 user, you don't need to select the HTML (.html) *option. Dreamweaver will write the necessary code for the SWF when it is imported into the Dreamweaver CS3 page.*

- GIF Image (.gif): Select this, and the Flash animation will be output as an animated GIF, or the first frame of the movie will be output as a static GIF image.
- JPEG Image (.jpg): The first frame of the Flash movie will be output as a JPEG image.
- PNG Image (.png): The first frame of the movie will be output as a PNG image. Be careful with this one because not all browsers can handle a PNG image.
- Windows Projector (.exe): Think of this as being a desktop SWF that is best suited to playback from a Windows desktop or CD, not from the browser.
- Macintosh Projector: The same thing as the Windows projector. Just be aware that a Mac projector won't play on a PC, and vice versa.
- QuickTime with Flash Track (.mov): Select this, and the Flash movie is output as a QuickTime movie, providing you have chosen Flash Player 5 as your target player. Why Flash Player 5? That is the only version of Flash Player the current version of QuickTime supports.

We suspect the addition of the ability to publish to QuickTime from the File *menu will make this choice even more infrequently used than it currently is.*

The Navigate buttons (they look like folders and are located beside each file type) allow you to navigate to the folder where the SWF will be saved (see Figure 14-7). If you see a path, click the Use Default Names button to strip out the path from the file name.

Figure 14-7. Strip out any paths in the file name to avoid problems.

3. Select all of the types except for QuickTime. Notice how each file type kicks out its own tab. Deselect everything but the Flash (.swf) option, and click the Flash tab to open the Flash settings shown in Figure 14-8.

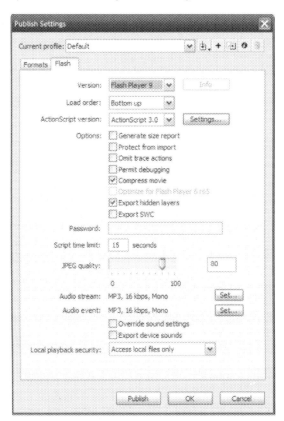

Figure 14-8. The Flash settings in the Publish Settings dialog box

There is a lot here, so let's review each of the areas in this panel:

14

- Version: This drop-down menu allows you to choose any version of Flash Player from Versions 1 to 9 (the current version) and any version of Flash Lite Player from versions 1 to 2.1. If you have the Property inspector open, you will see the version chosen also appears in the Property inspector. It is extremely important you understand that if you change your Flash Player version and are using features in the Flash movie that aren't supported by the Flash Player version you have chosen, you will be greeted by the Alert dialog box shown in Figure 14-9—but this only happens when you return to the Flash stage and try to add or manipulate something that isn't supported. In the case of Figure 14-9, we tried to add a drop shadow to a movieclip, and that feature is not supported in our target player.

Figure 14-9. Flash will let you know you can't do that when you try to do something that isn't supported by the version of Flash Player you have targeted.

- Load order: Your choices are Bottom up or Top down. This is the order in which Flash will load timeline layers into Flash Player. ActionScript is not affected by this setting: no matter what, ActionScript is performed in order of the highest layer to the lowest.

- ActionScript version: There are three versions of the language. If you are publishing to Flash Player 9, you are safe with ActionScript 3.0, ActionScript 2.0, or ActionScript 1.0 (we recommend ActionScript 3.0). If you are publishing to Flash Player 8 to 6 or Flash Lite 2 or 2.1, ActionScript 2.0 is your choice, though ActionScript 1.0 will work. Everything else uses ActionScript 1.0.

- Options: You have a number of options regarding the treatment of the SWF available to you. They are as follows:

  - Generate size report: Select this, and Flash will generate a .txt document that shows you where potential bandwidth issues may be located. When this option is selected, the .txt file is generated when you publish the SWF.

  - Protect from import: When this option is selected, the user will be prevented from opening your SWF in Flash.

  - Omit trace actions: Flash will ignore any trace() actions you may have added to your ActionScript (they will actually be removed from the SWF). You've used these to track the value of a variable and display that value in the Output window. Tracing is great for debugging, but enough such statements can affect performance.

  - Permit debugging: Select this, and you have access to the Debugger panel in Flash even if the file is being viewed in a web browser. You really should turn this off before you post the movie to the Web.

- Compress movie: Even though Flash compresses the FLA when it creates the SWF, selecting this allows Flash to compress the SWF itself—usually text-heavy or ActionScript-heavy—to an even greater extent during the publish process. If you are publishing to Flash Player 5 or lower, you can't use this option.

- Optimize for Flash Player 6 r65: Though this option is usually grayed out, you may select it when targeting Flash Player 6 to even further optimize the SWF. What's the r65? That particular release of Flash Player 6 introduced Flash Player enhancements that made it a "sneak peek" at Flash Player 7.

- Export hidden layers: All this means is that any layer with the visibility icon turned off will be compiled into the SWF. Developers often like to keep reference layers handy during authoring, but in previous versions of Flash, such layers would show in the SWF, even if they were hidden in the FLA. An old trick to "really" hide them was to convert such layers to guide layers—but that can get tedious. If you really want those layers gone, just delete them. If you're a little lazy, use this feature instead.

- Export SWC: Select this if you are an absolute code jockey and create your own custom components for Flash. That sort of thing is way out of the scope of this book.

- Password: This option works in conjunction with the Debugger panel. If you add a password to this text entry box, whoever opens the Debugger panel will be prompted to enter the password if debugging the SWF in a browser. If the plan is to test and debug your Flash app remotely, this is a "must do" option.

- Script time limit: Sometimes your scripts will get into a loop, sort of like a dog chasing its tail, and these things can go on for quite a long time before Flash sighs and gives up. Enter a value here, and you are telling Flash exactly when to give up.

- JPEG quality: This slider and text field combo specifies the amount of JPEG compression applied to bitmapped artwork in your movie. The value you set here will be applied to all settings in the Bitmap properties area of the library unless you override it for individual bitmaps on a per-image basis.

- Audio stream: Unless there is a compelling reason to do otherwise, leave this one alone. The value shown is the one applied to the Stream option for audio in the Property Inspector.

- Audio event: Same warning as the previous choice but for event sounds.

- Override sound settings: Click this and any settings—Stream and Event—you set in the Sound properties area of the library are, for all intents and purposes, gone.

- Export device sounds: Use this only if you are using Flash Lite and publishing to a mobile device.

- Local playback security: The two options in this drop-down menu—Access local files only and Access network only—permit you to control the SWF's network access. The important one is the network choice. Access networks only protects information on the user's computer from being accidentally uploaded to the network.

14

4. Click the Formats tab and select the HTML (.html) file type. When you do that, the Publish Settings dialog box sprouts an HTML tab. Click the HTML tab to open the HTML settings shown in Figure 14-10.

Figure 14-10. The HTML tab in the Publish Settings dialog box in Flash CS3

The important thing about this dialog box is to be aware that it does not convert your SWF to HTML. The best way to consider this option is like buying a hamburger at a large international chain. When the hamburger is finally ready, it will be wrapped in paper or placed in a colored box that identifies the contents. For example, you have ordered the MegaBurger, and the burger is wrapped in blue paper that has the words "MegaBurger" printed on it. The HTML option performs the same job: it provides the wrapper that tells the browser what's inside.

If you are a Dreamweaver CS3 user or prefer to "roll your own" HTML code, it still won't hurt to review this section, but Dreamweaver CS3 does this job for you.

If the Flash movie is to appear in a CSS-based layout, a lot of the options in this dialog box will not be used by the coder. Still, the HTML page to be created is a good starting point for a code jockey.

Let's review the main features of this panel:

- Template: This drop-down menu contains 11 options, but they all specify the type of HTML file you want the SWF to be embedded into. The Info button will give you a brief description of the selected template (see Figure 14-11). These templates can be found in C:\Program Files\Adobe\Adobe Flash CS3\en\First Run\HTML on your PC or HD:/Applications/Adobe Flash CS3/First Run/HTML on your Mac. If you are a hardcore coder and know exactly what you are doing, feel free to change them only after you have made a backup of the files. Though there are a number of templates, the Flash Only template will most likely become the one you use most often.

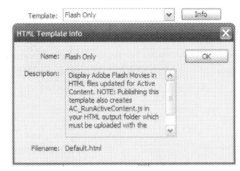

Figure 14-11. The Flash Only template description

- Detect Flash Version: This option determines whether the JavaScript code for this purpose is added to the HTML. What this does is to check to see whether the user's Flash plug-in will work with the version of Flash Player you have targeted. If the user has the version, life is a wonderful thing and the movie will play. If not, the user will see an error message along with a link to the location where the latest plug-in can be found.

> If you are a JavaScript wizard, feel free to customize the detection JavaScript to react differently if the wrong plug-in version is detected. For instance, if the IT boys have decreed "Thou shalt not add software to our machines," you could rewrite the code to load and play an alternate version of the SWF instead of suggesting the user do something that is forbidden.

- Dimensions: You get three choices—Match Movie, Pixels, or Percent—in this drop-down menu. Select one of the last two options, and you can change the physical size of your movie. If you choose Percent, you will discover the one circumstance that allows content positioned outside the stage to possibly show.

- Playback: These four choices determine what happens when the movie starts playing:

  - The first option, Paused at start, means the user gets things going. This is very common with banner ads, and you'd have to provide a button to tell the playhead to start moving, or the user would have to be smart enough to right-click and use the plug-in's context menu to select Play.

  - The Display menu option is actually quite important. It has nothing to do with menus in the movie and everything to do with Flash Player. If you test MoonOverLakeNanagook.fla and right-click (PC) or Ctrl-click (Mac) the SWF, the menu shown in Figure 14-12 appears. This menu allows the user to modify how Flash Player displays the movie. Many Flash designers and developers turn this off because they don't want people switching to low-quality graphics or zooming in on the stage. Still, there is a very important use for this menu. If your site requires visitors to use a web camera or a microphone, clicking the Settings option will allow them to choose the devices to be used. (The Settings option is always available, even if you hide the rest of the context menu.)

14

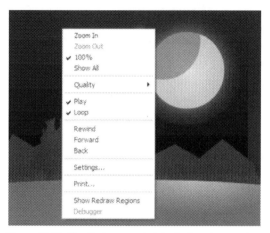

Figure 14-12. The Flash menu that is displayed at runtime

- The Loop option plays the movie continuously if it is selected or only once if deselected. The key point here is any stop() actions you may have in your ActionScript will override this selection.

- The Device font selection replaces any static text in your movie with a system font— _sans, _serif, and _typewriter—which can result in a significant file-size reduction. The downside to this choice is you have absolutely no control over which font is used because if the user doesn't have the three fonts installed, the machine will use one that is closest to the font, meaning the text may wrap or even change the "look" of your movie. Is this one of those things that falls into the category of things you should never do? Not really. It is your movie, and if you decide this is the way to go, you at least are aware of the potential hazards in the choice.

- Quality: This drop-down menu contains the six choices shown in Figure 14-13. These specify the render quality that your movie will play at, and the choice you make determines the speed at which your movie runs on the user's machine or device. We suggest you start with Auto High, which permits Flash to automatically drop the quality to maintain the frame rate and synchronization if needed. In many respects, this area is not one that should concern you because if Display menu is selected, the user can change this setting at runtime.

Figure 14-13. Try starting with the Auto High quality setting.

- Window Mode: The selection you make here will appear in the wmode settings in the <object> and <embed> tags used in the HTML. If you are unsure as to what the choices do, just leave the choice at the default: Window.

- HTML alignment: This selection allows you to specify the position of your movie window inside the browser window. The default will place the SWF in the center of the browser window.

- Scale: If you have changed the dimensions of the movie using the Dimensions option, the choices in the drop-down menu determine how the movie is scaled to fit into the browser window.

- Flash alignment: These two options permit you to set the Vertical and Horizontal alignment of your movie in its window and how it will be cropped, if necessary.

- Show warning messages: If this box is checked, any errors discovered when the HTML file is loaded—missing images is a common one—are displayed as browser warnings when the user arrives on the page.

Now that we have reviewed the major points, let's publish Lake Nanagook and look at it in a browser. Before you start, click the OK or Cancel button to close the Publish Settings dialog box and return to the Flash stage. Save the MoonOverLakeNanagook.fla to the Nanagook folder in your Chapter 14 Exercise folder. We'll explain why in a moment. Now open the Publish Settings dialog box and let's get busy:

1. Click the Formats tab and select the Flash and HTML formats.

2. Click the Flash tab and specify these settings:
   - Version: Flash Player 9
   - Load order: Bottom up
   - ActionScript version: ActionScript 3.0
   - Compress movie: **Selected**
   - Export hidden layers: **Deselected**

3. Click the HTML tab and specify these settings:
   - Template: Flash Only
   - Dimension: Match Movie
   - Quality: Auto High
   - Flash alignment: Center **for both** Horizontal **and** Vertical

4. Click the Formats tab and, when the panel opens, click the Use Default Names button to strip off any paths that might be associated with this movie.

5. Click the Publish Button. You will see a progress bar that follows the publishing process. Click OK to close the Publish Settings dialog box and return to your movie.

14

6. Minimize the Flash stage and open the Nanagook folder in the Chapter 14 Exercise folder. You will see that Flash has created four files, as shown in Figure 14-14. There are the FLA, SWF, an HTML file, and a JavaScript file named AC_RunActiveContent.js. This last file is used to prevent Internet Explorer from kicking out the "Click to activate and use this control" warning that has plagued developers since Microsoft changed how its browser displays active content such as Flash and even its own Windows Media Player. The only file that doesn't need to get uploaded to the server is the FLA.

Figure 14-14. The results of publishing the Flash movie

7. Open the MoonOverLakeNanagook.html file in a browser. The movie, as shown in Figure 14-15, starts playing. Congratulations!

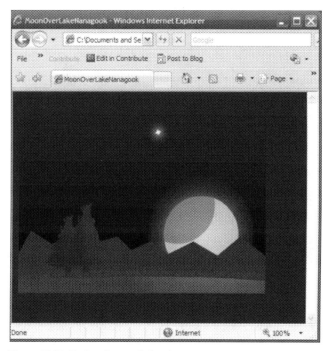

Figure 14-15. Playing the movie in a browser

> Hang on. How did the background color of the browser page turn blue? There was nothing in the HTML settings for that one. If you publish a Flash movie and use the HTML option, the background color of the HTML document will change to the stage color of the Flash movie.

Before we move on, there is one last option you may have noticed in the File menu that we'd like to talk about. The Publish Preview menu—File ➤ Publish Preview—contains the formats from the Publish Settings dialog box (see Figure 14-16). Selecting this will publish the movie and then launch the results in a browser if you select Default - (HTML). This menu reflects the choices made in the Publishing Settings window, which explains why a lot of the options are grayed out. If you are a Dreamweaver CS3 or Fireworks CS3 user, this menu item is the same as being able to do a browser preview in both of those apps. In fact, they all use the same key, F12, to launch the preview. The browser that opens will be the default browser used by your computer's operating system.

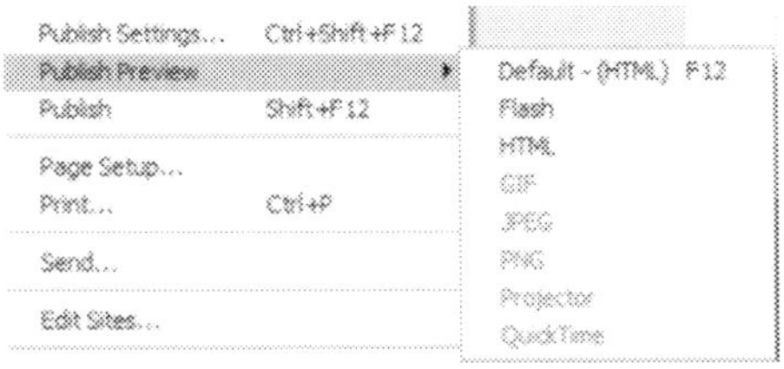

Figure 14-16. You can preview the movie in a browser without leaving the Flash interface.

Publishing Flash movies containing linked files

In Chapter 5, you created an MP3 player. Though you tested it locally, nothing beats testing on a remote server. The other aspect of that exercise, which we didn't review until now, is that of playing content located in another folder on the server. In the case of the MP3 files, this actually makes sense. Let's assume you are going to use the same MP3 soundtrack in five Flash movies over the coming year. If that MP3 is 5 MB in size, you will have used up 25 MB of server space if the file is slipped into the folder for each project that uses it. Doesn't it make more sense to upload it once and have the movies call it into the SWF from a single location?

In this example, we are going to assume the three audio files are located in a folder named Tunes in the mythical domain of mySite.com.

1. Open the Player.fla file located in your Exercise folder. When the file opens, open the Actions Panel and scroll down to the loadSong function in line 41 of the Script pane.

2. The critical line in this function is line 43, which uses the load() method to get the song. Change this line to the following:

```
song.load(new URLRequest("http://www.mySite.com/Tunes/" + thisSong));
```

Everything is straightforward if you use absolute paths, like you've seen so far. Absolute paths contain the full domain name, which means they're accessible from anywhere on the Internet. That's both a plus and a minus. If you hardcode all your file references as absolute paths, you know they'll work—until you decide to change your domain name, or until you repurpose your content for another project in another folder structure somewhere else. In cases like that, a relative path may suit your needs. Relative paths do not reference a domain

14

name, and because of that, they depend entirely on a very particular "point of view," namely, the physical location of the file making the reference.

You would think that a SWF looking for MP3s (or any external file) would consider itself as the beginning of the path—"Where is that file in relation to *me*?"—but that's not how it works. When a SWF references external files with relative paths, its point of view is actually that of the HTML document that contains it. If the SWF and the HTML file are in the same folder, this is a moot point, but keep it in mind if you decide to put all your SWFs in one folder and your HTML files in another.

To make matters even more interesting, there's an exception, and FLV video files are it. If you are using the FLVPlayback component, the path to the video, if it is a relative path, takes its cue from the location of the SWF itself. Same goes for a video object using the NetStream class. That said, the FLVPlayback component optionally uses skins, and skins are SWF files. If your movie uses relative paths to reference an FLVPlayback skin, set your point of view to the HTML document that contains this movie, but when referencing the FLV, set your point of view to the movie itself.

This "gotcha" often raises its ugly head if you have a custom controller or video skin or are using a server that dynamically loads the content. Either understand the "gotcha" fully, or enter the paths, as shown in Figure 14-17, as absolute paths.

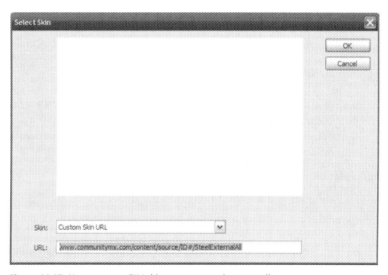

Figure 14-17. You can save FLV skins to remote sites as well.

What you've learned

- How to prepare a SWF for web playback
- How to export a Flash movie as a GIF animation and how to import a GIF animation into Flash
- How to deal with remote content needed by the SWF

This chapter dealt with the "end game" in Flash. We think you are now aware that preparing your Flash files for web output involves a lot more than simply selecting Publish in the File menu. There is a lot to consider, and those considerations range from what format will be used to output the file to a number of very important options that need to be addressed. We also dealt with remote content and how the SWF can grab it from elsewhere on your site and on the Web.

Speaking of the "end game," we are at the end of this journey that started and ended at Lake Nanagook. We hope you had fun and that you are inspired to explore Flash CS3 even further. As you do, you will discover a fundamental truth about this application: the amount of fun you can have with it should be illegal. We'll see you in jail.

14

INDEX

X

Z

friendsofed.com/forums

Join the friends of ED forums to find out more about our books, discover useful technology tips and tricks, or get a helping hand on a challenging project. *Designer to Designer* is what it's all about—our community sharing ideas and inspiring each other. In the friends of ED forums, you'll find a wide range of topics to discuss, so look around, find a forum, and dive right in!

■ **Books and Information**

Chat about friends of ED books, gossip about the community, or even tell us some bad jokes!

■ **Flash**

Discuss design issues, ActionScript, dynamic content, and video and sound.

■ **Web Design**

From front-end frustrations to back-end blight, share your problems and your knowledge here.

■ **Site Check**

Show off your work or get new ideas.

■ **Digital Imagery**

Create eye candy with Photoshop, Fireworks, Illustrator, and FreeHand.

■ **ArchivED**

Browse through an archive of old questions and answers.

HOW TO PARTICIPATE

Go to the friends of ED forums at **www.friendsofed.com/forums**.

Visit **www.friendsofed.com** to get the latest on our books, find out what's going on in the community, and discover some of the slickest sites online today!

friendsof

DESIGNER TO DESIGNER™

an Apress® company

DOM Scripting

1-59059-543-2 $39.99 [US]   1-59059-518-1 $49.99 [US]   1-59059-542-4 $36.99 [US]   1-59059-517-3 $39.99 [US]   1-59059-533-5 $34.99 [US]

EXPERIENCE THE DESIGNER TO DESIGNER™ DIFFERENCE

1-59059-306-5 $34.99 [US]   1-59059-238-7 $24.99 [US]   1-59059-149-6 $24.99 [US]

1-59059-262-X $49.99 [US]   1-59059-224-7 $39.99 [US]   1-59059-221-2 $39.99 [US]   1-59059-236-0 $39.99 [US]   1-59059-372-3 $39.99 [US]

1-59059-304-9 $49.99 [US]   1-59059-355-3 $39.99 [US]   1-59059-409-6 $39.99 [US]   1-59059-314-6 $59.99 [US]   1-59059-315-4 $59.99 [US]

   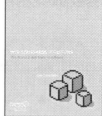 

1-59059-231-X $39.99 [US]   1-59059-408-8 $34.99 [US]   1-59059-428-2 $39.99 [US]   1-59059-381-2 $29.99 [US]   1-59059-554-8 $24.99 [US]